NBA's 50 Greatest Basketball Players of All-Time

- With an additional pick six? players projected to make the list -
- And one late addition making it a super seven! -
- Many other Hall of Famers also included -
- Player comparisons throughout -

The greatest basketball player of all-time is arguably Michael Jordan. Statistically, LeBron James is ahead of Jordan to becoming the greatest player ever. Just recently, Scottie Pippen said during the 2011 NBA Playoffs that Jordan was the "greatest scorer" of all-time and that LeBron had a chance to become the "greatest basketball player" of all-time. But as soon as LeBron and the Miami Heat collapsed in the 2011 NBA Finals against the well balanced and deep Dallas Mavericks team, he retracted his statement. For good measure, recently for those who missed it during one of the ABC halftime shows, in an interview with Mark Schwarz, Oscar Robertson was asked if LeBron was better than Jordan. He answered, "Come on, LeBron's in a class by himself." He went on to say that, "he is the face of the team now and wherever he goes he's going to be the face of the team!" In favor of Jordan, only Oscar so far has said publically that LeBron is the greatest while everybody else, I'm sure would pick Michael. Jerry West did say recently that LeBron has a chance to become the greatest player ever. He just needs to start winning championships to back it up. Well, I wrote those statements well over a year ago and sure enough; LeBron has begun to fulfill his legacy by winning consecutive NBA Championships including both Finals MVP awards. He also won his fourth MVP award.

Michael Jordan is the greatest player ever because he has the best individual *contributions* to the team's success in the regular season and postseason to go along with winning 6 NBA Championships. Wilt Chamberlain can match Jordan's individual accomplishments statistically in the regular season but not in the postseason, while Bill Russell surpasses him in championships but not in individual contributions, at least from a statistical point of view. If Jordan had not retired twice, had front office issues with ownership and management (read the book the Jordan Rules by Sam Smith) throughout the years, and by not having an equal peer to keep his drive going and from being bored with the game of basketball, he would have challenged Russell's 11 Championship Rings. So measuring greatness on Championships alone is only part of it. Basketball is a team sport just like baseball and football, albeit, played with just five 5 players. So there is obviously more chances for a player to make a significant impact with 5 players on the court vs. baseball and football, where there is 9 and 11 players on the field at one time. Individual contributions statistically and intangibly in the regular season and postseason, along with winning championships, determine player greatness. Contrary to public opinion, you don't necessarily have to win a championship to be considered great or even among the *elite* players of all-time. Here is a quick list of great individuals who never won a championship: Elgin Baylor, Karl Malone, Charles Barkley, Patrick Ewing, Dominique Wilkins, Reggie Miller, John Stockton, Steve Nash, Dan Marino, Barry Sanders, Earl Campbell, Randy Moss, Terrell Owens, Barry Bonds, Ted Williams, Tony Gwynn, Wade Boggs, Rod Carew, to name a few. Here is a quick list of players that only won one Championship: Jerry West, Oscar Robertson, Julius Erving (NBA) Moses Malone, Dirk Nowitzki, Peyton Manning, Hank Aaron, Willie Mays, Nolan Ryan, and Alex Rodriguez.

You could make the case that Barry Bonds and Alex Rodriguez are the greatest sluggers to ever play the game of baseball, or that Barry Sanders is the greatest running back of all-time, and that Peyton Manning and Dan Marino are among the top 5 quarterbacks of all-time. I know what you're probably thinking, is that one guy can make more of an impact in playing basketball than vs. the other sports! The Dallas Mavericks just proved that it takes 7 or 8 *solid* players to win a championship in 2011 and that basketball is very much a team sport. The Detroit Piston's also proved that team concept more than ever when they won the 2004 NBA Championship playing with one true superstar in Ben Wallace. To back up my point even further, during the playoffs before Dirk Nowitzki won his first NBA title, Magic Johnson and John Barry were asked the question on national TV - would winning a championship make Nowitzki a better player? And they both answered no! Magic did say it would put him in a VIP group though. You can interpret that as you wish. But in my opinion, by saying no, that's completely contrary to the public belief that you have to win a championship to be great or even better than another player when having debates or making player comparisons.

In the case with Nowitzki, all along I always knew how great Dirk was as a player and as a shooter because his best games even in the playoffs outnumbered the bad. Despite a few bad playoff games here and there, which happens to everyone, all a player could hope for, is for his team to pull him through to victory like the Dallas Mavericks did for Nowitzki in game 6 of the 2011 NBA Finals and the way the Los Angeles Lakers did for Kobe Bryant when he had a horrendous shooting performance in game 7 of the 2010 NBA Finals against the Boston Celtics two years ago. The best thing to do after a poor performance is to bounce back with another great game. Of course, if a player continues to fail repeatedly in big moments of big games throughout his playoff career, it would most definitely hurt his legacy. So it is best to judge a player over the long haul on individual contributions to the team success in the regular season, playoffs, and in the NBA Finals, whether it comes in a win or a loss. If a player, particularly a star player, plays well in a win he gets all the credit. If he plays well and loses he is often looked upon as a dog, choker, or a flat out loser. He shouldn't be discounted for having great games or for being a great player if the rest of the team, or key players on the team played poorly. And, he shouldn't get all the credit if he plays poorly and the rest of team plays great in victory. But winning period trumps everything in most everyone's mind. There is nowhere near, a fine line for this judgment as many great players of the past have failed to win championships. You just have to sit back and weigh the good with the bad (the individual contributions to the team's success and the strength of the supporting cast) as I have done throughout the book.

Jerry West for example, is ranked 9th all-time by Bill Simmons the man who wrote the best book (700 pages - 250,000 words) on basketball that I have read thus far, and he has only 1 championship ring. Simmons also ranks Elgin Baylor 15th and he never even won a championship. Even the great Wilt Chamberlain only won 2 and Simmons has him ranked 6th all-time, which is probably the lowest anyone would ever rank the "Great Chamberlain." Almost every Legend & magazine that I have read over the years including Sports Illustrated, Sporting News, ESPN The Magazine, Slam Magazine, and every article online that I could get my hands on, ranks Wilt Chamberlain at least in the Top 5, if not, either first or second at the top with Michael Jordan. So it is unfair to discount the Superstar of the past who did not win a championship or multiple championships.

This book contains: The Top 50 NBA Players of All-Time with exclusive projected rankings of LeBron James, Dwyane Wade, Chris Paul, Kevin Durant, Dwight Howard, Derrick Rose, and Blake Griffin as they approach their primes and where they might end up in the Elite Rankings of All-Time! On the cover of the book and on its title, instead of changing the subtitle from projected pick six, to a projected super seven. I have decided to keep both subtitles. When I first started writing the book in 2010, I left Blake Griffin out of my projected rankings in fear that he might not have the same explosiveness before his most recent injury and/or that the injury might reoccur. And as I was close to the completion of this book, Derrick Rose of the Chicago Bulls just tore his ACL in the first game of the 2012 playoffs against the Atlanta Hawks and is out for the rest of the year. This was the worst possible scenario that could have happened to the Bulls franchise, and for Rose as a player. The freak incident was a shock to all NBA fans around the world and we all just hope Rose has a successful recovery and regains the explosiveness he once had. With all the injuries around the league in a lockout shortened season, many players have gone down to injuries and you can only hope that it doesn't ever happen to one of your favorite players throughout the course of their playing career. Any type of injury, mild or severe, could happen to any player at any given moment and I hope it never happens *again* to Griffin after what he has already been through missing his rookie season due to a broken kneecap.

As I was at the halfway point of writing this book, I was following Griffin intently during the 2011 season and Kevin Love for that matter. And what I saw was even greater potential than what he showed beginning in his rookie season in 2010-11. I mean the way LeBron James has revolutionized the small forward position; Blake Griffin has the potential to do the same thing at the power forward position after I had already thought Karl Malone could take it as far as it could go. But in just two years in the league, Griffin seems to have added more versatility to the position than I have ever seen before. While my final pick of the projected 7 player rankings in which I have written about with each player having his own chapter, Griffin was my final selection over Love by a slight margin. But not to worry because throughout the book, well over 100 players are written about exclusively and extensively including Love in Griffin's chapter as potentially becoming the greatest power forward of this current era!

If I had to build three All-Time basketball teams based on *projected* rankings, it would look like this:

1st Team	2nd Team	3rd Team
Magic Johnson	Oscar Robertson	Stockton/ Paul
Michael Jordan	Jerry West	Kobe/ Wade
Kareem Abdul-Jabbar	Wilt Chamberlain	Hakeem Olajuwon
Larry Bird	Bill Russell	Tim Duncan
LeBron James	Elgin Baylor	Barry/ Durant

You don't have to jump to conclusions like I just did. This is *strictly a projected* ranking on my part. And, before any one gets bent out of shape, most of you I'm sure wouldn't put LeBron James in the Top 15, because up to the beginning of the 2012 season, the King was ringless! But think about it, Bill Simmons just said recently on national TV, that he would put James in his Top 10 players of all-time. In the middle of writing this book, he was just barely 27 years old and on the verge of winning his 3rd MVP award, and to becoming the youngest man in history to score 19,000 points. I also thought he might win his first NBA Championship (Jordan and Shaq were both 28 when they won their first) that season in 2012 and perhaps the year after. So once again, this is how I foresee the future rankings unfolding for some of the projected players above, who are barely in the prime of their careers and in the case of Kevin Durant, *approaching* his prime. If I didn't feel LeBron James had a legitimate *chance* to become the second or perhaps the greatest player ever, and that Larry Bird wasn't the *greatest Celtic* like many people believe (Red Auerbach once said Bird was the greatest player to put on a uniform), I would have to put Bill Russell at power forward on the First Team ahead of Wilt Chamberlain, not because I felt he was better, but because it would make a more *ideal* team with Kareem at center and with LeBron ranked ahead of Bird at the small forward position. Some might make the case for Shaq over Olajuwon on the third team. Also, I put Chris Paul and Dwyane Wade next to John Stockton and Kobe Bryant because they also have a legitimate shot to fill the *slot* someday, if they can get a few championship victories under their belt. But, I would lean more toward Stockton because of durability and longevity, and Kobe over Wade for that same reason, and because he has a 5 to 3 advantage thus far in NBA Championships won. Also, if Wade and Paul continue to have injuries, it is a scary thought in a very negative way, on how their futures might play out. If injuries *persist* for the rest of their careers, they might not make any ones Top 25. For Kobe, a lot of people would probably put him ahead of Jerry West on the second team, but I don't believe that is the case so far, as I have presented in the book and especially in West's Chapter. But the most intriguing thought of all, is how good Kevin Durant will end up becoming? Could he actually end up the better player over Julius Erving, Rick Barry and Elgin Baylor? At only 24 years old with a third scoring title already in his grasp, we will all have to wait and see!

So there are many ways to evaluate player greatness, and of course winning a championship in most people's eyes, weighs in the heaviest! But as I will mention throughout the book, individual contributions to the team's success are what I believe define a player's legacy. And many of those contributions can be measured by a player's individual statistics (and accolades), awards and honors, and intangibles.

Furthermore, if I had to create a point system to *help* measure the greatness of a player (awards and honors and individual accolades) that includes the MVP and Defensive Player of the Year awards, All-NBA First Team, All-Defensive First Team, scoring titles, rebounding and assists titles, etc. - the MVP in the regular season would be awarded the most points, followed closely by the All-NBA First Team selection (which means all five players are the best at their positions throughout the entire regular season). Of course, championship rings and just making it to the NBA Finals weighs in heavily as well; as do the other awards, honors, and individual accolades a player achieves when assessing player greatness.

Bear with me on this one, if you don't know where this going. Instead of creating a separate chapter for the MVP award and other individual awards, honors, and accolades, I have decided to insert this writing in the middle of the introduction part of this book.

The reasons I feel winning the regular season MVP, or even finishing second in the voting for that matter, weighs heaviest on a players resume (when evaluating a players greatness), even over winning an NBA Championship or Finals MVP award are: One, not every player can win the MVP award but up to 12 to 14 players can win an NBA Championship because it happens every year. Two, as I will explain in detail in Michael Jordan's chapter, winning MVP in my mind says a player is the best player in the league (statistically is the best objective way to measure this) for 82 games for that one particular season on a *top 4 or 5 team in contention to win a championship*, whereas with winning the Finals MVP; a player is awarded a trophy for being the best player for six or seven games in the NBA Finals (and the award doesn't even count toward the previous playoff series - with that being said, maybe they should have a playoff MVP as well). Of course, it is the most important set of games in the entire season, but it is a slightly *smaller sample size* of the greatness of a player compared to what another player has accomplished for a full season as NFL's Eli Manning would attest to. The younger Manning was recently indirectly asked by the media if he was the top quarterback in the NFL over his brother Peyton Manning because of his two Super Bowl victories that included two Super Bowl MVP awards vs. his brother with four regular season MVP awards. His answer was; well I was the MVP for two big games of my life, whereas my brother (Peyton who does by the way have one super bowl ring) was the best player in the *entire* league (over all the players on all 30 teams) for an *entire* 16-game season, four different times.

In fact, it is the *success of the entire team* that brings home a championship title. So contrary to what many people might believe, that the MVP is an individual award (which is when it's actually handed out to the player receiving it), and that it doesn't compare to a player who wins a championship or Finals MVP for that matter; but the truth is that the MVP award means a heck of a lot more than you might think. Which brings me to my third and final reason: more than any other sport, the MVP award in basketball is a *reflection* of individual success combined with team success. Do you see MVP winners on non-caliber championship teams in baseball and football over the years? Sometimes you do, and more often in baseball! But in basketball, if you go back to 1956 and 1959 when Bob Pettit won both MVP awards in the regular season, and when Bill Russell won 5 around the same time, and including all the winners in today's game, the MVP *almost always* comes from a top team (a top 4 team - which is usually the two best teams in either conference) in contention to win a championship.

So to put this into even *more perspective*, once again the MVP award in the NBA is a *reflection* of individual success with the emphasis on how a player's individual contributions (the most objective way to measure this is by statistics) translates into team success (wins), more than any other sport. So a person shouldn't be led to believe that the MVP award is not a good way to evaluate a player compared to winning an NBA title. Of course winning a championship is every player and every team's ultimate goal, but every player that has won the MVP award in the regular season is already in the Hall of Fame or eventually will be (when eligible) at 100 percent rate so far since 1956. So if players such as the most recent LeBron James (during his days with Cleveland) and Steve Nash who won the MVP award and didn't win a title, and even Dirk Nowitzki and Kobe Bryant the year they won MVP and didn't win the title the same year, it didn't mean they weren't deserving of the award or weren't winners, just because their respective teams weren't quite good enough *the entire* playoffs to bring home the biggest prize, which is an NBA Championship - their teams were simply among the *very best* for 82 games in the regular season and often most of the playoffs which equates to about 90 games in all.

Intangibles play a part in determining if a player is better than another usually when they are equal or near equal in talent. Being in the right place at the right time is the best virtue to winning championships, especially if you are a role player. Bill Russell and Tim Duncan are the best examples of players sacrificing their offensive game for defense, making the right pass, going after a key rebound, scoring in clutch situations, and doing all the little things to win championships. I think intangibles work far better in the Tim Duncan comparisons with Kevin Garnett, Karl Malone, and Charles Barkley than it does for Bill Russell vs. Wilt Chamberlain and Kareem Abdul-Jabbar. The reason: Duncan can match his peers on the offensive and defensive end while Russell would only be able to defensively but not offensively particularly in the scoring aspect of the game. Hal De Julio, Russell's high school scout that helped recruit him to the University of San Francisco, said that he was a meager scorer with atrocious fundamentals coming out of high school but sensed he had *extraordinary instincts* for the game especially in clutch situations. Even without a great cast of offensive players in Boston, Russell would have never come close to developing the offensive skills of Wilt and Kareem.

Many fans and some experts view role players as they do star players just because they have championship rings. Contrary to public opinion, role players of the past come and go either succeeding with championship teams or succeeding then failing after switching teams, while their former team continues to win titles. Or, they are sometimes fortunate enough to land on another championship caliber team such as in the case with Robert Horry. I could sit here all day and list players from every team the last thirty years who come and go at a dime a dozen. If a role player was that significant to the team with a nucleus of star players, it should have a huge negative effect on the team after his departure; instead another player gets acquired and fills in just fine. Many teams (with a strong nucleus in place) win repeatedly over the years. It's not to say that the role players don't matter in terms of their individual contributions on and off the court, or in terms of team chemistry, because it takes a total team effort to win a championship. However, due to their financial affordability and with the veteran's minimum, it is much easier to replace them (compared to a star player) with another player during the regular season or in the off-season. The key to all NBA Champions are the Superstars. You can't replace a Magic & Kareem, Bird & McHale, Isiah & Dumars, Jordan & Pippen, Shaq & Kobe, Duncan & Robinson, Nowitzki & Kidd, and LeBron James & Dwyane Wade.

Because of my extreme passion to follow sports for the past few decades including NBA basketball exclusively every chance that I could outside of work (I happen to be a light industrial clerk and work for my family business, Inspirational Family Books), has allowed me to write this book in my own words covering everything I have seen, heard, and read since the 1980s. Without fully realizing it, I was preparing to write this book all along learning, memorizing and retaining whatever visual images and knowledge I could over much of the thousands of games watched, everything I have read covering every conceivable basketball reference (including numerous opinion's on what great players of the past and present thought about other great players), and the statistics that have I tracked by way of the internet, newspapers, magazines, books, and abstracts. However, with that being said, I'm not a skilled writer by any stretch of the imagination, but have always wanted to put my basketball knowledge on paper and create a book with as much information (with player descriptions & analysis, and facts & stats) as possible - which in turn, allows you to judge the player rankings for yourselves, on as many great players as possible. In a nutshell, I wanted to build a mini Encyclopedia or miniature bible so-to-speak of the greatest NBA basketball players of all-time. But, without the help of the family (we all by the way happen to be half Asian and half Hispanic) around me (their encouragement and belief that I could put this book together), this project would not have been possible. And these people are my Dad, Mom, my brothers and sisters, my brother-n-law, a few friends, and my sibling's friends.

This book is filled with player introductions including a mini-biography, player attributes and skill sets, records and individual accolades, award and honors, player rankings and player comparisons throughout, and a player's chronological history year by year with interceding player evaluations of the NBA's elite and players outside the top 50. My book was actually completed (at over 190,000 words) *for the most part*, around this time last year right before LeBron James and the Miami Heat won their first NBA Championship. I also chose not to update some portions of the book, particularly some of the current players this past year, because I wanted to show the readers how I envisioned (or should I say predicted) the future of players such as LeBron James and Dwyane Wade to unfold. The most significant changes for the most part, would have been made for only two players in both James and Wade because they were able to reach the pinnacle of success two consecutive times winning back-to-back championships including a third title for Wade. LeBron was also able to capture two more regular season MVP awards and two NBA Finals MVP awards to add to his resume. Out of all the players in the book, these two are among the ones I have admired most, which actually *inspired me to fulfill* my dream of putting my basketball knowledge on paper. And finally, the most interesting part of this book, is that I have created a "one-of-a-kind" chart for individual accolades, honors and awards of the 50 greatest basketball players of all-time in which I have presented in the back of the book.

Michael Jordan

(Rank #1)

MVP (5-times), Scoring Title (10-times), Steals Title (3-times)

All-NBA First Team (10-times), All-Defensive First Team (9-times)

NBA Championships (6), Finals MVP (6-times), All-Star (14-times)

NBA Record: 63 points in a playoff game!

NBA Record: 8 50-point games in a playoff career!

NBA Record: 38 40-point games in a playoff career!

Michael Jordan was the most *incredible* human specimen the NBA has ever seen! As the greatest basketball player of all-time, Jordan was the Muhammad Ali of his sport not only with his athletic ability but with the popularity he brought to the NBA and around the world during the 1980s and 1990s. He helped make the NBA into what it is today by taking the sport to a whole new level of athleticism that we had never seen before. With a player of this stature and with the uncanny ability to soar and hang in the air longer and with more grace than anyone before him, he was simply given the nickname "Air Jordan" or "His Airness." The Chicago Bulls legend could do it all, beginning with his deft-defying acrobatic dunks in midair, his *ultra-quick* fadeaway shot from the low post or high post, and his *explosive* first step to the basket. Just looking at him, he seemed superhuman, something you could only dream of, someone of another planet, and he pranced around and shrugged his shoulders as though he would dominate you and everyone else with prolific scoring ease. Thinking back, it makes you wonder why he wasn't winning championships early on in his career. Watching him since 1985, I always marveled at how much he elevated his game over everyone else with his relentless scoring and his extreme will to win. And when he had you by the throat up in a playoff series, it proved almost impossible to come back and beat him! He and Tiger Woods had the *killer instinct* that is rare in today's sports - as they just so happen to be the greatest finishers since Bill Russell (never lost a playoff series after leading 2 games to 0) and Jack Nicholas who won a record 18 major golf championships. Even though Jordan didn't win his first championship until 1991 at the age of 28, he still seemed like he was playing at another level athletically and with a higher skill set over everyone else. I think *aesthetically*, playing the game with such ease and fluidity; he was the exact makeup of what you would want a basketball player to look like. You knew he was going to be great since his rookie season because he showed athleticism and skill at its highest level, being able to hang in the air longer than anyone else and detonate to the basket with his explosive first step finishing with some *ferocious dunk* or never seen before acrobat layup. It may have been an up-and-under reverse layup or right at the basket falling to the floor *and-one-finish* after the foul. He even had the spin moves, up-and-under moves, head fakes, and fadeaways when posting up either down low or in the high post. "Air Jordan" was even more spectacular than Dr. J and Elgin Baylor who were the great super high-flyers of the past. With his overall skill, you could see the greatness to come in his future including an improved jump shot he developed the second half of his career.

Born on February 17th, 1963 in Brooklyn, New York, Michael Jeffrey Jordan attended Emsley A. Laney High School in Wilmington where he was a three-sport athlete in basketball, football, and in baseball - like we all found out after his first retirement from the NBA. After a slow start to his high school basketball career, by his senior year, he showed his potential to perhaps becoming the greatest basketball player of all-time when he averaged a triple-double of **29.2 points**, **11.6 rebounds**, and **10.1 assists** per game, and was named a McDonald's All-American in 1981. He then received a scholarship to play basketball at the University of North Carolina under coach Dean Smith for three seasons before being selected by the Chicago Bulls in the first round 3rd pick overall of the 1984 NBA Draft. In need of a big man, the Portland Trail Blazers, who had the second pick in the draft, selected Sam Bowie ahead of Michael Jordan because they had landed shooting guard Clyde Drexler in the draft the year before. At North Carolina, Jordan played with other future NBA stars in James Worthy and Sam Perkins who were all part of the 1982 NCAA Championship Team.

While Magic Johnson, Larry Bird, and Isiah Thomas were winning all the championships in the mid to late 1980s, Michael Jordan was *assaulting* the league with his relentless scoring while at the same time being viewed by most as a selfish scorer, kind of the way Kobe Bryant was viewed for most of his career until recently. In his rookie season, Jordan averaged an impressive **28.2 points** per game, **6.5 rebounds**, **5.9 assists**, and **2.4 steals**, and started in his first All-Star game. He also beat out the number one overall draft pick in Hakeem Olajuwon for Rookie of the Year honors. But in the playoffs, the 38-win Chicago Bulls were ousted by the Milwaukee Bucks three games to one in the first round. In his second season, Jordan played in only 18 games but recovered in time for the playoffs where he averaged a *ridiculous* 43.7 points per game in three consecutive losses to the Boston Celtics, in another first-round exit. Despite the three losses, Jordan scored an **NBA record 63 points** in double overtime in game 2. In the 1986-87 season, Jordan followed up his incredible scoring escapade from the previous year's playoffs and averaged a **career-high 37.1 points** per game to go along with **5.2 rebounds**, **4.6 assists**, **2.9 steals**, and **1.5 blocks** - and was named to the All-NBA First Team. He also scored **40** or more points **37 times** and became the first player since Wilt Chamberlain to score 3000 points in a season and the first player in NBA history to record 200 steals and 100 blocks in the same season. But for the second straight year though, the Bulls were swept by the Celtics in the first round of the playoffs.

The following season, Jordan had his second best scoring campaign of his career averaging **35 points** per game, **5.9 assists**, **5.5 rebounds**, and a **career-high 3.2 steals**, on **53.5 percent** shooting. He also won his first MVP award and the Defensive Player of the Year award, becoming the first player to do so in the same season. In the 1988-89 campaign, Jordan had one of the greatest individual seasons in NBA history, in which I have ranked in the top five of all-time in the next chapter with Kareem. That season, he averaged a *gaudy* **32.5 points**, **8 rebounds**, **8 assists**, and **2.9 steals** per game - and shot **53.8 percent** from the field. He also averaged **34.8 points**, **7.6 assists**, and **7 rebounds** in seventeen playoff games as the Bulls made it all the way to the Eastern Conference Finals. This was also the postseason; Jordan hit the "famous shot" over Craig Ehlo at the buzzer to win the decisive game five in the first round of the 1989 playoffs that eliminated the Cleveland Cavaliers. The *indelible fist pumps by Jordan* that is still fresh in our minds today, gives us goose bumps every time we think about it!

The season after, Jordan had another stellar year averaging **33.6 points** per game and led the league in steals for the second time at 2.8 while leading the Bulls to a 55-27 record. That season, he also had a **career-high 69 points**, to go along with 18 rebounds, 6 assists, and four steals on March 28th, 1990 in Cleveland. In the playoffs, he *rocked the universe* once again averaging **36.7 points**, **7.2 rebounds** and **6.8 assists** per game, but the Bulls were eliminated once again by the Pistons in the conference finals. Two *notables,* over 4 of Jordan's greatest individual seasons statistically from 1987 to 1990, he lost to the Pistons three straight years in five games, six games, and seven games with the last two coming in the Eastern Conference Finals. Magic Johnson also won three of the four MVP awards during that same time frame. By that point, Jordan was on the brink of winning his first NBA championship and could have easily won an additional MVP award over Magic the last two seasons. Year after year in the playoffs and in the conference finals, Jordan and the Bulls kept losing to either the Celtics or Pistons, where it seemed like Jordan would never get over the hump to win an NBA Championship - kind of reminiscent to LeBron James for eight seasons. But after 7 years in the league, at 28 years old, Jordan finally won the 1991 NBA Championship over the powerhouse team in the Western Conference, the 1980s Los Angeles Lakers. Even though the Bulls lost game one, they came back strong and *thumped* L.A. in 4 straight games to win the series rather easily in five games. Following the Lakers closely at that time, hoping for Magic to win his 6th championship to tie Bob Cousy, it felt going in and throughout the series, that the aging Lakers were completely outclassed by the young and athletic legs of the Chicago Bulls.

In the 1992 Championship season, Jordan won his second consecutive MVP award and third overall. After improving their win total from 61 to 67 games, the Bulls had little *resistance* during their return to the NBA Finals. In what looked like a terrific matchup with the Portland Trail Blazers and their star Clyde Drexler, ended up not really being the matchup everyone anticipated, as Jordan put a stamp on game one with 6 three-pointers in the first half to set the stage for Portland's demise. The same thing happened the following season against Charles Barkley, Kevin Johnson, and the rest of the Phoenix Suns in the 1993 NBA Finals. To begin the series, the Suns put themselves in an even direr situation than Portland did the year before, by losing the first two games at home to all but put an end to the series. The odds of coming back in any playoff series let alone the NBA Finals down 2-0, is *slim to none*. Even though the Suns fought back hard, they never had control of the series after losing the first two games and then falling behind three games to one, before eventually winning game five and forcing a game six back in Phoenix. In the six games, Jordan *dominated*, scoring at least 30 points including four straight games of 42, 44, 55, and 41 points.

After winning back-to-back-to-back NBA Championships in 1991, 1992, and 1993, Jordan retired to play baseball. During the Bulls championship run, they won 61, 67, and 57 games. But, after an unsuccessful attempt to make the Major Leagues with the Chicago White Sox organization, Jordan returned to the NBA in 1995, late in the season, where he played in only the last 17 regular season games but played in the postseason. In the playoffs, the Bulls were not able to return to championship form in time and were eliminated by the Orlando Magic in the conference semifinals in six games. The following year, the Bulls were back on stride and finished off a three-peat as champions once again in 1996, 1997, and 1998. In those three seasons, they won 72, 69, and 62 games. At that point and even today, most people feel Jordan would have won 8 straight championships if he hadn't retired. But let's be realistic and fair to Hakeem Olajuwon and say he could have won, perhaps 7 out of 8 titles. Look at Shaq and Kobe, who were only able to win a total of 3 championships playing together, on paper; they looked like they were the better dual over Jordan and Pippen.

In Jordan's first three championship seasons from 1991 to 1993, he averaged 31.4 points, 6.4 rebounds, 5.7 assists, 2.6 steals, and 0.9 blocks per game, and won the scoring title all three years. He also won back-to-back MVP awards giving him a total of three for his career. And in the playoffs, he stepped up his game even further as only he could, and averaged 33.7 points, 6.6 assists, and 6.4 rebounds. The first half of his career before the retirement, Jordan shot 51.6 percent from the field, simply because he did more at attacking the basket rather than settling for jump shots, something I wished Kobe Bryant had done most of his career.

In player comparisons:

If you look at all the greats of the game ahead of Kobe in the elite rankings of all-time, almost all shoot a better percentage from the field with most players hovering around 50 percent. Even with Jordan becoming more of jump shooter the second half of his career, he still shot 47.7 percent from the field (not including his last two seasons at 39 and 40 years old with the Washington Wizards), tied with Jerry West and ahead of Bryant, Elgin Baylor, and Rick Barry. In his second stint during his championship seasons from 1996 to 1998, Jordan averaged 29.6 points, 6.1 rebounds, four assists, and 1.9 steals per game, and shot 48.2 percent from the field. He also won the scoring title all three years giving him a total of 10, and two more MVP awards giving him a total of 5 for his *astronomical* career. Despite Jordan no longer in his prime years, he still elevated his game in the playoffs averaging 31.4 points, 6 rebounds, and 4.1 assists in his final championship run.

Of note: Jordan did lose something, the Slam Dunk Contest his rookie year to Dominique Wilkins that nobody seems to remember. He averaged an astonishing 28 points as a rookie in 1985 before breaking his foot in his second season, missing a total of 64 games.

What separates Jordan from others during his time was his *extreme will to win* rivaled by no other. He and Scottie Pippen teamed up to form one of the greatest duals of All-time. Although, while Jordan may have been the greatest player of all-time, *as a dual* with Pippen, I have them finishing second behind Jerry West and Elgin Baylor, and potentially third behind LeBron James and Dwyane Wade. In Jordan's third season in the league in 1987, he averaged 37 points a game, more than any other player since Wilt Chamberlain's 44 points in 1963. In 1988, Jordan won his first MVP award and his only Defensive Player of The Year award in the same season before going on to win four more MVP's in 1991, 1992, 1996, and 1998. In the eyes of many, Jordan could have easily won the award six or seven times. A lot of times the MVP award voting, appears to be measured with more emphasis on what a player meant to his team rather than his individual statistical accomplishments that contributed to team success, such as in the case with Derrick Rose winning MVP award over LeBron James in 2010. I think most people thought Michael Jordan was in the same scenario when Charles Barkley and Karl Malone won their MVP Awards during the 1990s. Also, Jordan wasn't winning many MVP awards earlier in his career because Magic Johnson won three in 1987, 1989, and 1990 while posting great offensive numbers, and with his team finishing at the top of the standings.

MVP voting criteria:

In my opinion (as a great deal of the MVP results have went) the MVP should be given to the best player statistically for that one particular season playing for a top 4 or 5 team contending to win a championship. So for example, the Chicago Bulls finished the 2011 season with the best record in the Eastern Conference and the Miami Heat finished second but Derrick Rose won the award in a *landslide*. My belief that LeBron was the MVP over Rose was partially proven in 2012 when the Bulls were ultimately successful without him in the lineup - where he missed a great portion of the season. So Chicago's winning percentage was just as good without Rose as compared to with him. In fact, many experts are rethinking their original assessment and value of Rose winning the MVP from the previous season. LeBron had the best statistics out of the two by far even though playing with *two other* All-Stars. And, for those who think LeBron should be discounted for playing with two other all-stars, please do not! Larry Bird won three MVP awards playing with Robert Parish and Kevin McHale and Magic Johnson also won two MVP's playing with Kareem Abdul-Jabbar, and one more with just James Worthy.

I think the way the MVP is being selected in the minds of the voters has changed drastically once again over the last twenty years or so. Rose was clearly surpassed statistically by LeBron in 3 out of 4 major categories (tied for blocks per game), and in efficiency rating on Espn.com and NBA.com but the voters picked Rose for MVP *primarily* because he meant more to his team. He also shot a paltry 44.5 percent (lowest for an MVP winner since Iverson in 2001) from the field. For those of you who want to include his 50 or so last second shots at the end of quarters that the Chicago media claims lowered his shooting percentage, I already did. It only raised his field goal percentage from 44.5 percent to 46 percent which is still one of the lowest outputs ever for an MVP winner. He did shoot well from the free-throw line and from three-point range, and it is also understandable, *to some extent,* that his team had very few other scoring options. If Miami wasn't a top 4 team, let alone a top 2 team (the Heat had the second best record in the Eastern Conference with 58 wins, third overall behind the Bulls and Spurs) in 2010, than Rose definitely should have won the award. I believe the decisions were made by the voters long before the season ended, all but eliminating LeBron due to *his poor decision* in the off-season, blindsiding the Cleveland Cavaliers as he departed from his former team. LeBron easily could have won three straight MVP awards or should I say five straight including the last two MVP seasons.

Here are the stat comparisons for LeBron James vs. Derrick Rose for 2010-11:

LeBron: 26.7 pts, 7.5 rebs, 7.0 assists, 1.6 steals, .06 blocks, .510 FG%, .759 FT%, 33% 3PT

Rose: 25.0 pts, 3.9 rebs, 7.7 assists, 1.0 steals, .06 blocks, .445 FG%, .858 FT%, .33% 3PT

Chicago finished with the most wins in the NBA with 62 and Miami finished second in the conference with 58.

Here are the stat comparisons for Michael Jordan vs. Charles Barkley vs. Hakeem Olajuwon for 1992-93:

Jordan: 32.6 pts, 6.7 rebs, 5.3 assists, 1.9 steals, .08 blocks, .495 FG%, .837 FT%

Barkley 25.6 pts, 12.2 rebs, 5.1 assists, 1.6 steals, 1.0 block, .520 FG%, .765 FT%

Olajuwon: 26.1 pts, 13.0 rebs, 3.5 assists, 1.8 steals, 4.2 blocks, .529 FG%, .779 FT%

Phoenix finished with 62 wins, Chicago with 57, and Houston with 55.

As you can see the wins for Jordan combined with his overall numbers in two of the three major categories that increased from his previous MVP season's (see below), justify that he could have easily won the MVP award over Barkley just as LeBron could have over Rose. However, in 1997 the year Malone won the award over Jordan, I have it going either way as detailed in Malone's chapter.

Just like LeBron, Jordan was coming off back-to-back MVP seasons, and most likely in the eyes of the voters, especially in this day and age - with all the parity they have for all individuals, would most likely shy away from awarding the honor three years in a row. I would really be surprised if it happened any time soon. Here's a look at Jordan's and LeBron's MVP seasons compared to the *snub* season up above:

1991 and 1992

Jordan: 31.5 points, 6.0 rebs, 5.5 assists, 2.7 steals, 1.0 block, .539 FG, .851 FT, .31 3FG

30.1 points, 6.4 rebs, 6.1 assists, 2.3 steals, 0.9 blocks, .519 FG, .832 FT, .27 3FG

2009 and 2010

LeBron: 28.4 points, 7.6 rebs, 7.2 assists, 1.7 steals, 1.1 blocks, .489 FG, .780 FT .34 3FG

29.7 points, 7.3 rebs, 8.6 assists, 1.6 steals, 1.0 block, .503 FG, .767 FT, .33 3FG

For those of you who might not agree with the projected rankings of LeBron James as I have already mentioned in the intro and again in LeBron's chapter at the end of the book, even these stats above are in favor Jordan. In the next six seasons of his prime, LeBron would have to average near or maybe even above his own MVP numbers, and win a few championships before even being included in the conversation with Jordan as the greatest player ever.

Another example of the MVP voting: take Shaquille O'Neal or Kobe Bryant. A lot of the media and especially fans believe absurdly that these two players in their prime should have won the MVP award every year. This is totally preposterous for both facts: First of all if a player doesn't play the full season for whatever reason including injury, and plays lets say less than 70 games, usually (although Bill Walton in 1978 was one of the few exceptions) doesn't deserve to win the award vs. someone who put up better, equal or even near equal statistics for a full season. Second, if a player has a better or equal year statistically playing on a top 4 or 5 team in contention to win a championship, that player deserves the MVP for that one particular season over perennial greats like Bryant who put up his best statistical seasons when the Lakers finished a little above .500, with 45 and 42 wins. I believe, Dirk Nowitzki in 2007 had better statistics (by far efficiently wise) over Kobe, and had the best team in the league compared to Bryant's team at barely over .500. The only thing Kobe did significantly more of that season was in the scoring department but he did it with *less efficiency*. A lot of people thought he should have won the MVP that year including a lot of prominent sports writers and publicists for basketball, but the voters got it right in voting for Dirk.

So theoretically a player could be the best player every year, *in one's eyes*, or at least from a talent perspective, and not win a single MVP if he is not the best player for that one particular season statistically playing for a top four or five team in contention to win a championship. This is partly why Shaq and Kobe only have one career MVP each. So you ask, well why didn't the Diesel and the Black Mamba win multiple MVP awards during their championship run? Because, around that time, Iverson was torching the league with his four scoring titles while winning MVP in 2001 and Tim Duncan and Kevin Garnett were establishing themselves among the greatest power forwards of all-time (not only with their offensive game but their defensive, accumulating peak numbers in rebounding and blocked shots), winning three MVP awards from 2002 through 2004. Duncan and Garnett were a slight drop behind Shaq and Kobe in the scoring department, but had by far, the better defensive contributions in rebounding and in blocked shots. Even Garnett could come close to matching Kobe with his assists totals playing with the Minnesota Timberwolves where he averaged at least five assists from 2000 to 2005, including an *unbelievable* 6 assists in 2003. Finally, Steve Nash won the other two MVP awards in 2005 and 2006 because he single-handedly changed the identity of the Phoenix Suns and made his teammates better than anyone since Magic Johnson (or perhaps Jason Kidd). He led the league in assists in both seasons, *combined* record breaking efficiency numbers in field goal, free-throw and three-point percentage, and with his playmaking skills, elevated his teammates to a level rarely seen before while propelling the Phoenix Suns to the top of the Western Conference - and then came LeBron James!

Here are some of Jordan's astronomical statistical achievements: He has the highest career scoring average of **30.1 points** along with Chamberlain in NBA history. During his record setting (tying) 7 consecutive scoring titles from 1987 to 1993, he scored at least 30 points every season and averaged an incredible **33.2 points** per game on **.518** shooting. During that same span in the playoffs, he averaged an even more impressive **34.6 points** per game on **50 percent** shooting. With those types of numbers, it is no surprise; he has the highest career scoring average in the playoffs of **33.4 points** per game in NBA history. Jordan has won 5 league MVP awards and has made the All-NBA 1st Team 10 times and a league record 9 All-NBA Defensive 1st Teams. He won the **scoring title a record 10 times** while averaging over 30 points a game in 8 of those seasons, while winning 3 steals titles. What was equally impressive in which many people probably didn't realize, is that Jordan also led the league in points per game in the playoffs 10 times and averaged **30 points or more 12 times**. He won 6 NBA Championships and 6 Finals MVP awards in such a short career and retiring twice. In those Finals games he scored at least **30 points 23 times, 40 points 6 times, and 50 points** just the one time. Also, none of the other 4 players who accomplished the 50-point feat in the Finals did it more than once.

Outside of perhaps Wilt Chamberlain, nobody in NBA history posted greater scoring feats than Michael Jordan: This *lethal* scorer owns the NBA record for **30-point** games in the regular season with **562** and in the playoffs with **109**. He also had **173 career 40-point** games and **31 50-point** games in the regular season. In addition, he had **4 60-point** games in the regular and a record **8 50-point** games in the playoffs that included a single game record of **63** that came against the Boston Celtics in 1986. But his greatest feat of all might have been his *untouchable* record **38 career 40-point** games in the postseason. The next closest player on the all-time list is Jerry West at 20, and then other players including Kobe who trails by a large margin at 12, followed by LeBron at 11. Michael had more *combined* scoring accomplishments in the regular and in the postseason than any player in history. I'm sure he is in almost everyone's book, the greatest player to have ever played the game, and no player today with the possible exception of LeBron James will ever come anywhere close to what Michael Jordan accomplished throughout his career (in overall individual accomplishments combined with team success). In the elite rankings of all-time, who else would be ranked number one other than "His Airness?" Michael was simply the Greatest!

Career Totals

30.1 points, 6.2 rebs, 5.3 assists, 2.3 steals, 0.8 blocks, .497 FG%, .327 3FG%, .835 FT%

32,292 points, 6673 rebounds, 5633 assists, 2514 steals, 893 blocks, 581 threes

Kareem Abdul-Jabbar

(Rank #2)

MVP (6-times), Scoring Title (2-times), Rebounding Title (1-time)

Blocked Shots Title (4-times), All-NBA First Team (10-times)

All-Defensive First Team (5-times), All-Star (19-times)

NBA Championships (6), Finals MVP (2-times)

NBA Record: 38,387 career points

Also featuring:
Bob McAdoo

    Kareem Abdul-Jabbar could have been the greatest center of all-time. In twenty seasons with the Milwaukee Bucks and Los Angeles Lakers, Abdul-Jabbar won 6 NBA Championships and 6 NBA MVP awards, was named to 19 All-Star teams and finished his career as the NBA's All-Time leading scorer. At a towering 7-feet-2 inches tall, his sky-hook was the *deadliest* shot in NBA history. Growing up as a kid, we all knew who Kareem Abdul-Jabbar was probably for a lot of different reasons. For one, he always wore those famous goggles for protection, and two; his name was easily recognizable after changing his name from Lew Alcindor after his second season in the league, like when Cassius Clay changed his name to Muhammad Ali because of their Islam faith, and three; he had the most identifiable shot in history: the "Sky-hook." Like Michael Jordan, Kareem was something special. In his first six seasons with the Bucks, Kareem more than lived up to all the hype - since back to his high school days in New York City and in college at UCLA. Like Chamberlain, Kareem was ultimately dominant and had his best individual years during his first eleven seasons (six with Milwaukee and five with Los Angeles). During that period, he won an *unprecedented* six MVP awards that no one including Jordan has ever achieved. He also won more NBA Championships than most players in history not wearing a Celtics uniform, and won two Finals MVP awards during his career.

Kareem's signature shot, the Sky-hook, was legendary. Even to this day it has not been close to being *duplicated* (Kareem shot the sky-hook with full range of motion and with maximum extension releasing the ball at the tips of his fingers, and with more grace than anyone in history). The only hook shot in recent memory that makes it halfway to legitimacy is Magic Johnson's junior sky-hook or running hook. Every player that has used the hook shot over the years was actually shooting a swinging hook, running hook, jump hook usually off two feet or a push shot with half the motion. Ask any basketball fan today what stands out most about Kareem Abdul-Jabbar and they will usually mention one or two things: Kareem's the guy with the sky-hook and, or that he is the NBA's all-time leading scorer at 38,387 points.

The Sky-hook was the most *dependable* and *unblockable* shot in league history. Kareem could shoot it in the post position from either side of the court. With his back to the basket, he would either catch and shoot, catch and then take a couple dribbles before shooting, catch then take one dribble right and then left again before shooting, or post up on either block, drop step or fake right before shooting. To balance off his arsenal, he would occasionally shoot a jump shot with the same moves and positioning as his sky-hook or simply shoot a jump shot over an opponent facing the basket. And what might be most impressive is that at times, he would shoot the hook shot with the opposite hand. On the defensive end with his length and agility, Kareem was a formidable rebounder and shot blocker able to amass 17,440 rebounds and 3,189 blocks for his career which ranks third all-time in both categories. He could possibly have been number one on the career blocked shots list over Hakeem Olajuwon but shot blocking did not become an official stat until the 1973-74 season, his fifth year in the league. He was also a great passer out of the post and as an outlet passer to start the *Fast break*. Kareem has said he emulated the passing skills of Hall of Fame great Bill Russell.

Actually as a kid growing up, most of us thought the greatest player of all-time was either Kareem or Wilt Chamberlain, until Michael Jordan started assaulting the league with his 10 scoring titles during the late 1980s and early 1990s.

In player comparisons:

Dr. J once said, "In my opinion, Kareem Abdul-Jabbar was the greatest player to play professional basketball." If Kareem is ranked second in this book and third in Bill Simmons' (claims to be the most knowledgeable basketball expert) "The Book of Basketball," than he must be the greatest Laker of All-time or at least the greatest to *put on* a Lakers uniform. Kareem and Jordan combined the most individual success (statistics combined with regular and postseason awards and honors) and team success than anyone in history. Kareem's all-time statistics, honors, awards, intangibles for playing the game, and championships help prove that Kareem was better than Wilt Chamberlain and Bill Russell.

Ranking these two at the top of the list for all-time greats was made a little easier, at least for now (LeBron who just turned 28 still has the potential to get to #2), after reading what Kareem said in a letter about the flaws and lack of team concept of Wilt Chamberlain during his playing days. It reminded me of what was written by Bill Simmons' in his book about quotes from old-timers of the past believing that Russell was better than Wilt. Here are some of the things Kareem wrote in his letter from the book "Kareem" in response to all the aspersions and criticisms he took from Wilt throughout the years:

Kareem could not understand why Wilt was so jealous of him throughout the years with all Wilt's scoring records including his 100-point game, and two dominant seasons winning NBA Championships, with a 68-13 record playing for the Philadelphia 76ers and 69-13 Los Angeles Lakers team - that set a then record for wins including the still unbreakable record winning streak of 33 consecutive games in 1972. Wilt's Lakers also beat Kareem's Bucks in the Western Conference Finals in 6 games. After thinking it through Kareem mentions a plethora of reasons why Wilt must have been so jealous. He also mentions how frustrated Wilt was when he couldn't win the NCAA Championship playing with the University of Kansas - that ended up going into triple overtime and then afterwards, how he complained about the officiating, his teammates, and other things, and then quit, leaving college early to tour with the Harlem Globe Trotters to make his fortune. Kareem continued on and wrote the following to Wilt;

* After any tough test in which you didn't do well, you blamed those around you and quit. People who knew sports would wonder why someone with your talents could not provide the leadership to get to the top. An answer was never forthcoming.

Your personal career was marked by the same kind of pattern. Bill Russell and the Boston Celtics gave to you a yearly lesson in real competitive competence and teamwork. All you could say was that your teammates stunk and that you had done all that you could, and besides, the refs never gave you a break. Poor Wilt. You got all these rebounds and scored all these points and you were stuck with worthless teammates. What a shame! You had definitely outclassed the other centers in the league. But it doesn't surprise many people, considering that none of them were seven feet tall or agile enough to give you much competition - a twelve foot three–second lane was also a big help to you when you were establishing your scoring records. You didn't do very well against the Celts, which usually ended in frustration and loss.

In 1967, your team finally broke through, and in a real big way. That 76ers team established records that are still standing today. But the following year, things got tough the

76ers lost and, predictable as ever, you quit. You came out to L.A. and got with a dream team. No lack of talent there, with Jerry West and Elgin Baylor. The only lack that team had been leadership at the center position. Bill and the Celtics took one from you in '69 and the Knicks followed suit in '70. People are still trying to figure out where you disappeared to in that series. All that was necessary for a Laker victory was one win against a team who's injured starting center, Willis Reed, could not move. But Willis could still come out and compete and inspire his teammates. Yes the Knicks won with Dave Stallworth, six-seven and 200 pounds, and Nate Bowman, six ten and 215, playing most of the game at center. In that game you were a nonentity.

The same teams played for the world championship in 1973, and that time the Knicks didn't have any center! Jerry Lucas, six eight and 230, played high-post center that year. He was always considered a forward but he had enough guts and smarts to outplay you consistently. Yes, Wilt, we know you got umpteen rebounds per game, but no one really cares about those stats. The only significant stat is the New York Knicks's world championship. I guess that was the final straw for you because, true to form, you quit after that season and haven't been seen on the court since.

Of course, you come out every so often to take a cheap shot at me, and in those statements one can find the roots of your animosity. Somewhere, you must of thought I was personally trying to embarrass you. This was never the case. I only took advantage of your shortcomings, which you are still not aware of. When you were entertaining pipe dreams about fighting Muhammad Ali, he set the record straight on your attributes, saying to me, "Wilt can't talk, he ugly, and he can't move!" This says it all. So when I dropped those fifty points on you at the Forum it was not a personal attack. I was just taking advantage of your weak defensive skills to try to help my team win. By not admitting to any faults, it has been impossible for you to see how your play was missing necessary ingredients. You criticized people like George Mikan and Danny Manning in truly ridiculous ways, saying that your stats are so great compared to theirs. One thing they can point to is their leadership at times. They are winners. George Mikan is the man who had the pride and determination to show that big men could be great athletes. All of us big men should thank him for that. I know I do. But I digress. *

*Excerpt: from the book Kareem

Man, what a harsh letter by Kareem. Every hardcore fan should dig through the archives online to locate the 1989 book "Kareem" and read the full five page thrashing he gave to Wilt. I thought Bill Simmons was tough on Wilt; he now looks like a *saint* after the obliteration written by Kareem. I included the best portions of the letter to help prove that Kareem was better than Wilt particularly from the mental aspect of the game and intangibly, but at the same time hurts the debate I have in favor of Wilt over Russell. I agree with most of what was written by Kareem, except for when he said he dropped 50 on a far less dominate Wilt at the end of his career and the partial irrelevant and erroneous "ugly and he can't move" quotes by Ali. In fairness to Wilt, I mention in the next chapter, that in his prime, he could run circles around Shaq and would match up quite well if he played in his prime with Kareem. "Nevertheless, I am still in favor of Wilt being among the top 3 players of all-time," so much that I have flip-flopped him with Kareem over the years at #2 and #3 behind Jordan respectively. In a few more years, it might not even matter because I have LeBron James as the projected #2 in this book.

Kareem was born as Ferdinand Lewis Alcindor Jr. on April 16th, 1947 in New York City, New York and was drafted in the first round 1st pick overall of the 1969 NBA Draft by the Milwaukee Bucks. The young Alcindor grew up in Manhattan playing street ball while watching Earl Monroe dominate the playgrounds. Alcindor's high school team, Power Memorial Academy won three consecutive New York City Catholic championships, while going 79 and 2 including a winning streak of 71 straight games. Either Kareem or Bill Walton according to most basketball experts was the greatest player to ever play college basketball. After sitting out his first year at UCLA because the NCAA prevented freshman from playing at the varsity level, Lew Alcindor won 3 consecutive NCAA Championships and was honored as the Most Outstanding Player in the NCAA tournament 3 times from 1967 to 1969. He was also the inaugural winner of 1969 Naismith College Player of the Year award and was a two-time College Player of the Year in both 1967 and 1969. Elvin Hayes won the award over Alcindor in 1968. He was also selected First Team All-America in 1967, 1968, and 1969. As a testament to his *utter dominance*, college basket banned dunking after the 1967 season primary because of Alcindor, and it was not allowed again until 1976. Alcindor owns a lot of UCLA school records including career scoring average at 26.4 points per game, scoring average for a season at 29 points per game, and for a single game with 61 points.

In his rookie season, Lew Alcindor averaged **28.8 points**, **14.5 rebounds**, and **4.1 assists** - and **35.2 points**, **16.8 rebounds**, and **4.1 assists** in the playoffs, and of course won the Rookie of the Year Award. The Milwaukee Bucks finished with a 55-26 record and made it all the way to Eastern Finals where they would lose to the eventual champion New York Knicks. By his second season, Alcindor increased his offensive production mightily averaging **31.7 points** and **16 rebounds** and won his 1st NBA Championship in 1971 playing alongside newly acquired Oscar Robertson. After finishing with a record of 66-16 including a then record 20-game winning streak, the Bucks beat a Los Angeles Lakers team without Jerry West in the Western Finals and swept the Baltimore Bullets in four games to win the title. In only his second and third season in the league, Kareem won the scoring title and the NBA MVP award back-to-back becoming the youngest in NBA history to do so. In 1973, Kareem averaged **30.2 points**, **16.1 rebounds** and **5 assists**, but the Bucks were upset in the first round of the playoffs in six games to the Golden State Warriors. But, Milwaukee bounced back the following year and made it all the way to the NBA Finals in 1974 where they would eventually lose in heartbreaking fashion in seven games. Kareem was spectacular once again particularly in game 7 of the Finals and throughout the playoffs where he averaged an astounding **32.2 points**, **15.8 rebounds**, and **4.9 assists**. He also won his third MVP award in five years. With an aging Robertson and little help from his supporting cast, the Bucks never won another title and missed the playoffs entirely in 1975. Kareem did post one of the best games of his career in the regular season, a 50-point triple-double of **50 points, 15 rebounds and 11 assists**. At the time, apparently Abdul-Jabbar wanted out of Milwaukee mainly because he felt there were a lack of people who shared his religious and cultural views. The teamed obliged and traded him to the Los Angeles Lakers before the 1975-76 season. The Lakers missed the playoffs that year marking the only time Kareem missed the postseason in his Los Angeles career.

In 1976-77, Abdul-Jabbar won back-to-back MVP's for the second time in his career after leading the Lakers to respectability in his first of three seasons with Jerry West at the helm. Under West, the Lakers never made it back to the NBA Finals. In 1979, the Lakers drafted highly touted Earvin "Magic" Johnson out of Michigan State who was fresh off an NCAA Championship. With Kareem winning his 6th and final regular season MVP award and Magic Johnson blossoming in the playoffs his rookie year, the Lakers went on to win their first of 5 NBA Championships during the 1980s. The Lakers won the 1982 NBA Championship over the Philadelphia 76ers before losing to them the following year (At that point, the Lakers had drafted young *phenom* James Worthy out of North Carolina with their number one pick). They also had acquired **Bob McAdoo** before the start of the 1981-82 season to help bolster the frontcourt. While Worthy went on to become one of the greatest small forwards of all-time, McAdoo already was one of the great power forward/centers that was an established nine-year veteran, but was on the down side of his career.

In other player comparisons:

In my opinion, after the NBA/ABA merger from a *statistical* standpoint, McAdoo ranks right up there with Kareem in individual accolades during the 1970s. No other two players during that time posted better offensive numbers. Was he the best? Certainly not because every *superstar* who played for the New York Knicks and Boston Celtics had by far, more team success and won multiple championships. He didn't win 5 MVP awards in the decade like Kareem but he won one in 1975 and was runner-up the season before and the season after. He also was one of the few men in NBA history to win the scoring title three consecutive years from 1974 to 1976. If you sit back and look at his stats, he posted some of the best numbers in history during a six-year period from the 1974 to 1979 season averaging 29.1 points, 12.8 rebounds, three assists, and two blocks per game, on 51.6 percent shooting. In close comparisons over the same period, Kareem averaged 26.7 points, 14 rebounds, 4.6 assists, and 3.5 blocks per game, on 54.6 percent shooting. But if you take Kareem's best six years of his career which happened to be his first six in the league, he was even better averaging a Chamberlain/Jordan like **30.4 points, 15.3 rebounds**, 4.3 assists, and **3.4 blocks** per game, and shot **54.7 percent** from the field. Even though McAdoo did not make the Top 50 player rankings, I just wanted to *accentuate* his greatness as one of the league's great scorers even though he did play during the time the league was watered down - and had very little playoff success until he came to the Lakers for the 1981-82 season. Another drawback in comparisons to not only Kareem, but any other superstar, is that he was selected to only one All-NBA First Team and one All-NBA Second Team in his entire career. In terms of statistics vs. wins and losses, he was perhaps the Tracy McGrady at the power forward position during his time.

In addition, if you compared Kareem's best three seasons, two pre-dating McAdoo's arrival into the league vs. McAdoo's best three seasons the years he won the scoring titles, it gets even better for Kareem: McAdoo averaged 32.1 points, 13.8 rebounds and 2.8 assists, on 51 percent shooting and Kareem averaged **32.3 points**, **16.2 rebounds** and **4.3 assists** per game, on **57 percent** shooting as they didn't keep track of blocks during his first four seasons, which would have put him way over the top of McAdoo and over almost everyone else before or after.

In my opinion, Kareem had one of if not the best statistical seasons for a center or any player in history. Here are six *great noteworthy* seasons of some of the top NBA players of all-time:

Oscar: 1961-62   30.8 points, 12.5 rebounds, 11.4 assists, 47.8 FG%, 80.3 FT%

Wilt: 1961-62   50.4 points, 25.7 rebounds, 2.4 assists, 50.6 FG%, 61.3 FT%

Kareem: 1971-72   34.8 points, 16.6 rebounds, 4.6 assists, 57.4 FG%, .68.9 FT%

Bird: 1986-87   28.1 points, 9.2 rebounds, 7.6 assists, 52.5 FG%, 91 FT%

Jordan: 1988-89   32.5 points, 8.0 rebounds, 8.0 assists, 53.8 FG%, 85 FT%

LeBron: 2009-10   29.7 points, 7.3 rebounds, 8.6 assists, 50.3 FG%, 76.7 FT%

Kareem's season may have been the best in history even over Chamberlain's and Oscar's considering partly that they played more minutes per game and in an era of inflated offensive possessions. The bottom half, you can take your pick, but I am going with Jordan, LeBron, and then Bird. In McAdoo's MVP season in 1974-75, he averaged **34.5 and 14.1 rebounds**, on **51 percent** shooting but only averaged 2.2 assists per game. The year prior, he averaged a career-high 3.3 blocks and the year after he averaged a career-high 4 assists per game. If he had combined all of those numbers in one season, he would have had one of the 5 or 6 greatest seasons in NBA history.

McAdoo was one of the best scoring big men to play in the NBA. He was the old school/new school version of what we see in the NBA today with players like Nowitzki, Garnett, and Chris Webber of a few years back who could shoot proficiently from the perimeter and take their man off the dribble with their speed and quickness. Within his repertoire, McAdoo was an outstanding rebounder, formidable shot blocker, and a splendid passer. Born on September 25, 1951 in Greensboro, North Carolina, Robert Allen McAdoo Jr. attended Ben L. Smith High School in Greensboro. After two years at Vincennes Junior College, he went on to the University of North Carolina where he averaged 19.5 points and 10.1 rebounds per game, on 51.6 percent shooting. After one year at North Carolina, he was then selected with the 2nd pick overall of the 1972 NBA Draft by the Buffalo Braves. In only his second season in the NBA, McAdoo averaged **30.6 points** per game and had a **career-high 15.1 rebounds**, **3.3 blocks**, and shot 54.7 percent from the field - and was named to the All-Star team for the first of five consecutive seasons. He also won his first of three consecutive scoring titles. In his MVP season in 1975, he was named to his first and only All-NBA First Team. The following season, he capped off one of the best three-year runs in NBA history averaging **31.1 points**, **12.4 rebounds**, and **4 assists** per game.

In his first six seasons, including the last with the New York Knicks, McAdoo never made it past the second round of the playoffs. In the 1974 playoffs, the Braves lost to the eventually champion Boston Celtics in six games. In that series, McAdoo did his part averaging **31.7 points** and **13.7 rebounds** per game. In the 1975 playoffs, he averaged an incredible **37.4 points** per game and **13.4 rebounds**, but the Braves lost to Elvin Hayes, Wes Unseld and the eventual Eastern Conference champion Washington Bullets in a hard-fought seven-game series. In 1978, the Knicks were swept by the Philadelphia 76ers in the semifinals. McAdoo played for five different teams after the ABA/NBA merger but had very little playoff success until he was acquired by the Los Angeles Lakers during the 1981-82 season. McAdoo now on the downside of his career, was still a formidable player and scorer that backed up Kareem for four seasons, helping the Lakers to two NBA Championships. In the 1982 postseason, he came up big in the Western Conference Finals against the San Antonio Spurs in the decisive game, when he scored 26 points on 12 of 16 shooting. And in game five of the Finals against the 76ers, he contributed 23 points on 11 of 14 shots and had 5 blocks. So "Big Mac" at the end of his career, sacrificed his scoring to some degree and was still productive winning 2 championships. Even though he didn't make my top 50 players of all-time, Bob McAdoo will forever be remembered as one of the great scoring big men of all-time.

After losing a heartbreaking seven-game series to the Boston Celtics in 1984, in which the Lakers felt they should of won, by way of some bad inbounding plays near the end of game three that could have put them up 3 games to 1, the Lakers took avenge the following year winning the 1985 NBA Championship and their first against the Celtics in franchise history. Kareem was named Finals MVP at the age of 38. Even though the Celtics won the championship in 1986 against the Houston Rockets with one of the best teams in NBA history, the Lakers recaptured the throne for the 2nd time in three years to win their fourth championship of the decade. They went on to repeat as champion in 1988, becoming the first team since Boston in 1968-69 to do so. Kareem retired after the 1989 season with every team in every city giving their thanks and appreciation showering him with many gifts including a new Rolls Royce by all his teammates.

Kareem is the NBA's All-Time leading scorer at over 38,000 career points, 3rd in rebounding with over 17,000 rebounds, and accumulated over 5000 assists and 3000 blocked shots while be selected to the All-Star team 19 times. He won 6 NBA Championships and was the ultimate winner like his teammate Magic Johnson, and Celtics' Bill Russell. Even when he wasn't winning championships, his teams were ultimately competitive reaching an astounding 10 NBA Finals, and 14 Conference Finals, and his teams averaged 56 wins per season. He was also one of the most durable players in history missing only 80 games in 20 seasons and playing in at least 80 games in eleven seasons. He won league MVP a record 6 times with three coming with the Milwaukee Bucks and three with the Los Angeles Lakers. Kareem had 5 MVP awards before Magic entered the league and won his 6th and final MVP Magic's rookie season. During this time as a young Kareem and Lew Alcindor, he was a young, agile and athletic superstar as compared to what many young fans witnessed the latter half of his career. He also won the Finals MVP in 1971 and 1985, 14 years apart, which is an NBA record between MVP awards by any player in history. His two Finals MVP awards do not begin to tell the story because he played good enough to have easily won three or more to have possibly given him a total of five. We can almost count the one in 1980 when he dominated the series including scoring 40 points in game five on an injured ankle, then missing the crucial game six where Magic had the monster performance playing in his place. And he was easily the best player against the Celtics in the 1974 and 1984 Finals where his teams lost both times in heartbreaking seven games.

As I have already mentioned in the chart previously, Kareem had one of or *perhaps* the best statistical season for a center in NBA history in 1971-72 when he averaged **34.8 points**, **16.6 rebounds**, and **4.6 assists** per game, on **57.4 percent** shooting. To go along with his scoring achievements, he had **10 50-point** games, **70 40-point** games, and **429 30-point** games in the regular season which ranks 4th all-time. He also had **75 30-point** games in his playoff career which is good for 3rd on the all-time list behind Michael Jordan and Kobe Bryant - and **9 consecutive 30-point** games in the playoffs which ranks second all-time to Elgin Baylor. Furthermore, he is ranked second in playoff games played, 2nd in total points scored (behind Jordan), and 3rd in rebounding (behind Wilt Chamberlain and Bill Russell). In addition to his two scoring titles in the regular season, Kareem led the league in points per game in the playoffs 5 times and in blocks per game 6 times. He also had games of 11 blocks 3 times in his career, 10 blocks 4 times, and 9 blocks 8 times. As the NBA's All-time leading scorer and with his record 19 All-Star selections and 6 MVP awards to go along with 6 NBA Championships, one could make the case that not Michael Jordan, but Kareem Abdul-Jabbar was the greatest basketball player of all-time!

Career Totals

24.6 points, 11.2 rebounds, 2.6 assists, 2.6 blocks, 0.9 steals, .559 FG%, 721 FT%

38,345 points, 17,440 rebounds, 5660 assists, 3189 blocks, 1160 steals

Wilt Chamberlain

(Rank #3)

MVP (4-times), Scoring Title (7-times), Assist Title (1-time)

Rebounding Title (11-times), All-NBA First Team (7-times)

Field Goal % Title (9-times), All-Defensive First Team (2-times)

NBA Championships (2), Finals MVP (1-time), All-Star (13-times)

NBA Record: 100 points in a game!, NBA Record: 55 rebounds in a game!

    Wilt Chamberlain was one of the greatest players and most dominant centers of all-time. During his fourteen-year career, Chamberlain amassed more scoring and rebounding records than any player in history including the great Michael Jordan and Bill Russell. An *unstoppable* offensive force with a *devastating* inside game, The "Goliath" was a towering seven-foot-one with incredible strength and agility, able to dwarf and man-handle opponents in the low post for points, rebounds, and on defense to block shots. As testament to his legendary strength, in one particular game, Chamberlain blocked Gus Johnson's dunk attempt so hard he dislocated his shoulder. With his *smooth* finger-roll, *deadly* fadeaway, and *superior* rebounding, nobody has ever dominated the regular season the way "Wilt the Stilt" did. As the most imposing human specimen and offensive force of his era, if not ever, Chamberlain set incomprehensible scoring and rebounding records including the most famous and most talked about record of all-time; On March 2nd, 1962 in a 169-147 Philadelphia Warriors victory over the New York Knickerbockers, he set an **NBA record scoring 100 points** that still stands today. He also averaged an unfathomable **50 points** per game that same season in 1962, including having had **63 games** of at least **40 points** and **45 games** of at least **50 points.** The following year in 1963, he was nearly as spectacular when he averaged **44 points** per game. And, for his career, he scored **70 points** or more **6 times**, **60 points** or more **32 times**, and had **118 50-point** games and **271 40-point** games - all NBA records that will almost surely never be broken. Not only was he the most prolific scorer of his generation, he was also the *King of Rebounds* finishing his career with an **NBA record 23,924** and a **record 11 Rebounding Titles**. In addition, he had **40 rebounds** in a game **15 times** during his career including an **NBA record 55 rebounds** in one game.

Growing up as a kid, everyone knew who Wilt Chamberlain was. Other than the current all-time scoring champion Kareem Abdul-Jabbar and Julius Erving, when someone mentioned old timers, most of the boasting among fans was Oscar Robertson, Elgin Baylor, and Wilt Chamberlain. It was obvious that these three goliaths brought more to the game (in terms of offensive athleticism) than anyone else including Bill Russell. While Baylor was the *original* high-flyer that people came out to see and Oscar was the *ultra-athletic* guard, Chamberlain was the *monster* in the middle that dominated basketball statistically for 14 seasons from 1959-60 to 1972-73. Many of us have always felt Wilt was the greatest center of the past as Kareem was of the present, in the same way we viewed Michael Jordan as the greatest wing man of today to Elgin Baylor of yesterday. I think this was a fair comparison. As the years have gone by, I have learned the history behind Chamberlain's achievements and have followed the debates (based on facts, stats, and player analysis) about who the greatest center of all-time was. And, I have it this way after following basketball exclusively over the last few decades: Kareem Abdul-Jabbar, Wilt Chamberlain, Bill Russell, Hakeem Olajuwon, and Shaquille O'Neal.

In player comparisons:

Chamberlain was better in the regular season statistically than Kareem, even though Kareem won 6 MVPs to Wilt's 4. Chamberlain played against less "overall" competition and smaller bodies than Kareem whereas two thirds of Kareem's MVP awards came during the time when some marquee players played the early part of their career in the spinoff league: American Basketball Association from 1967 to 1976. Chamberlain played against Bill Russell and Walt Bellamy during his prime and Nate Thurmond, Willis Reed, Bob Lanier, Dave Cowens, Elvin Hayes, and Kareem near the end. Whereas Kareem played against 7 of the 8 including Wilt but not Russell in the beginning of his career (Wilt was MVP of the 1972 NBA Finals at 35 years old) - Bob McAdoo, Moses Malone, Robert Parish in the middle - and Ralph Sampson, Hakeem Olajuwon, and Patrick Ewing at the end of his. But the main difference was in the postseason. Kareem had a little better statistics in his postseason prime than Wilt with no significant drop off from the regular season. Kareem did it consistently for his first 18 seasons including winning 6 NBA

Championships; while Wilt, other than his rebounding and perhaps his passing numbers, dropped significantly particularly in the scoring department in the postseason. I don't think there is a superstar in NBA history whose career scoring dipped a whopping 8 points in the playoffs (22.5 points per game) compared to the regular season (30.1 points per game). This actually makes me feel better about LeBron James' chances of recovering from an atrocious 2011 NBA Finals that lowered his playoff average for that postseason to 23.7, by far the lowest of his career. At 28 points per game in the regular season, is still close to his 27.7 career playoff mark.

If Chamberlain had matched Kareem and Jordan's statistical contributions (particularly in the clutch) and intangibles in the postseason, he could have been ranked #1; and at the same time ending any kind of debate with Bill Russell. That is, providing his increased offensive production and clutch performances, translated into more wins and more championships. Wilt does have some notable records in the postseason. He had an NBA record 41 rebounds in the 1967 NBA Finals and led the league in rebounds per game average in the playoffs 8 times. Also, as a Philadelphia 76er, he had an incredible 30 points and 32 rebounds against the Celtics in Game 7 of the 1965 Eastern Finals; an eye-popping 29 points, 36 rebounds, and 13 assists against the Celtics in the clinching Game 5 of the 1967 Eastern Finals; and as a Los Angeles Laker, a near quadruple-double finishing with 24 points, 29 rebounds, 9 assists, and 8 blocks against the Knicks in the series ending Game 5 of the 1972 NBA Finals.

Here is Wilt's regular season and playoff averages vs. Kareem's and Jordan's:

Michael Jordan: 30.1 points per game, 6.2 rebounds, 5.3 assists, 50% FG, 83% FT

+ 33.4 points per game, 6.4 rebounds, 5.7 assists, 49% FG, 83% FT

Kareem A. Jabbar: 24.6 points per game, 11.2 rebounds, 3.6 assists, 56% FG, 72% FT

24.3 points per game, 10.5 rebounds, 3.2 assists, 53% FG, 74% FT

Wilt Chamberlain: 30.1 points per game, 22.9 rebounds, 4.4 assists, 54% FG, 51% FT

- 22.5 points per game, 24.5 rebounds, 4.2 assists, 52% FG, 46% FT

If Wilt had played his *entire* career in Kareem's era, he probably would have put up similar numbers as Kareem and possibly a little more. But would his mindset throughout his career allow him to be the ultimate team player Abdul-Jabbar was? Probably not, that's why he is safely ranked # 3 as the greatest to have ever played the game. Even

ESPN in 2007, ranked Chamberlain as the second greatest center to Abdul-Jabbar and ahead of Russell to help prove my *next* point.

Wilt had a jump shot and fadeaway shot that he could also use as a bank shot that was extremely effective just like Kareem's sky-hook. He had an equally effective finger roll that he shot as far out as the free-throw line. He also had the inside dominance (dunking over anyone or everyone in his path) like Shaquille O'Neal but with more mobility. And, because he was track star in high school and college, it enabled him to out finesse other centers with his speed and agility. Golden State Warriors color man Jim Barnett who played at the time Chamberlain did, once said, if Wilt played in today's game against Shaq, he would have ran circles around him scoring with ease! Which leads me to an even bigger debate, was Wilt Chamberlain better than Bill Russell? According to most people you ask, this has been a debate that has been going on for decades. Wilt had the better scoring statistics by a mile, but Russell has the 11 Championships. The way I look at it, if it takes 11 championships to 2 to make a debate on who was the greatest center, than it must have been Wilt, because of his individual accolades that contributed to his team's success. If the statistics were closer - I know the rebounds and assists were close and that they didn't keep track of blocks until 1973-74, you could make a better case for Russell, because his individual accomplishments were proven on the defensive end from a subjective point view, but were validated by his five 5 MVP awards. In fact, that's the only reason I put him ahead of Hakeem Olajuwon in the elite rankings, because "The Dream" was better than Russell by far offensively and not far behind on the defensive end.

Wilt demolished Russell statistically in the regular season. The rest of the numbers are not even close. Despite playing with fewer teams and smaller players in the era, Wilt accumulated 100 times more offensive records (I exaggerating a little or maybe not! He currently holds 72 career records and at the time of his retirement, I believed he held over 100) than Russell. Even in Russell's second to last season in 1968, Wilt at 31 years old, for the second time in his career, had a monster 50-point triple-double game of **53 points, 32 rebounds, and 14 assists.** And at the age of 35 he had recorded **124 30-30 games.** Also, Wilt was not a bad defensive center playing at 7-feet-1, three inches taller than his chief rival. Like Shaq, Wilt played defense inconsistently particularly the first half of his career. Besides, it has been said that a great offense always beats a good defense? Even after reading one of the biggest and best basketball books ever just recently, I am still going with Wilt. Not only am I going with Wilt, so are a lot of other people and books and publications including the credible Elliott Kalb (Espn.com), and NBA List Jam and Slam Magazine, who all rank Wilt ahead of Russell. Most magazines I have read in the past do the same (I wish more publications would officially list their top 50 players of all-time. Even Espn.com Hollinger ranking has Chamberlain statistically ahead of Russell by a long shot. Also, Chamberlain said in an interview a few years back before his death, that he was better than Russell, but that Russell had the better team.

Some people believe Russell played with an equal or slightly better cast of all-stars and Hall of Famers in his prime as Wilt. Untrue; Russell played with Bob Cousy, Bill

Sharman, Tommy Heinsohn, and Sam Jones in their primes, and John Havlicek in the beginning of his. Chamberlain played with only Hal Greer, Jerry West, and Gail Goodrich in their primes. He played with Paul Arizin the last three years of his career before he left to play basketball overseas, Nate Thurmond for only a year and a half (Wilt was traded to Philadelphia in the middle of 1965), Billy Cunningham his first three years in the league, and Elgin Baylor with bad knees for only two seasons in 1969 and 1970. Elgin played 2 games in 1971 and 9 games in 1972 before retiring early in the season. Wilt in his last three seasons, did play with Goodrich, but almost entirely without Baylor. So if you look at the duration of the time spent with each Hall of Famer it favors Russell by far. Just like in today's game, you need stability and time to grow as a team with the players, and with the head coach and his system. Russell played with the same coach and with more Hall of Famers, for a longer duration of time.

Both players played with nearly the same amount of All-Star players and Hall of Famers in their careers, but clearly, Russell played with more Top 50 players in their primes for a longer period of time than Wilt did. Russell also played with more Top 25 Hall of Fame Players in their primes. He won 6 championships with Cousy and Havlicek, 8 with Heinsohn and K.C. Jones, and 10 with Sam Jones. Even though Russell was at the end of his prime in the late sixties, so was Wilt. As things changed at the end of the decade with there being more black players and more teams, and with Chamberlain having a better mindset of team basketball, I think people take for granted that Wilt was the same dominant superstar in L.A. as he was with San Francisco and Philadelphia. Even though he was highly effective late in his career with scoring becoming less of a priority, because of age and injuries, he was not the same dominate and unstoppable force he once was in the early 1960s. Wilt was 32 at the end of his prime in 1969, playing with an injured Jerry West during the playoffs, and with a 34-year-old Elgin Baylor in his second to last full season. Like Chamberlain, Baylor was not the great player he once was before blowing out his knee in 1965. The trio lost the 1970 NBA Finals to the Knicks with a 33-year-old Wilt and 35-year-old Baylor in his final full season. In 1971, West missed the playoffs entirely because of injury, the year the Milwaukee Bucks won the NBA Championship. Chamberlain, who won the 1972 Finals MVP at the age of 35 about to turn 36, was playing with another great player in West, who was within a month shy of 34 years old and at the tail end of his prime, although you wouldn't know it judging by his statistics. West retired two years later. Also, two of the three were at the tail end of their careers with only West still in his prime. From a recent book of basketball on the shelf at your local book store, mentions that players from the past have all of a sudden, now agree that Russell was better. From what I can see, only about 5 or 6 players are quoted recently, whom they thought Russell was the better out of the two. If you're going to write a book with the most debatable subject in NBA basketball history in most people's eyes, maybe you should give at least 10 to 15 different clear cut opinions from past Hall of Famers. Not to sound contradicting, but I myself, have only given a few quoted opinions for each player, but my rankings in this book are based heavily on facts and stats along with *every conceivable basketball reference* I was able to get my hands on the last few decades!

If Russell was better than Chamberlain then why does he have only 3 First Team All-NBA selections and 8 Second Team All-NBA selections? First Team All-NBA at least today, means a player is the best at his position unless you're mixing guards and forwards (although, it did seem a few times they might have mixed a power forward with a center). I know it is a pre-playoff honor like the regular season MVP award, so if they had a playoff MVP or Finals MVP, Russell would have had many of those. If Wilt's supporting cast had helped pull his team through to victory in crucial games, there wouldn't be a discussion. As I mentioned in the beginning of the book, basketball is a team sport, as the Dallas Mavericks proved in this past year's NBA Finals in 2011. Dirk Nowitzki had an atrocious game six just like Kobe Bryant had in the decisive game seven the year before and both teams prevailed. Chamberlain, in his days, was swarmed with double and triple teams, and with fouling tactics that brought his overall production down at times.

Wilt was voted the better center at his position over Russell more times than not, but Russell was obviously looked upon as being the most valuable to his team. Hakeem Olajuwon for example, had more First Team selections than both David Robinson and Patrick Ewing during their playing days. Is Olajuwon known as the third best center? You would think not. Wilt was better for 80 games a year by a long shot over Russell, and was better statistically for an average of about 10 to 12 playoff games a year. Wilt showed his individual dominance for far more games during his entire career than Russell despite having far more losses in the regular season and in playoff games. Even head-to-head, including the playoffs, Wilt outscored Russell on average 28 to 14. If Wilt Chamberlain, Elgin Baylor, and Jerry West all played together in their primes in the early and mid-1960s, they would have most likely dismantled the Boston Celtics cast of all-stars despite Wilt's desire for individual accomplishments. If anything it makes more sense to say that Bill Russell was the greatest winner? Wilt wins the close debate, and if he had played with the right mindset most of his career, it wouldn't have even been close.

Take a look at the Great Chamberlain and his accomplishments throughout his career:

Wilton Norman Chamberlain was born on August 21st, 1936 in Philadelphia, Pennsylvania. Initially as a youth, Chamberlain was not interested in basketball and opted to become a track and field athlete where he competed in the high jump, broad jump, 440 meter and the 880 meter. Living in the Bay Area listening to Golden State Warriors color commentator Jim Barnett, a teammate of Chamberlain's, always mentions how track helped Wilt tremendously with his footwork playing in the NBA. At Overbrook High School, as a varsity player, he led the team to consecutive records of 19-2, 19-0, and 18-1. In his second season in 1954, Chamberlain set a school record 71 points in a game, won the Public League title and the Philadelphia City Championship. In his third and final year, he had scoring games of **74, 78,** and **90 points** and led the Panthers to the Public League title for the third time and the Philadelphia City Championship for the second straight year. Chamberlain finished his high school career with a 56-3 record and averaged a *gaudy* 37.4 points per game.

After being highly recruited by top collegiate programs, Chamberlain chose to play at the University of Kansas in 1955. In his varsity debut on December 3rd, 1956, he scored 52 points and grabbed 31 rebounds (breaking the old school record) and finished the season averaging 29.6 points per game and 18.9 rebounds. He also led his team to the NCAA Championship game. During the game, the North Carolina Tarheels used the "freeze-ball" technique by using multiple players to keep Wilt from scoring as the Jaywalks lost the game in triple overtime. Despite the loss, Chamberlain was honored 1956-57 NCAA Final Four Most Outstanding Player. In his junior year in 1957-58, Chamberlain averaged 30.1 points and 17.5 rebounds per game. But after another frustrating season in which Kansas did not make the NCAA tournament, Chamberlain wanted to join the NBA before his senior year. Because the NBA did not accept players into the league before the completion of their final year academically, he opted to play with the Harlem Globetrotters in 1958 for 50,000 dollars.

Chamberlain was selected as a territorial pick in the 1959 NBA Draft by the Philadelphia Warriors. Because there was no NBA team in Kansas, Warriors owner and NBA pioneer Eddie Gottlieb claimed that his franchise owned his draft rights due to his popularity of playing high school basketball in his hometown of Philadelphia. The NBA concurred marking an unprecedented territorial pick based on pre-college roots. Chamberlain began his pro career in 1959 with a bang. In his first NBA game he scored **43 points** and corralled **28 rebounds**. And in his fourth game, he outscored future rival and third year center Bill Russell 30 to 22. For the season, Chamberlain averaged an *unfathomable* **37.6 points** and **27 rebounds** per game as he set eight NBA records along the way and was honored with the MVP and Rookie of the Year award. In the playoffs, after defeating the Syracuse Nationals two games to one, the Warriors lost to the defending champion Boston Celtics in six games in the Eastern Finals. During the series, whenever the Warriors shot free throws, Tommy Heinsohn would grab and shove Chamberlain to prevent him from getting back on defense to halt the Celtics fast break. In game two, Chamberlain had had enough and threw a punch at Heinsohn but missed, actually landing a blow to his own teammate causing him to play with an injured hand the rest of the series. After returning for game five, Wilt dropped 50 points on Russell as the Warriors pulled out the victory. Philadelphia went on to lose game six at home on Heinsohn's last second tip-in.

Even as a rookie, Chamberlain had the golden opportunity to win his first championship if it weren't for this untimely mishap. So once again, it's what a player contributes to his team in the regular season and throughout the postseason that determines player greatness. For example, in the 2011, LeBron James carried the Miami Heat in the regular season and throughout the playoffs up until the NBA Finals similar to how Dirk Nowitzki did with the Dallas Mavericks in 2006. Just because the team as whole couldn't bring home the title, doesn't negate a players individual accomplishments for an 82-game season and for the entire playoff run. Without these cornerstone players, the Miami Heat and the Dallas Mavericks never would have even made it past the first round of the playoffs let alone making it to the Finals. However, as I continue to reiterate throughout the book, if a player comes up short time and time again in crucial moments of his career particularly in the NBA Finals, than naturally his legacy will begin to diminish or eventually become tainted. So I think it was unfair for the people to rip on Dirk in 2006 when he shot poorly in his first trip to the NBA Finals and on LeBron after he shot poorly throughout the 2011 Finals. Nowitzki came through in that series against the Heat and hopefully LeBron James does the same if and when he returns to the Finals in 2012 (in which he did - and also in 2013). So even though Chamberlain came up a little short more than once throughout his playoff career, he still was part of two of the *greatest* championship teams in NBA history in 1967 and in 1972.

In his second season, Chamberlain averaged similar numbers as the year before (**38.4 points** and a **career-high 27.2 rebounds** per game) becoming the first man in NBA history to amass **3000 points** and **2000 rebounds** (still no one else has reached those plateaus except Jordan in points - and Russell came really close once in the rebounding department). Chamberlain could have possibly reached those milestones as a rookie but he only played in 56 games. He also set the all-time record of **55 rebounds** in a single game against his greatest rival in Bill Russell. But in the playoffs, the Warriors took a step back as they were swept by the Syracuse Nationals in the first round. In the 1961-62 season, Chamberlain had the greatest individual scoring season in NBA history when he averaged **50.4 points** for the season and scored **100 points** in a game against the New York Knicks. He also set more *insurmountable* records including reaching the **4000-point** mark for the first and only time and the 2000-rebound plateau for the second time. He also led the league in scoring and rebounding for the third consecutive season. With a supporting cast of Paul Arizin, Tom Gola and Guy Rodgers, the Warriors made it back to the Eastern Finals by avenging the loss to Dolph Schayes and the Syracuse Nationals in five games in the semifinals. After splitting the first six games, the Warriors battled the Celtics in game seven to the very end until Sam Jones shattered Philadelphia's dream of a championship, when he hit the game-winning shot with two seconds on the clock. Time and time again, the 1960s Celtics somehow were able to eke out and win close playoff games throughout their championship run eliminating the dreams of many players and franchises along the way, similar to what the Chicago Bulls did to other teams during the 1990s. Some of the major differences during both team's title run, were that the Bulls played with at least twice the amount of teams in the league, won more championships *decisively* and *never faced* a seventh game in his Finals career. Whereas the Celtics played with fewer teams and needed some serious luck to win eleven out of thirteen championships. I know you make your own luck (like the Miami Heat did this year in 2013), and that's a good thing. But Russell's Celtics were pushed to the limit five times in the NBA Finals - where teams forced a seventh game.

Chamberlain followed up his monster individual campaign with another unbelievable scoring season when he averaged **44.8 points** and **24.3 rebounds** per game, and led the league in both categories for the fourth straight season. He also had his first 50-point triple-double of **51 points, 29 rebounds and 11 assists**. The next three seasons, he would win the scoring title three more times to give him a career total of seven in succession. But with Paul Arizin already retired, the Warriors missed the playoffs in their first season in San Francisco. In the 1963-64 campaign, Chamberlain had another terrific year averaging **36.9 points, 22.3 rebounds,** and a *superb* **5 assists** per game. With rookie sensation Nate Thurmond aboard to add strength to the frontcourt, the Warriors made it all the way to the NBA Finals. After defeating Bob Pettit, Cliff Hagen and the St. Louis Hawks in a tough seven-game series in the Western Final, the Warriors were outclassed in the NBA Finals by the six-time champion Boston Celtics four games to one. During the 1964-65 season with the Warriors having financial troubles and Thurmond improving as a prominent big man, Chamberlain was traded back to his hometown of Philadelphia. After another fine season with both clubs, Chamberlain averaged **34.7 points** and **22.9 rebounds** per game. After teaming up with future Hall of Famer Hal Greer in Philadelphia, the 76ers defeated the Cincinnati Royals in the first round of the playoffs three games to one before falling to the Celtics in seven games in the Eastern Finals. In game seven, Chamberlain posted a monster game of **32 points and 32 rebounds** including having had two clutch free throws and a slam dunk over Bill Russell in the final minute of the game. With a one point lead and five seconds on the clock, Russell flubbed the inbound pass that hit a guide wire over the back board giving the ball back to the 76ers. But what happened next is the famous highlight that's always shown during the NBA Finals when John Havlicek stole the ball on an inbound pass by Hal Greer. For the fourth time in six years, another Chamberlain led team was denied a championship bid by the Boston Celtics.

The following season, Chamberlain averaged **33.5 points** and **24.6 rebounds** per game. For the second time, he would begin a new streak and lead the league in rebounding for four consecutive seasons. He also won his second MVP award since his rookie year in the league. After finishing the regular season with 55 wins, the 76ers met their arch nemeses Celtics for the second straight year in the playoffs. After two convincing losses to begin the series, the 76ers won the next game at home behind Chamberlain's **31 points and 27 rebounds**. But after having issues involving practice with coach Dolph Schayes after game three; the 76ers lost the next two games and the series. In game five, Chamberlain did bring his A-game scoring **46 points** and corralling **34 rebounds**.

In the 1966-67 season, glory finally came to Wilt Chamberlain and the Philadelphia 76ers in historic fashion. With a 76ers team rostered with scorers Hal Greer and Billy Cunningham, new and former coach Alex Hanuum with his second stint with the franchise and with coaching Wilt in San Francisco, asked Chamberlain to focus more on the defensive end. As a result, Chamberlain led the 76ers to the best record in NBA history to that point at 68-13 which included the best start in league history at 46-4. He also won his second consecutive MVP award and third overall. Even though his scoring dropped to 24 points per game over the next two seasons, Chamberlain shot a then

career-high 68.3 percent from the field and handed out **630 assists** for an average of **7.8** per game. This was the first of two consecutive seasons; Chamberlain maximized his potential as the ultimate all-around team player. In the playoffs, the 76ers defeated the Cincinnati Royals in the semifinals before setting up the much anticipated rematch with the Boston Celtics in the Eastern Finals. In what looked to be a competitive series, Philadelphia took complete control by winning the first three games. In game one, the 76ers won convincingly 127-112 behind Hal Greer's 39 points and Chamberlain's unofficial quadruple-double of **24 points, 32 rebounds, 13 assists, and 12 blocks**. After a five point overtime victory in game two, Philadelphia dropped the hammer down and won game three 115-104 behind Chamberlain's 40 rebounds. With the series being all but over, the Celtics escaped with a four point victory at home before getting thumped in the clinching game five 140-116. Chamberlain posted 29 points, 36 rebounds and 13 assists, and put an end to the Celtics run of eight consecutive championships.

In the NBA Finals, the 76ers faced Chamberlain's old team from San Francisco and former teammate Nate Thurmond who was improving rapidly as an all-star center. But he wasn't the 76ers only concern because Rick Barry was coming off one of the greatest scoring seasons in NBA history at 35.6 points per game. After winning the first two games behind Chamberlain's defense and Greer's clutch shooting, the 76ers lost two of the next three games. Philadelphia was fortunate enough to have survived the scoring onslaught by Barry who averaged an eye-gouging 40.6 points for the series including a 55-point game. But in game six with 15 seconds on the clock and Philadelphia leading 123-122, Barry missed the potential game-winning shot with Chet Walker draped all over him as the 76ers went on to win the 1967 NBA Championship. In the series, Chamberlain averaged 17.7 points and 28.7 rebounds.

The following season, Chamberlain continued his solid team play by becoming the only center to lead the league in **assists at 702** edging out Lenny Wilkens by 23. He also had an incredible **31 triple-doubles** for a center and a **record 9 straight games with a triple-double** - was named to the All-NBA First Team for the seventh time, and won his third consecutive MVP award and fourth overall. In the regular season, the 76ers won 62 games and finished with the best record in the NBA for the third straight season. After coming off an NBA championship the previous season, Philadelphia looked to defend their title. In the playoffs, the 76ers beat the New York Knicks in the semifinals four games to two. But during the middle of a tough physical Eastern Finals series, Philadelphia lost *super sixth man* Billy Cunningham to a broken hand. With Chamberlain, Greer, and Lucious Jackson ailing with injuries, the 76ers lost the first game but won three games in a row putting the aging Celtics in a 3-1 hole, and on the brink of elimination for the second straight year. Knowing that no team had ever come back from a three to one deficit, the Celtics won the next two games convincingly. In game seven, an interesting set of circumstances happened, when Chamberlain only touched the ball 23 times in the low post, less than half of what he normally would have. With only seven touches in the third quarter and two in the fourth (kind of reminiscent of some of the games LeBron James had in the 2011 Finals), Chamberlain *disappeared* down the stretch as the 76ers lost game seven and the series 100-96. After the series, Coach Alex Hannum said Chamberlain should have been more assertive and demanded to have the ball. Because of the death of Martin Luther King before the series that affected the emotions of both teams, you would have to call the series a wash, in terms of which team should have come out victorious.

Prior to the 1968-69 season, Chamberlain was traded to the Los Angeles Lakers. He joined an already formidable Laker team that was in search of its first championship in the city of Los Angeles. In his first year with his new franchise, Chamberlain led the league in rebounding for the fourth straight season and eighth time overall. He also led the league in field goal percentage for the seventh time in his career. With the addition of Chamberlain, the 55-win Lakers felt going into the playoffs, this was their best chance at a title. After defeating the San Francisco Warriors in six games and the Atlanta Hawks in five in the semifinals and Western Finals, the Lakers faced their arch nemeses Celtics in the NBA Finals for the sixth time during the 1960s. After winning the first two games behind Jerry West's heavy scoring output, the Lakers lost the next two with little contribution from Chamberlain. But in game five, Chamberlain pitched in with 13 points and 31 rebounds as the Lakers won 117-104. In game six, Chamberlain reverted back to the way he played in the beginning of the series and in the Eastern Finals the year before, scoring only 8 points. Going into game seven, the Lakers felt confident that the final game of the series - at home was a game of destiny, after years of hard-fought battles with the Celtics. But after falling behind in the game, trailing by fifteen points after three quarters, the Lakers made a comeback despite Chamberlain twisting his knee on a rebound during the game. With West carrying the team, the Lakers closed to within 103-102 with three minutes to go. But the Celtics defense forced L.A. into multiple turnovers down the stretch ending the Lakers dream of a first championship on the West Coast. By that point, Chamberlain had already beaten the Celtics in the NBA Finals in 1967 playing for the Philadelphia 76ers, but if he had beaten Bill Russell one more time it would have further enhanced his legacy. But the real heartbreak was felt by Elgin Baylor and Jerry West, who never overcame the obstacle of beating the Boston Celtics.

The following year, Chamberlain seriously injured his knee and missed most of the regular season while West picked up the scoring slack and won his first scoring title. In the playoffs, with Baylor's bad knees and Chamberlain still hobbling, West carried the team as the Lakers defeated the Phoenix Suns in seven games and the Atlanta Hawks in a sweep, before facing off with the New York Knicks in the NBA Finals. This was where West hit the famous *buzzer-beater* from half court in game three to send the game into overtime where the Lakers eventually lost the 1970 NBA Finals. It was also the series where Willis Reed inspired his team to victory in game five hobbling on a bad leg. In a see-saw battle, the Lakers eventually lost the series in seven games. Despite the Lakers never leading in the series, Chamberlain and West came up big in game six to tie the series. Wilt scored 45 points and West pitched in with 31 points and 13 assists. Like the

Celtics of the 1960s, the Knicks had a well-balanced, great offensive and defensive team which included four Hall of Famers in Reed, Walt Frazier, Bill Bradley, and Dave DeBusschere. Like I mentioned earlier in the Wilt and Russell debate, if Baylor never blew out his knees, and West wasn't always injured, and Chamberlain played with the Lakers earlier in his career during his prime, the Lakers likely could have taken the Celtics and Knicks out in *some* of their NBA Finals matchups. And, at the same time, it would also have been interesting if the high powered Knicks teams had play against Bill Russell's Celtics when both teams were at their peak.

In Chamberlain's last three seasons in the NBA, he led the league in rebounding every year giving him a *staggering* total of 11 rebounding titles for his career. He also led the league in field goal percentage (including a career-high .727 in 1973) his last two seasons, giving him a total 9 FG percentage titles for his career. In the 1971 playoffs, the Lakers defeated Bob Love, Chet Walker, Jerry Sloan, and the Chicago Bulls in the semifinals but were eliminated by Lew Alcindor's Milwaukee Bucks in five games in the conference finals. That season, Baylor had a career threatening injury, playing in only 2 games, and West was lost for the playoffs with a knee injury. It wasn't until the 1971-72 season, that West, Chamberlain, and the rest of the Los Angeles Lakers would win the coveted NBA championship over the New York Knicks. It was too bad Baylor was not there to enjoy the celebration after he retired only nine games into the season. The Lakers finished with a then record 69 wins and a record 33-game winning streak that still stands today. With his scoring and rebounding contributions, Chamberlain was named the Finals MVP. What a way to cap off one of the great careers in the history of sports. Also to note: Wilt's Lakers did avenge the loss from the previous year and defeated Kareem's Bucks in the conference finals in 6 games.

For his career, Wilt Chamberlain averaged more points per game tied with Michael Jordan and more rebounds per game at **22.9** than anyone else in history. He also became the first man to reach the 30,000-point plateau and is still the all-time leader in total rebounds with 23,924. Out of his 7 scoring titles which ranks second to Jordan's 10, he averaged an *unfathomable* **39.6 points** per game, and **40.6** in his first six seasons in the league including an *unbelievable* **50.4** and **44.8 points** in back-to-back years in 1962 and 1963. And, in his 14-year career, he never averaged less than 18 rebounds and averaged at least 21 rebounds in his first nine seasons. But what was equally as impressive as his scoring feats, in 6 of his first 7 seasons, he averaged at least 24 rebounds per game including 27 in each of his first two years in the league.

Chamberlain came down to earth with his scoring in the playoffs, having only scored 50 points in game 4 times compared to 118 times in the regular season, but was just as dominate with his rebounding where he led the league in per game average in the postseason 8 times. In all 13 postseasons, Chamberlain averaged an unfathomable **24.5 rebounds** per game and never averaged less than 20 rebounds in any given postseason. He also averaged at least **24 rebounds** in 8 of his first 9 seasons in the playoffs including one five-year stretch, where he averaged **27.4 rebounds** and **5 assists** in 55 playoff games. It is mind-boggling just thinking about it, that the man averaged 27 rebounds for five consecutive seasons in the playoffs! Again, I know there were more offensive possessions in those days, but still. Most players in their lifetime will never have had even one 27-rebound game in their entire career let alone average that amount over 55 games. I'm still not sure what was more impressive out of all his scoring and rebounding feats because he was just as dominate in rebounding as he was in scoring, doing it for a longer period of time. Chamberlain finished his career with 11 rebounding titles in 13 seasons. Out of all the relevant categories in all of sports, I don't know if anyone led the league as many times as Chamberlain did in rebounding. Jordan had 10 scoring titles and I believe Ty Cobb in baseball, came the closest either matching or surpassing him with 11 or 12 batting titles - depending on the source, it is unclear how many titles Cobb actually won. Actually, I found out Babe Ruth led the league in home runs 12 times!

To help in adding to the justification of other player rankings in this book despite the fact they didn't mention or forgot about Kareem, in one interview with Ahmad Rashad before Chamberlain died, he was asked to pick his list of top 5 players ever not including him or Bill Russell, and he stated: Bird, Jerry, Oscar, Elgin, Jordan, and Magic - and if he could pick seven, Barkley! And in this same interview with Russell sitting next to him, Russell gave similar picks stating: Magic, Michael, Bird, Baylor, Oscar, Olajuwon or Pettit for a sixth.

Furthermore, even though he doesn't like to make comparisons between positions on the court, the great Rick Barry once said if he had to pick one player to start a team around, he would take Wilt Chamberlain. He also said on multiple occasions that Chamberlain was the greatest and most talented all-around center **(career 78 triple-doubles)** of all-time and it isn't even close. Larry Bird also has said; all you have to do is look at the numbers!

If Chamberlain had played with the same team concept the first half of his career as he did in the second half, there might not be any question - who the greatest basketball player of all-time is (And I'm referring to Jordan). His overall game would have been even greater than it already was, particularly in the playoffs, which most likely would have translated into more wins and more championships. Either way you slice it, Wilt Chamberlain was the Babe Ruth of basketball that put up *astronomical* scoring and rebounding numbers, in the way "The Babe" did with home runs and runs batted in. So with his 100-point and 55-rebound games, which I think are the greatest records in all of sports along with his 50-point scoring average for a single season, one could make the case that the *iconic* Wilt Chamberlain was the greatest basketball player of all-time!

Career Totals
30.1 points average, 22.9 rebounds, 4.4 assists, .540 FG%, 511 FT%
31,419 points, 23,924 rebounds, 4643 assists

Magic Johnson

(Rank #4)

MVP (3-times), Assist Title (4-times), Steals Title (2-times)

All-NBA First Team (9-times), All-Star (12-times)

NBA Championships (5), Finals MVP (3-times)

NBA Record: 11.2 career assists per game average!

NBA Record: 2,346 career assists in the playoffs!

Magic Johnson is considered by most the best point guard in NBA history. Gifted with a *unique blend* of size and ball-handling ability, Magic revolutionized the point guard position when he came into the league in 1979 playing for the Los Angeles Lakers. At six-foot-nine, he was able to dominate the dribble like a prototypical size point guard and at the same time, was a half a foot taller allowing him to pass *over the top* of the defense. As a rookie, Magic led the Lakers to the 1980 NBA Championship and was named Finals MVP. In game six, he had one of the most memorable games in the playoffs replacing the injured Kareem Abdul-Jabbar at center finishing with an astounding 42 points, 15 rebounds, and seven assists. Throughout his *illustrious* career, he would go on to have many more all-around games of this magnitude. But what made Magic so special, was his ability to make the players around him better. On the offensive end of the ball, I don't know if there has ever been a *selfless* player throughout history that made his teammates better than this man! Even though he was extremely talented offensively as a scorer, Magic was a pass-first point guard that set up everyone around him for easy scoring opportunities. He even carried the "Captain," Abdul-Jabbar the second half of his career, making sure he was the number one scoring option *by feeding* the big man in the post.

The Magic Man was well remembered for his passing accolades, and for retiring as the NBA's all-time assists leader. He was also known for his over-hand bullet pass and no-look zip passes on the fast break and in the half court. And aside from all that flash, he could make the thread-the-needle pass, behind-the-back pass, and the basic fundamental bounce pass that your typical six-foot-one point guard could make. But his greatest advantage was his enormous height for a point guard allowing him to see and pass over the top of smaller defenders while smaller point guards had to pass through or around. Overlooked at times as a scorer, Magic could score and finish at the basket with the best of them. He was in the same class as Jordan, Drexler, Barkley and Malone, but he just did it in a different way.

While a lot of his contemporaries were high-flying acrobatic dunkers, Magic stayed more grounded finishing drives to the basket with nifty layups and scoop shots in front of the rim. On the fast break or in the half court, he would either drive past or spin around defenders with his arms fully extended finishing easy layups directly at the basket, or on either side of the rim. Even though he wasn't elevating as much on his way to the cup as a lot of the high-flyers, he had this *uncanny* ability to *squeeze* in layups around his opponents outstretched arms in likes of the great George Gervin. Watching him in the 1980s, at times, he almost seemed as untouchable driving to the hoop as Jordan was dominating the paint with and-one finishes. Like Jordan, Magic was highly respected and was given the benefit of the doubt quite often by officiating. In addition to his dominate drive; he had a reliable set shot that kept on improving the second half of his career. In fact, it was so good that Magic became one of the all-time great clutch players/shooters in NBA history. He developed a *junior sky-hook*, which won the go-ahead game four in Boston during the 1987 NBA Finals to put the Lakers ahead in the series 3 games to 1. With his enormous height, Magic was perhaps the best rebounding point guard, or guard for that matter in history along with Oscar Robertson.

Earvin Johnson Jr. was born on August 14th, 1959 in Lansing, Michigan. He played basketball at Everett High School where as a fifteen-year-old sophomore; he recorded a triple-double of 36 points, 16 rebounds, and 16 assists. Afterwards he was given the nickname "Magic" by sports writer Fred Stabley Jr. In his senior year, Magic averaged 28.8 points and 16.8 rebounds per game, and led his team to a 27-1 record and a state championship. After being recruited by Indiana, Minnesota, UCLA and USC, Magic decided to play close to home, choosing Michigan State over Michigan because Spartan's coach Jud

Heathcote assured him of playing the point guard position. In two years of college, he averaged 17.1 points, 7.6 rebounds, and 7.9 assists per game. In his sophomore season, Magic led the Spartans to a 25-5 record and a berth in the 1979 NCAA Championship game against Larry Bird and Indiana State University. In the most watched game in college basketball history, Michigan State beat Indiana State 75-64 and Magic Johnson was voted 1979 NCAA Final Four Most Outstanding Player.

With nothing left to prove, Magic felt it was now time to enter the NBA draft as an underclassman. With the 1st overall pick of the 1979 NBA Draft, The Los Angeles Lakers selected Earvin "Magic" Johnson. In his rookie season in 1980, Larry Bird won the "Rookie of the Year Award" but Magic took home the *biggest prize*, when the Los Angeles Lakers finished the regular season 60-22 and defeated Dr. J and the Philadelphia 76ers to win the 1980 NBA Championship. During game five, Kareem sprained his ankle, and this is where Magic stepped up and had the memorable game six. While playing multiple positions including center, Magic rescued the Lakers with his forty-two-point, fifteen-rebound, seven-assist, and three-steal performance in the clinching game. He also became the only rookie in NBA history to win Finals MVP. In his second season, he injured his knee and missed 45 games but did return in time for the playoffs, but the Lakers lost to the 40-42 Houston Rockets behind Moses Malone, two games to one in the first round. In the 1981-82 season, Magic had his most balanced statistical season in only his third year in the league averaging a near triple-double of **18.6 points**, **9.5 assists**, and **9.6 rebounds** per game while leading the NBA in steals for the second consecutive year at 2.7 per game. He also became the third man in NBA history to record 700 points, 700 rebounds, and 700 assists (see the chart in Oscar's chapter for rebounds and assists) in the same season behind only Wilt Chamberlain and Oscar Robertson.

In the playoffs, the Lakers swept the Phoenix Suns in the conference semifinals and San Antonio Spurs in the Western Conference Finals before defeating the Philadelphia 76ers again in six games of the 1982 NBA Finals. After a triple-double in game six, Magic was named NBA Finals MVP for the second time in three years. The following year, Magic compiled **18 triple-doubles** and led the league in assists for the first time. He would go on to win the assist title three of the next four seasons. In the playoffs, the Lakers defeated the Portland Trail Blazers four games to one in the semifinals and the Spurs in six games in the conference finals, but lost convincingly to the 76ers in the 1983 NBA Finals in a four-game sweep. Before the season, Philadelphia was able to fill in the missing piece at center by acquiring Moses Malone from the Houston Rockets to neutralize Abdul-Jabbar at the center position. Julius Erving and the 76ers finally avenged the two previous Finals losses to the Lakers which came in 1980 and 1982.

The following season in 1983-84, heartbreak and disbelief came to the Los Angeles Lakers. After finishing the season with 54 wins, the Lakers coasted through the playoffs sweeping the Kansas City Kings in the first round, dispatching the Dallas Mavericks in five games in the semifinals, and finishing off the Phoenix Suns in six games in the conference finals before meeting their arch nemeses Boston in the NBA Finals. After shocking the

Celtics in game one 115-109 behind Kareem's 32 points, the Lakers lost game two that would have given them a commanding two games to none lead in the series. With the Lakers leading the game 113-111 with twenty seconds to go in regulation, Kevin McHale missed two free throws that would have tied the game. After the timeout, Magic inbounded the ball to James Worthy, who then made a bad crosscourt pass to Byron Scott that was intercepted by Gerald Henderson leading to an open layup at the other end. With thirteen seconds on the clock and the scored tied at 113, Magic carefully dribbled the ball up court looking for the open man, while at the same time enduring the pressure of the NBA Finals. After Kareem was denied the ball by Parish, Magic realized that there was only three seconds left on the clock and delivered a zip pass to Bob McAdoo. With McHale draped all over him, McAdoo wasn't able to get the shot off as time expired. Boston went on to win the game in overtime 124-121. In game three at home, Magic dished out 21 assists and the Lakers blew out the Celtics 137-104.

Before game four, Dennis Johnson was given the responsibility by Coach K.C. Jones to guard Magic the rest of the series. This was also the infamous game where the Celtics implemented *the-no-easy-layup-rule*, when Kevin McHale grabbed Kurt Rambis going for a layup and threw him to the floor. In game four, for the second time, the Lakers failed to take control of the series because of multiple miscues in the closing minutes down the stretch, when Magic had the ball stolen by Robert Parish and then missed two crucial free throws that would have won the game. The Celtics protected home court by winning game five. But in game six, the Lakers admirably defended their home court behind Magic's 21 points, 10 assists, and six rebounds but they eventually succumbed to Boston in seven games.

So from one perspective, the Celtics deserved to win the series going in because they earned the home court advantage in the regular season by finishing with a record of 62-20 but the Lakers felt that they had played well enough to have won the series. For the city of Los Angeles it must have felt like *déjà vu* all over again with a somber feel to it. *The pain, the agony of defeat*, and *the curse of the Leprechauns* haunted Los Angeles Lakers fans once again leaving doubt whether they would ever get past the Celtics in the Finals! The 1984 NBA Championship is the one that Magic said the Lakers let slip away. With the Boston win, it created a back-and-forth rivalry between Larry Bird and Magic Johnson going back to their college days. If the Lakers had won, it would have given Magic a two to nothing head-to-head advantage and three to one overall advantage against Bird in NBA championship games won. In the 1984-85 season, the Lakers finished the regular season with the same record as the Celtics the year before at 62-20 but still finished one game behind Boston overall for home court throughout the playoffs. After sweeping the Phoenix Suns in the first round, breezing through the Portland Trail Blazers in the semifinals and Denver Nuggets in the conference finals in five games, the Lakers got their long awaited rematch with the Boston Celtics. After being massacred by the Celtics in game one 148-114 on Memorial Day leaving Lakers fans thinking, *here we go again*, Los Angeles bounced back and won game two behind their captain Kareem Abdul-Jabbar's 30 points and 17 rebounds. The Lakers won two of the next three games in Los Angeles including the pivotal game five behind Kareem's 36-point outburst. In game six on the *mystical parquet floor* in Boston, the *curse* finally came to an end with the Lakers winning the 1985 NBA Championship 111-100 and Abdul-Jabbar was named NBA Finals MVP.

In the 1985-86 season, the Lakers finished the regular season at 62-20 and looked in cruise control on their way to the NBA Finals until they ran into the Houston Rockets in the Western Conference Finals. After winning game one, the Lakers crumbled losing four straight games that included the memorable last second game-winning shot by Ralph Sampson. If the Lakers had won the series, it probably wouldn't have mattered because the Celtics seemed almost invincible playing at home in the Boston Garden. During the Celtics championship years, players and fans, myself included, usually felt that the games were over before they even began - that's how strong the *mystique* was in the "Garden." Throughout a game the Celtics would play great team defense, slow the game down to their tempo, create good ball movement, and then shoot a high percentage shot with the shot clock running down possession after possession. The Celtics finished the regular season at 67-15 and set an NBA record 40-1 at home. They went on to win the 1986 NBA Championship in six games over the Houston Rockets.

Going into the 1986-87 season, The Lakers knew they had a lot of work ahead of them if they were to meet the reigning NBA champion Celtics in the Finals. They had to be up to the challenge of winning a road game in Boston knowing they had a dominate record at home. Magic was also up to the individual challenge of proving that he was just as deserving of MVP as Larry Bird who had just won the award for the third consecutive year. Magic did have his best scoring season of his career finishing with a **career-high 23.9 points** and **12.2 assists** and had a single-game high of **46 points**. He also led the league in assists for the fourth time in five years and ended up winning his first of three MVP awards. With an already improved jump shot, Magic worked with Kareem to develop a hook shot that would come to *fruition* in the 1987 NBA Finals against the Celtics. In a midseason trade to add depth behind center for the second half of the season, the Lakers acquired Mychal Thompson from the Portland Trail Blazers. After cruising through the playoffs with a first-round sweep against the Denver Nuggets, taking care of the Trail Blazers in five games, and sweeping the Seattle SuperSonics in the Western Conference Finals, the Lakers were primed and ready to regain their title over the defending champion Boston Celtics.

Finishing the regular season at 65-17, the Lakers had home court advantage over the Celtics in the NBA Finals and won the first two games at home in an up-tempo high scoring affair behind Magic's 29 points and 13 assists and 0 turnovers in game one, and Michael Cooper's plethora of three pointers in game two. In game three, Boston slowed the game to some extent and won by six. In game four, with the Lakers down by one point, Magic had the most iconic moment of his career when he delivered the game-winning hook shot over the outstretched arms of Kevin McHale and Robert Parish. At that point, the curse of the Boston Garden and their mythical leprechauns vanished into thin air forever!

For Los Angeles Lakers fans, Magic's hook shot has to be ranked at the top of the all-time greatest clutch moments in the city's history right up there with Kirk Gibson's improbable home run off Oakland A's great closer Dennis Eckersley in the 1988 World Series. Magic's shot of choice (which he called his "junior sky-hook") caught the Celtics by surprise as did Gibson's hobbling one-handed home run. Trailing three games to one, with the Lakers in complete control of the series, Boston showed its championship grit and took care of business rather handily in game five. While feeling confident with two home games left, the Laker's spanked the Celtics in game six 106-93 to win their 4th championship of the decade. Magic Johnson averaged **26.2 points** a game, **13 assists**, and **eight rebounds**, on **54 percent** shooting - and was named NBA Finals MVP for the third time. With all due respect to the Celtics, they were battling injuries all season long in which I mention in detail in the next chapter with Larry Bird. In the rivalry of see-saw battles with Bird and Magic throughout the years, Magic came out on top winning more championships. However, in my opinion, Bird had the slightly better all-around *statistics* throughout his career, often almost convincing me to flip-flop these two greats in the elite rankings of all-time.

At the rally during the victory parade, Pat Riley made a guarantee to repeat as champions. A few days later, Riley sat down with Magic and told him that this group of players will go down as one of the great teams in NBA history, but he said, "If you want to go down as one of the *greatest* teams that ever played, one way to do that is to repeat!" The Lakers went out and backed up his words by finishing with the best record in the NBA at 62-20 and earning home court advantage for the second year in a row. But in the playoffs, after sweeping the San Antonio Spurs in the first round, the Lakers battled two Midwest Division *heavy weights* the next two rounds in *grueling* seven-game series. In the Western Conference Semifinals, with Utah leading the series two games to one before losing three of the next four games, I felt like the aging Lakers were vulnerable to the younger *dynamic dual* of Stockton and Malone, but their championship experience proved to be too much for the inexperienced Jazz team. And in the Western Conference Finals, the Lakers took control of the series winning the first two games at home but were pushed to the limit by the pesky Dallas Mavericks. With prolific scorers Mark Aguirre and Rolando Blackman providing the scoring punch and with Derek Harper breaking down the Lakers defense, I felt Dallas was good enough to dethrone Los Angeles and win their first championship. With two gut-wrenching battles under their belt, it seemed fitting that the Lakers were pushed to the limit in the NBA Finals against the Detroit Pistons. After winning game one in L.A. and games four and five in Detroit, the Pistons felt they were ready to seize their first NBA championship from the Lakers until travesty set in when Isiah Thomas badly sprained his ankle during game six. Isiah returned to the game in heroic fashion by scoring 25 points in the third quarter. The Pistons stayed close the rest of the way and came within three points before the strange no-call at midcourt on the collision with Isiah and Magic, before eventually losing the game 103-102. With a hobbling Isiah, the Lakers went on to win game seven 108-105 behind "Big Game James" triple-double of 36 points, 16 rebounds, and 10 assists. The Los Angeles Lakers won the 1988 NBA Championship and James Worthy was named NBA Finals MVP. Many people felt the Pistons would have won the series if Isiah had never sprained his ankle.

The next year in Kareem's final season, the Lakers finished the regular season with 57 wins and steam rolled through the playoffs sweeping the Portland Trail Blazers, the Seattle SuperSonics, and the Phoenix Suns in the Western Conference Finals - before being swept themselves by the Detroit Pistons in the NBA Finals. It seemed too good to be true that the Lakers would three-peat as champions not only because it hadn't been done since 1966, but because I knew Detroit had the best record in the NBA and were the hungrier team after being so close the year before. After Byron Scott tore his hamstring prior to game one and Magic injured his during game two, the Lakers dream of a third straight championship and a going away party for Kareem was then shattered. In his last three years of his career before the HIV epidemic, Magic averaged **21.4 points**, **12.3 assists**, and **7.1 rebounds** per game, and shot over 90 percent from the free-throw line, twice in the regular season.

In the Lakers first season without Kareem, Magic and Worthy led the Lakers to the best record in the NBA at 63-19 record. But after defeating the Houston Rockets in four games in the first round, they bowed out to a terrific Suns team in five games that featured Tom Chambers, Kevin Johnson, Jeff Hornacek, Eddie Johnson and Dan Majerle. The next season, the Lakers finished with 58 wins and second place in their division to the reigning Western Conference Champion Portland Trail Blazers. After sweeping the Rockets in the first round of the playoffs, and the Golden State Warriors in an *epic* five-game series in the semifinals (that included the individual battle of forty-point games between Magic and Chris Mullin in the final game that went to overtime), the Lakers upset Portland in six games to return to the NBA Finals.

With Michael Jordan and the Chicago Bulls seeking their first championship in franchise history, the NBA now had its dream matchup with "Magic and Michael." Going into the series, in most people's eyes, it probably looked like it was going to be a competitive series especially after the Lakers stole game one in Chicago behind Magic's heroics and Sam Perkins big shot at the end of the game. But with Jordan and the hungry Bulls seeking their first championship and the way they destroyed every team in the playoffs including when they swept the two-time champion Pistons, I knew the Lakers and their old legs were in serious trouble. In the next four games, the Lakers were totally outran and outclassed by the younger, more athletic and superior defensive oriented Chicago Bulls team. Thinking back, it seemed like Jordan drove through the lane with more ease in the playoffs than in any time before. I mean Perkins and Divac looked like a pair of *immobile* Bill Laimbeer's with their hands up in the air every time Jordan floated passed them for easy layups and dunks. *I was saying to myself, do something, contest with more aggression, slide over and try and draw a charge, or just give a hard foul!* It just seemed like the Lakers big men were just standing around in a trance, admiring "Air Jordan" fly by them all series long. By the way, this was the series that Jordan had the *famous* highlight they show during every NBA Finals, when he was surrounded by three Lakers going for a dunk right at the basket but at the last second, switching the ball from his right hand to his left while coming down in midflight spinning the ball off glass on the left side of the basket. After retiring after testing HIV Positive in November of 1991, Magic returned in the 1992 NBA All-Star game where he led the West to victory and scored the last points of the game on a memorable three-pointer from 40 feet away. And, then in the summer he played sparingly (because of bad knees) for the 1992 USA Olympic Dream Team that featured the greatest collection of basketball players in history. A bulked up Magic made another comeback at the end of the 1996 season where he played in the last 32 games of the season and averaged only 14.6 points and 6.9 assists before losing to the Houston Rockets in the first round of the playoffs three games to one.

In player comparisons:

Magic was rated the greatest point guard in NBA history by ESPN in 2007. He led the league in assists 4 times in the regular season and 4 consecutive years in the playoffs from 1984 to 1987. He made All-NBA First Team 9 times while winning the regular season MVP award 3 times. He also won 5 NBA Championships and 3 Finals MVP awards including one his rookie season. Even though never making an All-Defensive Team, Magic did manage to lead the league in steals twice.

At the present day, in the minds of many, Magic Johnson is the greatest Laker of all-time by a slight margin over both Jerry West and Kobe Bryant. I can make the case for the following reasons: First of all, Bill Simmons who claims to be the greatest basketball mind, has Magic ranked as the 4th greatest player of all-time in his pantheon rankings, just as I do in my elite Rankings. So with Magic ranked ahead of Kobe for best all-time, he has to be the greatest Laker! Today we are often *prisoners of the moment* and get *sucked into* what a player or a team has done at the current moment, recently or within the last few years. By all accounts, that does entitle bragging rights for all to a certain extent. However, we should sit back, relax and look at the big picture for every great player and every great team of the present and the past, and don't go overboard on how much we boast. Even though Kobe's career is not yet complete, many people around league still say Magic was the greatest Laker. Even though West and Magic endorse Bryant as the greatest Laker, they are two of the most gracious people when it comes to giving credit to the franchise and its players. Even they are caught up in what Bryant has done recently and has given to the city of Los Angeles, including all his scoring accolades and two most recent NBA championships. Dennis Scott who works for NBA TV just said in the beginning of 2012, even if Bryant wins 6 or 7 championships, Magic is still the greatest Laker. For those who missed it, Kenny Smith of TNT said in 2011, that Magic Johnson was the greatest Laker of all-time. On the other hand, I'm sure a lot of fans would say Kobe is the greatest Laker. In my assessment, if Bryant does happen to win another championship or another MVP award, we can then open back up the conversation. Actually, we will in the next few paragraphs!

However, the same cannot be said about Kareem being ranked the greatest Laker over Magic because he had six of his best individual seasons with the Milwaukee Bucks including having had achieved one NBA Championship, one Finals MVP, his two scoring titles, and recorded his four best scoring seasons of his career before becoming a Laker. In support of Kareem, he did play fourteen seasons with the franchise as the best, second best, and third best player on the team - while winning five championships, three regular season MVP awards (the two in 1976 and 1977 were before Magic got there), and one Finals MVP.

Magic was the floor general during the "Showtime" days and did whatever it took for his team to win, whether it meant finishing at the basket or making the clutch shot, making the right pass to the open man, or using his enormous height to outrebound smaller guards to where he would often trigger his own fast break. Magic Johnson was the modern-day Oscar Robertson that could do it all. He could pass, rebound, and score when his team needed him to as he just so happens to be second on the all-time list for career triple-doubles behind only the Big O. In addition, his 4 career triple-doubles with at least 20 assists is tied for first with Rajon Rondo, who just tied Magic this season in 2012, which is one ahead of Oscar on the all-time list. As far as dribble penetration, Magic was not flashy in terms of flying through the air and dunking the ball, but he could drive to the basket and finish as good as any superstar to have ever played the game. He also had a highly effective set shot and was one of the greatest clutch shooters in NBA history right up there with Larry Bird and Jerry West. I would take Magic's open set shot in the clutch over any player he played with for the possible exception of Michael Cooper. Kareem was also a great clutch shooter in the low post but was thirty-three years old and less dominant when Magic entered the league in 1980.

In player comparisons with the greatest Lakers of all-time, Jerry West and Kobe Bryant were the better pure scorers/shooters, but Magic was the better passer, rebounder and free-throw shooter. Don't let Magic fool you for those of you who never saw him play or don't remember that far back! Like I have already mentioned in the beginning of the chapter highlighting his individual attributes, Magic might not have been as great a perimeter scorer and shooter, for that matter compared to West and Kobe, but he was equally as great a *clutch* player and shooter. In fact, he was just as effective driving and finishing at the basket as Kobe was, and maybe even a little better the second half of Bryant's career, due to the assumption that he so chooses to play more from the perimeter than by taking it to the rim. Magic was just as dominate finishing at the basket off dribble penetration as the other greats of the game, he just didn't jump as high and wasn't as flashy. If he wanted to, he could have averaged 25 points a game instead of being the ultimate facilitator and making his teammates better.

Defensively, Magic was underrated early on in his career. With his young legs and quick hands, he led the NBA in steals in back-to-back years. Kobe of course is an outstanding defensive player as was Jerry even though they didn't keep track of steals until West's last year in the league. West had great anticipation, extraordinarily long arms and quick hands. He would have made more than the four All-Defensive First Team selections but the honor wasn't inaugurated until the 1968-69 season. West averaged 27 points a game in the regular season and 29.2 in the playoffs while setting numerous scoring records, while Kobe is currently averaging 25.3 points in the regular season, and has plenty of high scoring games in his illustrious career including the second highest scoring game in NBA History with 81 points. But in the playoffs, Bryant is averaging 25.4 points and owns very few scoring records compared to West. I do understand Kobe was held back to a certain extent playing alongside Shaq but so was West during his early years playing with Baylor. So the statistics remain objective despite what everybody wants to think.

Magic Johnson owns just as much or more assists records in the regular season and in the playoffs (had 10 games of at least 20 assists in the postseason (ranks first), giving him 32 total - which ranks second to Stockton's 38) as West and Kobe do in scoring. He also holds the record for career assists per game in the regular season (11.2) and postseason (12.3) along with total assists in the postseason (2346). In addition, he also had the second most career triple-doubles in the regular season (138) and the most career triple-doubles in the playoffs (30) and NBA Finals (8).

Magic won five championships and three Finals MVP awards to Kobe's five and two. I felt Pau Gasol was the MVP of the 2010 NBA Finals because of his clutch scoring and rebounding and overall play coming in the four Laker wins - and because Kobe had his two highest scoring games coming in losses while shooting a *very low* 40 percent for the series including a *horrendous* 6 for 24 from the field for 25 percent in game seven. Although, Bryant did play superior defense, and rebounded a lot more than ever before. To be fair, I guess you can say Kareem could have won the 1980 Finals MVP with his scoring and rebounding numbers throughout the first five games of the series before injuring his ankle, while Magic averaged five turnovers per game.

So to summarize, Magic and Kobe won the same amount of championships but Magic was the best player on the best teams and set more playoff records. He also had the better career **winning percentage at .717** to .658 going into the 2012 season. In fact, in terms of overall winning percentage throughout his entire career in the regular season, he ranks ahead of Jordan, Bird, Russell, Kareem and Duncan. To hammer my point home even further from a winning perspective, Magic led the Lakers to 9 NBA Finals against the toughest competition in the history of the league, whereas Kobe helped lead his team to 7 NBA Finals against weaker competition. Magic won 5 NBA Championships against the mighty Boston Celtics twice with Larry Bird, Kevin McHale, and Robert Parish; the Philadelphia 76ers twice with Dr. J; and the Bad boys Pistons with Isiah Thomas, Joe Dumars, and Dennis Rodman. The four losses came against those same 76ers (with Moses

Malone), Celtics, Pistons, and Jordan's Chicago Bulls. Kobe playing second fiddle behind Shaquille O'Neal, won 3 championships in a row against the Indiana Pacers, Philadelphia 76ers, and New Jersey Nets. With Pau Gasol, Andrew Bynum and Lamar Odom, the Lakers beat the Orlando Magic and an aging Boston Celtics team with Paul Pierce, Kevin Garnett, and Ray Allen. The two losses came against lone superstar Ben Wallace and the Detroit Pistons and against an extremely formidable Celtics team with Pierce, Garnett, and Allen still in their prime. So in all Magic's wins and losses in the NBA Finals, came against the greatest players on the greatest teams of all-time. Whereas Shaq and Kobe's Lakers had to face only one all-time great team, the Boston Celtics in 2008. When the Lakers did win it all, it came against the 2010 Celtics on their last leg and against teams with only one true superstar in Reggie Miller, Allen Iverson, Jason Kidd, and Dwight Howard. Even if the number one seed Cleveland Cavaliers in 2009 and 2010 had faced the Lakers and lost, it would have come against a team with only one superstar in LeBron James - and by the way, if LeBron and the Cavaliers had faced the Lakers, I would have bet enormously that they would have won at least one of those championships!

West was the best out of the three overall statistically in the playoffs but only won one championship while taking the Lakers to nine NBA Finals. West and Baylor had to face the best team in the history of sports six times during the 1960s while often playing injured. In two thirds of the Finals appearances, Baylor had bad knees in the last four against the Boston Celtics in 1965, 1966, 1968 and 1969. Honestly, I think either "Mr. Outside" or "Mr. Inside" would have been the greatest Laker, if they hadn't been prone to injury most of their careers.

I did an article (on my former website JNBA@Allsports.com titled, LeBron James & Dwyane Wade "The Greatest Dual Ever"! on November 1st 2010 - and I ranked Jerry West and Elgin Baylor ahead of Jordan and Pippen, Shaq and Kobe, and Magic and Kareem proving how great they were individually playing together in their primes and stated that they were the only dual in NBA history to average 30 points in the *same season*. Baylor was just as prolific a scorer as West and Bryant but became less dominant the second half of his career due to chronic knee injuries. Baylor put up the *highest* regular and playoff scoring seasons out of any Laker in history in the first half of his career while having compiling terrific rebounding numbers, but never won an NBA championship. Shaquille O'Neal was the most physically dominant player in franchise history but only played eight of his nineteen seasons with the Lakers. He was the irreplaceable piece on their back-to-back-to-back NBA Championship teams from 2000 to 2002 and set his share of franchise scoring marks for a center in the regular season and the postseason. I left Wilt Chamberlain out of the conversation because he played only five years with the Lakers franchise.

The Celtics have the greatest franchise of all-time but the Lakers have the greatest *individual Superstars* of all-time that played throughout all the decades in NBA history including George Mikan in the 1950s. I could sit here all day and build a strong case for Baylor, West, Chamberlain, Kareem, Shaq and Kobe as being the greatest Laker of all-time, but Magic Johnson stills comes out on top. In fact, not only does Magic come out on top as the greatest Laker, I always felt in my youth, witnessing Magic and Jordan first hand, that Magic could have been just as great a player as Jordan. The way people view Bill Russell as the greatest *ultimate* team player, the same can be said about Magic. Like Russell, Magic won the NBA championship his rookie season and in his third season in the league. Even though he didn't win as many throughout his career, he still finished with five and only one less than Jordan who didn't win his first championship until his seventh season in the league at 28 years old. He also won 3 MVP awards to Jordan's 5 and was just as dominate in the passing aspect of the game as Jordan was in scoring. So basically, Magic had the upper hand the first half of his career, and wasn't too far behind in the second half.

So from a winning perspective, Magic was the *ultimate* facilitator who made his teammates better throughout his *entire* career compared to Jordan in mostly the *second half* of his. However, in player comparisons, you would still have to give a slight advantage to Jordan, because he has one more championship ring to his credit, and his individual scoring accolades for the betterment of the team, were backed up when he won the MVP award 5 times. Also, in head-to-head matchups, Jordan won more titles vs. Magic 1-0 and had the edge in total wins 11-7 (7-6 and 4-1 in the regular season and postseason) while Magic won more titles vs. Bird 2-1 and had the edge in total wins 22-15 (11-7 and 11-8 in the regular season and postseason). But before Jordan won his fifth and sixth championships at the age of 34 and 35, I felt you could make the case that Magic was the greatest basketball player of all-time or perhaps the second best player ever. Larry Bird even said during one of his press conferences; "Magic's [Johnson] just a great basketball player, he's the best I've ever seen," and that includes many of the players in this book, and you know who? That guy, the one that played on the Chicago Bulls!

Career Totals

19.2 points, 11.2 assists, 7.2 rebs, 1.9 steals, 0.4 blocks, .520 FG%, .848 FT%, .303 3FG%

17,707 points, 10,141 assists, 6559 rebounds, 1724 steals, 374 blocks, 325 threes

Larry Bird

(Rank #5)

MVP (3-times), Free-Throw Percentage Title (4-times)

Three-pointers made (2-times), All-NBA First Team (9-times)

NBA Championships (3), NBA Finals MVP (2-times), All-Star (12-times)

Also featuring: Dennis Johnson

Larry Bird was the *greatest clutch* shooter in NBA history along with Jerry West. Perhaps the greatest Boston Celtic of All-time, Bird was a marksman, deadeye assassin that brought terror to his opponents on a nightly basis. When the game was on the line, it seemed like he would not miss. A forward/power forward at six-foot-nine and one of the game's greatest scorers ever, "Larry Legend" probably made more big shots than any player in history. And, although well known for his lethal shooting, Bird was also one of the best *all-around* players to have played the game, winning 3 consecutive MVP awards from 1984 to 1986 right smack in the middle of the decade that had the most talented group of players in league history. At that point and even today, you could even make the case that he was the greatest basketball player of all-time. Longtime Celtics coach Red Auerbach once said that "Larry Bird was the greatest player ever to put on a uniform." With that being said, every basketball fan should watch "Larry Bird's 50 Greatest Moments" often shown on NBA TV. It might be the greatest assortment of plays ever assembled for any one player. The one hour special shows footage of his entire offensive repertoire that includes an array of jump shots, fallaway shots, twisting drives to the basket, rebounding and easy put-backs for layups, and *exquisite* passing that some players at the time had never seen before. To truly realize how great they were all basketball fans should watch old footage of NBA Hardwood Classics to relish the memory on Hall of Famers of the past.

Larry Bird's offensive arsenal included a jump shot from anywhere on the court, a fallaway shot that he could shoot from the low-post/high-post positions all the way out to the three-point line, and a stop-and-pop jump shot that he could shoot in the half court or on the fast break, where he would also come down court, stop on a dime like a shooting guard, and with his quick release, bury a jumper *right between the eyes* of his opponent. Bird could shoot with a *hand in his face* better than any player in NBA history partly because the starting motion of his shot release was way up behind his head. Because players had to honor his deadly jump shot, allowed him to take his man off the dribble and finish at the basket. He would also suck the defense in off dribble penetration and make the simple pass to Kevin McHale or Robert Parish inside the paint for an easy layup, or kick out to an open shooter on the perimeter. Despite, at times, being slow of foot, *particularly* in the second half of his career, Bird was a clever dribbler. It seemed like he could get to any spot he wanted on the court often scoring inside with some nifty, whirling layup finishing with either hand. He had to be ambidextrous, because a lot of his highlights throughout the years included him finishing equally with his left hand as he did his right. Some players in the NBA today can finish layups with either hand, but very few if not any, can shoot a jump shot, sweeping hook shot, or runner in the lane with their left hand the way Larry could. Bird was also a savvy rebounder, able to maneuver his way under the basket to get caroms (rebounds) and easy put-back layups. Underrated as a defensive player, Bird in his younger days from 1982 to 1984 made the All-Defensive Second Team three years in a row. He had great hands and anticipation on defense often making key steals and blocks throughout his career. He would pick off passes by reading the offense and then stepping in front of an opponent or by moving into the passing lanes. And in the low post, he had lightning-quick hands to deflect or strip the ball from a player when they least expected it. Despite the lack of leaping ability as a shot blocker when facing opponents straight up, Bird would take deceptive angles to the basket to block a player's shot from behind.

But what made Larry Bird special was that he was just as great a passer as he was a scorer. As a color commentator on CBS games during the 1980s, great Celtic Tommy Heinsohn always said that Bird was the greatest passer in the game along with Magic Johnson. As a youngster in the 1980s, I was always questioning what the heck he was talking about, saying to myself, well what about all the other great point guards in the league? Bob Cousy once said, "Bird was the best passer that he had ever seen." The more I watched Bird over the years, the more I realized how *special* he was. Even though LeBron James just broke the NBA record in 2010 for assists in a season for a forward and will accumulate more assists at his position than anyone in history, I am torn between which player will go down as the greatest passing forward of all-time. As far as pure passing, both players are spot on crisp passers that could make the simple pass into the post, bounce pass to a cutter, zip pass to the perimeter or across court, and the thread-the-needle pass between two defenders with the slightest bit of opening, in the mold of great point guards Magic Johnson, John Stockton, Jason Kidd, Steve Nash, and Chris Paul. But what separates the two thus far is that Bird was able to consistently make the more difficult, more spectacular pass that included a no-look zip pass over the shoulder with either hand, back-to-the-basket no-look over-the-head pass with one or both hands that only he or Magic could make, a variety of touch passes from the perimeter, out of the post or on the fast break, and a ridiculous assortment of behind-the-back passes from anywhere on the court. On a few occasions he was seen making the most difficult pass of all, the bounce pass underneath a player's legs. In favor of LeBron, aside from having the great court vision, fundamental passing skills and the ability to make the spectacular pass like a point guard, LeBron puts more velocity on his passes than any player ever including Magic. Using his immensely strong wrist and hands when making a skip pass, thread-the-needle pass, or cross-court pass, the ball is traveling faster thereby giving perimeter players more time to shoot when the defense rotates.

Bird's greatest attributes could have been his incredible basketball instincts, anticipation for the game and his mental and physical toughness. Bird was willing to give up his body for the sake of the team often diving into the stands and onto Boston's parquet floor (one of the oldest and most rugged courts in the league at the time) for loose balls. While battling in the trenches, he would fight hard by banging bodies and exchanging elbows in the like of past great Bob Pettit. After 13 seasons of immense back problems where bones were pushed into his nerves in the lumbar vertebra of his back, in 1992 he called it quits.

Larry Joe Bird was born on December 7th, 1956 in West Baden, Indiana and went to Springs Valley High School in French Lick where he led his team to 19-2 record as a junior. After leaving the school as the all-time leading scorer, in 1974 Bird attended Indiana University on a scholarship but left the school after 24 days because he broke his toe in a pick-up game that kept him from working for money he badly needed. After enrolling in Northwood Institute, he dropped out after two weeks because of the lack of competition. He then got a job for a year before playing AAU Basketball for Hancock Construction before enrolling at Indiana State. After scoring 43 points and grabbing 25 rebounds in one of the games against Indiana's finest players, he was noticed by Indiana State's assistant coach Bill Hodges and head coach Bob King. After the recruitment, in three years at ISU, Bird averaged **30.3 points**, **13.3 rebounds**, and **4.6 assists**, and was named NCAA College Player of the Year. He also won the AP Player of the Year and the John R. Wooden Award and left the school as the fifth highest scorer in NCAA history. In his final season, he led the Sycamores to a 33-1 record including a berth in the NCAA championship game in 1979 where they would lose to Magic Johnson and the Michigan

State Spartans. Prior to his senior year, Larry Bird was selected by the Boston Celtics as the 6th pick overall of the 1978 NBA Draft after becoming eligible after his junior season.

In his first year as a Boston Celtic, he led the team in scoring, rebounding, steals, and finished second on the team in assists and three-pointers made while making his first All-Star team and winning the 1980 Rookie of the Year. The Celtics finished the regular season at 61-21, but in the playoffs after sweeping the Houston Rockets in the semifinals, they were eliminated by the Philadelphia 76ers in five games in the conference finals. In the off-season, in one of the greatest trades in NBA history, the Celtics acquired Robert Parish along with the 3rd pick of the 1980 Draft from the Golden State Warriors in exchange for the draft rights to the first pick (Joe Barry Carroll) and the 13th pick (Rickey Brown). With that third pick, the Celtics selected Kevin McHale. In Bird's second season, he led the team again in points, rebounds, and steals while leading the Celtics to 62 wins and the best record in the NBA for the second consecutive season. In the playoffs, the Celtics swept the Chicago Bulls in the semifinals to set up a rematch with Philadelphia in the Eastern Conference Finals. This time behind Bird, Parish, McHale and Nate "Tiny" Archibald, the Celtics prevailed despite trailing in the series three games to one. In game 7, Bird gave a preview of his potential as one of the *game's great clutch shooters* by scoring 26 points including the game-winning shot. After the series Nate Archibald said, "I never heard the term 'point forward' until I met Larry." The Celtics went on to win the 1981 NBA Championship over Moses Malone and the Houston Rockets in six games.

The season after, the Celtics finished with the best record in the league at 63-19 for the third consecutive year. With Bird putting up similar numbers as his first two seasons, and with McHale and Parish jelling in their second season with the team, the Celtics were primed and ready to defend their title. After beating the Washington Bullets in the semifinals four games to one, the Celtics lost in the conference finals to the Philadelphia 76ers in seven games on their own home court. Boston won the first game but lost three games in a row to turn the table in favor of Philadelphia from the previous year. With a 3 to 1 deficit, Boston had slim chances of a comeback. But despite winning the next two games they eventually succumbed to Philly in seven games. After Los Angeles won the 1982 NBA Championship over Philadelphia giving Magic Johnson two titles in his first three years in the league, Bird wanted to get back to the NBA Finals and even the score. But the Celtics never even made it that far, losing in the conference semifinals to the Milwaukee Bucks in four straight games. In the 1983-84 season with newly acquired Dennis Johnson coming over from the Phoenix Suns, Boston wanted to avenge the loss in the playoffs from the previous two years to the Bucks and Eastern Conference Champion Philadelphia (who they lost to in 1982) that had just acquired Moses Malone in a trade with Houston. Bird would have his best season thus far in his career by increasing his scoring average to 24.2 points, his assist average to six and a half a game, and by winning his first of three consecutive MVP awards. The Celtics finished with the best record in the league at 62-20 for the fourth time in Bird's first five years in the league. With Bird entering his prime, the Celtics were overdue for a second championship of the 1980s. In the playoffs, Boston beat the Washington Bullets in five games in the first round before coming out victorious in a tough battle with the New York Knicks in the semifinals in seven games. And after defeating the Milwaukee Bucks in five games in the Eastern Conference Finals, they faced the Los Angeles Lakers in the NBA Finals for the first time in the "Bird vs. Magic" era. The Lakers surprised everyone by winning game one in the Boston Garden and had a good chance to win game two if they hadn't self-destructed in the closing seconds. In game three, Boston lost in L.A. by thirty-four points but regrouped and won a close game four in which the Lakers felt they should of won. The Celtics won game five and game seven at home decisively 111-103 to win the 1984 NBA Championship. Bird scored 34 points in game five and had 20 points and 12 rebounds in game seven. He also averaged 27.4 points and 14 rebounds, on 48 percent shooting for the series and captured his first Finals MVP award.

With Larry Bird evening the score with Magic Johnson in head-to-head championship games going back to their college days, Bird and the Celtics were ready to defend their title and win their third championship of the young decade. At the same time, Bird wanted to go up on Magic two titles to one in head-to-head matchups including college. In the 1984-85 season the Celtics were riding high coming off their second championship of the decade and with Bird taking his game to another level. Near the end of the regular season, Kevin McHale set the new Celtics record in scoring with 56 points on March 2nd, 1985 in which he was asked to be removed from the game because of exhaustion. Bird had questioned McHale after the game on why he didn't stay in and go for more points. You would assume it probably wasn't in his mentally to keep the scoring going when the other team was already down and the game was all but over. Ironically, nine days later, Bird showed McHale how to keep a scoring *flurry* going by torching the Hawks in *Hotlanta*, dropping 60 points to set a new franchise record. And to top it off, that same season, Bird took home his second consecutive MVP award. In the playoffs, the Celtics cruised to victory over the Cleveland Cavaliers three games to one in the first round, and then finished off the Detroit Pistons in six games in the semifinals, before dispatching the Philadelphia 76ers in only five games in the conference finals to set up the much anticipated Finals rematch with the Los Angeles Lakers. After obliterating the Lakers in game one at home 148-114 in the '"Memorial Day massacre," it looked like business as usual for the Celtics and their historical dominance over the Lakers. But it was not to be for Boston as they lost game two at home and got blown out in game three in Los Angeles. The Celtics bounced back in game four to tie the series at two but lost the pivotal game five in L.A. and the must win game six on their home floor 111-100. The Lakers finally beat the Celtics in the NBA Finals for the first time in their franchise's history.

The 1985-86 season was one of, if not the most *magical* season in Boston Celtics history. Larry Bird had just won his third consecutive MVP award and the Celtics finished the regular season as one of the greatest teams of all-time. After finishing with the best record in the league at 67-15 and the most *dominant* home court record in NBA history at 40-1, the Celtics were ready to *conquer* any team in its path. In the playoffs, Boston swept the Chicago Bulls in the first round, beat the Atlanta Hawks in five games in the semifinals; and then swept the Milwaukee Bucks in the Eastern Conference Finals. With the Lakers already out of the way in the Western Conference after they had lost in five games to the Houston Rockets, the Celtics had their eyes set on the twin towers and what was later known as "Clutch City." With Ralph Sampson coming off his miraculous game-winning shot and Hakeem Olajuwon emerging as a big-time star, the Celtics road to victory became a little more difficult. The Celtics had an additional big man of their own in Bill Walton to counter the size of the Rockets. Throughout the series, the combination of Parish, McHale and Walton were able to neutralize Olajuwon and Sampson inside freeing up Bird to perform his magic all over the court. But after taking the first two games at home convincingly, the Celtics were poised to complete one of the greatest seasons in NBA history. The Rockets won game three at home by two points but lost the crucial game four at home 106-103. With Boston in complete control of the series in the 2-3-2 format, the never-say-die Rockets came to play and blew out the Celtics in game five at home, forcing a game six. Boston then returned the favor on their home court with a 114-97 series clinching victory to win the 1986 NBA Championship. Larry Bird averaged **24 points**, **9.7 rebounds** and **9.5 assists**, and was named NBA Finals MVP for the second time in three years.

The following season, Bird averaged **28.1 points**, **9.2 rebounds**, and **7.6 assists** but with the Celtics hampered by injuries, made it back to the NBA Finals where they would lose to the Los Angeles Lakers in six games. After sweeping the Chicago Bulls in the first round of the playoffs, the Celtics faced two formidable opponents in the next two rounds that pushed them to the limit. The Milwaukee Bucks were so close to dethroning the Celtics for the first time behind Sidney Moncrief, Ricky Pierce, and Terry Cummings. Throughout the decade, the Bucks were the odd team out just like the Dallas Mavericks in the Western Conference. I felt Milwaukee was good enough to win a championship during the 1980s. With Don Nelson's five NBA Championship rings as a player and all his 7-50 win seasons as head coach, he was never able to lead Milwaukee to the Promised Land. In the Eastern Conference Finals, the Celtics beat the Detroit Pistons in a grueling seven-game series that featured the *improbable* steal in game five by Larry Bird that defined his legacy not only for being one of the most talented players of all-time, but for having one of the greatest basketball minds of all-time. With the Pistons up by two points and ten seconds on the clock, Bird faked right but drove left to the basket only to have his shot blocked out of bounds. On the inbound play with five seconds on the clock, Isiah Thomas tried to inbound the ball to the backcourt but Joe Dumars was being blanketed by Bird leaving Bill Laimbeer wide open under the Celtics' basket. After Bird bumped Dumars, he then darted down near the baseline anticipating the inbound pass from Isiah. As he stepped in front of Laimbeer to steal the pass, his momentum nearly carried him out of bounds, but at the last moment while tight roping the baseline, Bird made a quick pass underneath the basket to the cutting Dennis Johnson for the game-winning layup. It wasn't a coincidence that those two *heady* players completed the miracle play and that I just so included Dennis Johnson extensively in this chapter. Bird had the great sense to anticipate the steal and the quick instincts and vision to make the pass with a couple seconds on the clock as did D.J. who quickly cut to the basket anticipating the pass to lay the ball in over the trailing Dumars.

While Bird might have been the smartest basketball player ever to play the game, **Dennis Johnson** could have been the second, or at least he was on the 1980s Celtics. Larry Bird said D.J. was the best player he ever played with and that includes many of the all-time greats, McHale, Parish, Walton, and "Tiny Archibald." That speaks volumes even though Bird was probably heavily factoring in his mental aspect of the game to go along with his physical play. Because Bird thought so highly of D.J. who was just recently inducted into the Hall of Fame while *deceased*, was the deciding factor I included him in this chapter.

Born on September 18th, 1954 in San Pedro, California, Dennis Wayne Johnson attended Dominguez High School in Compton, Ca. After three years of junior college, he went on to play basketball at Pepperdine where in one year he averaged 15.7 points and 5.8 assists, on 56 percent shooting. Johnson was then selected in the second round with the 29th pick overall of the 1976 NBA Draft by the Seattle SuperSonics. After a slow start to his career coming off the bench with his production gradually increasing, by his third season he averaged 15.9 points, 4.7 rebounds, 3.5 assists, 1.3 steals, and 1.2 blocks per game. During this development stage, D. Johnson got a taste of the NBA Finals in dramatic fashion in both 1978 and 1979. The first year it wasn't so great because the Sonics had lost a heartbreaker to the Washington Bullets in seven games, despite the record (for a guard in the Finals) 7 blocks in game six by D. Johnson. After defeating the Los Angeles Lakers, Portland Trail Blazers, and the Denver Nuggets to win the Western Conference, Seattle took a three games to two lead in the Finals and were on the brink of their franchise's first championship until they lost the final two games of the series. Like most great champions you have to learn to fail at the highest level before you can win it all, and that's what happened to D.J. when he missed all 14 of his field goal attempts in game seven.

The very next season, Johnson and the *SuperSonics* bounced back and captured the 1979 NBA Championship. After finishing with 52 wins, Seattle eliminated the Lakers and the Phoenix Suns before winning the rematch with Washington in six games. Johnson was named NBA Finals MVP. For the entire postseason, D.J. averaged 20.9 points, 6.1 rebounds, and 4.1 assists per game. At that point, you knew he was going have a solid career because he blossomed in the postseason increasing his overall production significantly from the regular season and into the playoffs; In fact, those numbers were a prelude to the next three seasons. He had his best three years statistically in his last season with the Sonics and his first two with his new franchise in Phoenix; he averaged **19.1 points**, **4.9 rebounds**, and **4.1 assists** per game. And he almost matched those numbers in the playoffs despite never making it past the conference semifinals. After three years with the Suns, he spent his final seven seasons with the Celtics where he won two more NBA championships. Because the Celtics were such a deep and talented team, his overall numbers except for the assists began to decrease. At the same time, because he played with an exceptional cast of scorers and shooters in Bird, Parish, McHale and Danny Ainge, his assists rose to **6.4** per game.

In player comparisons:

Out of all the great defensive specialist (not including Jordan who was just as great but was best known for his relentless scoring and Pippen who played in only the last three years of the decade) during the 1980s, among guards and small forwards, Dennis Johnson was one of the top 4 or 5 along with Sidney Moncrief, Michael Cooper, and Joe Dumars. D.J. was one of the best defensive guards in history along with Moncrief, who won two Defensive Player of the Year awards in the early part of the decade. I think by winning the award weighs heaviest when making a player comparison because, it has been proven extremely difficult for any offensive player to win the prestigious award once in a career let alone twice. Look at today's game, using the example of Tim Duncan and LeBron James who are two of the best defensive players of this era, but they have never won the award. In comparisons it terms of man-to-man defense. I'm still not sure D.J. could have guarded Jordan in his prime as good as Dumars did. But then again maybe Dumars couldn't have guarded Magic as well as D.J. did. However, if you count Michael Cooper as a guard/forward, who also won the Defensive Player of the Year award in 1987, I think he was the best defensive player (despite often coming off the bench) of the 1980s, because he had a freakishly long wing span beyond belief and could guard Bird as well as anyone ever had. D.J. and Dumars did make the All-Defensive First Team 6 and 4 times respectively to Cooper and Moncrief's 5 and 4 times, but neither of the former two won Defensive Player of the Year.

Getting back to Larry Bird, unfortunately after defeating the Detroit Pistons in the conference finals, Bird and the Celtics ran into destiny but this time it wasn't on their side. The game-winning *junior sky-hook* in the Boston Garden that helped define Magic's career, gave the Lakers an *unthinkable* three to one series advantage in the Boston Garden on their way to winning the 1987 NBA Championship. After finishing the 1987-88 season with the best record in the Eastern Conference, the Celtics made it all the way back to the conference finals but would eventually lose to the Detroit Pistons in six games. Bird averaged a **career-high** in **scoring at 29.9 points** per game and field goal percentage at **.527**. In the playoffs, he had one of his best scoring games of his career in a back-and-forth shootout against Dominique Wilkins and the Atlanta Hawks in which he scored 20 points in the 4th quarter on 9 of 10 shooting as the Celtics won game seven 118-116.

From what I can remember, Larry Bird probably made more *buzzer-beaters* than any player in history. He has an impressive resume that includes: He is one of three players in history to win the NBA MVP ward three years in row and missed nearly winning a fourth in 1981 (Julius Erving won the award by 29 total votes which included 8 first place votes). The others are Wilt Chamberlain and Bill Russell. Bird also finished runner-up in the MVP balloting four times, either won the award or finished second in the voting six straight seasons, and finished in the top three eight consecutive seasons. During Bird's three year reign, he averaged: **24.2 points, 10.1 rebounds**, and **6.6 assists - 28.7 points, 10.5 rebounds**, and **6.6 assists - 25.8 points**, 9.8 rebounds, and **6.8 assists**. He scored 40 points or more in the regular season 47 times and 50 points or more 4 times which included 1 60-point game. In addition, Bird became the first man to shoot 50 percent from the field, 40 percent from the three-point line, and 90 percent from the charity stripe. Since then it has been accomplished eight other times; once more by Bird, once each by Dirk Nowitzki, Reggie Miller and Mark Price, and four times by Steve Nash. He also had **59 career triple-doubles** in the regular season (which ranks fifth all-time) and **10** in the playoffs.

At the time of his retirement, Bird either held or shared 27 Celtics records.

Larry Bird was the greatest forward to ever play the game. And he might retain that title, if LeBron James never reaches the level of team success that Bird did. And, no matter what LeBron does in the future, it will be awfully difficult for him, or anyone else for that matter to surpass Bird as a clutch shooter. Because I never saw Jerry West play, Bird was the greatest *clutch shooter* that I have ever witnessed, even over the great Michael Jordan. So not only was he the greatest when it counted most, he blended scoring/shooting, rebounding and passing, as well as anyone to have ever played the game. Also, just to throw it out there, in head-to-head career matchups vs. Jordan, Bird had the edge in total wins 23-12 (17-12 in the regular season and 6-0 in the playoffs).

While Bird was clearly the better player over Elgin Baylor, Rick Barry, and Julius Erving who all rank close behind him at the forward position, it is debatable on whether Magic Johnson was actually the better player over Larry Bird - even though Bird once said Magic was the best player he'd ever seen. The fact that Bird was the best, second best, or third best player in the NBA for eight straight seasons playing during one of the toughest eras of competition is objective enough for anyone to make the case that Bird was the fourth greatest player ever. But in this book, he will have to settle for fifth best by a *nose* as only Bird would have it based on his words of admiration for Magic Johnson as a player!

Career Totals

24.3 points, 10.0 rebs, 6.3 assists, 1.7 steals, 0.8 blocks, .496 FG%, .376 3FG%, 886 FT%

21,791 points, 8974 rebounds, 5695 assists, 1556 steals, 755 blocks

Oscar Robertson

(Rank #6)

MVP (1-time), Scoring PPG (1-time), Assist Title (6-times)

NBA Championships (1), All-NBA First Team (9-times)

All-Star (12-times), NBA Record: 181 career triple-doubles!

NBA Record: averaged a triple-double for a season!

Also featuring: Bobby Dandridge

    According to most, Oscar Robertson was the greatest all-around player to have ever played the game. He is the only man to average a triple-double for a season that included 41 actual triple-doubles in the 1961-62 season. During his prime playing for the Cincinnati Royals, Oscar took the point guard position to another level in the same way Wilt Chamberlain did at the center position, *dominating* his peers with his size and strength. He also brought a new level of excellence to the position in the three key aspects of the game: scoring, rebounding, and assists. The "Big O" had an outstanding jump shot from the high post, scoring over his opponents at will and in the low post, banging his opponents backwards creating space for a high percentage jumper/fallaway shot. With superior athleticism, he could take it to the rim and finish at the basket with the best that have ever played the game. With his 6'5" 220 pound frame, and plenty of *brawn*, he was able to outrebound smaller guards. Kareem gave him the highest of compliments in his autobiography; "Oscar Robertson was able to man-handle his opponents with his size and strength, by knocking you on your heels or fake knocking you on your heels, he would keep running in to you, doing it over and over again, he was the Jim Brown of basketball!" In addition to his scoring and rebounding *prowess*, Oscar was a gifted playmaker, distributing the ball to open teammates with precision passing. As the successor to the great Bob Cousy, Oscar picked up where Cousy left off, leading the league in assists multiple times including five times in a six-year period.

In player comparisons:

You could make the case, he was the greatest point guard to ever live, even over Magic Johnson for the simple reason; Oscar was the better pure scorer. He was the originator of the head fake and fallaway shot that great scorers use today. At the guard position, both Oscar and Magic *were as good as it gets* at rebounding and passing the ball. Because of the lack of team success, Oscar only won one MVP Award and one NBA Championship compared to Magic winning both multiple times. His only MVP award in 1964 came during the time when competition was at a premium. (Wilt Chamberlain and Bill Russell won 9 MVP's and 7 during Oscar's prime). Magic won more championships in his career in great part because he had the better supporting cast. From the intangible perspective, I think Oscar's teams overachieved and underachieved partly, because he played with an attitude of perfectionism that was often misunderstood. Many people felt his persona was due to the many scars left by all the segregation and racism he received throughout his career and especially early on, resulting in a lot of indelible bitterness, which perhaps made it hard at times for teammates to play with him and meet his expectations.

Oscar Palmer Robertson was born on November 24th, 1938 in Charlotte, Tennessee and was selected with the 1st territorial pick of the 1960 NBA Draft by the Cincinnati Royals. The territorial pick allowed the Royals to give up their number one pick in exchange for a local college player. Oscar had to grow up in poverty and as mentioned, segregation and had to deal with a lot of racism throughout his high school and college days. His Crispus Attucks High School went 31-1 and 31-0 and won back-to-back state championships in 1955 and 1956. His school also set a state record with 45 straight wins and became the first all-black school in the nation to win a state championship. To cap off a fabulous high school career, Oscar was named Indiana's "Mr. Basketball" his senior year.

In college, he led the University of Cincinnati Bearcats to two Final Four appearances and a 79-9 overall record, over three varsity years. Robertson became the first sophomore in history to lead the nation in scoring at **35.1 points** per game (during the season, he had two monster games of **56 and 62 points**). He then finished off a brilliant college career by leading the nation in scoring the next two years averaging **32.6 and 33.7 points** per game respectively. He was also named to the All-America First Team each season and won the College Player of The Year award, three consecutive years. Along the way, he set 14 NCAA College records including the career scoring mark that was eventually surpassed by Pete Maravich. As co-captain with Jerry West playing for the United States basketball team, Team USA went undefeated at 8-0 blowing out their opponents by an average of 42.4 points a game and won the gold medal in the 1960

Summer Olympics. This team which also included Hall of Famers Jerry Lucas and Walt Bellamy was regarded as the greatest group of amateurs ever assembled.

In his first season in 1961, the Cincinnati Royals finished the regular season at 33-46 and missed the playoffs but Oscar Robertson picked up where he left off in college averaging **30.5 points**, **10 rebounds**, and a league leading **9.7 assists** per game while winning Rookie of the Year. In only his second season, he had the best statistical season of his career and perhaps the best season in the history of the sport of basketball by recording the only triple-double for a season in NBA history. He averaged **30.8 points**, **11.4 assists**, and **12.5 rebounds** per game, and led the league in assists for the second straight year. In addition, he scored 40 points or more in a game 8 times, and had 17 games of at least 15 assists. He also corralled 20 rebounds or more in a game five times. After losing to the Pistons in the first round of the playoffs in 1962, the Royals finished the 1962-63 season with a paltry 42-38 record and defeated the Syracuse Nationals in the divisional semifinals three games to two before losing a hard-fought series to the Boston Celtics in seven games. With such a poor record in the regular season, Oscar should be given tremendous credit for taking a mediocre team to within one game of the NBA Finals in only his third year in the league. That year, he had his best season in the playoffs averaging **31.8 points** per game, **13 rebounds**, and **9 assists**. The following season in the playoffs, with a better supporting cast of Jack Twyman, Wayne Embry, Adrian Smith and rookie Jerry Lucas, the Royals beat the Philadelphia 76ers in five games but lost again to an overmatched Celtics team four games to one. The Celtics had gotten better from the previous year with Sam Jones coming into his own leading the team in scoring ahead of Tommy Heinsohn and with second-year John Havlicek having an immediate impact coming off the bench.

Individually, Oscar had one of the two best years of his career by winning the 1964 MVP, leading the league in assists for the third time, and finishing with a **career-high in scoring at 31.4 points** per game and averaged **11 assists**. He almost averaged a second triple-double, missing it by one tenth of a rebound finishing at **9.9** per game. We should just round up and give it to him. In fact, he averaged **30.0 points**, **10.5 assists**, and **10.5 rebounds** in his first five years in the league, and **30 points**, **10.5 assists**, and **9 rebounds** in his first eight years. Unfortunately a player has to average exactly double figures in three statistical categories for a season to get the credit. The same applies for a single game. However, *theoretically* a player could average a triple-double for a season and never actually record one. I wonder what the odds of that happening? To Oscar's credit as I have already mentioned, he did actually have 41 triple-doubles in the 1962 season.

The next three years from 1965 to 1967, the Royals never made it past the first round of the playoffs losing to the 76ers three games to one, the Celtics three games to two, and again to Philly three games to one. Oscar was equally productive during these three seasons as the previous four, averaging 30 points or more and winning two more assists titles. In fact, in 1968, Oscar led the league in assists per game, but Chamberlain won the assist title because he had finished with more total assists for the season. It wasn't until 1970 that scoring, rebounding, and assists titles were determined by per game averages over season totals. So if it wasn't for Guy Rogers in 1963 and 1967, and Chamberlain in 1968, Oscar could have won nine consecutive assists titles putting him one ahead of Cousy on the all-time list. He finished third in assists only one time in the first nine years of his career in 1968 behind Chamberlain and Lenny Wilkens partly because he played in only 65 games. Also in that same year, he did lead the league in points per game but Dave Bing won the scoring title based on total points. Once again, scoring, rebounding, and assist titles were based on total points instead of per game averages up until the 1969-70 season. In conclusion to his *out of this world* scoring, rebounding, and assist numbers, Oscar averaged **29.7 points**, **9.3 rebounds** and **9.4 assists** in his playoff career with the Royals before he was traded to the Milwaukee Bucks.

From the 1967-68 season to the 1969-70 season, Oscar played with Jerry Lucas and non-Hall of Famers Bob Love and Happy Hairston for the first year and Tom Van Arsdale for the last two and never made the playoffs. Oscar never had an *elite* supporting cast in Cincinnati to help him bring home a championship. He faced the stiffest competition playing with perhaps the weakest supporting cast of any superstar of the 1960s. While winning the individual matchup with Hal Greer and Bob Cousy, Oscar and the Cincinnati Royals were always losing alternating battles in the playoffs with the Philadelphia 76ers and Boston Celtics. Greer and Cousy had played with more elite Top 50 players in Chamberlain, Cunningham, Russell, Havlicek, and Jones - while Oscar just had Jerry Lucas who I just barley squeezed into the Top 50. Before the 1971 season, Oscar was traded to the Bucks for Flynn Robinson and Charlie Paulk. There was speculation that Coach Cousy was jealous of the attention Oscar was getting, perhaps because the Big O had just broken many of his records in Cincinnati. During a phone conversation, after Cousy told Oscar that he was going to trade him to Baltimore for Gus Johnson, Oscar told him that he'd better read his contract. Oscar said recently that the Royals attorney gave him the rights to veto any trade so Oscar's attorney asked him where he would want to go and Oscar said, "Since I am from the Midwest and I have always been in the Midwest, I would like to go to Milwaukee." At the time, Cincinnati did inquire about possible trades with the Lakers for either West or Chamberlain, but the Lakers said they would not consider trading either player. For the 1970-71 season, Oscar joined Superstar Lew Alcindor (who didn't change his name to Kareem Abdul-Jabbar until the end of the season) in Milwaukee in hope to capture his first NBA championship. At that point in his career, with Oscar no longer in his prime, he joined another Hall of Famer in **Bobby Dandridge** who had just recently been drafted by the Bucks (his smooth shooting stroke ranks right there at the top with other great shooters of the past in the likes of Sam Jones, Jerry West, Dave Bing, Lou Hudson, Pervis Short, and Joe Dumars). Of course, Alcindor was taken that same year with the first pick while Dandridge was selected late in the 4th round, 45th pick overall of the 1969 NBA Draft by the Milwaukee Bucks. He was also drafted by the Kentucky Colonels of the ABA.

Born on November 15th, 1947 in Richmond, Virginia, Robert L. Dandridge Jr. attended Maggie L. Walker High School in Richmond. In college at Norfolk State, Dandridge got off to a slow start playing in only ten games his freshman year. But, in the next three years, his production began to improve at a rapid pace. By his junior year in 1968, he raised his scoring average from 17.4 to 25.5 points per game while his rebounding average remained almost the same at 13.3. That year, he led the team to a 25-2 record and to the CIAA title but lost in the second round of the NCAA Division II tournament. In his senior season, Dandridge averaged an eye-popping **32.3 points** and **17 rebounds** per game. But in the Division II tournament, his team was eliminated in the first round. In the NBA, he had a solid career the rest of the way averaging 18.5 points, 6.8 rebounds, and 3.4 assists per game, on 48 percent shooting. He also won the NBA Championship with the Bucks in 1971 and again with Elvin Hayes, Wes Unseld and the Washington Bullets in 1978. The following year, he was named to the All-NBA Second team and All-Defensive First Team. During a 10-year span from 1970 to 1979, he was ultimately consistent averaging 19.6 points, 6.9 rebounds, and 3.4 assists per game, on 48 percent shooting. During that same span in eight playoff seasons, he averaged 20.1 points, 7.7 rebounds, and 3.7 assists, on 48 percent shooting. His career was highlighted with 4 All-Star selections and the finishing dunk in game 7 of the 1978 NBA Finals that sealed the game. Dandridge was also the 4th best small forward of the 1970s behind Julius Erving, Rick Barry, and John Havlicek. Known for making big shots throughout his career, Dandridge outplayed Erving in the 1978 playoffs, and hit the game-winning shot out of a triple-team, against George Gervin and the San Antonio Spurs the following year in 1979. That was the playoff series in which Dandridge helped slow down the great G. Gervin in the conference finals. The Bullets advanced to the championship round by coming from behind after being down in the series 3 games to 1.

The Milwaukee Bucks finished the 1970-71 season with a 66-16 record while setting the NBA record for consecutive wins in a season at 20. Though, the very next year, the Los Angeles Lakers shattered the record by winning 33 straight games. The Bucks waltzed through the playoffs beating the San Francisco Warriors and the Lakers without Jerry West in five games, before sweeping the Baltimore Bullets behind ironically Gus Johnson (the player that Cousy was going to trade Oscar for before the season) and Wes Unseld in the 1971 NBA Finals. The "Big O" finally got his long awaited NBA Championship and Alcindor was named Finals MVP. The following year, the Bucks finished with another sixty-win season at 63-19, but lost to the Lakers in the Western Conference Finals, who had just finished a historic record breaking season at 69-13. Chamberlain, West, and Gail Goodrich were too much for Kareem and the aging Robertson. After finishing the 1972-73 campaign with their third consecutive sixty-win season, the 60-22 Bucks lost to the Warriors four games to two in the conference semifinals. The next year in Oscar's final season, the 59-23 Bucks avenged the loss from two years previous to the mighty L.A. Lakers in five games, before sweeping the Chicago Bulls in the Western Conference Finals. This set up a showdown with Dave Cowens and the Boston Celtics in the 1974 NBA Finals. The favored Bucks fell behind three games to two before Kareem made the famous *clutch* hook shot in overtime to tie the series at three games apiece. But the Celtics prevailed in a decisive fifteen-point win in game seven behind Cowens' 28 points and 15 rebounds.

In 2006, ESPN named Oscar Robertson the second greatest point guard of all-time behind Magic Johnson, and the best post-up guard ever. Oscar might have had the best overall statistics in NBA history that included the prestigious, **181 career triple-doubles**. He also made the All-Star team 12 straight years and All-NBA First Team 9 times in a row. Oscar had the scoring ability of Wilt Chamberlain and Michael Jordan, the passing skills of Bob Cousy and Magic Johnson, and was a better rebounder than all guards and most small forwards. He is the only guard in NBA history to average 10 rebounds in a season and he did it three times. He led the league in assists 6 times and was the first player to average 10 assists for a single season. He also had games of 20 assists or more 8 times and 10 games of 19 assists. Oscar could have finished even higher on the all-time assists list, if he hadn't played in an era where assists were given less generously than in today's game.

Everything that I have written above and throughout the chapter illustrates how great Oscar Robertson really was. In the three major facets of the game - scoring, rebounding, and passing, he was at the top. I don't know if there is another player you can say that about. Here is what some of Oscar's numbers looked like on a nightly basis: **42 points, 18 rebounds, 15 assists - 40 points, 17 rebounds, 12 assists - 40 points, 16 rebounds, 15 assists**. Out of all Oscar's accomplishments, the one that stands out most to me are his 7 seasons of at least 500 rebounds and 500 assists that LeBron James might easily surpass someday (J. Kidd did it 8 times but never averaged 20 points). Here are some of the top members of the 500 rebounds and 500 assists club:

Oscar Robertson	Magic Johnson	LeBron James	Larry Bird
1960-61/ 716-690	1979-80/ 596-563	2004-05/ 588-577	1983-84/ 796-520
1961-62/ 985-899	1981-82/ 751-743	2005-06/ 556-521	1984-85/ 842-531
1962-63/ 835-758	1982-83/ 683-829	2007-08/ 592-539	1985-86/ 805-557
1963-64/ 783-868	1986-87/ 504-977	2008-09/ 613-537	1986-87/ 682-566
1964-65/ 674-861	1988-89/ 607-988	2009-10/ 554-651	1989-90/ 712-562
1965-66/ 586-847	1989-90/ 522-907	2010-11/ 590-554	
1968-69/ 502-772	1990-91/ 551-989	2012-13/ 610-551	

Jordan and Drexler had two seasons of 500 rebounds and 500 assists at 652-650 and 565-519, and 518-566 and 500-512 respectively. Chamberlain also did it twice with extraordinary rebound totals at 1,957-630 and 1,952-702. To put Oscar's amazing all-around game into *perspective*, He is the only man in NBA history to make the 600-600 club five times and the 700-700 club three times. Larry Bird never made either club, LeBron James so far hasn't either, and Michael Jordan did it once - while Magic Johnson and Wilt Chamberlain are the only other guys in NBA history to record at least 700 rebounds and 700 assists in a season. In addition, Oscar is the only man to make the 800-800 club and missed the 900-900 club by one assist. To recap, the "Big O" had **41 triple-doubles** in the 1961-62 season and **26 triple-doubles** in both the 1960-61 season and 1963-64 season. He also had **22 40-point triple-double** games throughout his entire career.

As an all-around basketball player in evidence of the numbers listed above, even going back to his college days, it's not surprising that one writer once labeled Oscar "basketball's Willie Mays." On the other side of the ball, former guard Dave Bing who played against Oscar, said "Oscar is without a doubt the all-time everything basketball player. His tremendous offensive ability has overshadowed his great defensive skills." And then there was his mindset as Elgin Baylor put it: "Oscar always made the big play, the right play. When you played against Oscar you not only faced an opponent with a tremendous amount of talent and physical skills, but you were also up against a finely tuned pro basketball mind. Oscar was smarter than any pro player I have ever faced. It was always a thrill to watch Oscar not only outplay but outsmart his opponents. The Big O was truly a basketball master, a performer without equal." Also, Wilt Chamberlain once said, "If I had my pick of all the players in the league, I'd take the Big O first. With all that said many people of today including Charles Barkley of TNT feel Oscar Robertson is the greatest all-around basketball player to ever play the game. It is hard to deny that judging from the numbers presented above!

Career Totals

25.7 points average, 9.5 assists, 7.5 rebounds, .485 FG%, .838 FT%

26,710 points, 9887 assists, 7804 rebounds

Bill Russell

(Rank #7)

MVP (5-times), Rebounding Title (4-times)

NBA Championships (11), All-NBA First Team (3-times)

All-Defensive First Team (1-time), All-Star (12-times)

Bill Russell was the greatest winner the NBA has ever seen. Playing for the glorious Boston Celtics franchise in the late 1950s through the 1960s, Russell won an unprecedented 11 NBA Championships in 13 years including his rookie year, 8 in a row from 1959 through 1966, and with his last two coming as a player-coach in 1968 and 1969. He also became the first African American superstar to play and coach in the NBA. While not being gifted offensively, Russell was the ultimate all-around team player excelling in man-to-man defense (there were no zone defenses allowed in the NBA in those days) and with relentless rebounding and shot blocking. He also was a *superior* shot blocker against penetration in the paint, where he was often seen swooping across the lane like a giant condor but with the speed of a peregrine falcon to block an opponent's shot (or maybe that's exaggerated a little or maybe not, because according to Bill Simmons, Russell really was *super-human*). With great court sense and vision, Russell was an outstanding passer in the half court and especially to start the fast break, by corralling a rebound and quickly outletting to the open man. Having massive hands and being fast on his feet ever since his high school days, he would often grab the rebound and race down the court on a one-man fast break. Russell and Wilt Chamberlain are the only players in NBA history to grab 50 rebounds in a game. He also had 2 more 49-rebound games and set an NBA record of 12 consecutive seasons of 1000 rebounds or more. As a testament of his durability; beginning after his rookie year, he averaged 76 games a season for the rest of his career. But what made Russell special were his intangibles, doing whatever it took for his team to win. Listed at 6-foot-9 and 6-foot-10, he was not a behemoth of a center compared to the king-size Wilt Chamberlain (although still big compared to a lot of the other big men), but relied on positioning, quickness, and anticipation to be a great rebounder and shot blocker.

William Felton Russell was born on February 12th, 1934 in Monroe, Louisiana. After moving to California, he played basketball at McClymond High School in Oakland where he was considered an offensive liability. He then went on to college at the University of San Francisco where he won two NCAA Championships in 1955 and 1956, and had a winning streak of 55 straight games. He was also named NCAA Tournament Most Outstanding Player in 1955 and averaged twenty points and twenty rebounds during his three years in college. UCLA coach John Wooden once said that Russell was the best defensive center he had ever seen. After college, the Harlem Globetrotters invited Russell to join their basketball team but after declining, he made himself eligible for the NBA Draft. Because the Boston Celtics were already well equipped with offensive scorers and needed a defense presence as a foundation in order to build a strong nucleus, Auerbach decided he wanted to draft Bill Russell. Russell was actually selected with the 2nd pick overall of the 1956 NBA Draft by the St. Louis Hawks. But the Celtics traded one of their top scorers in six-time all-star Ed Macauley and rookie Cliff Hagen for the number two pick in order to get Russell. The trade was negotiated because Boston gave up their 1st round draft pick for a territorial pick in order to draft star Tommy Heinsohn out of Holy Cross. In 1956, due to an Olympic commitment in which the U.S. national team won the gold medal at the Melbourne Games in November, Russell joined the Celtics in the middle of December. In his rookie season, he averaged 14.7 points and 19.6 rebounds per game - but lost the Rookie of the Year Award to teammate Tom Heinsohn. With Russell and Heinsohn teamed with offensive stars Bob Cousy and Bill Sharman, the Celtics went on to win the NBA Championship their first year playing together. This was where the Boston Celtics dynasty began!

The following year, college teammate K.C. Jones (who was also part of the 1956 Draft class) played in his first season after missing the year before due to military commitment. In Russell's sophomore season, he averaged 16.6 points and won his first rebounding title (most total rebounds) at 22.7 per game and led the league in rebounds per game for the second time. He also was selected to his first All-Star team and won his first MVP award despite finishing second, ending up on the All-NBA Second Team. During the regular season against the Philadelphia Warriors, Russell set an NBA record 32 rebounds in a half and 49 total for the game. But in the playoffs, after defeating the Warriors in five games, the Celtics lost in the NBA Finals to Bob Pettit and the St. Louis Hawks. Unfortunately for Boston, Russell had injured his foot in game three forcing him to miss virtually the rest of the series. In the 1958-59 season, Russell led the league in rebounding for the second consecutive time while Bill Sharman led the team in scoring for the third straight year. In the playoffs, the Celtics in a see-saw battle, defeated Dolph Schayes and the Syracuse Nationals in the Eastern Finals in seven games, before winning the 1959 NBA Championship over rookie Elgin Baylor and the Minneapolis Lakers in a four-game sweep. For the series, Russell snatched 30 rebounds in three straight games and set an NBA Finals record averaging **29.5 rebounds** per game (and **27.7** for the entire playoff run).

The following season, Russell increased his scoring, rebounding and assists for the fourth straight year to 18.2, 24, and 3.7 per game respectively and fellow rookie draftee Heinsohn led the team in scoring for the first time at 21.3 points per game. The Celtics finished the regular season with a then record 59 wins (only 16 losses) and a 17-game winning streak during the year. On November 7th, Russell's Celtics met *rookie phenom* Wilt Chamberlain and the Philadelphia Warriors for the first time with Chamberlain outscoring Russell 30 to 22, but Boston won the game 115-106. That season, Russell also set the league record for rebounds in a game with **51**. The one-on-one matchup that went on for the next decade between the two goliaths became known as "The Big Collision" and "Battle of the Titans." In the playoffs, the Celtics defeated Chamberlain's Warriors in the Eastern Finals in six games before surviving a tough seven-game series against the St. Louis Hawks in the Finals to win the 1960 NBA Championship. In Game two, Russell set an NBA Finals record with **40 rebounds** and in the winner-take-all game seven, he finished with 22 points and 35 rebounds. The following year, Heinsohn led the team in scoring once again as the Celtics returned to the Finals for the fourth time in five years. After eliminating the Syracuse Nationals in the Eastern Finals in five games, Boston defeated the Hawks handily in five games to win the title. In his first five playoff seasons and seven out of the first eight, Russell led the league in rebounds per game.

In 1961-62, Tom Heinsohn led the Celtics in scoring for the third consecutive season just as Bill Sharman did three years before him. Russell finished second on the team in scoring for the first time while setting a career-high at 18.9 points per game, and increased his assist average to 4.5. He also repeated as MVP as the Celtics became the first team to win 60 games in a season. In the playoffs, the Celtics defeated Chamberlain and the Philadelphia Warriors in seven games behind Sam Jones' game-winning shot in the finale. In the Finals, the Celtics faced a more formidable Western Division Champion Los Angeles Lakers that featured superstar Elgin Baylor and up-and-coming star Jerry West. After splitting the first six games, the Celtics won game seven in overtime despite Tom Heinsohn, Frank Ramsey, and Tom "Satch" Sanders all fouling out in regulation. In the series, Russell tied his own record of 40 rebounds and Baylor set the scoring record for points in the Finals at 61. In retrospect, this was the best chance for the Lakers to have created a back-and-forth rivalry similar to when the Celtics won the 1984 Championship and the Lakers took back the title the following year. Even though both teams won eight championships in nine years during the '80s, the *heated* rivalry didn't begin until both teams exchanged (and then flip-flopped) championships from 1984 to 1987. The following season, Bill Russell won his third consecutive MVP award and fourth overall. With Bob Cousy in his final season and John Havlicek in his first, Sam Jones led the team in scoring for the first time. In the playoffs, the 58-win Celtics battled for seven games against Oscar Robertson and the Cincinnati Royals in the Eastern Finals. This was the third consecutive series the Celtics won in seven games dating back to the previous year's playoffs. In a rematch from last year's Finals, Boston defeated Los Angeles in six games to win the 1963 NBA Championship. With Jerry West banged up and playing at less than a hundred percent, the Celtics depth proved to be the difference.

In the 1963-64 season, Russell led the league in rebounding for the third time and set a **career-high at 24.7** per game while second-year *sensation* John Havlicek and *sharp shooter* Sam Jones finished one-two on the team in scoring. The Celtics finished with the best record in the NBA at 58-22 and waltzed their way through the playoffs. After defeating the Cincinnati Royals in five games, the Celtics dismantled Wilt Chamberlain, Nate Thurmond, and the San Francisco Warriors four games to one in the NBA Finals. The following season, Russell won his fourth **rebounding title at 24.1** per game (that included another 49-rebound game against the Detroit Pistons) and fifth MVP award while S. Jones had a career year in scoring, leading the team at 25.9 points per game. Russell also finished fifth in the league in assists. The Celtics finished the regular season with a franchise record 62 wins and won their eighth title in nine years. For the second straight season, the Celtics defeated a Chamberlain led team in the Eastern Finals (Russell had a memorable game five posting 28 rebounds, 10 blocks (unofficial), 7 assists and 6 steals (unofficial), before winning the 1965 NBA title over the Los Angeles Lakers four games to none.

Prior to the 1965-66 campaign, Russell's scoring began to dip but his overall game of defense; rebounding and passing remained about the same. With Jones and Havlicek leading the way offensively, the Celtics won 54 games and returned to the NBA Finals. For the second straight season, the Celtics defeated the Philadelphia 76ers in the Eastern Finals before winning the 1966 NBA Championship over the Los Angeles Lakers in seven games. The following season, with Red Auerbach's retirement and the recommendation from Tom Heinsohn, Russell became the first African American head coach in NBA history. As a player coach, Russell and the Celtics had another solid campaign finishing at 61-21. But in the playoffs, Boston ran into a team that was well over due to win their first championship. After defeating the New York Knicks three games to one in the first round of the playoffs, the Celtics were eliminated handily by the eventual champion Philadelphia 76ers. The 76ers had just completed the most historic regular season run in NBA history in which they won 68 games and lost only 13. Wilt Chamberlain became the first player to beat the Celtics in the playoffs during the 1960s.

The very next season, Boston took back what was theirs for nine illustrious years, winning their tenth NBA Championship in 1968. After defeating the Detroit Pistons four games to two in the semifinals, the Celtics avenged the loss from the previous playoffs to the 76ers in the Eastern Finals in seven games. With both teams playing in the wake of Martin Luther King's death, the 76ers lost the first game before winning the next three. After trailing three games to one, the Celtics pulled the improbable like only they were able to do, and came back to win the next three games and the series. In their fifth meeting of the decade, the Celtics defeated the Lakers in six games to win the 1968 NBA Championship. At 35 years old in Bill Russell's final season in 1968-69, the Celtics finished in the middle of the pack in the Eastern Division. In what looked to be the end of a dynasty, the Boston Celtics made one last valiant run in the playoffs. After beating a Chamberlain-less (he was traded to Los Angeles) 76ers team, the Celtics defeated the Knicks in six games in the Eastern Finals. This set up an *epic* showdown for the ages! Not only was it Wilt vs. Russell one more time, it was one last chance for Elgin Baylor, Jerry West and the Los Angeles Lakers to beat the Celtics in the NBA Finals. With what looked like the Lakers best chance of coming out victorious with the decisive game seven at home, ended in *utter sorrow* for the city of Los Angeles but in *everlasting jubilation* for the Boston Celtics and their fans. After each team won on its own home court, the Lakers were still in good position to win the title with game seven back in Los Angeles. With extra motivation due to balloons hanging from the rafters in anticipation of a Lakers victory, the Celtics went out and took game seven, and that was that - Russell rode off in the sunset with his eleventh NBA Championship!

In player comparisons:

Out of the 5 MVP awards Russell won, only two came with 1st Team All-NBA honors. In 1961 and 1962, voters must have been convinced that Russell was more valuable defensively and intangibly over Chamberlain (and also over Pettit in 1958) who had won All-NBA First Team while averaging 38 and 50 points per game in both seasons. Also, Russell won MVP and made All-NBA First Team the following year over Chamberlain who had his second best scoring season of his career at 44 points per game. In determining who the greatest center of all-time is, you can make the case that Russell's 3 consecutive MVP awards during Chamberlain's best statistical seasons, weighs even more than his 11 Championships - of course; winning the MVP award is based heavily on how much individual contributions a player has in relation to its team's success, as I have explained in the beginning of the book. Russell did whatever it took to win with the greatest supporting cast in history, while Chamberlain, at times, seemed more focused on individual accomplishments. According to the many people around him during his time, you never heard Wilt talk about the team in the same way Russell did.

In the Bill Russell vs. Wilt Chamberlain debate, Russell held Chamberlain to 8 points in game 6 of the 1969 NBA Finals when the Lakers needed Wilt to score most. After Jerry West pulled his hamstring this was a golden opportunity for Wilt to enhance his legacy after already beating Russell once in the 1967 Eastern Finals. In favor of Russell, the criticism that I have already mentioned in detail in Kareem's chapter about the *shortcomings* of Chamberlain - which helps prove why Kareem was better than Chamberlain, also supports any arguments in favor of the Russell over Chamberlain debate. So, as I have already mentioned about Russell's MVP honors that translates his defense, rebounding, passing, and intangible values into team success, here is the rest of his impressive resume in the postseason that no one seems to really talk about: In his first 11 postseasons, Russell averaged at least **24 rebounds** per game including leading the league in rebounds per game in his first five seasons. He also averaged an *incomprehensible* **20 rebounds** per game in all 13 of his postseasons. So basically in rebounding, passing and on defensive, you could make the case that he was as good statistically as Chamberlain in the postseason. What most people are probably already aware of, are his regular season numbers: Russell averaged at least **21 rebounds** per game ten seasons in a row, and averaged at least **23 rebounds** in seven consecutive seasons. His **11 games** of at least **40 rebounds** and **130 games** of at least **30 rebounds** ranks second only to Wilt's 15 and 160. Other than Chamberlain's top ranked scoring and rebounding statistics and Michael Jordan's scoring accolades, Russell's rebounding numbers in the regular and postseason look nearly as impressive.

To continue on with the player comparisons: If you look at the rest of my Top 25 player rankings, every player is by far known for his offense over his defense for the possible exception of Kevin Garnett. Even as great an all-around player Garnett was in his prime with his rebounding, shot blocking and passing skills, even he ultimately was a terrific scorer, utilizing a jump hook and a killer fadeaway. I know they didn't keep track of blocks in Russell's days, and that's unfortunate. Even though many people have said Russell's shot blocking was off the charts, the same was to be said about Chamberlain's who was three inches taller. Also to note, in Kareem Abdul-Jabbar's case, he might have had more career blocks over Hakeem Olajuwon had they kept track of blocks his first four years. Even though Russell had incredible rebounding numbers, so did Wilt and Kareem. To offset Russell objectively, both were excellent all-around players that put up incredible numbers in all categories, except for of course the free-throw shooting for Wilt. In fact, only when you include scoring, which of course is the ultimate goal in basketball; Kareem and Wilt were by far the better all-around players.

You could argue that Russell has 11 championships and that Wilt and Kareem have a combined total of 8. But if that were the case, shouldn't Bob Cousy, John Havlicek, Sam Jones, and all the other Hall of Famers rank higher on most people's list? I mean if you look at the value of the other Celtics, they brought just as much to the game as Russell did but in other aspects. Some would make the case that Cousy was the best point guard of all-time with regards to his eight assists titles and six championship rings, and Havlicek blended offense and defense as well as any player of his generation, and that Sam Jones was the best clutch shooter of his time behind only Jerry West. Tommy Heinsohn also said "Cooz" was the offensive master and that what Bill Russell was on defense, Cousy was on the offensive end! So I rank Russell in accordance to the overall balance of the team, even though he was the second best *all-around* player next to Havlicek. He played with 8 Hall of Famers named Cousy, Havlicek, Jones, Sharman, Heinsohn, K.C. Jones, Ramsey, and Bailey Howell. If the Celtics had the best teams for 11 seasons in NBA history, because basketball is won as a team just like the Dallas Mavericks proved in 2011, then how could the rest of the Celtics Hall of Famers rank so far behind Russell. It's like saying Magic and Kareem should be ranked miles apart or West and Baylor or even Shaq and Kobe.

So was Russell more valuable than Duncan or Olajuwon that played with zero Top 50 players in *their prime* when they won championships? Drexler (who I have rank 41st on the all-time list), because he was out of his prime playing for the Houston Rockets, was not necessarily a top 50 player when Hakeem won his second championship. So when you look at Cousy, Havlicek, Heinsohn, and Sam Jones statistics during the championship years, they were almost as good as the other greats at their positions. That cannot be said for Olajuwon's supporting cast or Duncan's. Both played with one Hall of Famer each thus far. Aside from Drexler and Robinson, only Tony Parker has made the All-Star team more than twice, four times if you count the 2012 season. And, nobody made the All-NBA First Team or All-NBA Second Team during Olajuwon and Duncan's entire career. Actually, Sampson made Second Team Olajuwan's rookie year and Parker made Second Team the last couple of years as I was at the completion of this book. So if you take Duncan's supporting cast vs. Russell's, there's no comparison in talent. Not to sound contradicting, because I actually feel Manu Ginobili with his three championship rings, will eventually get into the Basketball Hall of Fame someday. But primarily because he is a foreign born player like Pau Gasol and Yao Ming - whom both might also eventually get in. Because of longevity and three championship rings, Parker also has a chance to make the Hall of Fame as well. Duncan played with one top 50 player (who was out *of his prime*) and Russell played with two top 25 players of all-time or three top 50 in anyone's book. So Russell can't be significantly, way better than Cousy and Havlicek and the rest of the cast of Hall of Famers? If that were the case, Duncan should be ranked ahead of Russell because his teammates, other than Robinson (who was out his prime in 1999 and nowhere near his prime in 2003), might not make anyone's top 100.

With that concept, in the 2003-04 season, Ben Wallace should be ranked significantly higher than Chauncey Billups and Rip Hamilton and that's just not the case. I mean Ben Wallace literally shut down the most dominant physical force in in the league in Shaq during the 2004 NBA Finals, and everyone else for that matter during an incredible five-year span (where he won the Defensive Player of the Year Award four times), but Chauncey Billups walked away with the Finals MVP. Also, based on defensive statistics, Ben Wallace could have easily won five straight DPOY awards if it weren't for Ron Artest in 2004 that averaged 2.1 steals and a measly 0.7 blocks per game. And, you know Wallace could easily be in the top 5 for all-time defensive players along with Bill Russell. So my point is that the rest of the Celtic Hall of Famers were *even more valuable* to the success of the Celtics dynasty than Duncan or Wallace's supporting cast during their championship runs. Furthermore, I know Wallace only won one championship and Duncan currently has four to Russell's eleven, and that Russell was even better than the four-time Defensive Player of the Year, but the same concept comes into play. His value to the Pistons was similar to the value of Russell's; he just didn't win all those championships.

You're probably thinking Bill Russell was ten times better than Ben Wallace. He was obviously better, but even if he was only twice as good, the Celtics should have blown out every team in every playoff series based on the superior supporting cast that featured 8 Hall of Famers throughout the years. Many times, the Celtics were pushed to seven games. I know Russell was the cornerstone and the best defensive player of all-time, but he was still one of the key pieces that fit into a *perfect puzzle*. I also realize that Russell was the most important player and key piece on the team, and that the offensive ran through Russell and K.C. Jones when Bob Cousy retired. Besides, the Celtics only played with 8 to the 13 teams from 1957 to 1969, which equates to playing far less playoff games against stiffer (more) competition. Even though every team had more star players with fewer teams in the league than in today's game, the Celtics still had by far the best group of Hall of Famers. If Russell had played with more teams and in more playoff series like in today's standards where they play four, instead of two or three, chances are he wouldn't have won as many championships. In his first 9 seasons, he played in only two playoff series to capture the title, and in his last 3 seasons he played in three playoff series. So 73 percent of the time he played in only 2 playoff series to win 8 out of his 11 championships. I think everyone gives Russell far more credit than the rest of his teammates, which they should to a *certain extent* because big men dominated in those days, but the gap should be a little closer. Can one man be that much better than eight solid players with many being Hall of Famers and three in the top 25 players of all-time? Once again, I know the Celtics would not have won 11 championships without Russell. But, I also think they wouldn't have won half the amount without the *perfectly knit* supporting cast of Hall of Famers.

So the all-around game of Russell on both ends of the floor is not enough to put him ahead Kareem or Wilt. But it is enough to put him ahead of Olajuwon because his defense and intangibles were validated with 5 MVP awards during the regular season. Also, despite the fact that Russell was voted the greatest player in the history of the NBA in 1980 by the Professional Basketball Writers Association of America, I would still put Oscar Robertson ahead of Russell because there are a lot of people out there that not only believe the "Big O" was the greatest basketball player of all-time, but the greatest basketball player of the 19th century! No matter how high or how low Russell ranks as the greatest of all-time, there no disputing that he was the greatest winner of all-time.

Career Totals
15.1 points average, 22.5 rebounds, 4.3 assists, .440 FG%, .561 FT%
14,522 points, 21,620 rebounds, 4100 assists

Hakeem Olajuwon

(Rank #8)

MVP (1-time), Defensive Player of The Year (2-times)

Rebounding Title (2-times), Blocked Shots Title (3-times)

All-NBA First Team (6-times), All-Defensive First Team (5-times)

NBA Championships (2), Finals MVP (2-times), All-Star (12-times)

Hakeem Olajuwon of the Houston Rockets according to the Basketball Encyclopedia could have been the greatest center of All-time and from what I can see that may very well be true, at least athletically and from a statistical point of view. During his prime, his skill set encompassed with an unprecedented amount of footwork took the center position to a whole new level. Olajuwon had more moves than a game of chess! Although listed at seven feet, he was probably closer to six-eleven but had great strength, speed, and agility. Ultimately in 1994, Olajuwon did what no other superstar accomplished, winning the NBA MVP Award, Defensive Player of the Year Award, and Finals MVP the same season he won his first NBA title. He is also the only man to record 200 blocks and 200 steals in a single season and is only one of four players to record a quadruple-double in league history. Not even Michael Jordan accomplished these three feats, but I still rank

Olajuwon 4th for all-time centers and 8th overall for the following reason: Hakeem had only one MVP award to Kareem's 6, Wilt's 4, and Russell's 5 - partly because he played with a more superior cast of centers and *non-centers* during his time. If he had won a couple of more regular season MVP awards or more championships, I would have most likely put him ahead of Bill Russell as the 3rd greatest center ever. Throughout his career, Olajuwon had to play against near equal talent in David Robinson and Patrick Ewing, aging Hall of Fame centers in Kareem Abdul-Jabbar, Moses Malone, and Robert Parish and an up-and-coming Shaquille O'Neal, Alonzo Mourning and Dikembe Mutombo. He also played during the time of Karl Malone, Charles Barkley, Michael Jordan, Magic Johnson, and Larry Bird who all won a total of 14 MVP's (15 including Robinson's in 1995). And for a few seasons, he must have felt like he was looking in the mirror with his only peer in Kevin McHale, in terms of low-post moves.

Growing up in Nigeria, playing soccer as a goal keeper - helped Olajuwon with his footwork in basketball. "Akeem the Dream" was the nickname he was given because of the "Dream Shake" he developed using his *world-class* spin moves and fakes in the low-post. He attributed this move to one of his soccer moves he translated to basketball. The Dream Shake would accomplish one of three things, it would misdirect the opponent and make him go the opposite way, it would freeze the opponent and leave him devastated in his tracks, or it would shake off the opponent and giving him no chance to contest the shot. Although my favorite Hakeem nickname of all-time is the Nigerian Nightmare! I have always viewed Olajuwon as the *King of All Moves* even over the great Kevin McHale or any other player. The reason: is because his moves were *superior* dominant. When Dream shook one way or the other, he was going at full speed with equal effectiveness. Out of his entire arsenal, his fadeaway baseline swish hitting bottom net stands out the most. All of Hakeem's spin moves, fakes, up-and-under moves, jump hooks and fadeaways were all dominant moves and performed with the highest - a dazzling array of skill, creating an unbelievable amount of separation from his opponents, with each, being a part of his repertoire of pet moves! Shaquille O'Neal said, "Hakeem has 5 moves than 4 countermoves - that gives him 20 moves." Michael Jordan even said, "If I had to pick a center [for an all-time best team], I would take Olajuwon. And the reason I would take Olajuwon is very simple: He is so versatile because of what he can give you from that position. It's not just his scoring, not just his rebounding or not just his blocked shots. People don't realize he was in the top 7 [in NBA history] in steals. He always made great decisions on the court. For all facets of the game, I have to give it to him." Magic Johnson also said, "In terms of raw athletic ability Akeem is the best I have ever seen."

When you get a chance to watch old film of NBA Hardwood Classics on ESPN Classic or NBA TV, you will be amazed of the overall skill Olajuwon exemplified! In some clips, Hakeem is often seen spinning one way and then the other, resulting in his patented baseline fadeaway, jump hook, or three-footer that he seemed to just drop in or finger role in, or a wide open top of the key jump shot he created from a spin move out of the post. He also could face and shoot - or drop step, spin baseline and throw down a power dunk. Olajuwon created more space of a spin move than any player in history - it seemed like he was covering 6 to 8 feet with his giant steps off each spin. I often think back of all the jump hooks and jump shots he created off a spin move over Shaquille O'Neal in the 1995 NBA Finals and the way he outplayed Patrick Ewing the year before in the 1994 NBA Finals outscoring him 27 points to 19 on average for the series, and blocking John Stark's game ending three-point attempt in game 6. And during seven years of his prime from 1989 through 1996, Hakeem outscored his closest rival David Robinson 26 to 22 in points per game during thirty head-to-head matchups. But what stands out most are the assortment of devastating up-and-under moves, spins moves, and fadeaways, he did on Robinson during the 1995 playoffs, merely demoralizing the Admiral. The final numbers for the series:

Olajuwon - 35.3 points, 12.5 rebounds, 5.0 assists, 4.1 blocks and 1.3 steals per game

Robinson - 23.8 points, 11.3 rebounds, 2.7 assists, 2.2 blocks, and 1.5 steals per game

Hakeem Abdul Olajuwon was born on January 21st, 1963 in Logos, Nigeria. Olajuwon by the way, in Yoruba means "always being on top." As a youth, his soccer skills as I have already mentioned, helped him with his footwork and agility that he would later use in basketball. After immigrating to the United States in 1980, Olajuwon played college basketball at the University of Houston with Clyde Drexler and was the #1 pick overall of the 1984 NBA Draft, going ahead of Sam Bowie and Michael Jordan. Charles Barkley and John Stockton also came out of this draft at #5 and #16 respectively. Coming from overseas, Olajuwon red shirted his freshman year in college because of lack of clearance from the NCAA. After the Cougars were eliminated in the Final Four in 1982 by the North Carolina Tar Heels, the team advised Olajuwon to workout with Moses Malone right next door, who at the time was the best center in the NBA playing for the Houston Rockets. The following year in 1983, heavily favored Phi Slama Jama (named for being an above the rim, slam dunking fraternity) lost the NCAA Championship game on a miraculous last second tip-in to North Carolina State. In his final season (he led the nation in field goal percentage at .675 and rebounding at 13.5 a game) in 1984, he lost in the championship game again, this time to Patrick Ewing and the Georgetown Hoyas. But he would avenge the loss to Ewing ten years later in the 1994 NBA Finals.

In his rookie season, Olajuwon averaged 20.9 points, 11.9 rebounds, and 2.7 blocks but finished second in the Rookie of the Year voting behind Michael Jordan. In his second season, he teamed with Ralph Sampson to form the dynamic dual known as the "Twin Towers" (the nickname they were referred by before September 11th, 2001). In the playoffs, after sweeping the Denver Nuggets in the first round and beating the Portland Blazers in five games in the semifinals, the Houston Rockets shocked the Los Angeles Lakers in the Western Conference Finals, winning in a short series rather handily four games to one. The series clinching victory came in game five at the Forum in L.A. when Ralph Sampson had the improbable game-winning shot at the buzzer that left the infamous Michael Cooper sprawled out all over the floor in disbelief. The Rockets went on to the NBA Finals but eventually lost to the Boston Celtics in six games. Like Magic Johnson's 1980 Finals performance in game six and Larry Bird's 1981 game-winning bank shot in game seven of the Finals, the game five victory (even though the Rockets eventually lost the series in six) was one of Olajuwon's most defining moments in the playoffs to that point, which gave a preview of his potential for years to come. In what felt like one against three at times, Hakeem in only his second year in the league, valiantly staved off elimination scoring 32 points, grabbing 14 rebounds, and blocking 8 shots. In hindsight, maybe Olajuwon would have won three championships if he hadn't faced a Celtics team that had perhaps the greatest season in NBA History, and the *All-Universe* frontcourt of Larry Bird, Robert Parish, Kevin McHale and Bill Walton.

In the 1986-87 season, after beating the Portland Trail Blazers in the first round of the playoffs three games to one, the Rockets lost to the Seattle SuperSonics in six games that featured a super scoring trio of Dale Ellis, Tom Chambers, and Xavier McDaniel who all averaged 24.9, 23.3, and 23 points per game in the regular season. Despite the loss, in game 6, Olajuwon shot a magnificent 19 for 33 (57 percent) from the field, scoring **49 points,** and collecting **25 rebounds** (11-offensive) and 6 blocks. Also, near the end of the regular season on Mar. 10th against the Sonics in what was probably the nearest someone had come to a *quintuple-double*, Olajuwon had **38 points, 17 rebounds, 12 blocks, 7 steals, and 6 assists**. In 1988 with chronic knee injuries, Sampson was traded to the Golden State Warriors and Olajuwon was left as the lone star - to try and take his team back to the Promised Land.

The Rockets won a total of three playoff games the next four years and never made it out of the first round losing to the Dallas Mavericks, Seattle SuperSonics, and twice to the Los Angeles Lakers in successive seasons. For the 4 games against Dallas in 1988, Olajuwon had games of **34-14, 41-26, 35-12 and 40-15**, and finished with an obscene stat line of **37.5 points, 16.8 rebounds, 2.8 blocks**, and **2.3 steals** per game. And according to ESPN's John Hollinger rankings, this was the highest player efficiency rating in NBA Playoff History. Hakeem's best teammates during that span were Purvis Short, Sleepy Floyd, Rodney McCray, Joe Barry Carroll, Otis Thorpe and Candice Wiggins' dad Mitchell Wiggins (who is now deceased), Vernon Maxwell and Kenny Smith. Olajuwon has always been active spiritually, but in 1991 he became a more devout Muslim and changed the first letter of his first name from Akeem to the proper Arabic spelling Hakeem.

Ramadan played a big part of Hakeem's life during his playing time in the NBA. Ramadan is the 9th month of the Islamic calendar which last 29 or 30 days. Compared to our calendar, the date's moves back *about* 11 days every year depending on the moon. A person will have fasted every day of the Gregorian calendar year over 34 years' time (Ironically Hakeem's jersey number). Ramadan is a time of spiritual faith and worship. A person takes part in fasting by abstaining from eating food and drinking during daylight hours for about a month to teach Muslims about spirituality, patience, humility, and submissiveness to god. I always thought that this strict observance of Ramadan interfered with Olajuwon's conditioning and energy level before and during games throughout his career, even though he noted as sometimes playing better during that month. In the 1991-92 season, the Rockets missed the playoffs entirely. Olajuwon had his best defensive statistics in his first eight years, leading the league in rebounding and blocks twice, while averaging an astounding 12.6 rebounds and 3.6 blocks per game. In the 1992-93 season, under new coach Rudy Tomjanovich, the Rockets finished with a franchise record of 55-27. Olajuwon would have his best scoring and assist season to that point at 26.1 points and 3.5 assists per game, while leading the league in blocks for the third time in his career. In the playoffs, the Rockets were pushed to the limit in the first round best-of-five, by the Los Angeles Clippers that featured stars Danny Manning and Ron Harper. But in the semifinals, the Rockets lost a hard-fought seven-game series to the Seattle SuperSonics that featured up-and-coming stars Gary Payton and Shawn Kemp, and sharpshooters Eddie Johnson and Ricky Pierce.

It took eight years for the Rockets to return to the NBA Finals since their disappointing loss to the Celtics back in 1986. In the 1993-94 season, the Rockets finished with the second best record in the NBA at 58-24, while Olajuwon took his game to a whole another level winning his first MVP award and second consecutive Defensive Player of the Year award. He also had a **career-high** in both **scoring at 27.3 points** and assists at 3.6 per game in the regular season. He also raised his level of play even higher in the postseason averaging **28.9 points**, **11 rebounds**, **4.3 assists**, and an *astounding* **4 blocks** in 22 playoffs games. The Rockets beat the Portland Trail Blazers in the first round three games to one before losing the first two games at home to the Phoenix Suns in the semifinals. This is where Olajuwon and the Rockets faced the daunting task of; having to win four out of the next five games to advance to the next round. The Rockets overcame incredible odds and showed their *true grit* by winning the next two games in Phoenix to tie the series, and then game five and seven at home to *survive* the series in seven games. Olajuwon had relied on his dominate low-post game and trust in his perimeter shooters. When double teamed in the post, he would kick out to the open man for jumpers or three-point shots. If the defense rotated fast enough, the Rockets had some of the best ball movement of all-time around the perimeter, where the ball fell into an often awaiting three-point shooter ready to knock down the big shot.

In my opinion, over the last 25 years, perhaps only Steve Nash's Phoenix Suns and Mike Bibby and Chris Webber's Sacramento Kings and Jason Kidd and Dirk Nowitzki's Dallas Mavericks had better ball movement around the perimeter *finding* open shooters. After coming from behind against a great Suns team that included Charles Barkley, Kevin Johnson and Dan Majerle, the battle tested Rockets made quick work of the Utah Jazz in the Western Conference Finals winning the series in five games. After defeating the Jazz, which had two great players in Karl Malone and John Stockton and two outstanding perimeter shooters in Jeff Hornacek and Jeff Malone, I felt confident on the Rockets chances of winning their first championship when faced up against the New York Knicks. This would set up a rematch between *two goliaths* going all the way back to their college days when Patrick Ewing's Georgetown Hoyas defeated Olajuwon's Houston Cougars in the 1984 NCAA National Championship game. At the time, the Knicks were hungry for their first NBA title in the Ewing era and their first since 1973, but the Rockets were even hungrier to win their first NBA Championship in franchise history. After the two teams split the first four games, the Knicks took control of the series by winning game five at home, giving the Rockets some doubt on whether they could pull off the comeback once again. By that point, I was starting to get concerned, but I thought back on how much grit they showed against the Suns in the semifinals and how six years earlier, the 1988 Los Angeles Lakers went through three gut-wrenching seven-game series on their way to the championship. I felt the Rockets had the same bit of destiny and determination to pull it off. At that point in time, I was disappointed that Olajuwon wasn't able to explode and have a break out game against the best center in the Eastern Conference, due in part because both teams played superior defense - not allowing the other to score over 100 points, and because Ewing did a good job containing Olajuwon all series long. But I guess you can say the same thing happened to Ewing on the other end. Despite the great defensive battle on both sides, Olajuwon still outscored Ewing in all six games averaging 26.9 points per game to Ewing's 18.9. He also shot 50 percent from the field (to Ewing's .363), had scoring games of 32 and 30 points, and had the huge block on John Starks at the end of game 6 with Houston holding to a 86-84 lead. The Rockets went on to win game seven 90-84 and the 1994 NBA Championship while Olajuwon was named Finals MVP. This was one of my all-time favorite NBA Finals, watching these two great *titans* go to battle. Though it was really too bad that one of these great teams had to lose!

The following season in 1995, Olajuwon would have almost an identical run as his MVP season the year before, but David Robinson walked away with the MVP. It was understandable before the postseason began because the San Antonio Spurs finished with the best record in the NBA at 62-20. The 47-win Rockets had gotten off to a slow start and had acquired Clyde Drexler in a mid-season trade with the Portland Trail Blazers for Otis Thorpe. "But never underestimate the heart of a champion" as Rudy Tomjanovich said during the Rockets improbable playoff run. The sixth seeded Rockets battled to the brink of elimination in the first two rounds against the Utah Jazz in five games and to the Phoenix Suns in seven just like the year before. In the conference finals, the Rockets went on to defeat the San Antonio Spurs in six games and won the 1995 NBA Championship over Shaquille O'Neal and the Orlando Magic in a four-game sweep. Of note: During the Rudy Tomjanovich era beginning in 1992, Olajuwon and the Rockets had an astounding 14-6 record in elimination games.

In both series, Olajuwon had his way with the second and third best centers in the NBA. He outscored Robinson in 5 out of the 6 games with games of **41, 43, 42, and 39 points** - and outscored Shaq in all four games finishing with **31, 34, 31, and 35 points** -

that equates to **32.8 points** per game to go along with **11.5 rebounds** and **5.5 assists** for the series. Also for the entire playoff run, he averaged a **career-high 33 points** and **4.5 assists** per game to go along with 10.9 rebounds and 2.8 blocks. In addition, out of the 23 playoff games, he had an astounding **16 30-point** games and **5 40-point** games, with three of those coming against his biggest rival Robinson in the conference finals. But, what's most impressive is that Olajuwon increased his scoring at every level of play, higher than almost anyone in history not named Jerry West. His scoring jumped from 21.8 in the regular season - to **25.9** in the playoffs - to **27.5** in the NBA Finals. You would be hard-pressed to find any superstar player who's averaged increased that much from the regular season to the playoffs - that is with a reasonable amount of games played. Still to this day, I often think back and marvel at how incredibly *super-human* "the Dream" was back in his day. I just wish Olajuwon had faced Jordan in the NBA Finals, because I think Olajuwon would have come out on top, especially that season in 1995!

After winning back-to-back championships with the Houston Rockets in 1994 and 1995, Hakeem went on to win the 1996 Gold Medal for the U.S. National team. It was too bad Olajuwon became a U.S. citizen after the 1992 Dream Team was assembled, because the greatest United States basketball team of all-time would have been even *greater* with the Dream on the Roster! In the 1995-96 season at the age of 33 (at season end), Olajuwon had his last great individual year when he averaged **26.9 points**, **10.9 rebounds**, 3.6 assists, and **2.9 blocks** per game - but the Rockets two year championship reign came to an end in the semifinals when they were swept by Gary Payton, Shawn Kemp and the Seattle SuperSonics. With Barkley aboard for the next two seasons, the Rockets were eliminated by the Utah Jazz in back-to-back years in six games in the Western Conference Finals and in the first round three games to two. For the 1998-99 season, Drexler retired and Pippen was acquired from the Bulls to make one last run at a title. But Houston was upset by the Lakers of all teams, in the first round of the playoffs three games to one. In his final five seasons, Olajuwon never played in more than 61 games due to injury.

In player comparisons:

Here are some more facts and stats to support the ranking of Olajuwon: Olajuwon, Michael Jordan, and LeBron James are arguably the most *talented* players ever. As mentioned in the beginning of the chapter, Olajuwon is the only man in history to win the NBA MVP Award, Defensive Player of the Year, and the Finals MVP in the same season. This accomplishment helps prove that he might have been the best offensive and defensive talent in NBA history. He is also the only man in history to combine **5000 blocks and steals** in a career (finishing with 5992), post **200 blocks and 200 steals** in the same season, and to average at least **14 rebounds and 4.5 blocks** for a single campaign (Kareem may have topped the list if they had kept track of blocks during his first 4 years in the league). In addition, he also led the NBA in blocked shots three times and rebounding twice, and retired as the all-time leading shot blocker in NBA history with 3830. And he recorded 25 rebounds or more in a game 4 times, and 10 or more blocks 12 times in his career. And, on top of all that, he stole the ball as often as some of the great guards to have ever played the game - that's why he had 12 seasons of 100 blocks and 100 steals which is by far the most of any player in history.

Olajuwon statistically, ranks up there as the greatest player ever in terms of his all-around contributions on the offensive end and on defense, right up there with Wilt Chamberlain, Oscar Robertson, Larry Bird, Magic Johnson, Michael Jordan and LeBron James. Unfortunately for the old timers, they didn't keep track of blocks and steals as an official stat until 1973-74. No player in NBA history *combined* better offensive skills with defensive skills. But because of the lack of *ultimate* team success in the first half of his career, other than the 1986 Finals appearance, despite the loss in which he played *extremely* well in the series, it's hard to justify ranking Olajuwon higher than eighth in the elite rankings of all-time. If Olajuwon's career scoring average were in the mid to high twenties and if he had won more than the one MVP award and two championships, he would have ranked even higher. And, if he had combined his best scoring seasons with his best rebounding, shot blocking, and steals seasons from the early part of his career - he would have easily had some of the best individual seasons of all-time, maybe even over Chamberlain, Kareem and the other players listed in the chart in Abdul-Jabbar's chapter. The case rest: for ranking Olajuwon as the fourth greatest center of all-time ahead of Shaquille O'Neal.

Career Totals

21.8 points, 11.1 rebounds, 3.1 assists, 3.3 blocks, 1.7 steals, .512 FG%, .712 FT%

26,946 points, 13,748 rebounds, 3058 assists, 3830 blocks, 2162 steals

Tim Duncan

(Rank #9)

MVP (2-times), All-NBA First Team (10-times)

All-Defensive First Team (8-times), All-Star (14-times)

NBA Championships (4), Finals MVP (3-times)

Also featuring: Tony Parker
& Manu Ginobili

Tim Duncan was one of the most fundamentally sound big men the NBA has ever seen. I guess that's why Shaquille O'Neal nicknamed him "The Big Fundamental." The San Antonio Spurs big man is believed by most, to be the greatest power forward of all-time! Skilled in every facet of the game, Duncan playing today is basically a power forward in a centers body and that's a scary thing to think about when making a player evaluation! During his prime, Duncan could do it all, scoring out of the low post with the best of them - with his *patented* jump hook and short fallaway in the lane or by driving or drop-stepping before spinning left or right finishing with a layup off glass with either hand. He could also shoot an *old school* bank shot from the perimeter on either side of the court. And from the top of the key, he could face and shoot right over the top of his opponent with an effective somewhat flat shot that always seemed to go in. Every once in a while, if you watched enough San Antonio games, he would do somewhat of a *Dream Shake*, fallaway shot from the baseline reminiscent of the great Hakeem Olajuwon. "I wish he had performed this sequence more often, because it would have made him a more *recognizable* scorer!" The *well-rounded* Duncan was also one of the great rebounding, shot blocking, and passing big men at the *power forward* position in NBA history. And from the passing perspective, there have been a lot of great ones throughout the years including the most recent Pau Gasol, Kevin Garnett, Chris Webber, Karl Malone, and Charles Barkley. But, Duncan ranks right there with them.

Duncan was the ultimate all-around player, ranking right there at the top with Olajuwon for all-time great big men. What separates the "Big Fella" from most of the other superstar *power forwards* is on the defensive end. During his prime, he along with Garnett, were the best rebounding and shot-blocking power forwards of his era and maybe before. He averaged double figures in rebounding thirteen straight years until the 2009-10 season. With his *impeccable* timing while keeping his feet grounded, Duncan was an outstanding shot blocker averaging 2.3 blocks per game for his career. He also owned the NBA Finals record for blocked shots in a game with 8 until Dwight Howard recently broke it with 9.

In player comparisons:

You would have to put Tim Duncan ahead of the other great power forwards of the past including; Malone, Barkley, Garnett, Dirk Nowitzki, and Bob Pettit ultimately because he had the best *blend* of offense and defense. On the offensive end, he was able to score with the best of them, *by pounding the ball* inside the paint where the percentage to score is highest. On the defensive end, he and Garnett stand *head and shoulders* above the rest at the top of the list. I didn't see Pettit play, but at six-foot-nine, I highly doubt he was as good as the 8-time All-Defensive First Team Duncan or the 9-time All-Defensive First Team Garnett defensively. In addition, from an intangible perspective, it always seemed like Duncan was in the right place at the right time to corral rebounds or to block an opponent's shot.

From a pure scoring standpoint, I always viewed Malone and Barkley as being the purest scorers at their positions. Malone had that *lethal* turnaround jump shot that got better with age and Barkley was well equipped with his own *killer* jumper, and fallaway shot that seemed almost automatic. Duncan was not as flashy with his outside shot but was nearly as effective shooting from 16 feet in, and especially in *clutch* situations. With a better low-post game, Duncan could match his peers offensively and could completely outplay them on the defensive end, *particularly* with his interior shot blocking. Although, I still *marvel* at how an aging Malone in his final season, with his still existent legendary strength and lightning-quick hands was able to man-handle Duncan in the 2004 Western Conference Semifinals by cutting off his drives to the basket and stripping him repeatedly in the low post. During the series, I was beginning to think that maybe Duncan was the one on the down side of his career. But Timmy made up for it by winning the NBA Championship the following year in 2005 and again in 2007. If you had to pick out a weakness for Duncan it would have to be his free-throw shooting, which hovers currently around 70 percent for his career.

Timothy Theodore Duncan was born on April 25th, 1976 in Christiansted in the U.S. Virgin Islands and went to St. Dunstan's Episcopal High School where he averaged 25 points per game as a senior. Prior to the ninth grade, Duncan was actually a swimmer before switching to basketball after Hurricane Hugo destroyed the Olympic sized pool on St. Croix. In college at Wake Forest, as a senior, he averaged 20.8 points, 14.7 rebounds, 3.2 assists, and 3.3 blocks per game - and won the Naismith College Player of the Year award and the John Wooden award. Duncan was then selected with the 1st pick overall of the 1997 NBA Draft by the San Antonio Spurs. In his first season, he made a *huge* impact averaging **21.1 points**, **11.9 rebounds**, and **2.5 blocks** per game - and shot a career-high 54.9 percent from the field, and won NBA Rookie of the Year. He also made his first All-Star team and was named to the All-NBA First Team for the first of seven consecutive seasons, and to the All-Defensive Second Team for the first time. In only his second away game of the season, he gave a preview of his potential as one of the leagues *next* great big men when he corralled 22 rebounds against Dennis Rodman and the Chicago Bulls. Because of Duncan's impact, living up to all the hype coming out of college, the Spurs went from the *dog house* to the *penthouse* in one season finishing with a record of 56-26. But after defeating the Suns in the first round, they were eliminated in the semifinals by Karl Malone, John Stockton, and the defending Western Conference Champion Utah Jazz who were on a mission to make it back to the NBA Finals. Despite the loss, Duncan was impressive in his first playoff game against the Suns and the first game in the next round against the Jazz scoring 32 and 33 points and grabbing 10 rebounds in both contests.

In the lockout shortened 1998-99 season, Duncan averaged similar numbers as his rookie year and was named to the All-Defensive First Team for the first of five straight seasons. During the shortened 50-game schedule, many of the teams were jockeying for playoff position within the conferences as three teams finished atop the East with 33 wins while the Spurs and Jazz finished tied at the top of the West with 37. Because the Spurs won the head-to-head battle two games to one during the regular season, they were awarded the #1 seed throughout the playoffs. It ended up paying tremendous dividends for San Antonio during the postseason as they completed one of the best playoff runs in history. The Spurs became the first team since the Chicago Bulls eight years before to lose *only* twice the entire postseason. After defeating the Minnesota Timberwolves three games to one, the Spurs swept the Los Angeles Lakers and the Portland Trail Blazers to win the Western Conference. In games 3 and 4 against Portland, Duncan came up big both times having monster games of 37 points, 14 rebounds, and four assists - and 33 points, 14 rebounds, and four assists.

In the NBA Finals, the Spurs did away with the first ever 8th seed New York Knicks in five games to win the 1999 NBA Championship. Without Ewing due to injury, Duncan and Robinson had their way throughout the series against New York's frontcourt of Larry

Johnson and Chris Dudley. After a bounce-back game 4 in which he had 28 points and 18 rebounds - in the clinching game five in New York, Duncan had 31 points and 9 rebounds, and was named Finals MVP. And for the series, he averaged 27 points and 14 rebounds per game. The following season, he had one of the best seasons of his career averaging **23.2 points**, **12.4 rebounds**, and **3.2 assists** per game. But with Sean Elliot banged up most of the year, worst came to worst as Duncan injured his meniscus at the end of the season causing him to miss the entire playoffs. As a result, the Spurs were not able to defend their title at full strength and were eliminated by the Suns in the first round three games to one.

The following season, Duncan had another outstanding year as the Spurs looked to rebound and make it back to the NBA Finals. But unfortunately, another Western Conference power had emerged in the Los Angeles Lakers, which had come off their first NBA championship in 12 years. After finishing with the best record in the NBA at 58-24, the Spurs looked to return to championship form in the playoffs - as they pounced on the Timberwolves once again three games to one in the first round, and then the Dallas Mavericks in five games in the semifinals. In what looked like a return to prominence, came to sudden halt in the conference finals, as the Spurs were swept in four games by defending champion Los Angeles who had now positioned themselves to begin a mini-dynasty behind dominant center Shaquille O'Neal and young up-and-coming superstar Kobe Bryant. In the 2001-02 season, Duncan had his best individual season of his career averaging **25.5 points**, **12.7 rebounds**, **3.7 assists**, and **2.5 blocks** per game - and won the NBA MVP award. By that point, I really felt the Spurs, would have bounced back and taken care of unfinished business against the Lakers, because after winning his first league MVP award, Duncan had proven that he was the best player the league had to offer. But it only got worse. After defeating the Seattle SuperSonics in the first round three games to two, the Spurs were trounced once again by the Lakers, this time in the semifinals in five games. In the fifth and final game, Duncan did come to play scoring 34 points and setting a franchise record in rebounds with 25. Despite the second round exit, Duncan was emerging into, not only the best power forward in basketball, but the best player in the entire NBA. To follow up what he did in the regular season, he was even more spectacular in the playoffs, averaging a **career-high 27.6 points** and **4.3 blocks** to go along with **14.4 rebounds** and **five assists** per game. He also outplayed Shaq in the five games averaging **29 points**, **17 rebounds**, and **five assists** to Shaq's 21 points, 12 rebounds, and three assists.

Over the last two seasons, in fairness to Duncan and the Spurs, Shawn Elliot was no longer with the team and David Robinson was 36 and 37 years old, and nowhere near the player he had used to be. With that being said, I still felt the Spurs of 2001 and 2002 were formidable enough to have given the Lakers more of a battle and potentially prevent a three-peat, but that didn't happen. The first year, the key acquisition of Derek Anderson showed his athleticism and flashes of brilliance as a scorer at the shooting guard position in 2001 and Steve Smith played like his old self at times during the 2002 campaign. So if I had to pick between which team had the better chance to recapture the title from the Lakers in those two seasons, I would take the 2001 Spurs because of Anderson's ability at times to neutralize Bryant at the two-guard position. And in 2002, had they gotten past the Lakers and met the Sacramento Kings in the playoffs, I believe the Kings would have won because they had the best team in the NBA that year and should have beaten the Lakers in the conference finals if it weren't for 6 or 7 horrendous calls that went against the Kings in game 6 in Los Angeles. At that point, even with just the one championship title under his belt, I along with many others felt Duncan was the best player in the NBA. But at the same time, it seemed like the majority felt a lot different believing Shaquille O'Neal was because he was in the midst of winning three consecutive NBA championships. But the following season, Duncan backed my belief and won not only his second MVP award, but his second NBA championship.

When the San Antonio Spurs won the NBA Championship in Duncan's second season (lockout shortened), later Phil Jackson arrogantly labeled that championship season as being an *asterisk year*. The Twin Towers, as they were once known, anchored a *formidable* San Antonio Spurs team in 2003 to stop Shaquille O'Neal, Kobe Bryant, and company from 4-peating as NBA champions. That postseason was Duncan's best of his career overall. In 24 playoff games, he averaged **24.7 points** per game and **3.3 blocks**, and a **career-high 15.4 rebounds**, and **5.3 assists**, on **52.9 percent** shooting. In the closeout game six against the Suns in the first round, he had a triple-double of **15 points, 20 rebounds**, and **10 assists** to go along with four blocks. In the second round against the Lakers in the matchup with Robert Horry, Duncan had a 36-point game early on in the series, and 37 points, 16 rebounds, and four assists in the clinching game 6 at home. Even when the Spurs were losing to the Lakers those last three years, they were always winning the power forward matchup (not just against L.A. but other teams as well). With Duncan's offensive and defensive *prowess* as usual, and with rising stars Tony Parker and Manu Ginobili, the Spurs were finally able to dethrone the 3-time champion Lakers. I was spot on with that series prediction and collected on my wager! In the next three games against the Dallas Mavericks in the Western Conference Finals, Duncan dropped 40, 32, and 34 points to give the Spurs a two to one series lead. And then unfortunately Nowitzki got injured in game three, forcing him to miss the rest of the series. After defeating Dallas in six games, the Spurs went on to win the 2003 NBA Championship over the New Jersey Nets four games to two. In the Finals, Duncan set the tone right off the bat once again, when he had one of the best all-around games in playoff history finishing with **32 points, 20 rebounds, seven blocks, six assists, and three steals.** To close out the series, he came ever so close to recording a quadruple-double, but settled for a triple-double finishing with **21 points, 20 rebounds, 10 assists, and eight blocks.**

In my opinion, this was San Antonio's best championship team despite Robinson being 37 years old about to turn 38 after seasons end. Duncan was coming off his second MVP season where he almost matched his numbers from the previous year (his points were slightly down two - to **23.3** per game but his rebounds, assists, and blocks were at a

career-high at **12.9**, **3.9**, and **2.9** respectively). Also, you had a great team when your fifth best player in the starting lineup was Stephen Jackson! Even though David Robinson was in his final year with the team, they had a second-year *speedster* in point guard Tony Parker, and a rookie in Manu Ginobili - who was about to turn 26 years old but was *more polished* than most first or second-year players in the league - because of his time spent in Europe. Also this was the only time the 4 best players during their championship run (Duncan, Robinson, Parker, and Ginobili) played together on the same championship team. In hindsight, outside of Duncan, you would think Robinson was the *integral* piece during the Spurs championship run. But it may have been Parker and Ginobili because they completed the inside-outside game, and were part of three championship title teams as compared to Robinson who was just on two. Both players fit the puzzle perfectly, kind of reminiscent to the old Boston Celtics of Cousy and Havlicek. Of course neither *is quite* the superstar the other two were. But, I can't remember a sixth-man (at the wing position) in recent NBA history since Havlicek, to have had this kind of an impact coming off the bench on *three* championship teams the way Ginobili has so far in his career. Including Robinson and Parker, he might have been the second most important player on the team - and he came off the bench.

Good enough to be a starter, the ultra-competitive **Manu Ginobili** was one of the most talented and *electrifying* players that I have ever witnessed play in the NBA. In fact, if I had to *model myself* and pick a player to play like, I would choose either him, Dwyane Wade or LeBron James! He was so good, that at one point before all the recent injuries, you could make the case that he was the second best shooting guard in the Western Conference next to Kobe Bryant. As a two-time All-Star, Ginobili was regarded by many as the *best player* ever to come out of Europe and was *tagged* the *Kobe Bryant* of the European League. Born on July 28th, 1977 in Bahia Blanca, Buenos Aires, Argentina, Emanuel David Ginobili was selected in the second round 57th pick overall of the 1999 NBA Draft by the San Antonio Spurs but decided to return to Italy and resume his career in the Euroleague. Playing over in Europe for 4 seasons from 1998-99 to 2001-02, and on South America's 2004 Argentine National Team that took home the gold medal, is where Ginobili became an *International Superstar*. His impressive resume before he entered the NBA in 2002 also includes Italian League MVP in 2001, Euroleague Finals MVP in 2001, FIBA Americas Championship MVP in 2001, Italian Cup MVP in 2002, and again Italian League MVP in 2002.

With all due respect to Drazen Petrovic, Arvydas Sabonis, and Dirk Nowitzki (until the 2011 playoff run), for a two or three year period, Ginobili was the best *one-on-one foreign player* I had ever seen. I mean he had no noticeable weakness. As great as Kobe was, Ginobili before the reoccurring injuries, might have been just as good or maybe even a little better at dribble penetrating attacking the basket (In fact, with his clever ball-handling skills, he along with Dwyane Wade of the Miami Heat, have perhaps the best *Euro step* or *1-2 step* in all of basketball). He was also just as great a clutch player and three-point shooter, and perhaps the better passer over Bryant during his prime. With his reckless abandon at times, Ginobili would do whatever it took to win at all cost. He would *utilize every ounce* of his body to corral rebounds, and to split the defense and dunk with *maximum extension* over taller opponents to assure a bucket. And, he would give up his body to dive for loose balls, and to draw (not including the notorious flops) *brutal* offensive fouls. So to reiterate, even though Ginobili was only a rookie during the Spurs 2003 championship season, he was an *experienced* player coming out of the European league.

Some of you may be in disagreement with the projected rankings because a lot of books and publications don't look that far ahead into the future due to the probability of a burn out, or major injury in one's career. But take my player projections five years ago with Parker and Ginobili. I told many people back then that someday both players would make it into the Basketball Hall of Fame. A lot of those people, flat out chuckled, probably because of what I have already mentioned above (trying to project too far into one's future). Or maybe they simply believed that there was no way Parker and Ginobili were Hall of Fame caliber players. Well, unlike other sports, one could make the Naismith Memorial Basketball Hall of Fame as a collegiate player or as an International player. So in the case of Ginobili, it was obvious to me, but maybe not to others, that at worse, if he did finish his career with inferior numbers (compared to other Hall of Famers) coming off the bench or due to injury, I knew he would still have a legitimate shot to make it into the Hall of Fame someday not only with his multiple championship rings, but with his *stellar* International play in which he was part of the 2004 Argentine Olympic team that brought home the gold.

The lightning-quick **Tony Parker** was and still is one of the top penetrating point guards in the NBA today. Born on May 17th, 1982 in Bruges, Belgium, William Anthony Parker was selected with the 28th pick overall of the 2001 NBA Draft by the San Antonio Spurs. The young and *explosive* point guard was the perfect complement to Tim Duncan in building a nucleus for multiple championship runs during the 2000s decades. In the most fundamentally sound set-offense in recent memory, Parker could score effectively out of the pick-and-roll with a jump shot, or by exploding to the rim finishing with a dazzling array of spin moves in the paint. In fact, this aspect of his game has always kept opposing defenses on their heels to where it makes the rest of the San Antonio offense flow gracefully, like running water in a river stream. And from my viewpoint, it seemed like Duncan relied on Parker a little too much during and after their 2007 Championship run. I wish at the time, Duncan was a little more assertive on the offensive end, but I guess that's what age does to you - because of this passiveness, Duncan has indirectly molded Parker into the leadership role of the team. And, although not gifted as a shooter, to his credit, Parker has continued to work on his jump shot throughout the years to where it has become extremely reliable in 2012.

Now after ten years in the league, with the Spurs still in contention to win another championship, Parker's offensive game is now complete. To go along with his ever improving jump shot, what has always made Parker great was his *uncanny* ability to finish at the basket with an *and-one* finish as good as any point guard in the league. In fact, this is his biggest strength and sole reason other than longevity and with having an excellent team with offensive schemes to fit his strong points; I believe he will someday make the Hall of Fame. He incorporates a lightning-quick first step to the basket, a crossover dribble, and spin moves in the paint to where he can finish on either side of the hoop. Or he can float in a shot with his *famous* and *unparalleled* tear-drop.

Even though, I predicted years back that Parker would someday make the Hall of Fame, I don't believe he is potentially a top 50 player, because he had more weaknesses (until the last couple of years) than any of the elite point guards I can think of. He has always been a solid assist man but an average to below average rebounder and defender at his position. Though he has always moved his feet well, he is somewhat deficient on the defense end. And aside from his dominant drive to the basket and an improved jump shot, he is still only an above average to good jump shooter and three-point shooter. Although, as we near the end of the 2012 season, he looks like he might be taking his game to a whole new level, perhaps elite status and as a serious MVP candidate. At only 30 years old in his prime, if he can have 3 or 4 more years like this one, he might be a *cinch* to make the Hall of Fame someday.

After David Robinson retired in 2003, the following season, the Spurs won 57 games but lost to the Lakers in the conference semifinals. Duncan's most memorable last second shot in the playoffs came in the game five loss in San Antonio that would have given the Spurs a three to two series advantage. This was just another clutch moment in Duncan's career that happened to be overshadowed by Derek Fisher's game-winning shot moments after. The Spurs thought they had the victory in the bank, and so did I, after Duncan launched a three-pointer with a couple of seconds left on the clock to give the Spurs a two point lead. But with .04 tenths of a second still remaining, it gave Fisher the opportunity to win the game on a catch-turn-and-shoot over Ginobili. The Lakers ended up winning the series back home in Los Angeles in six games but eventually lost to the Detroit Pistons in the 2004 NBA Finals. Notably, in my opinion, a player should not be able to score with less than half a second or maybe even eight tenths of a second left on the clock, unless it is an *extremely* quick catch-and-shoot, push-shot in one motion or a tip-in. Even though Fisher's shot seemed to be launched fairly quickly, he not only caught the ball and shot, he caught and turned before shooting. It was obvious, without the red light lit on the backboard, he got the shot off in time, but it probably took four tenths of a second just for the clock operator to start the clock. So in this scenario, at the very least, a player should be able to score on the catch-and-shoot if he's *already positioned* facing the basket. So for a player to catch, turn and then shoot, it is more realistic with at least eight tenth to a full second or more on the clock. Most players over the years will less than a half second on the clock, usually shoot a rushed or forced shot with no rhythm at all.

San Antonio made it back to the NBA Finals in 2005 and defeated Ben Wallace and the Detroit Pistons in a gutsy seven-game series, and then swept LeBron James and the Cleveland Cavaliers to win the 2007 NBA Finals. In the Detroit series, Duncan could thank

Robert Horry for saving the day in game 5 when he scored 21 of the teams last 35 points including five threes and the game-winning three-pointer with 9 seconds on the clock that gave the Spurs a 3 to 2 series advantage going back to San Antonio. This was the game Rasheed Wallace double teamed Manu Ginobili in the corner leaving "Big Shot Rob" for a wide open three! Duncan scored 26 points and grabbed 19 rebounds, but overall despite winning Finals MVP for the third time, had a subpar series (compared to his other Finals appearances) against an evenly matched and an equally tough defensive Detroit Pistons team. So without the big shot by Horry down the stretch, the Spurs would of gone back home having to win two games instead of just the one, and could have potentially lost the series.

Since Russell's Celtics 43 years ago, only Kobe's Lakers, Jordan's Bulls, and Magic and Kareem's Lakers, have led their teams to more championships than Tim Duncan. But perhaps Magic and for sure Michael won more as the best player on the team. That was one of the reasons; Duncan is ranked ahead of both Shaq and Kobe for greatest players ever. Also during that time, as good as Kobe was on the defensive end; Duncan was the best offensive/defensive player in my Top 25 behind only Hakeem Olajuwon and Michael Jordan. When Duncan won his second MVP award in 2003, I would have bet the house that he would have won at least one more to match Moses Malone with three, but that didn't happen. If he had, though already the best power forward ever, it would have rather easily elevated him past Olajuwon in the elite rankings and most likely put him ahead of Larry Bird. In players comparisons, while it is a close call between Duncan and Olajuwon, where most people might go with Duncan, I'm going with the "Dream," because he was the more talented (many felt he was the most skilled player ever), and was a little better than Duncan in almost every aspect of the game. He just won less because he had played against the toughest competition in the history of the league in the late 1980s and early 1990s, and with a less talented supporting cast during his prime. Olajuwon was basically a *one-man machine* in Houston that won two championships with less all-star caliber players than perhaps anyone in history. If it weren't for his *devastating* low-post game that opened up the perimeter for three-point shooting, the Rockets wouldn't have won any championships.

In player comparisons in the more recent era vs. Olajuwon, in favor of Duncan, he won more (third best winning percentage at .705 in the regular season among elite players) and he might have been the better *crunch-time* player overall, but it was really close. Also, Duncan had *more of a knack* to make all the clutch plays and elevate his teammates to greater heights for a *longer period of time*. In rebounding and in passing, some might call it a draw, but you would still have to give the edge to Olajuwon from an overall talent perspective. While Shaq and Kobe won more titles in a shorter time frame, Duncan won just as many or more as the *best* player on the team. It ranks this way: Duncan was the man on 4 title teams (even though they gave the last Finals MVP to Parker), while Shaq was the man on 3 and Kobe on 2 (from my view, It could have been justified as 1, based on how Gasol played in the Finals and if he had won Finals MVP in

2010), and Olajuwon on two. His teams were also more consistent and he won more games throughout the decade. Like Bill Russell, Duncan was the *ultimate* winner, and he played both ends of the court almost as good as you could ask in a power forward. If LeBron James never makes it into the Top 5 players of all-time, bumping Larry Bird out of position with a domino effect, Tim Duncan will bask in NBA glory as the second greatest forward of all-time. But even if he ends up at number three, one thing will always remain, he will forever be acknowledged by most as the greatest *power* forward of all-time!

Career Totals

20.2 points, 11.2 rebounds, 3.1 assists, 2.2 blocks, 0.7 steals, .510 FG%, .693 FT%

23,785 points, 13,219 rebounds, 3612 assists, 2652 blocks, 872 steals

Jerry West

(Rank #10)

All-NBA First Team (10-times), All-Defensive First Team (4-times)

Scoring Title (1-time), Assist Title (1-time)

NBA Championships (1), Finals MVP (1-time)

NBA Record: 6 consecutive 40-point playoff games!

NBA Record: 46.3 points average in a playoff series!

NBA Record: 40.6 points average in a playoff season! (min 10g)

Also featuring:
Gail Goodrich

Jerry West was the greatest clutch shooter in NBA history for a reason. Mr. West was given the nickname "Mr. Clutch" because he made memorable big shots throughout his illustrious career including the half-court heave in game 3 of the 1970 NBA Finals, that's often shown on TV during nationally televised games. A scoring machine for the Los Angeles Lakers during the 1960s, West was the Michael Jordan at the guard position in his days having made the All-Star Team all 14 years he played in the league - this is probably one of many reasons he is officially the silhouette of the NBA Logo. West was hands down, the greatest shooting guard of all-time behind Jordan not only in the regular season but in the playoffs. Objectively speaking, his overall numbers simply back this up as he is ranked either first or second to Jordan in many scoring feats including points per game at 27.0 in the regular season and 29.1 points per game in the postseason, where he ranks third behind only Jordan and Allen Iverson. In the postseason, he scored **30 or more points 74 times** and an incredible **40 points or more 20 times**. Out of all his plethora of 40-point games throughout his career, the most impressive streak came in the playoffs when he set an NBA record 46.3 points per game in a playoff series - that included 6 straight 40-point games in 1965. A consistent NBA Finalist, West took the Los Angeles Lakers to 9 NBA Finals while becoming the only man to win the NBA Finals MVP playing for the losing team in 1969. Even in the past games with most of them coming in wins, West in the NBA Finals had by far the most **30-point** games with **31** and **40-point** games with **10** than any player in history. He even had better numbers than the great Michael Jordan who had 23 and 6 respectively. West was a prolific scorer at either guard position and had a lightning-quick release and deadly jump shot from anywhere on the court. He could also back your best defender down and shoot right over him. He was also a good rebounder for his size at six-foot-three tops, with pinpoint passing skills, and was a tenacious defensive player. With his six-foot-nine wing span and quick hands, he was able to tip the ball away from opponents and get a lot of steals. Lenny Wilkens said in the book "Tall Tales," that West had hands as quick as a snakes tongue and if they had kept track of steals in his days, he and West would have been the league leaders. His greatest attributes was his perfectionism and intensity on the court and his extreme will to win.

Jerry Alan West was born on May 28th, 1938 in Chelyan, West Virginia and played basketball at East Bank High School. After growing six inches by his senior year, the six foot West led his team to the 1956 state title. In 1959, at West Virginia University, he led the team to the NCAA College Championship game but lost to the University of California despite averaging 32 points and 14.6 rebounds in five tournament games. West was selected #2 overall of the 1960 NBA Draft only to Oscar Robertson's territorial pick. Prior to the regular season, after West and Oscar played together on the 1960 Olympic team that went on to win the gold medal, the Lakers franchise moved from Minneapolis to Los Angeles for the 1960-61 season. After a modest rookie year by West, Elgin Baylor would lead the Lakers into the playoffs where they would lose in the second round to the St. Louis Hawks in seven games. In only his second season, West blossomed into one of the top 2 guards in the league, averaging an impressive **30.8 points**, **7.9 rebounds**, and **5.4 assists** per game - and was named to the All-NBA First Team for the first of six consecutive seasons. He also set a then record for a guard scoring **63 points** in a game against the Knicks. In the playoffs, the Los Angeles Lakers beat the Detroit Pistons four games to two in the Western Finals before eventually losing in the NBA Finals to the Boston Celtics in seven games. After West scored 40 points in game 2 to even the series at one game apiece, Baylor scored an NBA record 61 points in game 5 to give the Lakers a 3 games to 2 series lead. But Boston came back winning game six in overtime 110 to 107 to force the decisive seventh game. The Lakers had a chance to win game seven if Frank Selvey hadn't missed the potential game-winning shot at the buzzer and Baylor's missed tip attempt that would have given the Lakers their first title in the city of Los Angeles.

Despite losing in the Finals, West averaged 31.5 points during the entire playoff run. In the 1962-63 season, West played in only 55 games because of a hamstring injury, and was not in shape during the playoffs, as Baylor carried the Lakers to the NBA Finals. In the Western Finals, the Lakers avenged the loss to the Hawks from two years prior defeating St. Louis in seven games. But with West not in full force, the Lakers ended up losing to the Celtics in six games in the NBA Finals. Even with West playing at less than one-hundred percent, he still managed to score 42 points in the game 3 win, and 32 in the game 5 win with Baylor chipping in 43.

The following season, with Baylor suffering knee problems, West led the Lakers in scoring for the first time at **28.7 points** per game, but it wasn't enough to get out of the first round of the playoffs as they lost to the Hawks in five games. In 1965 Baylor had a career threatening knee injury and played in only one playoff game. This is where Jerry West showed his greatness with an *unprecedented onslaught* of record breaking 40-point playoff games that still stands today. In the Western Final series against the Baltimore Bullets, West had scoring games of **49, 52, 44, 48, 42 and 45 points**, but with an undermanned team, the Lakers ended up losing the NBA Finals to the Celtics in five games. After scoring 45 points in the game 2 loss in Boston, West scored 43 more points in game 3, which was the only Lakers win in the series. In the 1965-66 season, West averaged **31.3 points** and finished second in the league in scoring to Wilt Chamberlain. In the playoffs with Baylor playing at seventy-five percent, the Lakers beat the Hawks in a tough seven-game series, but lost again to the Celtics in the NBA Finals in seven games. Despite the loss, in the overtime game one win 133 to 129, West scored 41 points and Baylor pitched in with 36. In the game 4 loss 122-117, West scored an impressive 45 points. But after falling behind three games to one, the Lakers battled back to win the next two games behind West's 41 points in game 5 and Goodrich's 28 in game 6. In the decisive seventh game, West scored 36 points and fueled a fourth quarter comeback that brought the Lakers to within six points with 28 seconds left, and within 2 points with four seconds left, before eventually losing the game in heartbreak fashion 95-93. In the regular season in both 1965 and 1966, West averaged 31 points giving him 3 30-point seasons in his first six years in the league. He would end up with 4 30-point seasons for his career after winning the scoring title at **31.2 points** per game in 1970. Those same two seasons in the playoffs and two years later in 1968 and 1969, West led the league in scoring average in the postseason at **40.6, 34.2, 30.8, and 30.9** respectively.

In the 1966-67 season, West was injured playing in only 66 games and the Lakers were bounced out of the first round of the playoffs by the San Francisco Warriors in a three-game sweep. The following year, he missed 51 games, but the Lakers beat the Chicago Bulls and the Warriors to make it back to the NBA Finals for a fifth meeting with the Boston Celtics. With the series tied at two games apiece, West sprained his ankle while scoring 38 points in the game four win, but was not the same the rest of the series. Continuing on, playing through injury, West scored 35 points as the Lakers lost game five by three points. The Lakers were frustrated about the two losses they felt they should have won, eventually losing the series in six games behind forty points from John Havlicek.

The Lakers finished the 1968-69 season with 55 wins and defeated the Warriors and Atlanta Hawks convincingly in the playoffs before facing the Celtics in the NBA Finals for the sixth time of the decade. With the Celtics playing with Bill Russell in his final season and with Chamberlain in his first season in Los Angeles, in which he came over in a trade from the Philadelphia 76ers, the Lakers felt they were primed and ready to make one last stand against the 10-time champion Celtics. In the first two games, West lit up the score board scoring 53 and 41 points to lead the Lakers to a 2-0 series advantage. In the second game, Havlicek countered with 43 points but Baylor scored the last 12 points to give the Lakers a 118 to 112 win. But Boston made adjustments in game three, double teaming West and causing him to fatigue quickly to a point that he asked twice to be substituted for a long period of time. The Lakers lost game three by six points and game four on Sam Jones' buzzer-beater. West scored 39 points in a pivotal game five victory but severely pulled his hamstring during the game. Playing injured, the Lakers won game six by nine points in Boston with West scoring only 26 points. The Lakers franchise felt confident they would win game seven at home and decided to fill the rafters with balloons. This obviously motivated the Celtics to a 108-106 victory on L.A.'s home court. The Lakers dream of their first championship in L.A. vanished despite Jerry West's courageous triple-double of **42 points, 13 rebounds, and 12 assists.** The Lakers probably would have won the series before it even got to a seventh game if they had been playing with Gail Goodrich, who they had lost to the Phoenix Suns in the expansion draft before the season.

In the beginning of the 1969-70 season, Chamberlain seriously injured his knee and missed almost the entire season but was able to return for the playoffs. West picked up the scoring slack and won his first scoring title at 31.2 points per game. That season, West averaged 30 points or more in a playoff season for the 7th time in his illustrious career. And the two seasons prior he led the league in playoff scoring average for the third and fourth time in his career at 30.8 and 30.9 respectively. In the playoffs, after defeating Goodrich, Connie Hawkins, Dick Van Arsdale, and the Phoenix Suns in a tough seven-game series and sweeping the Hawks, the Lakers met the New York Knicks in the NBA Finals for the first time in the Baylor/West era. The Knicks were a team on the rise after the Celtics dynasty had ended in 1969. Playing with a loaded roster of four Hall of Famers in Willis Reed, Walt Frazier, Dave DeBusschere and Bill Bradley, and with the Lakers playing with a still hobbling Chamberlain, the two teams split the first four games. In the game three loss, West had one of the most famous shots in NBA history when he launched a half-court shot at the buzzer that tied the game in regulation to send the game into overtime. After spraining his left hand he missed all five of his shots in overtime as the game ended 111-108. In game four in which the Lakers won, West had a monster game scoring **37 points** and dishing out **18 assists**. In game five, Reed pulled his thy muscle but the Lakers were unable to take advantage. They committed 19 turnovers in the second half with West and Chamberlain only shooting the ball a total of five times. In one of the greatest comebacks in NBA Finals history, the Lakers ended up losing 107-100. In game six in L.A., with Chamberlain scoring 45 points and West scoring 31 to go along with 13 assists, the Lakers won in convincing fashion 135-113. This set up a favorable game seven in New York, but West now injured his hand, and had to take manual injections before the game. With Reed playing hobbled, he inspired his team to an upset victory and again brought more heartbreak for the championship starved Lakers. Reed walked away with the Finals MVP and Walt Frazier came up big in game seven having scored 36 points to go along with 19 assists.

For the 1970-71 season, **Gail Goodrich** was traded back to the Lakers from the Phoenix Suns for Mel Counts, but lost Baylor to an Achilles tendon rupture that virtually put an end to his career. They also lost West for the entire playoffs with a knee injury. The Lakers made it to the conference finals but got pounced by league MVP Lew Alcindor and the Milwaukee Bucks in five games. Without West, Goodrich averaged a **career-high 25.4 points** and **7.6 assists** in the playoffs. Afterwards, West actually considered retiring before the start of the next season, due to all the recent losses and a host of injuries throughout his career. But, glory finally came to Jerry West and the Los Angeles Lakers in the following year in 1972. After starting the season 39-3, the Lakers set an NBA record of 69-13 including a record 33-game winning streak, defeated the defending champion Bucks in the conference finals and won the 1972 NBA Championship over the New York Knicks, bringing the city of Los Angeles their first championship since the team arrived from Minneapolis. That season, Goodrich emerged as one of the best guards in the league averaging a **career-high 25.9 points** per game while West led the NBA in assists for the first time at **9.7** per game. He was stellar in the playoffs particularly when he had his way with Earl Monroe in the NBA Finals. During the winning streak, in 32 games (missed one game with Pat Riley taking his place in the starting lineup) West averaged **26.1 points**, **10.1 assists**, and **4.5 rebounds** per game. The *dynamic dual* of West and Goodrich formed one of the greatest backcourts in NBA history. Like West, Goodrich was a tenacious and fierce competitor. He was the Manu Ginobili of his day with the same energy and craftiness able to score off dribble penetration with deft one-on-one moves and could create his own shot from anywhere on the court. He also had an unorthodox low-post game able to punish smaller guards and was equipped with an exceptional quick-release jump shot. In addition, like West, he played both guard positions and had outstanding passing skills and quick hands on defense.

Born on April 23rd, 1943 in Los Angeles, Ca., Gail Charles Goodrich attended John H. Francis Polytechnic High School where he won the 1961 Los Angeles City basketball championship. In college at UCLA, he averaged 21.5 and 24.8 points in his junior and senior year and led the Bruins to its first two NCAA titles under Coach John Wooden in 1964 and 1965. He also set a then record 42 points against favored Michigan in the 1965 Championship game and was named to the All-America First Team. The left-handed Goodrich was then selected with a territorial pick of the 1965 NBA Draft by the Los Angeles Lakers but was lost three years later to the Phoenix Suns in the 1968 expansion draft. After a slow start in his first three seasons in Los Angeles, Goodrich blossomed in his first year with the Suns averaging 23.8 points, 6.4 assists, and 5.4 rebounds per game and was named to his first All-Star team. For eight straight seasons from 1969 to 1976, Goodrich was highly productive averaging 22.4 points and 5.5 assists per game and was named to the All-Star team five times. He was also named to his first and only All-NBA First Team in 1974, when West was in his final season. His three-year peak beginning in 1972 came when West was in his final three seasons with the franchise, where he averaged 25.1 points and 4.7 assists per game. In the 1972-73 season, the Lakers finished with 60 wins, and rematched the New York Knicks in the NBA Finals. After the Knicks took a 2-1 series lead, West had pulled both hamstrings in game four and the Lakers fell to the Knicks in five games. The following season, West played in only 31 games and one playoff game, and retired at the end of the year. Goodrich ended up playing two more seasons with the Lakers and his final three with the New Orleans Jazz, but never made it back to the playoffs.

West went to the NBA Finals 9 times, having to face the star-studded Celtic's team 6 times. His career scoring average is 27.0 points per game, 5th in history behind Wilt, Jordan, LeBron, and Baylor. It is somewhat misleading to measure Jordan's 6 and Kobe's 5 championship rings to just the 1 for West. Even though West had another star (Elgin Baylor the first half of his career, and an injury riddled out of his prime Baylor the second half - along with Chamberlain who was also at the end of his prime) as did Michael and Kobe, they had to face the greatest dynasty in the history of sports in the Boston Celtics which won 11 championships in 13 years - and the high powered Knicks team that included Willis Reed, Walt Frazier, Dave DeBusschere, Bill Bradley, and Earl Monroe that won 2 championships during this time. When West won his championship in 1972, Baylor had already retired in the beginning of the year. Despite his misfortunes of losing in the NBA Finals to the Celtics six times and the Knicks twice throughout his career - with a lot of those series going seven games, I believe that if Baylor had not repeatedly injured his knees beginning in 1964 and if Chamberlain wasn't out of his prime in 1969, and hadn't gotten severely injured in 1970; and West had not broken his nose at least nine times, broken his hands multiple times, injured his hamstrings and pulled all those muscles, he would have won more than one championship. Also, if Chamberlain had played with West and Baylor in their primes during the early sixties, despite his egotistical argumentative ways that he had with players (especially team captain Baylor) and coaches, I believe the Los Angeles Lakers would have won multiple championships. If Jordan and Pippen and Shaq and Kobe played during this era, the Bulls and Lakers also probably would have only won one or two championships.

In player comparisons:

Recently in the middle of 2011, The Herd syndicated radio show had on a guest speaker and during one of the segments he was asked the question: Who was the greater Laker, Jerry West or Kobe Bryant? He gave his arguments in favor of West and the callers gave their mixed opinions with many of the people favoring Kobe. I called the show to give my two cents but was not able to get through - so I did a recording on my former web site JNBA& Allsports.com to state the facts in favor of West. I made the case that he has 9 NBA Finals appearances and a Finals MVP award in 1969 in which he played for the losing team, and that he owns a significant amount of postseason records including **6 straight 40-point games, 46.3 point** scoring average for a playoff series and **40.6** for a playoff season. I also mentioned these other stats: West averaged **30 points or more 4 times in the regular season** to Kobe's 3. His career playoff scoring average is **29.1 points** (Kobe's 25.2 per game) which ranks 4th all-time to Jordan, LeBron, an Iverson. He also averaged over **30 points in the playoffs for 7 seasons** to Kobe's 4. He was a First Team All-NBA 10 times and All-Defensive First Team 4 times (All-Defensive teams weren't instituted until 1969). He was also a great passer averaging **6.7 assists** to Wade's 6.3, Jordan's 5.3, and Kobe's 4.8.

But out of all West scoring accolades in the regular season and the postseason, the one that stands out most to me is his career 40-point games in the playoffs which ranks second all-time only to Jordan. Here is the list of the top players with multiple 40-point playoff games: Michael Jordan 38, **Jerry West 20**, Elgin Baylor 14, Wilt Chamberlain 13, Kobe Bryant now has 13, Shaquille O'Neal 12, Hakeem Olajuwon 11, LeBron James now has 11, and Allen Iverson 10. I then emphatically, did a stat comparison of not only West and Bryant for the regular season vs. the postseason; I also included Dwyane Wade in the conversation as potentially becoming the second best shooting guard of all-time ahead of both players, and right behind Jordan. I strongly pointed out that both West and Wade have better statistics than Kobe in the regular season and postseason.

Here are the statistical comparisons (up to the end of the 2011 season at the time of this writing) for the four of them (keeping in mind that Wade just entered his prime while Kobe should be at the end of his) in the regular season and the postseason:

Jordan: 30.1 pts, 6.2 rebs, 5.3 assists, 2.3 steals, .83 blocks, 50%FG, 32.7% 3FG, 83.5% FT
33.4 pts, 6.4 rebs, 5.7 assists, 2.1 steals, .88 blocks, 49% FG, 33.2% 3FG, 82.8%FT

West: 27.0 pts, 5.8 rebs, 6.7 assists, 2.6 steals, 0.7 blocks, 47% FG, n/a 3FG, 81.4% FT
29.1 pts, 5.6 rebs, 6.3 assists, n/a steals, n/a blocks, 46.9% FG, n/a 3FG, 80.5% FT

Bryant: 25.3 pts, 5.3 rebs, 4.7 assists, 1.5 steals, 0.5 blocks, 45% FG, 33.9% 3FG, 83.7% FT
25.4 pts, 5.2 rebs, 4.8 assists, 1.4 steals, 0.7 blocks, 45% FG, 33.7% 3FG, 81.4% FT

Wade: 25.4 pts, 5.1 rebs, 6.3 assists, 1.8 steals, 1.0 block, 48% FG, 29.2% 3FG, 76.9% FT
25.9 pts, 5.7 rebs, 5.6 assists, 1.6 steals, 1.1 blocks, 48% FG, 32.7% 3FG, 78.9% FT

As you can see, both West and Wade (who had just entered his prime), had better numbers than Bryant. West has the 2nd highest average at his position in NBA history behind Jordan and the 3rd highest in the playoffs behind Jordan and Iverson. He is also a close 3rd in the NBA Finals behind Jordan and Wade but 4th overall with Rick Barry at the top of the list:

Barry: 36.3 points	Jordan: 33.6 points	Wade: 30.6 points	West: 30.5 points
(10-games)	(35-games)	(12-games)	(55-games)

At least statistically, Jerry West was the second best scorer at his position to Michael Jordan at every level of play, and at the same time ahead of Kobe Bryant. So from an objective point of view, West beats Bryant at his own game. While Bryant might have been the flashier more athletic scorer, the results for both players were near equal. Like Wade, he also had a better understanding of the team aspect of the game throughout his career. He played within the game and knew when to go on a scoring tear and when not to, unlike Bryant earlier in his career. It's kind of funny though, in his most recent book "West by West," West points out that he once joked with Kobe (in his earlier years), that in his younger days during his prime, he would beat him in a one-on-one, because he was too anxious to shoot. Come to think of it, fifteen years later, he still is to some extent where Kobe can get into that mode where he becomes too anxious and either rushes or takes an ill-advised shot. While many believe that his tendencies to score exclusively are for the betterment of the team, I disagree to some extent because out of all the great scorers in NBA history including Jordan and Allen Iverson particularly the second half of their careers, Larry Bird, LeBron James, Dwyane Wade, and Kevin Durant of today, all play within the game. Even though Durant for example has only one 50-point game so far in his career, it is partly due to the fact he plays within the game and doesn't try and play outside the game and run up the score. If he wanted to be a selfish scorer, or even if he chooses not to be, he has the talent to match or surpass Bryant's scoring accolades someday! Because of his size, you could give Bryant the advantage as a rebounder, but as a passer, I would give the advantage to West. Out of the four best shooting guards of all-time West has the highest assists average at 6.7 in the regular season and 6.3 in the playoffs. His last 9 seasons in the league, he averaged at least 6 assists per game and at least 7.5 in 4 of those in consecutive seasons. Any above average to good point guard would be happy with those career numbers. Just to throw it out there despite playing when rebounds were easier to come by during the era of more offensive possessions, West averaged at least 6 rebounds in his first 6 seasons in the league including 7 rebounds or more in 4 of those with the first three coming in succession to begin his career.

In my opinion, Jerry West and Elgin Baylor were the greatest scoring dual of all-time and both had a great all-around game to go along with it. In the 1971-72 season, West was asked to become more of a facilitator proving he was just as prolific a passer as he was a scorer. He had already been a terrific assists man his entire career averaging more at his position out of the four greatest shooting guards of all-time. But he was asked to do a little more that season with Chamberlain's low-post scoring and with Gail Goodrich having a career year from the perimeter. Even during the historic 33-game winning streak, West scored 30 points or more 7 times and finished in double figures in assists 18 times. He also had 13 assists or more in 9 out of those 18 games. Of course Bryant has the edge for his athleticism but even on the defensive end, you could call it a draw with West. And, many have said West was one of the great defensive players of all-time.

Through longevity, Kobe has been able to accumulate career totals that will rank among the greatest to have played the game. He also played with the most physically dominate player of this era in Shaq Diesel and the best supporting cast the last four years, enabling him to win 5 Championships in all with the Los Angeles Lakers. West played with Baylor for five years of his prime (before Elgin blew his knee out) but without a dominant big man until 1969. West teams were ultimately competitive for 9 Championship Finals appearances including the one title in 1972. When Bryant played with a lesser supporting cast between his championship seasons, his teams were barely over .500. Despite the frequent injuries and the one championship, West was ultimately great his entire career. In the eyes of many, he was just as good as or perhaps even better than Bryant in the regular season, postseason, and in the NBA Finals throughout his brilliant 14-year career. He also finished in the Top 2 for MVP 4 times to Bryant winning it once and finishing second in another. There are many great players to have worn a Lakers uniform including George Mikan, Elgin Baylor, Wilt Chamberlain, Kareem Abdul-Jabbar, Shaquille O'Neal and Kobe Bryant. But the greatest Laker of all-time has to be either Magic Johnson or Jerry West. And the second greatest shooting guard of time as of now is still Jerry West!

Career Totals

27.0 points, 5.8 rebounds, 6.7 assists, 2.6 steals 0.7 blocks, 474% FG, 814% FT

25,192 points, 5366 rebounds, 6238 assists, 81 steals, 23 blocks

Elgin Baylor

(Rank #11)

All-NBA First Team (10-times), All-Star (11-times)

NBA Record: 11 consecutive 30-point playoff games!

NBA Record: 61 points in a Finals game!

At a chiseled six-foot-five, Elgin Baylor was the original Dr. J and Michael Jordan and the godfather of hang time, defying gravity, and of the slam dunk. The high-flying, acrobatic superstar was the most *dominant* scorer at the forward position in his era if not ever. Growing up, in terms of skill and athleticism, I always viewed Baylor as the Jordan of the olden days. The Los Angeles Lakers legend along with Wilt Chamberlain, were the most prolific scorers of the 1960s. His 38.3 points per game scoring average in 1962 was the second highest scoring mark of any player in history behind Chamberlain, who surpassed the mark two more times, including in that year. But perhaps his greatest scoring feat came that same season in the 1962 NBA Finals when he set an NBA record 61 points against the Boston Celtics in game 5 that put the Lakers ahead in the series three games to two. Two other astounding feats in his career are his 18 50-point games (1 playoffs) and 102 40-point games (14 playoffs) that both rank fourth on the all-time list. Kareem Abdul-Jabbar said in his book "Kareem" in 1989 that when he was growing up, even though he played the center position, "he still wanted to be like Elgin." Baylor played during a time where a lot of his acrobatic moves were not captured on film. His teammate of six years and as an opponent for four, Tommy Hawkins said, "Elgin certainly did not jump as high as Michael Jordan. But he had the greatest variety of shots of anyone." Baylor was able to change the position of the ball in midair and the direction of his move while floating to the basket, and could shoot in all sorts of angles putting spin on the ball. To go along with grace and finesse, he also said: "Pound for pound, no one was ever as great as Elgin Baylor" and that, "He had incredible strength and could post up Bill Russell; he could pass like Magic and dribble with the best guards in the league." Bill Sharman in 1971 told the Los Angeles Times at Baylor's retirement that he was the greatest cornerman to have ever played pro basketball. My grandfather at 88 years old today said Baylor is the greatest basketball player he has ever seen. It is *credible* to take his word for it because he watches and listens on the radio to almost every Laker game since the teamed moved to Los Angeles for the 1960-61 season. Many other people feel the same way that saw Baylor play before the days of widespread television exposure.

Elgin Gay Baylor was born on September 16th, 1934 in Washington, D.C. He was selected by the Minneapolis Lakers with the #1 overall pick of the 1958 NBA Draft out of Seattle University. In three years in college including his freshman year at the College of Idaho, Baylor averaged 31.3 points a game and 19.5 rebounds, and led Seattle to the NCAA Championship game where they would lose to the perennial powerhouse Kentucky Wildcats. In the game, Baylor was playing with bruised ribs and got in foul trouble during the second half in which he may have been benched a little prematurely by his coach John Castelani. Despite the loss, he was named 1957-58 NCAA Final Four, Most Outstanding Player. With Lakers legend George Mikan retired and low ticket sales, the Minneapolis Lakers convinced Baylor to leave school after his junior year. In Baylor's rookie season, he averaged 24.9 points a game and 15 rebounds, and took the Lakers all the way to the 1959 NBA Finals where they would lose to the eventual champion Boston Celtics in four straight games. During his sophomore campaign, Baylor scored **64 points** on November 8th, 1959 to set a new NBA record for points (63), which was held by Joe Fulks since 1949.

In the 1960 and 1961 seasons, the Lakers (with rookie Jerry West aboard second time around) were defeated by the St. Louis Hawks in the Western Finals in a seven-game series twice. In the 1960-61 campaign, he averaged **34.8 points**, **19.8 rebounds**, and **5.1 assists** per game. And then the following year in a military duty shortened season, Baylor peaked averaging a **career-high of 38.3 points** per game to go along with **18.6 rebounds** and **4.6 assists**. During the regular season first time around, Baylor broke his own scoring mark by scoring **71 points** (he also had **25 rebounds**) against the New York Knicks on November 15th 1960. He also scored **63 points** in the same game against Wilt Chamberlain on December 8th, 1961 in which Wilt scored 78 points breaking Baylor's old mark. In the playoffs he averaged **38.6 points** per game and set an NBA record **61 points** in the go-ahead game five against the Boston Celtics in the 1962 NBA Finals. Unfortunately, the Lakers lost game six and then game seven on Frank Selvey's missed jumper at the buzzer. But his greatest feats could have been his two 50-point triple-double games in the 1961-62 and 1962-63 regular seasons: where he posted **52 points, 25 rebounds, and 10 assists** and **50 points, 15 rebounds, and 11 assists**. The next year with West having hamstring injuries, Baylor carried the Lakers to the NBA Finals but lost rather easily to the Celtics in six games despite averaging over thirty points or more (32.6) in the playoffs for the fourth straight year. In 1963, he also became the first player to finish the regular season in the top five in four statistical categories (points, rebounds, assists, and free-throw percentage) in NBA history. In the 1964 season, Baylor started having knee problems and averaged only 25.4 points per game, the lowest since his rookie year. The Lakers made the playoffs but lost to the Hawks for the third time in five years this time in the semifinals. After a career threatening injury in 1965, Baylor played in only one playoff game forcing Jerry West to take his game to another level. Behind West's record breaking 40-point scoring barrage in the playoffs, which included eight 40-point games in all, the Lakers beat the Baltimore Bullets in six games of the Western Finals before losing to the Celtics in five games in the NBA Finals. In the 1965-66 season, with Baylor playing at seventy-five percent, the Lakers made it back to the Finals after beating St. Louis in seven games in the Western Finals, but lost again to the Celtics (in 7 games) for the fifth time in eight years. The next season, with Baylor playing in only 70 games and West in just 67 including only one playoff game, the Lakers were swept in three games by the San Francisco Warriors in the first round (semifinals) of the playoffs. In 1968, the Lakers returned to the NBA Finals but lost in six games to the Celtics after West sprained his ankle in game four.

With Baylor's career slowing down in his final full seasons in 1969 and 1970, the Los Angeles Lakers were not able to capture the most coveted NBA Championship that had eluded them the entire decade. Even with newly acquired Chamberlain aboard to bolster the frontcourt, the Lakers came up short once again losing to both the Celtics for the sixth time in the decade and to the destined New York Knicks the following year. Because, Baylor and Chamberlain were moving up in age and were often recovering from injuries or playing injured, played a big part in Los Angeles coming up short once again. It was also one of the major reasons along with having to face the Celtics' dynasty during the 1960s, why Elgin Baylor never won a title in his magnificent career.

In player comparisons:

To try and stave off elimination throughout the decade, Baylor did have a few games where he scored in multitudes for the Lakers in many big games throughout his playoff career; after he scored 61 points in game 5 on the road of the 1962 NBA Finals against the Celtics, he scored 34 points in the follow-up game 6 at home (including 21 in the first half) and 41 points in game 7 on the road. There was no three-point line when Baylor scored 71 points, a Los Angeles Lakers record at the time. When Kobe Bryant scored 81 points against the Toronto Raptors, he had seven three-pointers to go along with it. Even though the game was close most of the way, the Lakers actually had a 20-point lead at the end of the 4th quarter in which he should have been pulled from the game. Bryant also played in one of the softest eras of defenses where players could fly around the court while not being touched without a foul or hand-checking call. Jordan also said just recently, that if he played in this era, he could score 100 points in a game.

The most impressive feat on Baylor's resume is his record 61 points (that came with 22 rebounds) he scored in the game five victory against the Boston Celtics in the 1962 NBA Finals that still stands today. In my opinion, it is the single greatest scoring game in NBA playoff history even over Michael Jordan's 63 points that came in the 1986 first-round playoff *loss* to the Boston Celtics. It took Jordan double-overtime to set the new playoff record. In the beginning of only his second season, Baylor scored an incredible 64 points in a game that broke the all-time record held at the time by Joe Fulks who set the mark 10 years earlier. And, in the beginning of his third season, he scored a Madison Square Garden record 71 points and followed that up with a 63-point game the year after in an epic battle with Wilt Chamberlain, and the 61 the year after (same season) in the Finals against the Celtics. So all four of Baylor's career 60-point games came in his second, third, and fourth years in the league from the beginning of the 1959-60 season to the end of the 1962 season.

You have to give it to Elgin; he was just as *lethal* in the postseason as he was in the regular season. From the 1961 season to the 1963 season he averaged 34.8, 38.3, and 34.0 points in consecutive years in the regular season and 33.4, 38.1, 38.6, and 32.6 in consecutive years in the playoffs from 1960 to 1963. He also owns the NBA record with **11 straight 30-point** games in the postseason. His first five years in the league from 1959 to 1963, before he started having knee problems in 1964, he averaged 32 points in the regular season and 33.6 points in the playoffs.

Here is a list of some of the greatest scoring seasons in the regular season and in the playoffs by the Top Players of All-time:

Regular season

*ABA

Wilt Chamberlain		Elgin Baylor		Kareem		Rick Barry		George Gervin	
50.4	1962	38.3	1962	34.8	1972	35.6	1967	33.1	1980
44.8	1963	34.8	1961	31.7	1971	34.0	1969*	32.3	1982
38.4	1961	34.0	1963	30.2	1973	31.5	1972*	29.6	1979
37.6	1960	29.6	1960	30.0	1975	30.6	1975	27.2	1978

Playoffs

37.0	1961	38.6	1962	35.2	1970	40.1	1970*	34.0	1975
36.9	1964	38.1	1961	34.7	1977	34.7	1967	33.3	1980
34.7	1965	33.4	1960	32.2	1974	33.7	1971*	33.2	1978
33.5	1966	32.6	1963	31.9	1980	30.8	1972*	29.4	1982

Regular season

Michael Jordan		Kobe Bryant		Iverson		Jerry West		LeBron James	
37.1	1987	35.4	2006	33.0	2006	31.3	1966	31.4	2006
35.0	1988	31.6	2007	31.4	2002	31.2	1970	30.0	2008
33.6	1990	30.0	2003	31.1	2001	31.0	1965	29.7	2010
32.6	1993	28.5	2001	30.7	2005	30.8	1962	28.4	2009

Playoffs

43.7	1986	32.8	2007	32.9	2001	40.6	1965	35.3	2009
36.7	1990	32.1	2003	31.7	2003	34.2	1966	30.8	2006
36.3	1988	30.2	2009	31.2	2005	31.5	1962	30.3	2012
35.7	1987	30.1	2008	30.0	2002	31.2	1970	29.1	2010

While Baylor can't match Chamberlain's scoring feats in the regular season, he matches or succeeds him in the playoffs. Furthermore, in Baylor's first six seasons (in the playoffs), he averaged 32.9 points per game and 21.6 his final six seasons, whereas Chamberlain averaged 32.8 points per game his first six seasons as compared to 17.6 his final seven.

With consideration to age (he started his career at the age of 24), maybe Baylor's numbers might have looked more like Jordan's (started his career at the age of 21) for a full career if he hadn't had all the knee injuries. Baylor still ranks in the top 4 all-time in the regular season at 27.4 points per game behind Jordan, Chamberlain, and LeBron - and 5th all-time in the playoffs at 27.0 points per game. With his four career 60-point games as I have already stated previously, he is 4th on the all-time list behind only the great Wilt Chamberlain, Michael Jordan, and Kobe Bryant. Within the scope of his scoring accolades, Baylor had 343 30-point games, 88 40-point games, and 17 50-point games (14 from a different source) in his regular season career. He also had 60 30-point games, 14 40-point games, and the one 50-point+ game (61 points in the finals) in his playoff career. In addition, he had **19 30-point** and **5 40-point games** in the NBA Finals which ranks third all-time behind West and Jordan.

Baylor was also selected to 10 All-NBA First Teams and 11 All-Star Teams.

Comparing Baylor to West is more difficult than comparing Baylor to Chamberlain or any other forward, power forward or center, because although undersized, not only could Baylor score from the perimeter, he could score from the post-position and rebound with the best of them. Those are the two main reasons; I have him ranked ahead of Rick Barry, John Havlicek and Julius Erving in my elite rankings of all-time. It also helps in comparisons to power forwards Bob Pettit, Charles Barkley, and Karl Malone. While both dimensions elevate his game ahead of most small forwards, the fact that he was one of the most prolific scorers of all-time, elevates him past most power forwards such as Pettit, Barkley and Malone. And, although Baylor and West's offensive production were similar playing together during all their excruciating title runs (seven in total) that fell short, West was the better clutch scorer during his playoff career.

In addition, in evidence of his old highlights (you see many of these on NBA Hardwood Classics, NBA TV and You Tube) - backed by player interviews, Baylor was also an excellent passer and defensive player, where he was often seen making precise zip-passes, stealing the ball and blocking an opponent's shot. Along with his rebounding prowess, Baylor had some of the strongest hands - as Jerry West once said that he never lost a bet that someone could rip the ball out of Baylor's hands because his *grip* was so strong! His other former teammate Rod Hundley once said in making a player comparison with Dr. J, "If Julius Erving ... is a doctor, then Elgin Baylor was a brain surgeon when he played."

Also, as a testament to Elgin Baylor's legacy, from the book Tall Tales, longtime Los Angeles Lakers announcer and now the late Chick Hearn had this to say about Baylor: I had never seen a player like this - all his high-flying moves and how he used reverse English on the ball to make a layup from unbelievable angles. He would hang in the air for so long that you'd worry that he'd get hurt when he came down. He was the pioneer for the kind of athletic players we see today. A lot of the moves people say were invented by Michael Jordan or Julius Erving, I saw Elgin do first. People ask me how good was Elgin ... well, he may have been the greatest player ever.

The great Tommy Heinsohn has once said he would put Baylor on his starting-five all-time team of greatest players ever and so has Jerry Sloan recently in the current book NBA List Jam! When once asked about their top 5 players ever not including themselves, Wilt Chamberlain and Bill Russell both mentioned Baylor 5th on their all-time list. And many people that played during his time as I have already mentioned in the beginning of the chapter, feel the same way. With all the evidence stated above and throughout the chapter, if Elgin Baylor isn't the greatest athletic scorer, and small forward of all-time over Michael Jordan and Larry Bird, than he was real close!

Career Totals

27.4 points aver, 13.5 rebounds, 4.3 assists, .431 FG%, .780 FT%

23,149 points, 11,463 rebounds, 3650 assists

Rick Barry

(Rank #12)

All-NBA First Team (5-times), All-ABA First Team (4-times)

Scoring Title (1-time), Steals Title (1-time), All-Star (8-times)

NBA Championships (1), Free-Throw % Titles (6-times)

NBA Record: NBA Finals 36.3 points per game (career)

Also featuring: Chris Mullin

At six-foot-seven, Rick Barry was one of the great small forwards to play professional basketball. Perhaps the greatest scorer at his position in history, Barry was an *unstoppable* scoring machine that possessed a deadly jump shot from anywhere on the court - as the San Francisco and Golden State Warriors legend had versatility in his offensive arsenal that included slashing drives to the basket and a highly effective fallaway shot and hook shot in the lane. A prolific scorer at every level of his career, Barry is the only man in history to lead the NCAA, ABA, and the NBA in scoring. His career-high 35.6 points per game average in 1967 ranks 4th all-time for a player behind only Wilt Chamberlain, Elgin Baylor, and Michael Jordan. In addition to being a lethal scorer, Barry was also a phenomenal all-around player with great court vision, rebounding and passing skills, and was a solid defender with good hands and anticipation, allowing him to average two steals per game during his outstanding professional career. He also had an in-depth knowledge on how to execute his team's defense. However, out of all his attributes for playing the game of basketball, the one he is most known for was his underhand free-throw shooting where he retired as the top free-throw shooter in NBA history at 90 percent efficiency. Also, being that Barry played in the Bay Area of Northern California most of his career, I don't think he ever got the recognition he deserved to let's say a Jerry West, who played in a big market of Los Angeles, even though he was equally as great a player. I don't think his reputation helped him out either, because he didn't use a lot of tact and was not an easy person to get along with. Being much of a perfectionist on the court, Barry often complained about what his teammates didn't do right, often rubbing them the wrong way. And, opposing teams viewed him as a very unlikable person to put it mildly.

In player comparisons:

If you listen to syndicated Bay Area talk shows of today, you will hear a lot of sportscasters mention the "true greatness" of Rick Barry. In fact, prominent radio sportscaster Gary Radnich often mentions his true greatness, stating that in his opinion, Barry is ranked in the top 10 or 15 players of all-time, maybe even the top 5. He even said you can make the case he was better than Larry Bird. In my opinion, I have always felt he was *really, really*, close - as does the great Jerry West. In his latest book "West by West," he mentions to a friend twice that as much as he admired Bird as player and for his *competitive drive*, he wasn't sure if Barry wasn't as great as Bird. As we already know, he also mentioned that Barry never got the recognition he deserved due in part because of his surly attitude. Even the great Bill Walton once said, "Until Larry Bird came along, Barry was the best forward I ever saw play basketball!" But you would have to say, in a nut shell, in terms of pure scoring and passing, they were about even, and the two best at their position in history. And, of course, Bird was the better rebounder because of his height at six-foot-nine. Although to note; throughout Barry's career and especially in the first half, he did grab his share of rebounds: 10.6 his rookie year, 9.2 the year after, 9.4 and 7.0 his first two seasons in the ABA, and 8.9 his first season back to the NBA. In fact, for a 9-year span in which he played eight seasons from the 1965-66 season through the 1973-74 season in both leagues, he averaged **8.3 rebounds** per game.

While Barry could have been the better scorer, Bird was the better rebounder and passer by a slight margin. Take for example this *jaw-dropping* stat line on March 26, 1974. Barry had one of the greatest performances in NBA history finishing with **64 points, 10 rebounds, 9 assists, and 5 steals** (he was the third player to score over 63 points after Chamberlain and Baylor) and coming within one assist of recording the first 60-point triple-double in history. For one, Bird's career-high in scoring was 60 and while Baylor's was 71, but could either of them put together an all-around performance like Barry did? Perhaps Baylor could have (or did) with his rebounding numbers and if they had kept track of blocks and steals in those days. And perhaps Bird did too if you focus on his rebounding and assists numbers. Barry and Bird were the two best passing forwards in NBA history even ahead of Baylor until LeBron James came into the league. In player comparisons overall, even though it is very close between Barry and Bird, based on what

I have written above, you would still have to go with Bird as the greatest ever, followed by Baylor - by a slight margin. The other reasons, are not necessarily because he won 3 NBA championships and Barry and Baylor only won a total of one, but because he had the best skill set backed by the best overall statistics in scoring, rebounding, and assists; And because he won 3 consecutive MVP awards to Barry and Baylor who never won one. I would also have to put Barry just slightly *behind* Elgin because he was not the rebounder or inside scorer that Baylor was (though Barry did say he attributed all the moves he learned from watching Baylor). He was also in and out of basketball, changing leagues including missing a full season due to a court order, and for accumulating 4 years of statistics in the ABA. Here are their career professional numbers:

Rick Barry: 24.8 points, 6.7 rebounds, 5.1 assists, 2.0 steals, 45%FG, 89.3%FT

Larry Bird: 24.3 points, 10.0 rebounds, 6.3 assists, 1.7 steals, 49%FG, 88.6%FT

Elgin Baylor 27.4 points, 13.5 rebounds, 4.3 assists, n/a steals, 43%FG, 78% FT

Based on these numbers, you could make the case that Baylor had the best career averages out of the three, even though they did not keep track of blocks and steals until the 1973-74 season. Arguments for Barry are that Baylor played his prime years in an era with about half the amount of teams in the league, very few black players, and where there were more offensive possessions allowing him to put up more points and corral rebounds.

Perhaps the second greatest Warrior of all-time at the *small forward* position was **Chris Mullin** (now an ESPN analyst and color-man) who was just named to the Basketball Hall of Fame this year in 2012. Growing up in New York, Mullin learned a lot while watching Walt Frazier and Earl Monroe play for the Knicks, and was also an admirer of the great Larry Bird. At the same time he wore number 17 in honor of John Havlicek. While Mullin wasn't as great an all-around player that Barry, Bird, and Baylor all were, he was nearly as great a shooter and passer as the first two - and a better shooter and perhaps a better passer over Baylor. Born on July 30th 1963 in Brooklyn, New York, Christopher Paul Mullin attended Power Memorial Academy and catholic Xaverian High School in Brooklyn where he was a McDonald's All-American. In college at St. Johns University, Mullin averaged 22.9 points, 4.4 rebounds, and four assists per game in his junior year, and won the gold medal in 1984 playing for the United States Olympic Team. In his senior year, he was also named to the All-America First Team and won the John R Wooden Award and USBWA Player of the Year in 1985. He was then selected with 7th pick overall of the 1985 NBA Draft by the Golden State Warriors. In the pros, the six-foot-seven Mullin began his career as a spot-up shooting guard feeding off of Eric "Sleepy" Floyd at point guard where his point production would increase over his first three years to 20.2 per game. He was also an outstanding passer averaging 4.8 assists and had very quick hands averaging 1.9 steals per game.

When Don Nelson took over as head coach in 1988, Mullin began to play the small forward position. By his fourth season in 1989, Mullin blossomed into a premier shooter similar to Larry Bird before him, when he averaged a **career-high** in **scoring at 26.5 points** per game, **rebounds at 5.9**, **assist at 5.1**, and **steals at 2.1** - and was named to the All-NBA Second Team. The next three years he would be named to the All-NBA Third Team, All-NBA Second Team once again, and the All-NBA First Team in 1992. He would later match those averages in rebounds and assists once more during his career and in the steals category two more times. At that point, he was as close to a *Larry Bird* that I thought we would ever see in the NBA during our lifetime until the *Big German* showed up for the 1998 NBA Draft. A Bird-like player, Dirk Nowitzki showed up decades earlier than I think anyone could have ever imagined - even though we didn't know it yet (because it took Dirk almost his entire career to close the gap with Larry as a player - and he still came up short, probably only 70 to 80 percent of the player Bird was). Like Larry, Chris was a clever ball handler with quick hands and mind, and he was fun to watch. Even though he was slow of foot at times, Mullin would outsmart opponents with his ball-handling and passing skills and would pickpocket players on defense when they least expected it.

He was also named to the All-Star team in 1989 for the first of five consecutive seasons. During that span, Mullin was spectacular, putting up numbers that are up there with the all-time greats of the game - averaging **25.8 points**, **5.6 rebounds**, **4.1 assists**, and **1.9 steals**, and shot 52.3 percent from the field. In addition, he was one of the all-time great free-throw shooters averaging .896 percent his rookie season and .865 percent for his career. In four postseasons between the years of 1989 to 1994, Mullin was nearly as impressive averaging 24.9 points, 5.7 rebounds, and 3.6 assists per game - and shot 52.5 percent from the field and 44.4 percent from three-point range. By the end of his five-year peak, Chris Webber had just come into the league and was traded to the Warriors on draft day prior to the 1993-94 season. At that point, Mullin's body began to break down and he began a downward trend statistically. If he had been healthy the second half of his career he may have been an even greater player than he already was.

In his playoff career with the Golden State Warriors, Mullin never made it past the second round primarily because the Western Conference was loaded with teams with more size and more talent. However, "Run TMC," featuring Tim Hardaway, Mitch Richmond, and Chris Mullin held their own and played "small-ball" under Coach Don Nelson with surprising success. Because I live in the Bay Area, it wasn't a shock to me as it probably was for many others around the nation because most people didn't realize Don Nelson was a *matchup genius*, for what little size and talent he had to deal with. If the Warriors were playing a team with a big lineup, Nelson would try and reverse the matchup in his favor by using the speed and quickness of a smaller lineup (usually an athletic big or two with the exception of Manute Bol), usually a third wing player (think

Sarunas Marciulionis) and two big men, or four wing players and one power forward (think Tom Tolbert) or center to score quickly and more often than the opposing team. With speed and shooting from the perimeter and just enough rebounding, and perhaps occasional shot blocking, time and time again it worked in the regular season and in the playoffs. Over the years, "Nellie" has pulled off more upsets against the number one or number two seeded teams (I believe 3 in total) more times than any coach in history including the latest victim, the Dallas Mavericks in 2007. Because of this innovation and that he has been a winner everywhere he has coached; he deserved to be named into this year's Basketball Hall of Fame. Many people have forgotten that he won 50 games or more 7 consecutive seasons with the Milwaukee Bucks and led them to 6 straight Central Division titles.

In three of the five playoff seasons, Mullin and the Warriors upset the Utah Jazz twice in 1987 and 1989 and the San Antonio Spurs once in 1991 before losing in the second round to the Los Angeles Lakers, Phoenix Suns, and to the Lakers again. In game 2 of the Laker series, second time around, Mullin had his signature game in the postseason scoring 41 points to Magic's 44 with the Warriors winning the game 125-124. It wasn't until Mullin's three seasons with the Indiana Pacers; he would make it past the second round of the playoffs. But by that time, Chris was at the end of his playing days with his minutes and overall production way down. Throughout his career, Mullin was an excellent shooter that perfected his jump shot from the perimeter and from three-point range due to all the hard work he put into the off-season. He was known for being a *gym rat* and for putting in hours and hours of shooting. In some stories, he was known for practicing shooting 100 three-pointers in a day, making at least three quarters of them on a consistent basis. He also was a gifted passer and had lightning-quick hands, able to steal the ball from an opponent when they least expected it. For his sixteen-year career, Mullin averaged 18.2 points, 4.1 rebounds, 3.5 assists, and 1.6 steals per game. He also shot a remarkable 50.9 percent from the field, 86.5 percent from the free-throw line, and 38.4 percent from three-point range. As a testament to his greatness, he was part of the "greatest team" ever assembled playing for the 1992 United States Dream Team that brought home the gold medal. Chris Mullin will forever be remembered for his deadeye shooting in the class of fellow Warriors legend Rick Barry and the great Larry Bird.

Richard Francis Dennis Barry III was born on March 28th, 1944 in Elizabeth, New Jersey and attended Roselle Park High School. He then went on to play basketball at the University of Miami where he averaged 29.8 points and 16.5 rebounds per game. In his junior and senior year, he averaged an incredible 32.2 points and 16.6 rebounds and 37.4 points and 18.3 rebounds respectively - and was named to the AP All-America First Team in 1965. After college, he was selected with the 2nd pick overall of the 1965 NBA Draft by the San Francisco Warriors. In his first two seasons in the league, he won the scoring title, was named to the All-NBA First Team twice - and took the Warriors to the 1967 NBA Finals, before losing in six games to Wilt Chamberlain and the Philadelphia 76ers. In that series, you could see what was to come in the future of the young *prodigy* - in his first trip to the *Big Dance*! Barry averaged a then record 40.8 points for the series to go along with three monster scoring games of 55, 44, and 43 points.

After playing in the NBA for two seasons, Barry signed with the Oakland Oaks of the ABA for the 1967-68 campaign, because his father-in-law was the coach of the team. Unfortunately he was forced to sit out that season due to a court dispute with the Warriors who claimed that the Oaks were the only team in the ABA to locate in the same market as an NBA team. So Barry opted to broadcast for the Oaks in their inaugural season. Because of this Connie Hawkins won the ABA's first scoring title. After winning the scoring title the next year at 34 points per game and the ABA Championship in 1968-69, the franchise moved from Oakland to Washington where Barry played in only 52 games due to injury. After that season, the Washington Caps became the Virginia Squires, but Barry was traded to the New York Nets in September 1970 for a number one draft pick and 200,000 dollars. Because Squires owner Earl Foreman was having expense predicaments, was the reason he said he sold Barry to the Nets. After playing the next two seasons with the Nets, Barry signed back on with the Golden State Warriors where he would play another six years from 1973 through 1978 before finishing out his final two seasons with the Houston Rockets. In Barry's first year back, he helped lead the Warriors to a semifinals victory over Kareem's Bucks, won the title in 1975, and in 1976 forced a seventh game in the conference finals against the Suns. As a testament to his dedication as a passer the second half of his career from 1974 to 1979, he averaged **6.1, 6.2, 6.1, 6.0, 5.4,** and **6.3 assists** per game respectively.

Behind head coach Al Attles, Rick Barry and a scrap team full of role players including rookie Jamaal Wilkes (who by the way just made the HOF), the Golden State Warriors won the 1975 NBA Championship over the Elvin Hayes and Wes Unseld led Washington Bullets in a four-game sweep. This was considered by many as the greatest upset in NBA Finals history. Barry was spectacular as always averaging **29.5 points** per game (and **28.3 points** the entire playoff run) while winning Finals MVP.

In other player comparisons:

Barry is the 4th man on the all-time scoring list for points per game in a season at 35.6 (2775) just edging out Kobe Bryant at 35.4. He has the highest scoring average in NBA Finals history at **36.3 points** a game, ahead of Michael Jordan's 33.6, Dwyane Wade's 30.6, and Jerry West's 30.5. He also had the second highest scoring game of 55 points (tied with Jordan) in NBA Finals history, right behind Elgin Baylor's 61. If you include his ABA stats, he had **115 40-point** games (with 70 coming in the NBA) which would rank 3rd all-time to Wilt Chamberlain and Jordan and slightly ahead of Kobe, who will most likely pass him this year or in 2013. In addition, he had 14 career 50-point games (13 and 1 in the playoffs from a different source) and 1 in the playoffs, which ranks 5th all-time. So as a pure scorer, Barry could have been the greatest *perimeter* scorer in history behind Jordan and ahead of everyone else including Bird, Baylor, West, and Kobe. He also had a higher career scoring average in the ABA over Julius Erving 30.5 to 28.7 and in the NBA 23.2 to 22 points per game.

I value Barry's ABA's scoring statistics more than any other player because he proved he was just as great a scorer in both leagues. In his rookie season in the NBA, he scored 57 points on Dec. 14th 1965 and 56 points the following year on Oct. 29th 1966. In his second season, at only 23 years old in 1967, he torched the Association for 35.6 points per game (finishing 5 points higher than 2nd place Oscar Robertson) and became the first man to win the scoring title over Chamberlain. He also had **28 40-point** games and **6 50-point** games. That same season in the playoffs, Barry nearly equaled his performance averaging **34.7 points** per game. And, to top that off, in the NBA Finals he had scoring games (that I have already mentioned) of **55, 44, and 43 points** (**47 and 41 points** in the previous series against the Hawks) and set an NBA record **40.8 points** average for the series that was later broken by Jordan's 41 points per game in the 1993 NBA Finals. If they had a Finals MVP at that time, he might have been the first player to win the award playing for the losing team. West pulled the trick in 1969 against the Boston Celtics the first year of its inauguration. Even when Barry came back to the Warriors from the ABA, he was still a dominant scorer as he proved in his third year back in 1975, when he led Golden State to the NBA Championship. That year, in the regular season, he averaged **30.6 points** per game (good for second) and led the league in **steals at 2.9** and free-throw percentage at **90.4 percent**. So from a scoring perspective, Barry was the great scorer Chamberlain was in those days, but at the small forward position. To compliment his points from the field, from the charity stripe at the time of his retirement, Barry was the best free-throw shooter to have ever lived, where he shot *exactly* 90 percent for his entire NBA career. In addition to his scoring accolades in which he left the game 6th on the all-time ABA-NBA scoring list, he was one of the great all-around players ever.

A lot of people probably wouldn't rank Barry this high for three reasons: He played four seasons in the ABA and sat out one season entirely, won one championship in the NBA, and because according to most, he wasn't a very likable person. With all that said, he was still among the greatest players ever as the numbers above speak for themselves. In a way, Barry was Jerry West at the small forward position but was not quite as great of a defensive player. And in comparisons to Elgin Baylor, he was not as great a rebounder or low-post scorer. The same could be said in the comparisons to Larry Bird. But as scorer and a shooter, he might have been at the top even over Kobe Bryant and Julius Erving as I have stated above. His **career-high** of **35.6 points** average for a single season is slightly higher than Kobe's 35.4 but currently trails Bryant in career average 23.2 (24.8 if you include the ABA) to 25.4. If you take away the last two seasons that Barry played in Houston when he was washed-up, including his ABA stats, he averaged **26.9 points**, **7.3 rebounds**, **4.8 assists**, and **2.3 steals** per game. Also, If you include his ABA stats in the postseason; he averaged **27.3 points** (24.8 NBA/33.5 ABA) and 30 points or more his first 4 playoff appearances **(34.7**, **40.1**, **33.7**, and **30.8)**. And the first three of those which came in 1967, 1970, 1971, he led the league in points per game in the playoffs.

Despite his negative vibe on the court that may have rubbed his teammates the wrong way, Barry's *perfectionism* and his *will to win* will never be questioned as he was as mentally tough as anyone to have ever played the game. The clincher for me, for ranking Barry so high for greatest players ever, was what many people have said about how great Rick Barry *really* was. His greatness as a scorer and as a shooter was as "good as it gets." If many people including Jerry West, feel Barry might have been as great as Larry Bird that says something! It says a hell of a lot coming from the master of evaluating talent. Since Bird is one of the Top 5 players of all-time and the fact that some people think Barry might have been almost or as great as Bird, he has to be ranked in at least the top 15 to 20 players of all-time in anyone's book. In fact, if Barry was almost or just as great as Bird in the eyes of many including West, he must have been better than West himself. I certainly don't think that was the case based on the comparisons that I have already made throughout the chapter. But at the same time like I have mentioned throughout the book, that dominance in one or two key aspects of players game (with the rest being good to very good) is better than another's whose *overall game* is very good to great but not dominant in any one aspect. And, that's what Barry was throughout his NBA and ABA career - a dominant scorer, shooter, and passer! So in a nutshell if we don't include LeBron James, the great Rick Barry might have been the greatest scoring (over 25,000 points in his NBA and ABA career) small forward of all-time and the second greatest passing forward of all-time right up there with Larry Bird.

Career Totals

23.2 points, 6.5 rebs, 5.1 assists, 2.0 steals, 0.5 blocks, .449 FG%, .330 3FG%, .90 FT%

18,395 points, 5168 rebounds, 4017 assists, 1104 steals, 269 blocks, 73 threes

Shaquille O'Neal

(Rank #13)

MVP (1-time), Scoring Title (2-times), FG% Title (10-times)

NBA Championships (4), Finals MVP (3-times)

All-NBA First Team (8-times), All-Star (15-times)

Also featuring: Andrew Bynum
& Yao Ming

Shaquille O'Neal was the most dominant center of his era, but not necessarily the most talented. After winning back-to-back-to-back championships with the Los Angeles Lakers from 2000 to 2002, Shaq became the greatest player in the NBA since Hakeem Olajuwon and Michael Jordan. In fact, by that point, many observers felt he had a chance to surpass Jordan as the greatest player ever. But as time went on, he was only able to win one more championship in 2006 playing for the Miami Heat. An *extremely* powerful specimen and a *behemoth* of a man weighing well over three hundred pounds, Shaq looked like he could move trees. His ability to back down or go through an opponent finishing with a ferocious slam dunk was his trademark. After watching him live, I was blown away by how much he stood out over everyone else. Even from a distance Shaq looked *gargantuan*. Playing out of the low post, he was a man among boys, able to body-up and move opponents around at will. Players would bounce off him like they would a brick wall. His size and strength allowed him to back down opponents for easy slam dunks, layups, or three-foot jump hooks that he would often bank in. For a man of his magnitude, he was surprisingly nimble on his feet when in transition and in the half court - maybe all that dancing over the years did him good. He was able to quickly drive past defenders by utilizing a drop-step or off a spin move to the basket for easy dunks, or he could face up and shoot an eight foot jump shot over the top of an opponent.

Shaq was just as intimidating on the defensive end as he was on the offensive end. Despite his sometimes lack of effort and instincts as a shot blocker, psychologically, the intimidation factor he *bestowed* upon his peers helped Shaq out on the defensive end. He was also a good rebounder because of his massive girth. He was a half a foot or more with an extra fifty plus pounds, an inflated Charles Barkley without the great timing. With his massive size at seven-foot-one, he was a formidable shot blocker throughout his career and played great defense when he wanted to, one time swatting 15 shots in game. Like many of the other great big men of the past, Shaq was an outstanding passer out of the low post. Able to see easily over the top of the defense, he would often use the over-the-shoulder pass to a cutter going to the basket.

Shaquille Rashaun O'Neal was born on March 6th, 1972 in Newark, New Jersey. He led his high school team, Robert G. Cole from San Antonio, Texas to the state championship his senior year and had a 68-1 combined record the last two seasons. In college, at Louisiana State University, he was a two-time All-American and AP Player of the Year in 1991. After being selected with the first pick overall of the 1992 NBA Draft by the Orlando Magic, O'Neal averaged **23.4 points**, and what ended up being a **career-high 13.9 rebounds** and **3.5 blocks** per game. He also won the 1993 Rookie of the Year award but the Magic missed the playoffs by a sliver due to a tiebreak with Indiana. In his second season, he led the franchise to a 50-32 record, but the Magic were swept in the first round of the playoffs by the same team that edged them out of the postseason the year before, the Indiana Pacers. But Shaq emerged as a big-time star finishing second in the league in scoring to David Robinson at **29.3 points** a game. Robinson scored 71 points on the last day of the season to win the scoring title at 29.8 points per game, as there was talk that his teammates intentionally fed him the ball in the post all game long just for the individual accomplishment. I was hoping for the game to be televised but settled for minimal highlights at the end of the day. Not knowing it at the time, Shaq had two other memorable feats that season, when he had a career-high 15 blocks in the same game he recorded his first triple-double. His **24 points**, **28 rebounds**, and **15 blocks** on November 20th, 1993, was one of the best games of his career and one of the best all-around games for any center in history.

In the 1994-95 season, Shaq won the scoring title averaging the same amount of points he did the previous season when he finished second to Robinson in the scoring race. But at the same time, he finished second to the "Admiral" in the most *prestigious* individual honor one can receive, the NBA MVP Award. In the playoffs, the 57-25 Orlando Magic dispatched the Boston Celtics, the Chicago Bulls with Michael Jordan (coming back from retirement), and the Indiana Pacers with Reggie Miller on their way to the Finals but lost the 1995 NBA Championship to Hakeem Olajuwon, Clyde Drexler, and the Houston Rockets in four straight games. In only his third season in the playoffs, Shaq gave a preview of his potential as the games next great dominating center in multiple games: In game 5 of the conference semifinals against Jordan and the Bulls, Shaq scored **23 points, corralled 22 rebounds, including 14 offensive rebounds** (a record for a regulation game), and had five blocks, four assists, and two steals. In the clinching game 6, he had 27 points, 13 rebounds, four assists, and four steals. He also had 35 points and 13 rebounds in the go-ahead game 5 against the Pacers in the conference finals that no one seems to remember. Despite the loss in game one of the NBA Finals (the Magic might have won the game if Nick Anderson hadn't missed four straight free throws), Shaq almost posted a triple-double finishing with 26 points, 16 rebounds, and nine assists.

And despite the loss to Houston, and the fact that O'Neal was outscored by Olajuwon in all four games, Shaq posted outstanding numbers in the series averaging 28 points, 12.5 rebounds, and 6.3 assists, on .595 percent shooting. The next two seasons, Shaq played in only 54 and 51 games respectively due to injury and averaged 26.4 points, 11.8 rebounds, and three assists per game - and won the 1996 Olympic Gold Medal playing for Team USA in Atlanta. With words swirling all summer long that Shaq was unhappy playing in Orlando, during the first day of the Olympics, Shaq announced he would join the Los Angeles Lakers. He signed a seven-year, $121 million contract. After being swept by Jordan and the Bulls in the second round of the playoffs in 1996, and by Olajuwon and the Rockets in the NBA Finals the year before, must have factored heavily in his decision to bolt Orlando for Los Angeles. At the same time, he probably felt he had done all he could do to bring a championship to the franchise.

In the 1996-97 season, the Lakers won 56 games in Shaq's first year in L.A. In the playoffs, after defeating the Portland Trail Blazers in the first round three games to one, the Lakers lost to the Utah Jazz in five games in the semifinals. Shaq did impress in his playoff debut with his new franchise when he scored 46 points against the Blazers. In Shaq's second season with the Lakers, he averaged **28.3 points** and **11.4 rebounds**, and led the league in field goal percentage for the second time and first of five consecutive seasons. He also was named to the All-NBA First Team for the first of 8 times during his magnificent career. With Shaq having his best individual season in three years, the Lakers finished tied for first place in the division with the Seattle SuperSonics at 61-21. But after eliminating Portland in four games for the second straight year and division foe Seattle in the semifinals in five games, the Lakers lost again to the Jazz, this time in the conference finals in four straight games. During the 1998-99 season, Los Angeles made a key trade that involved Eddie Jones and Elden Campbell for Glen Rice. With Kobe Bryant developing his game at a rapid pace in only his third year, Shaq and sharp shooter Glen Rice were primed and ready to make a championship run. But it was not to be. After eliminating the Rockets three games to one, the Lakers were swept by the eventual champion San Antonio Spurs with up-and-coming superstar Tim Duncan. Shaq did get his revenge against his old rival Olajuwon throughout the first round and in the clinching game four scoring 37 points.

The Los Angeles Lakers, under first year coach Phil Jackson, finished the 1999-00 season with the second best record in franchise history at 67-15 and won their first of three consecutive NBA Championships. That year, Shaq was honored with his first and only MVP award. In the regular season, Shaq had his best *all-around* season of his career, winning his second scoring title at **29.7 points** per game to go along with **13.6 rebounds**, **3.8 assists**, and **three blocks**. He also was named to the All-NBA First Team for the second time in his career and the first of seven consecutive seasons. In the playoffs, the Lakers were pushed to the limit in the first round by the up-and-coming, feisty and fast tempo Sacramento Kings that featured fancy dribblers Jason Williams, Chris Webber, and Vlade Divac. After breezing past the Phoenix Suns in the semifinals, the Lakers were pushed to the limit once again, this time by the Portland Trail Blazers in the Western Conference Finals.

Going into the series, Portland was loaded with stars and semi-stars in the likes of Scottie Pippen, Rasheed Wallace, Steve Smith, Damon Stoudamire, Arvydas Sabonis and Bonzi Wells. Despite falling behind three games to one, the Blazers stormed back and won game five in Los Angeles and game six at home convincingly setting up a decisive game seven back in L.A. Because Portland had such tremendous depth, had the momentum, and was taking it to the Lakers, I felt Portland was going to make Shaq and Kobe wait another year for their first NBA championship. And that almost happened if it weren't for an unusual set of circumstances. After outplaying the Lakers through the first three quarters, Portland blew a 15 point lead after being up 75-60 in the fourth quarter. It seemed *inconceivable* to watch Portland miss almost every shot down the stretch and have *hardly* any calls go in their favor. In the NBA Finals the Lakers played a formidable Indiana Pacers team that featured Hall of Famer Reggie Miller along with Jalen Rose, Rik Smits, Dale Davis, Travis Best, and Mark Jackson. The Pacers were able to neutralize Bryant with Miller and Rose, but Indiana's big men were completely outclassed and *man-handled* by the "Diesel" all series long. Shaq had **3 40-point** games including **43 points and 19 rebounds** in the first game, and **40 points and 24 rebounds** in the second game to set the tone for the series. He also averaged a gaudy **38 points** and **16.6 rebounds** for the entire six-game series as the Lakers won the 2000 NBA Championship.

In the 2000-01 season, Shaq followed up his MVP season averaging similar numbers of **28.7 points**, **12.7 rebounds**, **3.7 assists**, and **2.8 blocks**. From 2000 to 2004, Shaq averaged at least three assists per game. By that point in his career, Shaq had become an adept passer out of the low post and had complete trust in his teammates to score off an assist. He was like the many great passing big men of the past that had great vision and could see and pass over the top of the defense finding open cutters to the basket or out on the perimeter. During the season, disagreements between Shaq and Kobe began to surface having a negative effect on the outcome of the *regular season* as the Lakers finished with the second best record in the Western Conference at 56-26 behind the San

Antonio Spurs. But in the playoffs, the Lakers put aside any distractions and played like defending champions by trouncing the Portland Trail blazers, Sacramento Kings and the San Antonio Spurs of the Western Conference in four-game sweeps.

In the Finals, the Lakers got a *scare* from the Philadelphia 76ers and MVP Allen Iverson by losing game one on their own home court. Despite Iverson putting on a show for the ages scoring 48 points, the Lakers showed their *championship grit* and swept the next four games to win the 2001 NBA Championship. Throughout the series, Kobe was able to hold his own against Iverson as the series was won at the center position. Shaq was nearly as dominant as Iverson averaging **33 points, 15.8 rebounds, 4.8 assists**, and **3.4 blocks** and literally *destroyed* Dikembe Mutombo in the individual matchup. In both championship title runs, Shaq had the best two postseasons of his career averaging **30.6 points, 15.4 rebounds**, and **3.1 assists** per game. In the 2001-02 season, with the Shaq and Kobe feud beginning to escalate, the Lakers managed to improve their win total from the year before to 58 wins but still finished second in the conference, this time to the Sacramento Kings. In the playoffs, after sweeping Portland for the second straight season in the first round, the Lakers handily defeated the Spurs for the second consecutive year, this time in the semifinals in five games. In the Western Conference Finals, the Lakers met their biggest challenge ever in the Shaq/Kobe era. With *the best passing* team I have seen in my lifetime, the Sacramento Kings gave the Lakers all they could handle, coming within seconds of going up in the series three games to one if it weren't for the miraculous three-point shot by Robert Horry.

During the Lakers three-year reign, I always felt Shaq was clearly the centerpiece and the most valuable, *irreplaceable* Superstar on the team even over the sensational Kobe Bryant. He backed this up by winning the MVP award, scoring title, and the first of three consecutive Finals MVP awards (he had the highest scoring average for a center in Finals history), and by outscoring Bryant in the playoffs in three straight seasons from 2000 to 2002, **30.7 points** a game to 30.4, **28.5** to 21.1 and **29.4** to 26.6. Even though Bryant was in the beginning of his career and Shaq was in his prime, many people felt Kobe was just as valuable to the team as Shaq. Even though it did take the both of them to win multiple championships with Bryant sometimes carrying a great deal of the scoring load especially at the end of games when Shaq was in foul trouble, I still felt Shaq was easily the most valuable player on team. If you had replaced Bryant with 2001 MVP Allen Iverson (During the playoffs, Shaq marveled at his toughness and killer instinct) who took the 76ers to the NBA Finals against the Lakers - torching everyone who tried to guard him or two-time scoring champion Tracy McGrady in his prime, Shaq still would have won multiple championships. At the time, Iverson was as good as or slightly better than Bryant, and McGrady was nearly as talented. Ok, maybe these combinations would not have registered three titles, but at least one or two. No one could have replaced "The Diesel," and that's why Shaq beat Kobe to a fourth championship in 2006 playing alongside Dwyane Wade in Miami.

Aside from all his individual accolades and NBA Championships in the early part of the decade, for me, the most intriguing time I watched Shaq, were the couple or so times a year he matched up against the young and talented **Yao Ming**, who had just entered the NBA coming over from China. It was a real treat for me and probably for everyone else, to watch the two *titans* go at it in the low post like *two barbarians fighting in a grudge match!* In the beginning of his career, Shaq would obviously get the better of Yao in head-to-head matchups, but as the years went on it began to balance out to where Ming would hold his own. The way Shaq dunked on Robinson and Duncan during his prime, he would do the same to Yao in the early meetings, but Yao would get a piece of Shaq soon after with a couple of dunks of his own that shocked many observers and fired up the arena crowds. In their first meeting, Yao had 10 points and 10 rebounds, and blocked six shots including two against Shaq. But Shaq poured in 31 points and 13 rebounds, and won the game.

Born on September 12th, 1980 in Shanghai China, Yao played basketball for the Shanghai Sharks of the Chinese Basketball Association (CBA). After being pressured into entering the NBA Draft in 1999, behind a group of advisers, Yao decided to enter the 2002 NBA Draft where he was selected with the first pick overall by the Houston Rockets. In his rookie season in the NBA, he averaged a modest 13.5 points and 8.2 rebounds per game, but lost the Rookie of the Year award unanimously to high school phenom Amar'e Stoudemire. But, with all the fan popularity not only in the United States but also in China, Yao was named to the All-Star team for the first of 8 consecutive seasons he did play (voted to the All-Star team his final season in 2011 despite playing in only 5 regular season games). In his second season, he increased his scoring four points and showed his potential as the next great center behind Shaquille O'Neal where he had a **career-high 41 points and 7 assists** in a triple-overtime game in February of 2004. That season, the Rockets did make the playoffs as the seventh seed but lost in the first round to the Los Angeles Lakers in five games. Prior to the following season, Houston acquired Superstar Tracy McGrady in a seven-player trade that sent Steve Francis and Cuttino Mobley to the Orlando Magic. Yao was solid once again and averaged 18.3 points per game on 55.2 percent shooting, and was named along with McGrady, starters to the 2005 All-Star game. The Rockets won 51 games and returned to the playoffs for the second straight season but lost a heartbreaking seven-game series in which they blew a 2-0 series lead.

With Yao and McGrady looking to rebound from a crushing playoff loss from the year before, the most unfortunate thing happened when Yao developed osteomyelitis in his big toe on his left foot causing him to miss 21 games. With McGrady injured a good portion of the season, the two of them played in only 31 games together as the Rockets missed the playoffs. Yao did blossom in his fourth season in the league averaging 22.3 points and 10.2 rebounds per game, and was named to the All-NBA Third Team for the second straight year. In the 2006-07 campaign, Yao had the best season of his career averaging **25 points** and **9.4 rebounds** per game, and was named to the All-NBA Second Team for the first time but broke his knee early in the season on December 23rd 2006. Up to that point, Yao was having an MVP type of year averaging 26.8 points, 9.7 rebounds, and 2.3 blocks per game. With injuries beginning to mount, I was just hoping Yao would recover quickly and continue to blossom into the league's premier center over Shaquille O'Neal, who was moving up in age and was on a gradual decline averaging 17.3 points per game that season playing for the Miami Heat.

In the playoffs, for the second time in three years, the Houston Rockets were eliminated in seven games, this time to the Utah Jazz. Yao and McGrady both averaged 25 points for the series, but it wasn't enough as one or the other missed the playoffs the next two seasons due to injury. Even to this day, I am completely disappointment that the Rockets didn't become the next great team because I really felt Yao and McGrady would become the greatest dynamic dual in the NBA for at least the next four to five years, but that didn't happen. And even before the arrival of T-Mac, I also felt with the young nucleus of Yao, Steve Francis and Cuttino Mobley, the Rockets were talented enough to win an NBA championship or two, but that never panned out either.

While I may have *overestimated* the talent of Francis a little despite the knee injuries and Mobley with the bad heart condition (that wasn't well known until he decided to retire around the same age as Yao), I was *correct* on my player evaluation of Yao and McGrady. It was just one of those things where bad luck (with injuries) derailed and ultimately ended the career of two great players, who believe it or not, should eventually make it into the Hall Of Fame someday (See George Gervin's chapter for more on McGrady). If they had stayed healthy, McGrady (who has had chronic back spasms most of his career) who is trying to revive his career currently coming off the bench for the San Antonio Spurs, would have continued his great all-around play particularly as a scorer/facilitator similar but not quite at the level of the LeBron James in Miami. And, Yao despite not being as quick on his feet as some people would of liked, would have kept on improving his overall game while making the All-NBA First Team or Second Team for years to come. All in all, it was obvious that the Rockets did need to tweak their roster a little and find a third star player in order to have made a deep playoff run and win an NBA Championship.

In his eight seasons in the NBA, Yao averaged 19 points, 9.2 rebounds, and 1.9 blocks per game, and shot 52.4 percent from the field. If he hadn't been seriously injured four out of his last five years forcing him to retire prematurely, in my opinion, he would have been the best center in the Western Conference over Andrew Bynum for the upcoming next five years. It was unfortunate after playing in only five games; Yao had to retire at the end of the 2010-11 season at the age of 30. Because the "Great Wall of China" was something special in his own right - before the injuries started to mount, Yao was playing at a level even higher than Shaq, who was on the downside of his career. At the time, he was a unique big man that could score out of the low post with a fallaway shot and jump hook, and from the perimeter with a *soft* shooting touch. From the interior, he could dominate as a scorer in the likes of Shaq, Hakeem Olajuwon, David Robinson, and Patrick Ewing - and from the perimeter like centers of the past in Rik Smits, Jack Sikma, and Dan

Issel. Compared to Shaq, Yao was always the better shooter and free-throw shooter, and was actually the better passer. I even felt Yao had a chance to close the gap with Shaq as a dominate scorer, rebounder, and shot blocker as he was entering his prime. Even though he was a little slow at times, he actually moved pretty well before the injuries considering his tremendous height at 7-feet-5 or 7-feet-6 (depending on the source). If you can remember that far back or have watched old footage of Yao, he had a very good low-post game that had some similarities to Pau Gasol, where he could shoot with either hand (at times) around the basket, had an assortment of up-and-under moves, and could take his man off the dribble with a spin move like many of the great pivot-men of the past. Despite a short career, Yao Ming should make the Naismith Memorial Basketball Hall of Fame because of his years as an International player and for his stellar seven *near* complete seasons in the NBA.

When Shaq left Los Angeles, the Lakers finished with records of 34-48, 45-37, and 42-40 before Pau Gasol showed up in 2008. Kobe Bryant ended up winning consecutive championships in 2009 and 2010 thanks to All-Star Gasol and perhaps the best supporting cast in the league the last three to four years. Albeit, Bryant did win back-to-back Finals MVP's, even though my vote would have gone to Gasol in 2010 because I thought he outplayed Kobe in the four games out of the seven the Lakers won. Furthermore, the way Andrew Bynum has blossomed in 2012, we might look back at Bryant's last two championship campaigns and give even more credit to the frontcourt of Gasol, Bynum, Odom, and Artest (who played on the 2010 Championship team). Even though Bynum was very young and often injured in 2009 and 2010, he was a tremendous defensive presence throughout the playoffs and against the Boston Celtics in the NBA Finals. So if Bryant were to win a 6th championship ring down the road, Bynum might have become the most valuable player on the team. But now that Bynum, and Dwight Howard for that matter, are no longer with the team, it will be awfully difficult for Bryant to win one more ring.

Andrew Bynum reminds me a lot of Robert Parish, Shaquille O'Neal, and Kobe Bryant but in different ways. I decided to include him in this book at the last minute because he might end up becoming a better player than I originally predicted. He did have a chance to become the next great Laker center after Shaq, but with all the injuries throughout his career and with the lack of true centers in the NBA today, I kind of believe Bynum was acknowledged as the best center in the Western Conference by default! And, I still believe he is one injury away from having an average to an above average career. If so, the next best center on the way up could be DeMarcus Cousins. After what everybody was saying recently during the 2012 season, including now TNT analyst S. O'Neal and Skip Bayless on ESPN First Take, that Bynum was already the best center in the league over Dwight Howard, made me rethink my original assessment and his potential as a player. In fact, I am even questioning my evaluation even more after he pulled down 30 rebounds against Tim Duncan and the San Antonio Spurs on April 11th becoming the fifth Laker ever to record 30 rebounds in a game along with Wilt Chamberlain (who did it 14 times), Kareem

Abdul-Jabbar, Elgin Baylor, and Shaq. He also had his first triple-double of his career in the first game of the playoffs against the Denver Nuggets which included 10 blocks that tied the NBA playoff record with Hakeem Olajuwon and Mark Eaton. Also, his triple-double was the first for a Laker since Magic Johnson in 1991. This means in the playoffs, Shaq never did it as a member of the franchise and Kobe has never done it throughout his entire career to date.

At the same time, I believe Shaq is *biased* in favor of Bynum succeeding him as the next great Laker center just like he is toward acknowledging Bryant as the greatest Laker over Magic. I think Shaq was a prisoner of the moment, as Skip Bayless would say - whom by the way, I question his basketball knowledge to begin with. Not that I believe either one of them, about Bynum being the better center over Howard, because he probably never will be, it's just Bynum might end up being a little or perhaps a lot better than I originally thought.

Bynum also reminds me of a young Kobe in *terms of his immaturity* as a young player. While many (myself included), believe his recent actions (including the forearm to the face of J.J. Barea that resulted in a five-game suspension) are detrimental to the team, Kobe along with many others feel it gives Bynum the same edge it gave Bryant in his youth, with having the *don't-back-down type of attitude* and *killer instinct*. So we will just have to wait and see if it hurts the Lakers (or perhaps the next team he plays for), or helps them in the near future. As a player, Bynum reminds me of Parish more than anyone else, which is not necessarily a bad thing. He might even have more spin moves from either direction and might be able to shoot with more versatility over his left or right shoulder in the low block. Even though he has long arms, can shoot effectively with either hand, and has an assortment of spins moves, I don't think he'll ever be as great as any of the top 10 centers to have played the game. Not because he is a finesse player, but because I feel he doesn't *dominate* enough on either end of the court. Even though he may have the great height and length, more spins moves and more versatility on the offensive end even over Howard; he doesn't get to the free-throw line nearly as much, at least not yet. He also, is not nearly the defensive player or shot blocker that Howard is because he lacks the great timing.

Although young at 24 years old about to turn 25 this season, Bynum has already been injured to many times during his career and is miles away from Howard in career scoring and rebounding. With all Bynum's wasted seasons due to injuries, he will be lucky to finish his career with a scoring average of at least 18 points per game. More than likely he will finish with at least 10 rebounds per game but will trail many of the all-time great centers in career points and rebounding categories. And, on top of that, he has the poorest assist and steals per game averages of any elite center in history to date including Howard of today. So what that tells me, as of now, he is not yet a great passer averaging 1.2 assists for his career, and doesn't have quick hands on the *defensive end* to create steals averaging a paltry 0.3 per game. So from a longevity perspective, many centers are way ahead of him. But who knows, Bynum may continue to improve his overall game as he gets closer to his prime and may never have a major injury again, allowing him to become a perennial All-Star.

In 2003, Shaq waited until just before training camp to have surgery on his chronic big toe. The Lakers started the season off slow and ended up with the fifth seed where they were finally dethroned by the eventual champion San Antonio Spurs in the second round of the playoffs in six games. In the 2003-04 season, the Lakers acquired Karl Malone and Gary Payton for the veteran's minimum to make another run at a fourth championship in the Shaq and Kobe era. Looking to avenge the loss from the previous year, the Lakers beat the Spurs on Derek Fisher's miraculous shot at the buzzer in game 6 of the 2004 Semifinals, and then defeated the number one seed Minnesota Timberwolves led by Kevin Garnett in the Western Conference Finals. The Lakers won game one of the NBA Finals but Shaq and the rest of the Lakers were suffocated by Ben Wallace and Detroit's stifling defense the rest of the series and lost in five games. In the summer of 2004, Shaq was traded to the Miami Heat on July 14th for Lamar Odom, Caron Butler, Brian Grant, and a future first-round draft pick. Shaq had demanded a trade because the Lakers didn't want to pay him what he was asking for. In only his second season in Miami, he won his fourth and final championship playing alongside Superstar Dwyane Wade and aging Hall of Famers Alonzo Mourning and Gary Payton.

In player comparisons:

"The Diesel" was one of the greatest *offensive forces* to ever play the center position. Shaq came into the league when Hakeem Olajuwon, David Robinson, and Patrick Ewing were near the end of their primes. Many felt that if Shaq was more dedicated to health and fitness (Kobe must of been right all along when it seemed like he was bad mouthing him over the years for always being out of shape - Shaq only played in 75 games or more 5 times in his 19-year career) and played defense more consistently, he could have been the greatest center ever. I disagree, despite his physically dominate power game and highly effective jump hook; he still didn't have the overall skill offensively as Chamberlain, Abdul-Jabbar and Olajuwon, and not nearly the defensive instincts and timing of Bill Russell. However, I do give Shaq a slight edge over Bryant in the elite rankings of all-time for three reasons; One, he was the centerpiece and the more dominant player on the Lakers Championships teams winning all three Finals MVP awards. Two, he gave three franchises a face lift, including taking the Orlando Magic to the NBA Finals while posting tremendous offensive numbers, and by later winning championships with the L.A. Lakers and the Miami Heat. Third, he had no equal peer or near equal peers during his prime.

In addition, Shaq won the scoring title twice and could have won it four more times finishing second to David Robinson, Michael Jordan, and Allen Iverson two other times. He also led the league in field goal percentage a record 10 times (breaking Chamberlain's mark of nine), and won 4 NBA Championships and 3 Finals MVP awards. Shaq did have only 1 MVP award in the regular season but was the best player on three Finals teams where he played alongside one of the greatest perimeter scorers of all-time. Shaq's career scoring average ranked up near the top of the all-time list most of his career until recently. Most players, who stay in the league past their prime, tend to see their career averages dip especially in the scoring department where Shaq finished at a modest 23.7. To put his tremendous scoring ability into perspective, he averaged almost thirty points in a season three times - at **29.3**, **29.3**, and **29.7** respectively, and averaged 11 rebounds per game or more 12 straight seasons. And, his **28.8 points** average in the NBA Finals is the fifth highest in history behind Rick Barry, Michael Jordan, Dwyane Wade, and Jerry West. In those Finals games, he ranks third on the all-time list with **16 30-point** games tied with Kareem Abdul-Jabbar and third with **5 40-point** games tied with Elgin Baylor.

If Shaq had kept up his conditioning over the years, during the Lakers championship run and after the age of 35, he would have gone down as even greater than he already was. After winning three consecutive championships from 2000 to 2002, many people thought he would stand at the top with Jordan as the greatest player ever. But that never happened. In hindsight, I can see why many felt that way because at his peak, he actually had the higher career scoring average of **34.2 points** per game in the NBA Finals slightly ahead of Jordan's career mark of 33.6, and won three championships in a row in a dominate fashion similar to when Jordan won his first three titles. But Jordan had already played in 35 games of six Finals appearances as compared to Shaq's 19 games and 4 Finals appearances. And, in a way, you could say Shaq underachieved in his career based on all that potential. Instead of being a top 15 player, Shaq could have easily been a top 10 maybe even a top 5 player of all-time. In this book he will have to settle at number 13 behind his contemporaries he played with in Olajuwon and Tim Duncan. On the upside, you could always look back to how dominate Shaquille O'Neal was when he three-peated as NBA Champion and was Finals MVP each season. No matter where you rank Shaq among the all-time greats we can always remember for a three or four year period, he was once as *dominate* as the great Michael Jordan!

Career Totals

23.7 points, 10.9 rebounds, 2.5 assists, 2.3 blocks, 0.6 steals, .582 FG%, .527 FT%

28,596 points, 13,099 rebounds, 3026 assists, 2732 blocks, 739 steals

Kobe Bryant

(Rank #14)

MVP (1-time), Scoring Title (2-times)

All-NBA First Team (11-times), All-Defensive First Team (9-times)

NBA Championships (5), Finals MVP (2-times), All-Star (15-times)

Also featuring: Vince Carter
& Pau Gasol

Kobe Bryant will go down as one of the greatest scorers in NBA history as he is already the Los Angeles Lakers all-time leading scorer. Known for his *prolific* scoring, particularly from the perimeter, Bryant has the second highest scoring game of 81 points in history to only Wilt Chamberlain's 100. Even though it came against a Toronto Raptor team buried at the bottom of the standings, it was still an astonishing feat. During his prime, he backed this up with two other monster games when I saw him score 62 points (also 2005-06) in 3 quarters against Dirk Nowitzki and the Dallas Mavericks before resting in the 4th quarter because Los Angeles was up huge - and another 65 points (2006-07) at home against the Portland Trail Blazers. Even though Kobe was the best high school player in the country in 1996, and had an incredible pre-draft workout, I don't think most people felt he would be this good coming directly out of high school and into the NBA. The nation was more sold on Allen Iverson coming out of Georgetown at the time, and rightfully so. After averaging an astonishing 25 points a game as a sophomore, Iverson was the #1 pick in the 1996 NBA Draft, followed by Ray Allen at #5, Kobe at #13, and Steve Nash followed right behind him at #15. And honestly, other than the Lakers general manager Jerry West, I don't think anyone thought (initially) Kobe would blossom into this great of a player (top 10 or 15 player of all-time). Despite his *tendencies* to score *exclusively*, Bryant has a phenomenal all-around game. With Kobe now moving up in age, back in his prime he had an explosive first step and could get to the basket almost at will, often scoring with an acrobatic layup or slam dunk. Although blessed with this ability, Kobe prefers to score from the perimeter with a lethal fadeaway shot than to take punishment driving through the lane. I think this *preference* helped him sustain a long career to this day, along with being one of the top fitness guru's in the league. Kobe is known for having one of, if not the best work ethic in all of basketball.

Kobe Bean Bryant was born on August 23rd, 1978 in Philadelphia, Pa., and was the 13th pick overall of the 1996 NBA Draft by the Charlotte Hornets, but was traded on draft day to the L.A. Lakers. The name Kobe was given to him by his parents because of the famous beef of Kobe, Japan - and by the way, I also have loved the name because my family's nationality is half Japanese. Playing for Lower Merion High School, Kobe was regarded as the best high school player in the country. His rookie season, he won the 1997 Slam dunk Contest with Michael Finley and Ray Allen being his main competition.

By that point the dunk contest was becoming an old fad so the NBA cancelled the most coveted exhibition in NBA All-Star weekend the following year. But brought it back in 1999-00 at the Oakland Coliseum in dramatic fashion with "Vinsanity" **Vince Carter** putting on the most electrifying display of power and ariel artistry the league has ever seen, with his four memorable dunks including the *sick reverse windmill-360*; the *underneath-the-backboard windmill-180*; *the lob-and-catch underneath-the-legs windmill jam*; and the *straight-at-the-hoop elbow jam*, that Gerald Wallace tried and *botched* a few years later. Despite Carter's insanity with his exhibition and in-game dunking throughout his career, including the monster dunk over Frederick Weis in the 2000 Olympics, in the eyes of many, he has underachieved throughout the years to perhaps an even lesser extent (in terms of individual accomplishments) than his cousin Tracy McGrady. Having never made it out of the second round of the playoffs (until recently) including the series in which he had a 50-point dual with Allen Iverson in games three and four of the 2001 Eastern Conference Semifinals as a Toronto Raptor, Carter has come up short in the postseason on more than one occasion playing for the New Jersey Nets and with the Dallas Mavericks in 2012. But despite the mishaps and the injuries that took away his explosive leaping ability, I believe Carter will eventually make the Hall of Fame someday. During his prime, he was the ultimate showman and perhaps the greatest slam dunk artist in NBA history, even over the great Dr. J, Michael Jordan, and Dominique Wilkins. He was also an All-Star player for 8 consecutive seasons and scored at least 20 points per game for 10 straight years that included at least 24 points per game in 6 of those seasons. Here are his career totals through this season: 21,135 points, 5016 rebounds, 3836 assists, 1145 steals and 665 blocks. He also shoots 44 percent from the field and 37.4 percent from three-point range.

At Lower Merion High School, as a freshman, Kobe played for the varsity team, and was coached by his father his sophomore year. In his last three seasons, with Bryant playing at every position, his team (the Aces) finished with a 77-13 record. In his junior year, Bryant averaged 31.1 points, 10.4 rebounds, and 5.2 assists per game, and was named Player of the Year in the state of Pennsylvania. And as a senior, the young prodigy averaged an astounding **30.8 points**, **12 rebounds**, **6.5 assists**, **4 steals**, and **3.8 blocks** per game. After leading his team to 31-3 record and their first state championship in 53 years, he was named Naismith High School Player of the Year, McDonalds All-American, and to the USA Today All-USA First Team. In Bryant's first season in the NBA, he played in limited minutes in a reserve role behind Eddie Jones and Nick Van Exel. Bryant, at the time, became the youngest player to start in an NBA game. While playing shooting guard and small forward with his minutes gradually increasing in his second season, Bryant began to sharpen his skills, resulting in a scoring increase at 15.4 points (highest among non-starters) and a runner-up finish for the Sixth Man of the Year award. He would also become the youngest NBA All-Star starter in history and was one of four players including Shaq, Jones, and Van Exel, to be selected as an All-Star from the same team since 1983. In the lockout shortened 1998-99 season, with Jones and Van Exel no longer with the team, Bryant started every game and began to blossom as one of the top shooting guards in the league. During the regular season, the Lakers traded for Glen Rice to make a playoff push, but it wasn't enough as they were swept in the conference semifinals by the San Antonio Spurs.

During the Lakers championship run from 2000 to 2002, Bryant had his best individual season in 2001. During that three-year span, he averaged 28.5 points, 5.9 rebounds, five assists, and 1.7 steals per game - and shot 85 percent from the free-throw line. He was also named to his first All-Defensive First Team in 2000. In 2002, he was named to the All-NBA First Team for the first of eleven seasons. Despite averaging a modest 21 points during the 2000 playoffs, Bryant came up big when it mattered most: in game seven of the Western Conference Finals against the Portland Trail Blazers, he finished with 25 points, 11 rebounds, 7 assists, and 4 blocks to help the Lakers come back from a *potential season ending* 15-point deficit in the fourth quarter. In the NBA Finals against the Indiana Pacers, he gave a preview of his potential to someday reach the level of Michael Jordan. After spraining his ankle in game two in which the Lakers went on to win, Bryant returned for game four with a two to one series advantage. With a little over two and a half minutes left in the fourth quarter, Shaq fouled out with a 115-112 lead and Kobe took care of the rest. In the overtime period, he scored 8 of the Lakers 16 points to put the series out of reach at 3 games to 1. In the closing minutes of regulation, he hit a key jump shot and tipped in Brian Shaw's miss with 5.9 seconds on the clock to send the game into overtime where the Lakers eventually won. Before you get to the end of the chapter where Bryant's downfalls are exposed, it is always best to give credit where credit is due. Even though many of us have been extremely critical of his shot selection over the years, he gave a glimpse of his phenomenal all-around game and will to win at the young age of 22, about to turn 23. The way he pulled out game four of the 2000 NBA

Finals with his clutch scoring and *rebounding* to give the Lakers a 3 to 1 series lead, was kind of reminiscent of what he did in game seven and throughout the 2010 NBA Finals against the Boston Celtics where he went *berserk* not only with his poor shot selection, but with his *relentless* rebounding. In fact, even though I felt Gasol was the MVP, without Kobe's aggressive play (intangibly great chasing down and swarming over every loose ball), and *out of this world* rebounding at the shooting guard position, the Lakers would have lost the series rather easily. So despite the subpar shooting, you have to give Bryant his props for the other *aspects* of his game.

Bryant also came up big in the 2001 playoffs averaging **29.4 points**, **7.3 rebounds**, and **6.1 assists** per game. In my opinion, it was the best postseason performance of his career. Shaq even called him "the best player in the world" at that point. While Shaq was still dominating as the team's best player, Kobe was not far behind. In the clinching game 4 victory against the Sacramento Kings in the semifinals, he had the second highest scoring playoff game of his career with **48 points**, and then followed that up with **45 points** in the opening game against the San Antonio Spurs in the conference finals. For the four-game series, he averaged 33.3 points, 7 rebounds, and 7 assists per game. In the NBA Finals, after losing game one and surviving the scoring onslaught by Allen Iverson, Bryant held his own scoring 31 and 32 points the next two games to help the Lakers take a 2 to 1 series lead. An interesting point during the 2001 NBA Finals is that I was under the *impression* that Shaq felt he and Allen Iverson were not only the toughest players in the league, but also the two best players that endure the most punishment inside the painted area. I also thought he was referring to himself and Iverson as being the best players in the league at the time, and that maybe Shaq was taking back his statement about Kobe being the best player in the world. Around that time, there were a lot of rumors of the ongoing feud between the two of them. All in all, maybe I was just *incorrectly* reading between the lines. Even if I was reading it wrong, I wasn't wrong about Iverson being the best player in the NBA for that season in 2001 over both Shaq and Kobe, because he had just finished his most impressive season of his career winning the NBA MVP award. Finally, in 2002, Bryant scored 36 points in game 3 of the 2002 NBA Finals, to all but put an end to the series for the New Jersey Nets - putting the Nets down 3 games to 0. He also became the youngest man at 23 years old to win three NBA Championships.

The following season at 24 years old about to turn 25, Kobe in my opinion had his best all-around season. He averaged **30 points** per game for the first time and a **career-high 6.9 rebounds**, **5.9 assists**, **2.2 steals**, and shot **38.3 percent** from three-point range. He also had 9 consecutive 40-point games to tie Michael Jordan for second all-time behind Wilt Chamberlain's 14. On top of that, he also had 13 straight games of scoring at least 35 points. In the postseason, he was equally as impressive, averaging **32.1 points** in 12 playoff games but the Lakers mini-dynasty came to an end against the San Antonio Spurs as they were eliminated in six games in the semifinals. The next two seasons, Bryant's scoring dipped due to injuries, and because he had to share the scoring wealth with two other Hall of Famers in Karl Malone and Gary Payton. The Lakers were also in the rebuilding stages the second year, when Shaq was traded and Payton and Malone were no longer with the team. In the 2006 and 2007 campaign's, Bryant had two of the best scoring seasons in history when he averaged **35.4 and 31.6 points** per game respectively and won back-to-back scoring titles, but the Lakers fell into mediocrity finishing with the seventh seed in both seasons. To note: his 62-point game on December 20th, 2005 against the Mavericks, was the first time a player outscored an entire team through 3 quarters (62-61) since the inception of the shot clock.

After acquiring **Pau Gasol** in a lopsided trade with the Memphis Grizzlies the following season, Kobe played team basketball as good as he ever had in his career. That year, I felt he had his second best *all-around* season of his career averaging **28.3 points**, **6.3 rebounds**, **5.4 assists**, and **1.8 steals** per game, and shot 36 percent from three-point range and won the 2008 MVP award. He was definitely worthy of the award, but I felt it should have gone to Chris Paul of the New Orleans Hornets. Both players had great seasons with their respective teams finishing one game apart in the standings, but I felt C. Paul had the better overall numbers, leading the league in assists and steals (something Steve Nash never did in the same season), and because he meant more to his team. Outside of David West, he played with an inferior supporting cast of players in the same way Derrick Rose did with the Chicago Bulls in 2011. Not to take anything away from Bryant, but from my perspective, it actually felt Gasol was the most valuable player on the Lakers the second half of the season. After losing to the Celtics in the 2008 NBA Finals, the Lakers used that season as a building block for the next two as they captured the 2009 NBA Championship over Dwight Howard and the Orlando Magic, and the 2010 NBA Championship in a rematch with the Celtics from two years prior. In those two seasons during the Lakers championship run, Bryant averaged **29.8 points**, **5.7 rebounds**, and **5.5 assists** per game in the playoffs and back-to-back seasons of **30.1 and 32.8 points** in 2008 and 2009.

Bryant, the 2-time scoring champion, does have an impressive scoring resume of **27 40-point** games in the 2005-06 season and **10 50-point** games, including 4 straight in the 2006-07 season. His career total of **117 40-point** games and **24 50-point** games is the third most (his only 50-point game in the playoffs came in a loss against Phoenix) in NBA history to Jordan's 38, and to Wilt's unfathomable totals. He also trails Jordan in career 50-point games in the playoffs 8 to 1 and 40-point games 38 to 13. But as a model of consistency as a scorer in the playoffs, Bryant has an impressive **88 30-point** games. In his ongoing career, Kobe has already made the All-Star team 15 times, and has been selected to the All-NBA First Team 11 times and All-Defensive First Team 9 times.

In player comparisons:

Throughout Kobe's career, he has shown flashes of Michael Jordan. A lot of fans around the country and especially Los Angeles Lakers fans, believed at one point that Kobe was as good as or better than Michael. But I never thought that was the case.

Although, I will give Kobe this much, at one point in his career, I thought the Black Mamba (the nickname he actually gave himself) actually had a more lethal jump shot from the perimeter. Let me make this clear, I believed that his pure stroke from the outside and from three-point range could have been a little better than Jordan's at the same stage of their young careers (I would say from age 21 to 27). But under *duress*, I always felt Jordan was the deadlier scorer, especially shooting fadeaways from the low post or high post. Honestly, as great as Kobe was, his fadeaway, like everyone else's, looked almost in slow motion compared to Jordan's during and after his prime. Even at 40 playing with the Washington Wizards, even though he did not have the *spring* in his legs he once had, it was hard to believe that Jordan's spin and release, actually looked a little *quicker* than Bryant's. Jordan was also more dominant at attacking the basket in the half court and on the fast break, finishing with some never seen before acrobatics (his longer hands compared to Kobe's allowed him to control the ball better when making athletic scores around the basket). Both players were similar passers and rebounders - like Jordan, when Kobe committed his mind to passing and stuck his nose in the paint for rebounds, he was as good as we have ever had at the position. So from a skill set, both players were able to sky high and grab rebounds over taller players and make the spectacular pass like a great point guard could. But, what also separated Jordan from Kobe was on the defensive end. Jordan was just as relentless defensively as he was offensively. He amassed far more steals and blocks than Kobe ever will in his career. He played defense at full speed while Kobe has more of a tendency to pick his spots.

When Kobe was in his prime, I always felt he was about 80 percent of Michael and only about 70 percent from a statistical standpoint. During his better years, I believe he had the talent to close the gap with Jordan's greatness, but I didn't think Kobe could ever, consistently find the balance between being a dominant scorer and the ultimate team player the way Michael was. Take for example, the 2004 NBA Finals against the Detroit Pistons with Shaq, an injured Karl Malone, and with Gary Payton on the down side of his career. With three NBA titles under his belt, he should have put the team on his shoulders, and pulled the Lakers through to victory. When Shaq was being smothered defensively by Ben Wallace all series long and with Malone playing injured, this was the time for Kobe to take over the offensive load like he had in past postseasons. Instead of asserting himself with his proficient shooting or by attacking the basket like we know he can, like they have said recently about LeBron James, he disappeared somewhat in the series. Of course, we have to give part of the credit to the stifling Detroit Pistons defense. In the four losses against the Pistons, he shot 29 of 86, 34% from the field.

Also, when Kobe scored his only 50-point game in the playoffs against the Phoenix Suns in 2006, the Lakers ended up not only losing the game, but the series in seven after being up three games to one. Kobe in game seven, could not find the balance in scoring and making his teammates better, so he chose to play *hot potato* and take only 2 shots from the middle of the third quarter to the end of the game. So as a relentless scorer in game 6 to try and clinch the series, and as the ultimate facilitator in game 7, the Lakers ended up losing both games. In comparisons to LeBron James up to the 2011 season, he has five championships titles to LeBron having had zero. But compared to Jordan, on paper - objectively, his career just doesn't add up in any capacity except for the five championships that he achieved playing alongside possibly the most physically dominant player of all-time in Shaq the first half of his career, and with one of the best frontcourts in recent history, the second half - in Pau Gasol, Andrew Bynum, Lamar Odom, and Ron Artest. Even though Bynum was not ultimately productive offensively at the time, he was a tremendous defensive presence.

Between the times he played with Shaq early on in his career, to the arrival of Gasol in the middle of the 2008 season, Kobe finally learned, to the best of his capabilities, how to make his teammates better. He often deferred to Gasol as the first option in the triangle offense for easy baskets, and to create ball movement out of his double team from the post. He also learned to trust his teammates and find the open man more often than in any point in his career. Even with Bryant playing the last four seasons with the most talented team overall, he still had a little bit of trouble balancing out his scoring with ultimate team play. Take another example, the 2010 NBA Finals. He had some of the most atrocious shooting games you could imagine, including in game seven, where he shot 6 of 24 (25%) from the field, even though the Lakers still managed to close out the Celtics. Jordan never really had as many poor shooting games in the playoffs, partly because he had a better shot selection and dominated attacking the basket, resulting in a higher field goal percentage. Jordan's career playoff scoring average of 33 points per game on 50% shooting is a whopping 8 points higher than Kobe Bryant's 25 points on 45% shooting. Even Jerry West, who might be the second best shooting guard of all-time behind Jordan, has a huge 4-point advantage in the playoffs averaging 29.1 points per game. From my eyes during the 2012 season, Bryant looked like he had reverted back to his old self, often taking twice as many shots per game on some nights as Gasol and Bynum combined. I'm not sure this is a good idea for himself and for the Los Angeles Lakers going forward.

To continue on with the player comparisons, Bryant prefers to score from the perimeter while Jordan dominated at the basket. Jordan was far more dominant than Bryant in the paint, dunking over opponents *at will* or by finishing with some spectacular layup, often shooting and finishing when falling to the floor after a foul. Also, Kobe does not always play relentless defense on a consistent basis the way Jordan did having never amassed 200 steals in a season or 100 blocks (Jordan had 200 steals in a season 6 times). Again, their assists and rebounding numbers are not far apart. Honors wise, Kobe trails Jordan *immensely* in all these key categories: MVP's 5 to 1, Finals MVP's 6 to 2, and scoring titles 10 to 2 but leads his rival Dwyane Wade 1 to 0, 2 to 1, and 2 to 1 respectively. Jordan averaged 30 or more points in a season 8 times and won 10 scoring titles and still won 50 to 60 games a year. Kobe averaged 30 points or more just 3 times. While other teams wilted under Jordan's relentless scoring escapades, teams got up for Kobe. When Bryant had his onslaught of 50-point games (10 to be exact in 2007) and 27 40-point games in 2006 (also scored 50 points or more 6 times), his teams finished a little above .500. Although, in fairness to Kobe, he did play with a weak supporting cast and obviously felt it was better to take difficult shot at times than to pass the ball off.

Other notables, is that when Jordan destroyed every opponent in almost every game situation, Kobe often came up a little short against some of his greatest peers. Although, he just said in 2012, that he never really had a rival, which leads me to believe he's making a similar comparison to Jordan during his playing days. I realize timing at the wing position plays a big part with LeBron James being six and a half years younger and Dwyane Wade at three and a half. But the truth of the matter is, if you don't ever face one of your peers in the playoffs or in the NBA Finals, then your bragging rights to a greater extent should be based on *head-to-head* matchups (of course Championship Rings often weigh heaviest on a players resume) that include wins and individual contributions to the team success. Jordan won most of his individual matchups with his greatest peers in the regular season and in the postseason. For example: Bill Russell leads in the head-to-head matchup over Chamberlain in terms of wins in the regular season and postseason but not in the individual matchup. Of course, Russell often gets the nod and all the props because the wins are the most important goal. But they came behind the help of a great supporting cast. But in Kobe's case, through 2011, LeBron has had the career lead in wins 11 to 6 and in the individual matchup including points per game, rebounds and assists. LeBron also had a 6 to 1 advantage over Kevin Durant for that matter. Although in the Kobe vs. Durant matchup, Kobe does have the heavy advantage against Durant in the regular season and a modest advantage in the playoffs.

Even in the Kobe vs. Wade matchup, where it is much closer, Kobe still trails in wins and in the individual matchup statistically. Over the years, from my point of view, Wade with perhaps a slightly better *skill set* (Bill Simmons also agrees with this assessment in his book) won the individual matchup with Bryant more times than not - also, Kobe complemented Wade on "The Best Damn Sports Show Period" a few years back, mentioning his name first in regards to which players were the most explosive in the league at the time! The times, when I felt it did go the other way in favor of Bryant, it seemed like Kobe outplayed Wade (after Wade had the shoulder and knee surgery), and just recently at home in 2012. I also noticed that he had his way against inferior opponents (although he did have some of his best scoring games against elite defensive players) far more often than against an equal or near equal peer at the *wing position*. I'm not saying he can't perform against the best, it's just that he seldom had a *monster* game in term of points, and overall statistics against an MVP type of player. But in fairness to Kobe, you could come to the conclusion that he was held back from a statistical point of view, because he played with a better supporting cast as compared to other elite players such as Wade's Miami Heat and James' Cleveland Cavaliers.

In Jordan days everyone was inferior and only one could hope to contain him. Even in losses, he always had monster games, notably when he set an NBA record of 63 points against the Boston Celtics in the 1986 playoffs. Although: Gary Payton, Nate McMillan, and the rest of the SuperSonics, did contain Jordan as well as any team ever had during the 1996 NBA Finals. Even though Bryant scored 65 points against a Dirk Nowitzki led team in the regular season a few years back, Dirk now has the advantage over Bryant (and over LeBron 4 games to 2) in head-to-head matchups in the playoffs 4 games to 0, after defeating the Lakers in their only playoff meeting in 2011. I am not saying that *head-to-head* win totals and overall individual numbers alone win the argument for which player is better, but it certainly adds weight.

In other player comparisons:

Another good example is that even though LeBron hadn't won a championship just yet (through the 2011 season), LeBron won the individual matchup in terms of victories and individual contributions with almost all of his peers. In fact, from the individual matchup, he has outscored and has outplayed every big name star throughout his career including Carmelo Anthony. Aside from his slightly over five hundred record against Paul Pierce and the Celtics, the only notable downfall is his atrocious win-loss total against Anthony during his playing days with the Denver Nuggets. But the way the league designs road trips for Eastern Conference teams with many of the trips ending in the high altitude of Denver, many teams come out on the losing end, including the Dwyane Wade led Miami Heat teams of the past.

So what the readers are probably thinking, are what *relevance* does the last few paragraphs have with Kobe Bryant and the fact he won five championship rings vs. everyone else? *Nothing* if LeBron, Wade, Anthony and the rest of his peers never even approach Bryant's five championship rings. However, if Wade can add to his one championship title and LeBron can add a few of them, the bragging rights vs. Kobe would be even more favorable if they never meet in the NBA Finals.

Arguments for Bryant during his .500 days with the Lakers, is that he didn't have a good enough supporting cast he could trust, and that he played in a tough Western Conference. But, it should end right there! It is better to live and die by trusting your teammates - even if they are so-so good, than to take a low percentage shot that looks spectacular. The percentages are higher for a lot of players to take a wide open shot than for Kobe to pump fake, double, triple, or quadruple pump fake like only he did (Kobe has played this way most of his career particularly before the Gasol trade). Larry Bird said in his book "Larry Bird Earvin Magic Johnson - When the Game Was Ours" that Kobe and Jordan were most deadliest when they came down in a half court set, gave the ball up in the half court, went through the defense, and had the ball swung around to them. This is true when Kobe wasn't holding the ball too long with multiple defenders draped all over him. When Jordan got the ball in the low post and was double teamed, he would find the open man, pump fake or double pump fake and shoot a fadeaway over the double-team or pass the ball out to a teammate and quickly reset himself, only to have the ball zipped right back to him for another drive or fadeaway shot. When he was feeling it, he would do this possession after possession. With Kobe during his ball-hogging days, he would often hold the ball too long and take a low percentage shot out of a double or triple team often taking quadruple, quintuple, and sixtuple - *if that's even a word*, pump fakes before shooting it. Or who knows, maybe Kobe felt his teammates would not *mandatorily* cycle the ball back to him like the way they did for Jordan!

Although, it did seem like a lot of those shots went in during his run of forty and fifty-point games in 2006 and 2007. But the percentages and *basic* basketball logic says, if a double and triple teams occur, it is far better to pass the ball out to the perimeter and have the offense *cycle* the ball back to you the way Jordan did. Kobe should have, when the shot clock runs out, taken the next possession to satisfy his scoring thirst with a higher percentage shot. This is partly why Kobe didn't start winning championships again until Gasol arrived. Even though it may sound like it, I am not taking anything away from what Kobe Bryant has accomplished because he will go down as one of the greatest scorers of all-time.

I'm rehashing the Kobe vs. Jordan comparisons of the past few years because I want to illustrate what I have seen during all the hype of Kobe's prime and throughout his career. Today, it seems like fans, media, and many experts for that matter, *become prisoners of the moment* and buy into what a team or player has done at the current moment or recently. Everyone deserves to live in the moment but many people take it too far. After watching thousands of NBA games the last few decades, has allowed me to stay patient before making an intelligent comparison between current and former players. Not to sound contracting, but my projected rankings are based on what a player has done so far today and where he could end up if he stays at the current pace with health permitting. With Bryant's career not yet complete, he might end up ranked a lot higher than what he is in this book (maybe even eventually the Top 8), if he can play at a high level the next four or five years. I believe his greatest accomplishment that he will achieve during the next few years, is the record for career playoff scoring. However, he might just come up a little short in his quest to catch Kareem's all-time scoring mark and in his bid for a sixth championship to tie Michael Jordan. It is almost hard to predict how many championships a player will end up with, so in comparisons to LeBron James right now, and just about everyone else in the league outside of Tim Duncan, Kobe stands superior! After belting home the negative probably more than any other player, I wanted to revise the end of this chapter on a more positive note by mentioning Bryant's attributes (that I'm sure you all know defines his legacy) For one, we all know about Kobe's killer instinct, in which by the way, I reference several times throughout some of the other players' chapters. He also, along with Dwyane Wade has perhaps the highest skill set since Michael Jordan. And despite his tremendous scoring ability, Kobe is also one of the great all-around players ever with excellent passing, rebounding, and defensive skills.

Career Totals

25.5 points, 5.3 reb, 4.8 assists, 1.5 steals, 0.5 blocks, .454 FG%, .336 3FG%, .838 FT%

31,617 points, 6575 rebounds, 5887 assists, 1828 steals, 619 blocks, 1418 threes

Julius Erving

(Rank #15)

MVP (1-time), All-NBA First Team (5-times), All-Star (11-times)

NBA Championships (1), All-ABA First Team (4-times), ABA MVP (3-times)

ABA Championships (2), ABA Playoff MVP (2-times), ABA All-Star (5-times)

Also featuring: Connie Hawkins

Dr. J of the Philadelphia 76ers was one of the most spectacular, high-flying, gravity-defying, and athletic basketball players of all-time. Julius Erving was the "ultimate showman" and everything you could dream of in a *Superstar*. As an ambassador of the game, charismatic and humble at the same time, Erving brought nothing but class on and off the court. Playing for the Virginia Squires and the New York Nets of the ABA, his athletic prowess took the game of basketball to new heights with his innovation of never seen before slam dunks and spins in midair. Thinking back to all his highlights in the ABA and with the Philadelphia 76ers, watching him soar through the air for a slam dunk with his arm extended high above the rim, *left you breathless*. Whether it was on dunks or on crafty layups, the spinning, whirling and the contortion of his body, or with his swooping long arm high up above in mid-flight, *left you in awe*. His five greatest highlights that stand out most and often seen on NBA Hardwood Classics are: the dunks where he is soaring toward the rafters and then slamming it down over Bill Walton in the 1977 NBA Finals and the swooping cuff-tomahawk jam (or "Rock the Baby" cradle slam) over

Michael Cooper in 1983. His other memorable highlights were: when he drove right side with his arm up soaring for a dunk over Mark Landsberger and Kareem (with his arms extended), and then dropping his arm down at the last moment, as he floated underneath the opposite side of the basket for a scoop bank shot in the 1980 NBA Finals, and another time when he drove baseline on Kareem, bumping him in mid-flight with his arm in the air ready to cuff and throw down a slam, but at the last second switched the ball to his left side while floating past Kareem and then spinning it high off the glass from underneath the basket. And of course, he had the dunk from the free-throw line in the 1976 ABA Slam Dunk Contest that set the standard for greatest dunks of all-time. Erving electrified the crowd to new heights and paved the way for other slam dunk artist to showcase their aerial talent for the years to come.

Julius Winfield Erving II was born on February 22nd, 1950 in East Meadow, New York and attended Roosevelt High School where he was supposedly given the nickname Dr. J from a friend. He then went on to the University of Massachusetts where he averaged 26.3 points and 20.2 rebounds per game his two varsity seasons. He is also, only one of five players to average 20 points and 20 rebounds per game in NCAA Men's college basketball history. In 1971, he left school early as an undergraduate to sign with the Virginia Squires. Can you believe he was drafted the following year (the year of his graduation class) by the Milwaukee Bucks in the first round, 12th pick overall? If he had landed in Milwaukee, he would have teamed with Kareem Abdul-Jabbar and Oscar Robertson forming a trio for the ages. In his rookie season with the Virginia Squires, Erving averaged **27.3 points** per game. And, in his second season he led the ABA in scoring at **31.9 points** per game. After two stellar seasons of that magnitude, it was hard to believe that he was traded to the New York Nets before the 1973-74 season, due to financial restraints. After leading the Nets to two ABA Championships and winning three MVP awards, Erving was sold to the Philadelphia 76ers for about 3 million. He picked up where he left off in his first year with the 76ers, by putting on an exhibition of aerial acrobatics in the 1977 NBA All-Star game and winning MVP honors. At that point, he was leaving an inferior league, but a league that had a tremendous *influence* on what we are seeing in the NBA today. The ABA not only influenced the three-point line, because they used it first, but also the free-flowing open court basketball that brings excitement to the fans in today's game on a nightly basis. The ABA provided some of the greatest athletes, and acrobatic high-flying, slam dunk artist the league has ever seen. Next to Dr. J, the other slam dunk artist that made his way into the NBA from the ABA was **Connie Hawkins.**

C. Hawkins was one of the most talented forwards to have ever played the game. A great one-on-one player that could create his own shot, he was also one of the first modern-day power forwards that played *above the rim* before his knee injuries began to settle in. Like Dr. J and George Gervin, Hawkins had incredibly long hands that allowed him to palm the ball like a grapefruit and wave it high above his head, often in anticipation of making a zip pass to a cutter diving to the basket. As the ABA's first superstar (Rick Barry sat out the first season with the Oakland Oaks because of a legal ruling), he made his impact felt immensely throughout the basketball world as he dazzled fans with his soaring and swooping slam dunks that quickly became his trademark. He and Dr. J set the stage for aerial artistry for many of the super high-flyers that have graced upon the NBA scene over the years. Even before he played in the ABA, his legend began on the playgrounds of New York where he earned the nickname the "The Hawk." Today, you could almost call him a folk hero going back to his playground days at Rucker Park where he battled against some of the best basketball players in the world, and the time he spent performing with the Harlem Globetrotters. As one had said, "Hawkins could have been the greatest playground legend of all-time."

Cornelius L. Hawkins was born on July 17th, 1942 in Brooklyn, New York and went to Boys High School in Brooklyn where he didn't play much until his junior year. And that year, he led the team to an undefeated season and won the New York's Public Schools Athletic League title in 1959. In his senior year, he averaged 25.5 points per game and had a magnificent 60-point game. That season, he capped off a fabulous high school career by leading the team to another undefeated season and (PSAL) title. Because of the point-shaving scandal in which he never admitted to any wrong doing, Hawkins was expelled from the University of Iowa before ever playing on the varsity team. Because no other NCAA or NAIA college would offer him a scholarship and NBA commissioner J. Walter Kennedy would not approve any contract to play in the league, Hawkins began his career playing for the Pittsburg Rens of the American Basketball League from 1961 to 1963 where in his first season, he won the league MVP award. He then moved on to play basketball for the Harlem Globetrotters from 1963 to 1967. During that time, when his class was eligible for the draft, because of his alleged involvement with the previous scandal, he was passed up by the NBA teams in both 1964 and 1965 before formally getting banned from the league in 1966.

In his first two seasons after playing for the Globetrotters in 1967, Hawkins played for the Pittsburgh Pipers, which moved to Minnesota following the ABA's inaugural season in 1967-68. In his rookie year, Hawkins averaged a league leading **26.8 points** per game, **13.5 rebounds** and **4.6 assists**, and was named ABA MVP. In the playoffs, he was even more impressive averaging **29.9 points**, **12.3 rebounds**, and **4.6 assists** per game, and shot **59 percent** from the field. The following season, in only 47 games, he peaked averaging a superb **30.2 points** (second to Rick Barry), **11.4 rebounds**, and **3.9 assists** per game, and was named to the All-ABA First Team for the second straight year. After the season, he made a cash settlement with the NBA which assigned his rights to the expansion Phoenix Suns. In his first season (at 27 years old), he averaged 24.6 points, 10.4 rebounds, and 4.8 assist per game - and was named to the All-Star team for the first of four consecutive seasons. He also was named to the All-NBA First Team. In the playoffs, playing alongside Dick Van Arsdale and Gail Goodrich, the Suns were defeated by the Los Angeles Lakers in the Western Semifinals in seven games. In Hawkins' only playoff run in the NBA during his prime, he averaged **25.4 points**, **13.9 rebounds**, and **5.9 assists** per game. The Suns without home court advantage, actually stole the home court from the Lakers in game two winning three games in a row before eventually losing the next three and the series in Los Angeles. The next two seasons, he averaged about 21 points per game and 16 the year after, with a gradual decrease in scoring for the remainder of his career. Sad to say, he only made the playoffs in his first of two seasons with the Los Angeles Lakers in 1973-74, where he was considered washed-up. Judging from his ABA days and his time with the Phoenix Suns, Hawkins could have finished his career in the same class with the great Dr. J, if he hadn't gone through all the mistrials early on in his career.

After beating the Boston Celtics and Houston Rockets in the Eastern Conference, the 76ers made the Finals in Erving's first year but lost (despite leading in the series two games to none) to Bill Walton, Maurice Lucas, Bobby Gross, Lionel Hollins, and the Portland Trail Blazers - who proved to be the more destined team. Although, on paper, it somewhat appeared Philadelphia's roster of Erving, George McGinnis, Caldwell Jones, World B. Free, Doug Collins, and Henry Bibby were evenly matched with Portland except for the fact the Blazers played more as a team as opposed to playing as great individuals.

In that series, Julius averaged **30 points, seven rebounds**, and **five assists**. The next two seasons, the 76ers played second fiddle to the Washington Bullets in the East, but in 1980, they returned to the NBA Finals against the Los Angeles Lakers as they lost the series in six games - behind the heroics of Magic Johnson's spectacular outburst of 42 points, 15 rebounds and seven assists in game six, in which he played in place of the injured Kareem Abdul-Jabbar. Despite the loss, Erving averaged 26 points, 7 rebounds and five assists for the series. The following year, Erving had his best individual season as a 76er, where he averaged **24.6 points, 8.0 rebounds, 4.4 assists, 2.1 steals**, and **1.8 blocks**, and shot **52.1 percent** from the field. He also won his only NBA MVP award. Philadelphia finished tied with the Boston Celtics for the best record in the east at 62-20. But after taking a 3 to 1 series lead against Boston in the Eastern Conference Finals, the 76ers wilted, losing three straight games and the series in seven. The next year, Erving almost duplicated his individual season from the year before and shot a career-high 54.6 percent from the field. He also looked to take his team even deeper into the playoffs. In the postseason, the 76ers met their arch rival again in the 1982 Eastern Conference Finals, but this time they took avenge and beat the Celtics in seven games. But unfortunately, in the NBA Finals they lost again to the Lakers for the second time in three years. Prior to the 1982-83 season, the 76ers traded Caldwell Jones and a number one draft pick for Moses Malone to help neutralize Abdul-Jabbar, probably with the assumption they would meet the Lakers again in the NBA Finals. After finishing the regular season at 65-17 and then waltzing through the playoffs, glory finally came to the Philadelphia 76ers as they dispatched the mighty Los Angeles Lakers in a four-game sweep to win the 1983 NBA Championship. The combined inside/outside dominance of Malone, Erving, and guard Andrew Toney along with defensive stalwarts Bobby Jones and Maurice Cheeks, proved to be the difference overwhelmingly in the series. The next four years with a competitive but aging team, the 76ers never returned to the NBA Finals as Erving retired at the end of the 1986-87 season.

Julius Erving was the key figure in the ABA-NBA merger in 1976 where he won two ABA Championships, three MVP awards, and three scoring titles amazingly enough. Erving accumulated over 30,000 points in his career in both leagues, which ranked 5th on the all-time ABA-NBA scoring list. He averaged an astounding **28.7 points**, **12.1 rebounds**, 4.8 assists, 2.4 steals, and **2 blocks** per game in the ABA and **31.1 points**, **12.9 rebounds**, and **5.1 assists** in the playoffs. He even averaged an incredible **20.4 rebounds** and **career-high 6.5 assists** in eleven playoff games in his first season in the newly formed league playing for the Virginia Squires. To give you more of an idea how great Dr. J was in the ABA, he had nights like this during one six-game stretch in the 1976 ABA Finals: **45 points and 12 rebounds - 48 points and 14 rebounds - 31 points and 10 rebounds - 34 points and 15 rebounds - 37 points and 15 rebounds - 31 points and 19 rebounds**. Based on his statistics in the ABA and what many people have said about "the Doctor," warrant a high ranking in anyone's book. He was simply the fourth best small forward of all-time.

In player comparisons:

In player evaluations, I couldn't put Erving ahead of Shaq and Kobe because of a drop in individual accomplishments and the lack of team success in the NBA. In his best statistical season overall in the NBA, he averaged a **career-high 26.9 points**, **7.4 rebounds**, 4.6 assists, 2.2 steals, and **1.8 blocks** per game - and **shot 51.9 percent** from the field. I couldn't put Erving ahead of Rick Barry either, even though a lot of people may disagree, because Barry proved that he was just as dominant of a scorer in the ABA as he was in the NBA. From all the references studied, it is awfully close though, and if you focus on Julius Erving's ABA career, he was incredibly spectacular not only as a player but as a *showman*. So one could argue that with his 3 ABA MVP awards, 3 times leading the ABA in points per game, 2 ABA Championships and 2 ABA playoff MVP's, and how he *transcended* the game with his high-flying athleticism, he was a little better than Barry and his former teammate Moses Malone. The clincher is that Barry was the more *prolific* scorer and passer, and because many people including Jerry West felt that Barry could have been just as great as Larry Bird. I just think he really never got his due because of his personality issues on and off the court. Nevertheless, ABA and NBA star Dan Issel once said, "that if fans in the NBA had seen Julius Erving play in the ABA, they would have thought he was the greatest player to ever play the game!" And I'm sure many other people felt the same way too.

Career Totals

22.0 points, 6.7 rebounds, 3.9 assists, 1.5 blocks, 1.8 steals, .507 FG%, .777 FT%

18,364 points, 5601 rebounds, 3224 assists, 1293 blocks, 1508 steals

Moses Malone

(Rank #16)

MVP (3-times), Rebounding Title (6-times), All-Star (12-times)

All-NBA First Team (4-times), All-Defensive First Team (1-time)

NBA Championships (1), Finals MVP (1-time)

Also featuring: Bob Lanier & Dave Bing

Moses Malone of the Philadelphia 76ers was one of the all-time great centers in NBA history. A *relentless* offensive machine, the *big and burley* Malone was one of the great scoring and rebounding centers ever and perhaps the best offensive rebounder in NBA history. He is ranked 5th on the all-time list for rebounds with 16,212 and owns the NBA record for most career offensive rebounds with 6731. That equates into 41.5 percent of his rebounds coming on the offensive end. If you factor in his ABA days, he finished third in his professional career with 17,834 total rebounds behind only Wilt Chamberlain and Bill Russell. Not only was Malone dominate inside the paint as a *ferocious* rebounder, he was equally dominate as an inside scorer as many people would attest to, and in evidence of his career totals. He even ranked fifth all-time in career scoring at 27,409 in the NBA until Shaquille O'Neal and Kobe Bryant past him up on the list just recently. And, he is second on the all-time list for free-throws made with 8531 behind only Karl Malone. Watching him at the end of his career was impressive enough, and I can only imagine how great he was when he first came into the league and during his prime. Along with Chamberlain, Russell, Tim Duncan, Dennis Rodman and maybe a few others, his knack for rebounding was the best in NBA history. And along with Charles Barkley, his instincts and incredible feel for the ball to collect offensive rebounds was the best we have ever seen. Moses was basically a *bear* on the offensive glass! In addition, he might have been the toughest and one of the most physical centers (along with Shaq) to have played the game. He also had *great technique* in positioning himself for rebounds and was quick and light on his feet; all of these attributes are what made Malone special!

Moses Eugene Malone was born on March 23, 1955 in Petersburg, Virginia and went to Petersburg High School. Although signing a letter of intent to play for the University of Maryland, Malone was drafted by the ABA's Utah Stars in 1974 becoming one of the first basketball players to go from high school directly to the professional ranks. In his rookie season, Malone made a splash by averaging 18.8 points and 14.6 rebounds, on 57 percent shooting. By his second season, his contract was sold to the Spirits of St. Louis. After the ABA folded at the end of that season in 1976, Malone was selected with the 5th pick overall of the ABA Dispersal Draft by the Portland Trail Blazers. With the original rights to draft Malone, the NBA allowed the New Orleans Jazz to place Malone into the draft pool in exchange for their first-round pick in 1977 which turned out to be Gail Goodrich. Prior to the first game of the 1976-77 season, Malone was traded to the Buffalo Braves for a 1978 first-round draft choice. And after only two games with the Braves, he was traded to the Houston Rockets where he was reunited with Coach Tom Nissalke who coached him his rookie season with the ABA's Utah Stars.

Malone joined a Houston team that rostered two outstanding players in Rudy Tomjanovich and Calvin Murphy. During the regular season, Malone made an immediate impact by averaging 13.5 points and 13.4 rebounds per game, finishing third behind Bill Walton and Kareem Abdul-Jabbar. He also set an NBA record for offensive rebounds with 437 breaking Paul Silas' mark of 365. With a strong nucleus now in place, the 49-win Rockets defeated the Washington Bullets in the semifinals before falling to the Philadelphia 76ers in the conference finals. In twelve playoff games, Malone averaged 18.8 points and 16.9 rebounds, and set a playoff single-game record with 15 offensive rebounds. The following season, Malone vastly improved his offensive production by averaging 19.4 points and 15 rebounds per game. He also was named to his first of twelve consecutive All-Star games. Tomjanovich averaged 21.5 points and *super* point guard **Calvin Murphy** increased his scoring average from 17.9 to **25.6 points** per game. But, with Malone missing the last 23 games of the season with a stress fracture in his foot, the 28-win Rockets missed the playoffs.

In the 1978-79 season, Malone took a *giant leap* toward super stardom and increased his scoring to 24.8 points per game and set a career-high in rebounding at 17.6. Along the way, he set an all-time NBA record for offensive rebounds with 587. He was also named to the All-NBA First Team, All-Defensive Second Team, and won his first MVP award. With Rick Barry in his final two seasons, the Rockets were eliminated in the first round of the playoffs by the Atlanta Hawks two games to zero. In his fourth season in the NBA, Malone had another stellar campaign averaging **25.8 points** and **14.5 rebounds** per game. But in the playoffs, after the Rockets defeated the San Antonio Spurs two games to one in the first round, they were eliminated in a four-game sweep by the Boston Celtics in the conference semifinals. In the deciding game three against the Spurs, Malone scored 37 points and corralled 20 rebounds.

In the 1980-81 season, Malone averaged **27.8 points** and **14.8 rebounds** per game, and led the league in rebounding for a second time and for the first of five consecutive seasons. He also had a career-high in rebounds in a single game with 37 and finished second in the league in scoring to Adrian Dantley. His **51 points** in March that came in a game against the Warriors, was the most points scored in Rockets history up to that point, behind only Calvin Murphy's 57 and Elvin Hayes' 54.

With Malone in his prime, and Murphy and Tomjanovich at the end of theirs, the Rockets settled in mediocrity finishing the regular season at 40-42. But in the playoffs, Houston made an improbable run on their way to the NBA Finals. In the first round, the Rockets eliminated the Los Angeles Lakers two games to one and the San Antonio Spurs in the semifinals in seven games, before defeating division rival Kansas City Kings in the conference finals in five games. However, Houston's "Cinderella" season came to an end after losing to Larry Bird and the Boston Celtics in the NBA Finals in six games. In Malone's final season with the Rockets, he set a **career-high** in **scoring at 31.1 points** per game and points in a single game with **53**. He also broke his own record for offensive rebounds in a game with 21 and won his second MVP award. With the trade acquisition of Elvin Hayes, the Rockets improved their win total to 46 games in the regular season but were eliminated in the first round of the playoffs by the Seattle SuperSonics two games to one.

Prior to the 1982-83 season, Malone as a free agent, signed an offer sheet with the Philadelphia 76ers. But after Houston matched the offer, he was traded to Philadelphia for Caldwell Jones and their 1983 first-round draft pick. Malone joined an already formidable team that had just lost a heartbreaking seven-game series the year before to the Boston Celtics in the conference finals. With key pieces of Julius Erving, Andrew Toney, Bobby Jones, and Maurice Cheeks already in place, the 76ers were primed and ready to unseat Boston in the Eastern Conference. After sweeping the New York Knicks in the semifinals, the 76ers made quick work of the Milwaukee Bucks in the conference finals. In the Finals, after trailing at halftime in all four games, the 76ers avenged the loss to the Los Angeles Lakers from the year before by thumping Los Angeles in a four-game sweep to win the 1983 NBA Championship. After scoring 27 points and grabbing 18 rebounds in game 1 and 24 points and 18 rebounds in game 4, Moses Malone was named Finals MVP. He won his third regular season MVP award, becoming the first man in the four major sports to win the award in back-to-back seasons with a different team. The following season, Malone playing in only 71 games due to an ankle injury, and with

Erving's career slowing down, the 52-win 76ers were eliminated in the first round by the New Jersey Nets three games to two.

But in the 1984-85 season, Philadelphia looked to return to prominence as they finished the season 58-24 and waltzed their way through the playoffs defeating the Washington Bullets three games to one and sweeping the Milwaukee Bucks in the first two rounds. But what looked like an easy path back to the NBA Finals ended abruptly in the conference finals as the 76ers were dispatched in five games by Larry Bird and the Boston Celtics.

I wanted to include **Bob Lanier** somewhere in this book because, like many of the great stars of the past that played for losing teams (and in his case, 8 different coaches including the famous Dick Vitale), he never really got his due in terms of how great a player he really was, and because he became the National Chairman for the NBA's Stay in School Program. Like all great players, their peers always new how great they were. Not to say Lanier was the equivalent, or even within striking distance to Malone as an all-time great (particularly in terms of individual achievements, awards and honors, and championships won), because he wasn't or maybe he was from a talent and basketball ability perspective, but was often injured or playing injured. And he didn't even make my Top 50. But, because he played the center position superbly, and posted outstanding numbers during his prime, I included him in this chapter with Moses Malone. In player comparisons with Malone, at 6-feet-11, Lanier was actually the better shot blocker, and passer for that matter. But Malone was the more dominant scorer and rebounder. Lanier's offensive arsenal included an outstanding outside shot and a deadly left-handed hook shot. Malone won many individual honors including 3 MVP awards as Lanier never even made First or Second Team All-NBA. Despite only winning one NBA Championship, Malone had a lot more success in the postseason than Lanier.

Born on September 10th, 1948 in Buffalo, New York, Robert Jerry Lanier Jr. attended Bennett High School. In college, at St. Bonaventure in Albany, he put up impressive numbers in three varsity seasons averaging 27.6 points and 15.7 rebounds per game, on .576 shooting. In his senior year in 1970, he averaged 29.1 points and 16 rebounds, and led the team to the NCAA Final Four where they would lose to Artis Gilmore and Jacksonville University. Unfortunately, Lanier did not play in the semifinals because he got injured during the regional finals. He also was named Converse All-America for the third time and to the AP All-American First Team. After an outstanding college career, Lanier was selected with the 1st pick overall of the 1970 NBA Draft by the Detroit Pistons. After playing in limited minutes his rookie season, he *blossomed big time* in his second season increasing his scoring ten full **points to 25.7** per game, and his rebounding by six to **14.2** per game. He was also selected to the All-Star team for the first of seven consecutive seasons, with the eighth and final selection coming in 1982 playing for the Milwaukee Bucks. During that seven-year period, Lanier averaged 23.9 points, 12.8 rebounds, 3.6 assists, and 2.1 blocks per game - and shot 51 percent from the field. *Not* *too shabby* for a guy who the voters thought was not good enough to have made at least a couple All-NBA First Team or Second Team selections.

Despite posting similar numbers during his postseason prime, Lanier had very little playoff success primarily because he played with a weak supporting cast. His best teammate as a member of the Detroit Pistons was great scorer and Hall of Famer **Dave Bing**, who finished second on the team in scoring five straight seasons after Lanier's rookie year. Selected with the 2nd pick overall of the 1966 NBA Draft by the Detroit Pistons, Bing was one of the league's most athletic and explosive guards that could distribute the ball and score in abundance. After winning the Rookie of the Year award, the following year he won the scoring title averaging **27.1 points** and **6.4 assists** per game, and **28.2 points** in the playoffs. He also made the All-Star team for the first of seven seasons. In his first four campaigns, Bing had established himself as a true scorer and by his fifth season (Lanier's rookie year) in the league, he matched his career-high in scoring at 27 points per game. For twelve seasons, Dave Bing was a solid performer averaging 20 points and 6 assists per game. After making the playoffs just once before Bob Lanier got there (with Dave DeBusschere being his best teammate for less than two and a half years), Bing would go on to make the postseason four more times in consecutive seasons.

As a tandem, Lanier and Bing were not quite good enough to take the Pistons deep into the playoffs without a better supporting cast. After missing the playoffs in Lanier's first three seasons, the Pistons finally made it in 1974 but were eliminated in the first round in seven games to Bob Love, Chet Walker and the Chicago Bulls. The next *three* seasons, they were eliminated by the Seattle SuperSonics in the first round two games to one, in the semifinals to the Golden State Warriors four games to two, and again to the Warriors - this time in the first round two games to one. After the Pistons missed the playoffs the next two seasons, Lanier was traded in the middle of the 1979-80 season to the Milwaukee Bucks joining *super stud* Marques Johnson out of UCLA and *future star* in Sidney Moncrief. In what looked to be a promising end to his career playing alongside two mega talents in Milwaukee, it was not to be, as the Bucks lost two consecutive heartbreaking seven-game series in the first round to both the Seattle SuperSonics and the Philadelphia 76ers. And in his last three playoff seasons, the Bucks were eliminated by those same 76ers in the first round in six games and the year after in five games, before losing to the Boston Celtics in five games in the conference finals.

For the remainder of Moses Malone's career, his teams either missed the playoffs entirely or never made it out of the first round losing twice with the Washington Bullets in 1987 and 1988 and twice with the Atlanta Hawks in 1989 and 1991. Malone was more than productive in the first three of those years in the postseason averaging 20 points and 11.8 rebounds before he began a downward trend his last five years in the league. And, he was still very much productive in five years in the regular season from 1986 to 1990 averaging 21.4 points and 11.2 rebounds per game. His best teammates during that span were Julius Erving for one year, Bernard King for one and Jeff Malone for two, and

Dominique Wilkins for two. If Malone had been playing at a level near his prime at that stage of his career with Wilkins still at the top of his game, the Hawks would have made a deep run in the playoffs. With age and injury creeping up, Malone retired at the end of the 1995 season after playing only 17 games with the San Antonio Spurs.

In player comparisons:

Malone was the 6th best center of all-time. He was perhaps an even better player over Kareem Abdul-Jabbar from 1979 to 1983, where he won the NBA MVP award three times in five years. He also finished his career 5th on the all-time list for rebounds, 3rd if you count his ABA days with **17,834**, and won six rebounding titles in seven years (he also led the league in total offensive rebounds seven times including six years in a row). In fact, in his first nine seasons in the NBA, he averaged almost 24 points and an astounding 14.6 rebounds per game. He also averaged that exact amount in rebounding for eight playoff seasons during that same span of his career. Only Wilt Chamberlain and Dennis Rodman won more rebounding titles. As a testament to his low-post dominance as a scorer, Malone finished his NBA and ABA career with **29,580 points** and made more free throws than any player in history outside of Karl Malone. His three MVP years in five seasons - that signified dominance, was more than enough to put him ahead of Karl Malone and Charles Barkley in the elite rankings, but not enough to put him ahead of Julius Erving because the "Doctor" was equally dominate for one season and for three seasons playing in the ABA. Moses also had his best seasons when Kareem was at the end of his prime and when Larry Bird and Magic Johnson had just entered the league. Moses Malone will always be membered for his scoring and relentless rebounding, and for being the key piece to the only team (the Philadelphia 76ers) to win the 1983 NBA Championship during (between) the 1980s decade of the Los Angeles Lakers and Boston Celtics dynasties.

Career Totals

20.6 points, 12.2 rebounds, 1.4 assists, 1.3 blocks, 0.8 steals, .491 FG%, .769 FT%

27,409 points, 16,212 rebounds, 1796 assists, 1733 blocks, 1089 steals

Bob Pettit

(Rank #17)

MVP (2-times), Scoring Title (2-times)

Rebounding Title (1-time), All-NBA First Team (10-times)

Championships (1), All-Star (11-times), All-Star MVP (4-times)

Also featuring: Ed Macauley, Cliff Hagen
& Lenny Wilkens

Bob Pettit was the NBA's original power forward. The St. Louis Hawks great won the 1958 NBA Championship and became the first player to beat Bill Russell and the Boston Celtics in the NBA Finals. A two-time MVP and two-time scoring champion, Pettit was one of the league's all-time great big men that dominated the game in both scoring and rebounding. Although not athletically gifted, Pettit worked hard to excel in every facet of the game. He was the *workhorse*, the *gladiator*, and the *ultimate warrior* that was willing to outwork, out-bang, and outhustle his opponents for points, rebounds and loose balls. Bill Russell gave him the highest of compliments; He said, "Bob made 'second effort' part of his sports vocabulary. He kept coming at you more than any man in the game. He was always battling for position, fighting you off the boards." Being heavily into statistics growing up as a youth and not having much television coverage of the old-timers, I always envisioned Bob Pettit as the "pound it inside," Tim Duncan type, before finding out that he was actually a determined slasher playing from the perimeter equipped with an eighteen-foot shot, a turnaround shot, and a leaner coming off screens. He had to transition and fight hard from the perimeter to the interior to get position to corral rebounds. Without seeing much footage of his skill set as a youngster, I always felt from a statistical standpoint, Pettit could have been the greatest power forward of all-time. In comparisons with todays athlete, physical conditioning supported by performance enhancing nutritional supplements, to go along with improving technology of sports equipment, make it hard to compare eras. Even though Pettit at 6-feet-9 200 pounds perhaps would not have matched up well defensively against the Tim Duncan's and Kevin Garnett's of the world, from an objective view point offensively, you would have to give him his props, based on his *impressive* scoring and rebounding accolades.

In player comparisons:

Because we use Chamberlain, Baylor, Oscar, West, and Cousy's statistics in comparisons to current players to help evaluate their elite rankings of all-time, we must include Pettit's. Here are the career numbers of the five greatest power forwards:

Pettit: 26.4 pts per game, 16.2 rebounds, 3.0 assists, n/a blocks, 43.6%FG, 76.1%FT

Malone: 25.0 pts per game, 10.1 rebounds, 3.6 assists, 0.8 blocks, 51.6%FG, 74.2%FT

Barkley: 22.1 pts per game, 11.7 rebounds, 3.9 assists, 0.8 blocks, 54.1%FG, 73.5%FT

Duncan: 20.6 pts per game, 11.4 rebounds, 3.1 assists, 2.3 blocks, 50.8%FG, 68.8%FT

Garnett: 19.5 pts per game, 10.7 rebounds, 4.1 assists, 1.5 blocks, 49.8%FG, 78.0%FT

As you can see, Pettit ranks the highest in two of the three major categories for power forwards. His 26.4 points per game ranks 6th all-time and his 16.2 rebounds per game ranks 3rd on the all-time list behind Chamberlain and Russell. He also averaged at least 20 points and 12 rebounds per game in all eleven seasons he played and finished with 1000 rebounds or more 9 times.

Robert E. Lee Pettit Jr. was born on December 12th, 1962 in Baton Rouge, Louisiana and attended Baton Rouge High School, where he led the team to its first state championship in over 20 years. And, in college at Louisiana State University as a junior, he led the team to its first NCAA Final Four. As a senior, he averaged 31.4 points and 17.3 rebounds per game and was selected to the All-America First Team. But, because of his slender build there was some doubt whether he would make a successful transition from the collegiate ranks to the NBA. Pettit was selected with the 2nd pick overall of the 1954 NBA Draft by the Milwaukee Hawks. In the pros, he had to play forward for the first time facing the basket vs. playing the "standing pivot" in college. Even though he was slim, he was in great condition, and was willing to outwork his opponents on the court. In his first season, Pettit averaged 20.4 points and 13.8 rebounds per game, and won the 1955 Rookie of the Year award. In his second season after the franchise moved to St. Louis, he averaged 25.7 points and 16.2 rebounds per game - and won the rebounding title, the scoring title, and the league MVP award in 1956. Only Wilt Chamberlain would claim all three in the same season. But in the playoffs, with Pettit operating as a one man show, the Hawks beat George Mikan (in his final season in the league) and the Minneapolis Lakers two games to one in the semifinals before falling to the Fort Wayne Pistons in the Western Finals in five games. The Hawks actually won the first two games but lost three games in a row to end the series.

Prior to the 1956-57 season, the Hawks traded their #2 pick of the 1956 NBA Draft to the Boston Celtics to acquire **Ed Macauley** and **Cliff Hagen**. Of course that pick became Bill Russell. Because the Hawks were now more equipped with better balance scoring, Pettit's scoring dipped about a point the next two seasons to a shade over twenty four and a half per game. But he still finished second in the scoring race to Paul Arizin and in third place the year after to George Yardley and Dolph Schayes. New acquisition Macauley was a six-foot-eight forward/center that would out-quick and frustrate bigger defenders with his gliding moves around the basket. He was the odd-man-out that never got a chance to win a championship as a Celtic playing alongside Russell. Despite this misfortune, Ed Macauley was still one of the many great Celtics to have played the game, and the youngest in NBA history at 32 years old to be inducted into the Naismith Memorial Basketball Hall of Fame in 1960. In college at St. Louis University, he and future teammate Frank Ramsey were two-time First Team All-Americans. After four years of college, he was then selected with a territorial pick in the 1949 NBA Draft by the St. Louis Bombers where he played only one season. For the next six seasons, playing alongside Bob Cousy and Bill Sharman, he was a six-time all-star (his 7th selection came in his first season with the St. Louis Hawks) and the All-Star MVP in 1951. He was also named to the All-NBA First Team three years in a row from 1951 to 1953.

As for Hagen, who was a rookie the same year as Russell and K.C. Jones, became an instant scorer in only his second season in the league averaging 19.9 points per game and 10.1 rebounds. As a testament for being a terrific scorer with a deadly hook shot, he finished second on the team to Pettit in scoring seven consecutive seasons from 1958 to 1964. One of the best scoring guard/forwards of his time, Cifford Oldham Hagen was born December 9th, 1931 in Owensboro, Kentucky and attended Owensboro High School. In college at the University of Kentucky, Hagen helped the Wildcats win the 1951 NCAA Championship over Kansas State 68-58. The following year, he averaged 21.6 points and 16.5 rebounds per game, and was named to the All-America First Team. Because of a scandal involving three players over a four year period, Kentucky was forced to forfeit the 1952-53 season. In Hagen's senior year, he scored 51 points in the opening game against the Temple Owls and led the school to a 25-0 record. For the season, he averaged 24 points and 13.5 rebounds per game and was selected to the All-America First Team for the second time.

Hagen was selected in the third round, 24th pick overall of the 1953 NBA Draft by the Boston Celtics. In the same draft, the Celtics also selected Frank Ramsey in the first round and Lou Tsioropoulos in the seventh. But after serving two years in the military, upon returning, he was traded with Macauley before draft day in 1956 for St. Louis' number two pick which we already know became Russell. Holstering a proficient hook shot, Hagen averaged 18 points per game for his NBA career including a career-high 24.8 points in the 1959-60 season. For four straight seasons between 1959 and 1962, Hagen averaged an impressive 23.4 points, 9.7 rebounds, and 4.3 assists per game. He was also a solid shooter for his career averaging 45 percent from the field and 80 percent from the free-throw line. In the postseason, like many of the great players do, he raised his level of play from the regular season averaging 20.4 points, 8.3 rebounds, and 3.4 assists per game. He also put up staggering numbers in 17 playoffs games during the Hawks championship run and the year after averaging 28 points, 11 rebounds, and three assists, on 50 percent shooting. In both years he led the league in points per game in the playoffs. After spending ten years in the NBA, he played his last three seasons in the ABA for the Dallas Chaparrals.

With a strong nucleus now intact, the Hawks made a deep run in the playoffs. After defeating the Lakers in the Western Finals, they made it all the way to the NBA Finals only to lose a heartbreaking seven-game series to the Boston Celtics. But the following season with Pettit, Hagen, and Macauley in their second full season playing together, the battled tested Hawks would avenge the loss to the Celtics and capture the 1958 NBA Championship. After eliminating the Detroit Pistons in the Western Finals four games to one, the Hawks defeated the Celtics in six games with two wins coming on the road. In the clinching game six victory, Pettit had one of the greatest games in NBA playoff history when he lit up the Leprechauns, scorching them for a then playoff record 50 points. In retrospect, it was a huge accomplishment for two reasons: The Hawks were the first team to beat the Celtics during the Russell era and they did it without home court advantage.

Pettit was the one-man show in St. Louis until Hagen and Macauley got there. With a championship now under their belt, the Hawks looked to be championship contenders for years to come. The following season with Macauley playing in only 14 games, and newcomer Clyde Lovellette picking up the scoring slack, Pettit regained his mojo winning MVP, and led the league in scoring for the second time at **29.2 points** per game. He also averaged **16.4 rebounds** and career-high 9.3 free-throws made per game. In their title defense, the Hawks finished second to the Celtics in the regular season with 49 wins, but didn't get a chance at a rematch against their arch nemesis in the Finals, because they were eliminated by the Minneapolis Lakers in the Western Finals in six games.

In the 1959-60 season, Pettit had another stellar year averaging 26.1 points, 17 rebounds, and 3.6 assists per game as the Hawks looked to make it back to the Promised

Land once again. In the playoffs after, defeating the Pistons two games to zero, the Hawks looked to avenge the loss to the Lakers in the Western Finals from the previous year. After coming out victorious against, up-and-coming superstar Elgin Baylor and the Lakers in seven games, the tables were turned against the Hawks in the NBA Finals. In another gut-wrenching battle, the Hawks were defeated by the defending champion Celtics in seven games. In the 1960-61 season, Pettit averaged **27.9 points** and a **career-high 20.3 rebounds** per game, and led the Hawks to 51 wins. Despite the loss to the Celtics in the Finals the previous season, there was no let down by the Hawks as they returned to the NBA Finals. In the playoffs, for the second straight year, they grinded out another seven-game series victory against the Lakers in the Western Finals. But like in today's game, the window of opportunity to win an NBA championship is very narrow. With the Celtics' depth and championship experience, for the second straight year, the Hawks were eliminated by the Celtics in the Finals, this time in five games.

The following season, Pettit averaged a **career-high 31.1 points** and 3.7 assists per game. He also had his second best rebounding season of his career averaging 18.7 per game. But the Hawks settled in mediocrity winning a measly 29 games partly in due to Clyde Lovellette playing in only 40 games. Despite missing the playoffs, one of the upsides during the season other than Pettit's stellar individual year, was sophomore sensation **Lenny Wilkens**. In only 20 games during the season, Wilkens game a preview of what was to come in the future for the magnificent point guard when he averaged 18.2 points, 6.6 rebounds, and 5.8 assists per game. The *lightning-quick* Wilkens was one of the great point guards to ever play the game. In fact, during his time, perhaps only Oscar Robertson was better at the point guard position. Leonard Randolph Wilkens was born October 28th, 1937 in Brooklyn, New York and attended Boys High School in Brooklyn. At Providence College he made a name for himself averaging 14.9 points and 7.3 assists per game and was named to the All-America Second Team as a senior in 1960. In the NBA he played for four teams but became an All-Star playing for the St. Louis Hawks and the Seattle SuperSonics.

Wilkens was selected with the 6th pick overall of the 1960 NBA Draft by the St. Louis Hawks. He was the third great guard taken behind Oscar Robertson and Jerry West. After a slow start to his career, Wilkens became an All-Star by his third year in the league. For the next three seasons, he improved his overall production in every facet of the game and was named to the All-Star team each season. By his sixth season in the league in what ended up being a typical good year, he averaged 18 points, 5.5 assists, and 4.7 rebounds per game. In fact, from that point on, for eight straight seasons including his last three with the Hawks, four with the Sonics, and his first with the Cleveland Cavaliers - he averaged an impressive 19.3 points, 8.1 assists, and 5 rebounds per game. He also made the All-Star team 6 out of 8 eight seasons and a total of 9 out of an 11-year stretch of his career.

During the Hawks bid to recapture the NBA Championship twice during the early 1960s with Pettit leading the way, Wilkens was one of the key contributors during the playoffs. During the postseason, he was ultimately consistent, averaging 16.1 points, 5.8 assists, and 5.8 rebounds per game in 64 playoff games from 1961 to 1968. At the time of his retirement, he was ranked second all-time to Oscar in career assists. He averaged nine assists or more three consecutive seasons and eight or more in six different seasons. He also won the assist title in 1970 and finished runner-up to Wilt Chamberlain in the MVP balloting in 1968. So from a pure passing standpoint during his time, he was second only to the Big O. Unfortunately, Wilkens never won a championship with the Hawks and never made the playoffs with the SuperSonics.

In Pettit's last three seasons, he averaged 28.4, 27.4, and 22.5 points per game respectively as the Hawks got back to their winning ways, but unfortunately, they never made it back to the NBA Finals. In 1963, after beating the Pistons in the semifinals three games to one, Atlanta lost to the Lakers in the Western Finals in seven games, after they had defeated their arch rival the previous two meetings in the playoffs. However, in 1964, they returned the favor and beat Los Angeles in the semifinals three games to two before losing another tough seven-game series in the Western Finals to the San Francisco Warriors. In 1965, they lost in the first round to Walt Bellamy, Bailey Howell and the Baltimore Bullets three games to one. So in a nutshell, Pettit led his team to four NBA Finals in 1957, 1958, 1960, and 1961, but won the title just once in 1958. And, his teams were ultimately competitive in the playoffs having played in 7 different seven-game series: Three times they lost to the Boston Celtics, and one time to both the L.A. Lakers and Warriors. The two times they won both seven-game series, it came against the Lakers twice in the Western Finals, which happened to come in the last two years they lost to the Celtics in the NBA Finals.

During his postseason career, Pettit averaged an incredible 25.5 points and 14.8 rebounds per game, and 28 points and 16 rebounds from 1957 to 1963. He also averaged 8.9 free-throws made and 11.7 free-throws attempted at a 76 percent clip. To complete his resume, Pettit made the All-NBA First Team every season of his career until the last season. Even then he was named to the All-NBA Second Team. He also was named to the All-Star team all eleven seasons he played in the league. Even though he made it back to the Finals in 1960 and 1961, he never won another championship in his final seven seasons. During his stellar career, he did win a second MVP award and scoring title in 1959. Also, after winning his only championship in 1958, he averaged an astounding 27.8 points per game and 16.6 rebounds his final seven seasons, which ranks among the best seven year scoring and rebounding streaks of any forward in history. Over the years, the great Bob Pettit has been honored on the 25th, 35th, and NBA 50th Anniversary All-Time teams since his retirement in 1965!

Career Totals

26.4 points average, 16.2 rebounds, 3.0 assists, .436 FG%, .761 FT%

20,880 points, 12,849 rebounds, 2369 assists

Karl Malone

(Rank #18)

MVP (2-times), All-NBA First Team (11-times)

All-Defensive First Team (3-times), All-Star (14-times)

NBA Record: 8 years leading free-throws made!

NBA Record: 9,787 career free-throws made!

Also featuring: Adrian Dantley

Karl Malone was one of the greatest power forwards of all-time. In eighteen seasons playing for the Utah Jazz franchise, in the first half of his career - Malone redefined the power forward position with his *unprecedented* physicality and *brute* strength able to overpower opponents for points in the paint in the same manner Shaquille O'Neal did at the center position ... as I always viewed Malone as *the machine*, in terms of scoring at will from the low post and high post. Later on in his career "The Mail Man" developed one of the most *proficient* mid-range jump shots of any big man during his time if not ever. Overtime, his turnaround jump shot became almost as automatic as Jordan's fadeaway. Along with running-mate John Stockton, he was also famous for running the pick-and-roll and for finishing on the fast break. In his era, he was the second best scorer to Michael Jordan and is fittingly ranked second on the all-time scoring list behind Kareem Abdul-Jabbar at 36,928 career points. If he wanted to stick around a couple more years, he would have broken Kareem's all-time scoring mark. The first half of Malone's career, he was the most dominating inside player at *bulldozing* through opponents and scoring at will. He was so dominant in the paint, that he was often *grabbed and mugged* from behind before he was able to shoot to prevent easy baskets. When he was fouled after the shot, he was strong enough to finish the three-point play. Both sequences resulted in more free-throws made and attempted than any player in NBA history. He was also an outstanding rebounder during his time, able to use his size (at six-foot-nine) and strength to overpower and move around opponents on the low block. He amassed 14,968 career rebounds which ranks 2nd all-time among forwards and 6th overall behind Wilt Chamberlain, Bill Russell, Kareem Abdul-Jabbar, Elvin Hayes, and Moses Malone. And, although he was on the receiving end more times than not, Malone was an outstanding passer as well - out of the low post or high post finding cutters to the basket, and off the screen-roll. Not only was Malone on the receiving end of an assist from Stockton out of the pick-and-roll or pick-and-pop, he was sometimes the facilitator, but usually the *rock-solid* screen-setter to where Stockton, after deciding not to pass the ball off a screen, would pull up for a wide open jump shot. His unselfishness as a player enabled him to amass 5248 assists for his career. Defensively, Malone was underrated despite being on the All-Defensive First Team three times. He had quick hands, and was able to strip players trying to shoot or dribble out of the post. And, with his strong and powerful frame, he was able to push post-players further away from the basket.

Karl Anthony Malone was born on July 24th, 1963 in Summerfield, Louisiana and attended Summerfield High School where as a sophomore; he led the team to three consecutive Louisiana Class C Titles from 1979 to 1981. In college, Malone was then recruited by Coach Eddie Sutton at the University of Arkansas, but chose to play closer to home at Louisiana Tech University where he had a modest college career after missing his freshman season due to academic ineligibility. In his sophomore season, Malone averaged 20.9 points and 10.3 rebounds per game. The following year, he averaged 18.8 points and 8.8 rebounds, but his team would miss the NCAA tournament for the second consecutive time. In his senior season, with his individual numbers slightly down, he led the Bulldogs to a 29-3 record and a berth in the NCAA tournament for the first time in school history but were eliminated in the Sweet 16.

Malone was selected with the 13th pick overall of the 1985 NBA Draft by the Utah Jazz. In retrospect, Malone was one of the best sleeper picks (so-to-speak in terms of Superstar potential) in the history of the NBA Draft along with Kobe Bryant who was also selected at number 13 in 1996. In his rookie season, Malone finished second on the team in scoring at 14.9 points to Adrian Dantley. In the playoffs, the Jazz would lose to the Dallas Mavericks in the first round three games to one. In his second season, without Dantley who was traded before the season, Malone increased his scoring average significantly to 21.7 points per game and led the team in scoring and rebounding, but the Jazz lost again in the first round of the playoffs to the Golden State Warriors three games to two. In the 1987-88 season, Malone blossomed into a *premier* all-star averaging **27.7 points** and **12 rebounds** per game, and was selected to the All-NBA Second Team. With Stockton emerging as the top assist man in the league, the Jazz would make it out of the first round by defeating the Portland Trail Blazers three games to one, before eventually losing a hard-fought seven-game series to the defending champion Los Angeles Lakers in the semifinals. In the elimination game, Malone had 31 points and 15 rebounds, and averaged **29.7 points** and **11.8 rebounds** per game for the entire playoff run.

The following year, Malone and Stockton would increase their scoring averages to **29.1** and **17.1 points** per game respectively. Malone would also be selected to his first of eleven consecutive All-NBA First Teams. After winning the division title, the Jazz were upset in the first round of the playoffs for the second time in three years to the pesky Warriors in a three-game sweep. Unfortunately, Utah was the victim of one of Don Nelson's "Upset Specials" twice more than any other team. Actually, it was once since George Karl was the Warriors' coach back in 1987. The Warriors under Nelson, have pulled off more upsets as a seventh seed or eighth seed than any team in NBA history, with the latest coming in 2007 to the Dallas Mavericks. The Warriors have had a history of implementing "small ball" with an undersized but quick lineup, which includes two big men and three wing players or one center and four wing players to create mismatches in their favor on the offensive end. Living in the Bay Area, I have always been in favor of the system for two reasons: Bigger and more talented teams often succumbed to the *offensive flurry* and quick tempo offense of the Golden State Warriors resulting in many blowouts at the Coliseum arena in Oakland, including what happened recently against the Mavericks in 2007. In fact, on occasion, the Warriors were even able to *outgun* Steve Nash and the Phoenix Suns when they were at their best. Second, with its tremendous fan base for a small market team, Golden State plays an exciting *brand* of basketball and has one of if not the loudest arena in the NBA. The Warriors have always played as an *underdog* going back to Rick Barry's days in the 1970s. Despite the fact, they haven't gotten past the second round of the playoffs in recent years, and were eliminated by bigger and more talented championship caliber teams; I still believe the system can work to a maximum if the Warriors can someday acquire an athletic and talented big man or two.

Malone increased his scoring average for the fifth consecutive year to a career best **31 points** per game but finished second in the league to Michael Jordan. He also had one of the great and most efficient scoring exhibitions in NBA history when he scored a **career-high 61 points** on **21 of 26 shooting** for an *unfathomable* 81% from the field, and 19 out of 23 from the free-throw line, en route to 144-96 victory over the Milwaukee Bucks. Despite never winning a scoring title, Malone finished second in scoring five different times and first seven times in the Western Conference. Just to throw it out there hypothetically, if they had separate awards for both conferences like they do in baseball (with separate leagues), Malone would have won 7 Scoring titles instead of coming up empty with zero. That in itself *exemplifies* how great of a scorer he really was. Ultimately consistent every year, Malone finished with a career scoring average of over 25 points per game. Another great scoring Jazz player to score 30 points or more in a season other than Malone and Pete Maravich was **Adrian Dantley**, who did it four times including winning two scoring titles in 1981 and 1984. Dantley was one of the great scorers in NBA history that had a unique and unorthodox style - an undersized but deadly post-up player that never really got his due until recently when he was inducted into the Basketball Hall of Fame.

Born on February 28th, 1956 in Washington D.C., Adrian Delano Dantley attended powerhouse DeMatha Catholic High in Hyattsville Maryland. In his freshman year at Notre Dame University during the 1973-74 season, he was part of the Fighting Irish team that upset the mighty UCLA Bruins in 1974, ending their 88-game winning streak. That Bruin's team featured legendary coach John Wooden and stars Bill Walton and Keith (Jamaal) Wilkes. The next two seasons, he would average a remarkable 30.4 and 28.6 points per game to go along with 10 rebounds and was named AP All-America for the second straight year. He would also go on to lead the U.S. Olympic team in scoring as they captured the gold medal at the summer Olympics in Montreal. Dantley was then selected with 6th pick overall of the 1976 NBA Draft by the Buffalo Braves where he averaged 20.3 points and 7.2 rebounds. After winning the Rookie of the Year award, he became the first player in any of the major sports to be traded the following season after winning such an award. And, he was actually traded three times in two years after playing for the Braves and five times total during his career.

In his fourth season after playing for the Braves, Indiana Pacers, and Los Angeles Lakers, he finally found a home in Utah where he made a huge name for himself as one of the league's great scorers. For seven years straight from 1980 to 1986, Dantley scorched the NBA averaging 29.6 points and 6.2 rebounds per game, and shot an incredible 56 percent from the field. He also scored 30 points in a season 4 times, won two scoring titles, and was named to the All-Star team 6 times out of 7 years despite making the All-NBA Second Team just twice in 1981 and 1984, which happened to be the same years he won both scoring titles. He did have four sensational playoff seasons beginning in 1984 and 1985 where he averaged 28.9 points, 7.5 rebounds, and 3.1 assists per game, and shot 51 percent from the field. After defeating the Denver Nuggets and the Houston Rockets in the first round three games to two, the Jazz were eliminated in the semifinals in six games by the Phoenix Suns and in five games to the Nuggets in a rematch from the previous year's playoffs. His best postseasons, in terms of team success, came during his two-year tenure with the Detroit Pistons in which in the 1987 and 1988 playoffs, he averaged 19.8 points on 53 percent shooting. In both years, the Pistons came up a little short in crushing seven-game defeats to both the Boston Celtics in the Eastern Conference Finals, and to the Los Angeles Lakers in the NBA Finals. Detroit had eliminated the Washington Bullets in the first round in both seasons, and the Atlanta Hawks and the Chicago Bulls in the semifinals in five games. Dantley was one of the key pieces and primary scorers on the team that helped the Pistons once and for all dethrone the mighty Celtics in the conference finals before coming up a little short in Los Angeles. It was too bad he was traded after the season for Mark Aguirre, who ended up with the two championships - that had eluded Dantley his entire career. Though a great scorer during his time, I guess the only two All-NBA Second Team selections and the lack of playoff success signified why it took so long for him to make it into the Hall of Fame.

In the 1989-90 season, Utah increased their win total to 55 games but after a disappointing loss in the first round of the playoffs the previous year, the Jazz were eliminated once again in the first round this time by the Phoenix Suns three games to two. The next season, Malone averaged at least 29 points for third consecutive year and the Jazz would avenge the lost to the Suns from the previous playoffs by eliminating them three games to one in the first round. But the Jazz continued their early round exits by losing in the semifinals to the Blazers in five games. In the 1991-92 season, Utah finished with 55 wins, won their division, and appeared ready to make a deep playoff run with Stockton and Malone playing in their seventh season together. In the first two rounds, the Jazz beat the Los Angeles Clippers and the Seattle SuperSonics in five games, before losing to Clyde Drexler and the Portland Trail Blazers in the Western Conference Finals. Throughout the playoffs, Malone averaged outstanding numbers of 29 points and 11 rebounds per game including a career-high 52 percent from the field. Malone savored the year by winning the 1992 Gold Medal as a member of the U.S. Olympic Team.

The next season, the Jazz would take a step back as they were defeated by the SuperSonics in the first round of the playoffs three games to two, partly due to Mark Eaton's ineffectiveness playing in his final season in the league. In the 1993-94 season, Malone set a career-high in rebounds for a single game with 23. Despite finishing third in the division, the Jazz would rebound and make it back to the conference finals for the second time in franchise history. But after defeating the Blazers three games to one and the Nuggets in seven games in the first two rounds of the playoffs, they would go on to lose handily to the Houston Rockets behind MVP Hakeem Olajuwon. The Rockets seemed destined to win the title after defeating the Suns in one of the most miraculous comebacks in NBA playoff history. The following year, Utah set a franchise record in the regular season with 60 wins, but was defeated once again by the Rockets in heartbreaking fashion three games to two in the first round of the playoffs including the decisive game five on their own home court. The year after, the Jazz beat the Blazers in the first round of the playoffs in five games, which included a 38-point blowout in the decisive game five in Utah. In the next round, the Jazz defeated the San Antonio Spurs in six games but lost to the SuperSonics in a tough seven-game series in the conference finals. Malone capped off an outstanding year by winning the gold medal playing for the 1996 U.S. Olympic Dream Team.

In the 1996-97 season, Karl Malone won his first MVP award and led the Utah Jazz to the best record in the Western Conference at 64-18. That season, while many felt Jordon should have won the MVP award, I felt the voters made the right choice in voting for Malone. Here are the stat lines for both players whose teams finished in first place in their respected conferences:

Malone: 27.4 points, 9.9 rebounds, 4.5 assists, and shot 55 percent from the field

Jordan: 29.6 points 5.9 rebounds, 4.3 assists, and shot 48.6 percent from the field

So even though Jordan's team won 72 games the year before, his team still won slightly fewer games finishing with 69 wins to Malone's team finishing with a *franchise* record 64 wins. Also, Jordan's stats dipped slightly from the year before while Malone's increased every season *overall* over the past four years since his last great season in 1993. He also nearly matched his career field goal percentage at a whopping 55 percent and had a career-high in assists to that point (despite playing with the best assist man in the game in John Stockton). If Jordan was the best all-around player that season, there is no way a power forward of that size and physique in Malone, should have out assisted one of the greatest passing shooting guards of all-time. In fact, not only did Malone outplay Jordan in two major aspects of the game in rebounding and assists, he was nearly as great a scorer and defensive player having been selected to the All-NBA Defensive First Team for the first of three consecutive seasons. In addition, he led the league in player efficiency rating by ESPN.com for the first time in his career. In fairness to Jordan, he did have plenty of rebounding help in Dennis Rodman and shared the facilitating duties with Scottie Pippen.

In the playoffs, the Jazz turned the corner for the first time in franchise history by making it all the way to the NBA Finals. The Jazz swept the Clippers in the first round and did away with the other L.A. team in five games in the semifinals with Shaquille O'Neal and Kobe Bryant in their first season with the franchise. In the Western Conference Finals, John Stockton would show his *true grit* as an elite performer by knocking down the biggest shot in franchise history with a buzzer-beater in game six at home to bury their arch nemeses Houston Rockets once and for all. The Rockets had acquired Charles Barkley before the season to form a *Super Trio* in hope of winning a third championship - in which it would have been a first for "Sir Charles." In the Finals against the Chicago Bulls, the Jazz split the first four games with each team taking care of home court. In game five, Utah had an opportunity to take a three to two series lead but lost at home (in the 2-3-2 format) 90-80 before dropping the decisive game six in Chicago.

The tough minded Jazz came back the next season knowing how close they were to an NBA Championship. After finishing the season tied with the Bulls for best record in all of basketball, the Jazz marched through the playoffs defeating the Rockets three games to two and the San Antonio Spurs in five games in the first two rounds, before sweeping the Los Angeles Lakers in the conference finals. This set up a rematch with the top two teams and the two best players in the NBA. But after another tough six-game series, Malone and Stockton came up short once again. The following season, Malone recaptured the MVP award (his second) from Jordan who he had split the award with from 1996 to 1999. But in the playoffs of the lockout shortened season, the Jazz were eliminated by the Portland Trail Blazers in the semifinals in six games ending Utah's run at an NBA Championship. The very next season, with Malone at the age of 36 about to turn 37, averaged an impressive 25.5 points and played in all 82 games, but the Jazz were eliminated once again by the Blazers in the semifinals this time in five games. With Malone and Stockton clearly on the downside of their careers, but with Malone still averaging 20 points per game, the Jazz never made it past the first round losing in three consecutive seasons to the Dallas Mavericks and the Sacramento Kings twice. It wasn't until the 2004 season where Malone would get another chance at a championship. After teaming up with Gary Payton and joining Shaquille O'Neal and Kobe Bryant in Los Angeles, the Lakers came ever so close to winning a fourth championship for Shaq and Kobe, and a first for Malone and Payton. In what looked like a triumphant run to the title, Malone was injured in the conference finals against the Minnesota Timberwolves and was not himself in the NBA Finals against the Detroit Pistons, as the Lakers were eliminated in five games.

Despite never winning an NBA championship, Malone *revolutionized* the power forward position and set the standards for excellence, consistency and durability at his position over his incredible 19-year career. With all his attributes already described above, Malone from a statistical point of view was equally as impressive. He is the only man in history with **12 2000-point seasons** and to score 2000 points 11 years in a row. He also averaged 25 points or more in a season 12 times including 11 straight. In eight of those seasons, he averaged at least 27 points per game including six years in a row beginning in his third season in the league. During a 14-year stretch from 1988 to 2001, he averaged 27 points, 10.6 rebounds, and 3.6 assists, and shot 52.6 percent from the field. And, he nearly matched those numbers in the playoffs over that same period averaging 27 points, 11.3 rebounds, and 3.2 assists. Out of all the players in history, no one was more consistent on a regular basis than Karl Malone because "The Mail Man" always delivered.

In player comparisons:

With all that being said, it is no coincidence that Malone is ranked 18th in this book, Bill Simmons' Book, and Slam Magazine's in 2009. Partly for the same reasons; I think a lot of people view Malone like they viewed Dirk Nowitzki before he won his first championship - in which many felt he did not come through when it counted most, especially during the NBA Finals. Malone reached the Finals three times and twice in his prime and was so close to winning it in 1998, if it weren't for Michael Jordan's heroics in game 6; the famous steal and last second shot - if weren't executed, could have extended the series to 7 games. In player comparisons, Tim Duncan is ranked ahead of Karl Malone for greatest power forward of all-time, primarily because of his superior defensive and shot blocking skills, anchoring the San Antonio Spurs to 4 NBA Championships. But from a pure scoring standpoint, Malone had the better shooting touch and go-to-move with his turnaround jump shot. Although from a passing standpoint, you could call it a draw.

Malone, Duncan, and Barkley were all great passers at the power forward position during their time, but it ends right there. With his impeccable timing, Duncan was the better rebounder at seven-feet tall, and by far the better shot blocker. So despite the intangible perspective that also heavily favors Duncan, and the fact Malone shot 46.3 percent in the playoffs vs. 51.6 in the regular season and never won a championship, if it weren't for the *defensive side* of the ball (that includes rebounding and shot blocking) which also favors Duncan, Karl Malone might have gone down as the greatest power forward of all-time, because of his *dominance* as a scorer and for also having an *outstanding* all-around game. Instead of being a top 10 or 15 player ever - like he probably could have been, he will have to settle at number 18 in this book, at least until LeBron James finishes up his prime!

Career Totals

25.0 points, 10.1 rebounds, 3.6 assists, 1.4 steals, 0.8 blocks, .516 FG%, .742 FG%

36,928 points, 14,968 rebounds, 5248 assists, 2085 steals, 1145 blocks

Charles Barkley

(Rank #19)

MVP (1-time), Rebounding Title (1-time)

All-NBA First Team (5-times), All-Star (11-times)

Also featuring: Kevin Johnson
& Tom Chambers

Charles Barkley was one of the great power forwards of all-time. Back in his playing days with the Philadelphia 76ers, Barkley was one of the most *prolific* offensive forces the league has ever seen. While a lot of his spectacular moments and best individual accomplishments came as a member of the 76ers, it wasn't until he was traded to the Phoenix Suns, where he would reach the NBA Finals. That season in 1993, Barkley led the Suns to the best record in the NBA and was awarded the league MVP trophy. Throughout his stellar career, Barkley was one of the most gifted all-around players that could do it all, becoming one of four players in NBA history to amass 20,000 points, 10,000 rebounds, and four thousand assists joining Wilt Chamberlain, Kareem Abdul-Jabbar, and Karl Malone. During his prime, he was a *relentless* scorer and *ferocious* rebounder with point guard passing skills. Listed at six-feet-six, he was probably closer to six-foot-four and had a dominant low-post/high-post game. With his wide body and strength and agility, he could post up *any* power forward or center by backing them down underneath the basket for an easy layup or step-back fallaway shot, or he could pull his opponent away from the basket and shoot his patented jumper or three-point shot.

"Sir Charles" was such a good ball handler he would often dribble down court, stop on a dime and pull up in a player's eye at will, similar to the way Larry Bird used to. He also had a great jab-step that he used in isolation from anywhere on the court. He would simply fake left or right as though he was going to drive to the basket, causing the defender to take a step back, freeing himself up for an easy jump shot; or he would pump fake as though he was going to shoot the ball, baiting the defender into contesting his shot and then blow right past him for a dunk or layup. In one-on-one situations or when he had the ball in crucial moments during or at the end of games, he made opponents and fans hold their breath in *terror* the same way Michael Jordan used to, with teams hoping they wouldn't fall victim to his offensive arsenal. At the forward position, he could also finish on the break as good as or better than anyone in history, not named LeBron James. He will always be remembered for his famous cocked-behind-the-head two-handed slam dunk on the fast break that charged up fans in arenas throughout the league.

Barkley was just as great at rebounding as he was at scoring. Not including what Blake Griffin might turn out to be, "The Round Mound of Rebound" and Moses Malone were the greatest offensive rebounders of all-time. On a missed shot, often his own, players were at his mercy trying to outrebound him. With his wide body, big behind, and incredible feel for the ball, Barkley was able to out-box and outwork his opponents *relentlessly* to get position for easy rebounds and put-backs. Like some of the other great power forwards, he was an outstanding passer with the unique ability to dribble and run the floor like a point guard. I would have to rank him as the best true passing power forward ahead of Tim Duncan, Kevin Garnett, Karl Malone, and even Pau Gasol of today. Although not gifted on the defensive end, Barkley had good anticipation and quick hands for stealing the ball in key moments, and for coming out of nowhere when you least expected it to block a shot emphatically. As a testament to all these skills, Bill Walton once said in Slam Magazine, "Barkley is like Magic [Johnson] and Larry [Bird] in that they don't really play a position. He plays everything; he plays basketball. There is nobody who does what Barkley does. He's a dominant rebounder, a dominant defensive player, a three-point shooter, a dribbler, a playmaker."

During his later years with the Philadelphia 76ers and early years with the Phoenix Suns, you could make the case that "Sir Charles" was the greatest player in the NBA behind Michael Jordan not only because of his overall talent, but because he played with the same swagger, killer instinct, and an extreme will to win. In isolation plays, he would often take the other team's best player to school with his jab-step and fallaway shot (often with a player right up in his face), or he would bully and back down his opponent in the low post for easy layups a 'la Shaquille O'Neal. As a result of his tremendous swagger, he would often hold the dribble too long just to let his opponent know who was boss and that it was his game to win. It gave fans an adrenaline rush, watching Barkley go one-on-one, and when he would bang bodies and trade baskets with other superstars in the likes of Bird, Malone, and Dennis Rodman. But the difference between the two is that Barkley didn't know his limitations and was not nearly the defensive player that Jordan was. Really, he was versatile like M.J. in every way offensively, except he was not as great on the defensive end. In fact, he was so versatile and so good, I thought he was a sure bet to win at least one championship during his prime, but the same misfortune happened to him as to almost everyone else who played in the Jordan era.

Charles Wade Barkley was born on February 20th, 1963 in Leeds, Alabama and went to the University of Auburn for three years. He was then selected with the 5th pick overall by the Philadelphia 76ers in the 1984 NBA Draft. Prior, as a senior in prep school, he led Leeds High School to a 26-3 record and to the state semifinals, while leading the team in scoring at 19.1 points per game and rebounding at 17.9. In high school, Barkley was heavy set and struggled with his weight. After seeing him recently on TNT as a studio analyst throughout the years, I'm definitely not surprised. This is partly why he didn't get much recognition by college recruiters until the end of the state semifinals where he outplayed Alabama's best player. Throughout college, he played the center position at Auburn University where he showed off his versatility and athleticism to the fans, just as he did in the NBA with his high-flying monster dunks on the fast break, and with his rebounding and emphatic shot blocking. He made his only NCAA tournament appearance his junior year and finished college averaging 14.8 points, 9.6 rebounds, 6 assists, 1.7 blocks, and had a *center-like* shooting percentage of 68.2. Despite a promising college career, Barkley did not make the 1984 U.S. Olympic team, but did so as a professional in 1992 and 1996 winning the gold medal with Team USA and finishing both campaigns with a combined 16-0 record. Perhaps the best player that year on the greatest team ever assembled, the "United States Dream Team," Barkley led Team USA in scoring (71.1 field goal percentage) in 1992 while setting a record 87.5 percent from the three-point line. He also led Team USA in scoring, rebounding, and field goal percentage (81.6 percent) in 1996. The 1992 Dream Team finished 8-0 and averaged a record 117.3 points a game and had a point differential of plus 43.8.

In 1984 as a rookie, Barkley joined aging stars Dr. J, Moses Malone, and Maurice Cheeks in Philadelphia. This was the best season Barkley's team would have in his eight years as a member of the Philadelphia 76ers, winning 58 games and making it all the way to the Eastern Conference Finals where they would eventually lose to the Boston Celtics in five games. With his weight staying under control, he posted his best overall numbers in the 1986 playoffs (in only his second season in the league), averaging **25 points, 15.8 rebounds**, 5.6 assists, and **2.2 steals** per game, on **57.8 percent** shooting. But the 76ers lost in seven games to the Milwaukee Bucks in the semifinals. Before the 1986-87 season, Moses Malone was traded to the Washington Bullets and Dr. J retired at the end of the year. Naturally, Barkley picked up the slack for lack of size and talent up front, and led the league in **rebounding at 14.6** per game, **offensive rebounding at 5.7** per game, and made his first all-star team. But the 76ers lost again in the first round of the playoffs to Milwaukee in five games. The next season (his fourth year in the league), he had his best scoring campaign of his career averaging **28.3 points** per game and making the All-NBA First Team for the first time. But unfortunately, his team failed to make the playoffs for the first time. Barkley would go on to make First Team All-NBA four out of the next five years. He averaged 25.5 points per game and 12 rebounds the next two years, including shooting an eye-popping 60 percent from the field, and finishing second to Magic Johnson in the MVP award in 1990. Many felt Barkley was the MVP that year including "The Sporting News" and "Basketball Weekly," which honored him with the Player of The Year Award. After getting swept in the first round of the playoffs by the New York Knicks in 1989 and losing to the Chicago Bulls in the semifinals the next two seasons, the 76ers finished the 1991-92 campaign with a putrid 35-47 record prompting Barkley to begin trade demands.

Prior to the 1992-93 season, Barkley was traded to the Phoenix Suns for Jeff Hornacek, Tim Perry and Andrew Lang, where he joined a young and competitive Suns team that featured sensational point guard **Kevin Johnson** and "Thunder" Dan Majerle. At that point (Barkley averaged **25.8 points**, **12.5 rebounds**, and **4.1 assists** and won the MVP award), like most great championship teams equipped with two or three superstars, the Suns were now in position to make a title run. With Barkley now on the team, the Western Conference had three *dynamic duals* that featured a superstar point guard and power forward. The Utah Jazz had a seasoned John Stockton and Karl Malone and the Seattle SuperSonics had a *young and on the rise* Gary Payton and Shawn Kemp. While all three duals were devastating combinations, K.J. and Barkley were the most explosive. All three point guards were reliable scorers, excellent passers, and had quick hands on defense. While Malone was dominant using his *legendary* strength and Kemp was the *Explosive Boy Wonder*, Barkley at the time was a little bit of both. Like I mentioned earlier, Barkley was the second best player at that time to Michael Jordan.

To complement "Chuck," Kevin Johnson was also the most explosive point guard in the NBA at that time (By the way, Tim Hardaway was the second - see Iverson's chapter for crossover comparisons). Also, until I saw possibly Stephon Marbury before his career fizzled, and Derrick Rose and Russell Westbrook of today, I always felt K. Johnson had the most explosive first step to the basket that I had ever seen. I mean he destroyed guys off the dribble to where it almost became *second nature* for players to back pedal from the get go, to try and keep K.J. from obliterating the paint. If he had played in this day and age, with no hand-checking fouls and where they stopped whistling moving screens, he might have posted better scoring and assists combinations than any point guard since Nate "Tiny" Archibald. K.J. was the near equivalent to Rose and Westbrook with his explosiveness driving the basket, but had a better mid-range jump shot and passing skills. If he had played in today's game, Johnson could have possibly averaged between 25 to 28 points, and 12 to 14 assists. Despite the lack of three-point range, to complement his deadly drive to the basket, K.J had an *almost automatic* mid-range jump shot that was the best at his position during his time. With all that being said, I do realize, his two so-called weaknesses were the three-point shot and the lack of great defense. But during his prime,

I thought he had the potential to end up as one of the top five, or even top three point guards of all-time. As it turns out, he might barely make anyone's top 10 lists. The two things that went against K.J. were that in terms of age, he started off his career a little late and was hit with the injury bug, where he missed 15 games or more five times in eleven seasons. He also shrank in the clutch during the first two home losses of the 1993 NBA Finals that didn't help his legacy either.

Kevin Johnson actually began his career when he was selected with the 7th pick overall of the 1987 NBA Draft by the Cleveland Cavaliers. At that point, Johnson was already 23 years old (at years end), splitting time on the Cav's bench backing up Mark Price before being traded to the Phoenix Suns his rookie season. Born on March 4th, 1966 in Sacramento, California, Kevin Maurice Johnson attended Sacramento High School before heading to the Bay Area to play college basketball at the University of California (the same school Jason Kidd went to). In his senior year at Cal, he averaged 17.2 points and 5 assists per game before moving on to the NBA. In his first full season with the Suns he went from night to day and averaged an impressive **20.4 points**, **12.2 assists**, **4.2 rebounds** per game, and was named to the All-NBA Second Team for the first of three consecutive seasons. He also was honored with the NBA's Most Improved Player Award. With his elite point guard play in only his second season combined with Tom Chamber's **25.7 points** and 8.4 rebounds, and gunslinger Eddie Johnson's 21 points per game, the Suns shocked a lot of people and finished the regular season with 55 wins, 27 better than the previous year's 28. In the postseason, K.J. continued to impress averaging **23.8 points**, **12.3 assists**, **4.3 rebounds**, and 1.7 steals per game, on .495 percent shooting as the Suns would go deep into the playoffs. After sweeping the Denver Nuggets in the first round and taking care of the Golden State Warriors in the semifinals in five games, the Suns remarkable playoff run came to a screeching halt as they were swept by the Los Angeles Lakers in the Western Conference Finals. The following season, K.J. had another spectacular year averaging **22.5 points** and **11.4 assists** per game, and Chambers had a **career-high 27.2 points** per game on 50 percent shooting. He was also named to his first All-Star team. Phoenix finished third in the division with 54 wins and made another valiant run in the playoffs. In the first two rounds, after defeating the Utah Jazz three games to two and avenging the loss to the Lakers from the previous playoffs in five games, the Suns lost in the conference finals once again, this time to the Trail Blazers.

In the 1990-91 season, K.J. completed a sensational three-year run individually averaging 22.2 points, 10.1 assists, and a career-high 2.1 steals per game, on .516 shooting. After finishing with 55 wins for the second time in three years, the Suns were stunned in the first round when they lost to the Jazz three games to one. Even with Xavier McDaniel, the Suns were beginning a downward trend because Chambers was getting close to the downside of his career and because they didn't have a dominant inside presence. The next season, the Suns remained ultimately consistent finishing with 53 wins, but it wasn't enough to get back to the conference finals. After sweeping the San Antonio Spurs in the first round, the Suns were eliminated handily by the Portland Trail

Blazers in the semifinals in five games. All-star forward and veteran Tom Chambers, although he did not know it yet, was about to play his last season with the Suns in his quest for the most coveted NBA Championship. Barkley, who was also in search of his first NBA championship, looked to be the missing piece for the Suns to become title contenders. As one great power forward was coming into his prime, another was going out. By that point, Chambers had eleven fantastic seasons under his belt averaging 20.6 points and 6.7 rebounds per game, and 21.6 points and 7.1 rebounds in 63 playoff games (His last five seasons, he played in limited minutes as his overall production began to drop significantly). Born on June 21st, 1959 in Ogden, Utah, Thomas Doane Chambers went to Fairview High School in Boulder, Colorado before coming back to his roots to play basketball at the University of Utah. He was actually selected with the 8th pick overall of the 1981 NBA Draft by the San Diego Clippers where he spent his first two seasons. In his next ten seasons, five with the Seattle SuperSonics, and five with the Phoenix Suns, he averaged 20.5 points and 6.6 rebounds per game. Playing during the time of the toughest competition in NBA history from 1986 to 1993, Chambers was the main scoring option who led his teams deep into the playoffs in 1987 with the Sonics and in 1989 and 1990 with Suns. To give you an idea of how good Chambers was at that stage of his career, or for what it is worth, he even had 34 points during the 1987 All-Star game outscoring Jordan, Wilkins, Barkley, and Olajuwon.

In 1993, the Suns finished with the best record in the NBA at 62-20 earning home court advantage throughout the playoffs, and Barkley was rewarded with his first and only regular season MVP trophy. After a first-round scare, falling behind to the Los Angeles Lakers 2-0, the Suns battled back to win the series three games to two. They then went on to beat the San Antonio Spurs in six games in the semifinals and the Seattle SuperSonics in a hard-fought seven games in the Western Conference Finals (In game 7, Barkley had 44 points and 24 rebounds). In the franchise's first NBA Finals since 1976, the Suns gave up home court advantage by dropping the first two games at home (K.J. did come up small in both games at home) before taking two out of three games on the Chicago Bulls home court. Despite the loss in game four, Barkley posted a triple-double of **32 points, 12 rebounds and 10 assists**. We all know what happened after that. Jordan came to the rescue once again and crushed Sir Charles and the Phoenix Suns' dream of their first championship in franchise history.

The Suns won 56 and 59 games the next two seasons but were eliminated in the conference semifinals both years in seven games by Olajuwon and the eventual two-time champion Houston Rockets. The Suns blew a 3-1 lead after winning the first two games in Houston and a 2-0 advantage after winning both games at home. For three consecutive years, the Suns were good enough to contend for a championship but ran into the two best players (Jordan and Olajuwon) in the world in consecutive years. In fairness to Barkley, he was battling injuries in 1994 and 1995. And in 1993, a determined Bulls team took on the challenge despite not having home court advantage for the first time in their three trips to the NBA Finals. Also, the Rockets were hungry for a title and determined to repeat, showing their championship heart coming from behind in tough seven-game series in back-to-back years. Despite the reoccurring back spasms and a torn right quadriceps tendon in the middle of the year, Barkley had his best playoff game of his career, literally toying with the Golden State Warriors, torching the undersized and less athletic defenders for 56 points on seventy-four percent shooting in the clinching game three of the 1994 first-round playoffs in Oakland. Thinking back, this series makes a mockery of what Barkley has said recently when the Warriors upset the number one seed Dallas Mavericks in 2007 with what he called a "midget" lineup that has always tried to beat teams playing small ball.

After a .500 season in 1996, The Suns traded Barkley to the Rockets for Sam Cassell, Robert Horry, Chucky Brown, and Mark Bryant. In what was known as "Clutch City," he joined Olajuwon and Clyde Drexler to form a super-trio that became instant title contenders. The what-looked-to-be *mighty* Houston Rockets went 56-25 and made it to the 1997 Western Conference Finals only to lose to the Utah Jazz in six games. This is where John Stockton showed his true grit and shattered Barkley's dream of a championship by battling all series long and hitting the game-winning shot in game six at home. The very next season, the Rockets collapsed, finishing with a five-hundred record and barely making it to the playoffs, only to lose again in the first round to the Jazz in five games, and in the 1999 lockout shortened season to the Lakers three games to one. Barkley missed 113 games the last four years with the Rockets and played in only 20 games of the 1999-00 season because of a ruptured left quadriceps tendon, which forced him to retire at the end of the year. Barkley will be remembered for two things his final year in the league; his altercation with Shaquille O'Neal where he threw the ball at him after his layup was blocked, and when he came back for one last game at the end of the season after missing four months.

Charles Barkley is one of four players to score 20,000 points, record 10,000 rebounds and 4,000 assists in NBA history. He became the shortest man to win the rebounding title in 1987 and led the league in total offensive rebounds three years in a row from the 1987 season to 1989. He also ranks 2nd all-time in steals at the power forward position behind Karl Malone and first ahead of him in steals per game average. And perhaps his greatest individual feat came in the playoffs, when he posted a tying - third best scoring output in NBA history of 56 points in game 3 of the first round of the 1994 playoffs against the Warriors as stated previously.

In player comparisons:

Ranking Barkley behind Malone was somewhat difficult because Sir Charles was the more versatile offensive player, had the better nose for the ball, was a better offensive rebounder, a slightly better passer, and he had more of a swagger to where he thought he was better than everyone else. Sometimes being dominant with less versatility is better than more versatility and less dominance such as in the Shaq vs. Yao, Nowitzki vs. Gasol, LeBron vs. Carmelo, and Malone vs. Barkley comparisons. Shaquille O'Neal in his prime could spin, back down and dunk on anyone, and had a go-to jump hook that he would often bank in, while Yao could do the same with less quickness and less effectiveness while sometimes having his shot clank off the rim or having it rejected by an even smaller player. But Yao had more range on his jump shot, was likely the better passer, and was by far the better free-throw shooter. In the case of Nowitzki, despite the fact he plays both the power forward and small forward positions, the last few years, fans and media kept saying that Gasol was the best power forward in the league. I never thought that was the case, because even though Gasol is the better rebounder, passer, and defensive player by a slight margin, and has by far more offensive low-post moves, he still lacks the dominant go-to move that most superstars have. Nowitzki (who does have a very good all-around game) has the single most dominant fallaway shot off one foot or two since Larry Bird.

Not to sound contradicting but it appears LeBron does not have a go-to move just yet (prior to the 2012 season) and that is scary for a player as dominant as he is at only the tender age of 26 years old. Being the biggest of LeBron James admirers, maybe that's partly why he hadn't taken his team to the next level? Despite Carmelo Anthony's lightning-quick first step, dominant jab-step that is the best in the NBA today, along with his unlimited shooting range; LeBron is still the better player because he has the better overall game (dominate at his position as a rebounder and a passer) to go along with superior defense. To substitute for a go-to move, LeBron makes up for it with one of the most dominant drives to the basket since Michael Jordan. From a pure physical standpoint, he is simply "Shaq Diesel" from the perimeter. Even though the talent level is much closer with Barkley and Malone, the same theory applies. Malone was almost even with Barkley as a rebounder and passer, and had less offensive moves in his arsenal. On the other side of the ball, he was a slightly better defensive player, where he was selected to the All-Defensive First Team three times. The key was that Malone, with his extraordinary strength, was just as dominant as an inside player in the half court and on the break (often drawing fouls with and-one finishes), as he was from the outside (the second half of his career) having had one of the most deadliest turnaround jump shots in NBA history at the power forward position. During his time, it was almost as automatic as Jordan's fadeaway. In the last 25 years, you would have to rank Malone's turnaround jump shot at the forward position as the third best - *almost* automatic shot behind Bird's and Nowitzki's fallaway.

With all that being said, Barkley was dominating in some years, but just not as dominate on *both ends* of the court as the great power forwards ranked ahead of him. In my opinion, Barkley was the fourth best power forward of all-time. And, if he had been an elite defensive player, he could have been the greatest power forward to ever live. Because during his prime, in terms of skill set and versatility *offensively* for a player his size, he was as close to Michael Jordan as any player in history!

Career Totals

22.1 points, 11.7 rebs, 3.9 assists, 1.5 steals, 0.8 blocks, .541 FG%, .266 3FG%, .735FT%
23,757 points, 12,546 rebounds, 4215 assists, 1648 steals, 888 blocks, 538 threes

John Stockton

(Rank #20)

All-NBA First Team (2-times), All-Star (10-times)

Assist Title (9-times), Steals Title (2-times)

Other Feats: NBA Record 15,806 career assists!

NBA Record 3,265 career steals!

John Stockton was the most prototypical point guard to play in the NBA. Playing all nineteen seasons with the Utah Jazz, Stockton finished his career as the NBA's All-Time leader in assists at 15,806 and steals at 3265, and he led his team to the playoffs every single year. The 10-time All-Star won a record 9 consecutive assists titles while averaging at least 12 assists per game in eight straight seasons. Perhaps the exact make-up of what you would want in a point guard at six-foot-one; Stockton had *superior* court vision and passing skills, with quick hands and feet. His skill set at the point guard position - *combined* with *exquisite* passing during his time was rivaled only by the great Magic Johnson. Former Warriors' great Rick Barry said a few years back on his California Bay Area syndicated radio show, that if he had to build the perfect all-time basketball team he would choose Stockton as his point guard over Magic Johnson. Despite not being a fan favorite, Barry is one of the most knowledgeable basketball analysts ever. Living on the

West Coast and always listening to the late Los Angeles Lakers broadcaster Chick Hearn who usually seemed *unbiased*, always praised and marveled at the talent level of Stockton. He always said nobody in history runs the pick-and-roll better than "Stockton and Malone." Out of the pick-and-roll, Stockton would pull up for a jump shot off the screen or deliver a pass to the "Mailman" on the roll to the basket finishing with a power dunk or layup; and on the pick-and-pop, Malone would shoot his *patented*, almost automatic, turnaround jump shot from almost anywhere on the court.

Although being well known as the NBA's All-time assists and steals leader, Stockton was a reliable scorer able to knock down big shots when they mattered most. He also had extended range as an efficient three-point shooter. Defensively, he was underrated, but had lightning-quick hands and feet allowing him to accumulate a lot of steals, and had great anticipation for drawing offensive fouls. It was no coincidence that he was selected on the All-NBA Defensive Second Team five times. Stockton's greatest attribute, like many of the great superstars of the past, was perhaps his mental and physical toughness. He and teammate Malone set more *brutal* picks than probably anyone in history. Whether setting the *vicious* pick or being on the receiving end *absorbing the blow*, Stockton would often end up spilled on the floor only to hop back up as though it was part of his game routine. It reminded me of the old-timers in baseball when they would fall down after a brush-back pitch, time and time again, only to hop back up and finish the at bat. Ironically this was part of the beauty of setting picks and of the most successful pick-and-roll in NBA history. As a testament to his durability, Stockton missed only 22 games in his entire career with 18 coming in one injury riddled season. Perhaps his greatest feat of all was that he played in all 82 games, 17 out of his 19 seasons in the league - which is outright unheard of! In my eyes, you can make the case that he was the most durable player of all-time not only in basketball but in any sport.

Watching Stockton during the mid-1980s and 1990s with his precision passing was *awe inspiring*. He would often make the perfect pass in the half court by feeding the ball in the post or to a cutter slashing to the basket, or on the fast break with a *slick* half court pass to Malone for an easy slam dunk. I don't think any point guard in history had the wrist and hand strength of Stockton. It seemed like he could make just about any pass with just the flick of his wrist, hands, or even fingertips. The most impressive attribute of Stockton's passing skills was his flip-the-wrist no-look pass that is always shown on NBA Hardwood Classics. He did this on the fast break and in the half court often after penetrating to the basket, and then kicking to a perimeter shooter for an open three-pointer. My favorite Stockton pass of all-time is when he would dribble underneath the basket in to traffic and make a 90 degree flip-the-wrist pass to the top of the key to an often wide open Jeff Hornacek, resulting in a three-point bomb that ignited the raucous Utah crowd.

Only basketball fans that truly love the game and not just for the entertainment, appreciate the Stockton's and Duncan's of the world. He wasn't a fancy dribbler or passer, but Stockton was the most fundamentally sound point guard of all-time. Watching the game within the game, as it is often said in baseball, are what these to superstars are all about. Just like fundamental hitting; being able to work the count, base running; knowing when to take the extra base, and fielding; positioning to the hitters tendencies, the same is to be said about Stockton and Duncan making the perfect pass to right player at the right time, positioning for a rebound, and being *patient* to take the high percentage shot. So while many fans may have viewed Duncan and Stockton as being boring to watch, many of us would beg to differ. The great UCLA Coach John Wooden once said Stockton was the NBA player he enjoyed watching most and the only one he would pay to see. That is one of the greatest compliments any player could ever receive, coming from the greatest coach of all-time. Sorry Red Auerbach and Phil Jackson, but you're ranked 2nd and 3rd respectively. Even Dr. Jack Ramsey called Stockton the ultimate team player and best point guard ever in the *half court*.

John Houston Stockton was born on March 26, 1962 in Spokane, Washington. He went to high school at Gonzaga Preparatory and then to college in his hometown at Gonzaga University. Stockton would have a modest career in college until his senior season when he averaged 20.9 points and 7.2 assists, on .577 percent shooting. Stockton was selected with the 16th pick overall of the 1984 NBA Draft by the Utah Jazz behind fellow Hall of Famers Hakeem Olajuwon, Michael Jordan, and Charles Barkley. When Stockton arrived, his first coach Frank Layden said, "nobody thought he was going to be this good' 'but the thing was, you couldn't measure his heart."

Stockton started his NBA career off slowly by averaging about seven points and seven assists in his first three seasons, while his teams were eliminated in the first round of the playoffs by the Houston Rockets, Dallas Mavericks, and the Golden State Warriors. In the 1987-88 season, Stockton came into his own as an elite point guard, almost doubling his scoring average to 14.7 points per game and by leading the league in assists for the first time at **13.8** per game. In the playoffs, with teammate Karl Malone emerging into a perennial All-Star, the Jazz would defeat the Portland Trail Blazers in the first round in five games before losing a highly competitive seven-game series to the defending champion L.A. Lakers in the semifinals. In game five of that series, Stockton dropped **23 points**, dished out **24 assists**, and had **5 steals** - and in game seven: **29 points, 20 assists, and 5 steals**. The next season, Stockton led the league in **assists at 13.6** and **steals at 3.2** and increased his scoring average to 17.1 points per game. He would go on to win the assists title the next seven years for a record ninth straight, posting incredible averages of **14.5, 14.2, 13.7, 12.0, 12.6, 12.3**, and **11.2**. He also led the league in assists per game in the playoffs, 7 consecutive seasons during that same span and 10 times total during his playoff career. From 1989 through 1991 he peaked as a scorer averaging 17 points per game. In the playoffs, after falling to the seventh seed Warriors, the Jazz faltered again in the first round the following season to the Phoenix Suns before avenging the loss in the first round in 1991. But the Jazz would eventually lose in the semifinals to Clyde Drexler and the Trail Blazers.

In the 1991-92 season, Stockton led the league in steals for the second time as he saw his scoring slide a little due to Jeff Malone asserting himself as the number two scorer behind Karl Malone at 20 points per game. The Jazz would make it all the way to the conference finals where they would lose to the Blazers in six games. After the disappointing loss, Stockton would join Malone during the summer on the 1992 U.S. Olympic "Dream Team" and again four years later in 1996 on "Dream Team II." The following year in 1993, the Jazz would lose in the first round to the Seattle SuperSonics in five games. With Stockton and Malone remaining as consistent as ever, the Jazz ran into a team of destiny in the 1994 Western Conference Finals where they would fall to Hakeem Olajuwon and the Houston Rockets in five games. In only his 11th season in the league in 1994-95, Stockton passed Magic Johnson on the all-time career assists list with 9,921 and surpassed the 1000-assist plateau by seasons end, but the Jazz were once again eliminated in the playoffs by defending champion Houston, this time in the first round three games to two. The following year, Stockton passed Maurice Cheeks on the all-time steals list at 2,310 and completed a string of 9 consecutive assist titles breaking Bob Cousy's mark at 8. But in the playoffs, the Jazz were eliminated by the Seattle SuperSonics in the conference finals in seven games.

Stockton's biggest moment in playoff history came in game 6 of the 1997 Western Conference Finals against the Houston Rockets when he hit a three-pointer over newly acquired Charles Barkley to advance to the NBA Finals. Stockton's career started off slowly but erupted in his fourth season as a full-time starter. For ten years straight, he averaged at least 10 assists and for nine years straight at least 11. He also averaged 15.6 points and 2.6 steals, and shot .524 during that 10-year span. His last six seasons in the league, he averaged 8.2 assists and shot 50 percent from the field.

In player comparisons:

Stockton is the All-time assist and steals leader in NBA history finishing his career with 15,806 and 3265 respectively. He won 9 straight assist titles from 1988 to 1996 breaking Bob Cousy's record at 8. He also has five of the six best assists seasons in NBA history and has recorded 1000 assists or more 7 times. In addition, he also owns the NBA record for assists per game in a single season at 14.5 and the playoff record for assists in a game at 24 tied with Magic Johnson. Throughout his career, he was equally as impressive having recorded **20 assists** or more a *staggering* **38 times** with four coming in the playoffs (to me, that's the near equivalent to Jordan's 39 career 50-point games that included 8 in the playoffs) and led the league in assists per game average 10 times, including 7 straight seasons from 1988-1994. Those mind-boggling statistics alone in the postseason help prove his utter dominance in the most important aspect of the point guard position. His assist per game average in the playoffs is second only to Magic's at 10.1.

So for 19 seasons, Stockton was very good to great overall as a player, and was dominant in one (two, if you count steals) key aspect, passing! And, equally as important, he along with Magic Johnson, Jason Kidd, Steve Nash and Chris Paul, controlled the tempo of the game and made their teammates better than any other point guards in history. Those intangibles alone, along with his *utter dominance* as a passer, are the reasons for ranking Stockton third all-time behind Magic and Oscar Robertson. Like I mention throughout the book, less is sometimes more if a player is great to dominate in *key aspects* of the game vs. being just very good to great as an all-around player. For example, Dennis Rodman is a Hall of Famer because he dominated one of the three major aspects of the game: rebounding - which is actually a part of defense. Whereas there were certainly plenty of players that had by far a more all-around game than Rodman but weren't better - or even Hall of Famers because they didn't dominate in one key aspect of the game. There are loads of examples throughout history, but here are a few: Horace Grant, Chris Webber, Buck Williams, Jerome Kersey, Pau Gasol (although he'll probably make the HOF as an International player), and Tom Chambers. What Rodman did as rebounder, Stockton did as a passer. In addition, Stockton's overall game was very good to great and superb efficiency wise compared to Rodman's. Other than his exceptional ability to move his feet on defense and rebound, he was pretty much one dimensional compared to Stockton. Contrary to what one might believe, Stockton was a great all-around player, he just put more *emphasis* on what mattered most as a point guard, passing! So in conclusion, Rodman was better than most non-Hall of Famers including the players I mentioned above for his dominance in one key area, and Stockton was better than most of the great Hall of Fame point guards including Isiah Thomas for the same reason, and for having an exceptional all-around game (including efficiency statistics), comparable, but slightly ahead of Bob Cousy.

For those who felt Stockton wasn't as good as some of his peers during certain key playoff games, it was very minimal compared to what he accomplished over 19 seasons with his leadership and passing accolades. Stockton played within the makeup of the team while not focusing on individual matchups similar to the way Steve Nash ran the offense in Phoenix. Even though he wasn't as athletic to lets say Isiah Thomas, Kevin Johnson, Gary Payton or Tim Hardaway, as the greatest assist and steals man (in terms of pure numbers) in history, he did his job better than any point guard not named Magic Johnson. He didn't win a championship because the Jazz never had a legitimate third key Hall of Famer. Magic had Worthy, Bird had McHale or Parish, Isiah and Jordan had Rodman. And players like K.J., Payton, and Hardaway fell into the same scenario as Stockton. So to rehash and drive home the point on how great and dominate a player Stockton was, during the nine seasons he led the league in assists between the ages of 26 to 34, he averaged an incomprehensible 13.1 assists per game and 2.6 steals, and shot a proficient/efficient 52.2 percent from the field and 38.8 percent from three-point range. If any point guard averages 13 assists for one season, he would have a *Hall of Fame* type of year - By the way, I'm not necessarily buying into anyone who believes assists were easier to come by during the years Stockton played. During that same span in the playoffs, he averaged 11.8 assists and led the league in assists per game 8 times. Out of all the numbers and accolades in NBA history, Stockton's assists totals the 9 seasons he won the assists titles stand out almost like Jordan's scoring titles with 10. But, on the great John Stockton's resume, what might look equally as impressive, are his 7 seasons of at least 1000 assists!

Career Totals

13.1 points, 10.5 assists, 2.7 rebounds, 2.2 steals, .515 FG%, .826 FT%, .384% 3FG

19,711 points, 15,806 assists, 4051 rebounds, 3265 steals, 845 threes

Steve Nash

(Rank #21)

MVP (2-times), All-NBA First Team (3-times)

Assist Title (5-times), All-Star (8-times)

Free-Throw Shooting Title (2-times)

NBA Record .904 career Free-Throw percentage!

Also featuring: Paul Westphal

    Steve Nash is the consummate team player in NBA history along with Magic Johnson. The two-time MVP and five-time assists leader led a high powered Phoenix Suns offense to five fifty-win seasons (including two sixty-win seasons) deep into the playoffs on multiple occasions during the latter half of his career. As the *ultimate facilitator* and team player, Nash elevated the play of his teammates to extraordinary heights by controlling a fast tempo game and by making the perfect pass. Over the years, out of all the players in history, I don't know if there has ever been a player that made his teammates better than this man - and, if basketball is a team sport, then Nash should rank higher on most people's list for greatest players of all-time! Is there any one player in this era that makes his team better and gets his teammates more involved than Steve Nash? Maybe Jason Kidd, Chris Paul and LeBron James, and that's about it - and of the players of the past, perhaps just Magic Johnson and John Stockton! Winning back-to-back MVP's is proof enough what Nash meant to the Phoenix Suns, the rest of the league, and to the game of basketball. Over the last few years, Nash has been like *fine wine* that gets better with age! He even *peaked* at an age where most stars are on the down side of their career. After reviewing the all-star players of the past, at the age 32, 33, and 34 their overall production begins to drop gradually, and by the age of 35 and 36 their numbers start to fall off the charts. Look at Shaquille O'Neal's career recently that ended abruptly into retirement after playing one season with the Boston Celtics. Even at 37 years old, Nash's numbers had barely dipped. In 2011, he just won his fifth assist title and missed having his fifth season of shooting at least 50% from the field, 40% from the three-point line, and 90% from the free-throw line. Only stars Larry Bird, Dirk Nowitzki, Reggie Miller, and Mark Price are in this exclusive club. But only Nash and Bird have accomplished it multiple times. It is too bad Nash had back problems early on in his career and was a late developer, because if he had played like an MVP earlier on alongside Dirk Nowitzki, he could have possibly won a championship or two.

Aside from being such a great team player, Nash has a flare to getting his team to play at a pace never seen before by igniting the Suns' offense, on the fast break and in a quick tempo half court - launching a barrage of three-point shots. Under former coach Mike D'Antoni's system, Nash as a clever ball handler is able to create ball movement off dribble penetration, off the screen-roll finding cutters to the basket, or by kicking out to the perimeter for wide open jump shots. What's most exciting about Nash is that after a failed possession on a Suns' missed shot and rebound, he *recycles* the offense in a *frenetic*, exciting pace! After getting the ball back and resetting the offense, he keenly looks for the open man awaiting a wide open jump shot or three pointer, or dribble penetrates sucking the defense in often dumping the ball off on a *thread-the-needle* or *wrap-around* pass to a wide open big man for an easy layup, or drives and kicks back out to the open shooter. If the defense rotates fast enough, then the ball keeps moving around the perimeter (or sometimes back and forth between the elbows, interior, or to cutters) until someone becomes open, usually resulting in a three-point bomb to finish off the rally. If Nash gets the ball back during the ball movement, he can shoot it with great proficiency, dribble penetrate or pass to the open shooter to start the cycle all over again. To watch this repeatedly with each 24-second possession is truly a spectacle for NBA fans. Two of my favorite Steve Nash shots are: the underhand scoop shot off glass for a layup on either side of the lane and his fallaway shot over taller players - where he penetrates the lane as though going for a layup, and then all of a sudden dribbles back, pulling the big man away from the basket, before shooting his signature high-arching fallaway shot. Both shots, even under the most difficult of angles always seem to go in. This is all part of the flare Steve Nash gives to basketball fans on a nightly basis.

It is sad that he doesn't have an NBA Championship ring. I think what was lacking from the Phoenix Suns over the years was a consistent defense and the fact that the Suns were not playing with a *completely* healthy Amar'e Stoudemire (the Suns second best player), who had microfracture surgery on his knee to repair damaged cartilage. To this day, Amar'e, now playing for the New York Knicks, does not quite play with the same explosiveness he once had. Before the injury, he looked like he could've ended up being in the class of Tim Duncan and Kevin Garnett, but now that probably won't end up being the case. If he hadn't injured himself in 2005, I believe Phoenix probably would have gotten over the hump and won at least one championship. On the defensive side of the ball, although most people probably view Nash as a defensive liability, you would have to give him a pass because the teams he played for did not *emphasize* defense and did not have good defensive players protecting him the way Tony Parker has today and Magic Johnson of yesterday. At this stage of his career, it would be nice to see Nash finish his career as a Phoenix Sun, but it wouldn't surprise me to see him sign with a team in contention to win a championship - and at the end of this writing, who would have thought he'd end up a Los Angeles Laker.

Stephen John Nash was born on February 7th, 1974 in Johannesburg, South Africa. At St. Michaels University School (private boarding school in British Columbia) in his senior year, he averaged **21.3 points**, **11.2 assists**, and **9.1 rebounds** per game, and led his team to the championship title. He was also named his province's Player of the Year. Nash was not drafted by any college university until Santa Clara's coach Dick Davey requested and saw footage of him. He was then awarded a scholarship to Santa Clara University in Northern California, where he would eventually lead the Broncos to an upset against the #2 seed Arizona Wildcats in the first round of the 1993 NCAA Tournament. He left Santa Clara as the all-time leader in assists and free-throw percentage, and with having won West Coast Conference Player of the year twice. After being selected with the #15 pick overall of the 1996 NBA Draft by the Phoenix Suns, Nash spent the first two years playing behind Kevin Johnson, Sam Cassell and Jason Kidd, before being traded to the Dallas Mavericks before the 1998-99 season. Nash missed the playoffs in his first two seasons with Dallas while averaging similar numbers in the regular season as in his first two in Phoenix. In limited playing time (partly due to reoccurring back injuries), during his first four years in the league, he averaged less than ten points a game. But in the 2000-01 season, Nash and future Superstar Dirk Nowitzki had breakout seasons together averaging 15.6 points and 7.3 assists per game; and 21.8 points and 9.2 rebounds per game respectively. Teamed with Michael Finley and newly acquired Juwan Howard, the Mavericks made the playoffs for the first time since 1990. After beating the Utah Jazz three games to two in the first round, the Mavericks lost in five games in the semifinals to the San Antonio Spurs. In the 2001-02 season, Dallas won fifty games for the second straight year. But in the playoffs, after sweeping the Minnesota Timberwolves in the first round, the Mavericks lost again in the semifinals, this time to the Sacramento Kings in five games. In his sixth year in the league, Nash blossomed into an all-star averaging 17.9 points and 7.7 assists per game in the regular season while making his first All-Star team. He would join potent scorers Nowitzki and Finley to form "The Big Three in Big D." My favorite off the court moment involving the "Big Three" was the cameo in the tunnel of the animated movie Space Jams! Nash would nearly duplicate those numbers the following season while being selected to his second consecutive all-star game.

In 2003, Dallas would go deep into the playoffs for the first time in Nash's fifth year with the team. After finishing tied with the San Antonio Spurs for the best record in the NBA at 60-22, the Mavericks beat the Blazers and the Kings in seven grueling games in the first two rounds of the playoffs before meeting their interstate rival San Antonio in the Western Conference Finals. After a promising victory in game one in San Antonio, Dallas would go on to lose the series in six games with three of the last four losses coming on their own home floor. In Nash's sixth and final season with the team, despite acquisitions to Antawn Jamison and Antoine Walker, the Mavericks finished with only 52 wins (good for fifth place in the Western Conference), but exited in the first round of the playoffs in five games to the Sacramento Kings. With more offensive weapons to spread the ball around, Nash's scoring averaged dropped over three points to 14.5 per game in the regular season while his assists went up a point in a half to 8.8 per game - but he missed making his third consecutive all-star team.

Before the 2004-05 season as a free agent, Nash signed a six-year contract with the Phoenix Suns after Mark Cuban passed on the offer to match the deal. In his first season, Nash help turnaround a 29-win Suns team from the previous year into the best team in the NBA. Under Mike D'Antoni, the Suns finished the regular season with a record of 62-20 and led the league in scoring at 110.4 points per game. With emerging Superstar in Amar'e Stoudemire (before the micro–fracture surgery) and a good supporting cast in Shawn Marion, Joe Johnson and Quentin Richardson, the Suns swept the Memphis Grizzlies in the first round of the playoffs, before dismissing Nash's former team, the Mavericks in six games in the semifinals. In the Western Conference Finals, Nash would face the Spurs for the second time in three years, but this time it was in a Suns uniform. But the Spurs scored 100 points or more in all five games and beat the Suns handily at their own game four games to one. Despite a disappointing ending to a fabulous season, Nash was selected to his first of three consecutive All-NBA First Teams and awarded his first MVP trophy edging out Miami's Shaquille O'Neal. He also led the league in assists for the first time (and first of three consecutive seasons) while shooting a career-high 50 percent from the field.

The following year, the Suns finished with a modest 54-28 record, mostly due to a serious knee injury to Stoudemire and the departures (via trade) of Johnson and Richardson. With Nash leading the way, facilitating to Shawn Marion, Raja Bell, Boris Diaw, Leandro Barbosa and Tim Thomas, the Suns almost equaled their offense output from the year before by leading the league in scoring again at 108.4 points per game. In the playoffs, the Suns seemed destined to win it all for the first time, after a miraculous comeback in the first round against the Los Angeles Lakers. After falling behind three games to one to seventh seeded Los Angeles, the Suns pulled of the impossible by coming from behind to beat a Phil Jackson led team that had never lost a playoff series after leading 3 games to 1. I guess there's a first time for everything! With Kobe Bryant coming off one of the greatest scoring seasons in NBA history at 35.4 points per game, I figured he would have clenched the throat the way Jordan would have and finished off the Suns with a scoring flurry in the final three games. But this is where Kobe could not find the balance between being a great scorer and the ultimate team player. During the second half (mid-third quarter to the end of the game) of game seven, Kobe chose to shoot the ball only twice while simply deferring the offensive scoring load to the rest of his teammates. Even without Kobe's indecision or mind games (so to speak) during the series, and with Phil Jackson's legacy at stake being up 3 games to 1 in the series, I always felt the Suns with their *never say die attitude* were mentally tough enough to pull off the comeback. In that series, Nash showed his *true grit* by bringing the Suns from behind, facilitating with a flurry, finding open shooters at the end of quarters and games, and for fighting to the very end finishing off the last three games with his clutch free-throw shooting.

After watching this series, it reminded me of another terrific Suns guard of the years past that had some of Kobe's scoring ability and some of Nash's shooting and passing ability. Perhaps the Suns best guard since Nash, **Paul Westphal** was one of the great guards of the 1970s. A *dynamic* scorer, Westphal could score from the perimeter with a deadly jump shot and from the interior off dribble penetration. He also incorporated a fadeaway shot that he could shoot off the glass which looked similar to Kobe Bryant's. If you don't believe it, go to You Tube and watch the highlights of the 1976 NBA Finals to get a glimpse of his remarkable fadeaway. Westphal was able to create the most difficult of shots off the dribble, and though right-handed, had somewhat of a similar style to Gail Goodrich who played his best during the 1970s and Manu Ginobili of today. While his fadeaway was his best shot from the perimeter, his best and most famous shots off the dribble were his 360-degree bank shot from eight feet off a plant after driving to his left at full speed, and his absurd reverse layups often resulting in three-point plays. Like Nash, he was also an outstanding passer and an efficient shooter. In addition, although unlike Nash, he had very quick hands and was able to swipe the ball away from opponents and accumulate a lot of steals. Born on November 30th, 1950 in Torrance, California, Paul Douglas Westphal attended Aviation High School in Redondo Beach in southern Cal. In college at USC, as a senior, he averaged 20.3 points and 5.3 rebounds per game, and was named to the All-American Second Team.

Westphal was then selected with the 10th pick overall of the 1972 NBA Draft by the Boston Celtics. In a back-up role, he got off to one of the slowest starts for a perennial All-Star in league history playing in limited minutes. He averaged less than 10 points and three assists his first three seasons in the league and won a championship coming off the bench with the Celtics in 1974. With a championship already under his belt, Westphal was traded to the Phoenix Suns before the 1975-76 season. That year, the *slick* shooting guard blossomed into one of the best guards in the NBA averaging 20.5 points, 5.4 assists, and an astounding 2.6 steals per game. His uncanny ability to steal the ball from an opposing player was *magnified* more than ever in game 5 of the 1976 NBA Finals. With the series tied at two games apiece, Westphal had two key steals, one at the end of regulation against Jo Jo White, and another at the end of double-overtime against John

Havlicek to help keep the game extended. He also had two big shots down the stretch in triple-overtime to cut the lead to 128-126, but unfortunately the Suns lost the game and eventually the series. During the playoffs, he averaged 21.1 points and 5.1 assists, and led the Suns to their first ever NBA Finals appearance.

In his second season with Phoenix, Westphal averaged a **career-high 25.2 points** per game on 51 percent shooting, and was named to the All-Star team for the first of five consecutive seasons. He was also named to the All-NBA First Team for the first of three times in a four-year span. But the Suns took a step back and missed the playoffs entirely. Phoenix had actually overachieved the previous year when they finished at 42-40 and made it all the way to the Finals. The second best player on the team was eighteen point scorer Alvan Adams. In his five seasons with the Suns, Westphal averaged 22.5 points, 5.6 assists, and 1.8 steals per game, and shot .518 from the field. Prior to the next season, the Phoenix Suns selected Walter Davis with the 5th pick overall of the 1977 NBA Draft. At that point, the Suns instantly had two great scorers, especially with Davis having his best scoring season of his career as a rookie averaging 24.2 points per game. After losing in the first round of the playoffs to the Milwaukee Bucks, the Suns won 50 games the following year and made a deep run into the postseason. With the *dynamic dual* of Westphal and Davis, the Suns defeated the Portland Trail Blazers two games to one and the Kansas City Kings in five games to reach the Western Conference Finals where they would lose a heartbreaking seven-game series to the eventual champion Seattle SuperSonics.

After Nash and the Suns defeated the Lakers, they had to face the other L.A. team in the next round, and were pushed to the limit once again by a formidable Clippers team that included 25-point scorer Elton Brand, Sam Cassell, Corey Maggette, Cuttino Mobley and Kris Kaman. In the Western Conference Finals, the Suns faced another familiar foe in the Dallas Mavericks. With Dirk Nowitzki, Jason Terry, Jerry Stackhouse, and Devin Harris providing the scoring punch and Eric Dampier and Josh Howard anchoring the defense, the Mavericks avenged the loss to the Suns from the previous year in the semifinals by winning the series in six games. With or without Joe Johnson, I believe that if twenty-three-year-old Amar'e Stoudemire never injured his knee after coming off a career best 26 points per game in 2005, the nucleus of Amar'e and Nash would have been good enough to defeat the Mavericks that season and San Antonio the next. Nash led the league in assists for the second consecutive year and was awarded his second straight MVP trophy.

Even though currently Stoudemire is putting up similar numbers today as he did before the injury, he still doesn't have the explosiveness he once had. He can still dominate finesse players such as Pau Gasol and perhaps Dirk Nowitzki, by facing and knocking down his patented mid-range jump shot or by taking his man off the dribble like a small forward for an easy layup or dunk. But the difference between "Baby Shaq," (his nickname before the injury) before the injury vs. today, is that within three feet of the basket, he would elevate not only over players such as Gasol and Yao Ming, he would *man-handle* and *dwarf opponents* soaring high above the rim throwing down a ferocious dunk in the face of any player in the league today, similar to the way Blake Griffin has done the last couple of years. If Stoudemire's rebounding and shot blocking keeps improving playing for the New York Knicks, he still has an outside chance to finish as one of the great power forwards of all-time. But for now, I left him off the projected player rankings, because for whatever reason (perhaps because he's not the explosive player he once was), I sense a downward trend in his career which will definitely make it interesting to see how his future unfolds.

In the 2006-07 campaign, the Suns defeated the Lakers once again in the first round of the playoffs, this time four games to one, while Nash had one of the best regular seasons of his career averaging **18.6 points** and a **career-high 11.6 assists** per game but finished second in the MVP voting to Nowitzki.

Over the years, even though Nash got outplayed by Mike Bibby in the 2002 and 2004 playoffs - and by Tony Parker in 2007 and the year after in 2008 for that matter, he still had great playoff performances. In 2003, he took the Dallas Mavericks to the Western Conference Finals - by avenging the loss from the year before to Sacramento, dismissing the Kings in seven games. In 2005, his first year with Phoenix, he took the Suns to the Western Conference Finals only to lose to an experienced San Antonio Spurs team. In 2006, without Amar'e Stoudemire (out for the entire playoffs due to injury), Nash led Phoenix to the Western Conference Finals before losing to an up-and-coming Mavericks team.

Nash could have made it to the NBA Finals throughout his career if it weren't for a few mishaps; In 2006, if Nash had played with an explosive Amar'e (If Baby Shaq never got injured) in their second year together, the Suns could have been good enough to get pass Dallas and the Spurs the following seasons. Amar'e went from being a potential superstar to just an all-star after the injury. During the game 3 (the swing game) semifinals of the 2007 playoffs against the Spurs, Amar'e and Boris Diaw got ejected for leaving the bench and received one game suspensions, therefore changing the entire complexion of the series. In 2008, Tim Duncan made an improbable three-pointer in game 1 that crushed the Suns spirit, after Phoenix felt they had as good a chance as any to take the first game of the Western Conference Finals and eventually dethrone the defending champs. In a heartbreaking defeat in 2010 against the Lakers, the Suns left Ron Artest wide open for a three pointer in game 5 at home that would have given them a 3-2 series lead. Coming so close, this could have been Nash's last chance to make it to the NBA Finals. Four out of the last six years, the Phoenix Suns were good enough to play for an NBA Championship and it never transpired. I believe the Suns would have overcome all these scenarios, if Baby Shaq (Amar'e averaged 26 points a game at 22 years old) had never suffered a major knee injury.

Objectively speaking, Steve Nash led the NBA in assists five times, had at least 20 assists in a game 9 times (which ranks third all-time behind Stockton and Magic), is shooting more efficiently than any player in history from the field, three-point line and free-throw line, and is playing better than any point guard in history over 35 years of age. He also became, only the third point guard in NBA history to win the MVP award behind Magic Johnson and Bob Cousy and is one of nine players to win the award twice (He and Magic are also the only point guards to win the award twice). Ultimately, out of all the great players in history, the numbers don't begin to tell the story of the "greatness" of Steve Nash as a team leader and how he elevated the level of play of his teammates (stars and non-stars) throughout his playing career as I have described throughout the chapter. And that's why in this book he warrants such a high ranking as the 21st greatest basketball player of all-time!

Career Totals

14.4 points, 8.5 assists, 3.0 rebounds, 0.7 steals, .491 FG%, .904 FT%, .428 3FG%

17,285 points, 10,249 assists, 3613 rebounds, 892 steals, 1677 threes

Kevin Garnett

(Rank #22)

MVP (1-time), Defensive Player of The Year (1-time)

All-NBA First Team (4-times), All-Defensive First Team (9-times)

Rebounding Title (4-times), NBA Championships (1), All-Star (15-times)

Also featuring: Chris Webber

Kevin Garnett is one of the greatest power forwards of all-time. For most of his career playing for the Minnesota Timberwolves, Garnett accomplished almost everything you could ask for in a player including winning the NBA MVP Award in 2004, and later the Defensive Player of the Year award in 2008. He also won four consecutive rebounding titles beginning in 2004 on through to his final season in 2007 with the franchise. It wasn't until the following year, his first season with the Boston Celtics teamed with Ray Allen and Paul Pierce, he would finally capture the most coveted NBA Championship that had eluded him his entire career. A ferocious defender with a long wing span, tremendous agility (for a near 7-footer) and outstanding leaping ability, Garnett *epitomizes* what the modern-day great interior offensive/defensive player is all about (tall, slender and athletically built, and could shoot deep from the perimeter). But his greatest quality of all was seen on a nightly basis, where you were able to see his determination to play physical on both ends of the court and compete at all cost. With *eyes of a predator* staring down his prey, his intensity on the court was *unparalleled*. Garnett was the heart and soul of the 2008 Boston Celtics Championship team that did whatever it took to win including sacrificing his offense game for the betterment of the team. With a near flawless all-around game, Garnett was an *efficient* scorer, a *superior* rebounder and shot blocker, and was a *terrific* passer. To some, probably closer to six-feet-eleven but acknowledged by most as a seven-footer just like his peer and chief rival Tim Duncan, both were a forward in a centers body. And that's what made Garnett special during his prime to go along with having the athleticism, speed and mobility of a smaller player, and the size and strength of a power forward.

In player comparisons:

In fact, he was often seen guarding shooting guards at one time or another. Being very skilled offensively as well, "The Big Ticket" (his nickname that Wolves fans paid to see), had a variety of moves out of the low post and high post, which included a jump hook and fallaway shot that he could shoot as far out as eighteen feet. During his prime, his spin move to create space for his patented fallaway reminded me of Kobe Bryant's fadeaway shot but for a big man. This was the most impressive part of Garnett's offensive arsenal that I felt was more superior to any of Tim Duncan's one single move. However, he didn't use this weapon often enough and particularly in clutch situations (until his recent playing days). Also, if he had incorporated a more dominant inside game, there would have been a debate on who the greatest power forward of all-time was. While Garnett could match Duncan on the defensive end with his rebounding and shot blocking, he could also do one better and close out on shooters while guarding the perimeter much more effectively. As a testament to his greatness on the defensive end of the court, Garnett was selected to an NBA record tying 9th All-NBA Defensive First Team in 2011.

Aside from his superlative defensive skills, what sets him apart from most forwards was his passing ability. Garnett was one of the most unselfish players and splendid passers out of the pivot. He currently averages four assists for his career down from five before he came to the Celtics. Criticism of him most of his career, was that he was to passive offensively, giving up the ball to open players, instead of shooting in clutch situations and at the end of close games. I do agree to some extent to where I wish Garnett had taken more big shots early on in his career and played more in the low post by backing down his man and pounding it inside the paint. I think this was the main difference between Garnett's game and Duncan's. Although you could call it a draw on the defensive end, Duncan kept his feet more grounded to block shots and had slightly better overall timing. But, Garnett was easily the better perimeter defender - and, if he had had more team success early on in his career and won a couple more championships, he would have *certainly* been ranked even higher on most people's list for greatest power forwards of all-time.

Kevin Maurice Garnett was born on May 19th, 1976 in Greenville, South Carolina and attended Maudlin High School his first three years before transferring to the Farragut Career Academy in Chicago Illinois for his senior year. Due to a break out with the law involving lynching between races in which he was not directly involved, he decided it was safest to transfer schools. As a senior, Garnett averaged **25.2 points**, **17.9 rebounds**, **6.7 assists**, and **6.6 blocks** per game - on **67 percent** shooting and led the team to a 28-2 record. He also was named Mr. Basketball for the State of Illinois and National High School Player of the Year by USA Today. After foregoing college, Garnett was then selected with the 5th pick overall of the 1995 NBA Draft by the Minnesota Timberwolves and was the first player drafted out of high school since Moses Malone in 1975. This helped pave the way for other prep-to-pro *phenoms*, until recently when the league mandated for a player to attend at least one year of college (or play some type of organized ball up to the age of 19) before becoming eligible for the NBA Draft. In his rookie season, Garnett averaged only twenty-eight minutes because he began the season coming off the bench until Flip Saunders took over as head coach. Before the 1996-97 season, the Minnesota Timberwolves had made a draft-day trade for Stephon Marbury out of Georgia Tech at #4 overall of the 1996 NBA Draft. At the time, this looked to be one of the two key pieces in building a strong nucleus for years to come. In his sophomore season, Garnett increased his scoring average seven points to 17 points per game and made his first All-Star team along with teammate Tom Gugliotta who was also a first time selectee. He also showed his potential as a defensive specialist by blocking 8 shots in a game twice.

The following season, Garnett continued to improve at a rapid pace averaging 18.5 points, 9.6 rebounds, 4.2 assists per game - and had a career-high 1.7 steals, but many wondered if the athletic and talented Garnett could co-exist with the young and explosive Stephon Marbury who seemed to always want the ball in his hands. This sign of selfishness or an apparent lack of a positive attitude so-to-speak, led to a fall-out with management on disputed issues in which Marbury had with coaches regarding his role in the offense. During the lockout shortened season after demanding to be traded, Minnesota obliged and dealt Marbury to the New Jersey Nets in a three-way trade that sent Terrell Brandon from Milwaukee to Minnesota and Sam Cassell from New Jersey to Milwaukee. At the time, I thought the Timberwolves were one of the teams of the future that would battle Shaquille O'Neal and Kobe Bryant for the Western Conference crown for years to come. Unfortunately for Marbury, he battled off-the-court issues and became a head case for the other teams the rest of his career. It was really too bad, because I felt Marbury was the second coming of Allen Iverson, but in the Western Conference. It gave you goose bumps every time Marbury exploded to the basket or stopped on a dime in the same way it does watching Monte Ellis, Derrick Rose, and Russell Westbrook of today. In his fourth season, Garnett took his game to new heights when he averaged **22 points**, **11.8 rebounds**, and **5 assists** per game. During an eight-year span beginning in the 1999-00 season, Garnett averaged **22.5 points**, **12.7 rebounds**, and a **whopping 5 assists** per game.

But in the playoffs, from 1997 through 2003, the Timberwolves were ousted in the first round in a three-game sweep to the Houston Rockets, five games to the Seattle SuperSonics and three games to one by the San Antonio Spurs. In the second half of that seven-year span, the Timberwolves were eliminated three games to one by the Portland Trail Blazers and by those same Spurs, and then swept by the Dallas Mavericks before losing in six games to the Los Angeles Lakers in the league's first seven-game format. In 2003, Garnett averaged a **career-high 6 assists** and would collect a thousand rebounds for the first of three consecutive seasons. In retrospect, because Garnett signed a massive and unprecedented 126 million dollar contract before the new collective bargaining agreement in 1999, didn't allow Minnesota much leeway to sign other big name players or let alone retain their own. His contract, to the highest degree was similar to the mammoth contract Kobe Bryant signed before the current CBA expired in 2011.

In the 2003-04 season, Garnett had a career year averaging **24.2 points**, **13.9 rebounds** and **2.2 blocks** per game, and won the NBA MVP award as the Timberwolves finished with a franchise record of 58 wins and the number one seed in the Western Conference. With the acquisitions of Latrell Sprewell and Sam Cassell before the season, Garnett was now surrounded with a formidable supporting cast to help the Timberwolves go deep into the playoffs for the first time. After defeating the Denver Nuggets in five games in the first round and the star-studded Sacramento Kings in seven games in the semifinals, the Timberwolves met their fate in the conference finals against the Los Angeles Lakers. In the prior round, the conference semifinals not only paired two great teams in the Timberwolves and the Kings (who were title contenders at that time), but also two of the great power forwards of this generation in Garnett and **Chris Webber**.

In other player comparisons:

At that time, it was obvious that Tim Duncan was the best power forward in the game having won two MVP awards back-to-back, with Garnett closing the gap after he won the award in 2004. But what was equally intriguing to me was which player was the better passer out of Duncan, Garnett, and Webber? While Duncan had the better inside game and was about even with Garnett as a rebounder and shot blocker, Webber had the best pure jump shot (that developed over time) and was perhaps the best passer out of the three. I know there were so many other great passing power forwards including Charles Barkley and Karl Malone of the past, but Webber was so good it was almost mind-boggling watching him facilitate with Vlade Divac, Doug Christie, Peja Stojakavic and Mike Bibby. Even though the assists numbers between Garnett and Webber were really close, I would have to give the edge to Webber as the best passing power forward of all-time. I don't like to make this distinction to a player that wouldn't make anyone's top 50 but he was that good. It's kind of similar to Vlade Divac being the best passing center that I have ever witnessed and not making the top 50 either. Though, perhaps Arvydas Sabonis was better back in his prime playing over in Europe. Like I have mentioned in the LeBron James vs. Larry Bird comparisons, a lot of the great power forwards could make the simple fundamental bounce pass, the thread-the-needle pass, and the behind-the-back pass and no-look pass. But Webber like Bird - and Divac for that matter could make the most difficult of passes on a consistent basis. It was too bad; Webber faced multiple injuries throughout his career, because I believe he would have squeaked into the Hall of Fame. But what was most disappointing other than never winning a championship, was that Webber never maximized his potential as a player. Either, he wasn't the player we all thought he was, or he just didn't work hard enough on his weakness as an inside player on both ends of the floor. I know he had a little jump hook in the lane, but that was about it. Or maybe he wasn't talented enough to have played down on the block the way Tim Duncan did and develop an assortment of inside moves. Or maybe he was before he began having all the injuries? In the latter half of his career, he relied on step-back jumpers or wide open face-up jump shots, which in fairness, did fit the Kings offense to perfection. He was also a little down on his free-throw shooting and didn't use enough aggression on the defensive end for rebounding and shot blocking. "I always like to say, man what could have been for Chris Webber!"

Born on March 1st, 1973 in Detroit, Michigan, Mayce Edward Christopher Webber III attended Detroit Country Day School where he was the highest recruited high school player since Magic Johnson. In his senior year, he averaged 29.4 points and 13 rebounds per game, and led the team to its third MHSAA State championship. He was also named Michigan's Mr. Basketball and National High School Player of the Year. At the University of Michigan he joined a group of players in Jalen Rose, Juwan Howard, Jimmie King and Ray Jackson that became known as the "Fab Five." In two stellar years, he averaged 17.4 points, 10 rebounds and 2.4 assists per game, on 59 percent shooting - and led the Wolverines to NCAA Championship game in 1992 and 1993 where they would lose to Duke and North Carolina. At that point in his career, he was one of the most coveted high school and college players in history with great potential and expectations entering the draft. Webber was selected with the first pick overall of the 1993 NBA Draft by the Orlando Magic becoming the first sophomore since Magic to be selected at number one.

He was then immediately traded to the Golden State Warriors for Anfernee Hardaway and three future first-round draft picks. In only one season with the Warriors he averaged 17.5 points and 9.1 rebounds per game, and won the 1993-94 NBA Rookie of the Year Award. With all the hype surrounding him, in only three playoff games, he averaged 15.7 points, 8.7 rebounds and 9 assists, on 55 percent shooting. I mean nine assists in any game for a power forward is outstanding enough - LeBron James like. Up to that point, living in the Bay Area at the time, I and the rest of the fans were looking ahead to the bright future of Chris Webber as a member of the Golden State Warriors. But with continuing conflicts throughout the year with Coach Don Nelson, Webber exercised his one-year escape clause in his contract and agreed to a sign-and-trade with the Washington Bullets that brought the Warriors Tom Gugliotta and three first-round draft picks. Now joined with college teammate and good friend Juwan Howard, the Bullets now bolstered one of the most talented frontcourts in the league. With injuries beginning to mount in his first four seasons with the Bullets, Webber averaged a steady 20.9 points, 9.7 rebounds, 4.4 assists, 1.7 blocks and 1.6 steals per game - on 50 percent shooting. Unfortunately, the Bullets missed the playoffs his first two seasons. In his third season, for the first time in nine years, the Bullets made the playoffs but were swept by Michael Jordan and the eventually champion Chicago Bulls in the first round.

It wasn't until he played for the Sacramento Kings did he make a name for himself (in terms of his stellar play and greatness as a player during a six-year period). In six glorified years despite not winning the NBA Championship even though they should have eventually in 2002 (where in game six of the conference finals in Los Angeles at least seven horrendous calls went against the Kings), Webber averaged **23 points**, **10.5 rebounds**, **4.7 assists**, **1.5 steals**, and **1.4 blocks** per game, on 47 percent shooting. He also led the Kings to 55, 61, 59, and 55 wins from 2001 to 2004 and to the playoffs in all six seasons with the franchise. In the postseason, he averaged similar numbers as the regular season. In 1999 and 2000, the Kings (Vernon Maxwell in the first year) with Webber, Jason Williams, Vlade Divac, Peja Stojakovic, Nick Anderson, and John Barry - were feisty competitors pushing both playoff teams to decisive game fives. Throughout the years, at one time or another, the Warriors and the Kings were extremely exciting to watch. And, during this six-year span, they were most likely the best passing and most exciting team in the NBA. In 2001, with Bobby Jackson aboard, the Kings defeated the Phoenix Suns in the first round before getting swept by the Lakers in the semifinals. In their best season in 2002 after acquiring Mike Bibby, Sacramento defeated the Utah Jazz and Dallas Mavericks in the first two rounds before losing to the Lakers for the third straight year, this time in the Western Conference Finals in seven games. Despite the miraculous three-pointer by Robert Horry in the closing seconds of game four in Los Angeles, many people even today, felt the Kings were robbed of a chance to make it to the NBA Finals. Among other calls that went against the Kings including the elbow by Kobe Bryant to the face of Mike Bibby near the end of the game, on at least three occasions, Webber was hammered by Shaq and the gang while shooting layups in the low post, and the calls were never made. In 2003 and 2004, the Kings beat the Jazz and Mavericks in the first round in five games but were eliminated in the semifinals by the Mavericks and the Timberwolves in heartbreaking seven-game series. For his career, Webber only won one rebounding title in the lockout shortened season in 1998-99 and was named to his only All-NBA First Team. He was also a five-time All-Star.

With extra motivation to avenge the loss to the Lakers from the previous year's playoffs, the Timberwolves seemed up to the daunting task despite the injuries to Sam Cassell and Troy Hudson. But the Lakers behind their cast of future Hall of Famers; Shaq, Kobe, Karl Malone and Gary Payton, proved to be way too much for the injured and undermanned Timberwolves to overcome. In the next three seasons, Garnett would win the rebounding title three more times and for the fourth straight season, but the Timberwolves never made it back to the playoffs. In the off-season prior to the 2008 season, Garnett was traded to Boston for Al Jefferson, Ryan Gomes, Sebastian Telfair,

Gerald Green, Theo Ratliff and cash considerations. At the time, he had the longest current tenure with one team in the league. It was extremely difficult for Garnett to leave the Minnesota Timberwolves because of his loyalty to the fans and to the franchise. A lot of players of today feel the same way about leaving their respective teams via free agency including Dirk Nowitzki and Steve Nash prior to his recent decision on a sign-and-trade to Los Angeles. Fortunately for Dirk, who decided to stay with his team, won the championship ironically over LeBron James who chose to leave his team for another team that included two other star players.

When Garnett came over from the Timberwolves for the 2007-08 season, the Celtics won the championship almost instantly when he teamed with Paul Pierce and Ray Allen to form one of the greatest trios in NBA history. Doc Rivers was also a huge part of the Celtics' success. He implemented a defense first mentality to go with a "don't be a hero on offense" state of mind. That meant for everyone to play as a team at all times, on both ends of the floor, and to create ball movement offensively until someone becomes open to shoot. "Doc wanted no individuals to try and take over and become the star of the team." Also on the defensive end, Garnett was the anchor in the middle of that dominate defense which led the NBA in defensive field goal percentage and points allowed. At the time, many experts felt that it would have taken more than a year for the Celtics to win a championship, but the *Big Three* already in their thirties, were determined to win now and bring back the glory years of the Boston Celtics. Joining each other at a late age and not sooner, motivated them, knowing that they had just a couple of years left in their primes to capture the ultimate prize. I predicted that the Celtics would win the championship their first year with Pierce, Allen, and Garnett playing together, and that they would win at least two championships with this trio, including in 2010 against the Los Angeles Lakers. Unfortunately, I was only half right as the Celtics were only able to win one championship in the last four years. If Garnett, Pierce, and Allen had gotten together earlier in their primes, they probably would have won at least two or three championships or more.

In player comparisons:

In closing, I would have to put Garnett slightly ahead of Nowitzki in the elite rankings of all-time because of his all-around game - and slightly behind Barkley, Malone, and Bob Pettit for the direct opposite reason. Even though Nowitzki was the more dominant player (in terms of scoring) with his unstoppable fallaway shot, Garnett was the more dominant player from the defensive aspect of the game and was the better all-around player even though Dirk was a pretty darn good an all-around player himself. If Garnett had played more in the low-block with a more effective inside game similar to Tim Duncan and had been more assertive on offense, or let's say selfish in a good way particularly at the end of games, perhaps we would be talking about not only Duncan as the greatest power forward of all-time, but Garnett too.

As a testament to his defensive accolades, Kevin Garnett along with Michael Jordan, Gary Payton and Kobe Bryant are the only players in NBA history to be named to 9 All-Defensive First Team selections in their career. But in comparisons to Barkley, Malone, and Pettit, he was *less dominate* on the offensive end, but could certainly match his peers from an all-around perspective. In due part to his longevity and for coming into the league out of high school, Garnett has been able to accumulate some *worldly* numbers, including becoming only the third man in NBA history behind Kareem and K. Malone to amass 20,000 points, 10,000 rebounds and 5,000 assists. If Garnett can extend his career a few more years and be reasonably productive, he can only move up in the elite rankings of all-time. And no matter how the rest of his career unfolds, Garnett will go down as either the best or second best *two-way* offensive/defensive power forward of all-time.

Career Totals

19.1 points, 10.5 rebounds, 3.9 assists, 1.5 blocks, 1.3 steals, .498 FG%, .790 FT%

25,274 points, 13,843 rebounds, 5224 assists, 1970 blocks, 1742 steals

Dirk Nowitzki

(Rank #23)

MVP (1-time), Finals MVP (1-time), All-Star (11-times)

All-NBA First Team (4-times), NBA Championships (1)

NBA Record: 24 of 24 free-throw % without a miss in a playoff game!

Also featuring: Jack Sikma & Dan Issel

Dirk Nowitzki of the Dallas Mavericks is arguably the greatest shooting big man since Larry Bird. He has the same deadly fallaway shot that Bird had except he doesn't release the ball as way far behind his head. Dirk makes up for it with an *unconventional* one-of-a-kind, one-foot fallaway shot that no one in league history has ever used on a regular basis as its main weapon. Even though he has used the shot in recent years, he perfected it in the 2010-11 season and during the playoffs when he led the Dallas Mavericks to the 2011 NBA Championship. That's why LeBron James said during the NBA Finals that Nowitzki's fallaway is the single greatest shot next to Kareem's Sky-hook. I was beginning to believe that at least for this year, after watching him *mesmerize* all playoffs long; Dirk was hitting shot after shot. He reminded me of someone named Jordan. He was unstoppable especially against the Los Angeles Lakers and Oklahoma City Thunder when he averaged 28 points on 48 percent shooting, 46 percent from three-point range, and an astonishing 94 percent from the free-throw line. Honestly, since watching basketball the last four decades, I have never seen a shooting performance this efficient. Dirk was incredible, especially against the Thunder when he scored 48 points on 80 percent shooting and set an NBA record 24 for 24 from the free-throw line. You would have to say he is the greatest scorer/shooter ever since Larry Bird. Dirk has replaced Kobe Bryant as the best closer in the Western Conference, if not in all of basketball. My best new era rankings for Best Clutch Shooters over this past *decade* are: Chauncey Billups, Jason Terry, Mike Bibby, Ray Allen, Paul Pierce, Dirk, Dwyane Wade, Derek Fisher, and Kobe.

The knock on Nowitzki his entire career until 2011, was that he couldn't win the big one and that he choked in the clutch, especially in the NBA Finals in 2006. In player comparisons in a recent article for Espn.com by Alok Pattani in July of 2011 showed that Bryant for example is 7 of 25 for 28 percent from the field in very close playoff games with a few seconds on the clock, lagging behind several other players, while Jordan was an impressive 9 of 18 for 50 percent. Dirk is currently 5 of 13 for 38 percent (at the time of this writing), not too shabby. So for all those writers, especially those with books out who say Dirk didn't come through in big games were only partially right, particularly when he had four consecutive bad playoff games to finish the 2006 NBA Finals and the following year when he won the 2007 MVP award but lost in the first round to the Golden State Warriors. Timing is everything, and in the eyes of many, without winning a championship, everything is either dismissed or overlooked - even past great performances such as in the 2006 playoffs, when Nowitzki torched the San Antonio Spurs and Phoenix Suns but ended up losing in the Finals to the Miami Heat. As bad as most people think LeBron James played in the 2011 Finals, it made everybody forget how great he was closing out games against Boston and Chicago. Of course, if he continues to struggle in future NBA Finals, his legacy will most definitely become tainted. LeBron is also decent in these clutch situations going 8 of 20 for 40 percent (also at the time of this writing) when taking shots in the final seconds of playoff games. Nowitzki has always been one of the great scorers in this era right up there with Kobe Bryant. I have always said recently that out of the Western Conference teams, with the game on the line in the fourth quarter, I would want Dirk, Kobe, or Jet Terry to take the last shot.

Everybody thinks Nowitzki is a great player now that he won a championship. Dirk Nowitzki has always been a great player. He is currently ranks 15th on the all-time player efficiency rating by Espn.com. Magic Johnson and John Barry said during the 2011 NBA Finals, "that if Nowitzki wins a championship this year, it would not make him a better basketball player." A person's talent and skill doesn't change because you win a title. I believe it can only give a player more confidence going forward. There are many athletes who just win one championship and never win another (partly because of timing, injuries, or for the lack of a sufficient supporting cast) and there are some that take advantage of that confidence and win multiple. Magic did say though, "Nowitzki would be in a special group, a VIP group!" I totally agree. Just like I said in the beginning of the book, winning championships is not the only thing that determines player greatness. Win or lose, it's your individual contributions to the team's success that define a player - the more impact tangibly as well as intangibly. For example, Derek Fisher with 5 championships, who shoots 40 percent or less for his career (worst among active guards, right up there with Jason Kidd) and Robert Horry, with 7 championships (who could rebound and defend ok, but was known for hitting wide open jump shots), were both great clutch shooters for the Rockets, Spurs, and Lakers but overall, were just two above average players that played with the three best players outside of Michael Jordan in the past 30 years. So if you were ranking them in this book or any other listed ranking, they shouldn't make anyone's top 100. So by a gigantic margin, you would have to rank Karl Malone (second all-time leading scorer to Kareem) with 0 championships over Robert Horry with 7, and John Stockton (the all-time assists leader and steals leader) with 0 championships over Derek Fisher with 5. Without Malone and Stockton the Jazz would have never even made the playoffs all those years let alone contend for a title.

Dirk Werner Nowitzki was born on June 19th, 1978 in Wurzburg, Germany. He was drafted 9th overall by the Milwaukee Bucks in the 1998 NBA Draft and was immediately traded to Dallas where he has played his entire career. Dirk grew up playing handball and tennis but switched to basketball because he was tired of being labeled a freak for his height. Nowitzki played in Germany from 1994 to 1998 DJK Wurzburg before heading to the NBA. Dirk won the Euroscar Player of the Year Award 6 times and was the first European to win the MVP award in the NBA but not the first foreign born player. That honor goes to Hakeem Olajuwon followed there after by Tim Duncan.

Two other players (power forward/center) that kind of reminded me of Nowitzki were **Jack Sikma** and **Dan Issel**, but with a little less speed and with not as pure of a shooting stroke. Sikma even possessed an efficient three-point shot his final three years in the league. Like Nowitzki, Sikma and Issel were outstanding shooters and rebounders, as well as good passers. Sikma was only in his second season in the league playing alongside Dennis Johnson when the Seattle SuperSonics won the 1979 NBA Championship. In fact, the bulk of his playoff success came in his first three seasons with the Sonics, when he came ever so close to winning the title in his rookie year. After defeating the Los Angeles Lakers, Portland Trail Blazers, and Denver Nuggets in the Western Conference, the Sonics lost to Elvin Hayes, Wes Unseld, and the Washington Bullets in a heartbreaking seven-game series. For eight straight seasons from 1979 to 1986, Sikma was ultimately consistent averaging 17.6 points and 11.1 rebounds per game, and was named to the All-Star team seven consecutive seasons. In his five playoff seasons with the Milwaukee Bucks from 1987 to 1991, he lost to Larry Bird's Celtics in seven games, Dominique Wilkin's Hawks three games to two, Isiah Thomas' Pistons in a four-game sweep, Michael Jordan's Bulls three games to one, and Charles Barkley's 76ers team in a three-game sweep. So every year each team's biggest star was superior to Milwaukee's best player Sydney Moncrief! What was most interesting in Jack Sikma's career, was in his last three seasons in the league with the Bucks, he developed a formidable three-point shot, that I wish he had early on in his career. After making 7 three-point shots during his first eleven seasons, he made 196 in his last three. If he had developed the shot early in his career, maybe he would have been an even better scorer, in the class of Nowitzki or Issel.

In terms of his ability to score from the outside with a smooth shooting stroke within the three-point arc, and the *awkward* ability to drive to the basket, Dan Issel ("The Horse") was the Dirk Nowitzki of the ABA. Born on October 25, 1948 in Batavia, Illinois, Daniel Paul Issel was a legend even before his professional days, playing basketball at the University of Kentucky where he averaged 25.8 points and 13 rebounds per game. In his senior year, he averaged an astounding 33.9 points and 13.2 rebounds per game, and was named to the AP All-America First Team. He also set the school record for points in a game with 53, breaking Cliff Hagen's old mark of 51. But it was later broken at 54 by Jody Meeks in 2009. Issel was then selected in the 8th round, with the 122nd pick overall of the 1970 NBA Draft by the Detroit Pistons and the Kentucky Colonels of the ABA. Issel chose to play in the ABA where he was *The Show* as the most prolific scoring big man from the perimeter for six seasons. In his first season in the ABA, he led the league in scoring at **29.9 points** per game (edging out New York Nets Rick Barry's 29.4), had **13.2 rebounds**, and won the 1971 Rookie of the Year award. He also was named to the All-Star team for the first of seven consecutive seasons. In his second season, he was even more spectacular averaging **30.6 points** per game while being named to the All-ABA First Team. And, because of his durability (Only missed 24 games in 15 seasons), he led the ABA in total points three different seasons.

In 1975, Dan Issel won the ABA Championship with the Kentucky Colonels playing alongside Artis Gilmore and Louis Dampier. In his six seasons in the ABA including one with the Denver Nuggets, Issel averaged 25.6 points and 10.9 rebounds in the regular season and nearly duplicated those numbers in the playoffs. Although during his days in the NBA with the Nuggets, his overall numbers took a dip. I am assuming the reason was, partly because he played with better competition. In those nine seasons, he averaged 20.4 points and 7.9 rebounds per game, and scored a combine 27,482 points in both leagues, which is awfully high by anyone standards. In fact, at the time of his retirement, he ranked fifth on the all-time combine ABA/NBA scoring list behind Kareem, Wilt, Dr. J, and Moses Malone. In his NBA playoff career, he averaged nearly the same numbers as in the regular season but his team only went deep into the playoffs twice, losing both times to the eventual champion. In 1977, the Nuggets were eliminated in the semifinals by Bill Walton and the Portland Trail Blazers in six games, and in the 1985 conference finals in five games to Magic Johnson and the Los Angeles Lakers.

In Nowitzki's first five years in the league, he improved his overall game every season. After averaging eight points as a rookie playing in limited minutes, he literally doubled his scoring to 17.5 points per game and averaged 6.5 rebounds. By his third season in the league, he averaged 21.8 points and 9.2 rebounds and made his first playoff appearance with the franchise, where he averaged an impressive 23.4 points in his first 10 playoff games. In the 2001-02 season, he averaged the same amount of points in the regular season as he did in the playoffs the year before, and was named to the All-Star team for the first of eleven consecutive years to date. But the Mavericks were eliminated two years in row in the semifinals in five games to both the San Antonio Spurs and the Sacramento Kings. By that point, you knew Nowitzki was *something special* coming out of Germany because he kept improving year after year, especially in the postseason. Even in the 2002 playoffs, he averaged a **career-high** in **points at 28.4** and **13.1 rebounds** in 8 playoff games.

The following season, Nowitzki emerged into a big-time star averaging **25.1 points**, **9.9 rebounds, three assists**, and a career-high 1.4 steals per game. He was also named to the All-NBA Second Team. After beginning the season with 11 straight wins, he along with teammate Steve Nash, were voted co-Western Conference Player of the Month in November of 2002. The super tandem led the Mavericks to a franchise 60-22 record (tied with the Spurs) and made a deep run into the playoffs for the first time. With Nash, Michael Finley and Nick Van Exel aboard, Dallas looked like the next great team. With a rising Superstar in Nowitzki and a terrific three-guard rotation, the Mavericks defeated the Blazers (after winning the first three games, then losing the next three, before winning game 7 behind Nowitzki's heroics) and the Kings in the first two rounds of the playoffs in seven games, before losing to the eventual champion Spurs four games to two in the conference finals.

In 2003 playoffs, this was the first *real* chance for Nowitzki and Nash, for that matter, to have won their first championship. But it wasn't to be after Dirk got injured in game three, when Manu Ginobili collided into his knee forcing him to miss the rest of the series. In the game one victory, Nowitzki dropped 38 points on Tim Duncan before getting in early foul trouble in game two. The very next season, after losing Nick Van Exel and Raef LaFrentz, the Mavericks acquired Antawn Jamison and Antoine Walker in separate trades, but the new look Mavericks were bounced in the first round of the playoffs by the Kings in five games. With an aging Shawn Bradley and without LaFrentz, Nowitzki played more at center and focused more on the defensive end. As a result, he saw his scoring average dip considerably. In the 2004-05 season, Nowitzki emerged into one of the top two forwards in the league averaging **26.1 points**, **9.7 rebounds**, **3.1 assists**, and career-high **1.5 blocks** per game - and was named to the All-NBA First Team for the first of three consecutive years and the first of four in five seasons. Dirk also had a **career-high 53 points** in an overtime victory against the Houston Rockets.

In the playoffs, the Mavericks looked to bounce back after an early first-round exit from the year before. But they had to do it again in the first round against the Rockets after falling behind 2 games to 0. For the second time in Tracy McGrady's career going back to his days with the Orlando Magic, he lost again in the first round in seven games after having had a three to one and two to zero series advantage. After Dallas pulled off the most improbable comeback, they were not able to build on the momentum and were dispatched by MVP Steve Nash and the Phoenix Suns in the semifinals in six games. In the 2005-06 season, Nowitzki had perhaps his best statistical season of his career when he averaged a **career-high 26.6 points** per game, had **9.7 rebounds**, and shot **90 percent** from the free-throw line. He even finished 3rd behind Nash and LeBron James in the MVP voting. In the playoffs, Dirk had the best postseason of his career to that point averaging **27 points** and **11.7 rebounds** per game.

In fact, including the 2011 playoff run, he might of had his best postseason of his career in 2006 if he hadn't come up short against the Miami Heat in the NBA Finals. The 60-win Mavericks, swept the Memphis Grizzlies in the first round, finally got past the San Antonio Spurs in the playoffs (semifinals in seven games), before eliminating the Phoenix Suns in the conference finals four games to two. In all three playoff series, Dirk torched the Grizzlies with **3 30-point** games including **36** in game 3 which put Dallas up 3 games to 0, and against the Spurs with **2 30-point** games, including **37 points and 15 rebounds** in the decisive game 7. In that game, after Manu Ginobili hit a three-pointer in the finals seconds of play to give the Spurs the lead before, Nowitzki completed a three-point play to tie the game at 104, in which the Mavericks would go on to win. He also had **2 30-point** games against the Suns including **50 points** in game 5 to give the Mavericks a 3-2 series advantage. For Nowitzki's career, he has 45 30-point games in the playoffs, which ranks behind nine players on the all-time and ahead of Larry Bird's 43 and Wilt Chamberlain's 42. He also has 7 40-point games tied with Dwyane Wade and Bernard King, which ranks behind eleven other players including Barry's 8. To round out the list, George Gervin had 6 40-point games in the playoffs and Bird, Charles Barkley, Dominique Wilkins, John Havlicek, Bob McAdoo, and Bob Pettit all had 5.

So before the Mavericks loss to the Heat in the Finals, Nowitzki was having one of the all-time great playoff runs. And in the NBA Finals, despite losing four games in a row after winning the first two, Nowitzki didn't play particular bad, except for in game 4 at home where he shot 2 of 14 from the field, which would have put the Mavericks up 3 games to 1 in the series. So for three full playoff series and the first two games of the Miami Heat series, Nowitzki was spectacular. Similar to LeBron James this past year, just because a player comes up a little short in one series (albeit, it was the NBA Finals), shouldn't *negate* all his other great playoff performances - especially if LeBron eventually wins a championship or two, or three, or four, or five, or six, or seven in the years to come. Even just one, would have off set his lackluster performance in the 2011 NBA Finals against the Dallas Mavericks. However, as I will reiterate, if LeBron continues to falter with his offensive production and assertiveness to score and shoot in the Finals for years to come, then his legacy will certainly start to diminish over time. So far, he has come up big more times than not over the years, playing huge with 2 game-winning shots against the Washington Wizards, 48 points against the Detroit Pistons, pushing the Boston Celtics to seven games as the primary superstar, and against Boston and Chicago in last season's playoffs.

The following season, Nowitzki became the 5th player in NBA history after Larry Bird Steve Nash, and two others to average 50 percent from the field, 40 percent from the three-point line, and 90 percent from the free-throw line. That season he won the 2007

MVP award, but the Mavericks were toppled in the first round of the playoffs by the Golden State Warriors in six games. That series, Nowitzki didn't shoot particularly badly except for in the decisive game 6 in Golden State, where he shot 2 of 13 from the field. It was just a bad matchup for Dallas as a whole, as they were the latest victim of one Don Nelson's "upset specials" that I have already mentioned in detail in Karl Malone's chapter. This time around Dallas had to face an extremely athletic small-ball lineup that included Baron Davis, Monta Ellis, Jason Richardson, Mickael Pietrus, Matt Barnes, and Stephen Jackson. They also had to face three mobile forwards who were all outstanding shooters in Mike Dunleavy, Al Harrington, and Troy Murphy with agile center Andris Biedrins anchoring the middle. At that time, I believe the Warriors might have upset any team they had faced in the first round - perhaps, because out of all the Warrior great teams of recent years, this team might have been the most explosive.

In fact, they had the great Baron Davis, who in my opinion, had the greatest dunk in the history of the NBA playoffs in the next round over AK47 (André Kirilenko) and the Utah Jazz. In this posterizing dunk it seemed liked B-Diddy's entire head and shoulders were about to go through the hoop with Kirilenko dwarfed underneath him like when Blake Griffin slammed over the helpless Pau Gasol twice in a regular season game in 2012. At that time, I strongly debated that Baron Davis (Allen Iverson once said that he was the toughest point guard for him to defend in his career) was the best point guard in the NBA that season and in the playoffs, even over Chris Paul. It was a tough call, but I think I made a good case choosing the thunderous Davis with his strength and speed to go along with great scoring and passing ability at the point guard position. It was too bad Davis was injury prone throughout his career and came into training camp, sometimes out of shape, because I really thought he was going to end up a Hall of Famer. And by the way, his backcourt mate at the time, Monta Ellis who now plays for the Milwaukee Bucks, also has great potential to hopefully eventually make it into the Hall of Fame someday because of his Derrick Rose/Russell Westbrook type explosiveness when driving to the basket.

To compound matters, the Mavericks were eliminated in the first round of the playoffs the following season in five games to Chris Paul and the New Orleans Hornets, and to the up-and-coming Denver Nuggets the season after in five games in the semifinals. In the early round, they had eliminated the Spurs in the playoffs for the second time in four years, this time in five games. But the Spurs also took avenge the following year as they defeated the Mavericks in the first round in six games despite scoring games of **36, 35, and 33** by Dirk. Despite three early round exits in the playoffs the last three seasons, Nowitzki did his part averaging 26.8 points and 10 rebounds per game. It wasn't until 2011; he would capture the most coveted NBA championship that eluded him his entire career.

In player comparisons:

For 11 straight years, Nowitzki led the Mavericks to 50 wins and into the playoffs. He also was one of five players to win an NBA Championship, while being the lone all-star the same season. He is arguably the greatest *scorer/shooter* at the forward position since Larry Bird and perhaps the best clutch shooter as well. When Coach Rick Carlisle said during the 2011 playoffs that Nowitzki is one of the Top 10 players of all-time, I shook my head a little bit. But then I thought about it, and came to the conclusion that Dirk was at least a Top 25 player of all-time - at least for now until LeBron James, Dwyane Wade, Kevin Durant, and Chris Paul move ahead of him after their prime years are complete. I also, without a doubt, believe he was better than John Havlicek, Kevin McHale, and Scottie Pippen, because he was more dominate as a scorer and holstered an unstoppable fallaway shot just like Bird. With his career not yet complete, he should pass the great Havlicek in many offensive categories before his career is over.

Once again, usually dominance in one or two key aspects of a players game and very good in the rest, is better than another's just being very good to great as an overall player (but not dominate in any one aspect). A good example of this is Nowitzki vs. Pau Gasol. While Gasol may have the better all-around game and has won more championships 2 to 1, he isn't dominate in anyone aspect of his game, like Nowitzki is as a scorer and as a shooter. By the way, Nowitzki does have a very good overall game to compliment his dominate scoring. Even though Elvin Hayes was dominate with his fadeaway shot and in rebounding, he was not the clutch shooter and as great a winner that Nowitzki is today. As great as I already knew Dirk was, I'm sure a lot of people will now rank Nowitzki a lot higher as one of the game's elite after he won the 2011 NBA Championship!

Career Totals

22.6 points, 8.2 rebs, 2.6 assists, 0.9 blocks, 0.9 steals, .475 FG%, .877 FT%, .381% 3FG

25,501 points, 9096 rebounds, 2923 assists, 1050 blocks, 964 steals, 1197 threes

John Havlicek

(Rank #24)

All-NBA First Team (4-times), All-Star (13-times)

All-Defensive First Team (5-times)

NBA Championships (8), Finals MVP (1-time)

Also featuring: Bailey Howell

John Havlicek was one of the great all-around players to have ever played the game. Bill Russell once said, "He is the best all-around player I ever saw." Solid on the offensive end and on the defensive end coming off the bench, Havlicek was considered the greatest sixth man in NBA history. In sixteen glorious seasons playing for the Boston Celtics, Havlicek won 8 NBA Titles and was the 1974 Finals MVP. Out of all the players in history, only teammates Bill Russell and Sam Jones won more titles. After beginning his career coming off the bench before eventually becoming a starter, Havlicek blossomed into one of the league's top scorers. He was also one of the league's hardest working and durable players enabling him to finish his career as the Celtics All-Time leading scorer at 26,395 points - good for twelfth on the all-time list. In addition, he once had the most career assists for a non-guard in NBA history with 6114. "Hondo," his nickname inspired by the John Wayne movie, was a terrific scorer that could score from the outside or on the run, in the half court and on the fast break. At a solid six-foot-five, he was also an outstanding rebounder and passer at the small forward position. But what made Havlicek special was his mental and physical toughness (most likely attained from being a part-time football player), ability to perform in the clutch, and his energy and stamina he possessed on both ends of the court - as his longtime coach would attest. Red Auerbach described him as being the "guts of the team."

When you think of Havlicek, the first thing that comes to mind is the famous play-by-play call by the late Boston Celtics broadcaster Johnny Most, who exclaimed at the end of the 1965 Eastern Finals "Havlicek steals it! Over to Sam Jones, Havlicek stole the ball!" It's all over, "Johnny Havlicek stole the ball." As one of the league's best all-around players, he was equally as good on the defensive end as he was on the offensive end. In fact, many have said that if they had kept track of steals before the 1973-74 season, Havlicek would have been the league leader.

Born on April 8th, 1940 in Martins Ferry, Ohio, John J. Havlicek attended Bridgeport High School where he was a three-sport star. As years past, the school gymnasium was later named the "John J Havlicek Gymnasium." Afterwards, he then went on to play basketball alongside Jerry Lucas at Ohio State University where in three years playing in the shadow of Lucas, he averaged 14.6 points and 8.6 rebounds per game. He was also named an alternate at the 1960 Olympic Games in his sophomore year. After winning the 1960 NCAA Championship, Havlicek was selected with the 7th pick overall of the 1962 NBA Draft by the Boston Celtics and by the Cleveland Browns of the NFL. And by the way, my good friend's uncle **John Rudometkin** was selected with the 9th pick by the New York Knicks out of USC, but only played in three seasons due to illness. Named the "Reckless Russian" by the great Chick Hearn, Rudometkin was an awesome center (forward in the NBA) in college, making the NCAA All-America Second Team with Havlicek in 1962. If it wasn't for this unfortunate mishap, he would have emerged as a star in the NBA. But after a short stint in training camp playing wide receiver alongside star Jim Brown in exhibition games, Havlicek opted to play for the Celtics. In his rookie season, he contributed with 14.3 points and 6.7 rebounds per game in a supporting role, and was part of the Celtics team that won its fifth consecutive championship and sixth in seven seasons.

In his second year in the league in 1963-64, he made even more of an impact, when he led the team in scoring at 19.9 points per game. Coming off the bench with that type of scoring production, and with the versatility to play the guard and forward positions on both ends of the floor, Havlicek *revolutionized* the sixth man role. However to note, the *original* great Celtic sixth man before "Hondo" was Frank Ramsey, who was part of seven title teams from 1957 through 1964. In John's first two seasons, the Celtics defeated the Cincinnati Royals twice in the Eastern Finals, and the Los Angeles Lakers and San Francisco Warriors to win the NBA Championship. After Bob Cousy retired, Havlicek helped Bill Russell carry the Celtics to five championships along the way. By that point, the Celtics were still loaded with great offensive players in Tommy Heinsohn and Sam

Jones, but with Cousy now gone - Russell, Havlicek, and K.C. Jones took on the passing assignments. The following two seasons, Havlicek averaged a shade over eighteen points per game as the Celtics continued their perennial dominance.

In 1967, Havlicek and newcomer **Bailey Howell** led the team in scoring. Howell (a forward) had just come over from the Baltimore Bullets, where he spent two seasons, and the five seasons before that with the Detroit Pistons. He also completed the cast of 8 Hall of Famers who won championships playing alongside Bill Russell. Bailey E. Howell was born on January 20th, 1937 in Middleton, Tennessee, and attended Middleton High School. In college at Mississippi State University, he was basically a "Bull Dog" legend averaging an astonishing 27.1 points and 17 rebounds per game in three seasons. He left the school as virtually the all-time leader in almost every *relevant* statistical category including career points and rebounds per game. Howell was then selected with the 2nd pick overall of the 1959 NBA Draft by the Detroit Pistons. By his second season in the league, he averaged a **career-high 23.6 points** and **14.4 rebounds** per game. Teamed with Gene Shue, the Pistons made the playoffs but were eliminated in the first round for the second consecutive year. The following season, the Pistons made it out of the first round but lost in the Western Finals to the Los Angeles Lakers (for the third consecutive time in the playoffs) four games to two. The next two campaigns in 1963 and 1964 without Gene Shue but with a young Dave DeBusschere, the Pistons lost in the Western Finals again this time to the St. Louis Hawks three games to one, and missed the playoffs entirely. For two seasons with the Baltimore Bullets, he teamed with Walt Bellamy, Don Ohl, Gus Johnson, and Kevin Loughery to lead the Bullets into the playoffs where they would lose to the Lakers in the Western Finals in six games, and in a three-game sweep to the St Louis Hawks in the first round the year after. It wasn't until he joined the Boston Celtics that he would win his first NBA championship. For his career, Howell averaged 18.7 points and 9.9 rebounds per game, and was selected to the All-Star team 6 times. He was also one of the key contributors on the 1968 and 1969 Celtic championship teams. For 10 straight seasons playing for the Pistons, Bullets, and Celtics, he finished either first or second on the team in scoring - and with his career winding down in his final season in 1970, he finished third on the team in that department.

By that point with Bill Russell retired, the Celtics were in the rebuilding stages of the franchise. Don Nelson became the second leading scorer on the team behind Havlicek, who had just led the team in scoring for the fourth straight year. Now the focal point of the offense and best player on the team, Havlicek had his best season of his career to that point, averaging 24.2 points, 7.8 rebounds, and 6.8 assists - and was named to the All-NBA Second Team for the fifth time. He also accomplished a rare feat particularly in today's game when he led the team in points, rebounds, and assists - something I hope LeBron James does again and again in the upcoming years. But the Celtics missed the playoffs for the first time in 20 years. In the 1970-71 campaign, Havlicek had a career-year averaging **28.9 points**, **9 rebounds**, and **7.5 assists** per game. He also led the league in minutes, and was named to the All-NBA First Team for the first of four consecutive seasons. With cornerstone players Dave Cowens in his rookie season and Jo Jo White in his second, the Celtics missed the postseason for the second straight year. The following season, Havlicek completed the best three-year stretch of his career statistically averaging **27.5 points**, **8.3 rebounds**, and **7.5 assists** per game - as the Celtics won 56 games and made the playoffs for the first time in three seasons. By that point, the Milwaukee Bucks behind Lew Alcindor and Oscar Robertson had just come off their first NBA championship and the New York Knicks were fighting to reclaim the title they lost from the season before. With Cowens and Jo Jo White improving at a rapid pace and Havlicek still in his prime, the Celtics looked to contend for an NBA title once again. In the playoffs, the young Celtics defeated the Atlanta Hawks in six games before losing to the mighty New York Knicks in the Eastern Finals in five games.

In the 1972-73 campaign, Havlicek had another terrific season as the Celtics took a giant step and increased their win total from 56 to 68. Much of this was due to MVP Dave Cowens emerging as one of the best centers in the NBA. But other than Havlicek (despite his injury) and Don Nelson, the Celtics were a young team that had not yet gone through the *growing pains* that all champions go through. After defeating the Hawks in the semifinals in six games the Celtics were eliminated by those same Knicks in the Eastern Finals in seven games. But, in the following season, the Celtics would have their glory. Havlicek would average 20 points for the eighth consecutive year and lead the Celtics in scoring for the ninth straight season. To cap off a *brilliant* four-year prime, Havlicek won the 1974 Finals MVP. After eliminating the Buffalo Braves in the semifinals four games to two and in the rematch with the Knicks in the conference finals in five games, the Celtics won the 1974 NBA Championship over a tough Milwaukee Bucks team that featured Kareem Abdul-Jabbar and Oscar Robertson in his final season. In 1976, Havlicek won his final NBA title and retired two years later in 1978.

In player comparisons:

From the 1970 to 1973 campaign, Havlicek had four of the best *all-around* seasons in NBA history for a non-center averaging an astounding **26.1 points**, **8 rebounds**, and **7.1 assists** per game - and made the All-NBA First Team four consecutive seasons around the same time from 1971 to 1974. With stats like this, if I hid the name, you might have thought those were the numbers of LeBron James of today. In fact, he just so happens to be tied with LeBron in career triple-doubles in the regular season with 31. Both players are considered among the best all-around players ever along with Larry Bird and Oscar Robertson. Despite not ever finishing in the top two in the MVP voting (which in my mind, definitely hurts his ranking), to give Havlicek his props as one of the great players of all-time, I used his best 4 years in *succession* compared to some of the other great players of the past and present. Obviously Michael Jordan and Magic Johnson were great all-around players and perhaps better than everyone else on the list, but I didn't include them because their *emphasis* was on scoring and as a facilitator. I also left Jerry West off the list, because he dominated *both aspects* of the games at different stages of his career. I included Grant Hill because I believe he would have been one of the all-time greats if it weren't for his reoccurring ankle injuries:

John Havlicek	1970-73	26.1 points, 8.0 rebounds, 7.1 assists
Larry Bird	1984-87	26.6 points, 9.9 rebounds, 6.9 assists
LeBron James	2008-11	28.7 points, 7.6 rebounds, 7.5 assists
Grant Hill	1996-99	20.9 points, 8.5 rebounds, 6.8 assists
Oscar Robertson	1962-65	30.2 points, 10.5 rebounds, 10.8 assists

Like a lot of great players, Havlicek raised his level of play even higher in the playoffs. In fact, for seven seasons in the postseason between the years 1966 to 1974 (the year he won the Finals MVP), he was just as great as he was during his four year regular season peak averaging **25.7 points**, **8.1 rebounds**, and **5.6 assists** in 104 playoff games. If you take away the 1966 season, in six consecutive seasons (the years the Celtics made the playoffs) it looks even better: **26.1 points**, **7.9 rebounds**, and **5.9 assists** in 87 playoff games. So basically he averaged 26, 8, and 6 during his playoff prime which is comparable to almost anyone's best all-around numbers in the postseason. Other than his **career-high 54 points** in a game, Havlicek was one of the most consistent players of all-time in every aspect of the game throughout his regular season and postseason career. Although, Havlicek finished his career with outstanding career statistics as you can see below, the numbers don't begin to tell the story on how great he really was. Like Jerry West and Larry Bird who I feel are two of the greatest *clutch players* of all-time, the great John Havlicek was in that same class!

Career Totals

20.8 points average, 6.3 rebounds, 4.8 assists, .439 FG%, .815 FT%

26,395 points, 8007 rebounds, 6114 assists

Bob Cousy

(Rank #25)

MVP (1-time), All-NBA First Team (10-times)

Assist Title (8-times), All-Star (13-times)

NBA Championships (6)

Also featuring:
Nate "Tiny" Archibald

    Bob Cousy, at six-foot-one, was one of the first pioneers and great point guards in NBA history that helped lead the Boston Celtics to 6 NBA Championships in the late 1950s and early 1960s. When basketball was played with less flash and more fundamentals, Cousy took the point guard position to a new level with his fancy ball-handling and playmaking ability. He was the original showman and the "Houdini of the Hardwood," that revolutionized the point guard position with his dazzling array of dribbling and passing skills that included an assortment of between-the-leg and behind-the-back dribbles and no-look passes with either hand. Like many of the great point guards throughout history, he could make the spectacular pass as far out as half court and on the fast break. Intense and passionate like the rest of the great Boston Celtics, Cousy was the *ultimate* floor general and the original mainstay that helped build the Celtics' dynasty. Along the way, he led the league in assists 8 consecutive times during the regular season and in assists per game in the playoffs during his *full* thirteen years of his career. The thirteen-time All-Star was also one of the top scorers and free-throw shooters of his era.

Robert Joseph Cousy was born on August 9th, 1928 in New York City, New York and played basketball for Andrew Jackson High School in St. Albans, Queens NY, before accepting a scholarship to attend the College of the Holy Cross in Worchester, Massachusetts which was forty miles outside of Boston and close to his home. In his first year in college, Cousy played in limited minutes due to six freshman splitting time coming off the bench. In a troublesome beginning to his career, he was accused by his coach Alvin Julian of being a "show boater," because at the time basketball during the middle of the 1940s was played at a slower pace with flat-footed shooting and with direct player movement similar to route running in football. In his sophomore year, he played limited minutes until the game against Loyola of Chicago when he was urged on by the Boston Garden crowd with the chant "We want Cousy." After entering the game, he scored 11 points including the game-winning left-handed hook shot at the buzzer. From that point, two years later in his senior year, Cousy led the Crusaders to 26 consecutive wins and a second place finish in the National Invitational Tournament. He averaged 19.4 points per game and was named First Team All-America for the first time after making the Second and Third Team the previous two seasons.

Cousy was selected with the 3rd pick overall of the 1950 NBA Draft by the Tri Cities Black Hawks. Red Auerbach and the Boston Celtics passed on him at number one due to the skepticism for having more flash than substance. After declining to play for less money with the Black Hawks, the Chicago Stags then picked up Cousy's contract. But after the Stags folded as a franchise, Boston drew him out of a hat from the dispersal draft that included Max Zaslofsky and Andy Phillip. Sooner than later, the Celtics became sold on Cousy as a player. In his rookie year, he averaged 15.6 points and 4.9 assists per game, and was selected to his first of thirteen consecutive All-Star teams. In the 1951-52 season, Cousy increased his scoring average to 21.7 points, and posted 6.7 assists and 6.4 rebounds per game. He was also selected to the first of ten consecutive All-NBA First Teams and would end his career posting 33 triple-double games.

In the playoffs, behind Cousy, Ed Macauley, and rookie and future scoring sensation Bill Sharman, the Celtics lost for the second straight season to the New York Knickerbockers despite Cousy's 31 points per game average. The following year, Cousy led the league in assists for the first of eight consecutive seasons and in scoring average in the postseason for the first of three straight years. In the playoffs, the 46-win Celtics swept the Syracuse Nationals in the first round with Cousy having scored **50 points** in a game including a **record 30 of 32** from the free-throw line. But in the Eastern Finals, Boston lost again to the Knickerbockers three games to one. After finally defeating New York twice in a most interesting round robin playoff in 1954, the Celtics lost to Dolph Schayes and the Syracuse Nationals in the next round. Even with newly drafted and eventual Hall of Famers Jim Lostcutoff and Frank Ramsey, the Celtics would go on to lose to the Nationals in the playoffs the next two seasons. As a testament to his individual greatness, in 1954, Cousy led the league in assists per game in the postseason for the first of eight consecutive seasons. And in 1957, he won his first and only MVP award. The Most

Valuable Player award wasn't inaugurated until 1956 in which Cousy could possibly have won more than just the one if it had existed during the first half of the 1950s.

For the 1956-57 season, the Celtics drafted talented forward Tommy Heinsohn for more offensive firepower, and defensive specialist Bill Russell to build a fortified defensive foundation of *superior* rebounding and shot blocking. With Bill Sharman leading the team in scoring and Cousy coming off another stellar year, the young and much deeper Celtics finished with the best record in the league. In the playoffs, after finally beating constant rival Syracuse for the first time in four years 3 games to 0, the Celtics defeated superstar Bob Pettit and the St. Louis Hawks in a hard-fought seven-game series to win the NBA championship. The Hawks also featured former Celtics Ed Macauley and Cliff Hagen. The next season, the same group of Celtics with one year more experience, returned to the Finals to face their arch nemeses St. Louis Hawks, only to lose the rematch from the previous year in six games. The outcome might have been different if the Celtics hadn't lost Russell to a foot injury in game three.

In the 1958-59 season, the Celtics would reclaim their title by eliminating an old foe, the Syracuse Nationals in seven games before sweeping rookie Elgin Baylor and the Los Angeles Lakers. Cousy set an NBA Finals record 51 assists for a four-game series. Also, in the regular season, he set a then **record 28 assists** in a game, including **19** in one half. The following season, Cousy set a **career-high** in **assists at 9.5** and Heinsohn would lead the team in scoring for the first time. The Celtics won 59 games including 17 in a row propelling them to their third title in four years - by defeating the Philadelphia 76ers in six games before taking out the Hawks in the Finals in seven games. In his final three seasons and Sharman at the end of his career, Cousy began to show his age and had a gradual drop in production particularly in scoring and rebounding. But, the Celtics with a strong nucleus of Russell, Heinsohn, and Sam Jones were bolstered enough to win the NBA Championship the next three years.

The Celtics over the years have had great point guards in Bob Cousy, Jo Jo White, Nate "Tiny" Archibald, Dennis Johnson, and Rajon Rondo of today. But perhaps the most dynamic and explosive point guard might have been **Nate Archibald**. Although, he only won one championship in 1981 with the Celtics at the tail end of his career, he was still a highly productive floor general. A famous youth playground legend in New York City, Archibald made his name playing for the Kansas City/Omaha Kings and Boston Celtics. In only his third season in the NBA, Archibald became the first man in NBA history to lead the league in scoring and assists at a *staggering* **34 points** and **11.4 assists** per game respectively. He was also the original lightning-quick point guard that could dominate off dribble penetration and with an outside jump shot. As great as Chris Paul, Deron Williams, Derrick Rose and Russell Westbrook are today, I highly doubt they could have pulled off what Archibald did that season. Maybe today and if times were different and they *wanted* to play a more selfish game the way Jordan, Kobe, and Iverson all have at one point in their careers taking the majority of the shots; they might still come up a little short. The reason, it is hard for any player to average 30 points in a season let alone 34 points. Jordon scored 34 points or more twice in his career, while Kobe and Iverson did it just once.

Nathaniel Archibald was born on September 2nd, 1948 in New York City, New York and attended DeWitt Clinton High School in the Bronx. He then went on to Arizona Western College for one year before transferring to the University of Texas at El Paso where for three seasons, he averaged 20 points per game. Ironically, this was the same school that another great *small* point guard played his college ball years later in Tim Hardaway, who I highly mention later in Allen Iverson's chapter as having the best crossover-dribble during his time if not ever. Archibald was selected in the second round, 19th pick overall of the 1970 NBA Draft by the Cincinnati Royals and by the Texas Chaparrals of the ABA. After a modest rookie year playing for the Royals, he increased his scoring from 16 points to 28.2 points per game in his second season. By his third season with the franchise moving to Kansas City/Omaha, Archibald exploded upon the NBA scene and led the league in scoring and assists. He also was named to the All-Star team for the first of six times and to his first of three All-NBA First Team selections. Despite not winning the league MVP award thanks to Dave Cowens, he was acknowledged as MVP by the Sporting News. The following season, his scoring was cut in half to 17.6 points per game due to injuries. Sadly enough, the Kings missed the playoffs in his first four years in the league. In his last two seasons with the Kings, he averaged 26.5 and 24.8 points and 6.8 and 7.9 assists respectively, and was named to the All-NBA First Team in both years. In his second to last season with the franchise, the Kings finally made the playoffs but lost to the Chicago Bulls in the Western Conference Semifinals in six games.

In player comparisons:

Out of all the great Celtics point guards in history, Bob Cousy was the best for the same reasons everyone else is ranked in this book. He combined more individual contributions and team success than any Celtics point guard in history, and won more championships than any point guard in NBA history including Magic Johnson. His 6 NBA Championships and 8 assists titles says it all. But it doesn't say it all when comparing him to John Stockton who won 9 assists titles and was the most dominant player in that one particular aspect of the game; passing. Stockton was also perhaps the better defensive player having led the league in steals twice and making the All-NBA Defensive Second Team five times. Stockton is also the NBA's all-time leader in assists and steals. That's comparable to Kareem as the all-time leading scorer. And, in any era, I don't think Cousy would have been nearly the proficient shooter of the Stockton's and Nash's of the world.

While you may disagree with the rankings, think of it this way. If you surrounded that type of talent around the most quintessential point guards in history in Stockton and Nash, the outcome of team success would have been just as good. I believe that because Stockton only played with one true superstar his entire career that didn't come up big in the clutch on some occasions, and because Nash was the ultimate team player, justified when he won two consecutive MVP awards and almost a third straight. Either way you look at it Cousy, Oscar Robertson, Magic Johnson, Chris Paul, John Stockton, Steve Nash, Isiah Thomas, and even Jason Kidd and Gary Payton, are all in the same class when it comes to all-time great point guards. But if you want to put Cousy near the top of the list that's ok with me, because he brought so much to the game in terms of individual contributions to the team's success, and revolutionized the game and paved the way for the all the point guards that we see in the NBA today! Bob Cousy will forever go down as one of the top point guards of all-time. And from a winning perspective, we may never see a point guard in our lifetime win 6 NBA Championships!

Career Totals

18.4 points average, 7.5 assists, 5.2 rebounds, .375 FG%, .803 FT%

16,960 points, 6955 assists, 4786 rebounds

Bill Walton

(Rank #26)

MVP (1-time), All-NBA First Team (1-time), All-Star (2-times)

All-Defensive First Team (2-times), Rebounding Title (1-time)

Blocked Shots Title (1-time), NBA Championships (2), Finals MVP (1-time)

Also featuring: Greg Oden & Arvydas Sabonis

Bill Walton was one of the greatest centers to ever play professional basketball. In fact, he was so good coming out of college at the University of California at Los Angeles, everyone banked on him to become the next great center in the likes of Wilt Chamberlain, Bill Russell, and Kareem Abdul-Jabbar. Walton, along with Abdul-Jabbar, are considered not only the two best centers in college basketball history, but the two best players to ever put on a college uniform. The center comparisons with Kareem began in college because it was also Kareem's alma mater. In perhaps, the best college career for any player in history under Coach John Wooden, Walton won a *remarkable* three straight College Player of the Year Awards and two National Championships. Coming into the NBA with the Portland Trail Blazers, Walton was destined to have a fabulous professional career until the chronic knee and foot injuries set him back early on. In only his third season in 1977, he won the NBA Championship; and the following year in 1978, the NBA MVP Award.

Walton was the *epitome* of a great all-around center, able to score in the clutch with a soft touch out of the low post and from the perimeter. He also had a jump hook with either hand. With his enormous size (inches above his listed height at 6'11") and strength, Walton was one of the great rebounders and defensive players the league has ever seen. But what made Walton even more special, was his *extraordinary* gift to pass the ball as good as or better than any center to have played the game. Both Walton and Russell were known for being among the greatest outlet passers in history. But many believe Walton was even one notch above the rest, with the extra mustard he put behind his passing especially on outlet passes. As a testament to his superior passing ability at the center position, Walton averaged 5 assists in his MVP season in 1978. In his prime, one could say he was basically Larry Bird at center, with less shooting range, but with a lot better defensive skills. And that's a scary thought to reminisce about!

William Theodore Walton III was born on November 5th, 1952 in La Mesa, California and attended Helix High School. At seventeen years old, Walton played basketball with the U.S. Men's National team at the FIBA World Championship in 1970. In his three varsity seasons at UCLA, he averaged: 21.1, 20.4, 19.3 points and 15.5, 16.9, 14.7 rebounds per game on 65 percent shooting. As the centerpiece and anchor of the powerhouse UCLA Bruins, Walton led the team to a 30-0 record (including a point differential of 30+ in 1972) in consecutive seasons. He was also part of the men's basketball record 88-game winning streak during his three varsity years. The streak actually began when Walton was a junior in high school and ended in his senior year in college. The Bruins won back-to-back NCAA Championships against Florida State in 1972 and in 1973 over Memphis State 87-66. In the title game (second time around), Walton scored **44 points** and shot an astounding **21 of 22 from the field** and was named in both 1972 and 1973 NCAA Final Four Most Outstanding Player. In the middle of his senior year, UCLA's 88-game winning streak came to an end came with a 71-70 overtime loss against Notre Dame. And in the semifinals of the NCAA tournament, the Bruins were defeated by North Carolina State 80-77 in double overtime ending UCLA's dynasty and record 7 consecutive national titles. Walton did win his third straight Naismith College Player of the Year Award and the James E. Sullivan Award as the top amateur athlete in the United States.

After being drafted by the San Diego Conquistadors of the ABA, Walton opted to play in the NBA after being selected with the first pick overall of the 1974 NBA Draft by the Portland Trail Blazers. Acknowledged as the premiere center and franchise player for years to come, Walton's pro career began in the worst possible way. In his first two seasons in the NBA, at different times, Walton was inflicted with multiple injuries which included a broken leg, foot, wrist, and nose. Despite the injuries, as he proved in college, Walton showed his great potential as one of the league's best all-around centers. In only 86 games he averaged 14.7 points, 13 rebounds, and 4.5 assists per game but the Blazers missed the playoffs both years. In the 1976-77 season, as his health began to improve, Walton averaged 18.6 points, and the led the league in rebounding at 14.4 and blocks at

3.2 per game. He also was selected to his first All-Star game (didn't play because of injury) and made the All-NBA Second Team and All-Defensive First Team. In the first two rounds of the playoffs, the 49-win Blazers defeated the Chicago Bulls two games to one and the Denver Nuggets in six games. In the Western Conference Finals, with the Blazers having a Cinderella-type season, unexpectedly, swept Kareem and the Los Angeles Lakers in four straight games. In the NBA Finals, after losing the first two games, the Blazers stormed back and won the next four games to win the 1977 NBA Championship in historic fashion. In the decisive game six, Julius Erving scored 40 points and Walton had a masterful game of **20 points, 23 rebounds, 8 assists, and 7 blocks** while winning the 1977 Finals MVP.

The following year, Walton averaged 18.9 points, 13.2 rebounds, and 5 assists per game - and was named to the All-NBA First Team and All-Defensive First Team. He also won the MVP award after missing the last 22 games of the season due to injury. To begin the season, the Blazers won 50 of their first 60 games and finished with the best record in the NBA at 58-24. But travesty struck in the second game of the playoffs when Walton reinjured his foot causing him to miss the rest of the postseason, as the Blazers lost in the semifinals to the Seattle SuperSonics in six games.

That was the beginning of the end (in terms of being a superstar) for the great Bill Walton, not only was it sad then, it's even sadder now not only for one of the two best centers to have come out of college, but for the franchise that had to endure it. The Portland Trail Blazers have had more misfortune than any franchise in history in terms of great players, whose careers were cut short due to injuries. Not only am I sick to my stomach as I'm writing about Bill Walton, I'm feeling the same nauseam for Greg Oden, Brandon Roy, Arvydas Sabonis, and Sam Bowie! We all know what happened to Sam Bowie's career after he was drafted second behind Hakeem Olajuwon and in front of Michael Jordan in the 1984 NBA Draft.

But what has happened this past year, is the absolute worst possible thing that could have happened to the Portland franchise. Brandon Roy retired after an attempted comeback after knee surgery and **Greg Oden** on Monday February 20th, 2011 was undergoing a minor procedure on his left knee to clear out debris when the surgeon determined that there was additional damage and performed microfracture surgery on his left knee for the second time in his career. It was then announced with heartbreak to everyone that his season had ended. With his career already in doubt after surgeries on both knees, the third one may have put an end to it. Even back when he had surgery on both knees, one of the doctors said it was highly unlikely that he would ever play again in the NBA. Everyone was just hoping that with rehab in 2012, he would eventually make it back and play again. Before the devastating knee injuries and at the time of the 2007 NBA Draft when Greg Oden was taken with the first pick ahead of Kevin Durant - based on his physique and the way he played in college, I felt Oden was going to be an Alonzo Mourning type defensive player with a little less shooting range but with more size and strength. I also felt he would become the most dominant inside physical force since Shaq but that did not materialize due to the devastating knee injuries. Like I mentioned in Shaq's chapter about Andrew Bynum becoming the best center in the Western Conference for the next few years by default thanks to Yao Ming's early retirement, I believe he would have played second fiddle to Oden as well, if it weren't for the career changing travesty.

And then there was **Arvydas Sabonis** who was one of the best International league superstars that was on the downside of his career when he came to play in the NBA. Bill Walton himself even gave Sabonis the biggest of compliments stating that he was a 7'3" Larry Bird with unique court vision, shooting range, rugged in-game mentality, and versatility.

Can you image that guy playing at full strength with 1990-92 Portland Trail Blazers?

Born in Kuanas, Lithuania December 19th, 1964 in the USSR, Arvydas Romas Sabonis played basketball for the Soviet national junior team at the age of 15 years old. In 1981, he began his pro career playing in his hometown for the Zalgiris Kaunas. Playing for several teams in Europe, Sabonis was a 6-time Euroscar Player of the Year. He also won a gold medal in 1988 at the Summer Olympics in South Korea playing for the Soviet Union and the bronze medal in 1992 and 1996 playing for Lithuania. Sabonis was selected with the 24th pick overall of the 1986 NBA Draft by the Portland Trail Blazers but was restricted by the Soviet authorities from playing in the NBA until 1989. From that point on, he had an exceptional career playing over in Europe but endured multiple injuries along the way including a devastating Achilles' tendon injury soon after he was drafted. By the time he played his first season with the Blazers in 1995, he would develop chronic knee, ankle and groin injuries that all but eliminated his mobility and explosiveness. However, he was still an outstanding player and part of a great Blazers team that pushed the Los Angeles Lakers to the brink of elimination in the 2000 Western Conference Finals.

In seven seasons with the Blazers, Sabonis averaged a meager 12 points, 7.3 rebounds, and 2.1 assists per game, and averaged almost identical numbers in seven playoff seasons. The assist per game average doesn't even begin to tell the story of how great a passer Sabonis once was. Like I mentioned earlier, about Divac being the greatest passing center that I have ever seen, many have said it was Sabonis. After a brilliant career in Europe he was inducted into the FIBA Hall of Fame in 2010 and the Naismith Basketball Hall of Fame in 2011. Now that Arvydas Sabonis and Drazen Petrovic (who scored an incredible 112 points in a European league game and won the Euroscar Player of the Year Award in 1986, 1989, 1992, and 1993) are now enshrined, this opens up many doors for international player such as Yao Ming, Pau Gasol, Manu Ginobili whom I believe will all make the Naismith Memorial Basketball Hall of Fame someday.

Walton, in the next four years (didn't play in 1981 and 1982), played in only 14 games all coming in the 1979-80 season for his hometown San Diego Clippers before having surgery on his left foot. In his last three seasons with the Clippers including the 1984-85 season in Los Angeles, he averaged only 11.7 points, 9 rebounds, and 2.2 blocks per game. Prior to the 1985-86 season, Walton was acquired by the Boston Celtics in a trade for Cedric Maxwell and a first-round draft pick. With perhaps the best frontcourt in history already in place, Walton added even more depth to the frontcourt coming off the bench. With Larry Bird, Kevin McHale, Robert Parish and Walton, and a solid backcourt of Dennis Johnson and Danny Ainge, the Celtics had one of the most historic seasons in history. The Celtics finished the regular season with the best record in the NBA at 67-15 and a record 40-1 at home. As the sixth man coming off the bench, Walton played in a career-high eighty regular season games. In limited minutes, he averaged a career low in all five major categories, but shot a career-high 56 percent from the field. In the first three rounds of the playoffs, the Celtics continued their dominant season by sweeping the Chicago Bulls in the first round and the Detroit Pistons in the Eastern Conference Finals. Their only loss came against the Milwaukee Bucks in the conference semifinals. In the NBA Finals against the Houston Rockets, Walton played an *integral* part in the team success by helping to neutralize the "Twin Towers," as they were called in those days in Hakeem Olajuwon and Ralph Sampson.

In player comparisons:

If Bill Walton had never gotten injured, to where *almost* his entire prime of his professional career was cut short, he might have gone down as the greatest center to have ever lived. One thing is for certain, he along with Kareem Abdul-Jabbar, were the greatest college basketball players in history. That statement was validated because it came from the mouth of the great UCLA Coach John Wooden, and he was one of three players in NCAA history to win the College Player of the Year Award 3 times. Ultimately, he and Kareem made more of an impact in college and perhaps coming out of college than any two players in history. But what was most impressive about Walton, was his phenomenal all-around game during his prime that could have potentially been better than all of the top centers in NBA history including Abdul-Jabbar, Wilt Chamberlain, Bill Russell, Hakeem Olajuwon, Shaquille O'Neal, and Moses Malone. At his best during the prime of his career, Walton *blended* scoring, rebounding, passing, and shot blocking *as well or better* than any center to have ever lived.

Career Totals

13.3 points average, 10.5 rebounds, 3.4 assists, 2.2 blocks, .521 FG%, .660 FT%

6215 points, 4923 rebounds, 1590 assists, 1034 blocks

Allen Iverson

(Rank #27)

MVP (1-time), Scoring Title (4-times), Steals Title (3-times)

All-NBA First Team (3-times), All-Star (11-times)

Also featuring:
Tim Hardaway

Allen Iverson was one of the greatest scorers ever to play in the NBA. At one point, I thought he and Michael Jordan would stand at the top of the list for greatest scorers of all-time, even over the great Kobe Bryant. Listed at only six feet tall, Iverson brought more to the game than anyone ever has for a man of his stature, able to dominate the painted area off dribble penetration with acrobatic layups and also with fallaway shots. He was even able to slam it home and dunk off missed shots or alley-oop passes early on in his career. As a sophomore at the University of Georgetown, Iverson was a *prolific* scorer averaging an astounding 25 points per game and was the obvious pick coming out of college as an underclassmen when he was drafted with the #1 pick overall by the Philadelphia 76ers in 1996. In his first 10 seasons with the 76ers, Iverson averaged 28 points, six assists, four rebounds, and 2.3 steals per game - and won the 2001 NBA MVP Award. In his prime, many believe Iverson was arguably the quickest player to ever play in the NBA. Throughout his career, he was the *ultimate* scoring machine winning 4 scoring titles, and averaging 30 points or more in a season 4 times. He can back this up in the postseason where he averaged 29.7 points and six assists for his career, ranking 2nd to Jordan on the all-time playoff scoring list in points per game. He also was the second player in history along with Jordan to score 50 points twice in one playoff series. Out of all his talents, his greatest attribute was his crossover dribble which may have been the best the league has ever seen!

Iverson is the co-master of the crossover dribble made famous by the originator himself "Mr. Crossover," **Tim Hardaway**. Still to this day, I don't know whose was better. Both were able to *freeze* their opponents and leave them in their tracks. Two famous crossovers that come to mind are often replayed on NBA TV (or watch on DVD titled "NBA Ankle Breakers volume 1"). In this package, Iverson does multiple crossovers juking Michael Jordan so hard at the top of the key he almost fell over, and then by capping it off with a jumper in MJ's face. He did a similar combination to Reggie Miller, top of the key right, leaving him almost spilled on the floor with his arms barely holding him up.

Hardaway's crossover was called the "Killer Crossover" because it usually included an underneath the leg dribble and then a hard left to right dribble. It was breathtaking even watching it live on TV, when I saw him leave Isiah Thomas frozen at the Oakland Coliseum. After the juke, it looked like Isiah's body remained immobile, as he was only able to turn his head behind him as Hardaway *exploded* past him for a layup.

Hardaway was more *compact* with his crossover dribble and with his ability to finish at the basket, while Iverson, because of his long arms, was able to crossover with more of a sweeping motion and finish at the rim with more extension. He was also able to soar high in the air and dunk in the face of an opponent early on in his career while Hardaway stayed more grounded. While Iverson often *endured* punishment on his way to the basket, Hardaway *shredded* it. Tim Hardaway was a *battering ram,* and when he drove to the hoop, players who made contact with him, bounced off him like they would a brick wall similar to when LeBron James drives to the basket. The major difference though, is that LeBron is a foot taller and can easily score over another player, whereas Hardaway was so small at five-feet-ten plus (although listed at 6'0"), that even without contact, bigger and taller players had more of a chance to block or alter his shot. If Hardaway had any size what so ever, he would have completely dominated the game of basketball! By the way, I think Hardaway should be in the Hall of Fame because he was among the great scoring/assist guards of all-time. Hardaway and Iverson were both streak shooters and could stop on a dime from anywhere on the court, including as far out as the three-point line, and knock down clutch jumpers *right between the eyes* of their opponents. While both players were physical, Hardaway was the "Walter Payton" of basketball and Iverson was the "Barry Sanders" because he was able to stop on a dime, weave his way through opponents, and shoot from the most difficult of angles!

Allen Ezail Iverson was born on June 24th, 1975 in Hampton, Virginia. At Bethel High School, he played point guard and quarterback, and led both his basketball and football teams to state championships. After a visit from Coach John Thompson in high school, Iverson was recruited to play basketball at Georgetown University. In his two years in college, Iverson averaged an astounding 25 points in his sophomore season and left the school as the all-time leader in scoring with an average of 23 points per game. He also won Big East Rookie of the Year and was two-time Big East Defensive Player of the Year. Iverson was selected with the #1 pick overall of the 1996 NBA Draft ahead of other future Hall of Famers Ray Allen, Kobe Bryant, and Steve Nash. In his first season, Iverson lived up to all the hype and won the 1997 Rookie of the Year award by averaging an impressive **23.5 points** a game, **7.5 assists**, **4.1 rebounds**, and **2.1 steals** - and shot a decent 34 percent from the three-point line. Along the way, he broke the rookie record scoring 40 points or more in 5 consecutive games breaking Wilt Chamberlain's old mark of 3. He would put up similar numbers in his second season, but the 76ers missed the playoffs for the second year in a row.

In the 1998-99 season, Iverson emerged into an elite scorer and averaged **26.8 points** per game, and won his first scoring title while being named to the All-NBA First Team. In the playoffs, Iverson averaged **28.5 points** and set a playoff record with **10 steals** in an upset victory over the Orlando Magic in the first round in four games. But the 76ers were swept by the Indiana Pacers in the semifinals. The next year, Iverson signed a six-year extension to remain with the team. He increased his scoring average to **28.4 points** per game and was selected to his first of eleven consecutive All-Star games. In the playoffs, the 76ers beat the Charlotte Hornets three games to one in the first round before losing again to the eventual Eastern Conference Champion Indiana Pacers in the semifinals. After falling behind three games to zero, the 76ers battled back and won the next two games before eventually losing the series in six games. The Pacers were one of the elite teams in the conference the last few seasons that featured stars Reggie Miller, Jalen Rose, and Rik Smits.

In the 2000-01 season, Iverson blossomed *big time* into the most prolific scorer in the NBA, torching his opponents on a nightly basis. Iverson averaged **31.1 points** a game and recorded **17 40-point** games. He also won his second scoring title and led the league in steals for the first of three consecutive seasons. The Philadelphia 76ers finished with the best record in the Eastern Conference at 56-26 and Iverson was awarded the regular season MVP. With *super* sixth man Aaron McKie, Eric Snow, and Iverson in their third season playing together, and with newly acquired defensive stopper Dikembe Mutombo, the 76ers felt they were formidable enough to make a deep run in the playoffs and win their first championship since 1983. In the first round, the 76ers would avenge the loss from the two previous playoffs to the Pacers by dispatching them in four games. In the semifinals and conference finals, the 76ers defeated the Toronto Raptors and the Milwaukee Bucks in tough seven-game series. I felt both teams were good enough to have won the series just as I felt the Utah Jazz and Dallas Mavericks were back in 1988 against the Los Angeles Lakers. Vince Carter carried the Raptors throughout the playoffs as did Ray Allen with the Bucks. But Allen had more star support in Glen Robinson and Sam Cassell. Usually the best player or the best two players on a team wins out in the NBA Finals. And that's what eventually happened against Allen Iverson and the Philadelphia

76ers. After shocking the Los Angeles Lakers in game one with Iverson scoring **48 points**, the 76ers lost the next four games and the series behind Shaquille O'Neal's demolition of Dikembe Mutombo. Iverson peaked in the 2001 playoffs with an astounding **32.9 points per game**, and in the 2001 NBA Finals (**35.6 points** per game) single-handedly torching Tyronn Lue, Derek Fisher, Kobe Bryant and everyone else who tried to guard him on the Los Angeles Lakers.

In player comparisons: "The Answer" was just as prolific a scorer as the "Black Mamba" winning 4 scoring titles to his 2 (Of course, playing with Shaq early in his career lessoned Kobe's scoring opportunities). The same crossovers Iverson did on Jordan and Miller in the past, he did onto Bryant and his entourage. All fans should watch games of NBA Hardwood Classics or at least the footage of the entire 2001 playoffs including the NBA Finals against the Lakers to refresh the memory of the *deadly arsenal* of "Allen Iverson" at his greatest! His scoring output was better than any of Bryant's playoff runs.

Coming off his best scoring season of his career in the playoffs, Iverson turned the momentum into a scoring escapade the next five years. In 2002, he led the league in scoring for the second straight season and third overall at **31.4 points** per game. He would go on to win his fourth scoring title three years later at **30.7 points** per game. And in the postseason, he averaged 30 points or more 4 consecutive playoff appearances from 2001 to 2005.

The following year in 2002, the 76ers were hampered by injuries and made it to the playoffs as a sixth seed but were defeated by Paul Pierce, Antoine Walker, and the Boston Celtics in the first round three games to two. During the playoffs, Larry Brown began to criticize Iverson about missing practices which led to the most hilarious post-game interview that I have seen where Iverson was later mocked by fans and media around the league. Even at work we were mimicking the phrases over and over again. This is what Iverson had to say: We sit-in here, I supposed to be the franchise player and we in here talkin' about practice. "I mean listen, we talkin' about practice! Not a game, not a game, not a game, we talkin' about practice! Not a game, not, not, not the game that I go out there and die for and play every game like it's my last, not the game, were talkin' about practice man! I mean how silly is that, I mean were talkin' about practice! I know I suppose to be there, I know I suppose to lead by example, I know that! And I'm not; I'm not shoving it aside you know like it don't mean anything. I know it's important. I do, I honestly do. But we talkin' about practice man, what are we talkin' about! Practice, were talkin' about practice man! Pause, were talkin' about practice, were talkin' about practice, we aint talkin' about the game, we talkin' about practice man! When you come in the arena and you see me play, you see me play don't you, you see me give everything I got right! But we talkin' about practice right now! We talkin' about, pause. Man look I hear you, I, pause, it's funny to me too, pause. It's strange; it's strange to me too. But we talkin' about practice man! We not even talkin' about the game, the actual game, when it matters, we talkin' about practice!" One of the reporters, than suggested if Iverson showed up for practice it might not necessarily make him better but maybe his teammates. Iverson responded by saying; "How the hell can I make my teammates better by practicing!" If one is going to talk about practice that much, it has to be a little detrimental. Maybe this is why Iverson never reached his full potential and won a championship. Nah, I don't think so because Iverson gave it 100 percent every night he was on the court and played with more *heart and guts* as any player to have played the game. So, I guess you can say the issue was probably a little overrated. Even Shaq during his championship run said that he and Iverson take more punishment and play with more heart than anyone in the league.

I think the real reason, is that Iverson never played with another superstar until he went to Denver but by that time, Iverson was almost 10 years older than Carmelo Anthony. Three years after leaving Philadelphia his career came to a sudden halt after switching teams three different times. He probably wasn't able to extend his career because he played way to many minutes including having led the league seven times in minutes per game, was often injured, and endured more punishment driving to the basket than any player in history.

In the 2002-03 season, Iverson continued to have issues with Larry Brown regarding missing practice, culminating in the coaches departure after the 76ers were eliminated from the playoffs at the end of the year. The 76ers would make one last playoff push by eliminating the New Orleans Hornets in six games before losing in six games to the Detroit Pistons in the semifinals. The following season, the 76ers under new interim coach Chris Ford missed the playoffs entirely before returning in 2005 only to lose again to the Detroit Pistons in the first round three games to two. In the 2005-06 season, the 76ers missed the playoffs for the second time in three years. In Iverson's final full season with the franchise, he averaged a **career-high 33 points** per game but lost the scoring title to Kobe Bryant. The next year, Iverson averaged 31 points in his first 15 games before he was traded - apparently he was being held out of games indefinitely after missing practice before supposedly demanding the trade.

After the Denver Nuggets acquired Allen Iverson in a trade, I felt Denver would become a title contender immediately. Iverson was able to adjust his game as the number two scorer for the first time in his career, and at the same time, become the team's new facilitator. He averaged 24.8 points and 7.2 assists per game the rest of the season, and **26.3 points** and **7.1 assists** in his first full season with Nuggets. In the playoffs, the Nuggets were defeated by the San Antonio Spurs in the first round in five games. After winning game one, the well experienced Spurs battled back and won four straight games and the series. I didn't expect Denver to wilt and lose the series in five games because I felt they were good enough to pull the upset and go deep into the playoffs. I felt the same way in 2008, and picked Denver to knock off the number one seed Los Angeles Lakers in six games. With a formidable team that included the dynamic Carmelo Anthony, J.R Smith, Linas Kleiza, and big men Marcus Camby and Nene, I was shocked when the Nuggets were swept by the Lakers in the first round of the playoffs. I also felt that season or the next would be Iverson's best chance to win a championship. The next two seasons, Iverson endured chronic back injuries as his career fizzled into oblivion playing for the Detroit Pistons, the Memphis Grizzlies, and back again with the Philadelphia 76ers.

In player comparisons:

If Iverson had been more durable throughout his career and had won at least one championship, he would have ranked higher on most people's list for greatest shooting guards to have played the game. Despite his small size (shortest player to be drafted #1 overall and win the NBA MVP award), it kills me to rank Iverson this low, because I really felt as a *pure* scorer, his *passion* for winning and his *heart* for the game, along with his killer instinct was second only to Michael Jordan. Iverson was labeled as a selfish scorer in the same way Jordan and Kobe Bryant were early in their careers. Even after the trade to the Nuggets, many people felt Iverson was the same player. But from my point of view, I thought Iverson (playing point guard at times) was making a *conscious effort* to distribute the ball and defer to C. Anthony as the number one scoring option. I guess in the eyes of many, he didn't facilitate enough. He was also an underrated defender much like Clyde Drexler was. Although one was taller than your average shooting guard and one was shorter, both players had lightning-quick hands and were able to get a lot of steals in the passing lanes. Statistically, Iverson ranks among the best two-guards in history (ranked the 5th greatest shooting guard of all-time by ESPN in 2008) with a solid 6.2 assists per game and is tied with Jordan and Alvin Robertson with three steals titles apiece behind only Chris Paul who won his fourth and fifth the last couple of seasons.

Here are some more of Iverson's scoring feats: He had **345 30-point** games, **79 40-point** games, and **11 50-point** games. He also had **36 30-point** games, **10 40-point** games, and **3 50-point** games in the playoffs with the latter ranking behind only Michael Jordan and Wilt Chamberlain. So in speaking for many, if Iverson had a better supporting cast throughout his career and won a couple of championships, he could have easily been ranked a top 25 player, if not a top 20, because he did everything you could ask for and more at the position he played. Like I mentioned in Shaq's chapter, if Iverson played with a more *dominate* big man such as Shaq, he most likely, would have won at least one or two championships rings. While some people may even rank Iverson a little lower than what is listed in this book, it is more than likely because of what I have already mentioned and because perhaps his work ethic such as practice, injuries, and the off-the-court issues that prevented him from prolonging his career and perhaps reaching the 30,000 point plateau. But no matter how you view "The Answer," Iverson was one of the most *dominating*, *relentless*, and *dynamic scorers* of all-time.

Career Totals

26.7 points, 6.2 assists, 2.9 rebs, 2.2 steals, 0.2 blocks, .425 FG%, .780 FT%, .313 3FG%

24,368 points, 5624 assists, 3394 rebounds, 1983 steals, 164 blocks, 1059 threes

Isiah Thomas

(Rank #28)

All-NBA First Team (3-times), Assist Title (1-time)

Championships (2), Finals MVP (1-time), All-Star (12-times)

Also featuring:
Joe Dumars

    Isiah Thomas was one of the all-time great point guards in NBA history. Coming off an NCAA Championship in 1981 with the Indiana Hoosiers, Isiah was one of the first underclassmen to come into the NBA following in the footsteps of the great Magic Johnson. But unlike Magic, Isiah was only six-foot-one and perhaps the best little man to enter the league since Nate "Tiny" Archibald. As the floor general for the Detroit Pistons, Isiah won two NBA Championships back-to-back in 1989 and in 1990, where he was named NBA Finals MVP. With the *oozing* talent to score at will and as a phenomenal passer, it didn't take Isiah long to become an elite point guard in the NBA. After making the All-Star team his rookie year, the very next season Isiah averaged a career-high 22.9 points per game. Two years later, he also set a then record 13.9 assists per game in the 1985 season and eventually became the 4th man in history to reach the 9000 assists milestone. As the best point guard in the Eastern Conference during the 1980s, Isiah would be named to the All-Star team 12 consecutive seasons beginning in his rookie year.

Offensively Isiah was one of the best all-around point guards in NBA history. As one of the games most skilled ball-handlers, Isiah was equipped with an *explosive* first step and had the uncanny ability to finish at the basket a 'la Allen Iverson. And from the perimeter, he was one of the *deadliest* streak shooters the league has ever seen. When he got it going, he would shoot the lights out of the building as he has shown many times, especially throughout his playoff career. In addition, like many of the all-time greats, Isiah's greatest strengths could have been his mental toughness, killer instinct and his extreme will to win. Like Magic, behind the smile was the ultimate competitor and cold blooded assassin that brought terror to his opponents during the biggest games when it counted most and the stakes were highest.

That intangible brought out the best in his teammates to where everyone competed (as a team) at the highest and did whatever it took to win. Although small in stature, and not necessarily gifted defensively, Isiah had some of the quickest hands and feet that allowed him to pickpocket an opponent and accumulate a lot of steals out of the passing lanes during his career. Because of his tenacity on both ends of the floor and his killer instinct, Isiah was the leader and catalyst to the perfect fit of the "Bad Boy" image during the Detroit Pistons championship years.

Isiah Lord Thomas III was born on April 30th, 1961 in Chicago, Illinois and attended St. Joseph High School in Westchester. In college at Indiana University, he averaged 15.4 points and 5.7 assists per game. In his sophomore season, he led the Hoosiers to victory in the 1981 NCAA Championship game and was named Final Four Most Outstanding Player. With nothing left to prove, Isiah declared that he would be eligible for the draft, becoming one of the first underclass men to do so. Thomas was then selected with the 2nd pick overall of the 1981 NBA Draft by the Detroit Pistons. In his rookie season, he averaged 17 points, 7.8 assists and 2.1 steals per game, started in his first All-Star game, and won the 1982 Rookie of the Year award. In only his second season in the league, he averaged a **career-high 22.9 points** and **2.5 steals** per game but the Pistons missed the playoffs in both years.

In the 1983-84 season, Isiah blossomed into the best point guard in the Eastern Conference when he averaged **21.3 points**, **11.1 assists**, **4 rebounds**, and **2.5 steals** per game, and was named to the first of three consecutive All-NBA First Team selections. With teammates Kelly Tripucka, John Long, and Bill Laimbeer playing in their third season together, the Pistons made the playoffs for the first time since 1977. But unfortunately, they lost a tough series to Bernard King and the New York Knicks in the first round three games to two. Despite the loss in game five, Isiah had one of his "signature moments" when he scored 16 points in the fourth quarter to extend the game into overtime. For the series, he averaged 21.4 points and 11 assists per game. That season, Bernard King was named to the All-NBA First Team and had the best season of his career in the playoffs averaging a whopping **34.8 points** per game. One of the league's all-time great scorers, King would win the scoring title the following year at **32.9 points** per game and was named to the All-NBA First Team for the second straight season. Also that year in 1985, Isiah averaged a **career-high** in **assists at 13.9** and led the Pistons back to the playoffs. After sweeping the New Jersey Nets in the first round, the Pistons were eliminated in the semifinals by the defending champion Boston Celtics in six games. The very next season, the Pistons took a step back and got eliminated in the first round three games to one by a formidable Atlanta Hawks team that featured emerging superstar Dominique Wilkins.

In the 1986-87 campaign, the Pistons made huge strides into becoming an elite team. With the acquisition of Adrian Dantley in the off-season, the Pistons now had a legitimate big-time scoring threat to compliment Isiah. After winning 52 games in the regular season for the first time since 1974, the Pistons made it all the way to the Eastern Conference Finals. In the first round, they swept the Washington Bullets and then avenged the loss from the previous year's playoffs to the Hawks four games to one in the semifinals. In the conference finals, the Pistons looked like they were ready to unseat and dethrone the Celtics as champions, until their misfortunes came about in game five. After losing the first two games in Boston, the Pistons won the next two games at home decisively. In both games, the Celtics showed their age in more ways than one. After they were demolished in game four 145-119, and with their aging legs and lingering injuries, I really thought the Pistons were going to put an end to Boston's championship run. After splitting the next two games, the Pistons battled the Celtics to the very end in game seven. And, we all know what happened in the closing seconds of game five in Boston that changed the series, as I have described in detail in Larry Bird's chapter. If you haven't already seen the complete sequence on NBA Hardwood Classics, well I'm sure you'll remember the end result, "the steal by Bird underneath to D.J." It was too bad Isiah was the one who inbounded the pass. Anyway, after the crushing defeat, the Pistons never lost their confidence and determination to reach their ultimate goal of winning a championship, as they bounced back even stronger the following season.

During the 1987-88 season, **Joe Dumars** continued to improve as one of the better shooting guards in the league. Because of this, Isiah's scoring and assists dipped below 20 and 10 for the remainder of his career. For the season, Isiah averaged 19.5 points and 8.4 assists per game, and Dumars averaged 14.2 points and 4.7 assists. Dumars was one of the great shooting guards of his time and the perfect complement to Isiah Thomas at the point guard position. He combined offense with defense as well as any 2-guard in NBA history. On the offensive end, he was a *deadly clutch shooter* that could create his own shot from anywhere on the court. With shooting range as far out as the three-point line, Dumars would deliver a *rainbow* jumper that was as pretty as any I have seen in recent memory. I would have to go back as far as Pervis Short of the Golden State Warriors to find a *sweeter* high-arching jumper than Dumars.

In fact, during the Detroit Pistons championship years, the trio of Joe D., Isiah and the "Microwave" (Vinnie Johnson's nickname given to him because he would come off the bench and heat up in a hurry) were all deadly perimeter shooters that could deliver the *dagger* in crucial moments in a game, and especially in the playoffs. To balance off their offense arsenal, Isiah and Dumars would break down the opponent's defense practically at will off dribble penetration and kick, or by dump-off passes to an open big man sliding to the basket. Also in isolation, they could show you a *dazzling array* of multiple crossover dribbles before splitting almost any type of defense and finish at the basket. Not only was Dumars a versatile 2-guard able to play the point, he was equally as versatile on the defensive end, able to guard multiple positions including the greatest player in history in Michael Jordan effectively. Jordan himself said Dumars was the toughest opponent for him to go against. As great as Dumars was it was hard to hear Jordan admit to this because in the eyes of most, he was ultimately *unguardable*. But let's just say during the Pistons championship years and with their devised defensive schemes, Dumars attempted to *contain* him as well as any player ever had.

Although as a tandem, it is fair to say that the *dynamic dual* of Isiah Thomas and Joe Dumars, might have been the greatest backcourt in NBA history - and with Vinny Johnson included, they might have been the best *3-guard rotation* of all-time! Born on May 24, 1963 in Shreveport, Louisiana, Joe Dumars III attended high school at Natchitoches Central. At McNeese State (a small school), Dumars averaged **26.4** and **25.8 points** in his junior and senior year. After an outstanding college career, Dumars was selected with the 18th pick overall of the 1985 NBA Draft by the Detroit Pistons. By his fourth season in the league, he averaged 17.2 points and 5.7 assists per game. And in his prime the next six seasons, he averaged **20.1 points** and 4.7 assists and made the All-Defensive First Team for the first time, and first of four out of five seasons. In addition to his two championship rings, Dumars won the NBA Finals MVP award in 1989. That accomplishment in itself says a lot, because nearly every player that's won the Finals MVP is either in the Hall of Fame or eventually will be. So if Chauncey Billups and Tony Parker eventually get enshrined someday, that would leave Cedric Maxwell as the only player to win the award in its 42 plus years of existence and not makes it into the Hall of Fame.

With Dantley leading the team in scoring and Dennis Rodman, Rick Mahorn, and John Salley continuing to improve with more playing time, the Pistons looked to build on the previous season's crushing defeat in the conference finals and unseat the Celtics as the best team in the East. Another important piece to the revival of the Detroit Pistons as championship contenders was Bill Laimbeer. The six-foot-eleven center was the steady anchor in the middle that had been with the Pistons since Isiah's rookie season. After finishing with a 54-28 record and the second seed, the Pistons knew their road to the Finals would have to go through Boston. In the playoffs, the Pistons defeated the Washington Bullets with Moses Malone in the first round three games to two. After defeating the young up-and-coming Chicago Bulls in the semifinals in five games, Detroit finally got rid of the jinx and dethroned the Boston Celtics in the conference finals four games to two. The Pistons took immediate control of the series by winning both game one and the pivotal game five in Boston. The victory over the Celtics put the *finishing touches* on the Larry Bird era in Boston after I had already thought the Los Angeles Lakers had done in the previous NBA Finals.

For almost every team to win their first championship, they have had to go through the *agony of defeat* time and time again. As they say, you usually have to learn to fail at every level before you can win at the highest level. And that's what the Pistons did in the 1987 conference finals against the Boston Celtics and in the 1988 NBA Finals against the Los Angeles Lakers. Despite the loss in their first Finals appearances, Isiah had another signature game that defined the type of player he was more than ever, when he courageously scored 25 points in the third quarter on a badly sprained ankle. With the Pistons eyeing their first title up three games to two on the road in Los Angeles and Isiah hobbling up and down the court, he scored 43 total points for the game including the 25 in the third quarter. But it wasn't enough, as the Pistons lost the final two games and the series in seven.

The following season, the Pistons made a questionable mid-season trade for Mark Aguirre giving up aging low-post scoring sensation in Adrian Dantley. The trade proved dividends as the Pistons made it back to the NBA Finals and won not only their first championship, but their second the season after. In the playoffs, the 63-19 Detroit Pistons steam rolled the *old and beat up* Boston Celtics and the Milwaukee Bucks in three and four-game sweeps, before taking down Michael Jordan and the *up-and-coming* Chicago Bulls in the Eastern Conference Finals. In an NBA Finals rematch with the Los Angeles Lakers, the Pistons took care of business and avenged their crushing loss in the Finals from the season before and thumped L.A. in four games straight to win the 1989 NBA Championship. Despite the apparent excuses by *Lakers Nation* and fans who wanted the Lakers to win, I felt Detroit was the more destined team and would have come out victorious regardless if Bryon Scott and Magic Johnson had gotten injured. At the same time, I'm sure the Pistons fans felt the same way when they were in position to have won three straight championships, if Isiah hadn't severely sprained his ankle in 1988. But injuries are part of the game and it can snake-bite any team in any given moment of the season when you least expect it.

The season after, the Pistons finished with a record of 59-23 and swept the Indiana Pacers in the first round of the playoffs, and the New York Knicks in five games in the second round to set up an Eastern Conference show down with those same Chicago Bulls. After a tough grueling seven-game series victory, the Detroit Pistons repeated as 1990 NBA Champions over an *extremely* physical and talented Portland Trail Blazers squad in five games. Because the Pistons were pushed to the limit the year before in the conference finals against a Bulls team that was destined to get over the hump in the same way the Pistons were when they finally dethroned the Celtics for the first time two years earlier, I knew Detroit's reign as champion was close to coming to an end. And, that's exactly what happened the very next season as they were swept out of the Eastern Conference Finals by the eventual champion Chicago Bulls. The Pistons never recovered from that devastating beat down by Jordan and his entourage as they were eliminated the following year in the first round of the 1992 playoffs by the New York Knicks three games to two. In Isiah's final two seasons with the franchise, the Pistons never made it back to the playoffs as Isiah retired at the end of the 1994 season after tearing his Achilles tendon during the year.

In player comparisons:

During the 1980s, Isiah was the best point guard in the Eastern Conference and the second best in the entire NBA behind Magic Johnson. He was also one of the top pure point guards ever! However, you might still have to put Isiah as the 6th best point guard of all-time behind Magic, the Big O, John Stockton, Steve Nash, and Bob Cousy for a lot of different reasons. Objectively speaking, you can justify the ranking from an individual standpoint because he never won an MVP award (Stockton didn't either) and was not selected to the greatest team in history, the 1992 Olympic Dream Team. Even though many felt he may have been "blackballed" and that his career burnt out sooner than expected perhaps due to injuries, the fact remains that he still didn't make the team and Stockton did. So, not only did he have very many individual awards, honors, and accolades except the one assist title and three All-NBA First Team nods, his career only lasted 13 seasons.

But, what he did do is lead the Detroit Pistons to two NBA titles and was the NBA Finals MVP in 1990. Also, the five straight seasons, beginning in his second year in the league when he averaged 20 points or more, he also averaged 10 assists or more four times, including 13.9 per game, which was the highest of any player in NBA history not named Stockton. And, although underrated as a defender, he averaged a very high 2.3 steals per game over that same five-year span. Like most great players with championship rings, Isiah played his best in the biggest games in the postseason where he averaged **20.4 points**, **8.9 assists**, and **4.7 rebounds** per game. He also was known for having *big scoring runs* within those *big games* throughout his playoff career. So for a point guard with virtually no weakness besides not having a prolific three-point shot, Isiah was one of the most complete point guards to ever play the game. But, he was only a dominate player for a short time and had very few individual honors to show for, except for what I already mentioned above and the one NBA Finals MVP award (Joe Dumars won the first one in 1989) in 1990. It wasn't difficult to *not* rank him any higher than 6th in this book for all-time great point guards, even though one could easily build the case for him ranking anywhere from number three all-time to number six. During his prime, until Chris Paul proves otherwise, Isiah Thomas was one of the top three greatest scoring point guards ever along with Oscar Robertson and Magic Johnson!

Career Totals

19.2 points, 9.3 assists, 3.6 rebs, 1.9 steals, 0.3 blocks, .452 FG%, .759 FT%, .290 3FG%

18,822 points, 9061 assists, 3478 rebounds, 1861 steals, 249 blocks, 398 threes

George Gervin

(Rank #29)

All-NBA First Team (5-times), Scoring Title (4-times)

All-Star (9-times), ABA All-Star (3-times)

Also featuring: Alex English
& Tracy McGrady

George Gervin was one of the all-time great scorers to ever play professional basketball and the first guard/small forward to win three scoring titles in a row. Given the moniker "The Ice Man," Gervin was as cool as they come on the basketball court with his persona translating into *silky-smooth* drives to the basket and a *feathery* jump shot. The San Antonio Spurs gunslinger was the *ultimate* scoring machine that could score with grace and creativity from the inside or the outside, shooting from the most difficult degree of angles. Gervin was also able to finish on the fast break or in the half court with the best that have ever played the game. With his signature shot the "finger roll" layup, he would spin the ball high up in the air with the tips of his fingers allowing it to swish through the hoop. He had a variety of finger rolls that he performed as far out as the free-throw line. In addition, he could spin shots in from the front, left or right side of the rim, and also off reverse layups from either side of the basket. Some of his finger rolls were taken with the most difficult of angles underneath the basket often around opponent's outstretched arms. He was also able to squeeze shots in between multiple defenders contesting in the paint. His offensive arsenal also included one of the best bank shots of his era. After watching him demonstrate the finger roll live a few years back on "The Best Damn Sports Show Period," I realized that the players today really don't have a true finger roll. His hands and fingers were so long it looked almost extra-terrestrial, like he could palm the ball not only with his hands, but within his fingers. I was actually in awe on how easy he made it look. Gervin finished his career as the San Antonio Spurs all-time leading scorer with 23,602 points.

George Gervin was born on April 27th, 1952 in Detroit, Michigan where he went to Martin Luther King High School and then attended college at Eastern Michigan University and Long Beach State. After an altercation in college, he tried out for the Virginia Squires at the end of his sophomore season and was selected in the first round of the 1973 ABA Special Circumstance Draft by the Squires. In 1974, the Squires sold his contract to the San Antonio Spurs of the ABA where they became part of the NBA in 1976-77. In Gervin's first season in the NBA, he averaged a modest 23.1 points a game. His scoring average for almost anyone else at that stage of their career would have to be considered very good to great, but not for a guy who won four scoring titles. In the playoffs, the Spurs lost to the Boston Celtics in the first round two games to zero. The following season in 1977-78, Gervin averaged **27.2 points** per game and won his first of three consecutive scoring titles. The Spurs improved to a 52-30 record and won their first division title but lost in the Eastern Conference Semifinals to the Washington Bullets in six games.

For the 1978-79 season, the Spurs would win 48 games and another division title while Gervin won his second straight scoring title at **29.6 points** per game. In the playoffs, the Spurs would make it out of the semifinals for the first time after defeating the Philadelphia 76ers in a tough seven-game series. But in the conference finals, the Spurs became one of the first teams to blow a 3-1 lead and lost the series in seven games to Elvin Hayes, Bobby Dandridge, and the Washington Bullets. Gervin did play well throughout the playoffs averaging **28.6 points** per game and scored a total of 71 points in games three and four at home against the Bullets. But after trailing three games to one, Washington made adjustments particularly in the game six by suffocating Gervin with Dandridge and Kevin Grevey, and by using a crafty and taller lineup to force Gervin to switch gears and play on the defensive end. Playoff games are won ultimately as a team. And it was too bad Gervin didn't have the supporting cast to pick up the scoring slack to pull the Spurs through to victory.

The crushing lost reminds me of what happened recently to **Tracy McGrady** in his career where in three different seven-game series, his teams blew a 3-1, 2-0, 3-2 games lead to the Detroit Pistons in 2003, Dallas Mavericks in 2005, and Utah Jazz in 2007. McGrady was the *modern-day* Gervin in terms of pure scoring with a touch of *silky-smooth-fluidity* that only Gervin exemplified. McGrady was often criticized for never making it out of the first round of the playoffs despite averaging **28.5 points** per game in 38 career playoff games. He never had a formidable supporting cast in Orlando and didn't quite have enough pieces in Houston to make a deep playoff run before chronic back and knee injuries ultimately ruined his career. Even teammate Yao Ming's coinciding injuries shortened his career and forced him to retire prematurely at 30 years old after playing in just five games in 2010.

Tracy Lamar McGrady Jr. was born on May 24th, 1979 in Bartow, Florida. In his senior year in high school at Mount Zion Christian Academy in Durham, North Carolina, he was named High School Player of the Year by USA Today. As one of the most talented players ever to come out of high school and into the NBA, McGrady was selected with the 9th pick overall of the 1997 NBA Draft by the Toronto Raptors. In his first two seasons playing alongside his cousin Vince Carter, McGrady got off to a slow start playing in limited minutes. But by his third season, he was averaging 15 points per game, showing off his potential as one of league's most promising players. He gave a demonstration of his *raw* athletic ability during the 2000 NBA All-Star game festivities by finishing third in the dunk contest behind Carter and Steve Francis. For the first time going in, I felt all three contestants were good and talented enough to have won the competition. But, with those three or four *obscene* dunks that I described in Kobe's chapter, Carter won the contest in a landslide because he simply performed head-and-shoulders above the rest. However, later on in his career, McGrady would perform one of if not the best slam dunk in All-Star game history when he, using his left hand, through a lob pass to himself off the backboard before slamming it home between Dirk Nowitzki and Tim Duncan.

At only 21 years old about to turn 22 in the 2000-01 season, McGrady blossomed into one of the league's elite players averaging **26.8 points**, **7.5 rebounds**, **4.6 assists**, **1.5 steals**, and **1.5 blocks** per game - and shot .386 percent from three-point range. He was also named to the All-Star team for the first of seven consecutive seasons, to the All-NBA Second Team, and was honored with the NBA's Most Improved Player award.

In player comparisons:

At that point in McGrady's career, I often debated that he was easily one of the top 5 players in the NBA and was a slightly better all-around player than Kobe Bryant (also mentioned in Shaq's chapter). Most people, I'm sure would have called it a draw and or had given the edge to Bryant based on his defense, similarity in style, and the potential to become the next Michael Jordan. While Kobe may have been a version of Jordan at least aesthetically, T-Mac looked like he was as well, but also looked like a *cross-version* of Gervin with a little less creativity with his shot-making ability, but with a lot more athleticism - if that makes any sense. He was also the first six-foot-eight guard with prolific three-point shooting range. In my evaluation, I had it the other way judging from watching both players and in statistical comparisons. Even in head-to-head matchups, I gave McGrady the slight edge after watching him on multiple occasions outscore and out defend Bryant. In fact, McGrady is one of the few players that were able to block Bryant's fadeaway shot on occasion. Defensively, during his prime, he guarded Bryant as well as anyone ever had similar to the way Dwyane Wade and Kevin Durant do today. But maybe as far as scoring numbers, this was a classic example of stats being overblown or overrated due to the fact Bryant may have been held back and had to share a lot of his offensive production early on in his career with Shaquille O'Neal? Not to make excuses for T-Mac, but in terms of age, McGrady's career was cut short due to injury causing him to fall through the roof, landing harder than any superstar in history not named Bill Walton, Grant Hill and Steve Francis. And that includes perhaps Clyde Drexler at 31 years old. I mean McGrady was barely 29 years old when his scoring dropped to 21.6 points per game and barely 30 when it fell off the charts at 15.6. The last few years including recently playing for the Atlanta Hawks, he averaged 7.8 points, 3.3 rebounds and 3.3 assists per game while Kobe Bryant at a year older, looks like he's still in his prime from a scoring standpoint, having a career year.

The downward spiral of McGrady's career is all due in part because of his career threatening chronic back (spasms) and knee injuries. I know his off-the-court issues in Houston were exploited, but there are many players that either do good or bad off the court throughout the years that still have great careers and win championships. I will have to admit though; I never questioned McGrady's attitude and work ethic until his last couple of years playing for Houston. So if he hadn't been injured, he would have still been a *shoo-in* Hall of Famer just not quite at the level of Kobe like I once thought. And, if he had been healthy, Kobe would have still ended up being the better player, but it would have been a lot closer than most people realize. Still to this day, even in a back-up role, I feel McGrady is the better passer with the better court vision, and in his prime with his legs under him, was the better rebounder and in-game and exhibition dunker - if the latter really matters. But what separated the two as the years went on, is not necessarily the killer instinct to score because McGrady had that too, but Bryant's defense and his extreme will to win - albeit his way. Just like I believe former teammates Yao Ming and Grant Hill will eventually make the Hall of Fame someday, so will McGrady and his underachieving cousin Vince Carter, for that matter. How many people can say they have recorded 18,000 points, 5000 rebounds, 4000 assists, 1000 steals, and 800 blocks in a career? If he sticks around long enough, he may end with 20,000, 6000, 5000, 1000, 1000, and an additional 1000 three-pointers made for his career. As a Superstar at the shooting guard position only Jordan, Drexler, and eventually Bryant and Wade will have posted at least 20,000 points, 6000 rebounds, and 5000 assists for a career. And only Bryant and perhaps Iverson were better at his position during his time. Also remember, not including current players, only Tom Chambers and Mitch Richmond are the only players who have scored 20,000 points and are not in the Hall of Fame.

The following season, McGrady averaged **25.6 points** and had a **career-high 7.9 rebounds** per game, and was named to the All-NBA First Team. In the 2002-03 season, he posted one of the best all-around seasons since Michael Jordan when he averaged **32.1 points**, **6.5 rebounds** and **5.5 assists** per game, and made **173 three-pointers**. He also became the youngest player in history to average 30 points since Bob McAdoo in 1975. The very next season, he won the scoring title at **28.0 points** per game while posting identical numbers as the year before in almost every other category. In his first three seasons with the Houston Rockets before the reoccurring injuries, he averaged 25 points, six rebounds, and 5.8 assists. He also had, in my opinion, the greatest finish in the regular season on Dec. 9th 2004 when he scored 13 points in 33 seconds which included four three-pointers (one of those threes was a 4-point play) against the San Antonio Spurs. The biggest knock on McGrady's resume is that he never made it out of the first round of the playoffs as a starter, losing in seven games three straight playoff appearances. Even though he played in only 38 playoff games, like most great players he increased his scoring from the regular season to the postseason averaging **28.5 points**, **6.9 rebounds**, and **6.2 assists** per game. I'm sure those numbers will come down assuming the team he plays on makes the postseason in the years to come. But, maybe McGrady can also prove he is a winner by helping the team he plays for go deep into the playoffs.

Despite playing his NBA career injury free, Gervin fell into a similar situation as McGrady in terms of playoff success, because he had to compete with more talented teams such as the Los Angeles Lakers, Houston Rockets (made it to the NBA Finals and lost), Boston Celtics, and Philadelphia 76ers during their championship years. In his first four seasons, his best teammates were Larry Kenon who consistently averaged twenty points and made two All-Star teams but was nowhere near the Hall of Fame player the other elite teams rostered. He also played with Johnny Moore and Mike Mitchell for six years, a broken down James Silas for three years, and a washed-up Artis Gilmore for four seasons before leaving the NBA in 1986 to play in Europe. Unfortunately for Gervin, his career burnt out at the age of 34. Gervin's Spurs averaged 48 wins in his first ten seasons with the franchise and won 50 games or more five times.

In the 1979-80 season, Gervin won his third consecutive scoring title averaging an astounding **33.1 points** per game. But the forty-one-win Spurs lost two games to one in the first round of the playoffs to the Houston Rockets behind Moses Malone, Calvin Murphy, Rudy Tomjanovich, Robert Reid and Rick Barry. The following season after the Spurs and Rockets moved to the Western Conference, despite winning the division for a third time, the Spurs lost again to the Rockets, this time in the conference semifinals in seven games. At the time, Malone was carrying the team and Reid was picking up the scoring slack left by Barry (who retired) and an aging Tomjanovich. In the 1982 and 1983 playoffs, the Spurs beat the Seattle SuperSonics and the Denver Nuggets in the semifinals in five games, but were overmatched by the Lakers in the conference finals losing both years in a four-game sweep and six games respectively.

The semifinals matched two of the greatest scorers in NBA history, George Gervin of the San Antonio Spurs and **Alex English** of the Denver Nuggets. Both players began their career around the same time with Gervin blossoming *early on* and English following as a *late bloomer*. That season in 1983 with Gervin coming off his fourth scoring title the year before, English made his name known by winning his first scoring title at **28.4 points** per game. Despite the one career scoring title to his credit, for eight seasons from 1982 to 1989, English averaged an astounding **27.3 points**, **5.4 rebounds**, and **4.7 assists** per game, and shot **51 percent** from the field. You would be *hard-pressed* to find anything more than a handful of guys that can average 27 points over 8 years while missing only three games. Over that same stretch in the playoffs, he nearly equaled those totals averaging **26.4 points**, **5.7 rebounds** and **4.8 assists**, on **48 percent** shooting. He also made the All-Star team 8 years in a row and the All-NBA Second Team 3 times.

In Gervin's last two seasons with the Spurs and one with the Chicago Bulls, his teams missed the playoffs and were eliminated in the first round by the Nuggets and Boston Celtics.

Gervin won the scoring title four times in five years including three straight from 1978 to 1980. He won his first title by a sliver over David Thompson by seven hundredth of a point 27.22 to 27.15. Ironically in 1978, Thompson scored 73 points on the last day of the season and lost the scoring title to a Spur and sixteen years later in 1994, another Spur in David Robinson scored 71 points and won the scoring title over Shaquille O'Neal by a half point 29.8 to 29.3. In his magnificent career, Gervin was also runner-up to the MVP award twice and could have easily won it in 1978 over Bill Walton who only played three quarters of the season. His 26.2 point career scoring average in the regular season ranks 8th all-time and his 27-point career average in the playoffs ranks 6th. On top of that, he scored 26,595 total points in his ABA/NBA career. While playing in minimal playoff games (39), he led the league in playoff scoring average five straight years from 1978 to 1982. In addition, he scored 40 points in a game 68 times, and 6 times in the playoffs. He also had 5 career 50-point games including a career-high of 63. After he surpassed Chamberlain's 31 points and Thompson's 32 points in a quarter in the same game he won his first scoring title, he now shares his own record of 33 points in quarter with Carmelo Anthony who tied the mark in 2010. But what stands out most to me and defined George Gervin's career despite the lack of playoff success, was the day he scored 63 points to win his first scoring title over David Thompson. Not only was it the most exciting scoring race in NBA history, it triggered and catapulted Gervin into the *pantheon* of greatest scorers of all-time list - because he won three consecutive scoring titles beginning that night and an additional 4th in 1982 - that puts him 3rd on the all-time list behind only the great Michael Jordan and Wilt Chamberlain!

Career Totals

26.2 points, 4.6 rebs, 2.8 assists, 1.2 steals, 0.8 blocks, .511 FG%, .844 FT%, .297 3FG

20,708 points, 3,607 rebounds, 2214 assists, 941 steals, 670 blocks, 77 threes

Elvin Hayes

(Rank #30)

All-NBA First Team (3-times), All-Star (12-times)

Scoring Title (1-time), Rebounding Title (2-times)

NBA Championships (1)

    Elvin Hayes was one of the most talented power forwards to play in the NBA. The versatile Hayes along with Kareem Abdul-Jabbar were the next dominating big men to come into the league after Bill Russell, Wilt Chamberlain, and Nate Thurmond. At six-feet-nine, "The Big E" was able to play power forward and the center position so effectively; he ended up 4th on the all-time list in total rebounds at 16,279 behind only Chamberlain, Russell, and Kareem. He was even ranked 6th all-time in total points at 27,313, until Shaquille O'Neal and Kobe Bryant passed him on the list. With his *famous* fallaway shot, Hayes dominated both the college ranks and in the NBA. On the defensive end, he was also one of the game's best rebounders (as mentioned above) and shot blockers. Like the *Iron Man* Karl Malone, Hayes was incredibly durable having missed only nine games in his sixteen-year career.

    Elvin Ernest Hayes was born on November 17th, 1945 in Rayville, Louisiana and attended Eula D. Britton High School, where he averaged 35 points as a senior and led the team to the state championship in 1964. In the championship game, he score 45 points and had 20 rebounds. In college under Coach Guy Lewis, Hayes and Don Chaney became the first African American basketball players at the University of Houston. In his sophomore year, he averaged 27.2 points and 16.9 rebounds, and led the Cougars to the NCAA Tournament. In the 1966-67 season as a junior, Hayes averaged 28.4 points and 15.7 rebounds, and took Houston all the way to the NCAA Final Four where he scored 25 points and had 24 rebounds, but lost to the eventual champion UCLA Bruins that featured college great Lew Alcindor. His rebounding total in the Final Four was second all-time to Bill Russell's 27. In his senior season, Hayes averaged an astounding 36.8 points per game and 18.9 rebounds, and avenged the loss from the previous year in the tournament to Alcindor and the Bruins by snapping UCLA's 47-game winning streak in the Astrodome 71-69. In the first national televised college game known as the "Game of the Century," with the Cougars on a 17-game winning streak, Hayes scored 39 points and corralled 15 rebounds, while holding Alcindor to only 15 points and 15 rebounds. He also made the game-winning free throws after being fouled on his *sweet spot*, down low on the left block. During this game, I wonder if Alcindor was having eye trouble from a recent eye injury or was he playing possum in the same way some claim Bill Russell did against Wilt Chamberlain during the regular season. I would have to say, I don't think so on both occasions! Either way, Alcindor and the UCLA Bruins would have the last laugh by winning the rematch in the NCAA Tournament semifinals 110-69 with Hayes being held to 10 points. "The Big E," which was the nickname given to him in comparison to a Navy aircraft carrier "Enterprise," did complete a fabulous college career by setting a career-high in rebounds at 37 and finishing with a career scoring average of 31 points per game to go along with 17.2 rebounds. He also was named Sporting News College Basketball Player of the Year.

Elvin Hayes was selected with the 1st pick overall of the 1968 NBA Draft by the San Diego Rockets. In his first season, Hayes scored a season-high 54 points and won his first and only scoring title at **28.4 points** per game, becoming the last rookie to do so. He also averaged a superb **17.1 rebounds** per game but lost the Rookie of the Year and the MVP award to future teammate Wes Unseld of the Baltimore Bullets. In the playoffs, the Rockets were eliminated in the first round by the Atlanta Hawks in six games. The following year, he nearly duplicated his rookie campaign averaging **27.5 points**, and led the league in rebounding at **16.9**. And one year later, he also set a **career-high** in **scoring at 28.7 points** per game and averaged **16.6 rebounds**, good for third best in the 1970-71 season. At that point, Hayes missed the postseason three years in a row playing for San Diego and the Houston Rockets, despite averaging 27.1 points and 16 rebounds during that span. The following year, the Rockets had moved to Houston where Hayes played his final season in his first stint with the franchise before he was traded to the Baltimore Bullets for Jack Marin and future cash considerations. In his first year in a Bullets uniform, Baltimore finished with 52 wins and lost in the first round of the playoffs to the eventual champion New York Knicks in five games.

The very next season with an imposing frontcourt of Hayes and Hall of Famer Wes Unseld in their second year playing together, the Capital Bullets lost to the New York Knicks in the Eastern Conference Semifinals in seven games. However, Hayes did set a **career-high in rebounding at 18.1** and **blocks at 3.0** per game. In the 1974-75 campaign, the Bullets finished tied with the Boston Celtics for best record in the league at 60-22. In the playoffs, they eliminated both the Buffalo Braves in seven games in the semifinals and the defending champion Celtics in the conference finals in six games. In the NBA Finals, the Bullets were heavily favored but were shocked by the fourth best team in the NBA record wise - "Cinderella" Golden State Warriors losing the series in four straight games. The Warriors as a team may have looked a little inferior, but they had the great Rick Barry who averaged almost 30 points for the series and won Finals MVP. Barry claimed the victory was the greatest upset in NBA Finals history. The next season, the Bullets won 48 games but lost in the semifinals to the Cleveland Cavaliers in seven games but avenged the loss the following season winning two games to one in the first round. However, in the semifinals the Bullets lost to Hayes' old team, the Houston Rockets in six games.

In the 1977-78 season, Hayes would complete a brilliant college and pro career by winning the prize that eluded him the most. After finishing with less wins with 44 than the previous two seasons, the Bullets in the playoffs played like a team destined to win its first championship. After sweeping the Atlanta Hawks in the first round and finishing off the San Antonio Spurs and Philadelphia 76ers in the semis and conference finals in six games, the Bullets made it back to the *Big Dance* against the Seattle SuperSonics. In an interesting playoff format that went 1-2-2-1-1, the Bullets in a see-saw battle won game one and game seven in Seattle to win the 1978 NBA Championship. The next season, the Bullets would improve their win total by ten games and make it back to the NBA Finals. After eliminating the Hawks and then the Spurs in seven games, they would succumb to Seattle in five games in the Finals. In his last two seasons in Washington, the Bullets lost in the first round of the playoffs to Dr. J and the up-and-coming Philadelphia 76ers two games to zero, and missed the playoffs the following year. After being traded, Hayes finished the last three seasons of his career in Houston where he played in only three playoff games.

In player comparisons:

For a player some claim to have disappeared in crunch time, Elvin Hayes was sure good enough to have helped lead his team to three NBA Finals. How many people can say they led their team to 3 NBA Finals as one of the primary guys? Not many! If his teammates had pulled him through to victory during the times he didn't play well, all would be forgotten. The same is to be said about every great player that has come up a little short in big moments of big games. I'm not excusing his lack of *clutchness* at times; I just think he had a little bit of the Wilt Chamberlain syndrome to where his attitude of wanting to do things his way interfered with not only his overall play but with the perception he left upon his teammates. However, Hayes brought more than enough to the game over the years and produced *more* at his position than almost anyone in history. In fact, he was the second best big man in the game to Kareem Abdul-Jabbar in the 1970s, where he scored 18,922 points that decade to Kareem's 22,141.

Elvin Hayes is eighth on the all-time scoring list with 27,313 points and fourth in rebounding at 16,279. How can a player of that magnitude as a scorer and a rebounder rank out of anybody's list of top 50 players of all-time? In fact, he was actually the 6th leading scorer in NBA history until Shaq and Kobe passed him on the list within the last couple of years. Notably, as a rookie, Hayes led the league in scoring at 28.4 points per game and averaged 17.1 rebounds. Those were his averages in his first three seasons in the league which at the same time happened to be his 3-year peak. Over his first six seasons, he averaged 25.4 points and 16.3 rebounds per game including a career-high 18.1 rebounds and three blocks in his sixth season, the first year they officially started keeping track of that category. During that same six-year span, he averaged at least 14.5 rebounds per game. Two of his most remarkable accomplishments are: in his first 12 seasons as an All-Star, he averaged at least 11 rebounds per game and; 22.9 points and 13 rebounds for his entire playoff career. In addition, he also led the league in rebounding per game during the playoffs three times with averages of 15.9, 13.3 and 14, and had 8 blocks or more in a game 10 times in his career. Based on numbers alone, Hayes is easily one of the Top 50 players of All-Time.

Career Totals

21.0 points, 12.5 rebounds, 1.8 assists, 2.0 blocks, 1.0 steals, .452 FG%, .670 FT%

27,313 points, 16,279 rebounds, 2398 assists, 1771 blocks, 864 steals

George Mikan

(Rank #31)

All-NBA First Team (6-times), All-Star (4-times)

Scoring Title (3-times), Rebounding Title (1-time)

NBA Championships (5)

Also featuring: Joe Fulks
& Max Zaslofsky

George Mikan was the *first dominating* big man and pioneers that revolutionized professional basketball when the game was previously played with adept ball-handling and finesse. In his first six seasons with the first one coming in the Basketball Association of America in 1949, Mikan led the Minneapolis Lakers to five NBA Championships. He also won the scoring title in his first three seasons in the league. An extremely large man and physical force in the early 1950s, Mikan was so dominant that the NBA had to widen the lane from six feet to twelve (which became known as "The Mikan Rule"). It also led the NCAA to outlaw defensive goaltending due to all the shots he swatted away from the basket. Mikan was also one the best all-around big men ever, proficient at scoring, rebounding, and passing - and could run the floor with surprising speed, so to speak. One coach said he was the "Babe Ruth of basketball" while another said "he's nothing but a monster." In those days, as a behemoth of a man at six-feet-ten, Mikan was bigger and stronger than the centers he played against. He used his bulk to great advantage by backing down defenders in the lane to launch a deadly hook shot and would use his elbows as lethal weapons to shield his hook shot and when in pursuit of a rebound or loose ball. In addition, he was a *fierce competitor* that did whatever it took to win including punishing opponents with hard fouls and by playing through injuries. During his career, Mikan was noted to have broken over ten bones and for receiving one-hundred and sixty stitches.

George Lawrence Mikan Jr. was born on June 18th, 1924 in Joliet, Illinois and attended DePaul University. Beginning his college career as a somewhat clumsy guy, twenty-eight-year-old rookie coach Ray Meyer saw the potential in Mikan during the time where it was believed that taller players were too awkward to play basketball at a high level. Meyer worked with Mikan intensely to teach him how to make hook shots accurately with both hands. He also made him punch a speed bag, jump rope and take dancing lessons to enhance his skills as an athlete. In college, Mikan dominated his opponents with his size and strength and with his unstoppable hook shot. As a junior, he led the nation in scoring at 23.3 points per game and his team to victory in the 1945 National Invitational Tournament. He averaged forty points in three games which included a **53-point game** (in which he equaled the entire score of the Rhode Island State team), and was named MVP for the tournament. In his senior year, he led the nation again in scoring at 23.1 points per game. He was also named Helms National Player of the Year in both 1944 and 1945. Bob Kurland won it in 1946.

After college in 1946, Mikan signed with the Chicago American Gears of the National Basketball League that would later merge with the Basketball Association of America to form the NBA in 1949. In his rookie year with Chicago, Mikan played in 25 games of the season while averaging a lofty 16.5 points per game. He then led the Gears to the championship of the World Basketball Tournament where he averaged twenty points in five games and was named MVP. Before the start of the 1947-48 season, president Maurice White of the America Gear Company and of the Gears pulled the team out of the league to create his own proposed league of 24 teams. But after folding after just a month, the players from White's teams were dispersed equally among the eleven remaining NBL franchises. The Minneapolis Lakers ended up with Mikan after every team had about a nine percent chance of landing the *phenom*.

In his first season in the BAA, Mikan led the league in scoring for the first of three consecutive seasons at 28.3 points per game unseating **Max Zaslofsky**, who became the youngest in history to win the scoring title the year before. Although, Kevin Durant of the Oklahoma City Thunder just broke the record in 2010. Runner-up **Joe Fulks** finished second to Zaslofsky that year after he won the leagues first scoring title. While Mikan may have been the original great center, "Jumping Joe" Fulks was the original high scoring forward/center before both Bob Pettit and Mikan. In fact, he was credited as the first player to use a jump shot and set the NBA record of **63 points** in a game in 1949 until Elgin Baylor broke it ten years later in 1959. He also happened to be the Superstar that led the Philadelphia Warriors to the BAA's first championship in 1947. In the NBA Finals, the Warriors won games one, two and three before eventually taking the series in five. Although, the following year, after winning game one of the 1948 Finals against player/coach Buddy Jeannette and the Baltimore Bullets, Philadelphia would go on to lose the next three games and the series in six. Of note: Mikan did lead the NBL in points per game in both 1947 and 1948.

Mikan also led the league in playoff scoring for the first of four consecutive seasons at 30.3 points per game. After sweeping the Chicago Stags and the Rochester Royals in the Western Division, the Lakers defeated the Red Auerbach coached Washington Capitals in six games to win the 1949 BAA Championship. After the Lakers took a commanding three games to none lead in the series, Mikan sustained a broken wrist in game four and had to play game five with a cast. The Lakers lost both games but fought back to win game six convincingly 77-56. Before the injury, Mikan came up big scoring 42 points in game 1 and 35 in game three. Behind the nucleus of Mikan, Vern Mikkelsen, Jim Pollard and Slater Martin, the Minneapolis became the NBA's first dynasty winning 4 more championships in 5 years. And for good measure, all four of those players are in the Hall of Fame.

In the NBA's inaugural season of 1949-50, Mikan averaged **27.4 points** in the regular season and **31.3** (including **32.2** in the six-game Finals) in the playoffs. After finishing with an impressive 51-17 record, the Lakers swept the Chicago Stags, the Fort Wayne Pistons in the Central Division, and the Anderson Packers in the NBA Semifinals before defeating Dolph Schayes and the Syracuse Nationals in six games to win the 1950 NBA Championship. The Lakers seemed destined to win the series after Bob Harrison hit a forty-foot shot at the buzzer in game one on the Nationals home court. The following season, Mikan won his third straight scoring title at **28.4 points** per game and finished second in rebounding to D. Schayes at **14.1 rebounds** per game in the first year the NBA kept track of rebounds. He was also involved in the lowest scoring game in NBA history, scoring 15 of the 18 Laker points in a 19-18 loss to the Fort Wayne Pistons. Playing in the pre-shot clock era, the Pistons kept the ball away from Mikan by passing the ball around without any intent to score a basket. This record low game played a part in the development of the shot clock for the 1954-55 season. In the playoffs, the Lakers defeated the Indianapolis Olympians in the semifinals two games to one before falling to the Rochester Royals in the Western Final three games to one. Mikan averaged twenty points per game while hobbling on a fractured leg. What was even more surprising, a few decades later in 1990, he revealed that he had played the game with a plate taped to his leg.

In the 1951-52 season, the NBA widened the foul lane under the basket from six feet to twelve and ruled that players could stay in the lane for three seconds at a time. In the regular season, Mikan led the league in rebounds per game for the first time but his scoring dropped almost four points to 23.8 points per game and field goal percentage to a career low .385 percent. However, he did manage to score a **career-high 61 points** in a double-overtime victory against the Rochester Royals. In the playoffs, the Lakers swept the Indianapolis Olympians and defeated the Royals three games to one in the Western

Division before winning the 1952 NBA Championship over the New York Knicks in seven. After losing Jim Pollard (who scored 24 points in the opener) in game 4 with a back injury, the Lakers bounced back in the pivotal game 5 behind **32 points** apiece, from both Mikan and Mikkelsen. In a most interesting series in which neither team lost two games in a row, the Lakers played their home games in St. Paul and the Knicks played theirs in the dim lit 69th Regiment Armory. The following season, Mikan won the rebounding title and led the league in rebounds per game for the second time. In the playoffs, the Lakers swept the Olympians for the second straight season and defeated the Fort Wayne Pistons three games to two in the Western Division, before winning their second straight title in a rematch with the New York Knicks in five games. As Mikan's career began to slow down, the Lakers went on to win their third consecutive NBA championship and fourth in five years. After defeating the Rochester Royals three times and the Fort Wayne Pistons twice in the Western Division, the Lakers battled a familiar foe in Dolph Schayes and the Syracuse Nationals to a seventh game to win the 1954 NBA Title.

In Mikan's nine-year career, he won five titles (6 and 7 if you include the NBL titles in 1947 and 1948) including three consecutive from 1952 to 1954. He also made All-BAA and All-NBA First Team six times while winning three scoring titles (5 if you include the two titles in the National Basketball League) and one rebounding title. The NBA's first dominating big man deserves a spot on anyone's list of top 50 players of all-time. And on mine, he almost cracked the Top 30.

Career Totals

22.3 points average, 13.4 rebounds, 2.7 assists, .401 FG%, .784 FT%

8458 points, 4167 rebounds, 1027 assists

David Robinson

(Rank #32)

MVP (1-time), Defensive Player of The Year (1-time)

All-NBA First Team (4-times), All-Defensive First Team (4-times)

Rebounding Title (1-time), Blocked Shots Title (1-time)

NBA Championships (2), All-Star (10-times)

Also featuring:
Artis Gilmore

David Robinson was one of the great centers to ever play the game. Coming out of Navy with perhaps more hype than any center entering the NBA since Lew Alcindor in 1969-70, many people felt Robinson was the second coming of Bill Russell but with a better offensive arsenal! Playing left-handed at a towering seven-foot-one with a lean and *chiseled* body, Robinson was the *epitome* of what you can imagine a basketball player to look like. Tall, strong and fast, quick and mobile, with the body composition of Michael Jordan at the center position, Robinson used his height and *leverage* to back down and shoot right over the top of an opponent, and his speed and agility to drive or spin around opposing big men like a shooting guard. Facing the basket, Robinson would either shoot a jump shot right over the top of a helpless defender, or blow past him for a thunderous two-handed slam dunk. In the low post, he would use a little jump hook and turnaround jump shot, or a spin move to get around an opponent for an easy layup or slam. On occasion, he would use the up-and-under move or a short fallaway shot. With exceptional rebounding instincts, Robinson would pursue missed shots from all different angles slamming the ball home for easy put-backs. Defensively, he was an outstanding shot blocker in the low block and from flying out of nowhere to block a shot from the weak side in the same manner; the great Ben Wallace has done recently playing for the Detroit Pistons. Even though other great centers of the past could run the floor, Robinson took it to another level.

David Maurice Robinson was born on August 6th, 1965 in Key West, Florida. After moving several times because his father was in the Navy, the family eventually settled in Virginia. Robinson attended Osbourne Park High School where he played basketball as a senior, after showing little interest for most of his youth. Anywhere between six-feet-four to six-feet-seven inches, he drew little interest from college basketball coaches. So after scoring brilliantly on his SAT scores, he decided to go to the U.S. Naval Academy where he would major in mathematics. By the time he played his first college game at Navy Midshipmen, he grew to six-feet-nine inches and to seven feet by the time he left. With only one year of high school experience, Robinson averaged a meager 13.3 points per game on minimal playing time during his freshman year in college. He blossomed in his sophomore year averaging 23.6 points and 11.6 rebounds, and 22.7 points in his junior year to go along with 13 rebounds per game, which led the nation. He also set a NCAA Division I record 5.91 blocks per game for the season and 14 blocks in a single game up to that point. By his senior year, his scoring average soared to 28.2 points per game drawing nationwide attention. He would score **50 points** in his last college game and go on to win the college Player of the Year award and the John R. Wooden award. After being selected with the 1st pick overall of the 1987 NBA Draft by the San Antonio Spurs, Robinson had to return to the Navy for two years to fulfill his duty as a reserve on call during the time of the Persian Gulf War. During that time he was able to play for the 1988 Olympic team that won gold. Throughout his basketball career, he chose to wear number 50 after his idol Ralph Sampson who by the way just got inducted into the Basketball Hall of Fame.

Robinson joined the Spurs for the 1989-90 season where he led the franchise to a then record thirty-five-game turnaround from the year before. The 56-26 win Spurs, swept the Denver Nuggets in the first round of the playoffs before losing in the semifinals to the eventual Western Conference Champion Portland Trail Blazers in seven games. Despite the heartbreaking defeat, the up-and-coming Spurs played good enough to have won the series, pushing the Blazers into overtime in both game five and game seven in Portland. Robinson put up almost identical numbers in the playoffs as he did in the regular season averaging 24 points, 12 rebounds and 4 blocks per game, and won NBA Rookie of the Year. The next season, Robinson averaged 25.6 points and would win the rebounding title at 13 per game, but the second seeded Spurs would fall victim to one of Don Nelson's "Upset Specials", by losing to the 7th seed Golden State Warriors. The Spurs won the first game in San Antonio but the Warriors swept the next three to win the series behind "Run TMC" juggernauts Tim Hardaway, Mitch Richmond, Chris Mullin and rugged scorer of the bench Sarunas Marciulionis along with workhorse/scrapper Tom Tolbert handling the dirty work. The Warriors over the years have always had tough, gutsy, gritty, and scrappy players throughout the years including one of the most recent, Brian Cardinal who played for the Warriors during the 1993-94 season. You don't get nicknames like "The Custodian" over the years, if you don't make a huge impact as a workhorse that makes all the tough plays and does all the dirty work.

In the 1991-92 season, his third, Robinson led the league in blocks for the first time at **4.49** per game and won the Defensive Player of the Year award, but the Spurs would follow up last year's debacle in the postseason by getting swept in the first round of the playoffs by the Phoenix Suns. Robinson would savor the year by being selected to the 1992 U.S. Olympic Dream Team in which Team USA brought home the Gold Medal in Barcelona. The next season, following Robinson's greatest professional accomplishments to date, the Spurs as a team would rebound and defeat the Trail Blazers three games to one in the first round, but would fall victim once again to the Suns and MVP Charles Barkley in conference semifinals in six games.

The following year in the 1993-94 season, Robinson had perhaps his best statistical season of his career, when he averaged **29.8 points**, **10.7 rebounds**, **3.3 blocks**, and a **career-high 4.8 assists**. He also had two huge feats on the last day of the season when he scored **71 points** (tied for the 5th highest scoring game in NBA history at the time) surpassing George Gervin's franchise record of 63 and by winning the scoring title over Shaquille O'Neal by a half point, **29.8 to 29.3**. He also had a quadruple-double against the Detroit Pistons finishing with **34 points, 10 rebounds, 10 assists, and 10 blocks**. Out of the four quadruple-doubles in history, Robinson's might have been the best because it included the loftiest amount of points with 34. But in the playoffs, the Spurs would revert back to their old ways and lose in the first round for the third time in four years, this time to the Utah Jazz three games to one.

In Robinson's first five years in the league, he played with only one all-star in Shawn Elliot (drafted 3rd in the 1989 NBA Draft) and with a young but often injured Rod Strickland. He also played with above average player Willie Anderson, semi-stars Terry Cummings and Dale Ellis near the end of their careers - Cummings and Strickland had come over in a trade the same year Elliot was drafted. In the 1995 season, the year Robinson won the MVP award, he averaged **27.7 points**, **10.8 rebounds**, and **3.2 blocks**, and shot **53 percent** from the field - and **25.3 points**, **12.1 rebounds**, and **2.6 blocks** in the playoffs. The Spurs finished with the best record in the league at 62-20 and were in great position to win their first championship in franchise history. But they had to go through defending champion Houston to do it. Robinson was coming off an MVP season with a chance to even out the score with Olajuwon with a championship apiece - and bragging rights - not only as the top center in the league, but the best player in all of basketball. After Robinson and the Spurs swept the Denver Nuggets in the first round of the playoffs and *dismissed* the Los Angeles Lakers is six games in the semifinals (he actually played pretty well in the Lakers series averaging **30 points, 15.7 rebounds, 3.5**

assists, and 3.7 blocks), they eventually *took a knee* (almost literally) to the Houston Rockets in the conference finals in six games. Throughout the series, Robinson was demoralized and humiliated by Olajuwon's assortment of *Out Of This World* head fakes, up-and-under moves, and spin moves out of the low block. He must of felt like a "bunny hop in a P-Patch" (as the immortal Chick Hearn would say) trying to guard Olajuwon. Perhaps in this series alone, as much as I love the "Admiral" and the "Dream," after the annihilation of Robinson, Olajuwon put to rest any center comparisons forever! With all due respect to "The Admiral," in his first five years with the Spurs, he had sidekick Shawn Elliot as the only legitimate all-star and the "Little General" in Avery Johnson who was in his first year back and second stint with the team. He did have help in the rebounding department with somewhat in his prime Dennis Rodman and Jr. Reid, but all in all, he played with an inferior support cast. The following year at only 31 years old, Robinson never recovered from the clinic he received from Olajuwon, and began a downward trend numbers wise and with team success.

With every player in history, it appears that certain peak seasons in the regular season or in the playoffs, affect the future of a player in a positive or in a negative way the rest of their career. It appeared to be negative in the case of George Gervin, Clyde Drexler, and David Robinson. But I think it was more of a timing issue and a mere coincidence because most players have the drive to compete at the highest level or they wouldn't have made it this far in the NBA to begin with - and because players fall out of their primes at different stages of their career usually between 31 and 34. Because Drexler and Robinson never had a legitimate superstar as a teammate in the prime of their careers, they shouldn't be penalized at the top of the list for all-time greats. Albeit, Drexler did play with a formidable cast that included Terry Porter, who was a top 5 point guard at the time - and Jerome Kersey, Buck Williams, Kevin Duckworth, and super sixth man Cliff Robinson. But we all know that it usually takes two or three superstars to win a championship especially during and after the 1980s and 1990s. Since then there has been a couple of exceptions with the Detroit Pistons of 2004 and the Dallas Mavericks of 2011. Tim Duncan played with superstar Robinson at the end of his career but had a seasoned European Superstar in Manu Ginobili and a lightning-quick young point guard in Tony Parker.

Another all-time great Spur that went through similar playoff woes as Robinson was center **Artis Gilmore**. Gilmore actually began his professional career in the ABA playing for the Kentucky Colonels where for five years he was highly proficient as a rebounder, shot blocker and with high percentage shots which included a lefty hook shot - and where his team won the 1975 ABA Championship. After the ABA folded in 1976, he went into the special dispersal draft and was selected with the first pick overall by the Chicago Bulls. Even though his prime years were with the Colonels and the Bulls, his most successful years in the NBA playoffs despite not winning the championship, came in his five seasons with the San Antonio Spurs. For that reason, and that he was the last great center to play for the Spurs before Robinson, made it fitting to include him in this chapter.

Born on September 21, 1949 in Chipley Florida, Artis Gilmore attended Carver High School in Dothan, Alabama. He then went on to play basketball at Gardner Webb University and Jacksonville University where as a junior; he led the Dolphins to the 1970 NCAA Championship game against the UCLA Bruins. Despite coming up short in victory, Gilmore had one of the best college careers for any big man in history. That season, he averaged an incredible **26.5 points** and **22.2 rebounds** per game and was named to the All-America Second Team. In his senior year, he averaged **21.9 points** and **23.2 rebounds** and was named to the All-America First Team. Upon graduation, he also became one of five players to average at least 20 points and 20 rebounds for his career and left the school with the highest rebounding average at **22.7** per game in Division I history.

In his five seasons in the ABA playing for the Kentucky Colonels, Gilmore averaged an astounding 22.3 points, 17.1 rebounds, three assists, and 3.4 blocks per game - on .557 percent shooting from 1971 to 1976. He also led the league in field goal percentage his first two seasons and rebounding in his first three including four times in five years. One of his most impressive stats other than his career-high 18.3 rebounds per game in his third season, was his 5 blocks per game his rookie year. His accolades in his five seasons with the Colonels included 5 All-Star selections, 5 All-ABA First Team and 4 ABA All-Defensive First Team selections. I know at the time, the ABA was looked upon as an inferior league, but it was a partial sample-size testament to the potential of the great players that eventually played in the NBA. In fact, if most of the players had played in the NBA before the ABA, their numbers probably would have been similar or at worse - estimating 25 percent less. I mean one prime example is Rick Barry, who was just as great a player or better playing in the NBA than in the ABA. This is the primary reason, I have Barry ranked higher than any other ABA player including Julius Erving, proving he was just as lethal in both leagues. As I have mentioned extensively in Barry's chapter, he never really got his due based on the way he was perceived negatively (as a person) by many. Also, many people today including Jerry West still believe that Barry could have been as great as Larry Bird. It is too bad Connie Hawkins, Dr. J and the rest the gang didn't begin their career in the NBA because it would have elevated their status to presumably greater heights - resulting in higher rankings in almost anyone's book.

In his first six seasons with the Bulls, Gilmore averaged 20.1 points, 11.5 rebounds, and 2.2 blocks - on an eye-popping .588 percent shooting. In fact, even today, if you don't include Andris Biedrins of the Golden State Warriors, who has played in limited minutes in eight seasons, Gilmore is the NBA's all-time leader in field goal percentage. But it was unfortunate that the Bulls made it to the playoffs just twice and never made it out of the first round. His playoff success came with the San Antonio Spurs the next five seasons. At that point he was still a formidable player but on the down side of his career averaging 16.1 points, 9.7 rebounds and 1.8 blocks, on 62 percent shooting. He was also highly efficient from the field leading the league four consecutive seasons including his last two with the Bulls and his first two with the Spurs. He did make the All-Star team 6 times and the All-Defensive Second Team once in 1978. In the postseason, he averaged similar numbers in two seasons with the Bulls and three with the Spurs (17 points, 11.3 rebounds, on .568 shooting).

I know my player rankings are often justified from a winning perspective, and in the case of Elgin Baylor and Jerry West, because they took their teams to the Big Dance eight and nine times respectively even though only winning a combined total of one championship. But look at how high John Elway ranks in football as one of the top quarterbacks of all-time. Despite the infamous playoff win against the Cleveland Browns when Earnest Byner fumbled at the goal line and of course the three Super Bowl appearances in which he lost convincingly, Elway never took home the biggest prize until he was out of his prime the last two seasons of his career when he won back-to-back Super Bowls. At that time Superstar running back Terrell Davis was by far the franchise player and cornerstone of the team. So it could be unfair to say that Drexler and Robinson could only win a championship as the second best player on a team even though that's what actually transpired. Elway lost three Super Bowls with the Denver Broncos before finally winning and Drexler did the same after losing in his first two trips to the NBA Finals.

So many people felt Robinson was a soft player before he won a championship and that his personality held him back from reaching his potential. That may be somewhat true because the same has been said about a lot of players including the most recent Pau Gasol of the Lakers. I am not buying that in full for two reasons: number one, there are many players that have been given the soft label including Tim Duncan, when he was man-handled and regularly dunked on by Shaquille O'Neal, during his prime. But Duncan has always been a *silent assassin* with a killer instinct deep within his soul; he just kept it inside similar to the way recent champions Dwyane Wade and Dirk Nowitzki did. A player who is often viewed as soft in most likely a finesse player in the mold of Kareem Abdul-Jabbar, or David Robinson. So if a player is labeled soft, it shouldn't be interpreted by the style he plays, or by the way he looks from the outside, or by his facial expressions. It only comes from how he feels from the inside, with the questions being asked; does he have the will to win? Does he have the will to compete at all cost? Does he have the will to sacrifice a part of his game for the betterment of the team? Does he have the Killer instinct? Second, timing plays such a big part in sports throughout history. I am not saying that Robinson in his prime playing with an inferior supporting cast was as good as or better than Olajuwon, because he wasn't. Olajuwon proved that in head-to-head matchups in the regular and postseasons. But what I am saying, is that Robinson in his prime played with one of the worst supporting cast of any player in my Top 25 and beyond in some cases.

In the 1995-96 campaign, Robinson had his last standout season of his prime averaging **25 points** and **12.2 rebounds**, and **3.3 blocks** per game - but after defeating the Suns three games to one in the first round in which Robinson posted 41 points and 21 rebounds against Barkley and company, the Spurs were eliminated by the Utah Jazz in six games in the Western Conference Semifinals. The following year, Robinson hurt his back in the preseason and broke his foot in the sixth game of the regular season, forcing him to miss the rest of the year. The Spurs finished near the bottom of the standings and missed the playoffs for only the second time in Robinson's tenure with the team. This was a blessing in disguise, so to speak, or the best thing that could have happened to the Spurs because it allowed them to draft cornerstone Tim Duncan in the 1997 NBA Draft. The first year with Duncan and Robinson playing together, the Spurs finished the 1997-98 season with a record of 56-26. But in the playoffs, after beating the Phoenix Suns three games to one in the first round, the Spurs were defeated by the defending Western Conference Champion Utah Jazz in five games in the semifinals. In the lockout shortened season, the Spurs would finally bring home the glory for David Robinson and for the city of San Antonio. After steam rolling through the playoffs dispatching the Minnesota Timberwolves three games to one in the first round, the Spurs swept the Los Angeles Lakers and the Portland Trail Blazers in the semis and conference finals, before trumping the underdog New York Knicks in five games to win the 1999 NBA Championship.

During the Los Angeles Lakers championship run the next three years, the Spurs were up and down in terms of playoff success but would eventually dethrone the three-time champion Lakers in 2003. After losing to the Suns in the first round of the 2000 playoffs (Duncan was injured and missed the postseason), the Spurs rebounded in the 2001 season finishing with the best record in the NBA at 56-26. After taking out the Timberwolves and Dallas Mavericks in four and five games respectively in the first two rounds of the playoffs, the Spurs were swept in the conference finals by the defending champion Lakers. The dominating Shaquille O'Neal and rising superstar in Kobe Bryant were too much for Tim Duncan and the aging David Robinson. For three consecutive years, O'Neal had his way with the "Twin Towers" by pushing and shoving around their lanky bodies and dunking over them at will. Pulling for the Spurs at that time, it was extremely frustrating watching Shaq *punk* Duncan and Robinson underneath the basket as though they were rag dolls or something. But I knew in the end Duncan would have the last laugh, not only as champion, but as the *better* player when his career was all said and done.

The next season, the Spurs beat the Seattle SuperSonics in five games in the first round of the playoffs before getting eliminated again by the Lakers, this time in the semifinals. In Robinson's final season, the Spurs finished tied with the Mavericks for best record in the NBA at 60-22. After losing to Los Angeles in the playoffs the last two years, San Antonio continued to grow as a team and by adding new pieces. With Antonio Daniels and Terry Cummings going out and Manu Ginobili coming in to the league, along with ever improving by Tony Parker and Stephen Jackson, the Spurs were primed and ready to recapture their title from 1999. After the Spurs won the 2003 NBA Championship Robinson decided to retire on top.

In player comparisons:

During the first seven seasons of David Robinson's career, I thought he had a chance to become as great as or possibly even greater than Hakeem Olajuwon. But that never happened as we already know after his debacle during the 1995 Western Conference finals. In fact, if you take the averages from his first seven seasons and compare it to Tim Duncan's, they look like this:

Robinson: 25.6 points, 11.8 rebounds, 3.1 assists, 3.6 blocks, 52.6 FG%, 74.7 FT%

Duncan: 22.8 points, 12.3 rebounds, 3.2 assists, 2.5 blocks, 50.9 FG%, 69.4 FT%

So on paper, Robinson's best regular seasons were better than Duncan's at any point of his career and as good as or perhaps better in comparisons to Olajuwon's first seven seasons:

Olajuwon: 23.0 points, 12.6 rebounds, 2.2 assists, 3.4 blocks, 51.4 FG%, 68.5 FT%

For his career, he even matched Olajuwon's one MVP award, and finished second in the balloting two other times to Olajuwon finishing second just once. Even though he was very good to great in every aspect of his game, he wasn't dominate for more than just a few years like the other guys ranked ahead of him. If Robinson had played the way he did in his first seven years to let say, 10 to 12 years, he could have easily made the list of Top 25 Players of All-Time regardless if he won any championships as the second best player on the team. Of note: The two other factors that could have enhanced Robinson's legacy in the beginning and at the end of his career were: As I have already mentioned, he finished his rookie season at almost 25 years of age due to his military commitment and his team was not able to defend their NBA title at full strength in 2000 because of Duncan's season ending injury at the end of the regular season. Also, as other great players of the past that have had a negative reputation in which could have hurt their legacy's intangibly, one might say the same about Robinson, but in a positive way. Did his Christian belief as being a *Mr. Nice* guy hold him back with having the toughness or killer instinct on the court? While many would say yes, I would say no as I have already stated in my argument in favor of Robinson as one of the all-time greats.

Robinson's resume (statistically) was nearly as impressive as just about anyone's. He was one of only four men (Hakeem, Alvin Robertson, and Nate Thurmond being the others) to record a quadruple-double in NBA history. He also had 300 blocks in each of his first three seasons in the league and had 10 or more blocks in a game ten times in his career. He and Kareem are the only players to have led the league in scoring, rebounding and blocks during the course of their career. That says a lot because those are the three most *important* categories for a big man. I'm sure you could have added Wilt Chamberlain to the list but they didn't keep track of blocks in his days. Also, if there was a downer for me in Olajuwon's career, it was the fact that he never won a scoring title. Furthermore, as great as Olajuwon was in the steals department, Robinson is also the only man in history to finish in the top five in rebounding (12.2), blocks (4.49), and steals (2.3) in the same season. As a testament to his terrific all-around game and to prove his career-high 71 points was not a fluke (in terms of being a top scorer), Robinson scored 40 points or more 22 times in his career including a 50-point and 52-point game. All of these feats are Olajuwon like! Contrary to what many people might think, I believe if Robinson had all the right pieces around him during his prime, and with particularly another bona fide superstar, he would have won the NBA Championship sooner and his career would be looked at a lot differently perhaps in the same light as Olajuwon. But no matter how you viewed David Robinson before he played with Tim Duncan or during, he will always be remembered as one of the all-time great centers on the court and off!

Career Totals

21.1 points, 10.6 rebounds, 2.5 assists, 3.0 blocks, 1.4 steals, .518 FG%, .736 FT%

20,790 points, 10,497 rebounds, 2441 assists, 2954 blocks, 1388 steals

Kevin McHale

(Rank #33)

All-NBA First Team (1-time), All-Star (7-times)

All-Defensive First Team (3-times), Sixth Man of the Year (2-times)

NBA Championships (3)

Also featuring:
Robert Parish

    Kevin McHale was one of the greatest power forwards and sixth-men of all-time. A terrific scorer for the Boston Celtics coming off the bench or as a starter, McHale helped lead the Celtics to three NBA Championships in six years from 1981 to 1986. Teamed with Larry Bird and Robert Parish, the trio formed the greatest frontcourt in the history of the game. While Bird played from the perimeter and the interior, McHale and Parish played a good portion of the time exclusively in the box (low post/high post) where they were the anchors in the middle on both ends of the court. Both big men were exceptional scorers but McHale had an assortment of *devastating* low-post moves that included multiple head fakes, pump fakes, up-and-under moves, capped off by a lethal turnaround fallaway shot, jump hook and a step-back jumper, all which resulted in many trips to the free-throw line throughout his career. He also could pull up from just about anywhere on the court or take his man off the dribble with his explosive first step, finishing at the basket with an easy layup or short scoop shot when contested in the paint. An outstanding rebounder and shot-blocker, McHale helped anchor the greatest frontcourt in NBA history for 13 seasons in Boston. All his talents were attributed to his *unique* physical make-up (flappable feet to go along with lanky legs and body at six-ten or six-eleven) that included an extremely long wingspan mixed with world-class footwork in the likes of the great Tim Duncan and Hakeem Olajuwon. Although, he has given much credit to his high school coach for helping him develop his entire offensive game. Bill Walton once gave McHale the highest of compliments saying, "He was the second-best post-player of all-time, after Kareem Abdul-Jabbar. In his strategy against bigger guys, he was brilliant-subtle finesse, deft fakes, and all. He was so complete as an offensive threat that a defensive player had no defense against him." Other than Celtic great John Havlicek and with all due respect for Billy Cunningham - the two-time Sixth Man of the Year in McHale might have been the greatest sixth man of all-time.

Kevin Edward McHale was born on December 19th, 1957 in Hibbing, Minnesota and attended Hibbing High School where as a senior; he led the team to a runner-up finish in the AA Minnesota State Championship and was named Minnesota's Mr. Basketball in 1976. In four years at the University of Minnesota playing alongside center Mychal Thompson (an eventual rival playing for the Los Angeles Lakers), he averaged 15.2 points and 8.5 rebounds per game - on 55 percent shooting, and left the school as its top player on its 100 year anniversary. McHale was selected with the 3rd pick overall of the 1980 NBA Draft by the Boston Celtics. With Red Auerbach as team president, the Celtics traded their #1 overall pick and the 13th pick to the Golden State Warriors on draft day for Robert Parish and the #3 pick which ended up being McHale. In his rookie season, McHale played limited minutes coming off the bench and averaged a meager 10 points and 4.4 rebounds per game for the season. But behind super sophomore Larry Bird, the Celtics finished with an NBA best 62 wins and defeated the Chicago Bulls, Philadelphia 76ers, and the Houston Rockets to win the 1981 NBA Championship. In game six of the conference finals in Philadelphia with the Celtics up by one point, McHale helped save the win when he blocked Andrew Toney's shot and corralled the rebound with 16 seconds left on the clock. He also averaged 8.5 rebounds in only 17 minutes per game throughout the playoffs. The next two seasons, McHale averaged 28.5 minutes while his overall production began to increase. At that point, Parish was the more seasoned and more productive player after being in the league seven years, with the first four coming as a member of the Golden State Warriors. As a result of the first four years of McHale's development from 1981 to 1984, Parish averaged 19.3 points, 10.4 rebounds, and 2.1 blocks per game, on 54.6 percent shooting. After failing to make it back to the NBA Finals the previous two seasons, McHale was ever improving on both ends of the floor averaging 2.3 blocks per game and was named to the All-Defensive Second Team in 1983. In both seasons, the Celtics lost a heartbreaking seven-game series to the 76ers in the conference finals and swept the year after by the Milwaukee Bucks in the semifinals.

In the 1983-84 season, McHale became an All-Star for the first time averaging 18.4 points and 7.4 rebounds per game - on 55.6 percent shooting, and was named NBA Sixth

Man of the Year. Like Parish, he would make the All-Star team seven consecutive seasons. In the playoffs, the Celtics defeated the Washington Bullets, New York Knicks, Milwaukee Bucks, and the Los Angeles Lakers to win the 1984 NBA Championship. The following season, McHale averaged 19.8 points and 9 rebounds per game - and shot 57 percent from the field. He also became the first player to repeat as Sixth Man of the Year. On March 3rd, 1985 he scored a **career-high 56 points** against the Knicks and **42 points** two days later against the Pistons (career second best). Even though the Celtics lost the rematch to the Lakers in the 1985 Finals, that season and in the playoffs, McHale took his game to a whole new level which included having two of the highest scoring games of his career. For seven straight seasons from 1985 to 1991, he averaged 21.7 points, 8.4 rebounds and 1.8 blocks, on 57 percent shooting. And the last 9 years of his career in the playoffs, he was equally impressive averaging 22 points, 8.4 rebounds, on 57 percent shooting.

While Kevin McHale was on the upswing with his monster scoring games in 1985, running mate **Robert Parish** was now 31 years old, about to turn 32 at seasons end - was beginning a downward trend after averaging at least 19 points per game the last three seasons. During his prime, Parish was one of the all-time great centers. Although underrated most of his career, "The Chief" was an outstanding all-around center that played in the shadow of Larry Bird and McHale most of the time. He also played during the time of some of the greatest centers ever in Kareem Abdul-Jabbar, Bill Walton, Moses Malone, Hakeem Olajuwon, Patrick Ewing, David Robinson, and Shaquille O'Neal (in his first five seasons). Parish was the workhorse and *stabilizer* of the Celtics during the 1980s. He did all the little things that Dennis Johnson did at the wing position. Maybe not the flashiest of centers at a towering 7'1", the always reliable Parish, anchored the Celtics defense with his *formidable* and *intimidating* rebounding and shot blocking. Even though he was an inch shorter than Kareem, and way before he infamously *clocked* Bill Laimbeer during game 5 of the 1987 Eastern Conference Finals, he looked like a person you just wouldn't want to mess with. I think the fierce and often stoic look on Parish's face added to his deception particularly on the *offensive* end of the floor. To fans and opponents, it always looked like Parish was awkward (which he was), old and slow footed, and a beast of a man that could apply the dirty work to corral rebounds and block shots. Where all of a sudden throughout certain stages of the game, particularly when the Celtics needed him most, he would explode to the basket as though he was James Worthy or something, using a quick spin move to drive baseline against opponents finishing with a powerful slam dunk. I mean as great as Kareem was offensively, that was the one move that Parish used that was nearly as impressive. In fact, for a lanky, clumsy looking (he really wasn't, he just looked that way) big man, he was often seen beating Kareem down the floor on fast breaks. He also had a highly effective and unblockable hook shot that he relied on in crunch time moments. To balance off his arsenal, he had a formidable high-arching face-up jump shot.

Born on August 30th, 1953 in Shreveport, Louisiana, Robert Lee Parish went to Centenary College of Louisiana where he averaged 24.8 points and 18 rebounds per game his senior year. After college, Parish was selected with the 8th pick overall of the 1976 NBA Draft by the Golden State Warriors. After a slow beginning to his career, with his production improving gradually, by his third season he would average 17.2 points, 12.1 rebounds, and a career-high 2.9 blocks per game, but the Warriors made the playoffs just once. Although in 1979, he did have perhaps his best game of his career statistically against the New York Knicks finishing with **30 points and 32 rebounds**. Prior to the 1980-81 season (in what would be McHale's rookie year and Bird's second season), Parish was traded to the Boston Celtics forming the *soon-to-be* greatest frontcourt in NBA history. Throughout his stellar career, I really couldn't *pinpoint* his greatest individual season because he was always so consistent. He never led the league in an anything during the regular season or in the playoffs except for total blocks and rebounds in separate playoff seasons. But, what he did do for 15 straight years beginning with the Warriors in 1979 through 1993 with the Celtics is average 16.9 points, 10.3 rebounds, on 54.8 percent shooting. If I had to pick a best season for The Chief, you would have to go with the year he was named to his only All-NBA Second Team in 1982 when he averaged a **career-high 19.9 points** per game to go along with **10.8 rebounds** and **2.4 blocks**, on **54.2 percent** shooting. It's hard to believe that Parish only made one Second Team his entire 21-year career. But that just shows you how great centers were during that era as I have already mentioned. Though, he should be given tremendous props for his reliable play throughout the years playing in 78 out of 82 games - 11 out of 14 seasons with the Boston Celtics.

The 1986 Championship team was the one to remember because the Celtics had perhaps the *best team* and the *best regular season* in NBA history, when they went 67-15 and incredible 40-1 at home! During that playoff run, McHale had his best season in the postseason averaging **24.9 points**, **8.6 rebounds** and **2.39 blocks** per game - while shooting **.579 percent** from the field, and was named to the All-Defensive First Team for the first of three consecutive years. He also demoralized Ralph Sampson with his assortment of pet moves during the NBA Finals, against the Houston Rockets. The following season, the Celtics despite the injuries throughout, looked like they might repeat as NBA champions once again with their dominating home court record. But after Magic Johnson hit one of the most *iconic* shots in NBA Finals history to put the Lakers up three games to one, the Celtics championship run came to a screeching halt as they lost the series in six games. Not to take anything away from the Lakers, but McHale literally played with a broken foot throughout the series. In the 1986-87 season, McHale had the best individual season of his career averaging **26.1 points**, **9.9 rebounds** and **2.2 blocks** per game, on **.604 percent** shooting from the field - and was named to the All-NBA First Team. He also became the first man in history to shoot 60 percent from the field and 80 percent from the free-throw line. A near 80 percent career foul shooter, McHale shot a remarkable 89 percent in 1990. After his memorable individual season in 1987, he scored 20 points or more three straight years before his final three seasons where his numbers began to fall off the charts due to age and injury. His injuries consisted of numerous lower leg, ankle and foot problems. As I have described in Bird's chapter, the aging and *decrepit* Celtics fought *tooth-and-nail* but never made it back to the NBA Finals as McHale retired in 1993.

In player comparisons:

Similar to Parish's one All-NBA Second Team selection, what is even harder to believe is that McHale was named to only one All-NBA First Team and zero Second Team selections? But we all know he came off the bench for many years for the great Celtics teams that played during the time of some of the greatest power forwards of all-time in Karl Malone, Charles Barkley, and teammate Larry Bird. But to bang home my point on how great Kevin McHale was as I have already illustrated at the beginning of the chapter - if Pau Gasol is the most skilled big man in the game today, McHale would make him look one dimensional. This is not a direct insult to Gasol, it is merely one of the biggest compliments you could give the legendary McHale. He was so great throughout his career especially in 1987, the year Magic Johnson won the MVP award; Larry Bird said you could have easily given the award to Kevin. His greatest individual accomplishment was when he led the league two years in a row in field goal percentage. In fact, he shot an astounding .554 percent for his career and his frontcourt mate Parish, shot .552 for his career as a Celtic. Furthermore, McHale shot at least 57 percent for four straight seasons and so did Parish. When McHale's streak ended in 1988, Parish's began.

McHale owns the Celtics record with 9 blocks in a game, and he did it twice. He also led the league in field goal percentage at .604 in back-to-back years while finishing tenth all-time in career field goal percentage. He also owned the Celtics scoring record of 56 points until Larry Bird broke it nine days later. But, what stands out most about the Legend of Kevin McHale, is his low-post moves. Most observers including Charles Barkley of TNT, always mentions that McHale was the greatest power forward he ever played against. The reason is because he had *unparalleled* low-post moves. Even though Olajuwon's moves were more dominate because of his athleticism and ability to create more space faster as I have already described in his chapter, McHale had the greater assortment. Although according to Shaquille O'Neal, Olajuwon had 20 moves if you count all the countermoves.

In McHale's case, he probably had even more if you count the left-hand variety, the different angles he shot them, and his complete arsenal of countermoves. Facing the basket he could utilize the triple-threat position with a jab-step and pull-up jumper over an opponent, or he could fake left and drive right to the basket. Then, he had his primary shots that I mentioned in the beginning of the chapter; the lethal fallaway shot, jump hook and the step-back jumper. On both the fallaway and the jump hook (in which he could shoot with either hand), he could use the up-and-under move scoring off the pivot and underneath the opponent with his patented scoop shot. He also could fake the fallaway and the jump hook, draw the contact and still finish the shot. Like Olajuwon, he had an assortment of countermoves but with more variations where he could combine his primary moves off fakes and pivots. So from his *skill set* offensively, McHale could have been the greatest.

While some might rank McHale ahead of Dirk Nowitzki, one of the toughest calls in this book, was putting McHale ahead of Scottie Pippen. First of all, Nowitzki is a more versatile player like Larry Bird, able to play the small forward and the power forward position, and he was the more dominant scorer, better shooter and could be the slightly better passer. But the clincher was: like Bird, his single best move was his deadly fallaway shot or one-step fallaway. McHale had by far more moves and was the better defensive player, but Nowitzki had Kobe Bryant's killer instinct (as he showed most of his postseason career and all playoff long in 2011) to put the ball in the hoop, and the more dominant jump shot. He also, was totally underrated defensively and as a rebounder. Not that it means a whole lot, because most likely Rick Carlisle was completely off base and a *prisoner of the moment* when he said in 2012 that Nowitzki was a Top 10 player of All-Time. I mean, you have got to be kidding! I guess to some, Dirk's ranking in this book (number 23) doesn't look so bad after all!

Could McHale as the lone Superstar, have led a team to an NBA Championship? With the right pieces around him, you would have to say, possibly yes. That's why he's ranked ahead of Pippen by a smidgen. I also have Elvin Hayes ahead of McHale despite the lack of an abundance of team success other than the one championship, because like Nowitzki, Hayes had a more dominate fallaway shot and was one of the great rebounders and shot blockers of all-time, not only at the power forward position but at the center position. Because Hayes shot away from the basket with his fallaway vs. McHale with deeper low-post moves, you would have to give McHale the edge in that aspect of his game, but Hayes made up for it with his ferocious rebounding and shot blocking. Because McHale and Pippen played different positions, makes it more difficult to compare the two, but at the same time, makes it easier to interchange the two if you had to, because their ranking is almost a wash at 33 and 34 respectively. I know Scottie had more team success by a two to one margin (6 NBA titles to 3) but Pippen played with the greatest player of all-time and with Dennis Rodman (Hall of Famer), Horace Grant, Tony Kukoc, and an underrated supporting cast. But I think Kevin McHale would be the pick to build a team around as the number one guy over Pippen!

Career Totals

17.9 point, 7.3 rebounds, 1.7 assists, 1.7 blocks, 0.4 steals, .554 FG%, .798 FT%

17,335 points, 7122 rebounds, 1670 assists, 1690 blocks, 344 steals

Scottie Pippen

(Rank #34)

All-NBA First Team (3-times), All-Defensive First Team (8-times)

Steals Title (1-time), NBA Championships (6), All-Star (7-times)

Also featuring: Grant Hill
& Dennis Rodman

Scottie Pippen was one of the great small forwards of all-time. As the perfect complement to Michael Jordan, the versatile Pippen played multiple positions including his natural small forward position, shooting guard, and point guard for the Chicago Bulls that won 6 NBA Championships in the 1990s. Because of his excellent ball-handling and passing skills at six-feet-seven, Pippen was often referred to as a *point-forward*, often taking on the responsibility of bringing the ball down court to set up the offense. In the half court, he was adept at setting up the entry pass to a post-player or by finding a cutter darting to the basket. In transition, with his athleticism and explosive leaping ability, Pippen was an outstanding rebounder and one of the all-time great finishers in the open court and in the half court slashing to the basket. He was also a solid spot-up shooter that was able to knock down clutch jump shots from the perimeter and from three-point range. But what made Pippen special was on the defensive end where he was able to *suffocate* and *lock-up* the opposing teams' best player. Many of his greatest highlights are shown with him pickpocketing an opponent or stealing the ball in the passing lanes before racing down court for his *signature* "swooping one-handed" slam dunk. Out of all the players in history, Pippen could have been the best - where he was able to guard almost every position from point guard to power forward. Many people have said including his former coach Doug Collins; "Scottie could shut down anyone and take away half the court." An eight-time All-Defensive First Team, as a testament to his greatness, after Steve Kerr made the winning shot to win the 1997 NBA Finals, Pippen was the one who stole the ball on Utah's ensuing inbound pass before flipping the ball to Tony Kukoc to seal the victory. In addition, Pippen redefined the point-forward concept during the 1990s and was one of the first players selected to the greatest team in the history of basketball, the 1992 U.S. Olympic Dream Team in Barcelona.

Scottie Maurice Pippen was born on September 25th, 1965 in Hamburg, Arkansas and attended Hamburg High School. As a walk-on in college at the University of Central Arkansas Conway, Pippen averaged 17.2 points, 8.1 rebounds, and 2.1 steals per game, and shot 56 percent from the field in four seasons. As a senior, he averaged 23.6 points, 10 rebounds, four assists and 3.1 steals, on 59 percent shooting - and was named NAIA All-American in 1987. Pippen was then selected with the 5th pick overall of the 1987 NBA Draft by the Seattle SuperSonics before being traded soon after to the Chicago Bulls for six-foot-eleven Olden Polynice out of Virginia. In his rookie year, he played in limited minutes coming off the bench as did fellow rookie Horace Grant on an up-and-coming Bulls team that won 50 games for the first time since 1974. But in the playoffs, despite losing to the Detroit Pistons in the semifinals in five games, Pippen got his chance to become a starter in the decisive game 5 victory in the first round against the Cleveland Cavaliers. At that point, Michael Jordan was having his second best scoring campaign and best all-around season (to date) of his career while winning his first league MVP award. In his second season, Pippen nearly doubled his scoring average and finished second on the team in scoring at 14.4 points per game. With Jordan leading the way, and with the young Pippen and Grant bolstering the frontcourt in only their second season playing together, the 47-win Bulls made a deep run in the playoffs. The Bulls defeated the Cleveland Cavaliers in the first round three games to two for the second straight time, before taking down Patrick Ewing and the New York Knicks in the semifinals in six games. But in the Eastern Conference Finals, the Bulls lost again to the mighty Detroit Pistons four games to two.

The following year, Pippen would continue to improve his overall game particularly on the defensive end, increasing his overall production to 16.5 points, 6.7 rebounds, and 5.4 assist per game - and his steals and blocks to 2.6 and 1.2 per game respectively. He was also named to the first of seven consecutive All-Star games. After a 55-win season, in what looked like a stepping stone for the Chicago Bulls after reaching the conference finals from the year before, instead, ended up being for the Detroit Pistons. After losing only one game in each of the first two rounds to the Indiana Pacers and the Philadelphia 76ers, the Bulls for the third consecutive season, were eliminated by the Pistons this time in the 1990 conference finals in a tough seven-game series. As the Pistons lost to the

Lakers in game seven of the 1988 NBA Finals with Isiah playing on an injured ankle, the same can be said for Pippen playing with severe migraines in this decisive seventh game. Especially in the Conference Finals, repeatedly over the years, many players and teams learn to fail at the highest level before reaching the mountain top to win an NBA Championship, and that's what happened to the Chicago Bulls the last 3 years. Even though the Bulls came up short once again, Pippen emerged as a force to be reckoned with throughout the playoffs as he increased his scoring output over 6 points to 19.3 points per game.

In the 1990-91 season, the Bulls would finally dethrone the Detroit Pistons just like they had done to the Boston Celtics two and three years earlier. Pippen had another stellar season shooting a career-high 52 percent from the field and .309 from three-point range, and was named to the All-NBA Second Team - while Jordan won his second MVP award, as the Bulls bulldozed the entire NBA finishing with one of the best regular seasons and playoff runs in history. After finishing with the best record in the Eastern Conference at 61-21, the Bulls swept the New York Knicks in the first round, defeated the Philadelphia 76ers in five games, and swept away the "Bad Boys" Pistons, once and for all in the conference finals. Usually there's a handshake at the passing of the torch in the NBA, but not with these sore losers. Despite losing game one to the Los Angeles Lakers, the Bulls went on to sweep the next four games and the series to win the 1991 NBA Championship. In the clinching game 5, Pippen came up big scoring 32 points and grabbing 13 rebounds. The next two seasons, the Bulls completed a three-peat and defeated both the Portland Trail Blazers and the Phoenix Suns in six games.

With Michael Jordan now in retirement, Pippen was in the middle of his prime when the talented **Grant Hill** was coming into the league. Hill was a *glorified* Scottie Pippen with perhaps a little less defensive presence but with a little more offense that could create his own shot. This was probably the simplest way to describe G. Hill. So in my eyes, even though Hill did say at one time that Pippen was the best all-around player in the game, Hill was actually the better all-around player by a smidgen over Pippen during his prime, at least for certain - particularly on the offensive end. In fact, many have said, if it weren't for those career shortening chronic ankle injuries, Hill would have went down as one of the greatest small forwards of all-time probably ranking slightly ahead of Pippen - providing he ended up with a little more team success the second half of his career. Even though Hill was an above average player the second half of his career (currently playing for the Phoenix Suns at age 39), he still has an outside chance, or should I say, a very slim chance of making the Hall of Fame (2 national championships will help his cause) if he can hang on and have a couple more productive seasons. Come on, other than Coach K, Duke needs someone someday to represent their school in the Basketball Hall of Fame.

Born on August 5th, 1972 in Dallas, Texas, Grant Henry Hill attended South Lakes High School in Reston Virginian where he was a McDonald's All-American in 1990. In his first two years at Duke University, he won two NCAA Championships in 1991 and 1992 becoming the first Division I college to win back-to-back championships since UCLA in

1973. In his junior year, he averaged 18 points, 6.4 rebounds and 2.5 steals per game, and was named the nation's top defensive player in 1993. And in his senior year, he averaged 17.4 points, 6.9 rebounds and 5.2 assists per game, and was ACC Player of the year. He also led the Blue Devils to their third national title game in four years but would eventually lose to the Arkansas Razorbacks. As a testament to his great all-around play even on the defensive end, Hill was the first player in ACC history to record 1900 points, 700 rebounds, 400 assists, 200 steals and 100 blocks for a career. And, in case you don't remember, in one of the greatest games in college history, he happened to be the inbound passer who threw the three-quarter court heave to Christian Laettner, who then in desperation, turned and shot the last second shot beyond the free-throw line to beat the Kentucky Wildcats in the 1992 regional finals.

After graduating at Duke, Grant Hill was selected with the 3rd pick overall of the 1994 NBA Draft by the Detroit Pistons. In his first season, Hill became an instant star when he averaged 19.9 points, 6.4 rebounds, 5 assists and 1.8 steals per game - and was selected to his first of seven All-Star teams. He was also named co-Rookie of the Year with Jason Kidd. The next 5 years of Hill's career looked like this: **20.2**, **9.8**, and **6.9 - 21.4**, **9**, and **7.3 - 21.1**, **7.7**, and **6.8 - 21.1**, **7.1**, and **6.0 - 25.8**, **6.6**, and **5.2**. But sad to say, during his prime with an inferior supporting cast, Hill never made it out of the first round of the playoffs until 2010, playing with Steve Nash and the Phoenix Suns. In his first six seasons in the league, I felt Grant Hill was the second best wing player to Michael Jordan and a sure bet to make the Hall of Fame until travesty struck in 2001 with an ankle injury that kept reoccurring. In comparisons to Scottie Pippen, Grant Hill in his prime was without a doubt the better talent and the better player similar to the way I viewed Tracy McGrady in prime over just about every star wing player (including Vince Carter and Allen Iverson) not named Kobe Bryant. It was too bad both players' careers were cut short due to injuries.

By the way: perhaps, the reason why Hill and Pippen made very few All-NBA First Teams was because the NBA mixes and matches forward and guard positions, I'm assuming to keep from penalizing the five greatest players for anyone season regardless of position, or because of the technicality that many players play multiple guard and forward or forward and center positions at some point throughout the season.

During the Bulls first championship run, Pippen had one of his signature moments in Game 7 of the 1992 semifinal series against the Knicks when he posted a triple-double of 17 points, 11 rebounds, and 11 assists - and another in the closeout game 6 of the conference finals against the Cleveland Cavaliers when he had 29 points, 12 rebounds, five assists, and four steals.

After Jordan retired, the Bulls were in high hopes of making it back to the NBA Finals with Scottie Pippen as their new leader. Expectedly, Pippen had his best season of his career averaging **22 points**, **8.7 rebounds**, **5.6 assists**, and a **career-high 2.9 steals** per game. He also won the All-Star game MVP and was named to the All-NBA First Team for the first time in 1994. This was also the chance for Pippen to show his greatness playing out of the shadow of Michael Jordan for the first time! After an outstanding 55-win season without his "Airness," the Bulls swept the Cleveland Cavaliers before losing a hard-fought seven-game series to the New York Knicks in the semifinals. In game three, in which many felt Pippen would take the last shot in the waning seconds, it was rookie Tony Kukoc who made the game-winning shot. As the second hand man who refused to come off the bench after the timeout, Pippen was actually supposed to be the inbounder on the play that Phil Jackson drew up. Why does this matter when the Bulls won the game? Because, for the skeptics, it was one more knock against Pippen becoming one of the elite players of all-time and for his team's lack of confidence in him as the number one scoring option to *closeout games at the highest level*. This is one of many reasons, I will detail at the end of the chapter on why Pippen is ranked a little lower than some might expect. Despite losing the series in seven games, Pippen did have one of his signature moments in game 6 against Patrick Ewing similar to Jordan's famous dunk on Ewing in the 1991 playoffs. While Jordan spun baseline, Pippen's dunk over Ewing came on the fast break flying down court directly at the basket.

Despite the loss, Pippen carried the team averaging similar numbers in the postseason as the regular season. During his best four years of his postseason prime from 1991 to 1994, Pippen averaged 20.7 points, 8.2 rebounds, and 5.9 assists per game in the playoffs. And in the eyes of many, Pippen should have finished runner-up to Hakeem Olajuwon in the 1994 MVP voting for all he had done for the Bulls during the regular season without Michael Jordan. But what was equally as impressive, over the last 9 seasons as a Chicago Bull from 1990 to 1998 he averaged 19.2 points, 7.8 rebounds, and 5.5 assists. So basically, the last five years after his prime, his numbers other than his shooting percentage barely dipped. The following season in 1994-95, Pippen nearly duplicated his statistics from the year before winning the steals title at 2.9 per game. He also became one of four players since the post-merger to lead his team in total points, rebounds, assists, steals, and blocks since Dave Cowens in 1978. Both Kevin Garnett and LeBron James accomplished that feat in 2003 and 2009 respectively. But the Bulls took a step back and won only 47 games, seven fewer than the previous year. But, fortunately for the Chicago Bulls, Jordan came out of retirement, ending his baseball sabbatical and played in the season's final 17 games. In the playoffs, the Bulls defeated the Charlotte Hornets before losing to Shaquille O'Neal, Penny Hardaway, and the Orlando Magic in the semifinals in six games. Despite the comeback by Jordan, the Bulls that season were not quite able to get back into championship form. In his final three seasons with the Bulls, Pippen was ultimately consistent averaging 19.7 points, 6.2 rebounds, and 5.8 assists per game.

Of course the next three seasons with Jordan back, the Bulls three-peated for a second time. It was fitting that the Bulls lost to the Magic in 1995, not only because Jordan had an unexpected return at the end of the season, but because Horace Grant had left for Orlando prior to the season via free agency. Grant was an important piece to the success of the

Bulls winning their first three championships. At a solid 6-feet-10, he brought scoring to the frontcourt, great defense, rebounding, and shot-blocking. For a big man, he also brought speed and quickness to Chicago's defensive scheme to where Jordan, Pippen, and Grant became the three-headed monster (octopus style) trapping and locking-up perimeter players, and suffocating and stripping players in the post. When Grant left the team, it left a huge hole up front for one season until they acquired **Dennis Rodman** to fill his shoes. Indeed, Rodman did just that. While, he wasn't able to provide the scoring and shot blocking of Grant, he was able to make up for it with his *out of this world*, rebounding and defense, often guarding the opponent's best big man (forwards and centers). In addition to dominating the offensive and defensive boards, and corralling big rebounds and loose balls during crucial moments of games, Rodman was also a great one-on-one defender where he was able to quickly move his feet laterally to cut off an opponent driving to the hoop or to draw offensive fouls. He did this as well as anyone to have played the game.

In player comparisons:

Rodman was perhaps the most one-dimensional or two-dimensional star that I have ever witnessed in NBA history and that includes the other Detroit Pistons great Ben Wallace. For that reason alone, I was wrong on one of my Hall of Fame predictions, that Rodman wouldn't eventually make the Hall of Fame. It was also puzzling that during two of his four best rebounding seasons playing for the San Antonio Spurs, he was not able to help pull his team through to the NBA Finals. If he had, he would have proven his worth even more, like when Pippen had the chance to take the Portland Trail Blazers to the next level in the 2000 Western Conference Finals against the Los Angeles Lakers. Despite his terrific rebounding numbers during the 1995 playoffs, Rodman *wilted* along with everyone else who faced Olajuwon and the Houston Rockets. In observation, it could also be said that in *this* series and throughout his career, he could have been too focused at times on rebounding to a point he wouldn't leave his spot on the floor as a help defender to assist players such as David Robinson. Also, we know one thing for sure; from here on out, a player's character will probably never keep him from making the Hall of Fame - because of his character on the court and off, aside from pretty much being a one-dimensional player; I thought maybe the NBA would have passed on him.

From a rebounding standpoint - Rodman's greatest attribute and accolade - you would have to go back years and years to find a player that posted dominate rebounding statistics the way Rodman did. In fact, to validate his induction into the Hall of Fame, objectively speaking, he owns the NBA record winning the rebounding title seven consecutive seasons. In those seven seasons, Rodman averaged an astounding **16.7 rebounds** (and **5.8 offensive rebounds)** per game, including **18.7** in 1992 and **18.3** in 1993. He also was named to the All-Defensive First Team seven times and won the Defensive Player of the Year award twice. And best of all; you could make the case that Rodman was one of the Top 3 rebounders of all-time along with Wilt Chamberlain and Bill Russell, and one of the Top 3 offensive rebounders of the current era. The reason and case for number one: perhaps many of his rebounds on the offensive end, a lot of the times came at the expense of somebody else's missed shot as compared to perhaps many of Moses Malone and Charles Barkley's coming off missed or multiple missed shots of their own.

Many people felt Pippen was the perfect complement to Jordan, which he was. But what was most disturbing to me besides some of his horrendous shooting performances in a lot of big playoff games (which happens from time to time with most great players), is that Pippen failed on a golden opportunity to make it to the NBA Finals for the second time (third time when you include the 1994 season after Jordan retired) without Michael Jordan - not only with the Portland Trail Blazers but with the Houston Rockets the year before. I will say in fairness, Pippen was 33 years old when he was traded to the Rockets in their last minute bid to capture a third championship for Olajuwon, and a first for Barkley. Also, you could even make the case that the supporting cast with Portland in 2000 was deeper and more talented than when he played for both the Rockets and the Bulls. But of course, one of the problems was that Pippen was even older than when he played in Houston. I also know his supporting cast did not include another true superstar, but it was good enough to have kept Shaq and Kobe waiting one more year for their first championship. This was the perfect scenario to prove how great or not so great Pippen really was. It potentially would have brought the city of Portland its first championship since 1977. Behind the supporting cast of Rasheed Wallace, Steve Smith, Damon Stoudamire, Arvydas Sabonis, Bonzi Wells (who did his job torching Kobe Bryant offensively in the post and off the dribble all series long), Detlef Schrempf, Brian Grant and Greg Anthony, if Pippen had mustered up enough of his old self and finished off the Los Angeles Lakers in the Western Conference Finals after having a 15-point lead in the 4th quarter of game 7, we would be looking at Pippen in a whole different light, or at least I would. In fact, he would have closed the gap between Jordan as a player and would have made most people's list of Top 25 players of all-time. Instead he widens the gap even further from Jordan, because the Blazers were talented enough in 2000 in which Pippen could have easily made the difference, considering the series went seven games; and even though the Blazers get props for coming from behind after being down 3 to 1 in the series.

The reason I have Pippen ranked in the 34th slot behind Jordan is because of what I have already mentioned, and that Jordan was simply that much better on the offensive end over Pippen and just about anyone else in history for that matter. Also, Jordan was more of a focal point over any player on any team in NBA history even over Bill Russell.

Pippen resume includes: 6 NBA Championships and 1 steals title, and he was named to the All-NBA First Team 3 times and the All-Defensive First Team 8 times. He also has two Olympic gold medals he attained playing for the United States Dream Team in 1992 and 1996. I understand Pippen's greatness can't be measured on his statistics alone, so he gets his props as one of the great all-around forwards ever on the offensive end and on defense. Also, some have said that he might have been the greatest perimeter defender ever (It's still debatable in comparisons to his teammate Jordan, his other teammate Dennis Rodman, and the great Gary Payton who all won the Defensive Player of the Year Award at least once). But that slot I believe will end up going to LeBron James as he has shown that potential the last two seasons. Sooner than later, James might win the Defensive Player of the Year as he has proven he could guard multiple positions including point guard, and the quickest player in the NBA in Derrick Rose. My only other knock on Pippen was that he couldn't create his own shot in a *dominating* fashion the way some of the other greats of the game could (lets just say LeBron James played in Pippen's place with Jordan regardless if he retired both times, the Bulls probably could have won 10 to 12 championships instead of just the 6). But aside from that one single, albeit, important aspect of the game, Pippen with his size, athleticism, rebounding, passing and ball-handling skills, to go along with his slashing and finishing abilities in the paint, and of course his great defense - was all you could ask for in a small forward and the perfect complement to Michael Jordan and the success of the Chicago Bulls dynasty!

Career Totals

16.1 points, 6.4 rebs, 5.2 assists, 2.0 steals, 0.8 blocks, .473 FG%, .704 FT%, .326 3FG%

18,940, 7494 rebounds, 6135 assists, 2307 steals, 947 blocks, 978 threes

Willis Reed

(Rank #35)

All-NBA First Team (1-time), All-Defensive First Team (1-time)

NBA Championships (2), Finals MVP (2-times), All-Star (7-times)

Also featuring:
Dave DeBusschere
& Walt Bellamy

Willis Reed was one of the great centers to play in the NBA. A New York Knicks legend, Reed was the anchor in the middle who led the Knickerbockers to two NBA Championships in 1970 and 1973, where he was Finals MVP in both years. As one of the great and most *fierce* competitors the game has ever seen, Reed had his biggest moment in the decisive game seven of the 1970 NBA Finals. After a thigh injury in game five, no one knew for sure if Willis would be able to go in game seven. Even though he had minimal contributions throughout the game except for, of course the first two baskets in the beginning, what fans remember most was when Reed *courageously* ran through the tunnel with a limp prior to the game that inspired his team to victory. Undersized at six-feet-nine, the burly Reed had enough bulk to hold his own in many of the battles with Bill Russell and Wilt Chamberlain at the end of their careers, and Kareem Abdul-Jabbar at the beginning of his. Rugged, physical, and tenacious on both ends of the court, the formidable Reed was a solid all-around player that could score, rebound, and defend with the best of them.

Born on June 25th, 1942 in Hico Louisiana, Willis Reed Jr. attended high school at West Side High in nearby Lillie. At Grambling State University as a senior, Reed averaged 26.6 points and 21.3 rebounds per game, and led his team to one NAIA title, and three SAC Conference Championships. He was then selected in the second round, 8th pick overall of the 1964 NBA Draft by the New York Knicks. In his rookie season, Reed averaged 19.5 points and 14.7 rebounds per game (5th in the league), and scored 46 points in a game against the Lakers. He was also named to his first of seven consecutive All-Star games and 1965 Rookie of the Year. The following season, Reed played the power forward position and had a drop in production statistically primarily because of the acquisition of **Walt Bellamy**. Despite a beefed-up frontcourt now in place, the Knicks missed the playoffs for the second straight season. Out of all the great big men of the 1960s, Bellamy name is mentioned the least. He just so happened to be a teammate of Oscar Robertson and Jerry West on the U.S. Olympic team that brought home the gold medal at the 1960 Summer Olympics. Bellamy was also selected with the first pick overall of the 1961 NBA Draft by the Chicago Packers. In his first year, he made his mark immediately when he had one of the best rookie seasons in league history averaging **31.6 points** and **19 rebounds** per game, on a league leading **51.7 percent** shooting. His scoring average was the second highest for a rookie in NBA history behind Wilt Chamberlain's 37.6 and his rebounding average was the third highest behind Wilt's 27 and Bill Russell's 19.6.

In the 1966-67 season, Reed returned to form averaging almost identical scoring and rebounding numbers as his rookie year. He was also selected to the All-NBA Second Team for the first of three consecutive seasons. In a five-year span beginning that season, Reed was ultimately consistent averaging **21 points** and **14 rebounds** per game. Despite the formidable frontcourt dual of Bellamy and Reed, the Knicks were eliminated in the first round of the playoffs by a deeper and more talented Boston Celtics team. Although, Reed was masterful in his playoff debut - averaging **27.5 points** and **13.8 rebounds** per game. The following season, the Knicks traded Bellamy to the Detroit Pistons for *defensive guru* **Dave DeBusschere**, who was one of the NBA's great two-way players of all-time. At 6-feet-6, DeBusschere played physical on both ends of the floor. Offensively, he had an outstanding mid to long range shot and could take his man off the dribble scoring inside. He was also a hard-nosed guard/forward that could play the power forward position underneath the basket fighting for rebounds and with enough extension to block shots. But he was best known for his tenacious defense making the All-Defensive First Team six consecutive seasons.

Born on May 16th, 1940 in Detroit, Michigan, David Albert DeBusschere attended Austin Catholic Preparatory School. In college at Detroit University, he averaged 24.8 points and 19.4 rebounds per game. He was then selected as a territorial pick of the 1962 NBA Draft by the Detroit Pistons. In his rookie year, he averaged a modest 12.7 points per game, but gave a preview of his offensive potential when he came up big in four playoff games averaging 20 points and 15.8 rebounds. Even with another star in Bailey Howell, the Pistons lost to the St. Louis Hawks three games to one in the first round. After an injury riddled second season playing in only 15 games because of a broken leg, DeBusschere averaged 16.7 points and 11.1 rebounds per game. He also became Detroit's player-coach in 1964-65 at the age of 24 (was also the coach the next two years after) and was named to the All-Star team for the first of 8 consecutive seasons. In the 1966-67 season, he averaged a career-high 18.2 points per game and 11.8 rebounds. The following year and his last full season with the Pistons, he averaged 17.9 points and a career-high 13.5 rebounds per game. And, in only his second playoff appearance with the franchise, he averaged 19.3 points and 16.2 rebounds as the Pistons were eliminated once again in the first round, by the Boston Celtics in six games. DeBusschere had very little playoff success until he came to the New York Knicks in the middle of the 1968-69 season in a trade for Walt Bellamy and Howard Komives. Despite playing in the shadow of the great Willis Reed and Walt Frazier, DeBusschere overall production barely took a dip. During his five and a half seasons with the Knicks franchise, he averaged 16 points, 10.8 rebounds, and three assists per game.

In 1968, with Reed putting up similar numbers as the year before, the Knicks lost again in the first round of the playoffs, this time to the Philadelphia 76ers in six games. In the 1968-69 season, with DeBusschere in his prime jelling with his new team, and with Bellamy no longer aboard, Reed moved over to the center position where he felt most comfortable. And with Frazier and Bill Bradley continuing to improve in their second season, and with defense becoming more of the focal point, New York improved their win total to 52. In the playoffs, the Knicks made it out of the first round for the first time since 1953. But after sweeping the Baltimore Bullets, the Knicks lost once again to the Celtics in the Eastern Division Finals. Willis Reed did have another outstanding playoff performance averaging **25.7 points** and **14.1 rebounds** in ten playoff games. As it turned out, the Knicks used the 1969 playoff run as a stepping stone to prominence.

In the 1969-70 season, New York set a franchise record of 60 wins including a then NBA record 18-game winning streak. After another stellar year, Reed was named to both his first All-NBA First Team and NBA All-Defensive First Team. He also was named league MVP. In the playoffs, the Knicks faced a formidable Baltimore Bullets team in the semifinals that featured Earl Monroe, Kevin Loughery, Jack Marin, Gus Johnson, and Wes Unseld. After surviving a tough seven-game series with the Bullets, the Knicks defeated young Lew Alcindor and the up-and-coming Milwaukee Bucks in the conference finals four games to one. In the NBA Finals, the Knicks faced a Los Angeles Lakers team that featured Hall of Famers Wilt Chamberlain, Elgin Baylor, and Jerry West. During the series the Lakers were playing with a hobbling Chamberlain and an injured West for much of the series after he had sprained his wrist in game three. But the Knicks were playing with Willis Reed who had a torn thigh muscle (in game five) that kept him from playing in game six. Doubtful for game seven, Reed inspired fans around the country when he walked on to the court during pre-game warm ups. With the series tied at three, behind the courageous performance of Reed, the Knicks rallied winning game seven 113-99 and the 1970 NBA Championship. Walt Frazier had an outstanding game finishing with 36 points and 19 assists. Despite only scoring the Knicks first two buckets, Reed took home the Finals MVP award after having had games of **37 and 38 points**. He also averaged 15 rebounds for the first four games, before the injury in game 5. Walt Frazier was worthy of the MVP similar to when Magic Johnson won the award over Kareem in 1980 after he got injured. But in this case, Reed proved just as worthy throughout the series and in the final game with perhaps the *most courageous* performance in NBA Finals history.

The following season, the Knicks looked to defend their title winning the division and finishing with a modest 52 wins. In the playoffs after beating the Atlanta Hawks in five games, the tables were turned in favor of the opposing team. In another tough series like the year before, the Baltimore Bullets avenged the loss to the Knicks by winning the Eastern Conference in seven games. The very next season, Reed played in only eleven games because of an injured knee. Fortunately, the Knicks brought in Jerry Lucas to bolster the frontcourt and Earl Monroe to add depth to the backcourt. Walt Frazier picked up the scoring slack averaging a career-high 23.2 points per game. But it wasn't enough to win the championship. After defeating the Bullets in the semifinals four games to two, and the Celtics in the conference finals four games to one, the Knicks lost to the Lakers in the Finals in five games.

Prior to the 1972-73 season, coming off an injury riddled season, Reed's career began to slow down with his production dropping significantly. But the Knicks still had a strong group of core players in Frazier, DeBusschere, and Bill Bradley that blended good offense with good defense. In the playoffs, the Knicks avenged their latest playoff losses the previous two years. In the semi and conference finals, they defeated the Bullets in five games and the Celtics in a tough seven. In the NBA Finals after losing the first game, the Knicks won four games in row over the Los Angeles Lakers to win the 1973 NBA Championship. Reed was named Finals MVP for the second time.

From my perspective, Willis Reed was slightly better than Patrick Ewing for the same reason Kareem Abdul-Jabbar was over Wilt Chamberlain. The same theory applies not only in the center matchups but in all player comparisons. As mentioned in the Bill Russell vs. Hakeem Olajuwon comparisons, Russell combined more team success with individual success. Even though Olajuwon blended offense and defense better than any center to have played the game, Russell's individual contributions tangibly and intangibly, as a rebounder and as a passer, and on the defensive end combined with his enormous team success were validated when he won 5 MVP awards. If they had a Finals MVP award in those days, he would have had many of those too. Without the regular season MVP honors, I would have most likely ranked Olajuwon ahead of Bill Russell. The same can be said in the case with Patrick Ewing and Nate Thurmond. Reed won two championships and an MVP award while Ewing and Thurmond won neither. In statistical comparisons between Willis Reed and Dave Cowens, if you were to hide their names, you might not know who was who because their numbers were so similar. Even though Cowens had better postseason numbers overall, You would still have to rank Reed slightly ahead because of his defense and by winning two Finals MVP's with the second one coming on one leg in historic fashion. While some may feel either Walt Frazier or Patrick Ewing was the greatest New York Knick, Willis has to be for his individual contributions on both ends of the floor and from a winning perspective. Reed was the Finals MVP on both of the New York Knicks championship teams in 1970 and 1973. It is really close between the three of them, but this part of the book is based on what a player brings to the game from an individual perspective in relationship to the team's success. The impact Bill Russell and Kareem Abdul-Jabbar, and even Wilt Chamberlain to a lesser extent, had for their respective teams during their championship runs, the same can be said about the great Willis Reed!

Career Totals

18.7 points, 12.9 rebounds, 1.8 assists, 1.1 blocks, 0.6 steals, .476 FG%, .747 FT%

12,183 points, 8414 rebounds, 1186 assists, 21 blocks, 12 steals

Walt Frazier

(Rank #36)

All-NBA First Team (4-times), All-Defensive First Team (7-times)

NBA Championships (2), All-Star (7-times)

Also featuring:
Earl Monroe

Walt Frazier was one of the great all-around guards to have ever played in the NBA. He was also one of the best big-game guards right up there with Jerry West, Sam Jones, Reggie Miller, and Joe Dumars. And behind his *cool and calm* demeanor on the court and off, was a silent assassin that brought out all the artillery during big moments of big games. Also, the New York Knicks legend blended offense and defense as well as any guard during his time and maybe ever. As recently as 10 years ago, Frazier was believed to be by many (including the great Bill Walton) the fifth best guard of all-time. And, that assessment at the time might have been accurate until recently when Kobe Bryant, Dwyane Wade, and perhaps Steve Nash and Isiah Thomas a few years back, past him up on the list. Offensively, Frazier was able to outscore opponents on a nightly basis where he would drive to the hole with either hand or shoot a jump shot, often coming off screens. His *bread and butter* was out on the high post where he would back down defenders, *shake and bake*, and then shoot a high arching jump shot. Similar to the great Oscar Robertson who used to back his man down before shooting, Frazier had perhaps the best high-post game during his time and was the first player to play with his back to the basket from the perimeter!

Though a proficient scorer, Frazier was even better known for his defense becoming the first player in history to the make the NBA's All-Defensive First Team seven times. And, although not necessarily a believer in contact defense, Frazier would lock down opposing guards by using his lightning-quick hands in the same way Jerry West and Lenny Wilkens used to by intercepting a pass or pickpocketing an opponent as they dribbled into his area of the court. Frazier said, "My specialty was trying to turn a game around by intercepting a pass or poking the ball away as they dribbled, 'Nothing would shatter a team's morale faster than a steal.' Stealing the ball and making a pass that led to a basket were the part of basketball I loved most." With that being said, steals become a major part of the game of basketball particularly when administered during crucial moments of the game like when Michael Jordan had the key steal against Karl Malone in game 6 at the end of the 1998 NBA Finals that help define his legacy. Also, this helps out in the assessment of the projected rankings where Chris Paul currently reigns as the game's best steals/theft leader.

Walter Frazier Jr. was born on March 29th, 1945 in Atlanta, Georgia and attended David Tobias Howard High School where he played basketball, quarterback on the football team, and catcher on the baseball team. As a multi-sport athlete, Frazier was offered many scholarships for football but chose to play basketball at Southern Illinois University. In 1965, his sophomore season, he led ISU to the NCAA Division II Championship game but lost to Evansville 85-82. In his second varsity season in 1967 (academically ineligible in 1966) as a point guard, Frazier led the team to victory in the National Invitational Tournament (NIT) beating Marquette University 71-56 and was named tournament MVP. He was also a two-time Division II All-American in 1964 and 1965. Frazier was selected with the fifth pick overall of the 1967 NBA Draft by the New York Knicks. In his first season with New York, he and rookie Bill Bradley averaged nine and eight points respectively in limited minutes. Even with Willis Reed coming into his own, the Knicks were eliminated in the first round (semifinals) of the playoffs by the Philadelphia 76ers in six games. In his second season, Frazier made huge strides in becoming one of the top guards in the league when he nearly doubled his scoring and assists averages from his rookie year to 17.5 points and 7.9 assists per game. And, he also made the first of seven consecutive All-Defensive First Teams. Underrated as a rebounder, Frazier averaged 6.2 rebounds per game for the season and at least 6 rebounds in eight straight seasons. With Reed anchoring the middle and Frazier coming into his own as a top notch guard, the Knicks made it out of the first round of the playoffs for the first time in 15 years. After a 52-win season and a four-game sweep over the Baltimore Bullets in the semifinals, the Knicks were defeated four games to two in the Eastern Finals by the eventual champion Boston Celtics.

In the 1969-70 season, Frazier blossomed into one of the elite guards in the NBA when he averaged **20.9 points** and had a **career-high** in both **assists at 8.2** per game, and in field goal percentage at **51.8**. He also was named to his first All-NBA First Team and first of seven consecutive all-star selections. Beginning that season, for seven consecutive years of his prime, Frazier averaged a stellar **21.2 points**, **6.6 rebounds**, **6.5 assists**, and **2.1 steals** per game, and shot .493 percent from the field. And, for his entire postseason career that included eight seasons, he averaged **20.7 points**, **7.2 rebounds**, **6.4 assists**, and **2.1 steals** per game, and shot .511 percent from the field. With Frazier, Reed, Bradley, DeBusschere, and Barnett in their third season playing together, the Knicks had their best season in franchise history at 60 wins. In the playoffs, after defeating the feisty Baltimore Bullets in seven games and the Milwaukee Bucks in five in the Western Division, the Knicks met the Los Angeles Lakers in the NBA Finals. With Willis Reed leading the way, the Knicks captured the 1970 NBA Championship. Even though Reed was named Finals MVP after the most famous game in which he came limping out of the tunnel, Frazier had the monster numbers in the decisive game seven. In his best game of his career in the postseason, he posted **36 points, 19 assists, 7 rebounds, and 5 steals**. And for the record, he posted a triple-double of 11 points, 12 rebounds and 11 assists earlier in game 2 of the series.

The following two seasons, the Knicks looked to defend their title playing with the same core group of guys but were not able to win the NBA Finals. They were eliminated in the conference finals in a rematch with the Bullets in seven games and by the Lakers the following year in the Finals in five games. In both seasons, Frazier peaked in scoring at **21.7** and **23.2 points** per game, and in the playoffs at **22.6** and **24.3 points** per game. In the 1972-73 season, the Knicks looked to make it back to the Finals and build on their loss to the Lakers from the previous year. With Reed's career slowing down, Frazier and **Earl Monroe** picked up the scoring slack. The dynamic dual formed one of, if not the greatest backcourt (nicknamed "Rolls Royce") in NBA history for six seasons.

Earl "The Pearl" Monroe was one of the most spectacular and flamboyant players in history that brought a *street ball* style from the playgrounds to the NBA. He also went by the nickname "Black Magic" or "Black Jesus" because he was Magic Johnson in essence before Magic. It was tough to leave him out of my top 50 players of all-time for many reasons. To begin with, Monroe helped *revolutionize* the way basketball was played in the same way Bob Cousy, Connie Hawkins, and Julius Erving all did. Even as a youth, his legend stood out to me as much or more than most Hall of Famers because he brought so much *flair* to the game. With all the dazzling spin moves, whirling in the lane, fancy dribbling and circus like shots, Monroe was one of the most exciting players of all-time. Ultimately, what set him back from having an ever greater career were all the knee injuries early on, and that he was not offered a scholarship from any major colleges. Because of this, even though he worked for a year soon after, he spent a lot of *wear and tear* show casing his talents on the playgrounds of Philadelphia and New York, and for four years at a small unknown college before playing in the NBA.

Vernon Earl Monroe was born on November 24th, 1944 in Philadelphia, Pennsylvania and was selected with the 2nd pick overall of the 1967 NBA Draft by the Baltimore Bullets. Even at John Bartram High School he was called "Thomas Edison" because of all of his spectacular moves he invented. In college at Division II Winston-Salem State University in North Carolina, Monroe averaged an *unfathomable* **41.5 points** per game his senior year. He also was named Division II College Player of the Year and led the Rams to the Division II NCAA championship. In the NBA, Monroe averaged 20 points or more 10 times and had a single best scoring game of **56 points** on February 13, 1968 against the Los Angeles Lakers. He held the franchise record for points in a game until Gilbert Arenas broke the record on December 16th, 2006 in an overtime game in Los Angeles, that I just so happened to have watched live on TV - On another note: In this game, Kobe Bryant was given a dose of his own medicine when Arenas took ill-advised shots including deep... deep... deep three-point shots lighting him and his teammates up for **60 points**. I clearly remember how discouraged and annoyed Bryant looked during the game and especially after. And even though Bryant finished with 45 points of his own, he was still very unhappy after the game. He said I don't know what he's doing taking those kinds of shots and went on to say, he's crazy. You think, coming from him. Anyway, as a testament to Monroe's greatness before the knee injuries took it's tow, the gifted Monroe averaged 24.5 points, 4.7 assists, and 4.1 rebounds in his first three years in the league. He also had his highest scoring games of **40, 41, 41, 42, 45, 46, 49,** and **56** all within the first three years of his career with the one 40-point game coming in 1970.

With a power packed lineup, the Knicks were formidable enough to recapture the championship that eluded them the last two seasons. But, they had to make it past the 68-win Celtics and potentially one of the two 60-win teams in the Western Conference. After defeating the Baltimore Bullets in the semifinals in five games, the Knicks were able to grind out a tough seven-game series against the Celtics in the conference finals. While the Celtics were playing game 4 without John Havlicek due to injury, and with Earl Monroe missing the game as well, Frazier played 57 of 58 minutes including overtime and carried New York to victory despite trailing by 16 points in the fourth quarter. For the game, he finished with 37 points, nine rebounds, and four assists. And, in the clinching game 7 victory in Boston, Frazier came up big once again finishing with 25 points and 10 rebounds. For the historic series, he averaged **26.1 points** and led the team in scoring in all seven games; also the New York Knicks franchise became the first team in history to win a game 7 in Boston. In the Finals, the battle tested Knicks made quick work by eliminating the Los Angeles Lakers in five games to win the 1973 NBA Championship.

The following season, Frazier had another stellar campaign averaging **20.5 points**, **6.9 assists**, **6.7 rebounds**, and **2 steals** per game. He was also named to the All-NBA First Team for the third time and the All-Defensive First Team for the sixth consecutive season. With Willis Reed playing in only 13 games due to injury, the Knicks finished second in the division with 49 wins. In the playoffs with Reed averaging only eleven minutes per game, the Knicks beat the Capital Bullets in the semifinals in seven games before losing to the eventual champion Boston Celtics in the conference finals four games to one. The three seasons without Reed, the Knicks settled in mediocrity, never winning more than forty games. In 1975, they were eliminated two games to one in the first round of the playoffs by the Houston Rockets, and in the next two seasons they missed the playoffs entirely. In his last three seasons with the Cleveland Cavaliers, Frazier's career was all but over. He played in only 66 games total as the Cavaliers missed the playoffs in every season.

In player comparisons: In retrospect, the Knicks were completely out of playoff contention after the retirement of Willis Reed, which validates Reed's value to the team when he won the 1970 MVP and the Finals MVP in both of the Knicks championship seasons. However, at the height of his career, even Reed complimented Frazier by saying that "its Clyde's ball," and that "He just lets us play with it once in a while." With that high regard, one could make the case that Frazier was just as valuable to the Knicks franchise as Reed not only from an offensive standpoint, but from the defensive side as well. In fact, if you look at their individual accolades (4 All-NBA First Team selections to 1 and 7 All-Defensive First Team selections to 1 in favor of Frazier) not including the one MVP award Reed won in the regular season and the two in the Finals, Frazier comes out on top. During his time, Frazier was simply the best or second best player on the Knicks and the second best shooting guard in the league next to Jerry West. He was also nearly the clutch player on both ends of the floor!

Career Totals

18.9 points, 6.1 assists, 5.9 rebounds, 1.9 steals, 0.2 blocks, .490 FG%, 476 FT%

15,581 points, 5040 assists, 4830 rebounds, 681 steals, 63 blocks

Nate Thurmond

(Rank #37)

All-Defensive First Team (2-times), All-Star (7-times)

Nate Thurmond was one of the great centers in NBA history and perhaps the best defensive center since Bill Russell. Thurmond was the heart and soul of the San Francisco/Golden State Warriors for eleven seasons where he averaged 17.4 points and 16.9 rebounds per game, and 15 rebounds per game for his entire career which ranks 5th on the all-time list. During his time, many people felt he was better than Russell on the offensive end and even better than Wilt Chamberlain on defense. Wilt after his retirement, *illustrated* with his two fingers that Thurmond, at two to three inches shorter, actually had a four to six inch reach advantage even over him at seven-foot-one. In fact, the 6-foot-11 Warrior center was so good; Chamberlain became expendable in 1965 and was traded to the Philadelphia 76ers. With the versatility to play center and power forward, Thurmond was the epitome of the team that drafted him; a *true warrior* in every sense of the word - Thurmond had an intimidation presence, and dominated the game with his *rugged* toughness and superior rebounding and shot blocking. Offensively, he was smooth from the perimeter equipped with a soft shooting touch. He was also an outstanding passer finding cutters to the basket, and an excellent screen setter. "Nate the Great" will always be remembered for being one of the great rebounders and shot blockers in NBA history. His greatest individual accomplishment came from every major aspect of his game, when he became the first man in NBA history to record a quadruple-double of **22 points, 14 rebounds, 13 assists, and 12 blocks.** In addition, he also owns the NBA record for most rebounds in a quarter with 18.

Nathaniel Thurmond was born on July 25th, 1941 in Akron, Ohio and attended high school at Akron Central where he was a teammate of future NBA star Gus Johnson. In college at Bowling Green, Thurmond averaged 17.9 points and 17 rebounds per game and was named to the All-America First Team by the Sporting News in 1963. He also set a school record of 31 rebounds in his last college game. Later that same year, he was selected in the first round, 3rd pick overall of the 1963 NBA Draft by the San Francisco Warriors. In his rookie season, Thurmond teamed with superstar center Wilt Chamberlain to form an *imposing* frontcourt. After finishing with the best record in the Western Division, and with Thurmond increasing his minutes to almost ten minutes per game from the regular season to the postseason, the Warriors were formidable enough to defeat the St. Louis Hawks in seven games in the Division Finals before losing to the much experienced Boston Celtics in the NBA Finals in five games. The next two seasons, Thurmond blossomed into an All-Star and averaged 16.4 points and 18 rebounds per game, and had a career single-game high 42 rebounds on March 9th, 1965. But the Warriors missed the playoffs mainly due to the fact; Chamberlain was traded during the season after playing with Thurmond for only a year and a half.

In the 1966-67 season, the Warriors returned to prominence behind *super sophomore* Rick Barry's scoring *onslaught* and with Thurmond anchoring the defense and finishing runner-up in the MVP voting. That season, he also increased his scoring and rebounding significantly to 18.7 points and 21.3 respectively. In the playoffs, the Warriors won the Western Division by sweeping the Los Angeles Lakers in the first round and defeating St. Louis in six games in the Division Finals. Unfortunately, the young up-and-coming Warriors ran into the mighty Philadelphia 76ers that had just completed the most historic regular season in NBA history to that point, finishing with an eye-popping 68-13 record. In the NBA Finals, after falling behind three games to one, the Warriors battled back to win the next game before losing the decisive game six on their own home floor. For the series, Barry carried the Warriors averaging 40.8 points per game while Thurmond averaged **23.1 rebounds** for the entire playoff run. The very next season, after Barry left the team to join the ABA, the Warriors had a subpar year, finishing with 43 wins despite Thurmond's **20.5 points**, and **career-high 22 rebounds** and **4.2 assists** per game averages during the season. It was also the first of five seasons he would average at least twenty points. In the playoffs without an injured Thurmond, the Warriors defeated the Hawks in the first round in six games before getting swept by the Lakers in the Western Division Finals. In both seasons in 1967 and 1968, Thurmond averaged **21.3** and **22 rebounds** per game becoming the third player in history to average at least that amount behind only Chamberlain and Russell.

In the 1968-69 campaign, the Warriors whirled in mediocrity finishing the regular season at .500 and with a second consecutive playoff exit to the Lakers - this time in the first round four games to two. This was the second meeting between "Nate the Great" and "Wilt the Stilt" in the playoffs but with Wilt playing in a different uniform. The following year, Thurmond averaged a career-high of 21.9 points to go along with 17.7 rebounds in only 43 games due to injury, but it wasn't enough as the thirty-win Warriors missed the playoffs entirely. In 1970-71, with Jerry Lucas in his first full season with the team, the Warriors finished the regular season at .500 and exited the first round of the playoffs for the second time in three years, this time to MVP Kareem Abdul-Jabbar and the Milwaukee Bucks in five games.

The following season, the franchise changed their *first name* from "San Francisco" to "Golden State" as the Warriors finished with 51 wins, but unfortunately, they had to face defending champion Milwaukee for the second straight season in the playoffs. Despite Thurmond's 25.4 points, 17.8 rebounds, and 5.2 assists per game against rival center Abdul-Jabbar, the Warriors lost in five games once again. In the 1972-73 season, the Warriors made the playoffs for last time with Thurmond as a member of the team. After avenging the loss from the previous two seasons, the Warriors turned the table and defeated the Bucks in the first round four games to two, before falling to defending champion Los Angeles in five games in the Western Finals.

After failing to make the playoffs in his final year with the Warriors, Thurmond was traded to the Chicago Bulls where he made an immediate impact in the first game of the season - when he recorded the first quadruple-double in NBA history on October 8th, 1974 against the Atlanta Hawks. In the playoffs, the Bulls defeated the Kansas City/Omaha Kings in six games in the first round before losing to Thurmond's former team and eventual champion Golden State Warriors in seven games. The following year, after playing in only thirteen games, Thurmond was traded to his hometown Cleveland where he would play his last two seasons. Although playing with limited production, Thurmond made an inspiring impact playing for his home crowd. After a 6-11 start, the Cavaliers finished the regular season 43-22, won the Central Division, and made the postseason for the first time in franchise history. In the 1976 playoffs, after defeating the Washington Bullets in seven games in the semifinals, the Cavaliers lost to the eventual champion Celtics in the conference finals in six games.

While Russell was the best defensive center of the 1960s, Nate Thurmond was the best during the early 1970s, as both Chamberlain and Abdul-Jabbar can attest to. During his prime, Kareem told Basketball Digest that Thurmond played him better than anyone ever had. Thurmond never made an All-NBA First Team because he played with the greatest group of centers in history in Russell, Chamberlain, Abdul-Jabbar, Willis Reed, and Dave Cowens. He never won a championship for the same reason, and because he played with an inferior supporting cast compared to the other great centers of his generation. His best teammates were Chamberlain for a year and a half in the beginning of his career, and Jerry Lucas for a year and a half in the middle. He also played with Guy Rodgers his first three seasons and Cazzie Russell in his last three. And to complete the *instability*, he played with Barry for two seasons in the beginning of his career and for only two near the very end, before he was traded to the Bulls. The only quality player Thurmond played with for a long duration of time was the consistent scoring Jeff Mullins for eight seasons.

In Thurmond's last season with the Warriors in 1973-74, the inaugural season of keeping track of blocked shots, he averaged an astounding **2.9 blocks** per game. Russell, Chamberlain, and Thurmond could possibly have accumulated the most blocked shots in NBA history if blocks were an official statistic during their playing days. In one's eyes, Thurmond could have been the third best center of his era despite never winning a championship. He also was never selected to an All-NBA First or Second Team, because he played in the heart of the greatest era of *dominating* big men in NBA history. If you were to ask Bill Russell and Wilt Chamberlain (before he passed away) in their prime years, who was the best all-around center outside of the two of them, there's a good chance they would say Nate Thurmond. But a great portion of this book is all about the individual contributions to the team's success, and Thurmond never won a regular season MVP award or an NBA Championship, something Willis Reed who ranks ahead of him had done. But if you want to flip-flop the two, that's fine, because they were two of the best centers of the late 1960s and early 1970s.

Career Totals

15.0 points, 15.0 rebounds, 2.7 assists, 2.1 blocks, 0.5 steals, .421 FG%, .667 FT%

14,437 points, 14,464 rebounds, 2575 assists, 553 blocks, 125 steals

Dave Cowens

(Rank #38)

MVP (1-time), All-Defensive First Team (1-time)

NBA Championships (2), All-Star (8-times)

Also featuring:
Jo Jo White

Dave Cowens was one of the all-time great centers and the second best center to play for the Boston Celtics franchise behind Bill Russell. As the anchor in the middle during the 1970s, Cowens won the 1973 MVP Award and helped lead the Celtics to two NBA Championships in 1974 and 1976. He was also one of the key pieces; in turning around a franchise that was rebuilding after the 1960s Celtics dynasty had come to an end. In fact, after the departure of Russell, in the 1971-72 season, Cowens' second year in the league, the Celtics improved their winning percentage three straight years before winning two championships in a three-year span. They also set a franchise record of 68 wins in 1973. During all of that winning, Cowens finished in the top 4 in the MVP balloting four consecutive years. And like his predecessor, he was an outstanding all-around player, filled with athleticism; that could score, rebound, pass, and defend. Bill Walton once said: "Dave Cowens was the only player successful versus Wilt Chamberlain and Kareem Abdul-Jabbar. He was only 6-foot-8 but he *outworked* and outran everyone. He was a complete player." Even his coach Tommy Heinsohn said for his team's running style of play, he would take Cowens over any center in the league except for only Kareem and Willis Reed (when healthy). But his greatest attributes might have been his durability, giant-size heart and his ultra-competitive will to win at all cost. At only six-foot-eight to six-foot-nine (tops according to some) and able to guard taller centers, he would outwork and out-hustle opponents for points and rebounds. As a testament to his scoring and rebounding prowess, during his MVP season in 1973, Cowens outscored the Great Wilt Chamberlain (in head-to-head matchups) in his final season **31.3** to 14.3 and out-rebounded him **20** to 14.5. Also, on the defensive end of the ball, he would play relentless defense up in the face of taller opponents in order to make up for his lack of size.

Born on October 25th, 1948 in New Port, Kentucky, David William Cowens attended Newport Central Catholic High School before attending Florida State University where he averaged 19 points and 17.2 rebounds per game in three varsity seasons. He also had a single-game high of 31 rebounds and set the school record in 1969 for rebounding in a single season at 17.5 per game. Despite the criticism for being undersized to play the center position, with the influence of Bill Russell, Cowens was selected with the 4th pick overall of the 1970 NBA Draft by the Boston Celtics. At that time, Paul Silas had come over in a trade and promising rookie **Jo Jo White** had been selected in the draft the year before. With the three of them along with stars John Havlicek, Bailey Howell and Don Nelson, the Celtics looked to have a promising future. In his second season after playing in limited minutes, White and rookie Dave Cowens started the 1970-71 season off with a bang. Cowens averaged 17 points and 15 rebounds, and won the Rookie of the Year award - and second-year sensation White exploded into stardom raising his scoring average almost nine points from his rookie season to 21.3 points per game. He also averaged 5 rebounds and 4.8 assists, and was named to the All-Star team for the first of seven consecutive seasons. Even with Havlicek having a career year averaging 28.9 points per game, the Celtics unfortunately missed the playoffs.

The following season, Cowens averaged 18.8 points, 15.2 rebounds and 3.1 assists per game, and shot 48 percent from the field. He too, was also named to the All-Star team for the first of seven consecutive seasons. Throughout the book, it seems like I have written the same sentence over and over again, because so many players around this era and after for that matter, played in 7 All-Star games or more with many coming in succession. Even with Havlicek leading the team in scoring again at 27.5 per game, that didn't stop Jo Jo White from having a career year when he averaged **23.1 points**, **5.6 rebounds**, and **5.3 assists** per game. That season began a string of playoff success for the Boston Celtics where they won 56 games and defeated the Atlanta Hawks four games to two in the semifinals, before losing to the New York Knicks in the Eastern Finals in five games.

By that point, the Celtics had someone *special* in White who was blossoming in only his third year in the league. His skill set included speed, great defense, and perhaps an *underappreciated* jump shot. He also was a tremendous leader. Born on November 16th, 1946 in St. Louis, Missouri, Joseph Henry White attended McKinley High School. In college at the University of Kansas, he averaged 15.3 points and 4.9 assists per game. And by the way for you basketball fans today, White was one of the guards on the Kansas team in the movie "Glory Road" that lost in the Midwest regional final of the 1966 NCAA tournament in double overtime to Texas Western, which is now named UTEP. In the title game Pat Riley and the Kentucky Wildcats were the final victim, so to speak, to one of the most historic runs in college history, where UTEP became the first team to win the NCAA Championship with 5 black players in the starting lineup. It is a *must-see* if you haven't seen it. And, it was one of the most inspirational basketball movies I have ever seen. Particularly, because it exemplified what black people had to go through during the 1960s with all the racism and segregation. Tim Hardaway was another great point guard that played for UTEP who is featured in the bonus material of the DVD format. After college in 1968, White played for the U.S. Olympic team in Mexico that went undefeated finishing with nine wins including capturing the gold medal after defeating Yugoslavia in the title game 65-50.

Jo Jo White was selected with the 9th pick overall of the 1969 NBA Draft by the Boston Celtics after they had won their eleventh championship in thirteen years - which means, he and Dave Cowens, never had the chance to play with Bill Russell who had just retired. But after Cowens was drafted the following year and a trade was made for Paul Silas, a new era of basketball began in Boston. After White's sensational start to begin his career, from the start of his fourth season in 1972 through the end of the 1977 season, for a five-year stretch during the Celtics championship run, he averaged 18.9 points, 5.7 assists, 4.3 rebounds, and 1.4 steals per game. But, what might have been most impressive was that he never missed a single game during those five seasons. During that same span including one year after in the postseason, he raised his level of play even higher and averaged 21.5 points, 5.7 assists, and 4.4 rebounds per game. He also won the 1976 NBA Finals MVP where he had 33 points and 9 assists in the game 5 triple-overtime victory against the Phoenix Suns.

After White's career-year in his third season, it was time for Cowens to do the same in his third season in 1972-73, when he averaged **20.5 points**, **16.2 rebounds**, and **4.1 assists** per game, and was named league MVP. With both Cowens and White peaking in back-to-back years, the Celtics almost made it all the way to the NBA Finals. In the playoffs, after finishing with an incredible 68-14 record, the Celtics defeated the Atlanta Hawks four games to two before losing a heartbreaking (I can't believe I'm writing these words for a Celtics franchise) seven-game series to the eventual champion New York Knicks. As you can see, I didn't use the word heartbreaking in Havlicek's chapter because he was fortunate enough to have won eight championships. Even though Havlicek was near the end of his career, he along with Cowens and White were the cornerstones to the revival of perhaps a new Celtics dynasty, winning two Championships in 1974 and in 1976.

Here are some of Cowens' best games in the NBA Finals:

In game one of the 1974 Finals victory against Kareem and the Milwaukee Bucks, he had one of his best all-around performances in the postseason finishing with 19 points, 17 rebounds, and seven assists. He also outscored his counterpart in game 3 in Boston 30 to 26. In in the pivotal game 5, Cowens posted 28 points, six rebounds, and six assists - and in the clinching game 7, he outscored Kareem once again, finishing with 28 points, 14 rebounds and four assists; In the 1976 Finals against the Phoenix Suns, Cowens was equally impressive where he posted a triple-double of **25 points, 21 rebounds, and 10 assists** in game one - and 26 points and 19 rebounds in the famous game 5 triple-overtime game. He also had 21 points and 17 rebounds in the clinching game 6 in Phoenix.

In player comparisons, putting Dave Cowens ahead of Patrick Ewing was even harder than putting Willis Reed and Walt Frazier ahead of him, because he had even less individual accolades and didn't even win a Finals MVP award, even though he was worthy enough on both of the Celtics championship teams in the 1970s. But like Reed, although undersized, Cowens was a *bull* on both ends of the court, and at times, battled *relentlessly* to his advantage against greater and taller centers such as Kareem and Wilt. And, he would have done the same against Ewing. Kind of like Wes Unseld and Reed for that matter, Cowens was unique in his own right and the 11th best center of All-time!

Career Totals

17.6 points, 13.6 rebounds, 3.8 assists, 0.9 blocks, 1.1 steals, 460 FG%, .783 FT%

13,516 points, 10,444 rebounds, 2910 assists, 488 blocks, 599 steals

Patrick Ewing

(Rank #39)

All-NBA First Team (1-time), All-Star (11-times)

Also featuring: Alonzo Mourning
& Reggie Miller

Patrick Ewing was one of the great centers and New York Knicks players of all-time. A *beast of a man*, Ewing was one of the most *coveted* and prototypical centers to ever come into the NBA in 1985 out of the University of Georgetown. At a towering seven feet and massive in girth, Ewing was able to back down, bully up, and pound opponents in the low post for points and rebounds. His tremendous size and strength allowed him to dwarf over opponents for monster dunks and ferocious blocks on the defensive end. His offensive arsenal included a short jump hook and a deadly jump shot from the perimeter making him perhaps the best jump-shooting center ever. He was also named the 16th greatest college player of all-time by ESPN. Although he didn't win the 1994 NBA Championship with the Knicks, Ewing won the NCAA Championship and the Olympic Gold Medal in 1984 and 1992 playing for the U.S. Men's National Basketball team.

Patrick Aloysius Ewing was born on August 5th, 1962 in Kingston, Jamaica and came to Cambridge, Massachusetts at the age of eleven. He attended Cambridge Rindge and Latin School where his coach Mike Jarvis proclaimed him as the next Bill Russell, but with a better offensive game. He then moved on to play basketball for Coach John Thompson at Georgetown University where he was one of the highest recruited freshmen ever. Because of the teams "in-your-face" style and Ewing's intimidating defensive presence, he was given the tag "Hoya Destroya." As one of the first freshman in history to start on the varsity team, he led the Hoya's to the NCAA Championship game where they would lose to the University of North Carolina Tarheels, that featured future NBA stars James Worthy, Michael Jordan, and Sam Perkins. Although two years later in his junior year, he led the Hoya's back to the title game where they would beat the Houston Cougars 84-75 to win the 1984 NCAA Championship. Ewing would be named NCAA Final Four Most Outstanding Player. During his senior year, Ewing was named College Player of the Year and led the Hoya's back to the championship game for the third time in four years. But they would eventually lose to underdog Villanova 66-64.

In the first ever year of the NBA Draft Lottery, Ewing was selected with the 1st pick overall of the 1985 NBA Draft by the New York Knicks. Despite missing a total of 51 games in his first two seasons due to injury, he made an immediate impact by averaging 20 points, 9 rebounds and 2.1 blocks per game, and was named 1986 Rookie of the Year. After a stellar sophomore season, but with Bernard King in his last days with the team, the Knicks missed the playoffs both seasons. The following year, Ewing averaged similar numbers as his first two and increased his blocks to 3 per game. He also made the All-Star team for the second time and first of 10 consecutive seasons. After the Knicks squeaked into the playoffs with two other teams tied with the same record, they were quickly eliminated by the Boston Celtics in the first round three games to one. In just his fourth season, Ewing continued to improve his overall game by averaging 22.7 points, 9.3 rebounds, 2.4 assists, and 3.5 blocks per game. He also had a career-high 1.5 steals per game and shot .567 percent from the field. The much improved Knicks won the division at 52-30 and made it out of the first round of the playoffs for the first time in five years. After sweeping the Philadelphia 76ers in round one, they were eliminated by MVP Michael Jordan and the Chicago Bulls in the semifinals four games to two.

In the 1989-90 season, Ewing had perhaps his best individual season of his career averaging **28.6 points**, **10.9 rebounds** and a **career-high 4 blocks** per game, and shot 55 percent from the field. His **career-high 11 40-point** games, included a **51-point and 18-rebound** game where he shot 69 percent from the field in a loss at home to the Celtics. He also had two other monster games that resulted in wins; a **44-point and 24-rebound** game at Golden State and a **44-point, 22-rebound, and 7-block** performance vs. the Clippers. As a result of a magnificent campaign, he was named to his first and only All-NBA First Team selection. With Ewing at the top of his game, and with Charles Oakley and Mark Jackson improving rapidly in their second and third year with the team, the Knicks were on the brink of becoming the Eastern Conference's next elite team. But there was only one problem; they kept running into the other elite teams in the conference. After losing to the Bulls and Celtics in back-to-back playoffs, the Knicks were finally able to get past the Celtics in the first round three games to two, but lost rather easily to the eventual champion Detroit Pistons in the semifinals four games to one (in the only win, Ewing had **45 points, 13 rebounds, and 6 assists**). Also, in game 4 in Boston to tie the series, Ewing finished with **44 points, 13 rebounds, 5 assists, and 7 steals.** He also had perhaps his best individual postseason averaging **29.4 points, 10.5 rebounds** and **3.1 assists** per game, and shot **52 percent** from the field. His points and assists per game averages were career highs. At that point, with the Celtics and Pistons aging as a team, you would think the only place for the Knicks to go would be up.

Ewing and the Knicks, along with Jordan and the Bulls, looked like the teams to beat in the Eastern Conference for the next few years to come. Things looked bright going in to the following season with Ewing having another magnificent year averaging **26.6 points, 11.2 rebounds, 3.2 blocks**, and a career-high three assists per game. The only thing that stood in the way of the Knicks reaching their ultimate goal of a first championship was the Chicago Bulls. Both teams were chasing the same dream but the Bulls appeared to be at a faster clip. After an unexpected subpar regular season at 39-43, the Knicks were swept by their biggest rival and eventual champion Bulls in the first round of the playoffs.

From the 1992 to the 1996 season, Ewing remained ultimately consistent averaging 24.2 points, 11.4 rebounds, and 2.4 blocks per game. In the 1991-92 campaign, with the acquisition of Xavier McDaniel, and John Starks improving into a potential all-star, the Knicks returned to prominence and finished the regular season tied with the Celtics at 51-31. But after defeating the pesky Detroit Pistons three games to two in the first round of the playoffs, the Knicks lost a heartbreaking seven-game series to the Bulls in the conference semifinals. In the series, Ewing came up big finishing with 34 points, 16 rebounds, and 6 blocks as the Knicks stole game one in Chicago 94-89. After losing three of the next four games, in the elimination game six at home, Ewing came up big once again, this time playing on a serious ankle sprain. Behind his 27 points, the Knicks won the game 100-86 but were trounced by those same Bulls 110-81 in the decisive game seven and *that was that*. At the time, because Jordan had the *savage thirst* for multiple championships, it appeared this was Ewing's best and perhaps only chance at a championship title.

The following season, the Knicks finished with the best record in the Eastern Conference at 60-22. In the playoffs, New York began to look so convincingly good in the first two rounds; I began to think that just maybe they could overcome the Bulls. After defeating the Indiana Pacers three games to one in the first round, they quickly took care of the Charlotte Hornets in five games despite the infamous and embarrassing block shot from 5-foot-3 "Muggsy" Bogues on Ewing. In the conference finals, the Knicks were in great position to finally dethrone Chicago and make it to the NBA Finals. With home court advantage and a 2 games to 0 lead in the series, the Knicks wilted into oblivion and lost the next four games and the series, leaving the franchise without hardly any hope of ever winning a championship. But you know what, something more improbable actually happened the following season, Jordan retired.

This literally changed the landscape of the entire NBA and for the New York Knicks. In the 1993-94 season, the Knicks made a key trade with Dallas to acquire Derek Harper to form a dynamic backcourt with John Starks. They also had a solid defensive guard and three-point shooter in Greg Anthony coming off the bench. With Ewing remaining as consistent as ever and Charles Oakley, Charles Smith and young Anthony Mason bolstering the frontcourt, the Knicks were *primed and ready* to take command of the Eastern Conference. After finishing the regular season with 57 wins, the Knicks road to the NBA Finals, ended up being a lot tougher than one would have expected. After dispatching the New Jersey Nets in the first round three games to one, the Knicks finally beat their arch nemeses Chicago Bulls (without Jordan) in the semifinals in seven games. Just as the Bulls were going out, another team was coming in. That team was the Indiana Pacers. Although young, they were a very formidable squad that gave the Knicks fits throughout the Eastern Conference Finals. After each team took care of home court winning two games apiece, the Knicks were given a scare when they dropped game 5 at home. Fortunately the battled tested Knickerbockers were able to pull through and win the next two games over the young and inexperienced Pacers team.

In the NBA Finals, it was a *battle for the ages*, the New York Knicks vs. the Houston Rockets! After both teams split the first two games in Houston, the Rockets retook home court advantage in game three in New York. But the Knicks fought back and won the next two games to take a three to two series lead before going back to Houston for game 6 and 7. Because the Rockets were able to overcome an even bigger deficit in the semifinals against the Suns, I felt they were the more destined team to win their first NBA championship. Besides, the Rockets had the *best player* on the *best team*, and you know how that goes over the years! Furthermore, as an Olajuwon admirer, I was hoping that the Rockets would win their first championship before Ewing and the Knicks did. But unfortunately, one of these evenly matched teams had to lose. In one of, if not the toughest seven-game series I have ever *witnessed*, the Knicks battled as hard as any team ever had before, and could have easily brought home Ewing his first title. Despite the center matchup in which Olajuwon who came out on top when comparing numbers, I felt Ewing did a heck of a job containing "The Dream" by not allowing him to go *ballistic* with all those spin moves. Contrary to what some people might believe, in that Olajuwon dominated Ewing, this was the best I have ever seen any one player guard Olajuwon over any stretch of games. Even though the Rockets won the series, I was actually disappointed that Hakeem didn't average at least 30 points, and dominate the way I know he can. In fact, he was held to 17 points twice in two games.

The following season, New York won 55 games, but the tables were turned in favor of the Indiana Pacers as the Knicks were eliminated in the semifinals in seven games. The Pacers were able to take *complete* control of the series by winning game one in New York and both games at home to take a commanding three games to one lead. They also survived a last second finger roll by Ewing in the final seconds of game seven that would have sent the game into overtime. The next three seasons, even with the same core group of guys and a couple late additions, the Knicks were eliminated in the semifinals by the Chicago Bulls in five games, the Miami Heat in seven games, and to the Indiana Pacers in five games. In the 1996-97 season, the Knicks won 57 games and looked to return to the NBA Finals until they ran into the Heat. In the conference semifinals, it was a matchup between two extremely physical teams and two *goliaths* at the center position, that both played their college ball at Georgetown University.

The Heat featured one of the great defensive centers of his generation in **Alonzo Mourning**, and one of the best point guards in league history in Tim Hardaway. Like Ewing, Mourning was a *beast of center* with a little less girth, but with even more physical and mental toughness. In fact, in my opinion, Alonzo and Kevin Garnett played with more heart and more fire than any player in history, or at least in recent history! That in itself, along with the fact he was one of the all-time great centers and should eventually make it into the Hall of Fame someday, inspired me to include him in this book. Everything that I have written so far about physical and mental toughness, heart, and the will to win, including what I wrote in Bob Pettit's chapter, epitomizes everything and more what Alonzo Mourning was all about. Out of all the catch phrases in recent memory, the one that sticks in my mind more than anything else is when Marv Albert uttered the phrase "Blocked by Mourning." Even to this day, it gives me goose bumps thinking about how exciting it was watching him *reject* opposing players throughout his career, and especially the Dallas Mavericks in the 2006 NBA Finals. While most people probably view the "Slam dunk" as the most exciting play in basketball especially on the offensive end, the "block shot" is the slam dunk on the defensive end. I call it, the exact inverse of the slam dunk, instead of *in-your-face*; we call it *back-in-your-face*. In today's game, I know people are probably hooked on Dwight Howard's shot blocking style and in-game heroics, but for me, no one brought more excitement to the craft than "Zo." I think the main difference between the two, was not necessarily the talent and athleticism, in which Howard probably has more of, but from the intimidating demeanor behind the shot blocking. On Howards blocks and dunks for that matter, they are either accompanied with a straight face or a smile (which is just part of his personality), whereas in the "Ultimate Warrior" of Mourning, it came with more tenacity and fire burning in his eyes. In addition to being the most *emphatic* and *ferocious* shot blocker of his generation if not ever. Mourning was an adept scorer with a good inside-outside game (equipped with a good mid-range jump shot) and an outstanding rebounder.

Alonzo Harding Mourning Jr. was born on February 8th, 1970 in Chesapeake, Virginia and attended Indian River High School where he led the team to 51 straight victories. In his senior year, he averaged **25 points**, **15 rebounds** and **12 blocks** per game, and was named Player of the Year by USA Today. In college, at Georgetown University, Mourning led the nation in blocks at 5 per game his freshman year. By his senior year, he averaged 21.3 points, 10.7 rebounds and 5 blocks per game, and was named All-American. Impressively enough, Mourning was selected right after Shaquille O'Neal with the second pick overall of the 1992 Draft by the Charlotte Hornets. In his rookie season, he made a major impact on both ends of the floor for the expansion franchise Hornets. In fact, it was one of the best rookie campaigns I have ever witnessed. Unfortunately, Shaq had a season a little better on his way to winning the NBA Rookie of the Year award. Mourning averaged 21 points, 10.3 rebounds and 3.5 blocks per game, and shot 51 percent from the field. Both players became the first rookies to average 20 points and 10 rebounds per game since David Robinson in 1990. His most memorable game of the season came in the first round of the playoffs when he knocked down a twenty-foot buzzer-beater against the Boston Celtics in the decisive game 4 victory. In his first eight seasons, Mourning averaged **21.1 points**, **10.1 rebounds** and **3.1 blocks** per game, and shot .526 from the field. His best seasons came in back-to-back years where he was named Defensive Player of The Year: In the 1998-99 season, Mourning averaged 20.1 points, 11 rebounds and 3.9 blocks per game, on 51 percent shooting and made the All-NBA First Team. And the following season in 1999-00, he averaged **21.7 points**, **9.5 rebounds** and **3.7 blocks** per game, on a career .551 percent shooting - and was named to the All-Defensive First Team for the second straight year.

Before all the career shortening injuries began to mount, Mourning made it past the first round of the playoffs only twice. After defeating the Knicks in a grueling seven-game series, the Heat lost rather handily to the Bulls in the Eastern Conference Finals in five games. In 2000, after the Heat swept the Pistons in the first round, they were eliminated by their bitter rival Knicks in the semifinals in seven games. It wasn't until the 2005-06 season that glory came to Alonzo Mourning. In a back-up role as well as a starter because of the injuries to Shaq, Mourning helped lead the Miami Heat to the Promised Land where they would win the 2006 NBA Championship over the Dallas Mavericks. Despite the minuscule numbers in limited minutes, Mourning and Gary Payton played a vital part in the success of the Heat winning the championship because both players anchored and solidified the defense in both a starting role, or by coming off the bench. If it weren't for the kidney disease that ultimately ended his career, Mourning's legacy would have easily warranted a Hall of Fame induction. But for now, out of all the great players that have played for the Miami Heat including Tim Hardaway, Shaquille O'Neal, Gary Payton, Dwyane Wade, LeBron James and Chris Bosh, Mourning will always be remembered for his hard work and dedication, and for being the first Miami Heat to have his #33 jersey retired.

After the loss to the Heat, the following season, Ewing's career almost came to an end due to injury. He played in only 26 regular season games and the last four playoff games of the semifinals against the Pacers as they were eliminated in five games. In the 1998-99 season, Ewing was plagued again with injuries but the Knicks made a surprise return to the NBA Finals. As the first number 8th seed in history to reach the Finals, the Knicks beat the Heat in the first round three games to two, swept the Hawks in the semifinals, and eliminated the Pacers in the conference finals in six games. Unfortunately, Ewing battled an Achilles tendon injury that kept him from contributing in the NBA Finals as the Knicks lost handily to the San Antonio Spurs in five games.

The following season, Ewing played in 62 games as the Knicks made one last run at a title. In the playoffs, the 50-win Knicks swept the Toronto Raptors in the first round, eliminated the Heat for the third straight season, this time in seven games, before losing to **Reggie Miller** and the Indiana Pacers in the conference finals four games to two. With Michael Jordan now in retirement, this marked the changing of the guard in the Eastern Conference, even though the Knicks never won a championship. Other than Antonio Davis, the Pacers rostered almost the exact core group of players that eliminated the Knicks in seven games five years before in the 1995 semifinals (this is the series where in game 1, Miller scored 8 points in a nine-second span). With Miller, Rik Smits, Dale Davis and Mark Jackson still with the team, the Pacers now had a more experienced and more formidable team with the inclusion of Jalen Rose, Austin Croshere and Travis Best. With Miller leading the way, I felt the Pacers had a legitimate shot at beating the Los Angeles Lakers in the NBA Finals. In a highly competitive series, the Pacers succumbed in six games despite the stellar backcourt play of Miller and Rose. Both guards on Indiana were able to neutralize Kobe Bryant, but the Pacers big men were eaten alive by Shaquille O'Neal all series long.

Playing on the 2000 Indiana Pacers team, Miller was one of the great *clutch* shooters to have ever played in the NBA. He retired with the most three-pointers made in NBA history until Ray Allen broke the record just recently. He was also known as a "*Knick Killer*" for his clutch performances against the New York Knicks. Even though he lacked the athleticism of most great two-guards, he still holstered one of the deadliest jump shots in NBA history. In fact, from a pure shooting standpoint and from three-point range, in my player comparisons, I would take only Ray Allen's jump shot over Miller's. Although as sweet as Miller's shot was, the rest of his game wasn't. That's why he didn't rank in the top 50 players of all-time. I would also have to put him behind Allen among greatest shooting guards ever, because Allen had the better all-around game that included being able to take his man off the dribble like a scorer/shooter. He was also the better passer and defensive player as he proved in his later years playing for the Boston Celtics. Allen would even stick his nose in the paint and grab a respectable amount of rebounds throughout his career. With all due respect for Miller, he didn't have to rely on rebounding and distributing the ball most of his career, because he played with a formidable frontcourt and with outstanding point guards. Despite his shortcomings, you have to give Miller a lot of credit, because he played with the upmost consistency for 18 seasons (with the same team), and that says a lot!

Reginald Wayne Miller was born on August 24th, 1965 in Riverside, California and attended Riverside Polytechnic High School. In college at UCLA, he averaged 25.9 points and 5.3 rebounds per game, on .556 percent shooting. He also shot 88 percent from the free-throw line. In his senior year, Miller averaged 22.3 points and 5.4 rebounds, on .543 percent shooting. Fittingly, the NCAA instituted the three-point line for the 1986-87 season where he would shoot .439 percent from deep. One of Miller's most memorable games came in a victory against the defending National Champion Louisville Cardinals in

1987 when he scored a record 33 points in the second half that still stands today. He left UCLA with the record for most points and free-throws in a single season. Miller was selected with 11th pick overall of the 1987 NBA Draft by the Indiana Pacers. After a modest two seasons in the NBA, in his third year in 1989-90, Miller exploded, averaging a **career-high 24.6 points** per game, a whopping eight and a half points higher than his previous seasons average. He also made his first of five All-Star games selections. Two years later in 1992, Miller scored a **career-high 57 points** against the Charlotte Hornets. The franchise record still stands today. He also finished his career averaging 18.2 points, three rebounds and three assists per game, and shot .395 percent from three-point range. As already chronicled above, Miller and the Pacers played their best in the playoffs against the New York Knicks in both 1995 and 2000 with Spike Lee always in attendance. Like many of the other great players, Miller stepped up big in the playoffs. In fact, his career averages don't begin to tell the story. Because his career lasted so long, if you don't count the last three playoff seasons, in his first 12 years, Miller averaged 23.5 points and shot .408 from distance.

In player comparisons:

You could make the case that Patrick Ewing was the greatest New York Knick of all-time. He was one of the toughest players to rank because he never won an NBA Championship (partly because of timing and injury), and at the same time had the best individual success in terms of numbers and longevity of any Knicks player in history. He also played during the time of not only one of the most talented group of centers, but with the most overall talent in NBA history as I have written about in the introduction to Hakeem Olajuwon's chapter. I actually flip-flopped Ewing with Willis Reed and Walt Frazier many times before finalizing the rankings. As you could take your pick in the order for which you wish to rank the New York Knick greats! But for me as explained throughout the entire book, a player should be rated on his individual contributions to the team success. If the talent is near equal, it is very hard to give a player the nod without at least one championship on his resume. In fact, that's why both Reed and Frazier are ranked ahead of Ewing in this book. Other than the scoring aspect of the game which favors Ewing, the other numbers are not far apart. You might even give a slight edge to Reed on defense, judging on how great he matched up against Kareem Abdul-Jabbar and other great centers of his time. If Ewing had won at least one MVP award or one NBA Championship, I would have most likely gone the other way. But still, all in all, Ewing was one of the all-time great (prototypical) centers ever that at one point in his career, was in the same class with Hakeem Olajuwon and David Robinson. And, at that same point in time, he was also at the peak of his career when he played for the greatest team ever assembled, the 1992 U.S. Olympic Dream Team!

Career Totals

21.0 point, 9.8 rebounds, 1.9 assists, 2.4 blocks, 1.0 steal, .504 FG%, .740 FG%

24,815 points, 11,607 rebounds, 2215 assists, 2894 blocks, 1136 assists

Sam Jones

(Rank #40)

All-Star (5-times), NBA Championships (10)

Also featuring: Bill Sharman
& Tom Heinsohn

Acknowleged as one of the league's best shooting guards in history; Sam Jones was also one of the greatest winners of all-time. His 10 NBA championships are the most by any player in NBA history except for his teammate Bill Russell. Known for his clutch shooting, Jones possessed one of the smoothest and best jump shots ever. Given the nickname "The Shooter" or Mr. Clutch because of his lethal outside shooting, the six-foot-four Jones had explosive quickness and could stop on a dime releasing one of the purest shooting strokes and killer bank shots of all-time. As a testament to his shooting attributes particular in the clutch, his teammate Russell said: Jones was deadly from either side of the court or anywhere around the perimeter. With that being said, whether it was his own shot or somebody else's, Jones himself said that after a rebound he would move to another spot on the floor looking for a shot when the defensive player turned his back - Red Auerbach always marveled his speed, shooting touch, reflexes, attitude and dedication to the game. "He'll do anything you ask him," said Auerbach, "He's always in shape and ready to play and nobody works any harder at basketball than he does." Jones, along with Elgin Baylor helped pave the way for athletic wing men that could run the floor.

Samuel Jones was born on June 24th, 1933 in Wilmington, North Carolina and attended high school at Laurinburg Institute. In four years at North Carolina Central University, he averaged 17.7 points and 9.1 rebounds per game. After flying under the radar playing for a small college, Jones was selected with the 8th pick overall of the 1957 NBA Draft by the Boston Celtics. In his first three seasons, he won two NBA championships while playing in limited minutes. At that point in time, the Celtics had three outstanding scorers in Bill Sharman, Tom Heinsohn, and Bob Cousy that could fill it up on a nightly basis. In fact, with the tremendous scoring depth of the C's which included sixth man Frank Ramsey, it took Jones six years to lead the team in scoring. The next two seasons, as Jones minutes began to increase, so did his scoring. In 1961-62 with Sharman now retired, he averaged 18.4 points per game and 20.6 in the playoffs while making his first all-star team. He would go on to average at least 20 points or more for 7 consecutive postseasons. The following year, with John Havlicek in his first season, Jones led the Celtics in scoring for the first time at 19.7 points per game. He also shot a career-high .476 percent from the field and contributed 23.8 points in the playoffs. As kind of a Red Auerbach tradition, players had to wait their turn coming off the bench before becoming a starter as long as the starter was doing his job. That's why it took almost four years and a Sharman retirement for Jones to get his chance!

As great as Sam Jones was, he had big shoes to fill moving into the starting lineup replacing the great **Bill Sharman** who was one of the first pioneers and great shooting guards of his time. William Walton Sharman was born on May 2nd, 1926 in Abilene, Texas and was selected in the second round, with the 17th pick overall of the 1950 NBA Draft by the Washington Capitals. Coming out of the same draft as Bob Cousy, the super-tandem became one of the great backcourts in NBA history. While Cousy was setting all the records in assists, so was Sharman at the free-throw line where he led the league in free-throw shooting 7 times (including five seasons in a row), and became the first man to shoot 40 percent from the field. He was also fantastic in the playoffs averaging 18.5 points per game and shooting 91 percent from the charity stripe. Still to this day, he owns the playoff record for most free-throws made in a row with 56. In the 1964-65 season, Sam Jones continued to pick up the scoring slack once again with Heinsohn in his final days with the team, when he averaged a **career-high 25.9 points** (4th best in the league - while his backcourt mate K.C Jones finished third in assists) in the regular season and **28.6 points** in the playoffs. He was also named to the All-NBA Second Team for the first of three consecutive seasons. After that season, Auerbach said Jones became a true Superstar and told the Sporting News that as a shooter, he was every bit as tough to guard as Jerry West and Oscar Robertson.

Tom Heinsohn along with Bill Sharman and Bob Cousy were the original trio of scorers that provided the offensive fire power during the first half of the Celtics' Dynasty. In fact, because Heinsohn was a rookie in 1956-57, the same year as Russell, he ended up with the most championships out of the three. Sharman won four, Cousy won six, and Heinsohn won eight. Born on August 26th, 1934 in Jersey City, New Jersey, Thomas William Heinohn was selected with the 1956 Territorial pick by the Boston Celtics. His brilliant career as a scorer began in college at Holy Cross where as a senior; he averaged **27.4 points** and **21.1 rebounds** per game. He also had a **51-point** game against Boston College and was named AP All-America in the 1955-56 campaign. And in his first year in the NBA, Heinsohn averaged 16.2 points and 9.8 rebounds per game, and won the Rookie of the Year Award over fellow teammate Bill Russell. For his career, he averaged 18.6 points and 8.8 rebounds per game in the regular season, and 19.8 points and 9.2 rebounds in the playoffs. Heinsohn was a solid rebounder and passer that contributed scoring punch from the perimeter as well as the interior. Sharman once said, "He had the most variety in his repertoire of anyone in the league and could use his agility and exceptional body control to his advantage." His offensive arsenal included an assortment of drives to the basket and a one-handed set shot. He could also shoot a long range jump shot from the corners and beyond the top of the key. From the interior, he featured a right-handed hook shot from five to fifteen feet and short range left-handed hook shot.

In the 1965-66 season, Jones led the team in scoring for the third time in four years at **23.5 points** per game. He also had a **career-high 51 points** against the Detroit Pistons on October 29th, 1965 which stands as the fourth best scoring output in Celtics history. In the playoffs, he had another sensational run averaging **24.8 points** and 5.1 rebounds as the Celtics captured their 8th consecutive NBA championship. The following season, Havlicek and newcomer Bailey Howell led the team in scoring. Out of the three, Jones actually had the higher per game average but played in only 72 games. Until the 1969-70 season, the league awarded the scoring title to the player that scored the most total points in favor of points per game average. With three Celtics averaging at least 20 points, the Celtics were loaded with more fire power than the year before when they won their ninth championship, but ran into a team of destiny in the Philadelphia 76ers that finally got over the hump, dethroning the Celtics in the playoffs and winning their first championship since 1955 with the Syracuse Nationals franchise.

Throughout his playoff career, Sam Jones came up big in key moments of big games and in series deciding games during the playoffs, particularly in game *sevens*. Here are a few examples of his big game moments: In game 7 of the 1962 Eastern Finals against the Philadelphia Warriors, he scored 27 points and hit the game-winning jumper with two seconds left, and in the crucial game 6 of the NBA Finals against the Los Angeles Lakers, he scored 35 points, and followed that up with 27 points (with 5 coming in overtime) in the decisive game 7. He also outscored Oscar Robertson 47-43 in game 7 of the 1963 Eastern Finals, and had 37 points in game 7 of the 1965 Eastern Finals against the 76ers (the famous game where Havlicek stole the ball). Then in the 1966 semifinals, he scored 34 points against the Royals in the deciding game five and hit the game-winning jumper at the buzzer in the must-win game four against the Lakers in the 1969 NBA Finals.

In Sam Jones last three seasons playing with Bill Russell who had become the new player/coach the season before the Celtics won two more championships - Jones was still more than productive in both seasons where he averaged 21.3 points and 16.3 his final year, including 22.5 points per 36 minutes played. His 10 NBA Championships was the second most of any player in history behind only his teammate Russell. While Jones averaged a shade under eighteen points per game in the regular season, it was his big moments in the playoffs, particularly in game 7's, for which he will be remembered: like in the 1962 Eastern Finals, in the deciding game seven with the score tied at 107 and two seconds on the clock, he hit the game-winning shot over a contesting Wilt Chamberlain - who later acknowledged Jones as the Celtics best player.

Like most big-time stars that raise their level of play in the postseason, Jones averaged 18.9 points per game in his playoff career. But, if you don't count his first four years in which he averaged less than ten points due to playing in limited minutes, he averaged 22.6 points per game his final eight years in the league. And, if you don't count his last season and just the seven before (where he averaged at least twenty points), he averaged 23.7 points per game. If you crunch the numbers even more, he averaged 25.3 points in a five-year span and 26.4 in his three-year peak. But his clutch shots in close games and in game sevens of the playoffs and the NBA Finals as stated above, define the *greatness* of Sam Jones!

Career Totals

17.7 points, 4.9 rebounds, 2.5 assists, .456 FG%, .803 FT%

15,411 points, 4305 rebounds, 2209 assists

Clyde Drexler
(Rank #41)

All-NBA First Team (1-time), All-Star (10-times)

NBA Championships (1)

Clyde Drexler, at a rock solid six-feet-seven inches, was one of the great all-around guards to have ever played the game. The Portland Trail Blazers sensation was best known for his *slashing* and *smooth glides* to the basket resulting in swooping slam dunks, and for his tremendous leaping ability and athleticism finishing in the half court and especially in transition. Out of all the great players in history, with the possible exception of Michael Jordan, no shooting guard was better at *finishing* on the fast break. This is how he got the nickname "Clyde the Glide" by being able to soar and dunk over helpless opponents in the open court. Dynamic and electrifying as ever, one of his most famous dunks of all-time was when he *posterized* Isiah Thomas in the 1990 NBA Finals. After streaking down the court on a one-on-one fast break, Drexler glided directly at the basket and toward the rafters and threw down a monster slam dunk over a stationary and helpless Isiah. As he dunked the ball, he looked as though he was still levitating as Isiah's head was down to his waist. Isiah was either trying to draw the offensive foul or was just frozen out of admiration, or both. Watching it live on TV was awe inspiring.

Another of Drexler's greatest attributes: was his size (lengthy arms to where he could change the angle of his shots in mid-flight) and strength at six-foot-seven, able to *manhandle*, *punish*, and *post up* smaller guards scoring in the paint and by shooting an unorthodox jumper that often seemed to go in. Even against his greatest peer, in the fourth quarter of a loss in the clinching game six of the 1992 NBA Finals against the Chicago Bulls, Drexler showed his offensive repertoire, off dribble penetration against Jordan on many occasions including two memorable ones: after being tightly defended, he drove the center lane muscling up a finger-roll layup over Jordan and when he took him off the dribble from the high post right side; On this dominant drive to the basket, Drexler drove left to the center lane with Jordan draped all over him, but after contact underneath the rim, Jordan went spiraling out of bounds with a no-call as Drexler scooped in an easy layup. Other times, he would take Jordan off the dribble shaking him for *uncontested* layups. The only regret is that he should have tried to dominate the paint with dribble penetration against Jordan more often in the first five games of their NBA Finals matchup instead of trying to match Jordan's scoring onslaught from the perimeter.

In player comparisons:

Drexler was not only a great scorer, but he was one of the best rebounding and passing two-guards in NBA history. With his *wiry* strength, *amazing* vertical leap and great feel around the basket, he was able to get offensive rebounds, follow-up dunks and easy tip-in baskets. He also had great vision and could pass the ball almost as well as any player, at any position. It *seemed* like he never missed an open cutter slashing to the hoop. Here are the career rebounding and assists comparisons of the all-time elite shooting guards:

Drexler: 6677(6.1) rebs, 6125(5.6) assists   Jordan: 6672(6.2) rebs, 5633(5.3) assists

Bryant: 6575(5.3) rebs, 5887(4.8) assists   West: 5366(5.8) rebs, 6238(6.7) assists

Wade: 3364(5.1) rebs, 4049(6.1) assists   Frazier: 4830(6.1) rebs, 5040(5.9) assists

Judging from these statistics, it might make one wonder why Drexler is ranked so low on many people's list of greatest players of all-time. You would assume the reason is partly because he played the same position and at the same time as the greatest player to have ever played the game in Michael Jordan. But at least he won a championship (albeit, as the second best player) something Karl Malone and Charles Barkley never accomplished. Because he was out of his prime, as the second best player with the Houston Rockets in 1995, proved his value even more. The toughest thing for a team to do is to repeat as champion, and that's what the Rockets did with Drexler. Most teams win championships when their second best player is near or still in their prime but the

1994 and 1995 Rockets were an exception for two reasons: Olajuwon was the best player on the planet and because he was supported with perhaps the most prolific group of three-point shooters in NBA history. No other center in history would have been good enough to win a championship with that team. The combination of unstoppable low-post moves, allowing the "Dream" to score at will, and the ability to pass with excellence out of double and triple teams - allowed the system to work at an optimum. Of course, it took a collective effort in all aspects of the game including Otis Thorpe doing his part cleaning up the glass during their first championship season in 1994. Not to sound contradicting after praising Olajuwon so highly, I don't think the Rockets could have beaten the star-studded New York Knicks team without Thorpe and repeated as NBA Champions in 1995 against Orlando without the Thorpe trade for Drexler. In his prime as the best player on the team, Drexler proved he could lead a team in the Portland Trail Blazers to the NBA Finals twice, only to lose both times in a highly competitive five and six-game series against the defending champion Detroit Pistons in 1990, and defending champion Chicago Bulls in 1992.

What separated Drexler behind Jordan, Wade, Kobe, Iverson, West, and Frazier, was that he did not have the deadly jump shot or fallaway to compliment his terrific inside game the way the others did. Although, he did have a highly effective midrange jump shot, it wasn't in the class of the other great shooting guards ahead of him. And, a lot of experts have criticized him, saying that he never had the killer instinct, especially against Jordan and the Chicago Bulls. Well, what about all the other teams he *dismantled* during his entire playoff career? I am not buying into that, because most players and especially star players have the competitive fire to compete at the highest level or they would never have made it this far, reaching the highest level of success - which is the NBA. Some stars *conceal* their fire or killer instinct and let it show with their play on the court - think Dwyane Wade, Ray Allen, Tim Duncan, and Pau Gasol. Others let it show on their face - think Isiah Thomas, Allen Iverson, Kobe Bryant, and Kevin Garnett. I have seen Drexler play with plenty of fire and will to win throughout his entire career, and even in the second half of game six of the 1992 NBA Finals, but of course by that point is was all too late. The Trail Blazers would have never made it to two NBA Finals without him as the lone Superstar. Most great players want the ball in crucial moments, and so did Clyde. It was too bad he was far more effective driving to the hoop then settling for a *sometimes suspect* mid to three-point range jump shot. When the game was on the line, Drexler would attack the basket as well as anyone to have ever played the game, but when it came to pulling up for a perimeter shot in *some* defining moments in the playoffs, he would sometimes overshoot or undershoot it. A good example came against the Bulls in the '92 Finals; he ended up pulling the string on some of his shots resulting in an ugly bounce off the front of the rim. His unorthodox jump shot didn't sit well with the public eye because it may have looked at times like he was shooting it two-handed.

Defensively, Drexler was *underrated*. With some of the quickest hands ever, he was able to amass 2207 steals (7th on the all-time list and 2nd to Jordan at the shooting guard position). And as a solid team defender with *great anticipation*, he was able to amass a lot of his steals out of the passing lanes. Other than the possible exception of Scottie Pippen, Michael Jordan, Allen Iverson, and current players Dwyane Wade and LeBron James, I don't believe another superstar ever anticipated and stole the ball in the passing lanes better than Clyde Drexler. As a testament to his ability to steal the ball from an opponent, he had 10 steals in a game twice in his career, 8 steals three times, 6 steals three other times, and 7 steals in only one half of a game twice. In man-to-man defense he could have been better moving his feet laterally, but was fast enough to stay with his man after getting beat off the dribble. He would often ride a player into the lane where help was usually waiting or, with his incredible length and leaping ability, he was able to get a hand up to block the shot or deflect a pass. During the 1992 NBA Finals against the Chicago Bulls, Drexler did a good job staying close to Jordan, causing him to take a lot of difficult shots and forcing him to pass the ball (more often than he would of liked) after driving into the lane. With his athleticism and incredible vertical leap, Drexler was able to block shots flying in off the ball in the same *emphatic* manner Charles Barkley used to. Back in the day, if I remember correctly, Drexler was known to have been able to dunk on an 11 foot-plus rim.

Clyde Austin Drexler was born on June 22nd, 1962 in New Orleans, Louisiana. He grew up in the South Park area in Houston and attended Ross Sterling High School where he tried out for the basketball team his junior year but was cut due to the lack of conditioning. In his senior year at nearly the height he played at in the NBA, Drexler began getting attention from college coaches after a 34-point and 27-rebound performance in a tournament game on Christmas Day in 1979. After being recruited by the University of Houston, Texas Tech, and New Mexico State, Drexler chose to stay close to home and play basketball for the Houston Cougars. In his second year, he averaged 15.2 points, 10.5 rebounds, three assists and 3 steals per game. And in his third and final year, he averaged 15.9 points, 8.8 rebounds, 3.8 assists and 3.3 steals per game. With the Dynamic duel of Drexler and Olajuwon, the Cougars made it all the way to the Final Four in 1982 but lost to the North Carolina Tarheels. In 1983, the Cougars made it back to the Final Four as the number 1 ranked team in the country. In the semifinals, behind a dunking exhibition by both teams, the Cougars defeated the number 2 ranked Louisville Cardinals 94-81. In that game, Drexler finished with 21 points, seven rebounds, and six assists and had a monster double-pump slam that was highly publicized by Sport Illustrated. For all the teams' dunking escapades, what I found most interesting was that for initiation into "Phil Slama Jama" basketball fraternity, players had to stand underneath the basket as Drexler drove in from half court to tomahawk slam over them. Unfortunately in the championship game, the University of Houston lost to "Cinderella" North Carolina State, large in part because Drexler was a non-factor after getting his fourth foul before halftime.

Drexler was selected with the 14th pick overall of the 1983 NBA Draft by the Portland Trail Blazers. In his first season in the NBA, Drexler got off to a slow start playing in limited minutes in back-up role, as the Blazers were eliminated in the first round of playoffs by the Phoenix Suns three games to two. But in his second season, Drexler took a giant leap and more than doubled his offensive production by averaging 17.2 points, 5.5 assists, 6 rebounds and 2.2 steals. With Kiki Vandeweghe, Mychal Thompson and Jim Paxson leading the way, the Blazers made it out of the first round of the playoffs. After defeating the Dallas Mavericks three games to one, they were eliminated in the semifinals by the eventual champion Los Angeles Lakers in five games. In the 1985-86 season, Drexler had another solid campaign averaging 18.5 points and a **career-high 8 assists**. He also averaged a lofty 2.6 steals per game and was named to the All-Star team for the first of ten seasons. Now after quickly becoming one of the top steals men in the league, he averaged at least two and a half steals in four consecutive seasons. With Drexler emerging as the second best scorer on the team behind Vandeweghe, the Blazers returned to the playoffs but lost in the first round to the Denver Nuggets three games to one. The following year, the Blazers improved their win total to 49, up from 40 and 42 the previous two seasons, but they were eliminated once again in the first round, this time by the Houston Rockets three games to one. That season, Drexler was one of three players along with Larry Bird and Magic Johnson to average at least 21 points, 6 rebounds and 6 assists. In the 1987-88 season, Drexler led the team in scoring at **27 points** per game, seven points higher than Vandeweghe who played in only thirty-seven games. He also made his second and first of seven consecutive All-Star game selections.

A lot of times throughout the years, when a team's top scorer goes down to injury, another, often younger player steps up and blossoms in a huge way. Most notably was Tracy McGrady, when Grant Hill was lost to a reoccurring ankle injury years back, McGrady developed into an elite scorer and won two consecutive scoring titles. In similar fashion after Vandeweghe's injury, Drexler averaged a career-high 27 points per game two years in a row. In the 1988-89 campaign, he had his best statistical season of his career when he averaged **27.2 points**, 5.8 assists, a **career-high 7.9 rebounds**, and **2.7 steals** per game. That year, he also had perhaps the two best games of his career back-to-back: On January 4th, 1989 in a loss against the Lakers in Los Angeles, he posted a triple-double of 33 points, 11 rebounds and 10 assists; and two days later at home in a double-overtime victory against the Sacramento Kings, he had **50 points, 7 rebounds, 4 assists, and 3 steals.** And, to top that off, less than three weeks later on January 22nd at home against the New York Knicks he tallied **48 points, 11 rebounds, 6 assists, and 4 steals.** Despite Drexler's two best scoring seasons of his career, the Blazers were eliminated in the first round of the playoffs in both years by the Utah Jazz three games to one and in a three-game sweep to the Los Angeles Lakers. For the Blazers, this marked the fourth straight season of first-round exits. Despite the loss to the Lakers in the 1989 playoffs, the Blazers had a bright future that came to fruition almost instantly the following season. With Sam Bowie's career slowing down to where you could almost call it a travesty (in terms of battling nagging injuries and never reaching his potential), and with the trades of Paxson and Vandeweghe in consecutive seasons, allowed the remaining group of young and talented players on the team to gel into a title contender.

Prior to the 1989-90 season, the Blazers acquired veteran power forward Buck Williams in a trade to bolster the frontcourt while Jerome Kersey, Kevin Duckworth, and Terry Porter were all making huge strides into becoming outstanding players at their positions. With a terrific balance of offensive talent now in place, Drexler's scoring dipped four points to 23.3 per game, but his other numbers remained nearly the same. In the regular season, Portland finished second in the division with a 59-23 record. But with the retirement of Kareem Abdul-Jabbar the year before and with the rest of the Lakers aging, the Blazers were in good position to make a deep playoff run. After sweeping the Dallas Mavericks in the first round, the Blazers grinded out a tough seven-game series against the San Antonio Spurs, in which they were fortunate enough to have survived overtime games in both the pivotal game five and game seven.

In the Western Conference Finals, the Blazers defeated the Phoenix Suns in six games before losing in the NBA Finals to the defending champion Detroit Pistons four games to one. In their only victory in game two, Drexler scored 33 points including the winning free throws in the final seconds of overtime. Going into the series, I felt Portland was the more talented, more balanced, and much deeper team. I also thought they were bigger, stronger, and perhaps even more physical, and the perfect matchup for the "Bad Boy" Pistons. On paper, they appeared to be the better team offensively - in rebounding, and not far behind on the defensive end. The Pistons were obviously the better defensive team overall, but the Blazers played good *team* defense and were able to get a lot of steals by double teaming and trapping, and in the passing lanes. I also knew that the Pistons had possibly the best *three-guard rotation* in history that included Hall of Famers Isiah Thomas and Joe Dumars, and streak shooter Vinny Johnson. In retrospect, I think this was the difference, despite the Blazers more talented frontcourt that included sixth man Cliff Robinson. Also, as much as I hate to admit it, the Pistons appeared to be the *stronger willed* team after winning the title the year before.

Not knowing it at the time, the Pistons actually had three Hall of Famers to Portland's one - because as it turned out just recently, Dennis Rodman was inducted into the Hall of Fame. I just never thought the NBA would put the most one dimensional (albeit, he was dominate in that aspect, rebounding) player in history in the Hall of Fame with a head case of that magnitude. At least Ben Wallace (when he eventually gets inducted) with four Defensive Player of the Year awards, was not only a better shot blocker than Rodman, but also a better offensive player having been named to the All-NBA Second Team three times. Pulling for the Blazers at the time, I was really disappointed that they were not able to complete their magnificent playoff run and win their first championship since 1977. I guess Blazers fans could blame it on the coach (the young Rick Adelman), the team's up-and-down temperament, and the lack of discipline. Furthermore, like Rodman, the Blazers had two head cases in Kersey and Duckworth. Also, Buck Williams, sixth man Cliff Robinson, and rookie Drazen Petrovic were in their first year playing together. On the upside, Drexler did do his part averaging **26.4 points** and **7.8 rebounds** per game, on **.543 percent shooting** for the series - and had the memorable *monster slam* over Isiah

Thomas. He also had one of the best all-around seasons in the playoffs ever when he averaged 21.4 points, 7.2 rebounds and 7.1 assists, and 2.5 steals in 21 playoff games.

The following season, the Blazers finished with the best record in the NBA at 63-19. With the addition of veteran guard Danny Ainge, the Blazers looked to make it back to the NBA Finals. In the playoffs, after defeating the Seattle SuperSonics and the Utah Jazz in the first two rounds in five games, the Blazers were upset by the aging Los Angeles Lakers in the conference finals. Although the Lakers were an old team, they were still very much formidable. With sophomore sensation Vlade Divac improving at a rapid pace and with the acquisition of Sam Perkins to bolster the frontcourt, the Lakers were able to make one last push for a championship. Drexler did have another phenomenal playoff run, topping the season before, averaging **21.7 points**, **8.1 rebounds**, and **8.1 assists** per game.

In the 1991-92 season, Drexler averaged **25 points**, **6.6 rebounds**, and **6.7 assists** per game as the Blazers had another fabulous regular season finishing with the best record in the Western Conference at 57-25. With the same team still intact from the previous year, the Blazers were primed and ready to return to the NBA Finals and win it all. In the playoffs, after taking avenge on the Lakers in the first round three games to one, Portland made quick work of the Phoenix Suns in the semifinals in five games. After taking down the Utah Jazz in the Western Conference Finals in six games, the Blazers faced the defending NBA Champion Chicago Bulls in the NBA Finals. With hopes of winning their first title since 1977, they had to face a Bulls team with, not only the best record in the NBA, but one that was coming off its first championship. While Portland was *hungry* for their first championship in the Drexler era, the Bulls were *even hungrier* to prove that they had the best team for years to come. In the individual matchup with Drexler, Jordan also wanted to silence any doubt; that he was simply the best player in the game.

We all know what happened in the 1992 NBA Finals that I already mentioned in the beginning of this chapter. Although, Portland did actually battle back after losing game one in Chicago - splitting the first four games, which forced the series to go six games. But after losing game five at home, they would eventually lose the next game in Chicago after blowing a fifteen-point lead in the fourth quarter. Despite the disappointing loss, Drexler averaged 24.8 points, 7.8 rebounds, and 5.3 assist per game for the series. Not too shabby. He also averaged **26.3 points**, **7.4 rebounds** and **7 assists** per game for the entire playoff run. In fact, as title contenders between 1990 and 1992 - over 58 playoff games, Drexler averaged 23.3 points, 7.5 rebounds, and 7.3 assists. After finishing with All-NBA First Team honors and second in the MVP voting to Michael Jordan, it was fitting that Drexler was selected to play for the U.S. Olympic Dream Team during the summer of 1992. As the two best shooting guards in the world, Drexler and Jordan helped the United States bring home the gold medal in Barcelona. The following season, it seemed the Blazers never recovered from their second Finals loss in three years. With ensuing injuries, Drexler's production began to drop and the Blazers were eliminated in the first round of the playoffs by MVP David Robinson and the San Antonio Spurs three games to one. The very next season, the same thing happened when they were swept in the first round by the Phoenix Suns.

Before the trade deadline in the middle of the 1994-95 season, Drexler was traded upon request to the Houston Rockets for Otis Thorpe. Joining the city where he played college basketball - and where he was also a teammate with Olajuwon, was the perfect scenario at that point in Drexler's career. After two sub-par seasons in Portland due to injury, Drexler had a solid regular season with both clubs, once again raised his scoring average above twenty points per game. He also had shot a career-high 36 percent from three-point range. Drexler left Portland as the all-time leader in scoring, rebounds, and steals. After finishing the regular season with the sixth seed at 47-35, from the outside looking in, it seemed improbable for the Rockets to make it back to the NBA Finals. But the sixth seed Rockets behind Hakeem Olajuwon's scoring onslaught, performed like defending champions in the playoffs. After defeating the Jazz (Drexler and Olajuwon scored 41 and 40 points in game 4), and Suns and Spurs in the Western Conference, the Rockets became the lowest seed in history (sixth) to win the 1995 NBA Championship over the Orlando Magic.

Even though Drexler was not the superstar he once was in Portland, he actually ended up retiring after the 1998 season at the age 35 (about to turn 36 at seasons end) as a reasonably productive player, unlike many of the Hall of Famers of the past, who wait too long before retiring and see their skills deteriorate more than we all want to see. In fact, in his last four seasons with the Rockets including the championship season in 1995, Drexler averaged a healthy 19.5 points, 6 rebounds, 5.4 assists and 1.9 steals per game, and shot 34 percent from three-point range. Not bad by anyone's standards. So after averaging 18.4 points in his final season, if he wanted to, he could have still been productive and played another two or three more years to pad his career stats.

Clyde Drexler has an excellent resume as an all-around player as described throughout the chapter, but he played the same position at the same time as the greatest basketball player of all-time in Michael Jordan. For all of us who saw "Clyde the Glide" play, we all know how special and unique he really was. I mean we all talk versions of Michael Jordan in Dwyane Wade, Kobe Bryant, and even Allen Iverson as a mini version, but it will be a long time before we see a player like Drexler anytime soon. I just wish he had a more dominate perimeter game and was a better one-on-one defender. Because if had been, he might have gone down as the second best shooting guard of all-time behind Jordan. Other than his lack of dominance as a perimeter scorer and on defense, Drexler might have been the best rebounding and passing two-guard to ever live!

Career Totals
20.4 points, 6.1 rebs, 5.6 assists, 2.0 steals, 0.7 blocks, .472 FG%, .788 FT%, .318 3FG%
22,195 points, 6677 rebounds, 6125 assists, 2207 steals, 719 blocks, 827 threes

Gary Payton

(Rank #42)

All-NBA First Team (2-times), All-Defensive First Team (9-times)

Defensive Player of the Year, NBA Championships (1)

Steals Title (1-time), All-Star (9-times)

Also featuring: Shawn Kemp

Gary Payton was one of the great all-around point guards to play in the NBA. He blended offense and defense as well as any point guard in history. With a shooting stroke not as pure as other point guards, Payton continued to improve his jump shot throughout the years to where it became highly effective as far out as the three-point line. Although, scoring in transition and off dribble penetration finishing at the basket with a *spin move* was his trademark. He also had a terrific low-post game where he would punish smaller guards. With a keen eye to see the whole court, Payton was among the best assist men in history. At six-foot-four, despite a slender build, he was one of the strongest and best rebounding point guards of his time. With all that being said, the lightning-quick Payton, was best known for his *suffocating defense* that he played on a nightly basis able to *blanket* and lock down opposing guards. Over the years, the ultra-competitive Payton backed up his trash talking personality by accepting the ultimate challenge of guarding Michael Jordan in the 1996 NBA Finals, in which he helped hold Jordan to his lowest point total in Finals history up to that point. One of my finest memories of Payton is when I saw him in person on a Saturday in 2000 at the Oakland Coliseum during the East and West

All-Star game workout mentoring the young Kobe Bryant on how to play defense. It also brings back on what could have been for my youngest brother who by the way, at one time, had the greatest basketball instincts and skill (at either guard position) on the defensive side of the ball that I have ever witnessed in my lifetime - where he could play the passing lanes and suffocating man-to-man defense at an equal level. Like a lot of late bloomers, if only he had pursed the sport of basketball at every level, I could only imagine how great he could have been.

Getting back to Payton, he was going through all the motions, showing Kobe how to play in the face of an opponent by quickly moving his hands and feet. Ironically, that season, Bryant was honored with his first All-Defensive First Team selection. Fittingly given the nickname "The Glove," Payton became the only point guard in NBA history to win the Defensive Player of the Year Award and to be named to a record 9 All-Defensive First Team selections.

Gary Dwayne Payton was born on July 23rd, 1968 in Oakland, California and played basketball at Skyline High School before attending Oregon State University. At OSU, Payton improved his game every year, and peaked in his senior year averaging **25.7 points**, **8.1 assists**, and **4.7 rebounds** per game, and was named to the All-America Team. He took the Beavers to three NCAA Tournaments and left the school as the all-time leader in field goals, three-point field goals, assists and steals (still owns the record), and was named to the Pac 10's All-Decade Team.

As the most coveted point guard coming out of college, Payton was selected with the second pick overall of the 1990 NBA Draft by the Seattle SuperSonics joining future star teammate **Shawn Kemp** who was selected out of high school at number 17 overall the year before. Both players started their careers off slowly but steadily improved their overall game every season up to the year they won the Western Conference in 1996. In the 1992-93 season, Payton improved his points, field goal percentage, and free-throw shooting significantly as Kemp made the All-Star team for the first time. With veteran sharp shooters Ricky Pierce and Eddie Johnson providing the scoring punch, the Sonics went deep into the playoffs. After beating the Utah Jazz and Houston Rockets in tough five and seven-game series in the first two rounds, they were defeated in the same manner in seven games in the conference finals by the Phoenix Suns - which featured MVP Charles Barkley and All-Star point guard Kevin Johnson. The next season, Payton was named to his first of nine consecutive All-Star selections (not including the 1999 season in which there was no All-star game) and Kemp led the team in scoring for the first time. Picking up where they left off as title contenders in Payton's fourth season, the Sonics finished the regular season with an NBA best 63-19.

At the time, I was hoping the *dynamic* Payton and the *ultra-athletic* Kemp would form as good or better dual than Stockton and Malone or K. Johnson and Barkley in order to unseat the Chicago Bulls as NBA Champions. Kemp was one of the most talented and explosive players to come into the league and was a Kevin Garnett type of player with a little less defensive skills (including timing to block a shot), but with more explosive leaping ability. Before the off-the-court issues that derailed his career, Kemp ran the floor as well or better than any big man ever and might have been the best dunker in traffic of all-time even over players such as Shaquille O'Neal, Dwight Howard, Amar'e Stoudemire (before the microfracture surgery), and Dominique Wilkins. In my opinion, one thing is for certain, he was the best finisher off an alley-oop lob pass in NBA history where he would fly in from incredible angles and dunk over anyone or everyone inside the paint.

Born on November 26th, 1969 in Elkhart, Indiana, Shawn Travis Kemp attended Concord High School where he led the team to the state championship as a senior. After his rookie season, Kemp gradually improved his production on both ends of the floor. By his fourth season, he averaged 17.8 points, 10.7 rebounds and 1.9 blocks per game, and was named to the All-Star team for the first of six consecutive years. During that span, he averaged 18.5 points, 10.5 rebounds, 1.5 blocks, and 1.4 steals per game - and was named to the All-NBA Second Team from 1994-96. In the playoffs during that same period beginning one year earlier, from 1992 to 1998, he was equally impressive averaging 19.5 points and 10.9 rebounds, and 1.8 blocks per game.

Going into the 1994 playoffs, it appeared that the Sonics were a lock to come out of the Western Conference until lightning struck in a way I never thought possible. The Denver Nuggets pulled off the ultimate upset and defeated the Sonics in five games becoming the first #8th seed in NBA history to knock off the #1 seed. After winning the first two games at home, the Sonics lost three games in a row including the last two in overtime, shattering Seattle's dream of their first championship since 1979. Wow, what a crushing loss for the franchise! I think it took just as long for me to get over the ultimate upset as it did the Sonics. Despite a 57-win season the following year, the city of Seattle never fully recovered from the *collapse* in the playoffs from the season before as they were eliminated three games to one in the first round by the Los Angeles Lakers.

In the 1995-96 season, with Payton and Kemp in the beginning of their primes, the Sonics were poised and ready to reclaim the Western Conference crown. After a franchise best 64-18 record in the regular season, the Sonics made quick work of the Sacramento Kings in the first round three games to one and swept the defending champion Houston Rockets in four straight games in the semifinals, before grinding out a seven-game victory over the Utah Jazz in the conference finals. With a dominating season to that point, the Sonics looked like they were ready to capture the NBA championship until they ran into the Chicago Bulls that posted the best regular season record in league history at 72-10. Despite Chicago's dominance similar to Seattle's in the regular season and the postseason, I was *shocked* as so were many, that the Sonics *fell into the abyss* and lost the first three games of the series to *virtually put an end* to their title hopes. Knowing that no team in history has ever come back from a 3-0 deficit in the playoffs let alone the NBA Finals, I was almost convinced that it might actually happen when the Sonics won the next two games. George Karl assigned Payton to guard Jordan in the middle of the series as the momentum changed in Seattle's favor. Jordan then became frustrated with

Payton's hounding defense, that he was held to just one thirty-point game and career lows to that point of 26, 23, and 22 points in the last three games of the series. While Jordon viewed the battle of the *trash talkers* as an annoyance, Payton fed off it. Unfortunately for Seattle, the series came to an end in game six in Chicago.

The very next season, the Sonics won 57 games and the division with the same group of players from the previous year. But in the playoffs after knocking off the Suns in five games, the Sonics ran into the Rockets again which was now rostering three Hall of Famers in Hakeem Olajuwon, Clyde Drexler, and Charles Barkley. After falling behind three games to one, the Sonics mustered up all their playoff grit from the previous four seasons and battled back before losing the series in seven games. Before the 1997-98 season, after Kemp requested to be traded, he ended up in Cleveland in a three-team trade which sent Terrell Brandon and Tyrone Hill to the Milwaukee Bucks and Vin Baker to the Sonics. With most of the team still intact, the Sonics had a terrific regular season finishing at 61-21. But after defeating the young Minnesota Timberwolves three games to one in the first round of the playoffs, the Sonics bowed out to the Lakers in five games in the semifinals. The following season the Sonics fizzled into mediocrity in a lockout shortened season finishing at .500 and missed the playoffs.

The next three years, Payton had his best three scoring seasons of his career as he single handily carried the aging Sonics, but Seattle never won more than forty-five games and made the playoffs just twice - as they were eliminated by the Utah Jazz three games to two, missed the playoffs the following year, and lost to the San Antonio Spurs in five games the year after. From 1996 to 2003, Payton averaged **22.2 points**, **7.4 assists**, **5.2 rebounds**, and **1.7 steals** - and made 99 three-pointers. He also was a member of the 1996 and 2000 Gold Medal U.S. Olympic Team. In the middle of 2002-03 season, Payton was sent to the Milwaukee Bucks in five-player trade that brought Ray Allen to Seattle. The following year with Payton searching for his coveted championship ring, he signed on with the Los Angeles Lakers for the veteran's minimum as did fellow All-Star Karl Malone. Both players sacrificed their offensive game and financial gain to reach the same common goal. Teamed with two other shoo-in Hall of Famers in Shaquille O'Neal and Kobe Bryant, the Lakers seemed invincible throughout the regular season and in the playoffs until Malone got injured in the conference finals. After defeating the Timberwolves in six games and winning game one in the NBA Finals, the Lakers lost four games in row to the Detroit Pistons behind their dominant defense.

In his second stint with three potential Hall of Famers in Dwyane Wade, Shaquille O'Neal and Alonzo Mourning - Payton played limited minutes in his last three seasons in the league including the last two in Miami, where he finally captured his first NBA championship in 2006.

In player comparisons:

Giving Gary Payton the nod over Jason Kidd was made a little tougher the last few years, not only because of the championship ring that Kidd just won, but because of his longevity playing at a decently high level late in his career. I mean the guys 39 years old. Just like Kidd, if Payton had had more team success and won a championship or two during his prime, he would have moved up several rankings perhaps even into the top 25 players of all-time. Because he was that good, maybe the best two-way point guard in history until Chris Paul eventually takes that mantle from him. But Payton will always be remembered for his whirling, twisting, and spinning drives to the basket - and for his snake-like suffocating defense. One could make the case that "The Glove" was the best *perimeter* defensive player of all-time. And you know what; he's got my vote even over those two stars in Chicago!

Career Totals

16.3 points, 6.7 assists, 3.8 rebs, 1.8 steals, 0.2 blocks, .466 FG%, .729 FT%, .317 3FG%

21,813 points, 8966 assists, 5269 rebounds, 2445 steals, 285 blocks, 1132 threes

Jason Kidd

(Rank #43)

All-NBA First Team (5-times), All-Defensive First Team (4-times)

Assist Title (5-times), NBA Championships (1), All-Star (10-times)

Jason Kidd is one of the great all-around point guards to ever play in the NBA. In eighteen seasons to date playing for the Dallas Mavericks, Phoenix Suns, and New Jersey Nets, Kidd is one of the few players in NBA history that could dominate the game of basketball by scoring very little or not at all. However, scoring on the fast break with *blazing* speed was one of his greatest attributes. He was an outstanding finisher and passer in the half court and in transition, excelling on the fast break in a way not seen since Magic Johnson. After a rebound or on an outlet pass to start the break, with the blink of an eye, Kidd would dash down the court with a dominate *hard* dribble finishing at the basket or he would make a slick pass or *alley-oop* pass to the open wing-man flying down court. Aside from his *specialty* as one of the greatest facilitators of all-time, he was one of the great rebounders at his position. Despite the lack of an efficient jump shot early on in his career, Kidd was able to score points off dribble penetration as well as any point guard in history. With a phenomenal overall game of being able to score, rebound, and pass - Kidd is the active leader in triple-doubles with 105, and is ranked third on the all-time list behind the great Oscar Robertson and Magic Johnson (he is also ranked second all-time in the playoffs behind only Magic). Like his close friend and rival Gary Payton,

Kidd was one of the best two-way point guards of all-time. On the defensive end, with his quick hands and feet, enabled him to accumulate a lot of steals throughout his career to where he is currently ranked 2nd on the all-time list behind John Stockton.

Jason Frederick Kidd was born on March 23rd, 1973 in San Francisco, California and then raised on the other side of the Bay in Oakland. He then attended St. Joseph Notre Dame High School nearby in Alameda, Ca. where he led the Pilots to back-to-back championships. As a senior, Kidd averaged **25 points, 10 rebounds, 7 rebounds**, and **7 steals** - and was named Player of the Year by USA Today and received the Naismith Award as the nation's top high school player. He was also a McDonald's All-American and was voted Player of the Year by the State of California for the second time. After being highly recruited by top-ranked colleges, Kidd chose to stay close to home and play for the University of California, Berkeley. During his freshman year in 1992-93, Kidd averaged 13 points, 7.7 assists, 4.9 rebounds, and 3.8 steals per game - and was named National Freshman of the Year. He also set a freshman NCAA record for steals with 110 and a school record for assists with 220. Without a conference title since 1960, the same year California went to the NCAA championship game (they won it the year before in 1959), Kidd and the upstart Bears hoped to return to prominence after upsetting the two-time defending Champion Duke Blue Devils in the second round of the tournament. Their title run was short lived though - after they lost in the Sweet 16 to the Kansas Jayhawks. In his sophomore season, Kidd had another stellar year averaging 16.7 points, 9.1 assists, 6.9 rebounds, and 3.1 steals per game - and broke his own school record for assists with 272. He was also the first Cal player since 1968 to be selected First Team All-America and the first sophomore to be named Pac-10 Player of the Year. Unfortunately in the NCAA tournament, the tables were turned against the number five seed Cal Bears when they were upset by the number twelve seed, Wisconson-Green Bay in the first round.

It was no surprise that Kidd opted to leave school early and enter the draft because he looked and played like the next great NBA point guard even in college. Living in the Bay Area, I witnessed firsthand the potential and all the hype of Kidd coming out of college. Except for the outside shooting, he was everything everyone imagined him to be in the NBA, dominating the dribble like no other since Magic Johnson. Kidd was selected with the 2nd pick overall of the 1994 NBA Draft by the Dallas Mavericks, behind Milwaukee's Glen Robinson and one pick ahead of Detroit's Grant Hill. In his rookie season, Kidd averaged a modest 11.7 points, a solid 7.7 assists, and 5.4 rebounds per game. He also led the league with 4 triple-doubles and was named co-Rookie of the Year with Grant Hill. In his second season, he increased his offensive production averaging 16.6 points, 9.7 assists, and 6.8 rebounds per game - and recorded 9 triple-doubles, but the Mavericks would miss the playoffs in his first two seasons. With a nucleus of Jason Kidd, Jamal Mashburn and Jim Jackson, the Mavericks looked like the team of the future until they disbanded within a couple of years. Because team success never materialized in Dallas, partly due to the fact the trio wasn't a good fit for the newly adopted triangle offense; Kidd was traded to the Phoenix Suns during the 1996-97 regular season. In his first two campaigns with the Suns, the team settled in mediocrity, losing in the first round of the playoffs to the Seattle SuperSonics in five games and San Antonio Spurs three games to one. Kidd did have two solid seasons averaging eleven and a half points and nine assists while making the All-Star team for the second time in 1998. At that point, Kidd was the primary point guard because Kevin Johnson was no longer with the team.

In the lockout shortened season of 1998-99, Kidd blossomed into the best point guard in the NBA averaging 16.9 points, 10.8 assists, 6.8 rebounds, 2.3 steals, and a career-high .444 percent from the field. He also led the league in assists for the first of three consecutive seasons, and was named to the All-NBA First Team for the first of four straight years. But the Suns were swept in the first round of the playoffs by the Portland Trail Blazers. The following year, with Kidd having another stellar season, the 53-win Suns upset the Spurs in the first round three games to one before losing to the eventual champion Los Angeles Lakers in the conference semifinals in five games. In his final season with the franchise, the 51-win Suns were eliminated in the first round of the playoffs three games to one to the Sacramento Kings. Unfortunately, Kidd never made it past the second round of the playoffs in five seasons with Phoenix, and was traded before the 2001-02 season to the New Jersey Nets with Chris Dudley for Stephon Marbury, Johnny Newman, and Soumaila Samake.

Kidd made a huge impact in his first season, transforming the Nets into an Eastern Conference power. After finishing with a 52-win season, doubling the win total from the year before, the Nets made it all the way to the NBA Finals. With a solid cast of players in Kenyon Martin, Keith Van Horn, Kerry Kittles and Richard Jefferson - the Nets defeated the Indiana Pacers and Charlotte Hornets in the first two rounds of the playoffs, and the Boston Celtics in the Eastern Conference Finals in six games. But in the 2002 NBA Finals, the Nets ran into the two-time defending champion Lakers on their quest to three-peat while armed with the most potent dynamic-dual in the league. The following season, Kidd averaged a **career-high** in **scoring at 18.7 points** per game and led the league in assists for the fourth time. After a disappointing NBA Finals in which the Nets didn't win a game, the Nets *competed* and fought hard as though they had won the championship the year before. After finishing with the second seed in the Eastern Conference, New Jersey defeated the Milwaukee Bucks in the first round and swept the Detroit Pistons and Boston Celtics in the semifinals and conference finals, before they would lose once again in the NBA Finals, this time to the San Antonio Spurs. Despite the two losses on the biggest stage, during his first seven postseason appearances from 1997 to 2003 his last year he went to the Finals, Kidd averaged an astounding 17.3 points, 9.1 assists, 7.1 rebounds, and two steals per game in 62 playoff games

It is too bad, that it appears some players, such as in the case with Clyde Drexler - who peak in one given year in the NBA Finals, but then happen to find themselves in a downward trend the rest of their career. But like I have said before, it is usually a timing issue more than anything else where age and the *quality of the team has peaked.* Just like

Kobe Bryant once said, you have to *seize the moment* when you have a chance to win a championship because those opportunities don't come around very often! With that being said, it is hard for any team to reach the NBA Finals and win it, let alone make it back and stay on top for more than a year. This is what happened to Jason Kidd after the 2003 season until this past year when he won his first NBA championship with the Dallas Mavericks.

The following season in 2004, Kidd led the league in assists for the fifth time in six years (Andre Miller of Cleveland won the assist title in 2002), but the New Jersey Nets came up short on their bid to make it to the Finals for a third straight year. After sweeping the New York Knicks in the first round of the playoffs, the 47-win Nets were defeated by the eventual champion Detroit Pistons in the semifinals in seven games - as the defending Eastern Conference Champions didn't go down easy! However, even with the acquisition of Vince Carter the following year, the Nets were swept in the first round of the playoffs by the Miami Heat. After the season on July 1st, Kidd had microfracture surgery to repair his damaged knee. With one year under their belt playing together, Kidd and Carter were named to the All-Star team and rebounded from the first-round exit the year before and then led the Nets past the first round of the playoffs the next two seasons. But after defeating the Indiana Pacers and Toronto Rapters in six games, New Jersey would fall in back-to-back years in the semifinals to the Heat in five games, and to the Cleveland Cavaliers in six games behind fourth-year superstar LeBron James.

In their final season playing together in 2007, Kidd and Carter became the first dual to record a triple-double in the same game since Michael Jordan and Scottie Pippen in 1989. In that game, Kidd finished with 10 points, 18 assists, and 16 rebounds. Also, in the playoffs he had 16 points, a career-high 19 assists, 16 rebounds, and 3 steals in game three of the first-round series against the Toronto Raptors. In that game, he tied Larry Bird for second place on the all-time list for career triple-doubles. In the very next series against the Cavaliers, he recorded his 11th career triple-double in the postseason, passing Bird on the all-time list. And, he actually averaged a triple-double against the Raptors and the Cavaliers, becoming the first player to average a triple-double in multiple playoff series since Wilt Chamberlain and Magic Johnson. He also became the second player to average a triple-double for one playoff season. I actually thought with Vince Carter and Jason Kidd teaming-up together in New Jersey, the Nets were formidable enough to have given the Cavaliers a run for their money, but neither team was able to win the NBA Championship during the 2000 decade. Also, if New Jersey had a healthy Richard Jefferson in the 2007 playoffs, maybe it would have been the Nets in the NBA Finals instead of the Cavaliers. The next season, Kidd returned to the team where he started his NBA career, the Dallas Mavericks. Over six seasons (five with the Nets and one with the Mavericks), his assists and rebounding numbers remained ultimately consistent at 9 and 7.2 respectively but his scoring dropped every season to where he was averaging 12.5 points per game. Over that same span, Kidd was ultimately consistent in the playoffs averaging 12.7 points, 8.6 assists, and 7.8 rebounds per game in 63 playoff games.

In Kidd's last four seasons to date playing alongside Dirk Nowitzki, the Mavericks were finally able to get over the hump and win their first NBA Championship for the franchise. It was *sweet* in every respect, for the players on the team, and for the city of Dallas after they swept the Los Angeles Lakers in the semifinals, fended off a *tough and talented* Oklahoma City Thunder team in five games in the Western Conference Finals, and by taking down the mighty Miami Heat in the NBA Finals. Even though Kidd had lost a step over the years, he was still a *cagey* veteran that knew what it took to win. Other than his domination over the years as a dribble penetrator that could score and dish in the lane better than anyone since Magic Johnson, Kidd was pretty much the same player without the explosive first step on offense. He maximized his abilities to the fullest, and with his new leadership role on the team. In fact, to this day at 39 years old at the point guard position, he still is an exceptional rebounder and passer with quick hands and feet on defense. Just recently in 2012 at the Oracle Arena in Oakland, California, where Jason Kidd happens to be from, I got a chance to watch him up close for the first time with my sister and her other half, along with three friends - thanks to Brian Cardinal of the Dallas Mavericks who got us the tickets. Even to this day, I marveled at how lightning- quick Kidd's hands were stripping Warriors' big men in the low post, as though he was still 26 years old in his prime.

In addition to his well-kept skills over the years, Kidd became a good perimeter shooter and outstanding three-point shooter over the second half of his career. If he had combined his ever improving shooting skills of today with his tremendous all-around game during his prime, we would be looking at him in a whole different light. Instead of being a top 50 player, he might have been a top 25 player that was able to lead his team to multiple championships as the main guy on the team, particularly during his playing days with the New Jersey Nets. It's too bad that never happened. Like Clyde Drexler, he won a championship later on in his career as the second or third best player on the team. It's interesting, even though both players played different positions, both have the same great attributes and all-around game in the half court and on the fast break - that could finish at the basket, and rebound and pass at their positions as good as anyone to have ever played the game. But at the same time, both players lacked the lethal perimeter scoring that a lot of the other greats of the game had. Nevertheless, Jason Kidd will forever go down as one of the all-time great point guards for all the reasons mentioned above, and because he is one of the few point guards in NBA history that could *dominate* a game without scoring - and that says a ton!

Career Totals

12.6 points, 8.7 assists, 6.3 rebs, 1.9 steals, 0.3 blocks, .400 FG%, .785 FT%, .349 3FG%

17,529 points, 12,091 assists, 8725 rebounds, 2684 steals, 450 blocks, 1988 threes

Wes Unseld

(Rank #44)

MVP (1-time), All-NBA First Team (1-time), Rebounding Title (1-time)

NBA Championships (1), Finals MVP (1-time), All-Star (5-times)

Wes Unseld was one of the great rebounding and passing big men in NBA history. Never the prolific scorer at the center position, at 6-foot-7 inches, Unseld *dominated* the game with his relentless rebounding and outstanding passing skills. In his first season in 1968-69 with the Baltimore Bullets, Unseld became just the second player behind Wilt Chamberlain to win the Rookie of the Year award and the MVP award in the same season. Nine years later, teamed with Elvin Hayes, he led the Washington Bullets to the 1978 NBA Championship and was named Finals MVP. Even before Hayes got there, Unseld's impact on the team was so tremendous; he led the franchise to the playoffs in all twelve of his seasons in the league. Along with Charles Barkley, Unseld was the best rebounder for his height in NBA history. He also had one of the all-time great outlet passes ever along with Bill Russell, Wilt Chamberlain, Kareem Abdul-Jabbar, and Bill Walton.

Born on March 14th, 1946 in Louisville, Kentucky, Westley Sissel Unseld attended Seneca High School where he led the team to two state championships. In college at the University of Louisville, he averaged 35.8 points and 23.6 rebounds on the freshman team. And, in three years on the varsity team, he averaged 20.6 points and 18.9 rebounds per game, and was named to the All-America First Team in 1967 and 1968. After his senior year, he was then selected with the 2nd pick overall (behind future teammate Elvin Hayes) of the 1968 NBA Draft by the Baltimore Bullets and by the Kentucky Colonels of the ABA. In his very first season with Bullets, Unseld had an exceptional year averaging 13.8 points and 18.2 rebounds per game, and was named to the All-NBA First Team. As already mentioned above, he also became the second man in history to win the Rookie of the Year and the MVP in the same season.

In his first five seasons with the Bullets, Unseld averaged 14 points, 3.9 assists, and an incredible **17.1 rebounds** per game. During that same span he averaged a mighty **18.2 rebounds** in 40 postseason games, including **23.6 rebounds** in seven playoff games his second season. But unfortunately, the Bullets made it out of the first round of the playoffs just once in 1971. That year, after finishing the regular season with 42 wins, the Bullets made one of the most improbable runs in postseason history, making it all the way to the NBA Finals. After defeating the Philadelphia 76ers and the New York Knicks in seven games to win the Eastern Conference, the Baltimore Bullets "Cinderella" season ended abruptly when they were simply outclassed and swept by Lew Alcindor, Oscar Robertson, and the Milwaukee Bucks in the NBA Finals.

In an injury riddled sixth season in 1974, the newly named Capital Bullets lost to the New York Knicks in the first round of the playoffs in seven games. The second half of Unseld's career was more successful during the postseason. After winning the **rebounding title at 14.8** per game in 1975, Unseld and Hayes once again, led the Bullets deep into the playoffs. After finishing with the best record in the NBA tied with the Boston Celtics at 60-22, the Bullets defeated both the Buffalo Braves and the mighty Celtics, before losing to Rick Barry and the underdog Golden State Warriors in the NBA Finals in four straight games. The next two seasons, with Dave Bing at the tail end of his career, the Bullets were eliminated in the playoffs by the Cleveland Cavaliers in seven games and to the Houston Rockets in six games. In the 1977-78 season, with Unseld's career winding down, the Bullets acquired Bobby Dandridge to provide more scoring punch with Elvin Hayes. As a result, the three stars along with Kevin Grevey and Mitch Kupchak led the Bullets to the 1978 NBA Championship over the Seattle SuperSonics. Throughout the playoffs, Unseld averaged 12 rebounds and 4.4 assists per game as the Bullets defeated the Atlanta Hawks and the San Antonio Spurs in six games to win the Western Conference. With the same core group of players still intact, the Bullets vied for the title again in 1979, but lost to the same team they beat the year before, the SuperSonics in five games. The following season in 1980, Unseld retired.

In player comparisons:

Although Wes Unseld was never a dominate scorer, he dominated the game as an undersized center in both the rebounding and passing aspect, particularly to trigger the fast break often to the dynamic Earl Monroe. The man was a *relentless* rebounder and an exceptional passer for a big man. Also, with his massive thighs, he was an *unmovable* tree trunk when setting a pick for his teammates. He was simply, one of those special players like Bill Russell and Bill Walton who did all the dirty work and all the little things to make his team better. To prove his value with his overall game and intangibly, he averaged the fewest points in NBA Finals history for a Finals MVP winner. He also pulled the trick in his rookie season when he won the regular season MVP award while averaging only 13.8 points per game (an all-time low for an MVP winner). He is also one of the few players in the top 50, whose greatness can't be measured heavily on just numbers alone. However, he did average a staggering 17 rebounds per game in his first five seasons and almost four assists per game for his career. Because Unseld was so instrumental as the centerpiece for his entire career with the Bullets, it warranted him a spot in my Top 50 players of all-time. And it is fair to say, there may never be another player as *unique* as Wes Unseld was for a very long time!

Career Totals

10.8 points, 14 rebounds, 3.9 assists, 0.6 blocks, 1.1 steals, .509 FG%, .633 FT%

10,624 points, 13,769 rebounds, 3822 assists, 367 blocks, 628 steals

Dominique Wilkins

(Rank #45)

All-NBA First Team (1-time), All-Star (9-times)

Scoring Title (1-time)

Also: featuring Pete Maravich
& Ricky Rubio

    Dominique Wilkins was one of the most *electrifying* dunkers the NBA has ever seen and one of the most explosive scorers in league history. He was one of the few showman people paid to see - as very few players fired up the home crowd the way Wilkins did. "The Human Highlight Film" was truly a one man show with the Atlanta Hawks for eleven years. Throughout his career, Dominique was equally as dynamic a dunker in a real game situation as he was in exhibition. His signature dunk, the *360-degree Windmill*, he could perform in the slam dunk contest, would be used in live competition, often with *devastating* results as he would *pummel* opponents who stood in his way. He also had a multitude of other dunks as well including the *double-clutch* monster jam, where it looked like he would violently rip the ball through the rim with a defender sulking underneath the basket! In addition, he had one of the purest shooting strokes for a small forward in the history of the game. His offensive arsenal included a *deadly* face-up jump shot that he could shoot over any opponent at will. Because he had a 44-inch vertical leap, it allowed him to add extra elevation on his jump shot when necessary and gave him plenty of spring to dunk over taller players when driving to the basket. He was *virtually unstoppable* in one-on-one isolations.

Jacques Dominique Wilkins was born on January 12th, 1960 in Paris France due to his father being stationed there in the U.S. Air Force. After moving to Washington, North Carolina, Wilkins attended Washington High School where he won two Class 3-A State Championships in 1978 and 1979. He was also named the MVP in both games and was a McDonald's All-American in 1979. In college at Georgia University, Wilkins averaged 21.6 points and 7.5 rebounds per game, and was named SEC Player of the Year in 1981. After leaving college after his junior year, Wilkins was selected with the third pick overall of the 1982 NBA Draft by the Utah Jazz. Before the season, due to financial restraints and the reluctance to play for the Jazz, Wilkins was traded to the Atlanta Hawks. In his first two campaigns, he averaged 17.5 and 21.6 points per game. But the mediocre Hawks lost in the first round of the playoffs in both seasons to the Boston Celtics two games to one and Milwaukee Bucks three games to two. In only his third year in the league, Wilkins continued to improve his scoring at a rapid pace averaging **27.4 points** per game. He also made his mark as one of the most spectacular dunkers in the NBA when he won the Slam Dunk contest over rookie Michael Jordan during All-Star weekend. But unfortunately the Hawks missed the playoffs for the first time in three years.

In the 1985-86 season, Wilkins blossomed into the NBA's *premiere* scorer when he won the scoring title at **30.3 points** per game. He also had a **career-high 57 points** and was named to the All-NBA First Team. The Hawks finished with 50 wins and won their first playoff series since 1979. After defeating the Detroit Pistons three games to one, the Hawks lost to the eventual champion Celtics in the semifinals in five games. In the postseason, Wilkins averaged **28.6 points** and 6 rebounds per game. The following year, Wilkins had another outstanding season finishing second in scoring to Michael Jordan at **29 points** per game and became the first Hawk to start an All-Star game since Eddie Johnson in 1981. The Hawks increased their win total to 57 and won the division over the 52-win Pistons. But in the playoffs, after defeating the Indiana Pacers in the first round three games to one, the Hawks were eliminated rather handily by the Pistons in five games. Like I have mentioned in Isiah's chapter, both teams were on the rise, chasing the Celtics for *bragging rights* in the Eastern Conference. Despite their record during the two year period, the Pistons were actually the ones ahead in the pace because they had a more *balanced* offense and were the better defensive team.

In the 1987-88 season, Wilkins had perhaps his best season overall in both the regular season and the postseason averaging **30.7 and 31.2 points** per game respectively. After another 50-win campaign, the Hawks returned to the playoffs looking to build on their semifinals loss to the Pistons from the previous year. After defeating the Bucks in the first round three games to two, the Hawks were eliminated by the Celtics in a gut-wrenching seven games. It was really too bad, because this would have set up a rematch with the Pistons in the Eastern Conference Finals. With the Pistons and the Bulls on a collision course for Eastern Conference supremacy for years to come, it was unlikely Atlanta with lone star Dominique, would have advanced any further than the conference finals. Despite the crushing defeat to an aging Celtics team that was in its final days, Wilkins did have an incredible postseason individually and in the decisive game seven, where he outscored Larry Bird (34 points), finishing with 47 points on 19 of 23 shooting in a losing effort.

With the Pistons and Bulls on the rise and the New York Knicks lurking, the Hawks never recovered from the devastating loss to the Celtics and were eliminated every other year in the first round of the playoffs for the next five years. They were ousted by the Bucks in five games, missed the playoffs, eliminated by the Pistons in five games, missed the playoffs again, and were swept by the Bulls. The next year, Dominique was traded in the middle of the season to the Los Angeles Clippers. Over the last nine seasons with the franchise, Wilkins would be named to the All-Star team nine consecutive years. In fact, if you count only his first 12 seasons with the Hawks including the last 25 games playing with the Clippers, he averaged a whopping **26.5 points** per game and **6.9 rebounds**. He also scored 36 points and had 10 rebounds against his former team in Atlanta on March 25th, 1994.

While Bob Pettit may have been the greatest Hawk of all-time, Dominique Wilkins has to be, at the very least, second on the list. But perhaps the third greatest player/scorer in Hawks history was **Pete Maravich** who mesmerized basketball fans in the college ranks and in his first four seasons with the Atlanta Hawks franchise. Out of all the players in NBA history, Maravich may have been the *ultimate* showman that brought more creativity to the game with his *razzle-dazzle* circus shots, *ultra-smooth* playground moves, *fancy* dribbling and his spectacular *hot dog* passing. He was the modern-day Bob Cousy at the shooting guard/small forward position. Even John Havlicek said recently, "The best ball handler of all-time was Pete Maravich."

Despite the skeptics by basketball purist that believe Maravich could have been more style than substance, the numbers speak for themselves. It wasn't like he was the modern-day Jason Williams who brought excitement to the game with his *unconscious* three-point shooting, sometimes *inappropriate* fancy dribbling during crucial moments of the game, or *erratic* passing often resulting in to many turnovers. Or maybe he was to a certain extent, based on his 5 and 4.1 turnovers per game in the first two seasons, as the NBA started keeping track of turnovers in the 1977-78 season. While Jason Williams (nicknamed "White Chocolate") made himself known playing for the Sacramento Kings his first three seasons, and for his never seen before "elbow pass" in the 2000 Rookie game at the Coliseum in Oakland California, "Pistol Pete" was simply in a class by himself. J. Williams averaged a paltry 10.5 points on .398 percent shooting for his career while Maravich averaged 24.2 points per game on 44 percent shooting. Maravich was an *elite* scorer and passer at every phase of his career dating back to his playing days at LSU, Atlanta Hawks for four years, and for five years with the New Orleans Jazz.

By the way, maybe **Ricky Rubio**, whom I've been following since he was 17 years old over in Spain, may become the closest thing to Pete Maravich in terms of *creativity* as a ball handler and as a passer, but not necessarily in terms of scoring - where he needs some *serious* improvement on his jump shot. But so far in Rubio's rookie season of 2012, I'm not sure if I have ever seen a player drive to the basket at full speed and then make a pinpoint bounce pass from behind the back to a perimeter player, waiting as though he had just received a routine fundamental bounce pass. It was absurd watching him do it *twice* in the same game. No other player in the league could make that pass cleanly without having the ball either skid to the feet of a teammate or drift away to either side of the body. And, half the time, the ball would most likely go out of bounds. When most players make a behind the back pass, they are usually stationary, changing speeds off the dribble, or on the fast break. But with Rubio, he has the *uncanny* ability to dribble at full speed directly at the basket, completely fooling the defense and at the same time, able to no-look, flip the wrist and make the perfect bounce pass to a player standing in a stationary position, anywhere on the court (and that includes the three-point line). It seems almost impossible to synchronize a perfect bounce pass while dribbling at full speed the way Rubio can do it.

Only a few players, including Larry Bird, could make that pass *almost* with regularly. But Bird wasn't dribbling at full speed as though he was going to finish at the basket. If Bird was at full speed, then he was way slow in foot speed compared to Rubio. To make this clear, almost any skilled player at one time or another, can throw a behind-the-back or wrap-around pass, either in the air or off a bounce to a teammate inside or to the perimeter, but Rubio can do it with the flip of the wrist similar to the same way John Stockton used to. Stockton often made the same bounce passes Rubio makes, he just didn't do it driving at full speed toward the basket or from completely on the other side of the court. As I have already mentioned in Stockton's chapter, with his strong hands and wrist, he could make the deepest of passes from anywhere on the court including from underneath the basket to a player waiting beyond the three-point line. But a pass from that distance was usually thrown in the air.

Rubio also has the adept ability to make any pass from anywhere on the court consistently. And, no one makes the most difficult of bounces look routine like Rubio does. As I am writing, at only 21 years old playing for the Minnesota Timberwolves in limited minutes, he is already leading the league in steals and is in the top 5 in assists. In other comparisons, while I believe Stephen Curry of the Golden State Warriors has the potential to become the next Steve Nash, I think Rubio has a chance to become a Pete Maravich *type* of player. Although a few years back, some scouts have said he actually looks like a cross between Nash and Maravich. While the upside looks good for Rubio, the downside could be that he ends up being just a very good player but not necessarily a great one. For example, Tyreke Evans of the Sacramento Kings, to me looks like a cross between Dwyane Wade and LeBron James in terms of style. So a player can look like a cross between two other players and not actually be as good as either one of them. This could end up being the case for both Rubio and Evans. Although, as I can easily see both players having very good careers while making a few All-Star teams, I can also see the both of them having great careers with each actually becoming a superstar at their respective positions. I hope it ends up being the latter for the both of them.

Peter Press Maravich was born on June 22nd, 1947 in Aliquippa, Pennsylvania and went to high school at Edwards Military Institute in Salemburg, North Carolina. At Louisiana State University, he was one of if not the greatest scorer in NCAA history. In fact, he still holds the NCAA Division I record for career points per game at 44.2 (it's still unbelievable in print every time I glance at it today) and total points at 3667. In his first game on the freshman team against Southeastern Louisiana College, Maravich posted **50 points, 14 rebounds, and 11 assists**. And in his sophomore year, he averaged an eye-popping **43.8 points** and 7.5 rebounds per game and followed that up with a *mind-boggling* season of **44.2 points** and 6.5 rebounds per game in his junior year. In his senior year, he capped off one of the most spectacular college careers in NCAA history when he averaged **44.5 points** and 5.6 rebounds per game and was named Naismith College Player of the Year and Sporting News Player of the Year in 1970. He was also named SEC Player of the Year and All-America First Team for the third consecutive season.

Maravich was selected with the 3rd pick overall of the 1970 NBA Draft by the Atlanta Hawks behind Bob Lanier and Rudy Tomjanovich. He had joined a Hawks team that featured super scorer Lou Hudson and big man Walt Bellamy who had just come over in a midseason trade. In his rookie year, Maravich picked up where he left off in college, becoming an immediate scoring sensation averaging 23.2 points and 4.4 assists per game. After a scoring slide in his sophomore season, Maravich rebounded in his third season in the league averaging 26.1 points and 6.9 assists per game. He also was named to his first All-Star team and to the All-NBA Second Team. But in his first three years with the franchise, the Hawks were eliminated in the first round of the playoffs by the New York Knicks in five games and twice by the Boston Celtics in six games in consecutive years. In three postseasons with the Hawks franchise, Maravich averaged 25.5 points, 5.4 assists, and 5.1 rebounds per game. Unfortunately, he never made it back to the postseason again until his final season in the NBA playing for the Boston Celtics in 1980. In his fourth and final season with the Hawks, he averaged a lofty 27.7 points per game before being traded to one of the league's newest expansion teams, the New Orleans Jazz. Although it was an ideal situation for Maravich to play in the same city where he went to college, he went from one bad team to the next. Despite never making the playoffs in New Orleans, he did have three of his best statistical seasons from 1976 to 1978 averaging 28.3 points, 5.7 assists, and 4.6 rebounds per game.

As a testament to his prolific scoring, Maravich scored 40 points or more in a game 35 times and 50 or more six times including a **career-high 68 points** at home against the New York Knicks on February 25th, 1977. In that game, he destroyed an aging Walt Frazier and would have scored 70 points or more if it weren't for two questionable calls in the final two minutes. And, in his best season in 1976-77 he averaged **31.1 points**, **5.4 assists**, and **5.1 rebounds** per game - won the scoring title, and was named to the All-NBA First Team for the second straight season.

In player comparisons:

Back to Dominique Wilkins, who has one of the most impressive scoring resumes in NBA history. During a 10-year span from the beginning of the 1984 season to the end of the 1994 season, he averaged 28 points and 7 rebounds per game and had 8 seasons of 2000 or more points. Only non-centers Michael Jordan, Larry Bird, Allen Iverson, along with Dominique were able to average between 26 and 31 points for an entire decade. During his era only Jordan and *possibly* Bird were better *pure* scorers - although, Bird was easily the better shooter and by far the better all-around player. Because of his scoring accolades including finishing second three times to Jordan for the scoring title, was the primary reason on ranking Wilkins ahead of Paul Pierce and James Worthy among the greatest small forwards of all-time. On top of that, he was just as good a rebounder as both Worthy and Pierce and even better when it came to following a missed shot for an easy put-back or slam dunk. So compared to Pierce and Worthy, Wilkins was the more *dynamic* player and a more *dominate* scorer, and was just as good a rebounder, shot blocker, and pickpocketer. Although underrated as a passer, from a passing standpoint, I would give Pierce the edge over the both of them, as he just so happened to have a career-high 14 assists this past season in 2012. Wilkins also was an outstanding perimeter shooter averaging 46 percent from the field, 81 percent from the free-throw line, and almost an even 32 percent from three-point range.

Under any circumstances on any other team, there is no way possible, Pierce or Worthy would have averaged 28 points over 10 consecutive seasons with a solid seven rebounds to boot. Just maybe the great Larry Bird would have if he hadn't played with two other stars in Kevin McHale and Robert Parish. Dominique had the highest three-year peak (including a high of 30 points) of any scorer during his time outside of Michael Jordan. He also averaged a more than respectable 25.4 points and 6.7 rebounds per game in the playoffs while competing at the highest level against Bird and Jordan during their primes. His resumes includes 346 30-point games which rank 8th on the all-time list next to Jerry West's 350. He also had **56 40-point** games which ranks behind eleven other players including West's 66 and McAdoo's 58, and ahead of Shaquille O'Neal and LeBron James (who both have 49), and Larry Bird's 47. I know in 1996, Wilkins was left off the league's list of NBA's 50 greatest players; one would assume primarily because of a lack of many playoff wins and zero championships. And the other, the list was chosen when he was at the tail end of his career, bouncing around from team to team, playing for the Hawks, Clippers (where he was traded for Danny Manning), Celtics, Spurs and Magic. He even missed a couple seasons in between playing basketball in the Greek League and the Italian League.

So Wilkins must have been looked at in the same way Tracy McGrady would be looked at today if we had a selection committee vote on a current list of all-time great players. Like McGrady, Wilkins played with one of the worst supporting cast in history with only Doc Rivers, a washed-up Moses Malone, Kevin Willis, and Mookie Blaylock all who have one all-star selection apiece. Of course, the difference is that Wilkins was a Top 50 player and McGrady currently isn't based on that he hadn't played at a high level for more than 7 or 8 full years. Wilkins more than deserved to be on the NBA's 50 Greatest Players list even over James Worthy who I have followed even closer during the 1980s Los Angeles Lakers championship run. But, what people will remember most about Dominique Wilkins was that he was one of the greatest scorers ever at a level with Michael Jordan, and one of the most famous slam dunk artist the league has ever seen! And until Blake Griffin proves otherwise, "The Human Highlight Film," will remain the greatest in-game dunker of all-time.

Career Totals

24.8 points, 6.7 rebs, 2.5 assists, 1.3 steals, 0.6 blocks, .461 FG%, .811 FT%, .319 3FG%

26,668 points, 7169 rebounds, 2677 assists, 1378 steals, 642 blocks, 711 threes

Paul Pierce

(Rank #46)

NBA Championships (1), Finals MVP (1-time)

All-Star (10-times)

Also: featuring Ray Allen

Paul Pierce is one of the great small forwards in the NBA today. In fact, during his prime in the early to the mid and even late 2000s, he was so good, many of the Boston media proclaimed him to be the greatest pure scorer in Celtics history even over the great Larry Bird. Although known for his scoring, Pierce has an adept all-around game on both ends of the court. Without the blessing of raw speed, what has made Pierce *unique* over the years is his clever ball-handling skills and his deceptive speed and quickness, where he is able to score off a shot fake with a direct drive to the basket and by dribbling in and out of traffic finishing at the rim with a nifty layup, or he could stop on a dime and pull up for a jump shot from anywhere on the court. His change of speeds and stutter-steps are as good as anyone that has ever played the game. In fact, this is the part of his game that makes Pierce special. While most other great players rely on speed and athleticism, Pierce takes the more subtle approach, using a craft of *patience and deception*. In addition, he is one of the game's all-time great clutch shooters at the small forward position. When the game is on the line, Pierce is the one you want taking the last shot! At a solid 6-feet-7 with his *wiry* strength, Pierce is an outstanding rebounder and facilitator. Without the great leaping ability, he works hard to position himself for rebounds and uses his keen court vision to make the adept pass to an open teammate. He is also an exceptional defensive player that fit the mold of Doc River's championship scheme in 2008.

Paul Anthony Pierce was born on October 13th, 1977 in Oakland, California. After moving down south, he was raised in Inglewood, California and attended Inglewood High School where he was a McDonald's All-American. In college, at the University of Kansas, Pierce averaged 20.4 points and 6.7 rebounds per game his junior year. After foregoing his senior year, Pierce was selected with the 10th pick overall of the 1998 NBA Draft by the Boston Celtics. In his rookie season, he got off to a fast start to his career by averaging 16.5 points and 6.4 rebounds per game. He also shot a career-high 41 percent from three-point range and made the All-Rookie First Team. Even watching him in his first season, I knew Pierce was going to be an outstanding shooter with great three-point range. But, what I didn't know was that he would blossom into one of the most versatile scorers and best all-around players in the league. In all honesty, my assessment on most players at times can be spot on, but in the case of Pierce, I was disappointed to have been so far off. In his second season, he increased his scoring to 19.5 points per game and by his third season, he blossomed into one of the league's elite scorers averaging **25.3 points** per game. But unfortunately, the Celtics missed the playoffs in his first three campaigns - when he first came to Boston, they were perennial losers and in the process of rebuilding the franchise.

In the 2001-02 season, Pierce had another outstanding season averaging **26.1 points** and **6.9 rebounds** per game, and was honored with his first of five consecutive All-Star selections. And as a team, the Celtics went from night to day, and made it all the way to the Eastern Conference Finals. With Pierce and Antoine Walker improving rapidly as a dynamic dual, the Celtics won 49 games in the regular season for the first time in ten years and defeated a tough Philadelphia 76ers team with Allen Iverson, three games to one in the first round of the playoffs. In the semifinals, the Celtics made quick work of the Detroit Pistons in five games before losing to Jason Kidd and the New Jersey Nets in the conference finals four games to two. If only Kidd hadn't transformed the Nets into an elite team in the same way Steve Nash did with the Phoenix Suns, maybe the Celtics that year, would have been the ones in the NBA Finals. In his first postseason, Pierce averaged **24.6 points**, **8.6 rebounds**, and **4.1 assists** per game.

The following season, Pierce averaged **25.9 points** and a **career-high 7.9 rebounds** per game. He also proved his worth as a complete player by averaging **4.4 assists** per game. He would go on to average at least four assists for the next five seasons. It wasn't until the middle stages of his career, did I believe he would emerge into an elite small forward. At that time, it occurred to me that even if he never wins a championship, based on talent alone, he was going to go down as one of the great small forwards of all-time. In statistical comparisons to other great small forwards to have played the game, he was right there at the top. It then occurred to me, that someday, he might become a better player than the great James Worthy, who I felt was one of the top true small forwards of all-time. The Celtics won 44 games in the regular season in 2003, good for third in their division. In the playoffs, after defeating the Indiana Pacers in the first round four games to two, the Celtics were swept in the semifinals by those same New Jersey Nets. Pierce did have an impressive all-around performance in only his second playoff season when he averaged **27.1 points**, **9 rebounds**, **6.7 assists**, and **2.1 steals** per game. Other than his shooting percentage at nearly 40 percent, this was the best season statistically of his postseason career. Also, because the Celtics didn't have a dominant big man, it allowed for Pierce and Walker to accumulate an abundant of rebounds.

The next two seasons, after failing to add sufficient pieces around Pierce and Walker, the Celtics settled in mediocrity. In both years, they were eliminated in the first round of the playoffs in a four-game sweep to the Nets, and in seven games to the Pacers with the final game coming on their own home court. This was only the beginning of a downward trend as the Celtics would miss the playoffs the following two seasons. Despite the lack of playoff success the last four years, Pierce did have another outstanding season in 2006 when he averaged a **career-high 26.8 points** per game, **6.7 rebounds**, and **4.7 assists**. He also set a **career-high for points** in a game with **50**.

Prior to the 2007-08 season, was one of the biggest free-agent signings in NBA history, the Celtics acquired two future Hall of Famers in Kevin Garnett and **Ray Allen**. Garnett had been the cornerstone of the Minnesota franchise for 12 seasons as Allen had been for the Seattle SuperSonics and the Milwaukee Bucks for 11 seasons. It was a perfect fit, because Garnett blended an excellent offensive game with a tremendous defensive game. He was able to score in the low post or out on the high post with his patented jump hook or fadeaway shot that was the best in league for a big man at the time. More importantly, he gave the Celtics a defensive presence they so badly needed. Now with Garnett anchoring the middle, Pierce could now rely on becoming more of a facilitator. He could now pick his spots when to score out of the high post, take his man off the dribble, or wait for the ball to rotate for an open jump shot or three-pointer. The same thing could be said for Allen except, he was the older statesman out of the three and was playing more from the perimeter than off dribble penetration as he had done more frequently earlier in his career.

The youngest player of the newly formed "Big Three" and in the midst of his prime, Pierce had his best season overall in the playoffs where he outdueled LeBron James in game 7 of the semifinals and took it to Kobe Bryant in the NBA Finals. I remember watching the series saying to myself, this is how great Pierce really is and how he is *almost* as great as Kobe in every facet of the game. And you know what, he was during that six-game series in which he took home Finals MVP. His *barbarian* type grit, mental and physical toughness, and extreme will to win - that he's had within him his entire career, helped in bringing the Celtics back from what looked like an insurmountable comeback in game 4 in Los Angeles, and then blowing out the Lakers in game 6 at home to mark the biggest margin of victory (39 points) in a clinching game in NBA Finals history. In fact, out of all the *current* superstar players (not including role players in which I would chose Chauncey Billups over just about anyone) including Kobe Bryant and perhaps Dirk Nowitzki, with the game on the line (like I mentioned in the beginning of the chapter), I would want Pierce with the *ice water* in his veins to take the last shot.

Walter Ray Allen was born on July 20th, 1975 in Castle Air Force Base near Merced, California. He attended Hill Crest High School in Dalzell, South Carolina where he led the team to the state championship. At the University of Connecticut, Allen averaged 19 points and 6 rebounds per game and shot an incredible 45 percent from three-point range. In his final college season, he averaged 23.4 points and 6.5 rebounds per game and won the Big East Player of the Year award. He was also named to the All-America First Team and USA Basketball's Male Athlete of the Year the year before in 1995. After foregoing his senior year, Allen was selected with the 5th pick overall of the 1996 NBA Draft by the Milwaukee Bucks. As a member of the Bucks in the 2000-01 season, Allen had his best season averaging **22 points**, **5 rebounds**, **4.6 assists**, and **1.5 steals** per game - and shot .433 from three-point range. After winning the Central Division at 52-20, the Bucks defeated the Orlando Magic in the first round three games to one and the Charlotte Hornets in the semifinals in a tough seven-game series. In the Eastern Conference Finals, the Bucks' faced the number one seed Philadelphia 76ers led by league MVP Allen Iverson. Even though the 76ers had the better record and the best player in all of basketball, that season, I felt the Bucks had as good a chance as any to win the series. In spite of the fact the league would rather have seen the 76ers in the Finals instead of the Bucks for television revenue purposes, I felt Milwaukee may have been the better team or at least had the three or four best players in Ray Allen, Glen Robinson, Sam Cassell, and Tim Thomas. With each team having victories on the others home court in the first four games, the series was tightly contested until Philadelphia put an exclamation mark on game seven with a 108-91 victory. Similar to the other Bucks teams and the Dallas Mavericks of the 1980s, the same two teams were never able to get over the hump and win a championship.

As a member of the Seattle SuperSonics, Allen averaged **24.6 points, 4.5 rebounds**, and **four assists** his last four seasons (and **25.1 and 26.4 points** per game in his last two) from 2003 to 2007. But the Sonics made the playoffs just once in 2005. With a pair of young sharpshooters in Richard Lewis and Vladimir Radmanovich, I felt the Sonics would go deep into the playoffs, just as I did when Allen played for the Bucks in 2001. After defeating the Sacramento Kings in five games in the first round, the Sonics were eliminated in six games in the semifinals by the eventual champion San Antonio Spurs. For his career, Allen averaged at least 22 points per game in eight consecutive seasons, and 40 percent from three-point range. As the best player on his team, in four seasons in the playoffs before he became a Celtic, he averaged **24.9 points, 4.8 rebounds** and **4.8 assists**, and shot **43.5 percent** on three-pointers in 37 playoff games. After his championship season in 2008, Allen proved he still had a lot left in the tank when he turned-backed-the-clock and dropped in an impressive **51 points**, including two game tying threes and the game-winning three-pointer in game 6 of the first round of the 2009 playoffs.

In player comparisons:

Before Kevin Durant came into the league, I always felt Allen blended scoring ability with unmatched shooting as well as any player ever right up there with Dirk Nowitzki and Larry Bird. And in a nutshell, that's the best way to describe Ray Allen for his career as a shooter/scorer. In addition, there is probably no debate out of all the great shooters in history, Allen probably had the quickest release where if you gave him an inch from anywhere on the court, he could stop on a dime and shoot the lights out of the building (right before the release of this book, look what he did in the closing seconds of game 6 of the 2013 NBA Finals). And finally, the other aspects of his game (passing and rebounding at six-foot-five) were also good, as he became a very good man-on-man defensive player and an outstanding team defender during his championship run with the Celtics.

Because of this instant chemistry and sense of urgency among Pierce, Allen, and Garnett, the Celtics were able to win a championship in their first season as I have reiterated dozens of times on my former web site JNBA&allsports.com. In team comparisons, at the time of this writing - as an admirer of the "Big Three" in Boston, that season, I felt the same way about the "Big Three" in Miami in their first season playing together. Unfortunately, the Heat lost in the NBA Finals in their first trip, even though I predicted they would win it all. The difference so far between the two teams and what makes the 2008 Celtics so special, is what I have already stated. Both teams were unselfish and hungry to win it all, but I think the Celtics Big Three were even hungrier due to the fact they were much older with the average age being around 32, whereas the Miami Heat were around the average age of 28 years old. What made the Celtics *special* was that they were the *ultimate* team willing to sacrifice and do whatever it took to win a championship and that's exactly what coach Doc Rivers implemented every single day. If the Miami Heat, are to win a championship, they must do the same thing with every player knowing their role. It will be a little more difficult than I first expected, not because of their lack of heart or the will to win, but for the willingness to sacrifice at all cost for the sake of the team. From a chemistry standpoint, Garnett, Pierce, and Allen were a perfect fit; While LeBron James, Dwyane Wade and Chris Bosh are not quite. Going forward, they will all have to tweak their game a little to be successful especially at the end of games and in the playoffs.

Putting Paul Pierce ahead of James Worthy in my player rankings was not too difficult for the following reason: Pierce had the slightly better all-around game and the loftier career numbers particularly in the regular season. While you could call it a draw it terms of scoring and rebounding, Pierce was the better passer and defensive player. Even though Worthy was taller and guarded Larry Bird exceptionally well, he did it within the team defensive scheme. Whereas in his prime, Pierce was the better one-on-one defender, able to guard most forwards including doing a good job of staying in front of

LeBron James. Although, I do think both players benefited from the interior defense that both teams devised. But what made the both of them great, was their clutch shooting. This is the closest call of all calls in player comparisons between the two of them, so let's call it a draw. "Big Game James" had a little better post-up game, but the "Truth" had a better long-range game. Worthy did it for more playoff games and won more championships with three, but I will give Pierce the nod by a *hair* because of his *overall* game.

Career Totals

22.8 points, 6.0 rebs, 3.9 assists, 1.4 steals, 0.6 blocks, .447 FG%, .806 FT%, .370 3FG%

24,021 points, 6651 rebounds, 4305 assists, 1583 steals, 668 blocks, 1823 threes

James Worthy

(Rank #47)

NBA Championships (3), Finals MVP (1-time), All-Star (7-times)

Also featuring: Carmelo Anthony

James Worthy was one of the great small forwards of all-time. As the second or third scoring option, playing for the Los Angeles Lakers, Worthy won three NBA Championships during the 1980s and was the Finals MVP in 1988. A tremendous scorer in the half court and in transition, Worthy is well remembered for streaking down court on the fast break and finishing with a swooping one-handed slam dunk *Statue of Liberty* style - and in the half court, with his *lightning-quick* first step and spin move, he could explode to the basket like no other finishing with the same swooping one-handed dunk or with his patented finger role. His spots to operate on the court were at the corners, at the top of the key, and from the baseline. In addition, he had smooth spin moves out of the post and an outstanding mid-range jump shot. Underrated as a rebounder, passer and on defense, Worthy fought hard to position for rebounds, made the entry pass into the low post and to cutters diving to the basket, and held his own defensively moving his feet quickly to stay in front of opponents. Worthy was one of the few great players who increased his scoring *significantly* from the regular season to the postseason. "Big Game James" lived up to his nickname more than ever in the 1988 NBA Finals. In the decisive game seven, Worthy had his first career triple-double of 36 points, 16 rebounds, and 10 assists.

James Ager Worthy was born on February 27th, 1961 in Gastonia, North Carolina and attended Ashbrook High School where he averaged 21.5 points and 12.5 rebounds per game his senior year. In college at the University of North Carolina, Worthy averaged 14.5 points and 7.4 rebounds per game. In his junior year playing alongside Sam Perkins and Michael Jordan, he averaged 15.6 points per game and led the Tarheels to a 63-62 victory in the 1982 NCAA Championship game against the Georgetown Hoyas. For the game, Worthy finished with 28 points on 76 percent shooting and was handed the key steal on an inadvertent pass that sealed the game. He was also named NCAA Final Four Most Outstanding Player and to the All-America First Team. After foregoing his senior year, Worthy was selected with the 1st pick overall of the 1982 NBA Draft by the Los Angeles Lakers. In his first three seasons, he averaged 15.2 points and six rebounds, and shot 57 percent from the field. After missing the playoffs his rookie season because of a broken leg, Worthy began his playoff career in 1984, the year the Lakers met the Boston Celtics in the NBA Finals for the first time since 1969. After replacing Jamal Wilkes in the starting lineup, James became a major contributor in the regular season and in the playoffs. After steamrolling the Kansas City Kings, Dallas Mavericks, and the Phoenix Suns in the Western Conference, the Lakers were primed and ready to capture their third championship of the decade. In a highly competitive series, the Lakers squandered multiple opportunities to take early control of the series in games two and four, before eventually losing to the Celtics in seven games. But unfortunately, as I described in detail in Magic Johnson's chapter, the inexperienced Worthy was part of the many mishaps throughout the series, when he threw the bad pass to Gerald Henderson that could have potentially sealed the game. But, in the following season, the Lakers would take avenge against the Celtics in the NBA Finals. After losing only two games total throughout the playoffs against the Suns, Portland Trail Blazers and Denver Nuggets, the Lakers had all the momentum going into the Finals rematch.

During the playoffs, Worthy proved his worth as a clutch performer averaging **21.5 points** and **5.1 rebounds** per game, on **.622 percent** shooting. He also set an NBA record for field goal percentage in a five-game series at **.721** against the Nuggets. In the 1985-86 season, Worthy increased his scoring for the fourth straight year to 20 points per game and shot a career-high .579 percent from the field. He would also be named to the All-Star team for the first of seven consecutive seasons. During that seven-year span, he would average 20.3 points, 5.4 rebounds and 3.5 assists per game, on .527 percent shooting. Worthy had another solid postseason, but that was the season the Lakers were upset by the Houston Rockets in the Western Conference Finals. The following year was the season the Lakers put a strangle hold on the rivalry with the Boston Celtics by defeating them in the NBA Finals for the second time in three years. It also gave the *Big Three* for the Lakers a two to one head-to-head advantage over the *Celtics Big Three* and all but put an end to the Celtics reign in the Eastern Conference during the 1980s. Worthy had one of his best postseasons of his career when he averaged **23.6 points**, **5.6 rebounds**, and shot .591 percent from the field.

In the 1987-88 season, the Lakers won their fifth NBA championship of the decade to complete one of the greatest runs in history, winning five championships in nine seasons. Worthy was a huge part of this as he proved by averaging **22 points, 7.4 rebounds**, and **4.4 assists** and winning the 1988 Finals MVP. During the playoff run, he averaged 21.1 points, 5.8 rebounds, and a playoff career-high 3.6 assists. With Kareem Abdul-Jabbar in his final season, the Lakers made it back to the NBA Finals for the third consecutive year hoping for a three-peat, but that never materialized. With injuries to Magic Johnson and Byron Scott early in the series, the Lakers were swept by the Detroit Pistons in the Finals. But Worthy was spectacular as always averaging **24.8 points, 6.7 rebounds**, and shot .567 percent from the field. The very next season, he nearly duplicated his scoring in the playoffs, but the Lakers were eliminated by the Phoenix Suns in the semifinals in six games.

In the 1990-91 season, the Lakers made it back to the NBA Finals for the fourth time in five years but they had to face the next great team in the Chicago Bulls who were seeking their first NBA championship. Even with their promising young center in Vlade Divac and with the addition of Sam Perkins, the Lakers were no match for the young legs of the Bulls. After shocking Chicago on their home floor in game one, the Lakers lost the next four games and the series in five. Just as the Celtics mini-dynasty came to an end in 1987, so did the Lakers decade-long dynasty in 1991 (I think the Pistons actually put the old legs of the Los Angeles Lakers to rest for good after the 1989 NBA Finals, they just didn't know it yet). After Kareem retired, two years later, Worthy led the team in scoring in 1991 and in 1992 the year Magic Johnson retired after testing positive for HIV. After missing the postseason for the first time in eight years due to a knee injury, in his last two seasons and with Worthy moving up in age and his career slowing down, the Lakers were eliminated in the first round of the playoffs in five games to the Phoenix Suns and missed the playoffs all-together in 1994, Worthy's final year in the league.

After Worthy retired, the player I compared him to the most was Paul Pierce until **Carmelo Anthony** came into the league in the 2003-04 season. While it could have been easier to combine the three players into one chapter because they are ranked side by side, I gave Pierce and Worthy their own, because of the way the book was designed with the Top 50 players of all-time having an exclusive chapter title to themselves, of course with many players interceding. Aside from Worthy's spin moves out of the low post and high post, and his trademark swooping one-handed slam dunk he made famous, what stands out most, was his lightning-quick first step that was the quickest that I had ever seen at the small forward position until Carmelo Anthony came into the league.

In player comparisons:

Potentially, Anthony might become the better small forward over Worthy, Pierce, and Dominique Wilkins - and perhaps eventually make it into the list of top 50 players of all-time. In fact, Anthony might end up having the better all-around game over the three of them, but needs to work on his defense and his passing ability to make that happen. At the young age of 28 years old, only six months older than LeBron James, Anthony statistically is on pace to surpass Worthy, Pierce, and Wilkins on the all-time list in most categories including surpassing Dominique on the all-time scoring list. Will he ever be the prolific scorer Dominique was and the passer and defense player Pierce was? Perhaps for the former and probably not for the latter, but he does have a lightning-quick first step like Worthy to go along with a tremendous all-around game on the offensive end, and is tough as a bull on the glass to corral rebounds. Many people today including Charles Barkley feel Anthony is the most versatile scorer in the NBA even over Kevin Durant and the aging Kobe Bryant. In fact, I would agree that he does utilize the triple-threat position *to his strength* as good as or better than anyone in the NBA. And in the playoffs, that comes in handy more than ever because the game tends to slow down into a half-court game. Today, a lot of great scorers use this stance to dribble out of, pass the ball or pull up for a jump shot. It is actually one of the most fundamentally sound aspects of the game that all of us were taught at a young age, as most notably my younger brother who was the starting point guard on our High School team would attest to - and by the way, he was also one of the most fundamentally sound players that I have ever seen at any level of play. Also, just to throw it out there, before he shattered his femur, he was able to finish in the paint scoring over forwards and centers as well as anyone by floating in the air, moving his arms from side to side with both hands protecting the ball, while almost always scoring or drawing the foul or both. Getting back to Anthony, he utilizes the triple-threat position to perfection in terms of scoring off the dribble and using his jab-step to trigger his lethal jump shot.

With all that being said, I left Anthony off the projected player rankings because LeBron James and Kevin Durant are both better players and more complete at the same position, and from the mental aspect of the game, where I have the gut feeling Anthony may underachieve the rest of his career. Like I mentioned, he still needs some work on the defensive end, and as passer. All four players were great clutch players, but perhaps this was James Worthy's biggest attribute and why he was given the nickname "Big Game James." Notably, out of the four of them, Worthy has the biggest increase in scoring from the regular season at 17.6 per game to **21.1** in the playoffs. He also won 3 Championships and one Finals MVP. Because of this, his ranking is more than justified and could easily be ranked higher in the minds of others. And that's fine, because you could make the argument that James Worthy was the greatest second scoring option at his position to have ever played the game!

Career Totals

17.6 points, 5.1 rebs, 3 assists, 1.1 steals, 0.7 blocks, .521 FG%, .769 FT%, .241 3FG%

16,320 points, 4708 rebounds, 2791 assists, 1041 steals, 624 blocks, 117 threes

Dolph Schayes

(Rank #48)

NBA Championships (1), All-NBA First Team (6-times)

Rebounding Title (1-time), All-Star (12-times)

Also featuring: Neil Johnston
& Paul Arizin

Dolph Schayes was one of the NBA's first great big men and pioneers who actually began his professional career during the pre-NBA era in the 1948-49 season with the Tri-City Blackhawks of the National Basketball League, where he won the Rookie of the Year award. Six years later, as a member of the Syracuse Nationals, Schayes led the franchise to its first NBA Championship in 1955. For six years up to the 1953-54 season, Schayes played his career without the benefit of a shot clock, which happened to be invented by his owner and former coach Danny Biasone. As one of the league's top scorers, Schayes was able to open up defenses with a highly effective high-arching set shot from the perimeter and was athletic enough to score driving to the basket. In addition, he was also one of the great rebounders and free-throw shooters in the history of the game. The 12-time All-Star was either the best or second best at his position throughout his NBA career making the All-NBA First and Second Team 6 times each. He also led the league in free-throw shooting three times and was one of the most durable players of all-time having only missed three games in his first twelve seasons.

Adolph Schayes was born on May 19th, 1928 in New York City, New York, and attended DeWitt Clinton High School in the Bronx, and then college at New York University from 1945 to 1948. He was then selected with the 4th pick overall of the 1948 BAA Draft by the New York Knicks and by the Tri-Cities Blackhawks in the NBL Draft. Prior to the NBA merger in the 1949-50 season, the Blackhawks traded Schayes' rights to the Nationals. In his first season in the NBA he averaged 16.8 points per game and made his first All-Star team. He also had ten of the league's fourteen best rebounding games. And after leading his team to 51 wins and into the playoffs, the Nationals beat the Philadelphia Warriors in the semifinals and New York Knickerbockers in the Eastern Finals, but lost to the Minneapolis Lakers in the NBA Finals in six games. With a chance to play in his hometown of New York, Schayes passed on a much lower financial offer to play for the Knickerbockers following the NBA Draft. In his sophomore season of 1950-51, he averaged 17 points and led the league in **rebounding at 16.4** per game. This so happened to be the inaugural year of the league officially keeping track of rebounds. For the next 10 years as one the league's most consistent performers, Schayes would average at least 12 rebounds per game. In the playoffs that year and the year after, the Nationals would go on to defeat the Warriors for the second and third straight time but were ousted in the Eastern Finals by the Knickerbockers in both seasons. To put a damper on the Nationals, the following season in 1953, they were swept in the first round by the Boston Celtics two games to zero.

In the 1953-54 season, the Nationals made huge strides into becoming one of the league's elite teams. After finishing third in the division, they took avenge on their arch nemeses, the Knicks and the Celtics. In a most interesting "Round Robin" to begin the playoffs, the Nationals defeated the Knicks twice and the Celtics four times including twice in the Eastern Finals. After making the NBA Finals for the second time, the Nationals lost to George Mikan and the Minneapolis Lakers in seven games. The following season, the pinnacle of success would finally come to the Syracuse Nationals. After beating the Boston Celtics three games to one in the Eastern Finals, the Nationals went on to win the 1955 NBA Championship over the Fort Wayne Pistons in seven games. In the 1955-56 season, Schayes averaged 20 points or more for the first of six consecutive seasons. Looking to defend their championship from the previous year, the Nationals fell into mediocrity winning less than half their regular season games. Although, in the playoffs, they kick-started their season by defeating the Knicks in the "Third-Place" game, and then the Celtics in the semifinals two games to one before falling victim to Paul Arizin and Neil Johnson and the Philadelphia Warriors in the Eastern Finals in five games. In that season, Schayes lost a chance for a repeat mainly due to the fact the Warriors rostered two Hall of Famers.

Paul Arizin was one of the great shooters at the small forward position and first pioneers that began the use of the jump shot. In addition, he was also an outstanding ball handler and a tough defender. Born on April 9th, 1928 in Philadelphia, Pennsylvania, Paul Joseph Arizin attended La Salle College High School (the high school shares the same campus with the college) where he was cut as a senior after playing sparingly in a few games. With little to no basketball experience, he continued on playing for multiple teams throughout the city including intramural, independent and church leagues. He then went on to play basketball at Villanova (where he got off to a slow start playing for the Catholic Youth Organization before making the team his sophomore year). By his junior year, he continued to improve at a rapid pace averaging 22 points per game. He also scored 85 points in game on February 12th, 1949 against Naval Air Materials Center which was the second highest scoring game in NCAA history to Frank Selvy's 100. The team finished 22-3 and made it to the NCAA Championship but lost to future All-Star and future teammate Alex Groza and the Kentucky Wildcats 85-72. In his senior year, he averaged 25.3 points per game which was the second highest in NCAA history at the time. He also led the team to 25-4 record and was named college Player of the Year by the Sporting News.

Arizin was selected with the first pick (territorial) of the 1950 NBA Draft by the Philadelphia Warriors. In his rookie season, he averaged 17.2 points per game and won the Rookie of the Year award. In his second season, Arizin exploded upon the NBA scene leading the league in scoring at **25.4 points** per game. He also won the scoring title for the second time in 1957 at **25.6** points and set a **career-high 26.4** points per game two years later in 1959. In those days, those numbers were extraordinarily high considering he played in the slow ball era where most players shot flat-footed. His 85 points in a game and an alleged 100-point game against a junior college that the NCAA did not recognize, was a preview of Arizin's potential as one of the game's elite scorers. Unfortunately, he missed the next two seasons because he had served in the Marines during the Korean War. But by his second season upon returning to the NBA, he along with Tom Gola and Neil Johnston led the 76ers to the 1956 NBA Championship.

Neil Johnston was the big scoring center in the middle that began his career one year after Arizin in 1951-52 and ended it three years before in 1959. Donald Neil Johnston was born on February 4th, 1929 in Chillicothe, Ohio and went to Ohio State University where he starred in baseball and basketball. In fact, he began playing baseball for the Philadelphia Phillies organization for two and a half years before deciding to switch to play basketball in the NBA. With his deadly right-handed hook shot that he would use in a sweeping motion, Johnson won three scoring titles from 1953 to 1955. He also led the league in field goal percentage three times and won the rebounding title once. In five seasons of his prime, he averaged 22.9 points, 13 rebounds, and three assists per game, and made the All-Star team 6 times and the All-NBA First Team 4 times. But his career was short lived when he retired after a serious knee injury in the 1958-59 season. When Arizin was serving military duty and during his first season after returning, this is where Johnston won three scoring titles with Arizin finishing second in his first year back. At that point in 1955, Arizin had missed two seasons and was obviously not the same player in his first season back from military duty. Because of this, and that Johnston had just come into the league, and based on his scoring output when both teammates played together afterwards, it is likely that Arizin could have won 4 or 5 scoring titles instead of just the 2. If that had happened, we would be looking at Arizin in whole different light. If he had won four or five scoring titles it would have tied or put him ahead of Allen Iverson and George Gervin and right behind Michael Jordan and Wilt Chamberlain with the most scoring titles in NBA history. In addition, he more than likely, would have retired with a higher scoring average that would have elevated him up among the list of all-time greats. With that being said, I was highly considering replacing Jerry Lucas with Paul Arizin at #50 in my player rankings.

In player comparisons:

In the next two chapters - the reason I kept Billy Cunningham and Jerry Lucas in the top 50 over Dave DeBusschere and Hal Greer is because they were more impactful as the second best player during their respective teams championship run (or in contention to win a championship) - even though Lucas didn't win a championship during his prime playing for the Cincinnati Royals. In fact, I was almost going take Paul Arizin over the four of them. I know Greer provided the much needed scoring punch from the perimeter but Cunningham did the same from the inside and the outside, in addition to being a major contributor on the defensive end. While DeBusschere was very good offensively and provided superior defense, his team was encompassed with other superior defensive players in the likes of Walt Frazier and Willis Reed. As for Lucas, he was the big man that provided scoring, rebounding and defense for Oscar Robertson and the Cincinnati Royals. His impact was obviously felt, not only because of the media publicity going back to his college days and in the pros, but five years later when he was quickly inducted into the Basketball Hall of Fame.

Getting back to Schayes, in their title defense, he averaged 22.1 points, 13.9 rebounds, and 3.4 assists per game in the postseason. For the remainder of his career, the Nationals never made it back to the NBA Finals, losing in alternating seasons in the playoffs to the Philadelphia 76ers and Boston Celtics. In the 1963 season, the Nationals were eliminated by the Cincinnati Royals in the semifinals three games to one. His best individual season came in the 1957-58 season when he averaged **24.8 points**, **14.2 rebounds**, and **3.1 assists** per game - and a league leading .904 percent from the free-throw line. He also finished second in the voting for the MVP award.

In his first 12 NBA seasons, Schayes made the First and Second Team All-NBA six times each and was named to the All-Star team every year. That in itself proves the greatness of anyone player in any one era. He was one of the first perennial All-Stars and pioneers along with George Mikan to have played in the NBA's inaugural season in 1949-50. Along with Bill Sharman, he was one of the NBA's first great free-throw shooters, leading the league three times. I know he played with fewer teams and fewer players than at any other time in history, but so did everyone else that played in that era and shortly after. Despite the one championship it was inconceivable for me to leave him out of the top 50 because of the *incredible* durability, consistency and individual accolades as mentioned above. Despite the fact he didn't have any scoring titles and just the one rebounding title, the clincher was that he was on the All-NBA First or Second Team in his first twelve seasons he played in the league. Besides, there was no MVP award given out before the 1956 season in which he would have more than likely won at least one of those. He also was outstanding and consistent in the postseason averaging 19.5 points and 12.2 rebounds per game, and had the monster **50-point** game against the Celtics. So because it's hard to compare eras, I'm not going to penalize the ranking in place of others that have never made, or have very few All-NBA First Team selections. Both First and Second Team honors simply mean you were the best or second best at your position. And, that's what Dolph Schayes was for 12 *straight years!*

Career Totals

18.5 points average, 12.1 rebounds, 3.1 assists, .380 FG%, .849 FT%

18,438 points, 11,256 rebounds, 3072 assists

Billy Cunningham

(Rank #49)

All-NBA First Team (3-times), All-Star (4-times)

NBA Championships (1), ABA MVP (1-time)

Also featuring: Hal Greer

Billy Cunningham was one of the great small forwards to ever play the game. In his prime, playing for the Philadelphia 76ers - during the late 1960s and early 1970s, he was the best small forward in the NBA. Born on June 3rd, 1943 in Brooklyn, New York, William John Cunningham attended Erasmus Hall High School where he became a Superstar and was the MVP of the Brooklyn league in 1961. That same season, he was also named First Team All-New York City. In four seasons at the University of North Carolina, Cunningham averaged 24.3 points and 15.1 rebounds per game. And, in his sophomore year in 1963, he set a school record for rebounds per game at 16.1. Although known for his scoring and rebounding, Cunningham was also a good leaper and defensive player. In his high school days he was given the nickname "the Kangaroo Kid" because of his outstanding jumping ability.

Cunningham was selected with the 5th pick overall of the 1965 NBA Draft by the Philadelphia 76ers. In his rookie season, the *multi-talented* and *ultra-competitive* Cunningham joined a 76ers team that was coming off a crushing seven-game series defeat to the Boston Celtics in the Eastern Finals from the year before. With a formidable team of Wilt Chamberlain, Hal Greer and Chet Walker, Cunningham looked to be the missing piece to get Philadelphia over the top. In a rematch in the Eastern Finals, with alternating home games, the top seed 76ers gave up home court advantage by losing the first two games of the series, before winning game three in Philadelphia. But with Chamberlain having coaching issues with Dolph Schayes, the 76ers lost the next two games and the series.

In the 1966-67 season, with a talented team still in place, and with another year of experience under their belt, the 76ers jelled into the best team in the NBA finishing with an incredible 68-13 record including a 46-4 start to the season. With Chamberlain and Greer seeking their first championship with super sixth man Cunningham coming off the bench, the 76ers were primed and ready to capture their first title since 1955 (Syracuse Nationals). After defeating the Cincinnati Royals in the semifinals three games to one for the second time in three years, the 76ers steam rolled the Celtics in the Eastern Finals in five games. Against Chamberlain's former team, the 76ers won the 1967 NBA Championship despite the scoring onslaught from Rick Barry. Star guard **Hal Greer** had been a big part of the Philadelphia franchise in the same way Sam Jones was for the Boston Celtics, providing scoring punch from the perimeter. The *smooth shooting* Greer was one of the great shooting guards of his generation that was ultimately durable and consistent throughout his career allowing him to average 19.5 points per game or more 10 straight seasons. He also had averaged 22 points or more 7 times in 9 seasons.

Harold Everett Greer was born on June 26th, 1936 in Huntington, West Virginia and attended Douglass High School. At Marshall University in his final year of college, he averaged 23.6 points and 11.7 rebounds per game before being selected in the second round with the 13th pick overall of the 1958 NBA Draft by the Syracuse Nationals. In his first four seasons, Greer gradually improved his points, rebounds, and assists every year to where he averaged 22.8 points, 7.4 rebounds, and 4.4 assists per game. The Nationals were a team that was still competitive after winning the 1955 NBA Championship but had a group of star players that were either at the end of their career or just beginning. While Hall of Famers Dolph Schayes and George Yardley were going out, Johnny "Red" Kerr and Larry Costello were coming in. So without a talented big man, Greer became far and away the best player and best scorer on the team until the 1965 season when Chamberlain got there. He led the franchise in scoring for two seasons with the Nationals and two with the newly named 76ers that had moved to Philadelphia for the 1963-64 season. So basically the city of Philadelphia did not have a team for the 1962-63 season because the Warriors had already moved to San Francisco. Greer had his best individual seasons the year before Chamberlain arrived, averaging **23.3 points**, **6.1 rebounds**, and **4.7 assists** - and the year after the 76ers won the championship in 1967, averaging a **career-high 24.1 points** per game, **5.4 rebounds**, and **4.5 assists**. In his postseason career, he was equally consistent averaging 20.4 points per game, 5.5 rebounds, and 4.3 assists. In his finest playoff run, he averaged **27.7** and **25.8 points** per game in back-to-back seasons in 1967 and 1968. In a brilliant thirteen-year career with the franchise, Greer was named an All-Star 10 consecutive seasons and to the All-NBA Second Team 7 straight years.

After winning the 1967 NBA Championship, the 76ers looked to defend their title, finishing with the best record in the league for the third straight season. In the semifinals, the 62-win 76ers defeated the New York Knicks in six games but lost Cunningham to a broken hand. Prior to the Eastern Finals, Martin Luther King had been assassinated, changing the entire mindset of the players for both the Philadelphia 76ers and the Boston Celtics. Despite what had happened, including Cunningham's broken hand and the rest of the team being banged up with injuries, the 76ers lost the first game before taking the next three, but lost the final three games and the series in seven. Much of the blame went on Wilt Chamberlain for not asserting himself in the decisive game 7, as I have described in detail in his chapter. After Chamberlain was traded to the Los Angeles Lakers, Cunningham blossomed into an offensive force averaging **24.8 points**, **12.8 rebounds** and **3.5 assists** - and was named to the All-NBA First Team for the first of three consecutive seasons. When Chamberlain left, Cunningham led the team in scoring four consecutive seasons including posting a **career-high 26.1 points** and **13.6 rebounds** per game in 1969-70. But the 76ers never made it past the first round of the playoffs again. After finishing with 55 wins the 76ers were eliminated each season from 1969 to 1971 by John Havlicek's Celtics in five games, Lew Alcindor's Milwaukee Bucks in five games, and Earl Monroe's Baltimore Bullets in seven games.

After the 1971-72 season, Cunningham jumped from the NBA to the ABA where he led the Carolina Cougars to the Eastern Division Finals. Despite the loss to the Kentucky Colonels, he was named 1973 ABA MVP for the regular season. After two seasons with the Cougars, and with his future in doubt due to injuries, Cunningham returned to the city he began his career, Philadelphia. With Hal Greer already in retirement, he had two productive seasons but the 76ers missed the playoffs both years.

In player comparisons: Billy Cunningham is ranked as the 49th greatest player of all-time for the same reason Jerry Lucas is at #50 as I have described in the previous chapter. Both were great players on championship caliber teams. In his prime, Cunningham averaged 24.3 points, 12.6 rebounds and 4.6 assists, and was basically the John Havlicek for the best Philadelphia 76ers teams while Hal Greer was the Sam Jones; whereas, Dave DeBusschere of the New York Knicks was somewhere in between. It was hard to even conceive leaving both Lucas and Cunningham out of the top 50 because out of all the players that missed the cut, they did not possess the great *combination* of scoring, rebounding and defense the way these two did, even though DeBusschere was real close!

Career Totals

20.8 point, 10.1 rebounds, 4 assists, 1.8 steals, 0.5 blocks, .446 FG%, .720 FT%

13,626 points, 6638 rebounds, 2625 assists, 115 steals, 45 blocks

Jerry Lucas

(Rank #50)

All-NBA First Team (3-times), All-Star (7-times)

NBA Championships (1)

Also featuring: Jack Twyman
& Wayne Embry

Jerry Lucas was one of the greatest big men to ever play in the NCAA and the NBA. In the first half of his career playing for the Cincinnati Royals alongside Oscar Robertson, Lucas was well known for his all-around game, and particularly in the rebounding department where he finished his career 4th on the all-time list in rebounds per game at 15.6 behind only Wilt Chamberlain, Bill Russell, and Bob Pettit. As a *blue collar* worker, Lucas was a complete player that could score, rebound, pass, and defend. On the offensive end, he had a reliable one-handed push shot, hook shot, and worked hard underneath the basket to score off missed shots with easy put-back layups. And, as a frontcourt player at only six-foot-eight, he worked hard to corral rebounds by banging bodies and crashing the offensive and defensive boards. Even early in his high school days, Lucas would use the skill of rebounding on the offensive end to score easy points off his teammates missed shots, and to limit his opponents to one shot on the defensive end. In fact, as a testament to his hard work and dedication as a rebounder, he became the fourth player in NBA history behind Chamberlain, Russell, and Pettit to average 20 rebounds in a single season.

After a short two-year stint with the San Francisco Warriors, it wasn't until his final three seasons playing for the New York Knicks he would win his first NBA Championship in 1973.

Born on March 30th, 1940 in Middletown, Ohio, Jerry Ray Lucas attended Middletown High School where his team won 76 straight games. In his sophomore year, he scored 55 points in the quarterfinals and 44 in the state finals in back-to-back games. He also led the team to straight undefeated seasons that included two championships in 1957 and 1958. In both years, he was named Player of the Year by the state of Ohio. After being offered over 150 scholarships, Lucas chose Ohio State University where he had one of the most coveted college careers in NCAA history. In his sophomore season, he averaged 26.3 points and 16.4 rebounds per game, on .637 percent shooting - and was rated second to Oscar Robertson for NCAA Player of the Year. The following year after Ohio State won the title; he averaged 24.9 points and 17.4 rebounds, and led the team to the NCAA Championship game undefeated. Unfortunately, OSU was upset by the University of Cincinnati. During the tournament, Lucas became the only man in NCAA history to record **33 points and 30 rebounds** in a single game against the Kentucky Wildcats. In his final year in college, the Buckeyes made it back to the *Big Dance* for the third straight year but lost with Lucas a nonfactor, as he tried to play on a badly injured knee. Despite the losses, Lucas was named College Player of the year in 1961 and 1962. During his three years of college, he led the team to a combined 78-6 record and was honored Final Four Most Outstanding Player in both 1960 and 1961.

Jerry Lucas was selected with a territorial pick of the 1962 NBA Draft by the Cincinnati Royals. After instead signing with the Cleveland Pipers of the American Basketball League in which his deal eventually fell through, Lucas sat out a year. In his rookie season (the year after in 1963-64), he averaged 17.7 points and 17.4 rebounds per game, and led the league with a .527 percent field goal percentage. He was also named to the All-Star team for the first of six consecutive seasons. In the playoffs, with MVP Oscar Robertson as the leader of the team, the Royals defeated the Philadelphia 76ers three games to two before falling to the Boston Celtics in five games. The following season, Lucas took his game to a whole new level when he averaged 21.4 points and 20 rebounds, and shot a career-high .814 from the free-throw line. That year, he was named to the All-NBA First Team for the first of two straight seasons. But in the playoffs, his team lost to Philadelphia in the first round. In his third year in the league, he duplicated the season before and even did a little better, averaging a career-high 21.5 points and 21.1 rebounds per game. But once again in the playoffs, the Royals lost in first round, this time to the mighty Celtics four games to one.

The next three seasons, he averaged 19.2 points and a *whopping* **18.8 rebounds** (including two seasons of 19 or more) but the Royals made the playoffs just once more in 1967 as they were eliminated in the first round by the 76ers three games to one for the second time in three years. Lucas did make the All-NBA Second Team for the second time and the following year, the All-NBA First Team for the third time in his career. Despite the lack of playoff success with the Royals, Lucas averaged 16.2 points and 16.8 rebounds in four playoff seasons in Cincinnati from 1964 to 1967. When Lucas came into the league with the Royals, the stars on the team - **Wayne Embry** and **Jack Twyman** - were near the tail end of their careers. Robertson played six seasons with the both of them while Lucas played just three. The Royals four best players were either too old or too young to overcome the super powers of the Eastern Division and win an NBA championship over either the Celtics or 76ers.

Jack Twyman who was a pure-shooting forward/guard that made a living shooting from the corners, played the first two years of his career with the Rochester Royals and then the next three with the franchise after the move to Cincinnati, which was right before Oscar and Jerry came into the league. Born on May 11th, 1934 in Pittsburgh, Pennsylvania, John Kennedy Twyman attended Central Catholic High School in Pittsburgh before moving on to play basketball at the University of Cincinnati, the same college Robertson attended. In his senior year, he averaged 24.6 points and 16.5 rebounds per game, and was later drafted in the second round with the 8th pick overall of the 1955 NBA Draft by the Rochester Royals. Twyman began his professional career in the same manner he did in college, with a gradual increase in production. After improving his scoring every season similar to his senior year in college, by his fourth season in the league in 1959, his scoring average jumped over 8 points from the previous year to 25.8 points per game. He also posted a career-high 9.1 rebounds per game and was named to his third consecutive All-Star team.

The following season, he would have a career year averaging **31.2 points**, **8.9 rebounds**, and a career-high 3.5 assists per game. By that point, with Oscar coming into the league the year after, Twyman scoring dipped six points. He averaged almost identical numbers as he did in the 1959 season, giving him a three-year average of 27.4 points, 8.8 rebounds and 3.1 assists per game, on 44 percent shooting. For his career, he was named to the All-Star team 6 times and the All-NBA Second Team twice. Unfortunately prior to the 1962 season, there wasn't much to talk about because he only made the postseason just once, losing to the Detroit Pistons two games to none in the 1958 Western Semifinals. Playing with Robertson, Lucas, and five-time All-Star Wayne Embry from 1961 to 1966, he was solid in the playoffs averaging 18.3 points and 7.5 rebounds per game despite never reaching the NBA Finals. As great as Twyman was on the court he was even greater off, as his family took care of former teammate Maurice Stokes after a career-ending illness.

The next four seasons with the Golden State Warriors and New York Knicks, Lucas averaged 17.1 points and 14.4 rebounds per game, and shot .505 percent from the field. Although highly productive playing in place of Willis Reed for almost the entire season in 1972, it wasn't until his second season with the Knicks in 1973; he would capture the most coveted NBA Championship that had eluded him his entire career. By that point, he was in his final two years in the league and was not nearly the same player he once was -

despite the fact in the series; he was noted to have done a heck of a job with helping guard Wilt Chamberlain.

In player comparisons:

Jerry Lucas was the final pick to complete my Top 50 players of all-time for a lot of different reasons including, he is one of five players to average 15 rebounds or more for a career and average at least 20 rebounds for a single season joining Chamberlain, Bill Russell, Bob Pettit and Nate Thurmond. But the main two reasons were that he was one of the *greatest* amateur Olympic players in history that won the gold medal in 1960. And, he was also one of the few players throughout history that made an impact from a *transcending* point of view, *so-to-speak,* as compared to his other statistical accomplishments (not including rebounds because he ranks among the top players in that category) and number of championships won. A good example of this was the impact he made in high school (among his scoring feats as well as rebounding), in college at Ohio State (outside of being the best player on the team over Havlicek), on the 1960 Olympic team (outside of having made the team over Havlicek, and that he scored as many points as Oscar Robertson), and when he first came into the NBA.

Regardless if you disagree with the final 7 spots in this book, it really won't matter in a few years because the last man standing should be Jason Kidd ranked at # 50. With my projected rankings of LeBron James, Dwyane Wade, Chris Paul, Kevin Durant, Derrick Rose, Dwight Howard, and Blake Griffin - most are almost a sure bet to fill the spots someday, unless of course, a few other players emerge and take their place. Even as of right now, one could put LeBron, Wade, and Durant in the top 50 and perhaps the top 25. But like I mentioned in the beginning of the book, I only wanted to include players in the *initial* rankings if they had *completed* their prime years. Wes Unseld at #44, Dominique Wilkins at #45, Paul Pierce at #46, James Worthy at #47, Dolph Schayes at #48, Billy Cunningham at #49, and Jerry Lucas at #50 will most likely be off the list and perhaps almost everyone else's in the next few years - which eases the guilt I had on leaving Paul Arizin out of the Top 50. It should also ease any disagreements anyone else has, who feel Hal Greer and Dave DeBusschere should be on the list. But for now the great Jerry Lucas will have his spot in the limelight for the readers to enjoy, at least in this book.

Career Totals

17.0 points average, 15.6 rebounds, 3.3 assists, .499 FG%, .783 FT%

4,053 points, 12,942 rebounds, 2732 assists

LeBron James

(Projected #2)

MVP (4-times), Scoring Title (1-time), All-Star (9-times)

All-NBA First Team (7-times), All-Defensive First Team (5-times)

NBA Record: youngest to make All-NBA First Team!

NBA Record: youngest to record a triple-double!

LeBron James of the Miami Heat is one of the most talented players to ever come into the NBA. Drafted with the #1 pick overall in 2003 by the Cleveland Cavaliers at the age of 18, LeBron was the most coveted high school phenom since Lew Alcindor and the only *sophomore* in high school history to be selected to the USA Today All-USA First Team. Today at the age of 27 (prior to the conclusion of the 2012 season), James has more than lived up to all the hype and expectations in every facet of the game, but has yet to win the most coveted NBA Championship! Now in his second season playing alongside Dwyane Wade, Chris Bosh, and with a formidable supporting cast in Miami - LeBron hopes to capture the trophy that has eluded him his entire career. Known for his great all-around play, LeBron's greatest attributes are his deadly combination of *size, strength and speed* that allows him to finish on the fast break or in the half court, as good as or better than anyone that has ever played the game! And aside from his tremendous athletic ability he *combines* scoring, rebounding, passing, and defense better than any player ever, and that includes the likes of past greats Oscar Robertson, Michael Jordan, Larry Bird, and Magic Johnson. After improving his low-post game in 2011 while working out in the off-season with Hakeem Olajuwon, LeBron virtually has no weakness in his repertoire going forward.

If he should capture his 3rd MVP award in 2012, giving him more than any player in the NBA today and the most since Jordan won his third back in 1992, the only thing left to complete his resume as one of the Top 5 basketball players of all-time is for him to win multiple championships. As a testament to his greatness for being the best, most outstanding, and most valuable player in the league every season, "Doc Rivers" gave LeBron the ultimate compliment. He said if LeBron doesn't win the MVP every year, usually the voters are just tired of voting for him! Coming from the great head coach of the Boston Celtics franchise that coached against the great Kobe Bryant in the NBA Finals twice in the last four years, it says a lot.

"King James" is ultimately the best finisher in the game today going to his left or to his right in transition or in the half court. To balance off his arsenal, he has recently incorporated a short jump hook with both hands and a runner in the lane, similar to the *tear drop* that his teammate Dwyane Wade uses and Tony Parker has mastered. Aside from his improved free-throw shooting and jump shot over the years, LeBron is already hands down either the *best or second best* scorer, rebounder, passer and defensive player at his position in NBA history. If it isn't within his grasp this year in 2012, one day he should capture the Defensive Player of the Year Award.

With the determination to improve his overall game every season including this years improved low-post game, LeBron has a chance to go down as, not only one of the top 5 players of all-time, but maybe even the top 2 when it is all said and done. To get to number one, four championships in a row (something Jordan and Kobe never accomplished - for two totally different reasons), with all his MVP's, accolades, life-time statistics, and all-around play, could put him in a *draw* with Jordan as the greatest player ever. He just needs to start winning some championships like the rest of the players ranked ahead of him. His statistics so far, are on pace to put him among the top of the list of all-time greats in all categories including points, rebounds, assists, steals, and blocks. Potentially, he could become the first man in NBA History to record **40,000 points, 10,000 rebounds, 10,000 assists, 2000 steals, and 1000 blocks.** If he doesn't break Kareem's record of 38,000 plus points, it is almost a given he will reach at least the 30,000 to 35,000 point plateau - because at 27 years old, he became the youngest man this year in 2012 to score 19,000 points. So realistically, barring injury, in six more years at the age of 32, he should be hovering around 30,000 points - whereas Kobe for example, won't reach that plateau until next season at the age of 34 about to turn 35. Of note: Kevin Durant is on pace to reach that milestone by the age of 33 years old. And the way he's going he might actually catch LeBron. Let me make this clear, Durant by the end of his prime has a legitimate shot to catch LeBron in the scoring department and possibly in blocks. But LeBron would still stand superior in rebounds, assists, and steals. See Kevin

Durant's chapter for a complete breakdown of the statistical categories of James, Bryant and Durant through their first four seasons in the league.

Watching LeBron over the years, I think he is equally the incredible human specimen that Jordan was while weighing 40 pounds heavier. Many people, who don't watch LeBron on a regular basis, feel he doesn't quite have the athleticism that Jordan had. I do agree to a certain extent, because Jordan was lighter and could hang in the air a little longer allowing him to contort his body in more ways, similar to Dwyane Wade and Derrick Rose of today. Even though Jordan could float in the air longer, as far as ball control finishing at the basket, I see them both similar. After watching over 300 games a year including ninety percent of LeBron's games since he was a rookie with the NBA League Pass, I have been able to witness LeBron first hand at his finest to *accurately* assess his maximum potential.

LeBron writes and does most things left-handed but shoots right-handed. Being ambidextrous, allows him to drive left and finish with a sweeping left-handed layup, or drive right slamming down the "hammer dunk." If contested in the lane, he has the uncanny ability to contort his body and alter his shot and finish with spectacular acrobatics. On his patented drives to the basket, he is able to finish with either hand by switching from his right to his left or left to his right by crossing over in the paint, or by staying with the original drive particularly on the left side than pirouetting to the opposite direction to finish the layup with his right hand. He can also keep the dribble left and pirouette on the same side with an incredible finish using his left or right hand. Basically, LeBron is built like Karl Malone (about 10 pounds lighter) but has Michael Jordan's athleticism and finishing ability with a touch of Julius Erving's dunking style. And to go along with it, he has Magic Johnson and Larry Bird's rebounding and passing ability, and basketball court sense. For a man his size at perhaps six-feet-nine 260, he is one of the game's great streak shooters and when he is feeling it, he can knock down three-pointers like a prolific shooting guard. In addition, LeBron does have tremendous finishing abilities in the low post or high post, that includes an up-and-under move from either side of the basket finishing with his left or right hand and a fadeaway shot from the post or anywhere on the court that Jordan, Kobe and Wade all have. He even incorporated an absurd left-handed jump hook from six to twelve feet that I have never seen him shoot before until the 2012 season. He just needs to work to refine his overall post-game by continuing to work hard and practice like he did this past off-season with Hakeem Olajuwon. In time, because of the Miami Heat's need for a low-post game, LeBron will potentially post up six to ten times a game like he has already shown early on in the 2011-12 season. It doesn't surprise me like it will the most of you, but LeBron has already proven his ability to post up occasionally and even shoot fadeaway jumpers during his first eight seasons in the league, but just needs to incorporate it into his offensive arsenal on a regular basis. Many highlights of a single player are often missed on Sports Center and on NBA TV. So a person looking to critique a player, shouldn't rely on just highlights in place of watching a full game because many times a player who scores 30 or 40 points for example, often only three or four of his made baskets from the field, or sometimes even zero, are shown on the highlight package due to many reasons including: One: time restraints, two: because of the assortment of multiple highlights from different players on the same or opposite team, and three: many of the highlights may come on the defensive end.

One example of LeBron's potential as a post-player was *exemplified more than ever*, when he scored **48 points, including 25 straight, and 29 of the teams last 30** against the Detroit Pistons in the 2007 Eastern Conference Finals at the age of 22 years old. If you missed it, in this game LeBron had multiple fadeaways (that weren't shown on the highlights, or at least the highlights that I remember) including a *devastating fadeaway* from the top of the key that was as fast as or faster than Jordan's during his heyday. If you watched it live, you would have been in utter disbelief! I have seen many fadeaways from LeBron over eight seasons that were of this speed. So again, if you haven't watched LeBron on a regularly basis, chances are you've missed his unbelievable fadeaway shots that he has used *on occasion*, until this seasons improved post-up game. In player comparisons, to be clear, Jordan had by far the better, more proficient and *consistently* quicker fadeaway shot as part of his offensive arsenal. But LeBron has shown the same ability on a few occasions over the years. So if he never perfects it as a regular part of his offensive arsenal, it will never be in the class of Jordan's or Kobe's, and Wade's for that matter. People who have criticized LeBron for not having a post-up game were inaccurate in their assessment. He always had it, albeit *unpolished*; because he never utilized it on a consistent basis until his second season with the Miami Heat. And of course, he still has not *mastered* the fadeaway shot just yet. So eventually, the overall substance and effectiveness of his low-post/high-post game (short-jump hook and fadeaway) will eventually rival the other greats of the game, but in terms of style and flash it may never look aesthetically pleasing to the eye like Jordan, Kobe, or Wade's. But that's expected for a man built like a *Mac Truck* in the mold of the great Karl Malone!

Born on December 30th, 1984 in Akron, Ohio as LeBron Raymone James, during his entire career going back to his high school days at St. Vincent-St. Mary, until this year, LeBron's dominance for the game of basketball has been off dribble penetration finishing with a thunderous dunk, his exquisite passing and outstanding rebounding for a small forward, and his suffocating defense. Although built like a power forward, until this year, LeBron has played most of his career like a small forward, shooting guard, or point guard. And at the age of 27, barely entering his prime, his game is still evolving and has been improving from year to year. First and foremost over the past few years, he has improved his jump shot, his defense, and his free-throw shooting. After the completion of an *improved* low-post game this year, the only thing left to complete his resume is for him to win his first of multiple championships, hopefully beginning this year 2012. There are still many people including the most famous Skip Bayless on ESPN First Take who feel LeBron is lacking the clutch gene and is not a premier clutch shooter or clutch player, for that matter. But I beg to differ because of his mastery in the previous year's playoffs against the Washington Wizards in three consecutive seasons to begin his young career, the Detroit Pistons in the Eastern Conference Finals in 2007, in game 2 of the 2009 conference finals against the Orlando Magic where he made the "Jordanesque" game-winning three-point shot at the buzzer, and last season in 2011 against the Boston Celtics and the Chicago Bulls. In every season except for last year, LeBron has played with an inferior cast of players that have made a total of two All-Star games - one in his second season in 2005 in Zydrunas Igauskas, and one appearance by default in 2009. It actually took two players including Ray Allen to get injured in order for Mo Williams to make the All-Star team three years ago.

I think people are basing what LeBron has done recently, fumbling the ball out of bounds and clanking baskets off the front of the rim on jump shots, or on runners throughout his horrendous (in terms of scoring) NBA Finals series in 2011 against the Dallas Mavericks. Most fans and even media are *prisoners of the moment* and either forget or don't care to remember how he demolished the Chicago Bulls and Boston Celtics in semifinals and conference finals, just weeks before. I will have to say this though, in a nutshell, despite LeBron's need for an improved low-post game for the 2012 season, he should have kept attacking Dallas' defense or zone defense whether he was able to or not. I know he was not able to penetrate and score off dribble penetration like he is accustomed to doing with Shawn Marion, DeShawn Stevenson and Jason Kidd draped all over him, but he should of "kept on coming." So it was a *lesson learned* by LeBron James, that going forward, he needs to stay in attack mode in big games and in playoff games, and set his teammates up for scoring opportunities even if he is not able to score himself. This simply means that he must operate out of the *triple-threat* position where he can pull up for a jump shot, pass if there is a wide open shooter, or dribble penetrate to the basket. If he is cut off like he was quite often in the 2011 Finals against the Mavericks, he must continue to attack (when collapsed on) and get rid of the ball at the last second even if it means falling to the ground like Jordan used to.

If you look back to Jordan's championship years, he was always in attack mode whether he was scoring in the lane and from the perimeter or creating shots for his teammates in Craig Hodges, John Paxon, Steve Kerr, and B.J. Armstrong. LeBron needs to do the same thing which he has done so far in this year's 2012 playoffs, instead of getting rid of the ball to soon and passing it around the perimeter. In fairness, which most people might not realize, is that not every play is drawn up for LeBron. So theoretically, and I'm not even including plays drawn up for Chris Bosh, you could say the ball should only be in LeBron's hand about half the time and in Wade's the other half because he was nearly as great a dominate scorer and facilitator for the Miami Heat as James was when he played for the Cleveland Cavaliers. When LeBron captures the most coveted NBA Championship (or multiple championships), he should easily finish his career ranked in the top 5 in anyone's book when it's all said and done. Most, if not all experts on TV, radio and the internet, including most polls have at least the number one ranking in agreement with Michael Jordan?

LeBron James, as a dual with partner Dwyane Wade, could be the most explosive tandem in NBA history excelling at taking the ball to the rim and finishing at the basket and potentially more dominant than Michael Jordan and Scottie Pippen were. The "Freight Train" and the "Black Mongoose," the nickname I gave Wade (find out why in Wade's chapter), both display tremendous scoring ability from the interior and from the perimeter, including a dazzling array of jump shots, fadeaways and three-point shots all within their arsenal. Both are outstanding rebounders at their positions and have pinpoint passing skills and keen court vision. I should have made this chapter Dwyane Wade and LeBron James! Their overall game is top notch, including relentless on the ball defense that only Jordan and Pippen exemplified. While I have personally nicknamed Dwyane Wade the "Black Mongoose" in Wade's chapter because of his collapsing defense he plays especially on the "Black Mamba," you can say LeBron is the "Human Octopus," able to put a strangle hold and lock down opponents on a nightly bases. In fact, Wade said in 2012 that LeBron can shut down any player on defense if he guarded him for a full game. In other words, he is basically saying that he could guard any player at all five positions. Who else can you say that about in NBA history? Derrick Rose even said, during last season's Eastern Conference Finals, that he was *extremely* impressed by how a man of LeBron's size was able to guard him. Wade and LeBron often block shots flying in off the ball or in transition with their incredible leaping ability. Both have made the All-Star team 9 years in a row and are on the All-NBA First Team or Second Team almost every year when Wade is heathy. After teaming up with the Miami Heat, both players are on track statistically to put up *big-time* Hall of Fame numbers.

Despite mixed opinions before and after the Miami Heat lost the 2011 NBA Championship to the Dallas Mavericks, a lot of people including many experts believe that LeBron James and Dwyane Wade couldn't and still cannot co-exist. I was one of the few people that predicted back in May of 2010 on my former website JNBA&Allsports.com that LeBron would leave Cleveland to join, either the New York Knicks or the Miami Heat. For one, I knew that LeBron and Wade were good friends going back to their draft days and became even better friends playing together for the U.S. Olympic Dream Team in 2008. Second, I knew both were dominate players but totally unselfish at the same time. Whereas, many people felt the both of them needed the ball and that they couldn't co-exist together. After watching almost all of LeBron and Wade's games the last few years, I knew what everyone was saying was actually the direct opposite. Most people assume that to be great scorers of this magnitude always need the ball to score. It is true that both players need the ball in their hands, but in *different capacities* throughout the game. Because LeBron and Wade were unselfish and let the game come to them while playing for their respective teams throughout their career, made it easy for me to envision them playing together and sharing all the responsibilities. In fact, from a scoring standpoint, players may not necessarily score as much but will feed off each other with better open looks from the outside and easy baskets inside off cuts or Alley-oop passes, therefore becoming more *efficient* scorers. And third, LeBron mentioned in an interview on "Larry King Live" prior to his decision to leave Cleveland, if his free agent class that included

Wade, Chris Bosh, Amar'e Stoudemire and Joe Johnson, were playing in Major League Baseball without a salary cap, they would all sign with the same team. So with that being said, "I took it as a hint," that if LeBron chose to leave Cleveland for another team and join forces with another star it would be with close friend Dwyane Wade over anyone else.

Thinking back, I believe without having any actual proof - LeBron, Wade, and Bosh all signed their *second* three-year contract in anticipation of possibly playing together in the future while *odd-man-out*, Carmelo Anthony signed the five-year. Anthony just said recently on the "Dan Patrick Show" that if he had to do it over again, he would have taken the three-year contract instead of the five. I assume he was implying, despite signing recently with the New York Knicks the year after Amar'e Stoudemire, it would have given him more options as a free agent to join forces with fellow draftees and an opportunity to leave Denver the *right way* so to speak. During the 2011 All-Star break, there were reports and rumors that Anthony wanted out of Denver and wanted to sign with the Knicks where he said he grew up, and not the lowly New Jersey Nets even though the franchise will be moving to Brooklyn in 2013. From what I understand he actually grew up in Jersey - go figure, or maybe it was New York.

LeBron chose Miami because it gave him the best chance to win not only one championship but multiple championships. There have been many *dynamic duals* in NBA history but none as similarly talented as James and Wade. There has always been a Robin to a Batman in the likes of Michael Jordan and Scottie Pippen, Shaquille O'Neal and Kobe Bryant, and even Elgin Baylor and Jerry West. Pippen differed to Jordan as the number one scoring option as did Kobe to Shaq early on in his career. Even West did, until Baylor started having knee problems the second half of his career. But with Miami, there is no such thing, because this is the first time that two *super heroes* with an identical skill set have played together in their *prime* in NBA history! I stated long ago that I believed before LeBron and Wade joined forces, they could co-exist and form the greatest "Dynamic Dual" the league has ever seen. In fact, this season in the 2012 playoffs against the Indiana Pacers, James and Wade became the first dual in NBA history to average 32 points each in 3 consecutive playoff games.

The Miami Heat in 2011, almost won the NBA championship playing with a lack of chemistry most of the season. So, all in all, I know Miami can win a championship playing the way they did this year but it would be easier, for LeBron James and Dwyane Wade to tweak their game a little particularly at the end games to improve the overall team chemistry. Both players are similar in terms of being able to dominate at the basket and both are used to having the ball in their hands. But because Wade is already in his prime and has made big shots throughout the 2006 the NBA Finals, I would designate him as the closer and LeBron as the facilitator because he is simply the better passer. This doesn't mean that Wade is the better player or that they can't *switch* their roles from time to time. It's just more *fitting* to run a team when everyone knows their role particularly at the end of games. Do you have to be the number one scoring option on a team to be considered the best player on the team? Absolutely not! Look at Bill Russell, Magic Johnson, Steve

Nash, Chris Paul and Jason Kidd throughout the years. Because Wade is almost three years older than LeBron and keeps having reoccurring injuries, LeBron will automatically become the number one scoring option sooner than you might expect. The way he is dominating the 2012 season in every facet of the game including scoring, and with Wade already being injured in the beginning of the year, LeBron has been the number one option. Maybe this will change the second half of the year and into the playoffs. But like I mentioned earlier, either player has the supreme ability and option to take over at the end of games when necessary.

If it isn't LeBron's team already, it will be soon because Dwyane Wade is the older statesmen, already in his prime and is not getting any younger. I just hope for the both of them, particularly for Wade, they can stay injury free the next few years during their championship run.

Here are LeBron's statistical achievements so far at 27 years old: LeBron has the 2nd highest efficiency rating by Espn.com in NBA history behind only Michael Jordan. He is also on pace to break Kareem's All-Time scoring mark of 38,356 points while finishing with over 10,000 assists and 10,000 rebounds, 2000 steals and 1000 blocks. Because LeBron is incredibly durable averaging 78 games a year, should allow him to break Abdul-Jabbar's scoring record by the age of 37 providing a career threatening injury, a lost season due to another NBA lockout, or at worst, a complete burnout of his career (where this would be the only non-legitimate reason for him coming up short). He also has two MVP awards and is on his way to a third, and has made All-NBA First Team 6 times and All-Defensive First Team 4 times. LeBron potentially could break Karl Malone and Kobe Bryant's record of 11 First Team All-NBA selections. Michael Jordan, Abdul-Jabbar, Elgin Baylor, Jerry West, Bob Cousy, and Bob Pettit have 10 selections; Oscar Robertson, Magic Johnson and Larry Bird have 9.

Before the transition to the Heat the King was shattering records at a historical pace including these astonishing numbers. The youngest to win two MVP's (back to back) at 25 years old tied with Kareem Abdul-Jabbar. All he needs is three more to tie Jordan. The youngest in NBA History to make First Team All-NBA, youngest to score 40 points, youngest to score 50 points (Brandon Jennings just recently broke the record scoring 55) including a 56-point game. He is also the youngest to score 5,000 points, 10,000 points, 15,000, 18,000 and now 19,000 points in 2012. If he stays healthy in 2013, he will become the youngest in history to reach the 20,000 and 21,000 point plateau at the ripe age of 28. After last year, he now has 9 career 50-point games at only the young age of 27.

After losing the MVP award to Derrick Rose, the NBA Championship to Dirk Nowitzki and the negative criticism he took all year long starting with "The Decision" to leave Cleveland, I expected LeBron to rebound mightily with a few monster games of 50 points or more in 2012, but that didn't happen. Despite the lack of scoring accolades this season, the young Kevin Durant and Kobe Bryant did not even come close to matching the scoring records that LeBron had at such a young age. In 2006, LeBron had the best season for a

21-year-old in NBA history when he averaged a gaudy **31.4 points, 7 rebounds and 6.6 assists** per game, and had **15 40-point** games (Durant at 23 years old had 13 total 40-point games and one 50-point game in his young four-year career). That season, he also became the youngest man in history to be selected to the All-NBA First Team. That means he was the best at his position at an earlier age than *anyone* in history. In addition, while many felt Kobe Bryant could have been the MVP over Steve Nash that season, I felt LeBron could have been the MVP over the both of them. Based on the criteria in the beginning of the book and throughout, LeBron had his best individual contributions and overall numbers even over Kobe, who had his best scoring season at 35.4 points, while the Cleveland Cavaliers finished with the 5th best record in the NBA. I said the MVP should go to the best player who has the best individual contributions statistically playing for a top 4 or 5 team that's in contention to win a championship. Cleveland was the fifth best team record wise, as they used that season as a stepping stone to make it to the NBA Finals the following year in 2007.

In the **2007-08** season, LeBron became the third man in NBA history behind Oscar Robertson and Michael Jordan to average at least **30 points**, **7.9 rebounds**, and **7.2 assists** per game. He also became the third man in 20 years to lead the league in scoring, and average at least seven or more assists per game (Jordan and Iverson were the others).

He also had two monster games:

On March 5th against the New Knicks he had: **50 points, 10 rebounds, 8 assists**

-Becoming the first player since Kareem in 1975 to average at least those numbers-

On Jan. 15th against the Memphis Grizzlies he had: **51 points, 9 rebounds, 8 assists**

-Becoming the first player since Rick Barry in 1978 to record at least those numbers-

During his first MVP season in **2008-09** he had two memorable games:

On February 4th against the New York Knicks: **52 points, 9 rebs, 11 assists, 2 blocks**

-Becoming the first player since Wilt Chamberlain in 1968 to record at least those

On March 17th against the Orlando Magic: **43 points, 12 rebs, 8 assists, 4 steals**

- **1 block** becoming the first man since Larry Bird in 1992 to record at least those numbers

Just of note: Between those two great all-around games all within a six-week period, LeBron had two other monster games of:

On February 20th in Milwaukee: **55 points, 9 assists, and 5 rebounds**

On March 13th in Sacramento: **51 points, 9 assists, and 4 rebounds**

Even in the playoffs, semifinals loss against the Orlando Magic in six games, James did his part with monster scoring games of **49, 35, 41, 44,** and **37 points**.

During his second MVP season in **2009-10** he had two more memorable games:

On February 6th against the New York Knicks: **47 points, 8 rebs, 8 assists, 5 steals**

   -Becoming the first man since Rick Barry in 1974 to have at least those numbers-

On February 18th against the Denver Nuggets: **43 points, 15 assists, 13 rebs, 4 blocks,**

   - 2 steals becoming the first player ever to record those numbers since the NBA began keeping track of blocks and steals in 1974-

Here are some other notables of LeBron James:

- He has the highest scoring average at over 30 points against the Celtics franchise in history as of 2011, while Michael Jordan finishes 2nd.

- He and Michael Jordan have 2 50-point games in Madison Square Garden, the Meca of NBA Basketball arenas. One more and he will stand alone in the record books.

- He is the only man in NBA History to have at least 50 points, 8 rebounds, and 8 assists twice in the same season.

- He is tied with Kareem as the youngest player in NBA History to win back-to-back MVP's and to win 3 in 4 seasons.

- He has the 3rd highest scoring average against the Knicks, only about a point and a half behind Michael Jordan.

- He is the only player in NBA History to win Player of the Month 4 times or more twice in two different seasons. He won Player of the Month 4 times in 2009 and 5 times in 2010.

- He has 31 career triple doubles, second out of active players to Jason Kidd.

- He has the highest scoring average in All-Star Game history ahead of Jordan and Kobe.

- He has the 3rd highest scoring average in NBA History behind Jordan and Chamberlain.

- His 25 career 35-point playoff games are 4th All-Time behind Jordan, Kobe, and Shaq

- He already has 53 career 30-point and 11 40-point playoff games

- He is on pace to break Karl Malone's record of 12 seasons of 2000 or more points/season

- He is also on pace to break his 11 All-NBA First Team selections

- He is the youngest man in NBA history at 21 years old to average 30 points in a season

In a game recently on January 19th, 2011 against Kobe Bryant and the Los Lakers, James had one of his best all-around performances finishing with 31 points, eight rebounds, eight assists, four steals and three blocks. He also had his 10th career 40-point game in this year's playoffs (2012). In game 4 of the semifinals against the Indiana Pacers (which is rostered with potential star players including Paul George - who could end up becoming a Scottie Pippen type player able to create his own shot in a dominate fashion, or maybe that player might end up being Kawhi Leonard), he finished with a remarkable **40 points, 18 rebounds, 9 assists**, two steals, and two blocks - becoming the first player in 25 years to reach at least those numbers. It was one of LeBron's signature clutch games in his quest to win his first NBA Championship. With Chris Bosh out indefinitely and Miami down two games to one on the road, the dynamic dual of LeBron and D-Wade finished with a combined 70 points on their way to evening up the series at two games apiece. The Heat also won the next two games to make it three straight victories to win the series in six games.

Here is the James vs. Jordan comparisons in terms of wins. As it stands, Jordan has 6 NBA Championships to LeBron's 0, but Michael never beat the Boston Celtics in a playoff series, going 0 for 6 (2-playoff series) all-time. LeBron and the Miami Heat just defeated the Celtics 4 games to 1 in the 2011 playoffs while knocking down clutch shot after clutch shot to finish games while posting 2 35-point games and 1 30-point game. His team just did it again in 2012 putting away the Celtics in 7 games in the Eastern Conference Finals. In that series, LeBron had 6 30-point games and one monster game 6 (that tied the series) in which he had one of the greatest playoff games in NBA history finishing with **45 points, 15 rebounds, and 5 assists** tying Elgin Baylor's exact stat line back in 1961. He also played the same way in the conference finals the year before, finishing off the number one seed Chicago Bulls in just five games, before unraveling against the Dallas Mavericks in the NBA Finals! The bad news for LeBron is that he will always have two defeats in the NBA Finals, something Jordan never did. The good news is that LeBron is still only 27 years old as I am completing this book. Jordan was 28 when he won his first of six championships. Providing LeBron doesn't lose in the Finals for a third time this season, two losses isn't such a bad thing, because almost every player outside of Jordan, Duncan, and the 1960s Celtics lost numerous championships: Kobe has 2 NBA Finals losses, Shaq has 2, Bird has 2, Kareem has 4, Magic has 4, Elgin Baylor has 7, Jerry West has 8, and Wade now has 1 thanks partly to LeBron. Who knows, hopefully LeBron will win his first championship in this year's lockout season just like Duncan did in 1999.

In closing, I added these segments from an article I wrote (Keep in mind that as one of the biggest LeBron James *admirer*, I was simply disappointed, or should I say frankly upset) after the Miami Heat lost the 2011 NBA Finals to the Dallas Mavericks. This is partly why I came up with a projected ranking for this book so that LeBron James, Dwyane Wade, Kevin Durant, Chris Paul and Dwight Howard, Derrick Rose, and Blake Griffin can *fulfill* their legacy *for better or for worst* in the Elite Rankings of All-Time.

Dallas' zone defense at times was just enough to throw the Miami offense off kilter during the 2011 NBA Finals all series long. This is the primary reason, among others, of the collapse of LeBron James 8.9 point differential in the NBA Finals vs. his regular season scoring average which I will literally blast at the end of this article. You will not here me mention a LeBron vs. Jordan comparison for a very, very, very............. long time and possibly ever with a performance like I just saw last night. Only a triple double average for one season or another 10 50-point games (he has 9 50-point games in his career already), or 3 to 6 Championships in the next six years will change my mind! After listening to all of the talk shows this morning (ESPN First Take, The Herd, Mike and Mike in the Morning, The Dan Patrick Show, and all Espn sportscasters throughout the Morning) I have come up with my own conclusions about every playoff minute I have seen this year and previous years of LeBron James: I Don't like the way he finished games in this year's NBA Finals. How could this be? LeBron has performed in the clutch in previous years and especially against the Boston Celtics and Chicago Bulls in this year's 2011 playoffs. He played 3 great games against the Sixers, 3 great games against the Celtics including 2 35-point games and 1 30-point game, and 1 35-point game against the Bulls. His career scoring average going in to this year playoffs was 29 points per game tied with Jerry West and right behind Jordan. Then the collapse, I mention in the beginning of the article. Everyone including Skip Bayless on ESPN First Take was saying just 2 weeks ago that LeBron James is turning the corner as a clutch player, now all of a sudden everyone is saying he is a bum and can't perform in the clutch. He just proved it with monster performances against Boston and Chicago, against Orlando in 2009, and with 2 game-winning shots against the Washington Wizards years before, a 48-point game performance against the Detroit Pistons, and taking the 2007 Cleveland Cavaliers team to the NBA Finals at just 22 years old. Kevin Durant and Derrick

Rose both turn 23 in a couple of months. Let's see if they have 2 NBA Finals appearances by 26 years old?

From my perspective, I agree, that it did appear LeBron shrank in the clutch like everyone in the world suggest, but I can see the big picture on why this happened, and what is to come from King James next year and for his future. Earlier in that same playoff season, Kobe averaged about the same amount of points against the Mavericks scoring 17 points in game 3 and game 4 and missed all of his 3 point shots going 0 for 8 and everybody was blaming Pau Gasol for flaming out. From a statistical standpoint, LeBron actually had better numbers against the Mavericks than Kobe did and nobody was saying anything. Owe wait, that's probably because he has 5 Championships on his resume in which he played with the most physically dominant big man of All-time and for playing with the best supporting cast the last two years. This year Dallas had the best supporting cast with 2 Hall of Famers in Kidd & Nowitzki and former All-Stars in Marion & Peja, and the second best clutch shooter of this era in Jason Terry. LeBron at only 26 now has two NBA Finals losses but so does everyone else except Jordan and Duncan. Kobe has 2 NBA Finals losses, Shaq's has 2, Kareem has 4, Magic has 4, Elgin Baylor & Jerry West have 8, Bird has 2, and now Wade has 1 thanks impart to LeBron. Most people know that it took Shaq and Jordan 7 years to win a Championship while going to college but did the ignorant out there know that Jordan was 28,29,30 when he won his first set of championship's and 33,34,35 when he won his next 3. Take that and look it up! If LeBron wins it next year as everyone originally predicted, he would be only 27 years old.

Of course you all know the Decision he made in the off-season is what this is all about! But how can a player of this magnitude play so well in all three playoff series except the Finals. Many factors can affect a player's performance and I noticed every one of them. In game 1 and 2 LeBron was in foul trouble which did not allow him to get in an offensive rhythm. In game 2 having 4 fouls, he probably didn't want to be aggressive at the end of the game by getting an offensive foul. Also defensively in the 4th quarter in which he could have help close out Dallas, he seemed to not play his usual tough defense in order to stay out of foul trouble. Also, as Jason Terry suggested, he could have fatigued throughout the series playing an average 45 plus minutes a night (More than any other player in the Finals). He still should have been more aggressive on both ends of the court because he hadn't gotten his 5th foul yet. In game 3 he appeared to become even more passive after celebrating a Dwyane Wade 3-pointer in front of the Dallas bench. Jason Terry took notice and LeBron was not the same the rest of the series. It just seemed like LeBron shrank after Terry's comments about not being able to chase him around for 7 games and for

DeShawn Stevenson saying that LeBron checked out of game 4 when Miami could have taken a 3 to 1 series lead. How can he score just 8 points in any game let alone a crucial game 4 in Dallas? This is where everyone started calling LeBron a choke artist and that he shrinks in big games. The team as a whole played terrible in game 5. LeBron showed a little more assertiveness offensively in this game but it was too late. The Heat had blown games 2 and 4 and put the series in Dallas' hands. Dallas headed to Miami and won the series in 6 games, finishing off the Heat the way they did in game 5.

Also, I have to admit that it did appear at times, LeBron did not want the ball. How could he be devastating in the clutch, finishing off games in Boston and Chicago and not in Dallas? Another explanation is he could have just lost confidence in that he was unable to open up his outside shot, due to not being able to penetrate through the Dallas defense. I understand that he needs to develop a go-to move and not rely on dribble penetration dunks and layups that he's been accustomed to his entire career. He has a fadeaway/fallaway shot that he uses every once in a while that nobody seems to realize. I know because I have watched almost every game of his career. All he needs to do is practice, practice, practice……...until he perfects it just like Dirk Nowitzki, Larry Bird, Michael Jordan, and Kobe Bryant all have done. He also needs to humble himself and pound out hard practices on his low-post game. Call Hakeem Olajuwon if you have to! Kobe did a couple of years ago and look what happened to him, he won another Championship.

LeBron James took my advice (not literally) and practiced with Olajuwon in the summer of 2011. Hopefully this aspect of his game will improve greatly and his team will get over the top to win an NBA Championship. It appears in the middle of the 2012 season that LeBron has completely changed his game into a legitimate low-post player shooting around 55 percent. And as the season is winding down, in the eyes of many, he has not let up with his use of a low-post game. Like I have already mentioned in the beginning of the chapter, he always had the game he just didn't use it on a consistent basis because of the make-up of the team in Cleveland (having Zydrunas Ilgauskas and Anderson Varejao in the low-block). Let's just hope his post-game keeps improving throughout the years and into this season's playoffs because low-post scoring is what the Miami Heat need most in their second season going forward. In addition, he has taken the defensive side of his game to new heights proving that he can guard all five positions like no man before him. With his transformation now complete (I always knew he had this post-up ability) in his overall-game, playing more on the box and the ability to defend all five positions in 2012, added to his already impressive overall game, he should win his third MVP Award in four years, which would put his in a special class of the all-time greats of the game. Because every player who has won at least three MVP's other than Moses Malone, you could make the case, is a Top 5 player of all-time or at the very least a Top 7. After another MVP type season this year in 2012, LeBron will move up on the all-time list for greatest players ever and his legacy will grow enormously, once he starts winning championships, hopefully beginning this year! And, after 14 pages of writing up to the end of the 2012 season and right before the book was published, LeBron (who also won his 4th MVP award), Wade, Bosh and the rest of the Miami Heat just won consecutive NBA Championships in 2012 and 2013.

Career Totals

27.6 points, 7.3 rebs, 6.9 assists, 1.7 steals, 0.8 blocks, .490 FG%, .337 3FG%, .747 FT%

21,081 points, 5553 rebounds, 5302 assists, 1323 steals, 649 blocks, 1020 threes

Chris Paul

(Projected #14)

All-NBA First Team (3-times), All-Defensive First Team (3-times)

Assist Title (2-times), Steals Title (5-times), All-Star (6-times)

NBA Record: 5 Steals Title!

NBA Record: 108 straight games with a steal!

Chris Paul of the Los Angeles Clippers has the potential to finish his career as one of the top three point guards of all-time ... as he already has posted comparable numbers to other great point guards of the past. Paul put up one of the most impressive stat lines ever for a point guard in the 2008-09 season when he averaged **22.8 points**, **11 assists**, **5.5 rebounds**, and **2.8 steals** per game - and shot 50 percent from the field, 36.4 percent from three-point range, and 86.8 percent from the charity stripe. This ranks up there with Magic Johnson's best season. But what stands out most, is that he is the only man to lead the NBA in assists and steals in back-to-back years and is currently 3rd on the all-time list in career assists per game average behind only Magic and John Stockton. In the early part of the 2012 season at the time of this writing on C. Paul, I had these things to say: At 26 years old, he already has 3 steals titles which ties an NBA record shared by Michael Jordan, Allen Iverson and Alvin Robertson, and is on pace to win a record 4th steals title which would put him alone at the top all-time. After watching Paul for the past six seasons, I truly realize how special he is! He is not only one of the greats of all-time; he might be the greatest from the mental aspect of the game. It did appear he lost a step after his injury riddled season in 2009-10 when he suffered a torn meniscus in his left knee, but after watching him this past year and against the Los Angeles Lakers in the 2011 playoffs, he seemed really close to the way he played before the injury. Playing with a *killer instinct* and an *extreme will to win*, Paul single-handedly dominated Los Angeles, putting a first-round scare into Lakers fans by helping the Hornets extend the series to six games. Overall, Paul played at a higher level in the playoffs and especially from a shooting standpoint over Derrick Rose, who won MVP that season. Paul was the one playing like the MVP (many felt he should have been MVP in 2008 over Kobe Bryant after it appeared the voters waited until the last week of the season to decide their vote based on the team that finished first in the standings), outplaying Bryant and the rest of the Lakers. He looked like the old "CP3" during the 2011 season and especially in the playoffs against L.A.

Chris Paul appears to have regained *most* of his explosiveness that made him the best point guard in the NBA three seasons ago. He has the *uncanny* ability to stutter-step and change speeds as good as or better than anyone in the NBA today, and the *explosive* killer crossover to change direction going to the basket at will in the same way Derrick Rose, Russell Westbrook, Deron Williams, and Dwyane Wade all do. He doesn't dunk the way the others can but can finish equally as well. He can even do one better with unmatched skill by changing speeds of the dribble, stutter-stepping or drop-stepping shooting a fallaway over the outstretched arms of a contesting big man, or he can pass with upmost *precision* out to an open teammate on the perimeter or to a cutter darting to the basket. He reminds me of John Stockton, Steve Nash, and Jason Kidd in this way except Kidd didn't have Paul's jump shot, while Nash and Stockton could not explode and finish at the rim the way Paul can. Another special quality that Paul has is that he seldom makes a mistake with his decision making. He controls tempo and holds the dribble in search for the open layup or perfect pass to the open man who has the best chance to score. He does his craft as good as or better than any point guard in history. I would say he along with Steve Nash have the highest IQ in the game today as it is proven with his assist to turnover ratio at 4 to 1 - which happens to be the best for a superstar point guard in NBA history.

Christopher Emmanuel Paul was born on May 6th, 1985 in Lewisville, North Carolina and was drafted out of Wake Forest University by the New Orleans Hornets with the 4th pick overall of 2005 NBA Draft. At West Forsyth High School in Clemmons, N.C., despite never winning the state championship, Paul had a memorable senior year scoring **61 points** in the first game after his grandfather's death, before pulling himself out of the fourth quarter before the game was even over - more on this story later. In his two years in college, Paul led the Demon Deacons to the NCAA tournament twice and was named ACC All-Defensive Team honors. In his rookie season, the New Orleans Hornets played only three games in New Orleans and the rest in Oklahoma City due to Hurricane Katrina. Paul won the 2006 NBA Rookie of the Year award over college rival Deron Williams (who was drafted one slot ahead of him) after averaging 16.1 points and 7.8 assists. He also had his first triple-double of **24 points, 12 assists**, and **12 rebounds** on April 6th, but unfortunately the up-and-coming Hornets missed the playoffs. The impact he made around the sports world as the next great NBA point guard was acknowledged when he won the ESPY Award for "Best Break through Athlete."

In his second season, the Hornets played their home games in Oklahoma City but missed the playoffs partly due to Paul playing in only 64 games because of injury. The following season in 2007-08, Paul blossomed into a Superstar by averaging a *superb* **21.1 points**, **11.6 assists**, and **2.7 steals** - and won his first of two consecutive assist and steals titles. He also was named to the All-Star team for the first of five consecutive years to date and finished second in the MVP balloting to Kobe Bryant, assuming *primarily*, because the Lakers edged out the Hornets for best record in the conference. Preliminary consensus by the media went back and forth the last two months of the season making a case for both players for MVP. But from my eyes, it looked like the voters waited until the last week of the season before coming to a conclusion based on which team would finish with the best record in the standings. I believe Chris Paul was robbed of his first MVP award for the following reasons: As I described in the beginning of the book in Jordan's chapter, the MVP should be given to the best player statistically on a top four or five team *contending* to win a championship. Paul clearly was the MVP because he led the league in assists and steals, had the highest player efficiency rating, and because he meant more to his team in the same way Steve Nash and Derrick Rose did when they won the award. It is merely an *illusion* that Kobe meant more to his team the way Paul did before or after the acquisition of Pau Gasol. If anything, from what I remember after following the season extensively, Gasol was just as valuable to the Lakers the second half of the season and in the playoffs as Bryant. So in a way, you could say it was absolutely *ludicrous* for the voters to make up their mind based on a couple games at seasons end.

In the 2008 playoffs, Paul averaged **24.1 points, 11.3 assists, 4.9 rebounds**, and **2.3 steals** per game. In the first round, the Hornets eliminated the Dallas Mavericks in five games behind Paul's heroics. In his first playoff game, he scored **35 points including 24** in the second half, dished out 10 assists and had 4 steals. He also set a franchise record of **17 assists** in game two to give the Hornets a 2-0 series lead. After splitting the next two games, Paul put the *exclamation mark* on the Mavericks by winning game five at home in dramatic fashion 127-103. Paul finished with his first career triple-double in the playoffs with **24 points, 15 assists, and 11 rebounds**. In the Western Conference Semifinals, two premier guards in C. Paul and Tony Parker met head-to-head for the first time. After the two teams split the first six games with each team winning on its own home floor, the young Hornets lost game seven at home to a more experienced Spurs team. Not only was I disappointed that Paul lost to his point guard rival Parker in the playoffs, it was even more disappointing that he didn't face Kobe Bryant and the Los Angeles Lakers in the

Western Conference Finals after finishing second to him in the MVP voting. The following season, Paul had another stellar year leading the league in assists and steals for the second straight season and made First Team All-NBA for the first time. He also set an NBA record with a 106 games with at least one steal. But in the playoffs with no surprise, the seventh seed Hornets lost to the second seed Denver Nuggets in the first round in five games. With a rejuvenated Chauncey Billups leading the way coming over from the Detroit Pistons and with Carmelo Anthony and Nene' coming in to their own, I felt the Nuggets were good enough to not only beat the Hornets, but the Lakers in the Western Conference and the Orlando Magic in the NBA Finals, but it was not to be.

The following year, is when the Hornets and the basketball world held their breath when it was revealed that Paul had torn his meniscus in his left knee. With Paul playing in only 45 games due to injury, the Hornets missed the playoffs. In the 2010-11 season, Paul posted modest numbers coming off arthroscopic knee surgery averaging 15.9 points per game, 9.8 assists, and a league leading 2.4 steals that tied the all-time record for steals titles with three. With the uncertainty on whether Paul would ever regain the explosiveness he once had, he was now being tagged by the media as the second best point guard in the league to Deron Williams. During the regular season, people were questioning why Paul's scoring output was down from the previous seasons despite already knowing he had successful knee surgery. In one interview, Paul answered by saying, "I have enough scorers on the team and that my job is to distribute and score when my team needs me to." During the season, along with a lot of people, myself included, I wasn't sure Paul had regained the *entire* explosiveness he once had before the injury. But in the playoffs, CP3 erased all doubts by dominating the first four games of the first-round series against the Los Angeles Lakers - but unfortunately it wasn't enough as the Hornets succumbed in six games. For the series, Paul averaged **22 points**, **11.5 assists**, and **6.7 rebounds** per game, which was a little better overall than the 2008 playoffs before the knee injury. But what was even more impressive was that he shot 54.5 percent from the field, and 47.4 percent from three-point range. In game one, he had **33 points, 14 assists, 7 rebounds, and 4 steals** - and **27 points, 15 assists, 13 rebounds, and 2 steals** in game four to tie the series.

Prior to the 2011-12 season, Paul was unofficially traded to the Los Angeles Lakers in a three-team deal that would have sent Pau Gasol to the Rockets and Lamar Odom, Kevin Martin, Luis Scola, unproven Goran Dragic, and a 2012 first-round pick to the New Orleans Hornets. But after David Stern and the league (owner of the Hornets) nullified the trade because they felt it wasn't a fair deal, Paul was traded to the Los Angeles Clippers within a few days. Before the trade, in all likelihood, it appeared by most that Paul was definitely going to be traded to the New York Knicks or sign with them as a free agent at the end of the season. As I have already mentioned, being spot on with LeBron's decision to leave Cleveland, I was caught completely off guard when Paul accepted whole heartedly to play for the Clippers. While many people, especially in Laker Land, felt the trade was a complete joke after it was nullified by the league, I felt it was rectified for two reasons: The relevant one was the same as Stern's because the Hornets received the best player in Eric Gordon compared to any of the proposed players in the Laker deal. The Hornets also received Al-Farouq Aminu, Kris Kaman, and a 2012 first-round pick from the Clippers. As mentioned, Stern said they were not getting fair compensation. Just with that statement, case closed! And two, while many felt Stern was doing injustice to the Lakers organization; he actually made it better for the rest of the league in the long run. The new collective bargaining agreement in 2012 is designed to give small market teams a better chance to keep marquee players such as in the case with Kevin Durant of Oklahoma City and Dwight Howard in Orlando (Hopefully Howard stays in Orlando or joins another small market team without a big name star - but I guess that didn't happen). Even though Paul went to a big market to play with Blake Griffin (potentially one of the best big men in the game) it still brought parity to the league because the Los Angeles Clippers have been *cellar dwellers* since their existence.

When I heard about Chris Paul and the **61 points** he scored in a high school game after his grandfather's death at the age of 61 years old in a gang related incident, I realized even more what a *relentless* competitor Paul truly is. He displayed the ultimate drive to dominate the game of basketball from a scoring standpoint in honor of his grandfather and showed the class to take himself out of the game when the game was already decided. It also showed me, aside from being a pass-first point guard, he has the *competitive drive* to accomplish anything his mind desires, including dominating from the scoring aspect of the game, and with motivation to eventually win the NBA Championship sooner than you might expect. If Paul didn't pull himself out of the game he could have possibly scored 70 to 80 points with the sheer determination he had inside of him. Just to emphasize, he could even score at will playing in today's NBA game if he so chooses in the likes of Derrick Rose and Russell Westbrook. But Paul is the ultimate pass-first point guard just like the great Magic Johnson.

They always talk about Kobe Bryant having the competitive drive and killer instinct, but in my opinion, there might not be a player in the NBA outside of maybe Kobe himself, that is more competitive, and plays with more heart and killer instinct than Chris Paul. He may be a nice guy off the court, but on the court, he is a cold-blooded assassin, that will do whatever it takes to win at all cost, whether it be scoring, controlling tempo, making the perfect pass, or on the defensive end getting a lot of steals with his cat-like quick instincts. That's why he made the right choice to play for the Los Angeles Clippers over demanding to go elsewhere and play for an organization that doesn't have a clubhouse full of players with good camaraderie. Hopefully, his persona will be a big contribution to the rest of the team as they set their sights on their quest to bring the franchise it first NBA championship in the coming years.

Though it will be tough to see anyone amass what Oscar Robertson did statistically. Chris Paul with his overall game including on the defensive end, should go down as one of the great point guards of all-time barring another major injury. He is the complete package that can score, rebound (for being only six feet tall), pass and defend. In fact, he might potentially be the best offensive/defensive point guard in NBA history even over all-time greats in Oscar, Magic, John Stockton, Bob Cousy, Isiah Thomas, and Gary Payton. With 2 assists and 5 steals titles already under his belt, if he can win a couple championships in the near future with Blake Griffin and the Los Angeles Clippers, Chris Paul will more than likely go down as the third or fourth best point guard in NBA history.

Career Totals

18.6 points, 9.8 assists, 4.4 rebounds, 2.4 steals, .473 FG%, .356 3FG%, .858 FT%

10,311 points, 5449 assists, 2426 rebounds, 1331 steals, 534 threes

Dwyane Wade

(Projected #15)

Scoring Title (1-time), All-NBA First Team (2-times)

NBA Championships (3), Finals MVP (1-time), All-Star (9-times)

Also featuring: David Thompson

Dwyane Wade of the Miami Heat is one of the most talented 2-guards to ever come into the NBA. But, I don't think anyone envisioned him to be this good though! After blossoming in his first three seasons and by continuing to improve his game every year, I believe Wade is potentially one of the top four shooting guards ever, right up there with Michael Jordan, Jerry West, and Kobe Bryant. I think from a skill set he is second only to Jordan. His overall balance of scoring, rebounding, passing, and the *uncanny* ability to steal the ball and block an opponent's shot with his *explosive* leaping ability and *unmatched* timing may be the best we have in the NBA today, not only at the guard position but at any given position. There are perhaps only two reasons that can slow down Wade from becoming the second best shooting guard of all-time and they are: He missed his first season of college at Marquette due to the NCAA's violation of Proposition 48 to where his pro career began at 21 when some other players in his draft class started at 18 or 19 years of age, and because he has been *injury prone* most of his career. He should have been nicknamed "Superman" or "Batman," instead of "Flash" given to him by Shaquille O'Neal. I know D-Wade is quick, but he is a lot more than just quick. He might be the most explosive player in the league. With his *jaw-dropping* strength and speed, quick and explosive leaping ability, incredible change of direction on dribble penetration, and spin moves in the post, make him almost impossible to defend in the paint as well as from the perimeter. His signature move off dribble penetration is his deadly "1-2 Step" that confuses the defender into which direction he will attack the basket similar to the "Euro Step" or Killer Crossover dribble that most great ball-handlers utilize. Until the last couple of seasons where he has been battling injuries, he was among, if not one of the greatest player in the league right up there with LeBron James, Chris Paul, Kevin Durant, and Dwight Howard.

Over the years, Wade has played in the shadow of Kobe Bryant (who plays in a big NBA market of Los Angeles) his first seven seasons. Now with this *Super Team* the Miami Heat put together in 2010, he is sure to get all the recognition he deserves, providing LeBron does not steal the spot light in a big way. Aside from being a great scorer and dribble penetrator, Wade has an outstanding mid-range jump shot and fadeaway, albeit not quite as good as Bryant's but he makes up for it with easy points in the paint (off dribble penetration and with a short jump hook) and from the free-throw line. And even though his shooting stroke is not as pure, he is equally the clutch shooter that Kobe is, as he has proven throughout his playoff career and especially in the 2006 NBA Finals. The pump fake he often uses off the "double-pivot" before releasing his deadly fadeaway, he also uses to freeze his opponent before detonating to the basket. So while Kobe might be a little more effective and flashier to some people from the perimeter with his outside shooting, Wade is the more effective and flashier player off dribble penetration. As I have already described above, Wade can maneuver and get to any point on the court with the speed and quickness of a point guard. In addition, when healthy, his crossover dribble when attacking the basket has always been a notch above Bryant's. With his explosive first step off the dribble, he is without a doubt, the best shooting guard at finishing at the hoop since Jordan! Of course, if Wade continues to have injury plagued seasons, Bryant will most certainly go down as the better player when it is all said and done.

His rebounding, shot blocking, and the uncanny ability to suffocate and steal the ball from an opponent, is also the best I have seen at his position since Jordan. He is so quick off his feet; he is able to block seven-foot centers occasionally as he did recently, during the 2011 regular season and throughout the playoffs. Look at what he did in the NBA Finals against Tyson Chandler, timing his blocks in one-on-one situations. In player comparisons: The difference between Wade and other players such as LeBron, Kobe and Durant, is when they block a big man's shot, it is usually coming weak side off the ball or from behind on the fast break. On the other hand, D-Wade at only six-foot-four, is so quick and explosive, he is able to time and block a players shot in a *one-on-one* situation facing them straight up or man up (which ever term you prefer). As a passer, Wade has been a great *facilitator* with high assists numbers his entire career until this year when LeBron took over the duty. At the time of this writing, if you look at his career assists average for all-time great shooting guards up until the last couple of years, he ranked second only to Jerry West at 6.1 assists per game and ahead of Michael and Kobe. Defensively, Wade is often overlooked, because I have watched him constantly every game that I could, and he is a *mongoose* on defense. In fact, I emailed Wade personally (although I didn't get a response) and told him his nickname should be the "Black Mongoose" because of the ultra-quick and often suffocating defense he plays (like when a mongoose clamps down on a snakes neck), locking-up opposing two-guards, and especially when he had locked down Kobe on Christmas Day in 2010, stealing the ball from him in the closing minutes and then blocking his three-point shot on the last possession of the game. I have a copyright on the nickname, so if he ever decides to go with it, I should get the credit! I believe Bryant has been selected to the All-Defensive First Team the last two times over Wade based on reputation over anything else, as Kobe had been injured a couple of years back forcing him to play fewer minutes to conserve his legs for the upcoming years.

Dwyane Wade reminds me a lot of Superstar center fielder Eric Davis, who played for the Cincinnati Reds back in the late 1980s and early 1990s that used to crash into the center field fence all the time chasing down fly balls only to come up limp or injured, and causing his career to be shortened. Wade attacks the rim, like no other in the NBA, the way Eric Davis attacked the baseball, diving for line drives or crashing into the center field fence to rob hitters of home runs. He is relentless at getting to the basket and drawing hard fouls, often resulting in banged up limbs - shoulders, back, legs, knees, hands and wrists. Fortunately for Wade, in the case he is hampered along the way with more injuries, he has established himself enough statistically to eventually make it into the Hall of Fame. He should have no problem getting to 20,000 points, if not 25,000. And if he can avoid major injuries for the remaining part of his career, he might challenge West and Kobe as the second greatest two-guard of all-time.

Out of the 29 players in NBA history (at the time of this writing) to score 20,000 points only 2 (that are eligible) *are not* in the Hall of Fame (Mitch Richmond & Tom Chambers). 20,000 points should get you into the Hall and that's why Wade and hopefully two other great players in Vince Carter and Tracy McGrady, should make the Hall of Fame especially if they should reach that plateau - because "Vinsanity" and "T-Mac" were the third and fourth best shooting guards of their era next to Kobe Bryant and Allen Iverson.

Wade is also on pace to finish with 25,000 points, 6,000 assists, and 5000 rebounds which would put him atop the all-time greats. He won an NBA Championship in 2006, his 3rd season in the league while winning Finals MVP honors. He also posted one of the greatest, most dominant NBA Finals performances in history finishing with a scoring average of **34.7 points** during the six-game series. It was the best scoring average since Jordan in the 1990s and better than any of Kobe's outputs in seven Finals appearances. His **33.8 player efficiency rating** by ESPN.com was the highest in the Finals since the ABA-NBA merger in 1976. Even after this seasons debacle losing to the Dallas Mavericks in the 2011 NBA Finals, Wade *just recently* had the 3rd highest scoring average at **30.6 points** per game in NBA history behind only Rick Barry and Michael Jordan! As of the end of the 2011 season, he also had the higher career scoring and assists average over Kobe while just entering his prime (25.4 to 25.3 and 6.1 to 4.8). Wade became the second player to record at least **50 points and 15 assists** or more in a game since Wilt Chamberlain did it in 1968. But the statistic that stands out most is that Dwyane at 6-foot-4 ranks first in blocked shots per game for all-time great shooting guards in NBA history, while Jordan ranks a close second. And, his overall defense *statistically*, at the two-guard position, ranks second only to Jordan.

Dwyane Tyrone Wade Jr. was born on January 17th, 1982 on the south side of Chicago and was drafted by the Miami Heat, 5th pick overall of the 2003 NBA Draft out of Marquette University. Growing up as a child, Wade idolized Michael Jordan and has patterned his game after him, but wears the #3 because it represents the Holy Trinity. At Harold L. Richards High School, Wade led the team to the title game and set school records in total points at 676 and steals at 106. In 2002-03 season, at Marquette he led the team to its first Final Four since the school won the National Championship in 1977, and was named All-American First Team by the Associated Press. During the NCAA tournament against the top seeded Kentucky Wildcats, Wade made his name known by recording only the fourth triple-double in NCAA tournament history finishing with **39 points, 11 rebounds, and 11 assists.** Although, he did have a modest rookie season in 2003-04 playing in the shadow of hyped up Superstars to be in LeBron James and Carmelo Anthony, finishing with a 16.2 scoring average on 46.5 percent shooting, and leading the Miami Heat into the playoffs with a 42-40 regular season record. Wade showed his brilliance early on in his young career by hitting the game-winning shot in game one of the first-round series against the New Orleans Hornets, in which they went on to win in seven games. But unfortunately, they lost a hard-fought series to the sixty-one win Indiana Pacers team in the second round.

The next year, the Miami Heat traded Caron Butler, Lamar Odom, and Brian Grant to the Los Angeles Lakers for Shaquille O'Neal. With the most unstoppable physical force in the NBA and a dramatically improved D-Wade, the Heat became titles contenders instantly finishing with a record of 59-23 and sweeping the Nets and Washington Wizards in the first two rounds of the playoffs, before losing to the reigning champion Pistons in the Eastern Conference Finals. Wade blossomed into an All-Star averaging 24.1 points in the regular season and a superb 27.4 points in the playoffs to go along with 5.7 rebounds and 6.6 assists. In the 2005-06 season, the Heat finished the season with a 50-32 record despite battling injuries and having a lack of chemistry, but played on another level at the end of the season and in the playoffs. In their title run, they finished off the Chicago Bulls with Wade badly injuring his hip in game five, and did the same to the New Jersey Nets and the Detroit Pistons, all in six-game series before beating the Dallas Mavericks in the 2006 NBA Finals. After falling behind two games to zero, D-Wade became the ultimate Superstar in *Jordan-esque* fashion by sweeping three straight games at home and finishing off the disheartened Mavericks in game six in Dallas. Wade easily took home NBA Finals MVP. This was the greatest Finals performance that I have ever witnessed in over four decades of watching NBA Basketball. Wade was absolutely *relentless* at dominating and attacking the basket at will thereby *scorching* Dallas with 2 40-point games and finishing with an eye-popping 34.7 scoring average (and 39.3 in the four wins) to go along with 7.8 rebounds per game and 2.6 steals for the series. He also went to the free-throw line an astounding but questionable 97 times. That's an average of 16 free throws a game. It may sound absurd even with the recent rule change for hand-checking, but that's how dominate D-Wade was. As a result, Wade became the number one selling jersey in the NBA for almost two years. And maybe his biggest honor of all that season, was when he won "Sportsman of the Year" by Sports Illustrated in 2006 after leading the Miami Heat to their first NBA Championship.

In the 2006-07 season, the Heat were dealt a *double-blow* when Shaq injured his knee in November causing him to miss thirty-five games, and Wade *scared* to death the organization by dislocating his left shoulder going for a steal in a game against Shane Battier, only to then be carried off in a wheel chair. Despite missing thirty-one games during the regular season, Wade made a go at it in the playoffs with a black sleeve on his shoulder but was not nearly a hundred percent. Even with a healthy Shaquille O'Neal leading the way, the Heat got swept in four games to the Chicago Bulls. After another injury riddled season and with multiple confrontations with Pat Riley, the very next season, Shaq was traded for Shawn Marion and Marcus Banks. But Wade played again in only 51 regular season games due to the games missed recovering from the shoulder and knee surgery the year before. With ailing knee pain and because the Heat had one of the worst records in the NBA, Riley held him out of the last 21 games of the season, as the Heat missed the playoffs for the first and only time since Wade has been with the franchise. In 2008-09 season, Wade had his best individual season of his career averaging a **career-high 30.2 points**, **7.5 assists**, **2.2 steals**, and **1.3 blocks** per game. He also won the scoring title and was named to the All-NBA First Team and All-Defensive Second Team for the first of two straight seasons.

In addition, like his current and fellow teammate LeBron James, Wade has had monster scoring games throughout his career that included great all-around numbers. There are a lot of great scorers in NBA history including Kobe Bryant and Allen Iverson whose monster games didn't fill the stat sheet in all the relevant categories outside of let's say just scoring. In fact, other than LeBron and D-Wade, no other current player combines scoring, rebounding, assists, steals, and blocked shots better than these two on a nightly basis or I would have listed them throughout this book. Here are six *monster* performances from Dwyane Wade the year he won the scoring title in 2009:

vs. the New York Knicks on Apr. 12th   **55 points, 9 rebounds, 4 assists**

- career-high 6-threes (50 pts.- 3 qrts.)

vs. the Utah Jazz on March 12th	**50 points, 5 rebounds, 5 assists**
at the Orlando Magic on Feb. 22nd	**50 points, 10 rebounds, 9 assists, 4 steals, 2 blocks**
vs. the Chicago Bulls on March 9th	**48 points, 12 assists, 6 rebounds, 4 steals, 3 blocks**
vs. the New York Knicks on Feb. 28th	**46 points, 10 rebounds, 8 assists, 4 steals, 3 blocks**
vs. the Cleveland Cavs on March 2nd	**41 points, 9 assists, 7 rebounds, 7 steals**

After his **35-point, 16-assist, 6-rebound** game on March 4th at home against Shaquille O'Neal and the Phoenix Suns and his **31-point, 16-assist, and 7-rebound** game Feb. 24th at home against the Detroit Pistons, Wade became the first Miami Heat player to record 2 30-point, 15-assist games in a career.

As a Wade admirer, after the career threatening injury, I was worried that he might never be the same. If his career had taken a dive, it would have been for the right reasons unlike the great **David Thompson** whose career was cut short primarily from what he did off the court. Because we live in today's era, it is easy to compare Wade to Jordan and Kobe, but in retrospect, Wade may have been (in terms of *physical comparisons)*, perhaps ahead of Bryant and closer to Thompson (during his prime), beginning with the fact both were listed at six-foot-four with explosive leaping ability. Listed as a guard/forward, with his 44 to 48 inch vertical leap earning him the nickname "Skywalker," Thompson was nearly as explosive jumping *vertically* as Jordan and Wade and definitely more than Kobe. But was he as skilled laterally, blessed to be able to incorporate *devastating* crossover dribbles and with the ability to finish with an *obscene* acrobatic layup like the other three? I would have to say, probably not!

David O'Neil Thompson was born on July 13th, 1954 in Shelby, North Carolina and attended Crest Senior High School. In college at North Carolina State University he averaged 35.6 points and 13.6 rebounds while playing on the freshman team. In his sophomore year, he averaged 24.7 points and 8.1 rebounds per game, and led the team to a 27-0 season in 1973. By his junior year, he led the team to the 1974 NCAA Championship over Bill Walton and the reigning champion UCLA Bruins. He was also named Final Four Most Outstanding Player and AP Player of the Year. Because other great teams of the past did not win their conference championships including that season's Maryland Terrapins, the following season, the NCAA decided to expand the tournament for teams other than the league champions. To cap off a brilliant college career, Thompson averaged an astounding 29.9 points and 8.2 rebounds per game his senior year, and was named to the All-America First Team for the third consecutive season. He was also named AP Player of the Year for the second straight year and NCAA College

Player of the Year in 1975. Thompson was then selected with the 1st pick overall of the 1975 NBA Draft by the Atlanta Hawks and by the Virginia Squires of the ABA. After foregoing both teams, he signed with the Denver Nuggets of the ABA. In his first season, he averaged 26 points, 6.3 rebounds, 3.7 assists, 1.6 steals, and 1.2 blocks per game - and won the ABA Rookie of the Year. He also finished second to Dr. J. in the slam dunk contest, but won the All-Star game MVP that was held at McNichols Sports Arena in Denver. He also led the team to the Finals where they would lose to the Kentucky Colonels. The following season, behind the impact that Thompson had *instilled* in Denver as a franchise, the Nuggets were one of four ABA teams that merged in to the NBA.

In player comparisons:

The next three seasons with the franchise, at a couple of months shy of his 23rd, 24th, and 25th birthday, Thompson would have the best seasons of his career. Because his career was cut short due to off-the-court drug issues and injuries, this is all we have to go on in comparisons to Wade, Bryant, and Jordan as the top athletic two-guards for any three-year period, ending within four and a half months of the age of 25. By all means, this three-year period does not prove Thompson was a top 50 player of all-time, because I left him off the list. But, it does illustrate what could have been for David Thompson if he had extended his playing career. With the chart down below, it also helps my case for Dwyane as potentially becoming the second best shooting guard of all-time, if he can avoid or sustain major injuries beginning this current season. His overall career statistical comparisons have already been presented in Jerry West's chapter for greatest shooting guards ever. Keep in mind, Wade's best season (most likely efficiency wise) could come within the next three years, but may be overlooked because he will be sharing the points, rebounds, and assists with teammates LeBron James and Chris Bosh. And his steals and blocks could actually go up as well with the help of having a great team defensive scheme. Ultimately, if Wade can win two, three, or four more championships, this will obviously close the gap with Kobe Bryant in terms of team success.

Thomp: 1977-79   25.7 points, 3.9 assists, 4.2 rebounds, 1.2 steals, 1.0 block, 51 FG%

Wade: 2005-07   26.1 points, 6.9 assists, 5.0 rebounds, 1.9 steals, 0.9 blocks, 49 FG%

Bryant: 2001-03   27.9 points, 5.5 assists, 6.1 rebounds, 1.8 steals, 0.6 blocks, 46 FG%

Iverson: 1998-00   25.4 points, 5.3 assists, 4.0 rebounds, 2.2 steals, 0.2 blocks, 43 FG%

Jordan: 1985-87   34.7 points, 5.2 assists, 5.2 rebounds, 3.0 steals, 1.3 blocks, 52 FG%

Because I think so highly of David Thompson, I decided to include him in the book extensively. And as you can see it was fitting to include him in Wade's chapter, because of his skill set and Thompson's best three years resemble Wade's three seasons at nearly the same age.

Prior to the 2008-09 season with the rehabilitation to his shoulder and knee at almost full strength, D-Wade was primed and ready for the summer Olympics. Behind the best group of players since the original U.S. Dream Team in 1992, the "Redeem Team" with Wade, LeBron, Kobe, Paul, and Howard - won the 2008 Gold Medal by going 8 and 0 in the tournament while blowing out the majority of the their opponents. I am not a fan of statistical data in the NBA All-Star game (particularly in this day and age) because it is an exhibition with the lack of all-out competitiveness (particularly on the defensive end) except for maybe in the 4th quarter, and that's why I seldom mention All-Star statistics or numbers throughout this book. Other than the All-Star selections, the game itself has very little influence on my elite rankings. However, I do highly consider the Olympic contributions and statistics because they are played with true competitiveness although with a natural *exhibition* style due the overall talent and athleticism of Team USA, resulting in front running leads in games and blowouts. I watched every game in its entirety and printed the box score of the composite total of all 8 games. A lot of people thought Wade was the MVP of the Olympic Team because he led the team in scoring. He did, but only by a slim margin of 16.0 to LeBron's 15.5 and Kobe's 15.0. In my opinion Wade and LeBron were co-MVP. Why does this all matter? Because it *helps* determine which players are the best in the league today.

My current top 7 player rankings were almost identical to ESPN's prior to the 2011-12 season posted during the NBA Lockout.

ESPN Rankings: LeBron James, Dwight Howard, Dwyane Wade, Chris Paul, Dirk Nowitzki, Kevin Durant, and Kobe Bryant

My Rankings: LeBron James, Dwyane Wade, Dwight Howard, Chris Paul, Kevin Durant, Dirk Nowitzki, and Kobe Bryant

Dwyane Wade had the best season of his career the following year he won gold while posting ridiculous numbers of 30.2 points a game, 7.5 assists, 5.0 rebounds, 2.2 steals, and 1.3 blocks - on 49 percent shooting, and winning his first scoring title. Not only did he post great all-around numbers in the Olympics, he had the best all-around season at the shooting guard position since Michael Jordan. So you can tell that the biggest star shines among the other stars and that's what Wade did! D-Wade and LeBron had the best statistics on the best team in the world at the Summer Olympics. In player comparisons, I know Kobe had the big clutch three-pointer in the gold medal game against Spain and played great defense on the other team's best player, but everyone else also pulled through on both ends of the court throughout the tournament. Bryant's shooting was subpar compared to many of the players on Team USA. At 30 years old, he may have had too many miles on his legs, thereby settling for jump shots, or maybe he just didn't want to attack the basket like a lot of the players did. He shot 46 percent from the field (17 of 53 on threes for 32%) and his buddy Carmelo Anthony shot 42 percent (14 of 37 on threes for 38%) compared to an *astronomical* 67 percent from the field for Wade (8 of 17 on threes for 47%), and 60 percent for James (13 of 28 on threes for 46%). I know in International play the three-point line is 21'9" compared to 23'9" in the NBA, but that should make it easier for everyone to shoot a higher percentage. For Team USA, LeBron finished the tournament ranked first in steals and blocks, second in points and assists, and third in rebounds while Wade finished first in scoring, second in steals and in field goal percentage. It is no coincidence that LeBron and Wade were ranked 1st and 3rd on ESPN's player rankings for 2011 and Kobe and Carmelo were ranked 7th and 12th respectively.

Wade followed up the 2009 season with a terrific 2010 season, particularly in the five games in the first round of the playoffs against the mighty Boston Celtics. Despite the loss in what seemed like a very long series, Wade played like he did back in 2006, single-handedly carry the team and its offensive scoring punch. For the series, Wade torched the Celtics averaging **33.2 points, 6.8 assists, 5.6 rebounds**, and shot 56 percent from the field - and 40 percent from three-point range. At that point in time, both Wade and LeBron-led teams were getting beat up in the playoffs by both the Celtics of the present and from the Pistons in previous seasons past, prompting two good friends to team up in Miami the following year to form potentially the greatest dynamic dual in NBA history and seize control over the NBA's elite teams in the Los Angeles Lakers and Boston Celtics, which at the time were recently stock piling stars and superstars. The Miami Heat followed suit by adding both LeBron James and Chris Bosh, but took inaccurate criticism from fans and media around the country who felt the two most athletic Superstars of our time took the easy way out instead of fighting and battling it out against one another the way Magic Johnson, Larry Bird, Isiah Thomas, and Michael Jordan all had done. To clarify this *misconception*, between LeBron and Wade - if one of the two were beating the other in the playoffs over the years, it would be like Jordan joining Isiah in Detroit or Bird in Boston for example, in order to win his first championship. That's not even close to what happened in Miami. Jordan was losing almost every season to either the Pistons or the Celtics before he finally got over the hump to win a championship. While a lot of the great teams including Jordan's Bulls, Bird's Celtics, and Magic's Lakers built a championship team through the draft, the Heat did it through free-agency or sign-and-trade the way the Celtics did in 2008 with Kevin Garnett and Ray Allen teaming up with Paul Pierce. Even Kobe Bryant, the second time around, won both championships via a *lopsided* trade for Pau Gasol. In fact, for good measure, LeBron and Wade never faced each other in the playoffs. Of course, the way the Heat went about celebrating their Superstar players coming together added negative criticism to the notion that the LeBron, Wade and Chris

Bosh took the easy way out teaming up in Miami. If anything, it was a brilliant move on all three of them in their quest to build the NBA's next great dynasty.

And, after a slow start to the 2010-11 season, due to a host of injuries that lingered into the playoffs, Wade returned to prominence in the 2011 NBA Finals where he carried the Miami Heat to a 2 to 1 series advantage before falling to the Dallas Mavericks in six games. For the series, Wade averaged 26.5 points, seven rebounds and 5.2 assists, on 54.6 percent shooting - bringing his career scoring average in the NBA Finals down a bit to 30.6 per game. After one year of experience playing together already under their belt, and after learning to fail at the highest level which is the NBA Finals, with the new "Big Three" in Wade, LeBron and Bosh now in their prime, history shows that the Heat will return to the big stage and win it all next season. And, if and when that happens as I have described in LeBron's chapter, D-Wade can play at the end of games as the *designated closer* to improve the team chemistry. If Wade should relinquish that title or defer to LeBron as the go-to-guy on the team, it will most likely be because James has earned the right with his stellar play every season, is the younger player by over two and a half years, and is almost always injury free compared to Wade who's usually playing *banged-up* most of the time. But all in all, both players can dominate the game (in all aspects including scoring), at any point throughout all forty-eight minutes, at the end of games, and still co-exist like we have seen just recently. And, if Wade can get anywhere close to 100 percent healthy someday, despite all the injuries he has been through, LeBron and Wade should remain a devastating combination (dynamic dual) for years to come resulting in the Miami Heat winning multiple championships. If Dwyane Wade was not the best player in the NBA before the last couple of years than he was really close. If he can stay injury free for the last two or three years of his prime and win a few more championships (which would put him close to Kobe Bryant's five), he still has an outside chance to go down as the second best two-guard of all-time!

Career Totals

24.7 points, 5.1 rebs, 6.1 assists, 1.8 steals, 1.0 block, .489 FG%, .289 3FG%, .767 FT%

16453 points, 3364 rebounds, 4049 assists, 1183 steals, 667 blocks, 341 threes

Kevin Durant

(Projected #16)

Scoring Title (3-times), All-Star (4-times)

All-NBA First Team (4-times)

NBA Record: youngest to win a Scoring Title

and back-to-back-to-back Scoring Titles!

Also featuring: Russell Westbrook

Kevin Durant of the Oklahoma City Thunder could be the purest scorer to come into the NBA since Michael Jordan. The young *phenom* has already won two scoring titles back-to-back in 2010 and 2011, becoming the youngest in NBA history to do so. And he is also well on his way to winning at least four or five scoring titles or more, which would put him third on the all-time list behind Jordan's 10 and Wilt Chamberlain's 7, and would most likely put him past George Gervin and Allen Iverson who have 4 scoring titles each, before his career is over. What makes Durant so special at the young age of 23 is that he has the athleticism and scoring ability of Michael Jordan, Kobe Bryant, Dwyane Wade, and LeBron James and at the same time, the pure shooting of a Larry Bird, Dirk Nowitzki, Reggie Miller, and Ray Allen. And that's a scary thought for a guy listed at six-feet-nine (who may be closer to 6-feet-11), and still hasn't added any muscle so far, being in the league only 4 years. His style and length reminds me of the great George Gervin, but from a shooting and statistical standpoint, more like the great Rick Barry who ranks 12th in this book. Both have averaged 30 points in a season while shooting close to 90 percent from the free-throw line. There was no three-point line until it was inaugurated for 1979-80 season, the last year of Barry's career. Durant also produces great ball-handling skills for a player his size, where he often explodes off the dribble to the basket for an easy layup or slam dunk. It is truly amazing watching Kevin Durant elevate on his dunks! With a seven-foot-five wing span, when he comes swooping in over an opponent for a hammer-dunk, it is jaw-dropping impressive. It leaves you in awe in the same way LeBron, D-Wade, Blake Griffin, Vince Carter, or any other high-flyer throws down a thunderous dunk. Because players have to *honor* his deadly outside shot, the lane often becomes wide open, which enables him to blow past defenders leaving them in their tracks. Being tall and athletic, Durant is an outstanding rebounder and shot blocker for a perimeter player. Overall, he is becoming an excellent defender, with his quick hands that enable him to get a lot of steals, and with his enormous length allowing him to get a hand on a shooter to block the shot. Aside from not yet having developed a low-post game, if there is a weakness in his overall game, it is from the passing aspect. He needs to work on dribble penetration and kick or finding the open man cutting to the basket instead of holding the ball too long before passing it around the perimeter. His 2.7 career assists per game average for the first four years he played in the league, was among the lowest at the time of any superstar small forward including Carmelo Anthony whose was at 3.1 per game. I know Kevin is a shooter first, but I think he needs to get his career assist average around 4.0 per game to be ranked up there with the all-time greats. And, so far the past couple of seasons, he is averaging over three assists per game.

Kevin Wayne Durant was born on September 29th, 1988 in Washington, D.C. As a youth, he won many championships under AAU coach Charles Craig who was murdered at the age of 35. Ever since then, Durant wears number 35 in honor of his deceased mentor. In high school at Montrose Christian Academy, as a senior, Durant led the team in scoring and steals, and was named the Washington Post All-Met Player of the Year. In college, Durant played one season at the University of Texas where he would average a lofty 25.8 points and 11.8 rebounds per game. He also became the first freshman in NCAA history to be named National College Player of the Year in 2007. ESPN analyst Dick Vitale gave high praise to Durant saying he is the "most prolific offensive skilled big perimeter player I've witnessed in many a year" and compared him to Dirk Nowitzki, Kevin Garnett and Tracy McGrady.

Durant was selected with the 2nd pick overall of the 2007 NBA Draft by the Seattle SuperSonics. In his first season, he averaged 20.3 points and won the NBA Rookie of the Year award. In his second season, the franchise would move to Oklahoma City where they would change their name from the Sonics to the Thunder. Durant's scoring increased significantly to 25.3 points while his rebounding improved to 6.5 per game, but the Thunder missed the playoffs for the second year in row. In the 2009-10 season, Durant would become the youngest man in NBA history to win the scoring title at **30.1 points** per game. Oklahoma City won 50 games and set a franchise record by increasing their win total by 27 games. In the first round of the playoffs, the eighth seeded Thunder lost the first two games on the road against the Los Angeles Lakers despite Durant's magnificent play, scoring 24 points in his first playoff game and 32 in a competitive game two loss 95-92. The young Thunder would take advantage of their home court and win the next two games with Durant having scoring games of 29 and 22 points. After getting blown out in game five in L.A., the Thunder would rebound and battle to the very end only to lose game six in heartbreak fashion at home 95-94. Before the series, I felt the Thunder had a real good chance to pull the upset, because all the playoff teams in the Western Conference were evenly matched from top to bottom while finishing only a few games apart in the standings.

In the 2011 season, Durant would win his second consecutive scoring title at **27.7 points** per game (and 3rd consecutive the year after at **30 points** per game) and the Thunder finished with a 55-27 record. The young and talented squad that included Russell Westbrook, James Harden, Jeff Green, and Serge Ibaka had improved from the season before simply because the core groups of players were in their second, third, and fourth season playing together. But midway through the season, the Thunder felt they needed another big man to compete with the other Western Conference Powers, particularly the Los Angeles Lakers and Dallas Mavericks, so they then traded one of their young core players in Jeff Green and veteran Nenad Krstic to the Boston Celtics for Kendrick Perkins to solidify the interior. At that point, Oklahoma City now felt they featured a team that had a legitimate shot at winning a championship. Westbrook came into his own as an elite point guard and Harden emerged as a super sixth man, while Ibaka continued to blossom into one of the better defensive forward/centers in the league. He has also improved his midrange jump shot that has come to fruition this season in 2012 and into the playoffs.

As the fourth seed in the playoffs, the Thunder made quick work of the Denver Nuggets winning in the first round in five games. As good as the Thunder were, I courageously picked the Nuggets to win the series in seven games based on the way they were playing going into the playoffs and because they were a deep veteran team that got even deeper when they traded Carmelo Anthony at the All-Star Break. In the conference semifinals, the Thunder ran into another hot team in the Memphis Grizzlies that were coming off a masterful series themselves. They had just defeated the number one seed San Antonio Spurs in one of the great upsets in playoff history. The Grizzlies featured one of the best young teams in the league that included all-star forward Zack Randolph, center Marc Gasol and Mike Conley who reminded me of a young Tony Parker. If Conley can someday develop as scorer and score at will in the painted area the way Parker does with perhaps explosive quickness and a variety of spins moves, he might end up becoming the better player - because so far, Conley is the better pure shooter, three-point shooter, and defensive player. In comparisons to Westbrook, Conley is not quite at that level yet and may never be with all the *ridiculous* new-age point guard talent that is coming into the league.

Russell Westbrook like Derrick Rose is one of the most explosive point guards in the NBA today, able to dominate off dribble penetration finishing at the basket with an *ultra-athletic* layup or slam dunk, or by kicking to the open man. The difference between the two in this dominant aspect of their games is that Westbrook is a more *straight-to-the-basket* finisher where he can finish in front of the rim or with either hand on either side of the basket. Whereas Rose is the ultimate finisher in the NBA since Michael Jordan, Kobe Bryant, Dwyane Wade, and LeBron James - because he can *contort* his body going in all different directions in mid-flight and shoot from the most difficult of angles as I have described later in detail in Rose's chapter. Compared to Rose, Westbrook doesn't finish his shot with the same *degree of difficulty* when contested in the paint. When Rose finishes at the basket it doesn't matter if one, two, or even three players are contesting his shot, he still seems to squeeze the ball in the hoop or draw the foul, or both.

Westbrook is also an outstanding rebounder, an improved passer, and steady on the defensive end. His only noticeable weakness is a consistent jump shot that will come in time. Like Rose, it is scary to see what he might become! As I have mentioned in LeBron's chapter about James and Wade becoming the greatest dynamic dual of all-time, well Durant and Westbrook could eventually be in the conversation. I will never doubt Durant as the next great Superstar, but for some reason as great as Westbrook is and is going to be, I don't ever see the two making anyone's top 5 for greatest duals of all-time. And to put it on record, I am making this statement after the two of them scored **91 points (Durant had 51 and Westbrook had 40)** at home against the high scoring Denver Nuggets on February 19th, 2012.

When it is all said and done, I do believe Durant will end up somewhere near LeBron among the all-time greats, but providing Wade remains healthy the next few years in order to play at high level as he has done in the past and to build more life time statistics, I don't foresee Westbrook becoming nearly the player Dwyane Wade is on either end of the floor. Though, I do think he might be able to match Wade's explosiveness driving to the basket and his quickness on defense, I don't think he will ever be the great all-around scorer that Wade is. D-Wade has proven his ability to score from the interior like Michael Jordan and from the perimeter like Kobe Bryant and Michael with one of the best fadeaway shots ever. He also incorporates a sweet bank shot from either side of the court and a short jump hook from either hand at close range. Also, I don't think Westbrook can match Wade's defensive skills as the best steals/shot blocker combination at the guard position in NBA history.

Born on November 12th, 1988 in Long Beach, California, Russell Westbrook Jr. attended Leuzinger High School where he averaged 25.1 points, 8.7 rebounds, and 3.1 steals per game his senior year. He also scored a career-high 51 points in a game. After being overlooked by many top colleges, Westbrook was offered a scholarship to play for the UCLA Bruins where he was a backup to Darren Collison his freshman year. In his sophomore year, he averaged 12.7 points, 4.3 assists, and 3.9 rebounds per game as the Bruins advanced to the Final Four for the second straight year only to lose to Derrick Rose and the University of Memphis. He also scored 22 points in the game and was named Pac-10 Defensive Player of the Year. Westbrook was then selected with the 4th pick overall of the 2008 NBA Draft by the Seattle SuperSonics which moved to Oklahoma City prior to the 2008-09 season. After two solid seasons in the league, Westbrook blossomed into an All-NBA Second Teamer averaging 21.9 points, 8.2 assists, 4.6 rebounds, and 1.9 steals per game. After improving every year of his first three seasons, by the tender age of just twenty-three, he averaged over 23 points per game in 2012.

It seemed like the young Grizzlies peaked just at the right time and played at a whole different level in the playoffs vs. the regular season under new coach Lionel Hollins. The Grizzlies had taken control of the series by winning game one in Oklahoma City and game three at home before the Thunder battled back and won three of the last four to win the series in seven games. This was one of the most *competitive* series I have ever witnessed in a long time with game three going to overtime and game four going to triple overtime. But in the Western Conference Finals the Thunder would eventually lose to the Dallas Mavericks in five games. The *prognosis* in by eyes is that the Oklahoma City Thunder this year in 2012 has all the ingredients to win a championship except one. They don't have a superior offensive post-up scorer, even though Kevin Durant could eventually become that guy similar to what LeBron James is doing in Miami. Because Durant is great perimeter player like Kobe Bryant, he doesn't need to score down low all the time, just on occasion. But in the playoffs, when the game slows down, it is more ideal to have a designated low-post or high-post player to relieve the pressure for creating shots from the rest of the team. Most of the championship teams over the years have had that including the Mavericks of last year. Even though Dallas had great defensive centers that weren't great offensive post players, similar to Oklahoma City's Perkins and Ibaka (although Serge's jump shot is continuing to improve), they had Nowitzki dominating the *high-post* which is a version of posting up. Durant has to do the same thing to be successful in the playoffs against bigger opponents unless they acquire an offensive post-presence down the road. I am not saying they can't win a championship with this team, but it would be awfully difficult.

With that being said, as the season goes on, it looks like maybe they can as the Oklahoma City Thunder just swept the Dallas Mavericks in the first round of the 2012 playoffs and spanked the Los Angeles Lakers in the semifinals in five games. They also completed an improbable comeback down two games to none to the San Antonio Spurs in the Western Conference Finals winning four straight games to win the series in six. In a way, it really didn't make sense because the Spurs were the favorite, had the best record in the NBA and had tons of depth (more than in 2011), and were on the most historic winning streak in the regular season going into the playoffs in NBA history. They had just won 20 consecutive games including 10 straight in the playoffs and had the great Tim Duncan down low. So much for the Thunder not having any low-post scoring!

In player comparisons:

At the time of this writing in 2012 a lot of people wanted to say it was Durant's league now, because Kobe Bryant is getting closer to the age of 35 and is on the down side of his career, and Dwyane Wade has been injury prone most of his. And, prior to the end of the 2012 season, the public usually disregards LeBron James because he had not won a championship. LeBron, who had been to the NBA Finals twice, was still only 27 years old and racking up incredible Hall Of Fame numbers that will eventually put him in the class with Wilt Chamberlain, Kareem Abdul-Jabbar, and Michael Jordan when it is all said and done. He should amass 10,000 assists by the end of his career putting him right up there with John Stockton, Jason Kidd, Steve Nash, and Magic Johnson. Despite Durant's two scoring titles at the time, he was still behind LeBron James' pace of reaching scoring milestones of 5,000, 10,000, 15,000, 20,000 career points. LeBron who is as *durable* as iron, would have to get hurt at some point during his career in order for Durant to match him statistically. He himself would also have to stay injury free. LeBron could sit out the next two years and still be ahead of Kobe Bryant's pace of breaking Kareem Abdul-Jabbar's all-time scoring mark. Kevin Durant is also ahead of Kobe's pace to reach that milestone but behind LeBron. If Durant should somehow catch LeBron in scoring, he would fall short in almost all other major categories except for blocked shots.

Here is LeBron vs. Durant vs. Kobe their first 4 seasons in the league:

LeBron - 8439 points, 2102 rebounds, 2033 assists, 555 steals, 231 blocks at 22 years old;

Durant - 8128 points, 1986 rebounds, 842 assists, 374 steals, 288 blocks at 23 years old;

Kobe - 4240 points, 1054 rebounds, 803 assists, 301 steals, 175 blocks at 21 years old

As you can see, after their first four years in the league, LeBron who is one year younger than Durant, has Oscar Robertson type numbers, while Durant is close in the scoring and rebounding categories, and is ahead only in blocks. Durant does beat LeBron in efficiency statistics in 2 out of the 3 categories (36% 3FG to 33% and 88% FT to 74%), but LeBron leads in field goal percentage 48% to 46%. But as both players battle for supremacy in the 2012 NBA Finals, Durant could have beaten LeBron to a championship giving him bragging rights in head-to-head competition where it matters most, and for best player in the NBA. If that had happened, it wouldn't have changed LeBron's status as the best player in the NBA in my mind like it might have for the most of you, because

LeBron is now a 4-time MVP proving his dominance in every aspect of the game, including dominating the paint off dribble penetration, rebounding, passing, and on defense. Durant is also great in all those aspects but is only dominant thus far as a scorer/shooter as he has proven winning three consecutive scoring titles to date. Although, as a testament to Durant's greatness already, Kobe Bryant just recently said that Durant is him at six-feet-eleven. What a scary thought on how great "Durant Ulla" might just become! With Kevin Durant closing the gap with LeBron James as the best player in the game today, it will most likely be debated for years to come on which player is the greatest in the NBA out of the two. Not by me, but by most everybody else.

Career Totals

26.6 points, 6.8 rebs, 3.1 assists, 1.3 steals, 1.0 block, .475 FG%, .373 3FG%, .884FT%

12,258 points, 3153 rebounds, 1447 assists, 578 steals, 470 blocks, 701 threes

Dwight Howard

(Projected #26)

Defensive Player of The Year (3-times), All-Star (7-times)

All-NBA First Team (5-times), All-Defensive First Team (4-times)

Rebounding Title (5-times), Blocked Shots Title (2-times)

NBA Record: 3 consecutive Defensive Player of The Year Awards!

Dwight Howard of the Orlando Magic is one of the most unique big men to ever come into the NBA. The new and improved "Superman," is not your prototypical center at seven feet, having a polished offensive game, and being able to stay grounded to block shots with his size and length. He is more like the six-foot-eleven; undersized pogo stick with incredible upper body strength, explosive leaping ability, great timing, and an offensive game that doesn't come natural to him without hard work. As he is about to enter his prime, Howards low-post game is rather simple. Other than his ability to back down and *overpower* his opponents for monster slam dunks a'la Shaquille O'Neal, his only two *go-to* moves is the sweeping right-handed hook shot in the middle of lane and his across the lane left-handed, layup. Although he could eventually become a *polished* offensive center someday, Howard has a chance to go down as one of the great centers to have ever played the game.

For certain, at least statistically, he is on pace to surpass the likes of the great Patrick Ewing and David Robinson. Will he reach Top 30 stature? I believe so, that's why I have him ranked potentially 26th on the projected rankings once his prime years are complete, which could put him as the 7th or 8th best center of all-time. To put him ahead of Bill Walton when it is all said and done will not be easy, but perhaps likely, because Walton's career was shortened immensely due to injuries. Because Howard started his career at the age 18 years old, this will enable him to accumulate some unbelievable Hall Of Fame numbers. He should easily surpass 20,000 points and 12,000 rebounds and will most likely end up with 25,000 points and 15,000 rebounds to go along with at least 2,000 blocks. If for some reason Howard never becomes a dominant scoring machine in terms of developing an overall low-post game, it will be hard to rank him among the elite centers of all-time. He may end up in the Top 40 to 50 players of all-time instead of the Top 25 to 30.

Dwight David Howard was born on December 8th, 1985 in Atlanta, Georgia and attended Southwest Atlanta Christian Academy where his dad has served as Athletic Director. As a youth with his quickness and versatility, he often played the point guard position until he made the varsity team as a freshman in 2000. Playing as a small forward and then a power forward at six-foot-nine as a junior, Howard averaged 20 points and 15 rebounds per game. As senior, he averaged **25 points**, **15 rebounds** and **8 blocks** per game, and led the team to the 2004 state title. He also won numerous awards including Naismith Prep Player of the Year, Gatorade National Player of the Year, and McDonald's National High School Player of the Year. After foregoing college like his idol and now fellow peer Kevin Garnett, Howard was selected with the number one pick overall of the 2004 NBA Draft by the Orlando Magic. In his first two seasons, with Tracy McGrady no longer with the team, Howard at such a raw age posted modest numbers but set several records. He became the youngest man in NBA history to average a double-double with 12 points and 10 rebounds, to average 10 rebounds for a season, and to record 20 rebounds for a single game. After gaining twenty pounds of muscle in the off-season, Orlando coach Brian Hill was responsible for helping Howard in his conversion to the center position by having him work on his low-post game and defense. As a result, Howard increased his scoring average to 15.8 points and his rebounding to 12.5 per game. With a plethora of records already under his belt, Howard added one more by becoming the youngest player to record 20 points and 20 rebounds in the same game. The following season in 2007, he continued to improve as the future of the franchise by averaging 17.6 points and 12.3 rebounds per game, on 60 percent shooting - and was selected to his first of six consecutive All-Star games. In his first postseason appearance, the young and inexperienced Magic were swept in the first round of the playoffs by the number one seed Detroit Pistons.

In the 2007-08 season, Howard's offensive game was in *full flight* when he averaged 20.7 points and led the league in rebounding for the first of three consecutive seasons. He also led the league in double-doubles with 69 and recorded 20 points and 20 rebounds eight times. With the addition of free agent Richard Lewis providing the scoring punch along with Hedo Turkoglu, the ever improving Magic finished with 52 wins and won the division for the first time in twelve years. As the number three seed in the playoffs, the Magic dispatched the Toronto Raptors in five games in the first round behind the stellar play of point guard Jameer Nelson and three dominant 20-20 games by Howard before losing in five games to the Detroit Pistons the next round. The following season, Howard emerged *big-time* as the league's most dominant shot blocker increasing his average almost a *full point* to 2.9 blocks per game. As an already established rebounder leading the league for the second straight season, Howard blossomed into the best defensive player in the NBA. He also won the Defensive Player of the Year award for an unprecedented first of three consecutive seasons. After a 59-win regular season, the Magic in the playoffs defeated the Philadelphia 76ers in the first round four games to two, grinded out a seven-game series against the defending champion Boston Celtics in the semifinals, and defeated the number one seed Cleveland Cavaliers in six games in the conference finals. After the world waited in anticipation for its dream matchup between LeBron James' Cleveland Cavaliers and Kobe Bryant's Los Angeles Lakers, Dwight Howard and the Orlando Magic said, *not so fast,* as they upset the number one seed on its way to the NBA Finals. Unfortunately the young Magic lost to the more experienced and deeper Los Angeles Lakers team that featured Bryant, Pau Gasol and Lamar Odom.

In player evaluations, I understand that Howard's rebounding numbers might be skewed a little or a lot, whichever you prefer. While it is fair to say he has been the only big man on the team over the years to swallow up all the rebounds playing with four perimeter players. It is also fair to say he has played with limited competition at his position in history compared to other great centers of the past. But, that doesn't take away from his *super-human* talents.

Dwight Howard may be getting the label that LeBron James had in terms of winning championships. Anyone who thinks Howard's smile or laughing ways, makes him less serious about winning a championship is sadly mistaken. I don't think he would be getting all those technical fouls out of frustration if he was not serious about winning and I certainly don't think he would have made it to the NBA Finals. If you have watched enough NBA games regularly via NBA League Pass, you can see the determination and will to win that Dwight Howard shows on a nightly basis. Magic Johnson carried a smile and he was dead serious about winning. All the attention that Howard appears to want, whether it be dunking on someone emphatically or blocking a shot in the stands, it is all part of the act and foremost his entertaining style. He is a unique shot blocker that depends on timing, quickness, and leaping ability to block shots as opposed to a typical center that stays more grounded relying on height and length. I do agree with his critics and with the book "Score Casting" that Howard should work on keeping the ball in play the way Bill Russell used to, instead of frequently swatting it out of bounds.

So Howard's mannerisms - the smiling or complaining is sometimes used to shrug of frustration as well as to draw attention and excitement during a game. If you watch enough of his games, you would notice a lot of horrendous calls going against Dwight by players double teaming him and being overly aggressive with a lot of grabbing and shoving. I think as he matures with better composure and more discipline, calls made against Howard in the future will result in better officiating. Look at Shaq Diesel; he got a lot of calls going his way during the Los Angeles Lakers championship years. Calls made against Howard for defensive fouls as well as offensive fouls should balance out in years to come as he will learn how to control his frustration better as he enters his prime. And, if for some reason they don't balance out in the future, we might look to the fact that Howard had to use more of his upper body strength to move players around in the paint as compared to Shaq and former players such as Barkley who have relied more on lower body strength and added weight. Therefore officials would probably be more inclined to call a foul on Howard's flailing arms than against Shaq or Barkley's lower body (big rear ends) movement to gain position down low.

Dwight Howard has led the league in total rebounds five straight years from 2006 to 2010. He also became the youngest player in history to reach 1000, 2000, 3000, 4000, 5000, 6000, and 7000 rebounds for his career - and post 1000 rebounds in six consecutive seasons since Bill Russell. But, what I believe will help define Howard's career for individual accomplishments are his career 20 point and 20 rebound games. In this day and age, those numbers are hard to come by. Since 1986, Howard in 2012 had more **20-20** games with 41 than most great players except for Charles Barkley and Hakeem Olajuwon who had 42 each. With a good 8 to 10 years left to play in his career, he already has more 20-20 games than Shaquille O'Neal who finished his career with 34. I know Howard has been pretty much the only big man on his team most of those years in Orlando, but it still says a lot about his *utter dominance* defensively as an inside player. In our lifetime, I believe only Kevin Love and perhaps Blake Griffin will ever approach Howard's accomplishments in those combined categories. He also became the fifth player in history to lead the league in both rebounds and blocks in the same season along with Kareem Abdul-Jabbar, Bill Walton, Hakeem Olajuwon, and Ben Wallace - and the youngest to lead the league in blocks. In addition, his most prestigious record of all might be that he became the first man ever to lead the league in rebounding, blocks, and field percentage in the same season.

Howard has been to one NBA Finals but is yet to get his team over the top. Like LeBron, Howard who is barely entering his prime, is accumulating statistics at a rapid pace. So no matter what happens in the future, his resume will always include overwhelming numbers in scoring, rebounding, and in blocks. Without multiple championships, Howard and James will go down as two of the greatest players to have ever played the game, but with them their overall legacy will be enhanced greatly!

Career Totals

18.3 points, 12.9 rebounds, 1.0 assist, 2.2 blocks, 1.0 steals, .577 FG%, .577 FT%

12,731 points, 9017 rebounds, 1043 assists, 1530 blocks, 710 steals

Derrick Rose

(Projected #27)

MVP (1-time), All-NBA First (1-time)

All-Star (3-times)

Also featuring: Rajon Rondo
& Deron Williams

Derrick Rose of the Chicago Bulls is one of the most talented and unique point guards to come into the NBA. The lightning-quick Rose blends great ball-handling skills of your typical point guard but adds *explosive* finishing ability of an athletic shooting guard in the likes of past and current greats Michael Jordan, Kobe Bryant, and Dwyane Wade. Out of all the players in the league today, he along with Russell Westbrook of the Oklahoma City Thunder and Monte Ellis of the Golden State Warriors, are perhaps the quickest players in the NBA since Allen Iverson. Even on TV, Rose looks like a blur when exploding past defenders on his way to the basket. With his explosive first step and multiple crossover dribbles, Rose can get to any point on the court finishing at the basket or he can stop on a dime and pull up for a wide open jump shot. On dribble penetration, he can also create incredible space off *ankle-breaking* jukes or by maneuvering between two players, splitting the double-team and finishing at the hoop with a dunk or an unbelievable acrobatic layup, *and-one* finish. The "Contortionist," he is often called, with his 40 inch-plus vertical and incomparable body control in midair, can contort his body from side to side in the most incredible of angles, finishing on either side of the basket. Watching Rose finish at the cup reminds me so much of Jordan of the past and D-Wade of today. And at such the young age of 23, it's freakishly scary how good Rose is at finishing at the rim. Could it be possible that he is equally as good as Jordan was at finishing at the basket with an obscene acrobatic layup? If not so than he is really close. In addition, he also has the *uncanny* ability to follow his missed shot for an easy tip-in or put-back layup.

As a testament to his greatness already, at the young age of only 23, during this year's 2012 All-Star weekend, LeBron James gave Derrick Rose the highest of praise saying that "Derrick has definitely evolved the point guard position. He's doing it; him and Russell are two guys with speed, athleticism, can score, can pass, can jump, can do everything at the point guard position. I think D-Rose from end to end, is probably one of the fastest, quickest guys we have with the ball in our game. It's always exciting to get out there with him." He is absolutely right! A better way to put it is that Rose has revolutionized the point guard position once again just like Magic Johnson did 32 years ago in 1980. What's even scarier, as I suggested in the comparisons to Michael Jordan above, is that Dwyane Wade thinks Rose has taken his athleticism even above his when he was in his prime. D-Wade also had this to say about Rose: "I see a lot of things I did when I was younger, probably on a little bit more athletic of a level with him," Wade said, "But I do see the things that he does and I'll be like, 'Man, I used to do that or 'Man, I've done that before' but he does it at another notch up than even when I did it. He's so athletic and so fast." Those are huge words coming from D-Wade, who I think is the best at attacking the basket since Jordan. It basically confirms what I and everyone else have seen with their eyes, how fast and quick Derrick Rose really is. Like I said earlier, could he actually be as athletic finishing at the basket as his predecessor Michael Jordan? Actually, I hope not, because it would be nice to see Jordan remain the best the game has ever seen in that *aspect* of the game.

Rose averaged a career-high of 25.0 points a game in 2011. In only his third season in the league at 22 years old, he became the youngest man in history to win the prestigious NBA MVP award. Though at times, a shoot-first point guard throughout the year, Rose had to carry the bulk of the offensive load for the Chicago Bulls simply because they had a roster full of minimal offensive talent. Nevertheless, even with an improved jump shot and three-point shot, Rose still needs to work on improving his shot selection. This should come in time when the Bulls acquire more offensive help to relieve some of the scoring pressure. In the 2011 playoffs, he got exposed by deeper more talented offensive teams where despite having averaged **27.1 points** per game, he shot a paltry 39.6 percent from the field and 24.8 percent from three-point range. His shot seemed suspect because he relied on it too often to match the scoring output of teams with more scoring depth such as with the Atlanta Hawks and Miami Heat. Rose is an outstanding rebounder for a point guard and an excellent passer. And, his explosive leaping ability, allows him to out-jump taller players a 'la D-Wade and corral rebounds for easy put-backs. He moves his quick feet well on the defensive end keeping the dribbler in front of him, but needs to work on synchronizing his hands with his feet to become an elite defender. He averaged only one steal a game in 2011 and 0.9 for his first three years in the league.

Derrick Martell Rose was born on October 4th, 1988 in Chicago, Illinois and played high school at Simeon Career Academy where he won two state championships in the state of Chicago. In his senior year, he averaged an impressive **25.1 points**, **9.1 assists**, **8.8 rebounds**, and **3.4 steals**, on 59 percent shooting - and was rated by scouts as the number one point guard in the country. After being recruited heavily by the University of Illinois and Indiana University, Rose accepted an offer to play for the University of Memphis where he led the team to the 2008 NCAA Championship game. And it's scary to think of; *what could have been*, if both Rose and Eric Gordon (of the Los Angeles Clippers) had decided to attend the University of Illinois. Rose elected to attend Memphis before his senior year while Gordon changed his verbal commitment from Illinois to the University of Indiana. The tandem, with the chemistry already intact after playing AAU basketball together, would have created one of the great backcourts in NCAA history. Gordon has one of the most explosive first steps and deadly jump shots in the league today and is quicker (because of his hybrid size at 6-feet-3) than most if not all the shooting guards in the league - and is as quick, and stronger than most point guards. He is a unique talent at six-foot-three built in the mold of past great Joe Dumars of the Detroit Pistons who was also six-foot-three. As I was in the midst of this writing, Gordon was the cornerstone for the Los Angeles Clippers franchise along with Blake Griffin until he was traded recently to the New Orleans Hornets. In a couple of years, Gordon is my sleeper pick as the next great two-guard in the Western Conference along with Tyreke Evans of the Sacramento Kings, rookie sharp shooter Klay Thompson of the Golden State Warriors, and James Harden of the Oklahoma City Thunder. One of the four should eventually unseat Kobe Bryant as the premier shooting guard in the Western Conference.

After moving up in the lottery with a 1.7 percent chance, Rose was selected with the first overall pick of the 2008 NBA Draft by the Chicago Bulls. In his first season, he averaged 16.8 points and 6.3 assists, and won the 2009 NBA Rookie of the Year Award. And, in the playoffs against the Boston Celtics, Rose tied Kareem Abdul-Jabbar's record of **36 points** in a playoff game debut and became the second player after Chris Paul to record at least **35 points and 10 assists** in his first playoff game. The young *upstart* Chicago Bulls shocked the basketball world when they pushed the defending champion Celtics to seven games in the first round of the playoffs. With Rose leading the way averaging **19.7 points**, **6.4 assists**, and **6.3 rebounds** per game, the rest of the league was given a preview of what was to come in the *great* future of Derrick Rose and the Chicago Bulls franchise. The next season the Bulls would finish with a .500 record and make the playoffs only to lose in the first round to LeBron James and the Cleveland Cavaliers in five games despite another terrific performance by Rose who averaged **26.8 points** per game and **7.2 assists**. In the regular season, Rose would increase his scoring average four full points to 20.8 per game and make his first All-Star team becoming the first Chicago Bull since Michael Jordan to do so.

In the 2010-11 season, Rose would flourish as the next superstar by becoming the youngest player in history to win the NBA MVP award. For the season, he finished with a career-high in almost all categories, averaging **25 points** per game, **7.7 assists**, and **4.1 rebounds** - while shooting 85.8 percent from the free-throw line and 33.2 percent from three-point range. He also was selected to start his first All-Star game and to the All-NBA First Team. His 2000-point, 600-assist season was accomplished only two other times in the last 30 years by Michael Jordan and LeBron James. So what that tells me, is other than Chris Paul at the point guard position, Rose might have the most potential to score and assist at the highest level in the likes of the great Nate "Tiny" Archibald.

In the years to come (barring injury), if Rose's outside shooting and defense keeps improving he might surpass Paul as the greatest point guard in the league today. And even If he doesn't improve those aspects of his game, he still might end up being the greatest point guard of his generation. It is flat out scary how good Derrick Rose might become, because he was already at the top of his peers when he won the MVP at 22 years old.

In player comparisons:

With Steve Nash and Jason Kidd at the tail end of their careers, the Top 5 point guards in the NBA today are in the following order: Chris Paul, Derrick Rose, Russell Westbrook, **Deron Williams**, and **Rajon Rondo** (and if you wanted to know, Tony Parker and Stephen Curry are ranked 6th and 7th). And for those of you who feel Parker should easily be in the top 5, you may have a point, but go back to Tim Duncan's chapter to read the complete break down on Parker's game. While Paul and Williams are more similar in comparisons as I have described in Paul's chapter. Rose and Westbrook at times seem like mirror images. In fact, if you looked at their recent statistics and covered up their names you wouldn't know who was who. As I described in the introduction to Rose, both players are the most explosive point guards in the league today that can drive to the basket with reckless abandon and finish with an assortment of acrobatic layups and slam dunks. Both are very good passers and rebounders. The only noticeable differences so far between the two, is that Rose's development as a jump shooter and free-throw shooter is ahead of Westbrook's. But I think Westbrook is slightly ahead on the defensive end able to anticipate and accumulate a lot more steals. With their incredible leaping ability, both players are exceptional shot blockers at the point guard position.

Even though Rondo is the best out of the five defensively with Paul slightly behind, he doesn't present nearly the offensive game that the other four point guards do. Although from a passing standpoint, Rondo is beyond Rose and Westbrook and right up there with Paul and Williams. If Rondo can someday develop a consistent jump shot and Rose and Westbrook eventually become elite defenders, we can then take our pick on whom the best point guard in the NBA today is. What's interesting to note, while many (including Stephen A. Smith) feel Deron Williams might be the best point guard in the league especially after Paul had surgery on his knee, he lacks a couple of things. For one; health, even though he has everything you would want in a point guard, size at six-three, lightning-quickness, speed and strength, outside shooting as far out as the three-point line, the ability to score inside with dribble penetration, and play good defense, he has been injury prone like Paul the last few years. Second of all, he lacks the dominance in one or two particular aspects of his game that the other four players have.

Like I have mentioned throughout the book, sometimes less is more and being dominant in one or two aspects of a player's game is better than another's being just very good to great in all other aspects. In player comparisons, using the example with power forward Pau Gasol, you could make the case that Gasol has the better all-around game than Nowitzki, but that doesn't necessarily make him a better player because Nowitzki has the deadly one-foot fallaway (to go along with a very good overall game).

Getting back to the point guard comparisons, Rose and Westbrook excel at dominating the paint off dribble penetration, and Rondo and Paul dominate on the defensive end where they are able to accumulate a lot of steals, and by facilitating to set up teammates for scoring opportunities. Williams is very good to great in all of those aspects but not necessarily dominant. Even though he has only one all-star and zero All-NBA First Team selections, with health permitting, he still has a slight chance of becoming the top guard in the league as he enters his prime. Look at what he did recently. Williams just had one of the great scoring games for point guard in history when he scored a franchise record **57 points** to go along with 7 assists and 6 rebounds in a 104-101 victory on March 4th, 2012 against the Charlotte Bobcats. He was also 21 for 21 from the free-throw line and came within 3 of Dirk Nowitzki's all-time mark set in the 2011 playoffs. So it just so happened to back fire on me, as Williams just proved he could be dominate in both the scoring aspect and the shooting aspect of the game. Even Rondo two days later, who I have currently ranked as the fifth best point guard, took his best shot to prove he is the top point guard in the league. On March 6, 2012, Rondo became the youngest man in NBA history behind Wilt Chamberlain and Oscar Robertson to record *at least* **20 points, 15 rebounds, and 14 assists** in a single game.

But even if Williams can stay injury free, because the point guard position is changing to a more athletic type of point guard and there is more talent coming into the league than ever before, maybe we won't ever have a clear cut pick for top PGs in the league for the years to come. Here are the career numbers for the current top five point guards (up to the time of this writing) in the league today:

Paul: 18.7 points, 9.9 assists, 4.6 rebs, 2.4 steals, .471FG%, .853 FT%, .359 3FG%

Rose: 21.1 points, 6.8 assists, 3.9 rebs, 0.9 steals, .468 FG%, .818 FT%, .311 3FG%

Westbrk: 18.1 points, 7.0 assists, 4.8 rebs, 1.6 steals, .425 FG%, .815 FT%, .276 3FG%

Williams: 17.3 points, 9.2 assists, 3.3 rebs, 1.1 steals, .459 FG%, .810 FT%, .354 3FG%

Rondo: 10.8 points, 7.6 assists, 4.4 rebs, 1.9 steals, .487 FG%, .620 FT%, .243 3FG%

As you can see, Paul has the best balance of statistics, ranking the highest in four of the seven categories and second in three others while Rose, Westbrook, and Rondo rank first just once and only Williams' ranks second twice. And, although Stephen Curry of the Golden State Warriors didn't make my list of current Top 5 points guards, in large part because he missed much of the 2012 season with injuries, the young sharpshooter might eventually do so sooner than later. From a shooting standpoint, Curry reminds me of a smaller version of Reggie Miller at the point guard position but as a facilitator, more like a young Steve Nash with incredible ball-handling skills but with more assertiveness to score. And if Curry can stay injury free for the years to come and reaches his potential as a Nash type of player, he might challenge Paul and Rose for the title of *best point* guard in the league.

After I have exhausted my thoughts on the 5 best point guards in the league today, the next wave is already on the way in, Brandon Jennings, John Wall (who had the best pre-draft workout at the combine that I had ever seen in terms of his quickness, speed, and agility), Kyrie Irving, and Ricky Rubio who I have been following since he was 17 (see Dominique's chapter), and soon-to-be draftee Damian Lillard. Also, K. Irving at only 19 years old, who is averaging 18 points per game and on his way to becoming the 2012 Rookie of Year, might eventually become the best point guard in the league. So while Chris Paul is currently the best point guard in the NBA, Derrick Rose, Russell Westbrook, and Deron Williams are not far behind. If Rose keeps improving his outside shot and his defense, *the sky's the limit* on how great he may become!

Career Totals

21.0 points, 6.8 assists, 3.8 rebounds, 0.9 steals, .464 FG%, .815 FT%, .310 3FG%

5858 points, 1911 assists, 1071 rebounds, 243 steals, 214 threes

Blake Griffin

(Projected #33)

All-Star (2-times)

Also featuring:
Kevin Love

In only his second season in the NBA, Blake Griffin of the Los Angeles Clippers was named to his second consecutive All-Star team and has put his stamp as the "poster child" of the league by way of the slam dunk as he is one of the most promising, up-and-coming power forwards along with Kevin Love of the Minnesota Timberwolves. Potentially great in every facet of the game including scoring, rebounding and passing, Griffin has made his mark on the league not only for his tremendous all-around talent but for his "out of this world" leaping ability and *monster* slam dunks. In only his second season this year in 2012, he already has four *memorable* dunks against Kendrick Perkins and Serge Ibaka of the Oklahoma City Thunder and two against Pau Gasol of the Los Angeles Lakers. With those four dunks alone, many feel Griffin will become the greatest *in-game* dunker of all-time. I feel the same way as of right now, even after reminiscing over past greats Dominique Wilkins, Michael Jordan, Julius Erving, and Vince Carter. I mean, what he did to K. Perkins and P. Gasol was completely demoralizing, pummeling the helpless power forward and center to the ground. In the case of Perkins, at least he was able to contest the shot with his arm way up in the air before eventually be dwarfed by Blake's levitation. But even then, it seemed he was still a foot or so below the towering extension on the dunk by Griffin. When Gasol was *humiliated* so-to-speak on both dunks, which by the way happened to come in the same game, he was forced to the ground with either the leverage (with perhaps the off arm extended) or the body weight of Griffin, like a ragdoll thrown to the ground from the mouth of Rottweiler or Pit bull.

Aside from Griffin's greatest attribute of being able to float through the air and levitate way above the rim with the *grace of a hot air balloon* and then explode at the last moment for a monster slam dunk like a *bomb about to detonate*, he is a skilled offensive player with unlimited potential. He has the entire offensive arsenal but needs to refine most of it which I believe will come in due time over the next couple of years. He may not have the three-point shot that his contemporary **Kevin Love** has, but has good range on his jump shot up to 18 to 20 feet. Over time, he may even extend his range to the three-point line, which he has done on a few occasions with nine three-pointers in his first two seasons. Is his outside shooting considered reliable this year and for years to come? Potentially yes, but right now it is very inconsistent whereas Love is more polished and has a better outside game shooting the ball, after being in the league four seasons. Even though Love has a polished inside game as well, I believe Griffin will eventually become the better inside low-post scorer and rebounder. With Love, perhaps slightly ahead in both aspects of the game right now, I believe Griffin has more of a chance to be the more dominate player in the likes of the great Karl Malone as he gets closer to his prime. His offensive arsenal includes: incredible leaping ability, spin moves down low to create scoring opportunities, and a fadeaway shot that he can create at any point on the court including the corners, baseline, and at the top of the key. He even has a reverse spin that is very difficult for any player to pull off in midair, where he finishes in the paint with a finger roll. With all that being said, so far in the last couple of years, Griffin has been very sporadic and for that matter, erratic at times with his shot selection and execution, but that should improve as he develops and matures as a player. He also needs to work on his defense where his blocks and steals are less than one per game for his career. Over time his size, strength, and athleticism, and work ethic, should allow him to become a formidable defensive player for years to come. My only major concern from a skill set offensively is his poor free-throw shooting that I hope improves over the upcoming years.

Even from the rebounding perspective of the game, Love is a little bit ahead of Griffin but not by much. Despite Love's incredible rebounding instincts and positioning, in due time, Griffin might become the better rebounder and offensive rebounder by a slight margin over Love due to his overall size and athleticism. But what also separates the two thus far, is that Griffin is the better passer and potentially could become one of the top all-around power forwards ever in the likes of the great Karl Malone and Charles Barkley.

Born on March 16th, 1989 in Oklahoma City, Oklahoma, Blake Austin Griffin attended Oklahoma Christian School where he won the state championship all four seasons under his Dad who was the head coach. In college at the University of Oklahoma, Griffin averaged **22.7 points** and **14.4 rebounds** per game, and shot 65 percent from the field in his sophomore year. He also won the Naismith College Player of the Year award and John R. Wooden Award. After two years of college, he was selected with the 1st pick overall of the 2009 NBA Draft by the Los Angeles Clippers but did not play that season after breaking his kneecap in the final preseason game. The following year, Griffin averaged **22.5 points**, **12.1 rebounds**, and **3.8 assists** per game, on 50 percent shooting - and won the 2011 Rookie of the Year award. Even as rookie he showed tremendous promise in the scoring aspect of the game and in rebounding. He scored a career-high and set a Clippers record with 47 points, and had 14 rebounds, and became the first man since Allen Iverson in the 1996-97 season to have 2 40-point games as a rookie. He also set a franchise record for consecutive double-doubles at 23 and became the first man since 1968 to record 27 straight double-doubles.

After becoming the first rookie to play in the All-Star game since Yao Ming, Griffin became a *mega-star*, "Bigger than Life", when he participated in the 2011 Slam Dunk Contest! The second half of the season, he had two triple-doubles of **33 points, 17 rebounds, and 10 assists** and on the last day of the season **31 points, 10 rebounds, and 10 assists**. In his second season in the league, Griffin had a similar year as his rookie season with his overall numbers just slightly down.

With Griffin entering his third season and Love his fifth, both players are already considered two of the three best power forwards in the game along with Pau Gasol of the Los Angeles Lakers. In fact, so far, he might be the best power forward out of the three after his explosive season in 2012.

Kevin Love of the Minnesota Timberwolves has been equally impressive as Griffin in only his fourth season in the league at only 23 years old. Born on September 7th, 1988 in Santa Monica, California, Kevin Wesley Love's family moved to Lake Oswego Oregon where he attended Lake Oswego High School. His dad Stan Love was a former NBA forward who showed Kevin tapes of the great Lakers and Celtics rivalries and of past Hall of Famers, including centers Bill Walton, Wes Unseld, Hakeem Olajuwon, David Robinson, Charles Barkley, and Michael Jordan. In high school, Love led the team to three consecutive state championship games in Oregon winning once his junior year. As a senior in 2007, Love averaged an incredible 33.9 points, 17 rebounds, and four assists. In only one season in college at the University of California at Los Angeles, Love averaged 17.5 points and 10.6 rebounds per game, and shot 55.9 percent from the field - and was named to the All-America First Team. He also led the Bruins to the NCAA Final Four where they would lose to the Memphis Tigers.

After only one year of college, Love was selected with the 5th pick overall of the 2008 NBA Draft by the Memphis Grizzlies behind former UCLA teammate Russell Westbrook who was taken fourth by the Oklahoma City Thunder. After the draft he was traded with Mike Miller, Brian Cardinal, and Jason Collins to the Minnesota Timberwolves for O.J. Mayo, Antoine Walker, Marko Jaric and Greg Buckner, in which former general manager Kevin McHale orchestrated. After a modest rookie season playing for a losing franchise, Love continued to improve his game in his second season averaging 14 points and 11 rebounds per game.

By his third season in the NBA, with big man Al Jefferson no longer with the team, Love blossomed in a big way averaging 20.2 points, a league leading 15.2 rebounds, 2.5 assists, and shot 41.7 percent from three-point range - and was named to his first All-Star team. But what stood out most that season, was when he set the franchise record for rebounds in a game with a **31-point** and **31-rebound** performance at home against the New York Knicks on November 12th, 2010. It was the first time a player had that many rebounds in a game since Charles Barkley snagged 33 in a game in 1996. At the same time, he became the first man since Moses Malone in 1982 to record 30 points and 30 rebounds in the same game. In one game on December 18th in a loss to the Denver Nuggets, he set a then career-high of 43 points to go along with 17 rebounds. And, he had another phenomenal game of 37 points and 23 rebounds against the Golden State Warriors on February 27th, 2011. In addition, he had four games of 30 points and 20 rebounds, and broke Kevin Garnett's franchise record of 37 consecutive double-doubles, finishing the streak at 55. It was the longest streak since the ABA-NBA merger in 1976 surpassing Moses Malone's 51-game streak from 1979 to 1980. With all his accomplishments that season he was named 2010-11 NBA's Most Improved Player.

In the 2011-12 season, Love just keeps on getting better, *scary* to a point, that it makes me rethink how good he is going to be in comparisons to Blake Griffin. With a concussion just recently, it looks like Love will finish the 2012 season with a **career-high 26 points** per game giving him a four-year average of 17.3 points and 12 rebounds per game. Even after his latest scoring and rebounding accolades in which he scored **42 points** in a game, **51 points** in another, followed by a **30-point and 21-rebound** game, and a **40-point and 19-rebound** game two games after that - which all coming in the month of March, I still believe Griffin will become the better player even though it might end up being really close.

Many people today feel Kevin Love is the best power forward in the game over Blake Griffin and Pau Gasol. While I tend to agree to some extent because Love is four years into his career with a more polished game as a scorer and as a rebounder, I still believe Griffin has potentially the better all-around game and is the more *gifted* passer at the power forward position - even though Love is darn good himself. Whichever one you choose (2012 #1 Draft pick Anthony Davis with a massive wingspan could eventually become one of those choices), both players are the best we have in the game today and should make the All-Star team for the next 10 years. While Love is unique in his own right, similar to Larry Bird in many respects including from the mental aspect (to some extent), rebounding and shooting from long range, so is Griffin as a versatile inside-outside scorer that can shoot effectively (but so far inconsistently) from mid-range, and can pass like many of the other great power forwards before him. But no matter how his career materializes in terms of where he will end up among the all-time greats of the game, Blake Griffin might end up becoming the best in game dunker of all-time!

Career Totals

20.4 points, 10.4 rebounds, 3.6 assists, 0.6 blocks, 0.9 steals, .529 FG%, .611 FT%

4653 points, 2368 rebounds, 821 assists, 143 blocks, 214 steals

Copyright © 2013 by Johnny Osaki

All dated references come from the National Basketball Association
Most of the recent quoted references have come from what I have listened
to or have seen quoted come from the National Basketball Association

Here are some of the sources and books that help me write this one:

Espn.com, NBA.com, Yahoo Sports, NBA Encyclopedia, Wikipedia, NBA Wikipedia, Sporting News Official NBA Register Book, Sporting News Official NBA Guide Book, Basketball Reference.com, ESPN Classic, NBA Hardwood Classics, You Tube, Sports Illustrated Almanac, Sport Illustrated magazine, The Sporting News magazine, Yahoo Sports Basketball magazine, Slam magazine, The Book Of Basketball (Bill Simmons) Who's Better, Who's Best in Basketball? (Elliot Cobb) Larry Bird Earvin Magic Johnson _When The Game Was Ours, KAREEM (Kareem Abdul-Jabbar), West By West (Jerry West), Red and Me (Bill Russell), Dream Team (Jack MacCallum), Score Casting

Here is a listing of more great basketball books (references) for your interest:

The NBA's Top 50 (Ken Shouler), Giant Steps (Kareem Abdul-Jabbar), Wilt (Wilt Chamberlain and David Shaw), Wilt, 1962 (Gary Pomerantz), Goliath (Bill Libby), My Life (Magic Johnson and Bill Novak), Drive (Larry Bird and Bob Ryan), The Big O (Oscar Robertson), Show-time (Pat Riley), Mr. Clutch (Jerry West), Second Wind (Bill Russell and Taylor Branch), Basketball My Way (Jerry West and Bill Libby), Confessions of a Basketball Gypsy (Rick Barry and David Wolf), The Drive Within Me (Bob Pettit with Bob Wolff), The Last Loud Roar (Bob Cousy), Hondo (John Havlicek with Bob Ryan), Give' Em the Hook (Tommy Heinsohn and Joe Fitzgerald), Maravich (Wayne Federman and Marshall Terrell), Pistol (Mark Kriegel), The Inside Game (Wayne Embry with Mary Schmidt Boyer), Life on the Run (Bill Bradley), Eleven Rings (Phil Jackson) Sacred Hoops (Phil Jackson), The Last Season (Phil Jackson with Charley Rosen), More than a game (Phil Jackson with Charley Rosen), The Perfect Team (Foreword by Chuck Daley)

Loose Balls and Tall Tales (Terry Pluto), 24 Seconds to Shoot (Leonard Koppett), Hang Time (Bob Greene), The Golden Boys (Cameron Stauth), The City Game (by Pete Axthelm), The Franchise (Cameron Stauth), Unfinished Business (Jack MacCallum), Auerbach on Auerbach; On and Off the Court; Red Auerbach (Red Auerbach with Joe Fitzgerald), The Game(Kenny Dryden), Wait' Til Next Year (William Goldman and Mike Lupica), The Breaks of the Game; Playing for Keeps (David Halberstam), Twentieth Century Treasury of Sports (edited by Al and Brian Silverman), Classic Wiley (Ralph Wiley), Tip Off (Filip Bondy), The Long Season (Rick Adelman and Dwight Jaynes), Only the strong Survive (Larry Platt), 48 Minutes (Bob Ryan and Terry Pluto), 07 Seconds or Less (Jack McCallum), Fathers Playing Catch with Sons (Donald Hall), The Fab Five (Mitch

Albom), The Best American Sports Writing of the Century (edited by David Halberstam), Everything They Had (David Halberstam), Best seat in the House (Spike Lee and Ralph Wiley), The Rivalry (John Taylor), Second Coming (Sam Smith), Evergreen; Seeing Red (Dan Shaughnessy), Rebound, (Bob Greene), The Punch (John Feinstein), The Jump (Ian O' Conner), Champions Remembered (Ray Fitzgerald), When Nothing Else Matters (Michael Leahy), The Pro Game (Bob Ryan), Black Planet (David Shields), Falling From Grace (Terry Pluto), But They Can't Beat Us (Randy Roberts), The Big Three; The Last Banner (Peter May), Covert: My Years Infiltrating the Mob (Bob Delaney), Out of Bounds (Jeff Benedict)

Top 50 2013	MVP	runner-up	All-NBA 1s	second	Defense 1s	second	All-Star	Champion	Finals MVP	Scoring	runner-up	League Rebound	Titles Assist	Steals	Blocks	PER	second
1. Michael Jordan	5	3	10	1	9		14	6	6	10				3		7	3
2. Kareem Abdul Jabbar	6	1	10	5	5	6	19	6	2	2	3	1			4	9	3
3. Wilt Chamberlain	4	2	7	3	2		13	2	1	7		11	1			8	2
4. Magic Johnson	3	2	9	1			12	5	3				4	2			1
5. Larry Bird	3	4	9	1		3	12	3	2				4	2			1
6. Oscar Robertson	1	1	9	2			12	1				1				2	2
7. Bill Russell	5	2	3	8	1		12	11				2	6				5
8. Hakeem Olajuwon	1	1	6	3	5	4	12	2	2			2	4		3		1
9. Tim Duncan	2	2	10	3	8	6	14	4	3			2			3		1
10. Jerry West		4	10	2	4	1	14	1	1	1	2		1			2	4
11. Elgin Baylor		1	10				11				3					1	1
12. Rick Barry			5,4	1			8,4	1,1	1	1,1	1			1		1	4
13. Shaquille O'Neal	1	2	8	2		3	15	4	3	2	4				5		3
14. Kobe Bryant	1	1	11	2	9	3	15	5	2	2	3						
15. Julius Erving	1,3	1	5,4	2,1			11,5	1,2	,2	,3						1,4	1
16. Moses Malone	3		4	4	1	1	12	1	1			6				2	
17. Bob Pettit	2	2	10	1			11	1			2	1				4	1
18. Karl Malone	2	1	11	2	3	1	14					5				1	1
19. Charles Barkley	1	1	5	5			11										2
20. John Stockton			2	6		5	10						9	2			
21. Steve Nash	2	1	3	2			8						5				
22. Kevin Garnett	1	2	4	3	9	3	15	1				4				2	
23. Dirk Nowitzki	1		4	5			11	1	1								
24. John Havlicek			4	7	5	3	13	8	1								
25. Bob Cousy	1		10	2			13	6				1	8				
	MVP	runner-up	All-NBA 1s	second	Defense 1s	second	All-Star	Champion	Finals MVP	Scoring	runner-up	Rebound	Assist	Steals	Blocks	PER	second
26. Bill Walton	1	1	1	1	2		2	2	1			1		1			
27. Allen Iverson	1		3	3			11			4	2			3			
28. Isiah Thomas			3	2			12	2	1				1				
29. George Gervin		2	5	2,2			9,3			4							,1
30. Elvin Hayes			3	3		2	12	1				2					
31. George Mikan			6				4	5		3	1	1				3	
32. David Robinson	1	2	4	2	4	4	10	2		1		1		1	1	3	1
33. Kevin McHale			1		3	3	7	3							1	3	1
34. Scottie Pippen			3	2	8	2	7	6					1				
35. Willis Reed	1	1	1	4	1		7	2	2								
36. Walt Frazier			4	2	7		7	2									
37. Nate Thurmond		1			2	3	7										
38. Dave Cowens	1	1		3	1	2	8	2									
39. Patrick Ewing			1	6		3	12										
40. Sam Jones				3			5	10									
41. Clyde Drexler		1	1	2			10	1									
42. Gary Payton			2	5	9		9	1						1			
43. Jason Kidd		1	5	1	4	5	10	1					5				
44. Wes Unseld	1		1				5	1	1			1					
45. Dominique Wilkins		1	1	4			9			1	3						
46. Paul Pierce				1			10	1	1								
47. James Worthy							7	3	1								
48. Dolph Schayes		1	6	6			12	1				1	1				1
49. Billy Cunningham	,1		3,1	1			4,1	1									,1
50. Jerry Lucas			3	2			7	1									
Projected	MVP	runner-up	All-NBA 1s	second	Defense 1s	second	All-Star	Champion	Finals MVP	Scoring	runner-up	Rebound	Assist	Steals	Blocks	PER	second
2. LeBron James	4	1	7	2	5		9	2	2	1	3					6	1
14. Chris Paul		1	3	1	3	2	6						2	5			1
15. Dwyane Wade			2	3		3	9	3	1	1							2
16. Kevin Durant		3	4				4			3							1
26. Dwight Howard		1	5		4	1	7					5			2		1
27. Derrick Rose	1		1				3										
33. Blake Griffin				2			3										

, = ABA